Wisdom Literature

WISDOM LITERATURE

A Theological History

Leo G. Perdue

Westminster John Knox Press
LOUISVILLE • LONDON

Scripture quotations from the New Revised Standard Version of the Bible are copyright © 1989 by the Division of Christian Education of the National Council of the Churches of Christ in the U.S.A. and are used by permission.

Book design by Sharon Adams
Cover design by Eric Walljasper, Minneapolis, MN

First edition
Published by Westminster John Knox Press
Louisville, Kentucky

This book is printed on acid-free paper that meets the American National Standards Institute Z39.48 standard. ∞

PRINTED IN THE UNITED STATES OF AMERICA

07 08 09 10 11 12 13 14 15 16—10 9 8 7 6 5 4 3 2 1

Library of Congress Cataloging-in-Publication Data

Perdue, Leo G.
    Wisdom literature : a theological history / Leo G. Perdue.—1st ed.
      p. cm.
    ISBN 978-0-664-22919-1 (alk. paper)
    1. Wisdom literature—Criticism, interpretation, etc.   I. Title.
   BS1455.P424   2007
   223'.06—dc22   2007012407

Contents

Abbreviations

AASOR	Annual of the American Schools of Oriental Research
AB	Anchor Bible
ABRL	Anchor Bible Reference Library
AGAJU	Arbeiten zur Geschichte des antiken Judentums und des Urchristentums
AnBib	Analecta biblica
ANET	*Ancient Near Eastern Texts Relating to the Old Testament*, ed. J. B. Pritchard. 3rd ed. Princeton: Princeton University Press, 1969
ANRW	*Aufstieg und Niedergang der römischen Welt*
AOAT	Alter Orient und Altes Testament
ATANT	Abhandlungen zur Theologie des Alten und Neuen Testaments
ATD	Das Alte Testament Deutsch
b.	Babylonian Talmud
BAR	*Biblical Archaeology Review*
BASOR	*Bulletin of the American Schools of Oriental Research*
BBB	Bonner biblischer Beiträge
BETL	Bibliotheca ephemeridum theologicarum lovaniensium
BGU	Aegyptische Urkunden aus den Königlichen Staatlichen Museen zu Berlin, Griechische Urkunden
BHK	*Biblia hebraica*, ed. Rudolf Kittel. 3rd ed. Stuttgart: Württembergische Bibelanstalt, 1937
BHS	*Biblia hebraica stuttgartensia*, ed. Karl Elliger and Wilhelm Rudolph. Stuttgart: Deutsche Bibelstiftung, 1983
BHT	Beiträge zur historischen Theologie
BibOr	Biblica et Orientalia
BJS	Brown Judaic Studies

BKAT	Biblischer Kommentar: Alte Testament
BN	*Biblische Notizen*
BO	*Bibliotheca orientalis*
BT	*Bible Translator*
BWANT	Beiträge zur Wissenschaft vom Alten und Neuen Testament
BWL	W. G. Lambert, *Babylonian Wisdom Literature.* Oxford: Clarendon, 1960
BZ	*Biblische Zeitschrift*
BZAW	Beihefte zur Zeitschrift für die alttestamentliche Wissenschaft
BZNW	Beihefte zur Zeitschrift für die neutestamentliche Wissenschaft
CANE	*Civilizations of the Ancient Near East,* ed. Jack M. Sasson. 4 vols. New York: Scribner, 1995
CBQ	*Catholic Biblical Quarterly*
CBQMS	Catholic Biblical Quarterly Monograph Series
CIS	Corpus inscriptionum semiticarum
COS	*Context of Scripture,* ed. W. W. Hallo, et al. 3 vols. Leiden: Brill, 1994–
CPJ	*Corpus papyrorum judaicorum*
CRINT	Compendia rerum iudaicorum ad Novum Testamentum
CTM	Calwer theologische Monographien
DSD	*Dead Sea Discoveries*
ETL	*Ephemerides theologicae lovanienses*
FAT	Forschungen zum Alten Testament
FOTL	Forms of the Old Testament Literature
FRLANT	Forschungen zur Religion und Literatur des Alten und Neuen Testaments
FS	*Festschrift*
HALOT	Ludwig Koehler, et al., *Hebrew and Aramaic Lexicon of the Old Testament,* trans. and ed. M. E. J. Richardson. Repr. 2 vols. Leiden: Brill, 2001
HAR	*Hebrew Annual Review*
HAT	Handbuch zum alten Testament
HBS	Herders biblische Studien
HBT	*Horizons in Biblical Theology*
HO	Handbuch der Orientalistik
HSM	Harvard Semitic Monographs
HTR	*Harvard Theological Review*
HUCA	*Hebrew Union College Annual*
HUCM	Hebrew Union College Monographs
IB	*Interpreter's Bible,* ed. G. A. Buttrick, et al. 12 vols. New York: Abingdon, 1951–57
ICC	International Critical Commentary

IDB	*Interpreter's Dictionary of the Bible,* ed. G. A. Buttrick. 4 vols. Nashville: Abingdon, 1962
IEJ	*Israel Exploration Journal*
Int	*Interpretation*
IRT	Issues in Religion and Theology
JAAR	*Journal of the American Academy of Religion*
JANES	*Journal of the Ancient Near Eastern Society of Columbia University*
JAOS	*Journal of the American Oriental Society*
JBL	*Journal of Biblical Literature*
JCS	*Journal of Cuneiform Studies*
JEA	*Journal of Egyptian Archaeology*
JEOL	*Jaarbericht van het Vooraziatisch-Egyptisch Gezelschap (Genootschap) Ex oriente lux*
JJS	*Journal of Jewish Studies*
JNES	*Journal of Near Eastern Studies*
JNSL	*Journal of Northwest Semitic Languages*
JSHRZ	Jüdische Schriften aus hellenistisch-römischer Zeit
JSJ	*Journal for the Study of Judaism*
JSJSup	Journal for the Study of Judaism Supplements
JSOT	*Journal for the Study of the Old Testament*
JSOTSup	Journal for the Study of the Old Testament Supplements
JSP	*Journal for the Study of the Pseudepigrapha*
JSPSup	Journal for the Study of the Pseudepigrapha Supplements
JSS	*Journal of Semitic Studies*
JTS	*Journal of Theological Studies*
KAT	Kommentar zum Alten Testament
LÄ	*Lexikon der Ägyptologie,* ed. Wolfgang Helck, et al. 6 vols. Wiesbaden: Harrassowitz, 1972–86
LD	Lectio divina
LXX	Septuagint
m.	Mishnah
MGWJ	*Monatschrift für Geschichte und Wissenschaft des Judentums*
MT	Masoretic text
MVAG	Mitteilungen der Vorasiatischen Gesellschaft
NF	Neue Forschung
NIB	*New Interpreter's Bible,* ed. Leander E. Keck, et al. 12 vols. Nashville: Abingdon, 1994–2004
NovTSup	Novum Testamentum Supplements
NTS	*New Testament Studies*
OBO	Orbis biblicus et orientalis
OBT	Overtures to Biblical Theology
OCD	*Oxford Classical Dictionary,* ed. S. Hornblower and A. Spawforth. 3rd ed. Oxford: Oxford University Press, 1996

OLA	Orientalia lovaniensia analecta
OTP	*Old Testament Pseudepigrapha,* ed. J. H. Charlesworth. 2 vols. Garden City, NY: Doubleday, 1983–85
Or	*Orientalia*
OrAnt	*Oriens antiquus*
OTS	*Oudtestamentische Studiën*
PTMS	Pittsburgh Theological Monograph Series
RB	*Revue biblique*
REJ	*Revue des études juives*
RevQ	*Revue de Qumran*
RHPR	*Revue d'histoire et de philosophie religieuses*
RHR	*Revue de l'histoire des religions*
RTL	*Revue théologique de Louvain*
SBFLA	*Studii biblici Franciscani liber annuus*
SBL	Society of Biblical Literature
SBLDS	SBL Dissertation Series
SBLMS	SBL Monograph Series
SBLSCS	SBL Septuagint and Cognate Studies
SBLSP	*SBL Seminar Papers*
SBLSymS	SBL Symposium Series
SBLTT	SBL Texts and Translations
SBS	Stuttgarter Bibelstudien
SHANE	Studies in the History of the Ancient Near East
SJT	*Scottish Journal of Theology*
SNVAO	Skrifter utgitt av det Norske Videnskaps-Akademi i Oslo
STDJ	Studies on the Texts of the Desert of Judah
SUNT	Studien zur Umwelt des Neuen Testament
Sup	Supplement(s)
SVTP	Studia in Veteris Testamenti pseudepigraphica
TDNT	*Theological Dictionary of the New Testament,* ed. Gerhard Kittel and Gerhard Friedrich. Trans. G. W. Bromiley. 10 vols. Grand Rapids: Eerdmans, 1964–76
TDOT	*Theological Dictionary of the Old Testament,* ed. G. J. Botterweck, et al. Trans. J. T. Willis, et al. Grand Rapids: Eerdmans, 1974–
TLOT	*Theological Lexicon of the Old Testament,* ed. E. Jenni and C. Westermann. Trans. M. E. Biddle. 3 vols. Peabody, MA: Hendrickson, 1997
TQ	*Theologische Quartalschrift*
TU	Texte und Untersuchungen
TUAT	Texte aus der Umwelt des Alten Testaments
VF	*Verkündigung und Forschung*
VT	*Vetus Testamentum*
VTSup	Vetus Testamentum Supplements

WBC	Word Biblical Commentary
WMANT	Wissenschaftliche Monograpahien zum alten und neuen Testament
WO	*Die Welt des Orients*
WUNT	Wissenschaftliche Untersuchungen zum Neuen Testament
y.	Jerusalem Talmud
ZÄS	*Zeitschrift für ägyptische Sprache und Altertumskunde*
ZAW	*Zeitschrift für die alttestamentliche Wissenschaft*
ZBK	Zürcher Bibelkommentare
ZTK	*Zeitschrift für Theologie und Kirche*

Chapter 1

Introducing
the Historical Theology
of Wisdom Literature

INTRODUCTION

Where Is Wisdom to Be Found?

Until the 1970s, wisdom literature had been marginalized in Old Testament (Hebrew Bible) research. Even now, this continues to be true largely of sapiential texts and themes in Old Testament theologies in spite of the revitalization of theological discourse beginning in the 1980s.[1] Since the rise of modern biblical scholarship shaped by the Enlightenment, wisdom and the sages were located in the Second Temple period, where they languished, largely ignored in scholarly discourse, until the late 1960s. While the past two generations have witnessed a steady outpouring of wisdom scholarship, a comprehensive social history of the sages and their literature has yet to be written.[2] This is due in part to the difficulty of dating individual texts, largely because of the paucity of historical references in the writings themselves, to the lack of specific indications of the identity of the shapers of the tradition, and to infrequent comparisons to equivalent literature and social institutions from other adjacent cultures.[3] Analyses have been limited mostly to the delineation of conceptual views of sapiential texts placed in the writings and poetic books of the canonical and deuterocanonical literature by various groups of the shapers of the different canons.

This lack of thorough treatments of the social history of wisdom has also hindered the study and articulation of wisdom theology. While numerous theologies of individual books and parts of books have been written, the only complete theology of wisdom literature is the one I wrote in 1994.[4] Gerhard von Rad's *Wisdom in Israel* is not so much a theology as it is an introduction to some of the major themes and concepts one discovers in this literature.[5] The older study by O. S. Rankin is also more of an attempt to articulate the intellectual ideology of the sages, and not their theology.[6] In my 1994 articulation of the theology of wisdom literature, I argued that creation was the center of wisdom theology that served as a unifying factor for all of its theological themes. The present study builds on the earlier one in several ways. In addition to rehearsing the salient features of the theme of creation in the five canonical and deuterocanonical texts, this volume will go beyond the traditional sapiential corpus to include discussions of the wisdom psalms, references to the sages and scribes in nonsapiential literature, and setting this developing theology of wisdom within the context of the theologies and cultures of ancient Near Eastern wisdom and Greco-Roman philosophy, rhetoric, and school texts. Thus this study will move beyond a literary analysis that explores the major metaphors of creation in order to discuss the historical development of wisdom theology within a social-historical framework. Obviously, historical judgments about the relationship of texts and traditions will vary. But the intent of this volume is to begin the task of the social and contextual location of wisdom texts and their diverse theologies.

Creation and Wisdom in Old Testament Theologies

The lack of interest in the theology of wisdom literature is noticeable in many of the Old Testament theologies that have been written, including even most of the recent ones. Indeed, comprehensive Old Testament theologies have given only slight attention to the sages and their theological points of view. This is due to two considerations. First, the initial three wisdom texts (Proverbs, Job, and Qoheleth) do not focus either on the acts of God in history or on other typical features of Israelite theology: covenant, the election of Israel, the election of the house of David, the Jerusalem temple, prophetic judgment and salvation, and eschatology. Indeed, two of these canonical texts, Job and Qoheleth, are even opposed to the traditional affirmations of Israelite and early Jewish religious belief in, for example, the justice of God. It is not until Ben Sira toward the end of the first quarter of the second century BCE that the typical faith of salvation history, election, and Torah are integrated into sapiential theology. This does not mean that Yahweh's control of history is ignored (cf. Job 12:13–25). But the lack of any reference to redemptive history makes it all the more difficult to speak of a wisdom theology that is in any fashion Israelite. But this raises the question of why it should be unique. Second, if wisdom theology does not give expression to the typical affirmations based on the ideology of the monarchy, court prophets, and priests of Jerusalem, then where should it be located? Some have argued that wisdom, particularly in its earliest expression, is secular and has no interest in theology. However, even a cursory reading of the wisdom texts indicates that they have at their theological core the theme of creation. In general, biblical theologians have placed the importance of this theme in the Second Temple. Many Protestant interpreters have expressed little interest in this period, choosing instead to regard salvation history in the Pentateuch and Psalms and the prophetic theology as the two areas of fundamental importance that shape the formative faith of the First Temple. Protestant Old Testament theologians and historians have stereotyped the religion of the Second Temple as Jewish legalism and therefore theologically peripheral.

Writing a History of Wisdom Theology

In writing a theology (or better, theologies) of the sages, I think that the best approach involves a combination of several factors:

1. *Religionsgeschichte* (history of religions), which examines the theological views present in the wisdom literatures of other cultures of the Eastern Mediterranean world: Egypt, Mesopotamia (Sumer and Akkad), Ugarit, Aram, and the Hellenistic empires of the Ptolemies and the Seleucids. Since wisdom was an international cultural tradition, it is clear that the Israelite and early Jewish sages were affected in their theological thinking by the region in which they lived and worked.

2. The methods involved in the writing of social history, ranging from historical criticism to cultural anthropological to sociology. The various developing theologies of the sages should be placed within the ongoing social-historical matrix of Israel, early Judaism, and the eastern Mediterannean world that affected their views.

3. The literary character of myth and the metaphors used by the sages in the articulation of their theologies. Creation myths, in particular, were the common reservoir of texts used by the sages in the construction of their own theologies.

4. Finally, the relationship of wisdom theologies to others in biblical and nonbiblical texts.

The History of Religions and Old Testament Theology[7]

One of the more substantial developments in recent years has been the appropriation of the methods of the history of religions in writing theologies of the Old Testament. Traditionally, the history of religions has been more concerned with the scientific and historical description of the beliefs, rituals (including purity), concepts of holiness in regard to sacred space and time, mythic and cultic literature, and cultic personnel. Value judgments concerning the validity of religion, including beliefs and practices, for contemporary religious life are often avoided. While this avoidance of truth claims by historians of religion is denied or questioned by many scholars, theology as an articulation of the faith of the church is more concerned with the veracity and authenticity of the Hebrew Bible's beliefs about God and moral behavior for contemporary Christian communities.[8] The focus has been primarily on beliefs about the Deity, moral behavior, and the relationship of humans, the elect, and creation to God.

In addition to the use of different theoretical models, another important feature of the history of religions is to see the religion of ancient Israel and early Judaism as influenced by and similar to other religions of the ancient Near East. These similarities may be explained in a variety of ways, including cross-cultural borrowing and the sharing of a common cultural context.

The history of religions and biblical theology, however, are different disciplines and, until recently, have gone their separate ways. However, this rigorous bifurcation of the two has been challenged by Otto Eissfeldt. For him, "the religion of the Old Testament [must] be investigated by the same means with which historical scholarship otherwise works: linguistic and historical-critical mastery of the sources, and analysis of their content on the basis of an empathetic personal reliving." This methodology reveals the major themes of Israelite religion. However, Old Testament theology requires that the interpreter then must move beyond the methods of historical criticism to assess these themes by the application of Christian faith and to use them in the articulation of biblical theology. In spite of their differences, Eissfeldt argued that the two methods are a unity and that they both strive to know the same truth "by which faith is grasped."[9]

The History of Religions and Old Testament Theology:
Differences and Relationship

One should not overlook the fact that many Old Testament theologians also wrote histories of Israelite religion, and a clear demarcation between the two undertakings was not always made. However, there are important differences between them. The first is in establishing the context of the interpreter: Old Testament theology is written from the perspective of the church, while the history of religions comes out of the scientific academy. The second is purpose: Old Testament theology is written for the faith and instruction of the church, while the history of religions is written more for an academic readership. Old Testament theology as carried out by Christians seeks to establish a close relationship with the theologies of the New Testament and the church, while the history of religions does not move beyond the cultural life of ancient Israel and early Judaism. The third is judgments made: Old Testament theology presents the teachings of the Hebrew Bible to be normative or at least renders certain teachings to be theologically relevant and true, while the history of religions does not expressly articulate normative evaluations. The fourth is the nature of the Bible: Old Testament theology regards the text as inspired revelation for believing communities, while the history of religions considers it a human document to be critically evaluated in the same ways that other literatures are assessed. The fifth is the view of comparable texts: Old Testament theology deals exclusively with the biblical text and sets forth its theological affirmations, while the history of religions examines all features of material culture in Israel and the ancient Near East and has the objective of presenting both the official and popular expressions of religious life in ancient Israel. Finally, the sixth is the agreement of the identity of the writers and traditionalists: both approaches share the view that the Hebrew Bible is written by the elite, who articulate theological and religious expressions of an ideology supporting their own interests and not by social inferiors and the marginalized of ancient Israel.[10]

In spite of these fundamental differences, there remain considerable similarities between the two undertakings. In more recent years, a number of scholars, while not blurring the distinctions between the two, have sought to use the history of Israelite religion to set forth the theology of the Hebrew Bible. The most recent example of this reemergence of the combination of the goals and methods of the history of religions and biblical theology is the continuing work of Rainer Albertz.[11]

The appearance of the major outlines of Israelite religion by Albertz has led to a significant discussion about several of his major contentions. In 1995 the *Jahrbuch für biblische Theologie* included detailed replies to his work from both Old Testament theologians and historians. While many scholars voiced their criticisms about his approach and the assumptions with which he worked, many of the respondents agreed that it was important to make use of the results of the history of religions to shape Old Testament theology. The scholar must participate in both disciplines, although with different objectives defined by the purposes of each approach.[12] This view is seconded by James Barr. Near the end of his treatment of the history of religion and Old Testament theology in *The Concept of Biblical Theology*, he remarks: "the relation between biblical theology and the history of religion is and should be one of overlap and mutual enrichment. And the ultimate reason for this is that the *stuff* of which biblical theology is built is really biblical religion, or . . . those elements of biblical religion which are commended, supported and advanced by the main currents of the Bible."[13] Indeed, the history of religions provides Old Testament theology with insights and understandings that otherwise would be impossible to obtain.

The Different Objectives of the Two Methods

The fundamental difference between the two methods is that they have different objectives. The approach of *Religionsgeschichte* seeks to set forth what is intended to be a descriptive account of the development of the religion of Israel, without allowing the theological or ideological perspectives of the interpreter to enter into these texts and into other elements of material culture and to exert undue influence. While interpreters work out of their own ideological perspectives, the historian still cannot simply make up sources or ignore those not compatible to personal taste. Old Testament theology, by contrast, emerges most often out of the context of the church and seeks to determine and interpret the major beliefs of ancient Israel that may be related to the theological concerns of the present. Of course, the church is not a monolithic institution; adjustments and differences are found among various hermeneutical applications and conclusions. The chief concern of Old Testament theology is to determine what is normative for the believing community (or communities), for the method seeks to ascertain what is fundamentally true to the church in expressing its faith.[14] This requires one to make value judgments, with dogmatic interests often overruling those of the text and its context, a legitimate enterprise as long as the interpreter is honest in admitting these. The history-of-religions approach is more inclusive and seeks to set forth the many different beliefs of ancient Israel in a diachronic portrayal in interaction with the different religions and cultures of the ancient Near East and early Greco-Roman world. The value of these extrinsic, cultural beliefs and practices for the church is not addressed by most theologians, who see them as possessing little significance for theological doctrines. In addition to avoiding value judgments, historians of religion make use of history as the structure for arranging material culture, including texts, and recognize and note the diversity that exists both intrinsic and extrinsic to the biblical text and its local and more expansive cultures of the eastern Mediterranean world. The historical-critical discovery of diversity, especially in matters of faith as well as ritual and moral enactments, is one of the greatest challenges facing the church's use of the Old Testament. Finally, the history of religions is as concerned with the features of popular religions in ancient Israel and early Judaism as it is with the official religions of the nation of Israel and its major social institutions that are set forth in the biblical text deemed to be authoritative Scripture. Indeed, to write a history of Israelite religion, the historian takes into consideration both the material culture and the text of the Old Testament.[15] One is not given preference over the other. Biblical theology from the context of the church tends to privilege the official religion expressed in ideologically shaped traditions and texts.

These differences between the two disciplines have produced a tension that has continued during the past two centuries for various reasons.[16] First, the diversity of beliefs and practices results in part from the fact that the Hebrew Bible was constructed over a millennium. This is the diachronic reality of this collection of texts. Furthermore, the intrinsic differences over matters of history, faith, morality, and ritual practice are not only diachronic but also synchronic. This internal diversity militates against finding a center or unity in the theology of the Hebrew Bible. Second, the final redaction occurred late in the history of Judah. This leads to the conclusion that later editors reshaped earlier texts and traditions to support their own theologies and ideologies and to reflect their different historical and social contexts. Third, it is doubtful that scholars will ever agree on a "center" that unites the diverse biblical texts, since there is none. Any "center" derives not from the text but from the constructive imagination of the theologian, who has moved into what I call the second phase of biblical theology: the shaping of the materials into a systematic whole that may be used by contemporary theologians, who have a variety of public audiences. Fourth, some would agree that "the Old Testament is a history book," although the meaning of the term "history" is used in a variety of ways, including not only what is reconstructed to have happened[17] but also the development of traditions of faith.[18] The description of the Old Testament as a "history book" fits the chronological development of the tradition complexes of the Hebrew Bible and reflects the fact that large parts of the Hebrew Bible are narratives (e.g., the Deuteronomistic History and the Chronicler's History) that are concerned with historical developments, and yet are guided by an intrinsic commitment to particular ideological understandings that shape their discourse. Fifth, histories of Israelite religion focus on beliefs and practices of ancient Israel in the context of the ancient Near East and the eastern Mediterranean world, while the theology of the Hebrew Bible deals especially with the idea of revelation. The question of revelation, outside the efforts to describe its various understandings in disparate texts, is not an issue for historians. Sixth, the relationship of the Old Testament to the New Testament in the history-of-religions approach is shaped not by speaking of the revelation of God reaching its culmination in the New Testament and especially the Word of God in Jesus Christ, but rather by a historical, chronological, and synchronic development that moved from early Israel through the variety of Jewish communities into the early church. There is, of course, no Hegelian dialectic that leads ever upward to the advancement and perfection of the moral character and religious worth. There is some continuity between ancient Israel and early Christianity, since the earliest Christians, including Jesus, were Jews who regarded the Hebrew Bible as Scripture to explain what was transpiring in God's new acts in their time. However, for historians of religion, there is no privileging of a text, a Testament, or a religious affirmation. Seventh, Karl Barth's disdain for religion as a human means to achieve salvation and his strong emphasis on theology as the Word of God that reached its culmination in Jesus Christ as the "Word made flesh" have served to intensify this tension between the two fields. For him, "religion is the concentrated expression of human unbelief."[19] For Barth Christianity is not a religion, but rather a community formed by revelation through the Word and the engagement of faith. This means that, for dialectical theology, the history-of-religions approach to Israelite religion and early Christianity is illegitimate. The Bible rather is the revelation of God to humanity demanding a yes or no. Barth's view, in effect, dispenses with the theological importance of history and results ultimately in an intrinsic docetism that culminates in the authority of ideas extracted from their social and human embodiment, including even the incarnation.

It is my view that biblical theology may legitimately claim a role for itself as a separate discipline of inquiry only when it takes seriously and utilizes many of the features of the method of the history of religions.[20] This approach plays an important role in helping to understand the faith of ancient Israel, even if it, taken alone, does not address issues of modern concern. In this volume, however, I am interested not in writing a hermeneutical theology for the contemporary church, but rather in setting forth the contours of the theology of Israel's sages that provides the basis for the shaping of contemporary theology. In using the method of the history of religions as an entrée into Old Testament theology in general and wisdom theology in particular, I agree with those who contend that one cannot exclude pseudepigraphical texts and material culture that provide insight into the religious worlds of ancient Israelite and early Jewish sages.

METAPHORS, MYTH, AND IMAGINATION

The Role of Language in Sapiential Theology

In the crafting of their spoken and literary traditions, the sages used language to construct a mythic world, which they invited the simple to enter and there take up residence. The door to this world was wisdom. The linguistic world of the sages is created, sustained, and revitalized by the power of words, particularly metaphors of creation, providence, and wisdom. These metaphors provided the theological center of sapiential imagination expressed artistically in the narratives, sayings, instructions, and poems of the wise that were the forms into which the meaning of theology and moral instruction were placed. In the shaping of these literary forms, the sages created an esthesis of order and beauty that was to compel obedience and to endure through the generations.

Metaphors in Human Discourse

At the center of the estheses shaped by the sages in their discourses were key metaphors that engaged the imagination of their hearers and readers and led them along the path to insight into understanding and moral action.[21] Cultural anthropologists have shown that "experience . . . is a function of culture, especially in its symbol-creating activity. Here, too, the prevailing modern practice of arguing from experience to concepts is reversed. Religion is a system of culturally-embedded symbols that gives birth to . . . both the world view and the ethos—that is, the experience—of the people living in that symbolic world."[22]

I have frequently mentioned metaphor and its importance for theological imagination. Now comes the point where it is necessary to define the term. According to John Murry, metaphor is "as ultimate as speech itself, and speech as ultimate as thought," being "the instinctive and necessary act of the mind exploring reality and ordering experience."[23] Metaphors are at the conceptual core of linguistic expression that gives rise to human thinking, experience, and emotions, including perception, reason, analysis, imagination, and feeling. Humans are able to think rationally, conceptually, and imaginatively. In so doing, they possess the capacity to create systems of captivating meaning and beauty that shape, define, interpret, and draw into their poetic embrace the offerings of their social and natural worlds. Metaphor resides at the center of this process of world building but also participates in its dissolution.[24] This means that theological language is metaphorical. In a sense it has to be, since God resides beyond the sphere of human perception and sense experience. Indeed, one may speak of revelation through inspiration, dreams, visions, enthusiasm, ecstasy, meditation, and sacred words spoken and written. But, in the final analysis, each of these depends upon the psychological capacity of imagination to determine their meaning. God and the world of the Divine must ultimately be imagined on the basis of perception arising from experience, and the key to the process of imagination and meaning is metaphor.

For the sages, the ultimate object of the quest for knowledge was God, believed to be revealed in the order and workings of the world and in acts of providence both in maintaining creation and in directing human history.[25] God was imagined to be a deity of creation and sustenance whose ongoing acts were based on justice and the reinvigoration of the forces of life. The sages considered themselves responsible for developing ways for existing in the world that would enable them to live in harmony with the world and the social order, and promote well-being for themselves. They articulated the manner of prudent behavior and proper speech that in general was designed to offset as much as possible disasters that overcame the unthinking fool. Although God, of course, resided beyond human perception, the sages assumed that God was good, caring, and just, for the world contained the materials necessary for human and other creatures' survival and even enabled the wise to love, find contentment, and experience joy. And they generally assumed, save for the Job of the dialogues and Qoheleth, that God could be trusted not only to support and bless with life those who lived wisely and justly and spoke properly and well, but also to continue to revitalize the powers of life inherent in creation and history that were constantly threatened by chaos and evil that would put the cosmos into disarray and collapse the justice that was at the basis of social and individual life.

Consequently, creation in wisdom literature requires an understanding of root metaphors, the literary tradition (narrative or poetry) in which they are found, the "voice" that is heard within the tradition, and the listening audience that may enter into the linguistic world created by the tradition.[26] Finally, the vitality and meaning of these root metaphors are shaped by the sociohistorical context in which they and their interpreters exist. Meaning is construed only when root metaphors and the literary texts or speeches in which they are placed are encountered by the interpreter standing in multiple social contexts. This does not suggest that interpreters are allowed to make the texts and their root metaphors mean anything they choose. An elegant, appropriate interpretation may be judged only by other views that compete for allegiance and the status of what was real and true for the sages.

Metaphors and the Metaphorical Process

As I noted in my earlier theology, which depended largely on metaphorical renderings, among the significant results that derive from the encounter with metaphors are engagement, absurdity, and destabilization. A metaphor depicts the object it describes in a way that, when engaged and taken literally, is absurd.[27] For instance, to refer to the beginning of creation as the activity of engendering and giving birth to child Wisdom and then providence as due to her childlike play are absurd when understood literally, and yet these birth metaphors are what one finds in the elegant poem embedded in Prov. 8:22–31. To describe chaos as the personified sea or as a sea monster in the form of Leviathan, or Canaanite Lotan (Job 38–41), is equally absurd. But it is the shock of the absurd that shakes the audience out of the frame of mind of mundane existence to consider new possibilities of reality. This shock leads to the destabilization of a comfortable worldview and awakens the imagination to new insights and meaning.[28] This anomie may become intense, for the former metanarrative that has directed one's faith and life has deconstructed and no new meaning system has yet emerged to take its place.

If the hearer engages in religious discourse and is induced to reshape traditions of faith, however, metaphors may result in mimesis, in new insight into the object described. This allows for hearers to determine from their own experience something that is true in the relationship between the tenor and the vehicle. This means there is a "second shock" for the hearer, but this subsequent shock is the "shock of recognition."[29] Metaphor, then, may transform the world of the audience, including its worldview and moral values, and reshape meaning, at least to a degree.[30] Traditions incorporate the major features of what communities understand, value, and believe. David Tracy notes that root metaphors bear the heaviest weight in the conveyance of the major ideas and ideals of a culture that are transmitted in oral and written traditions.[31]

From this one may conclude that a metaphor conjoins two distinct subjects within a sentence, usually called the tenor and its vehicle.[32] The tenor is the principal subject that is conveyed by a vehicle, or secondary subject.[33] By effectuating the relationship between the two, insight into the meaning and nature of the principal subject is given. For example, folly is a prostitute, or the mouth of the fool devours the neighbor. These descriptions of folly engage the imagination in order to intimate the immorality, wayward character, and destructive power of a foolish thought or way of acting. Thus the vehicle becomes the means by which the tenor is described, understood, and given meaning. In addition, the vehicle suggests that the tenor is, but also is not, something that is real. There is not a literal equation between the two, for invariably there continues to be tension[34] between what a metaphor sets forth and what is true and false.[35] Instead, in their evocative interplay the tenor and its vehicle offer a "strategy of discourse" that destabilizes the literal meaning of a statement and offers in its place a new insight.[36] They arouse human imagination that upon reflection may lead to a fresh worldview. When perceived as true, metaphors begin to allow the listeners to reshape the tradition of faith and moral virtue for the community in which they reside.[37] The metaphors selected by Israel to tell of divine creation were not new, but rather were taken from the mythic traditions of the ancient Near East. Israel encountered these metaphors and inserted them into the literary and rhetorical expressions of their social, cultural, and religious worlds. They become, as the essence of sapiential tradition, the organizing symbols for the extended community of sages and their adherents and sustain them through the processes of memory and actualization.

Finally, for the sages, metaphors are ambiguous, since they are capable of having a surplus of meaning that rejects concrete, simple, and unilateral understanding.[38] This variety of significations means that metaphors by nature reject any one-dimensional interpretation. They instead include a range of interpretations that result from the variety of human experience and the understandings of the sapiential community in which they take root.[39] Once they lose their power to convict, they die and threaten to collapse the world of meaning they have helped to erect. When they do die, the sages are required either to craft new metaphors to reshape their tradition or to revitalize the old ones that had been lost to disuse by injecting something dramatically new.[40] For example, the metaphor of day, signifying birth and the beginning of life, is destabilized in Job 3. Day, symbolizing life, light, and enlightenment, is replaced by an abysmal darkness of approaching death, the shroud of mystery, and nonbeing that collectively become for Job in the dialogues an oppressive and onerous burden that may be escaped only through the ultimate finality of nothingness and the descent into the infernal regions of the underworld where darkness and nonexistence reign supreme. Job escapes this imprisonment only by unmasking the tyranny and lack of compassion of Yahweh, and thus begins the search for a humanism in which meaning is created by reflective sages.

Metaphors are not eternal, however, for, like living creatures, they are born, live for a time, are active in shaping the world, and then eventually die. But through imagination, new ones are created to carry on the task of the conveyance of meaning. These metaphors die normally because of a change in the cultural and social experience of the mythmakers. Thus holocaust, tyranny, exile, and changing cultural formulations lead to new theological expressions.

Metaphors and Ancient Near Eastern Myths[41]

The sages of the eastern Mediterranean world drew on formative, mythical metaphors of creation that provided the literary core of major culture myths. These myths were cosmogonic or anthropocentric and included the activities of their prominent cultural deities: Marduk and Inanna in Babylonia, Baal and Anat in Ugarit and larger Canaan, Isis and Seraphis in Egypt and Syria, and Yahweh and Asherah in Israel and early Judah. Any examination of wisdom in Old Testament and early Jewish theology should begin by focusing on these mythological metaphors that shape and provide the meaning of the theological discourse of the sage's views of the cosmos, human nature, and the world and in turn the larger features of Israel's evolving religious culture and history.

Theological metaphors are present in many genres of ancient Near Eastern literature. However, the culture myth that supports the supremacy of a particular god, his/her city and temple, and his/her chosen ruler is the most important expression of theological metaphors. Myths have to do with the origins and continuation of the cosmos and its order and of humanity and its social structure, but myths are far more interested in the continuation of the present than the explication of the past. While they may express curiosity about beginnings, they are much more concerned to continue the processes of reality that enable life and the social world of the culture to endure. There are two types of myths in the ancient Near East that Israelite and other ancient Near Eastern poets and sages appropriate: myths of origins and myths of maintenance.[42] Myths of origins tell of the beginnings of the world and of humanity and the setting forth of the orders of the natural and human life that made existence possible. In addition, myths of origins often function to define the continuing responsibilities of social institutions (temple and cult, kingship, marriage, and culture) in shaping human culture. The primary concern of these myths, which are repeated and reenacted on a regular basis in liturgy and instruction, is not to respond to innocent inquiry about origins or to legitimate the way things are in the cosmos and society, but to secure the orders of life and to relieve the anxiety of people who fear a descent into oblivion. Thus myths of maintenance rehearse and reenact the drama of the divine story in order to strengthen and secure the orders that undergird all of life and the social institutions that reflect, guard, and preserve these orders. On occasion, the two types of myths, which actually are two separate functions, are combined into one major drama (e.g., Gen. 1–3). The rigid dichotomy between cosmological and anthropological myths set forth by Claus Westermann[43] and developed by two of his students (Rainer Albertz[44] and Peter Doll[45]) is simply wrong. The metaphors of myth were used by poets and sages to shape the content and the artistry of other genres of literature.

Theological Metaphors in Wisdom Literature

The sages of Israel use four major poetic metaphors to speak of the creation of the world: fertility, artistry, word, and battle,[46] while they describe the creation of humanity with the metaphors of artistry and birth. God is the one who makes the world fertile; who uses his artistic skills in creating reality; who, through the power of spoken wisdom, Torah, and word, gives shape to reality and its intrinsic righteousness; and who, as the Divine Warrior, defeats chaos prior to establishing the cosmos. These same metaphors are used to engage the imagination of the wise in their depicting of the continuing providence of the Creator. As for the creation of humanity, God is the parent (father/mother) who fathers or gives birth to human beings, or the artisan/architect who crafts in elegant form human creatures. Metaphors in the creation myths of the ancient Near East were also the organizing features of their literary formation. Myths, at their essence, are understood as stories about the gods to explain the origins of things and to secure their continuation through the power of spoken word and sacred drama, and are the enactment of certain literary, often dramatic, movements of a tale. Key metaphors provide the major themes and means of focusing the narrative description of creation. Thus, since these myths offer a plethora of metaphors from which the sages could choose, there seems to be little doubt as to the origins of these metaphors in their symbolic constructions. The sages use them to shape and construe their own understanding of the world and its continuation.

Imagination[47]

I should emphasize that the sociocultural world produced by the imagination does not transcend the influence of its social settings and the life experiences of the world builders. All literary texts that incorporate worldviews are shaped by their contexts and the later ones of their interpreters' world. At the same time, both the creator of the symbolic world and its future interpreters are affected by their contexts to redescribe the meaning of these imaginative worlds. This is the continuing hermeneutical circle that spirals its way forward into the future until it ultimately collapses through its loss of the power to convince and convict.

The sages engaged in imagination and perception to fashion, organize, and classify the images they formed. These images, placed into the rhetorical structures of sapiential texts, issued from and gave expression to the social experiences and institutions of their own world. These representations and their interpretations sculpted an esthesis that possessed and conveyed the teachings of the sages, and through their rhetorical forms the sages evoked the imaginations of their students, who thereby came to understand and then act on the basis of their forms and various construals.

The sages imagine God by reference to common objects that are attainable to ordinary perception. The sages do not often name God through specific epithets composed of metaphors, but in their description of divine character and especially activity they allude to specific roles common to Israelite and Jewish society as ways of molding their theological discourse about the nature and activity of the transcendent Deity hidden from direct observation or experience. These metaphors also serve as the lenses through which to imagine the character and activity of God, the relationship of the Deity to the world, and the connection of God to human beings and their social reality. The sages' rendering of God is a constructive, nonreferential enterprise. This simply means that God is active in the world of sapiential imagination, but at the same time remains outside this world, existing in an unknown, impenetrable sphere. This is the point at which idolatry or self-serving ideology should be avoided, but rarely is.

Metaphor, Imagination, and the Theology of the Sages: Conclusion

In the postmodern era, history and historians have been greatly criticized by postmodernists, who have denied the existence of objectivity and the commonality of epistemology based on reason and empiricism. If postmodernists are correct, then historians are engaged in illusory quests that are nothing more than the writing down of their own subjective notions. I still remain a historian and claim that history is a pursuit that may be undertaken to discover data and make plausible arguments that lead to the reconstructions of times, events, peoples, and cultures that are past. The data that allow this process of historiography to transpire are not created by the minds of the inquirer. In addition, historical plausibility is not an impossible goal to reach. History is the reconstruction of people, events, and times from the past by the rigorous application of scientific methods to documents and other elements of material culture that testify to the peoples and cultures of the past. This does not mean that the historian is freed totally from the influences of his bias and ideology. However, the claim for history is that the one analyzing cultural and intellectual data may construe them in ways that make sense in their respective contexts. And these construals are offered for critical response by others representing a broad cultural and ethnic spectrum. This allowance of intensive review and open criticism is one of the safeguards of modern historiography.

While it is important to trace the history of the tradition of wisdom and its theology through the centuries, one also needs to recognize that the language of the sages was metaphorical and the content was creation. I have continued to find helpful the twin metaphors of the Dionysian dance and the Apollonian vision.[48] While the sages searched for and even sought to create a harmonious order within the cosmos, society, and human behavior, this order was not static, but rather dynamic. This means that order was not created once and for all, but rather continued to change. Once these cultural metaphors are identified in the literature and material data and discussed, biblical theologians may then engage in articulation of a discursive presentation of this faith. Thus to capture the duality of creation and, later, history within the wisdom tradition is to recognize the metaphors for God, humanity, and the world in the literature that are located within the dominant myths of each culture. The rhetoric of the sages not only enhances the elegance of their linguistic expression, but also stimulates the imagination that sustains and continues to shape a world of beauty, justice, and meaning.

Chapter 2

Salvation History, Covenant, Creation, and Providence

INTRODUCTION

Creation, providence, and wisdom are the salient themes of wisdom theology.[1] Since the origins of modern biblical theology in the Reformation, however, these themes have often have been the stepchildren of salvation history, election, and covenant. For example, in the early work of the Old Testament theologian Gerhard von Rad, creation, providence, and wisdom received a soteriological interpretation in order to allow wisdom even a secondary place in his theology.[2]

The subordinate status of creation, providence, and wisdom in many of the biblical theologies of the twentieth century was due largely to four related factors. First, Karl Barth's dominance in European and American theological thought in the 1940s and 1950s led to the prominence of soteriology and special revelation, which found its principal expression in the incarnation.[3] The primary danger of the theology of creation and providence and religion based on human epistemology, not incidentally the two fundamental themes found in wisdom literature, was the possibility of their leading to a natural theology, an anathema in Barth's theology of revelation. Second, several important twentieth-century theologians of the Hebrew Bible prior to 1970, especially those in America, argued that what was

15

unique in the ancient Near East and therefore valid in Old Testament theology was its emphasis on history in general and the saving acts of God in history in particular. The acts of the gods in the ancient Near East were narrated in myths, particularly those having to do with the origins of reality, while Israel spoke of history and gave only limited consideration to the secondary theme of creation, providence in the guidance of the cosmos, and wisdom that is devoid of salvation history until the deuterocanonical literature was written much later. These themes were shared by other cultures in the ancient Near East, and thus did not point to the unique theology of the Hebrew Bible. This view of salvation history was combined with Palestinian archaeology in American scholarship, especially in the work of G. Ernest Wright, to shape a theology of salvation in history. Third, Old Testament theology was often differentiated from the history of Israelite tradition. This meant that important scholars who considered salvation history as unique in the ancient world disregarded parallels to myth, cosmic renewal, and wisdom in the literatures of Egypt and Mesopotamia and therefore obscured Israel's own contribution to faith. Fourth, and most importantly for this investigation, the theology of wisdom literature is strongly shaped by creation, providence, and wisdom.[4] This tended to marginalize wisdom literature in articulations of Old Testament theology. For example, creation theology was not considered to be a significant theological theme in biblical theology until more recently. As a consequence wisdom was regarded as an interloper in biblical theology, appearing toward the latter end of this form of faith and intellectual inquiry.

There is no need to rehearse the development of the first three factors or to describe their eventual collapse in theological analysis in any detail, for they are well known. First, while Barthian theology has continued to utter its voice through the revised theology of Neo-Barthians, it has lost its dominant theological position in contemporary theology. Neoliberalism, womanism, feminism, liberation, postcolonialism, and postmodernism, to name some of the newer approaches, not only rival but also have often superseded the once proud dominance of neo-orthodoxy. Second, numerous studies, including Bertil Albrektson's *History and the Gods*,[5] have demonstrated that the major cultures of the ancient Near East also viewed history as directed by their gods. This means, then, that instead of Israel's view of God acting in history as unique, it represented a common perspective in the other cultures of the ancient Near East as well. The assumed superiority of Judaism and Christianity began to subside as a wealth of data from the eastern Mediterranean world pointed to many common religious affirmations and practices. Third, the approach of the history of religions to the study of ancient Israel and early Judaism has regained methodological prominence in some of the more recent theologies of the Hebrew Bible. Thus the ancient Near Eastern and Greco-Roman influence on and parallels with Israelite and Jewish religious thinking, especially in the areas of creation mythology, providence, and wisdom, have been demonstrated time and again in the histories of religion of this part of the globe and thus have come to be recognized as important in theological formulations, not only in the Bible but also in many other religions. Fourth, and most significantly, the history of religions has enabled biblical theologies to take into consideration the major role of creation theology, providence, and wisdom in the faith of the Hebrew Bible. This, in turn, has led to providing a place of importance for wisdom literature in Old Testament theology, especially since the theology of the three canonical and two deuterocanonical wisdom texts give priority to these three related themes.

THE PRIMACY OF HISTORY OVER CREATION

Since the 1930s, the themes of creation (involving both origins and providential renewal of the cosmos) have been subordinated to those of covenant and saving history in most Old Testament theologies. Thus most Old Testament theologians have either ignored or made less of creation in the writing of their theologies.

Gerhard von Rad

As the most prominent Old Testament scholar of the twentieth century, Gerhard von Rad placed his indelible stamp on Old Testament theology that continues to have great importance. Strongly influenced by Barth,[6] von Rad subordinated creation theology to saving history in his provocative essay published in 1936. He argued in this programmatic essay: "The Yahwistic faith of the Old Testament is a faith based on the notion of election, and therefore primarily concerned with redemption."[7] Subsequently, von Rad viewed Israel's God as the one who acted redemptively in history on its behalf, from election to statehood to eschatology. At the same time, he attributed the conceptions of covenant, law, and creation to the later development of an originally solitary, historical faith, largely due to their absence in what he determined was the early credo of Deut. 26:5–9. Indeed, he noted that these themes were not incorporated into the creedal faith until the fifth century BCE (Neh. 9). But if salvation history, or "God's Mighty Acts," to use the language of G. Ernest Wright,[8] is the major focus of Israelite faith, what are we to do with wisdom literature that, previous to the deuterocanonical book of Ben Sira in the early second century BCE, makes no mention of this theology of redemption in history?

As early as 1936, von Rad recognized that wisdom literature presented a different theological emphasis: "A quite different strand of religious influence entered the Yahwistic faith in the form of wisdom-lore, a highly rationalised mode of speculation concerning the divine economy in this world which we may regard as being of Egyptian origin. At this point we were faced with unequivocal, self-justified statements of belief concerning the creation."[9] According to von Rad, however, a great many safeguards against this independent faith in creation and natural theology had to be established by the theologies of ancient Israelite and Jewish writers, especially in speaking of salvation history, before this wisdom speculation could be developed.[10]

According to von Rad, Deutero-Isaiah represents the most important reflection in the Hebrew Bible on creation faith, while election is understood in terms of the divine creation of Israel (see the verbs "create" and "redeem" that are associated in Isa. 43:1; 44:21, 24; 46:3; 54:5). Von Rad's soteriological understanding of creation is key to his thought. Only Psalms 19 and 104:8 do not find themselves positioned in this salvific understanding (cf. also Job 38–41). They instead witness to the power of God in the making of reality, and thus they speak of creation standing alone as a theological tradition.[11] However, these two psalms are on the periphery of the Old Testament, precisely because they do not speak of the soteriological function of creation. Von Rad thought that they likely derived from a foreign origin.

In his *Old Testament Theology*, von Rad argued that experiential (earlier) wisdom and even theological (later) wisdom stood on the periphery of Old Testament theology.[12] Proverbs was secular and handled theological themes in a rather limited way. This book sets forth the parameters of the orders by which human life is supported and to which humans are responsible. The name Yahweh in the sayings results from a later theologizing of experiential wisdom. According to von Rad, the transition to statehood eventually led to a Solomonic enlightenment. During this period of royal secularization, the human achieved primary importance in the world. This led to the ethos that promoted early, secular wisdom. Von Rad saw in the postexilic period[13] that wisdom sought to establish a connection between the creation that it confronted and the divine revelation that it received, something that eventuated in the reflective work of Jesus Ben Sira (Sir. 24; cf. Wis. 7–9). Thus wisdom became a primeval revelation to humanity, and engaged in self-praise.[14] This occurred during the late postexilic period when the interest in saving history had waned in some traditional circles due to the experience of Babylonian captivity. While he did not date Proverbs 8 to a preexilic period, he thought that its theme of creation did contain older elements.[15] Unlike Hans-Heinrich Schmid, von Rad did not think that the biblical sages developed the concept of an all-embracing world order; rather he contended that the wise observed and spoke of general ordinances that regulate natural and social phenomena.

Von Rad's *Wisdom in Israel* indicates a shift in his thinking when he pointed to the importance of creation (including the theology of providence in revitalizing the cosmos) in wisdom theology (see especially Job 38–41; cf. 9:2–3). In the last volume he wrote, von Rad even regarded creation as a theological doctrine that is parallel or perhaps an alternative to saving history. Faith in God the Creator came to be seen as the framework and foundation for talk about God, the world, Israel, and the individual. Creation became revelatory to those who trusted in it. Creation may be trusted because it was viewed as very good (Gen. 1:31). In contrast to the cult and the various canonical views of salvation history, wisdom's soteriology was based not on human agency or on God's acts of salvation effectuated by his entrance into history, but on the features inherent in creation itself. Practical wisdom was not stimulated by divine actions in history, but rather by the basic questions of humankind. How was one to live both actively and passively within the environment of the world so as to be successful? Later wisdom's view of the world called to humanity to listen. And what humans are to hear is the offer of salvation: life in abundance, but not the liberation of salvation history. Humans are to learn to trust the creation, its orders, and the Creator who established them and through them offers life.[16]

Von Rad recognized that many Old Testament texts mention the theme of creation in the Hebrew Bible, but it is not a topic that stands on its own merits. It is always subordinated to the interests and content of the doctrine of redemption. The Hebrew Bible even gives a "soteriological interpretation" to the doctrine of creation. However, "the doctrine of creation never attained to the stature of a relevant, independent doctrine."[17] Even in Second Isaiah, where the theology of creation appears frequently, creation and salvation are in essence one act of the universal redemptive purposes of God. This does not necessarily mean that creation was a late idea in Israel, since creation mythology in Canaan was well known in the Late Bronze Age, but it does mean that its theological importance in the Hebrew Bible derived only from its relationship to soteriology.

He noted that the ancient credo does not refer to creation theology (Deut. 26:5–9). Thus von Rad argued that creation is not a doctrine to be confessed, but rather a reality to be assumed, for it precedes the saving history. The Yahwistic (J) portions of Genesis 1–11 used its creation narrative as a preface to the history of redemption in which Abram and his offspring (Gen. 12:1–3) were called to be the conduit for the divine salvation of all the nations. This linkage is J's specific theological contribution, and von Rad doubted that J had any Israelite predecessors here. Instead, the Yahwist was responsible for bringing together the traditions of creation, primeval history, and the flood and linking these to the call of the ancestors.[18]

What von Rad argued about the primal history in J also pertained to creation in the rest of the Hebrew Bible until the very late books written in and after the exile. These themes of salvation history and creation were irreconcilable in their attempts to derive divine knowledge. The first assumes direct revelation through history, while the second is more indirect in gaining theological understanding through natural revelation. Creation especially became an important theological theme in hymns, wisdom literature, and Second Isaiah, texts that were late compositions from the exilic and postexilic periods. At a time when the earliest faith was thought to be the most important expression of belief, a view undoubtedly shaped by Romanticism, this meant that creation's late integration into the faith of the Old Testament pointed to its secondary status.

In his *Theology*, von Rad noted several new emphases about creation in these late texts. For example, he argued that history and creation were especially linked together in Deutero-Isaiah (e.g., Isa. 51:9–10) and the Psalter. In the Psalms he noted that the wondrous quality of creation issued forth in praise (Pss. 19; 145:10; 89:5; cf. Isa. 42:10–12). In a 1964 essay he concluded, "As the Hebrews saw it, man's situation in the world is thus a quite remarkable one: he lives within a created order from which ascends an unending hymn of praise, yet he himself hears nothing of it. He is rather in the position of Job, reasoning with God and at odds with him, yet needing only to be told that already at the time when God set about creating the world, the heavenly beings shouted for joy. He must be taught, as if he were blind and deaf, that he lives in a world which could be revealed to him, a world indeed in which, according to the remarkable teaching of Prov. 8, he is himself enfolded in the self-revealing secret of the created order."[19]

Evaluation

When creation is removed from the articles of Israelite faith in the so-called credo, or regarded to be of secondary importance, then major problems ensue. One of these is the negation of the importance of any theological contribution of many Old Testament texts, including wisdom literature, to the continuing formulation of the Old Testament from the beginning of the nation to the apocalyptic vision. Many traditions, including wisdom, are marginalized theologically.

Von Rad's analysis stands or falls on the legitimacy of his argument that Deut. 26:5–9 (= Deut. 6:10–13) was the Old Testament's earliest credo. Yet it is not possible to isolate these verses form-critically and then to conclude they formed the earliest creed. I submit they are more of a summary of the faith of Israel present in Deuteronomy and the Deuteronomistic History, an articulation that began in the eighth century BCE. His position privileges Deuteronomic texts, religion, and faith to the detriment of many other texts.

THE DIALECTIC OF HISTORY AND CREATION

Claus Westermann

Other theologians prefer to characterize Old Testament faith as the dialectic of history and creation. This provides a much more prominent theological position to creation, one equal to and independent of salvation history. Von Rad's colleague for many years at Heidelberg, Claus Westermann, sets forth an integrating dialectic between divine blessing (creation) and saving history that forms the structure of his theology.[20] Even so, he concludes that the two themes cannot be clearly divided. He notes that the Hebrew Bible continues to "break through the dividing line between these two realms."[21] For example, when God comes to save, the realm of nature responds, including the quaking of the earth or the crossing of the Red Sea. Saving history originates in the compassion of God who encounters his people, Israel, in history as a merciful Deity and then opens dialogue with them in order to become their God and to shape their destiny. With the exception of wisdom literature, all other sections of the Hebrew Bible speak of this memory of the saving God of history. Since this encounter goes back to the beginning of Israel's history, Yahweh continues to be Israel's savior. These saving deeds are actualized anew and in different ways to address changing situations.

Westermann notes that in both the beginning of time in primeval history and in the end of time with apocalyptic these saving deeds are extended universally to include all humanity and all other creatures. Thus salvation is an original design of human existence from primeval times. Westermann argues that the events of the primal history take on a fixed sequence: Israel's need, their summons from this need, their hearing, and their response that, if accepted by God, leads to their salvation. Israel's "election" (*bōrē'*, ברא) eventually results from their confession and proclamation of these divine acts of salvation (Deut. 7:6–8). But it is the totality of these acts, not simply election, that is central to the life of humanity in general and Israel in particular. This is also true of covenant (*běrît*, ברית). In the final analysis, it is the collation of divine actions of God's saving grace, not covenant, that is determinative for Old Testament faith. According to Westermann, covenant is a Deuteronomic creation that defined Israel's relationship with God as static, not active. In following von Rad, Westermann contends that the historical creed in Deut. 26:5–9 speaks of the whole of God's continuing acts of salvation, not his individual acts that are simply pieced together. It was not until the development of Deuteronomic theology that the divine revelation at Mount Sinai and the giving of the Torah transformed the saving event into "a condition, i.e., the continuing covenantal relationship."[22] Westermann's and von Rad's Lutheran dichotomy of grace and law becomes clearly exposed in this view.

Westermann differs from von Rad in establishing a dialectic of divine blessing, grounded in creation, with God's saving acts in history. For Westermann, blessing (or more concretely stated, creation) becomes an equally significant theological theme in the Hebrew Bible, even if it is not an object of confession. Saving acts continue to occur in history in order to effectuate salvation, even as blessing is a durative action that undergirds salvation and enhances life. Creation is neither the beginning of history nor the act of God that initiates history.[23]

According to Westermann, there are two traditions of creation: the creation of humanity (Gen. 2:4b–3:24), the older of the two, and the creation of the cosmos (1:1–2:4a). A religion that is only soteriological tends to ignore the human dimensions of birth, life, and death while blessing perpetuates the vital forces and stages of human life and indeed all of creation. The creation of the world also means that all things are in the hands of God, including the cosmos, nature, humanity, and God's people.[24]

Westermann argues that humanity understood the world as a whole, in spite of the fact that only a small part of it could be perceived by the senses. In speaking of the whole, Israel came to understand God as the one who was responsible for what happens from the beginning to the end of time and in every sphere of life, including the nations. The "new heaven and new earth" of apocalyptic corresponds to the creation of heaven and earth in the beginning of time. Thus one finds in creation theology the development of universalism, especially in the primeval history and in apocalyptic. Israel learned to understand God and its own purposes beyond the boundaries of its particularity. Thus God became the Lord of both universal history and the cosmos.[25] Creation continues in the Hebrew Bible to be related to the blessing activity of the Creator (see especially P). Blessing is given to the living creatures of the world during primal creation and continues to sustain life into the future. God's blessing was universal and served to preserve the well-being of all life. Divine blessing empowered the movement of the human generations through time and space in the continuing cycles of life.

Evaluation

This dualistic understanding of Old Testament theology, in which both creation and history played a substantial role, leads to the inclusion of all of the Hebrew Bible. This approach also provides an important theological place for the wisdom literature, since its theology of creation became a substantial part of ancient Israel's faith. One questionable facet is that Westermann still tends to make creation theologically less important than salvation history for Israelite faith.

COVENANT AND CREATION

Walther Eichrodt

Many Old Testament theologians have contended that central to Israel's faith was Yahweh's establishment of a covenant, not only with Israel, but also with the entire world, including its people and the inhabited cosmos. This covenant provided continuity to the theme of the divine covenant with Israel and the early church.

The theology of Walther Eichrodt was significantly influenced by his colleague in Basel, Karl Barth. Eichrodt's theology was the first important Old Testament theology to appear after Barth's epoch-making work, the *Epistle to the Romans*, appeared in 1919, only a short time following the horrors of trench warfare and human slaughter produced by advanced implements of war.[26] The Great War decimated liberalism's view, grounded in Hegel, that humans were progressing toward an increasingly higher level of morality. This uncompromising faith in progress suffered a mortal blow in the Great War and the Great Depression that followed in 1929. Eichrodt published his theology in three volumes that appeared in 1933–1939, the same time that the Western world had plunged into the depths of devastating economic depression. National Socialism was one of the extreme ideologies that took advantage of the despair in Europe, and, through the maniacal leadership of Adolf Hitler, it increased in strength and eventually assumed totalitarian power in Germany from 1933 through 1945. Teaching and writing in neutral Switzerland, Eichrodt, a clergyman of the Reformed Church, as was his colleague Barth, opposed National Socialism and sought to provide hope for the future by writing a theology that emerged out of the conception of the sovereignty of God.

Arguing against the developmental approach of historical criticism and rationalistic individualism, Eichrodt sought to find the constant, normative center of Old Testament theology that would give structure to what he thought was at the heart of the teaching of the Old Testament: the kingship of God and his entrance into human history. This integrating center he found in the theme of the covenant, both between God and Israel and between God and the world of creation and humanity. Eichrodt regarded covenant as "a convenient symbol for an assurance much wider in scope and controlling the formation of the national faith at its deepest level, without which Israel would not be Israel."[27] The covenant was both interactional and bilateral in that it involved the sovereignty of God and the obedience of human beings. He argued that creation was the work of the God of the covenant. Even the world (cosmology and creation) was not independent from God, but rather a created domain under divine providence. Thus Eichrodt articulated not only a covenant of God with Israel, but also gave a covenantal understanding to the relationship between God and the world. This meant that the world was placed under the sovereignty and direction of divine will and was not subject to the control of human use and abuse. In spite of his best efforts to include the wisdom texts within this rubric, covenant in effect ruled out this literature for any authentic role in the construction of Old Testament theology.[28]

Evaluation

The preceding theologians, insightful and provocative as their presentations may have been, do not present an adequate avenue for wisdom literature's entrée into Old Testament theology. Certainly, the sages spoke of the sovereignty of God and his control of history and the cosmos through the principle of retribution, but not of salvific acts (until Ben Sira). In addition, the wise men and women of Israel and Judah regarded Yahweh as the creator of humanity and, aided by Woman Wisdom, of the cosmos. Even the international scope of wisdom provides insight into God's relationship to the nations. However, missing in the writings of the canonical wisdom texts is the key theme of covenant. A theology based on covenant excludes these writings from Old Testament theology, and thus they are lost to the historical theology of wisdom and to contemporary hermeneutical reflection.

CREATION AND CANON

Brevard Childs

Since 1979, one theological consideration has been to give primary emphasis to the final form of both a canonical book and the canon as a whole. The canonical form has interpretive and authoritative precedence over the earlier stages of the redaction of the book. This approach has been developed by the prodigious theological books of Brevard Childs,[29] who was heavily influenced by the *Church Dogmatics* of Barth. However, Childs has insisted that the canonical approach is not a method with the proscription of certain steps and principles. Childs notes that the canonical process was in essence a hermeneutical one: bearers of tradition and their communities of faith transmitted the traditions that came to form the Hebrew Bible and the New Testament. The final decisions about which books eventually entered into the canon and the stabilization of the consonantal texts were also hermeneutical in nature. "Canon consciousness" involved the transmission and formation of books, their entrance into the collection of Scripture, and the stabilization of the consonantal text. This points to tradition bearers who were aware that they were shaping literature for present and future communities of faith that would affect the belief and practice of future generations. The canonical process is heavily theological and is not shaped by sociopolitical forces at work in the life of those in the community of faith who handed down the literature. This means that the canonical text is an authoritative one that is shaped for the later church. The Scripture is the theological context in which all valid theological work of the church is carried forth.[30]

Childs argues that the biblical texts leave traces of a canonical process at work in the shaping of the collection of texts, and he spends some time in pointing to textual indications of this process. This process also provided guidelines for interpretation of Scripture and earlier traditions by later communities of faith. For example, the book of Deuteronomy, written in the last years of the monarchy, provided the canonical means by which to interpret the laws of the Pentateuch.

Childs is not content to write only an Old Testament theology. Instead, he prefers to work out the major elements of a biblical theology, emphasizing that the New Testament does not destroy or replace the Old. The witness of the Old Testament, while understood as promise and not fulfillment, continues to utter its voice to the contemporary church. For Childs, biblical theology is not simply located in the New Testament's use of the Old. The Old Testament continues to have its own integrity and should "be heard on its own terms."[31] Thus the task of biblical theology is to reflect on both the Old and the New Testaments. The New Testament is something that is new, for it proclaims "the redemptive intervention of God in Jesus Christ." Thus the New Testament tends to approach the Old in terms of this new event and therefore assumes theological priority over the Old Testament for the faith of the church. Biblical theology has as one of its objectives the understanding of the variety of voices in the Bible, and yet also to see them collectively as "a witness to the one Lord Jesus Christ."[32] The discrete witnesses of both texts are not locked in the past, but continue to confront believing communities in the present. When it comes to contemporary theology and biblical theology, Childs encourages systematic theologians to be more biblical and biblical theologians to be more systematic, not simply in the structuring of their theological themes, but also in addressing the demands of faith for the contemporary church.

Childs follows closely the major view of von Rad that Israel's earliest faith was redemptive theology that historically began with the exodus from Egypt. Creation was a secondary element that developed later as a dimension of Israelite faith. However, Childs contends that while this is true historically, it is not true canonically, for the shaping of the corpus begins with creation. Childs notes that the beginning of history (Gen. 1–11) does not start with Israel (Gen. 12–50), but rather with "the preparation of the stage for world history."[33] While noting the difficulties entailed by efforts to set forth the relationship between the Yahwist and Priestly sources, Childs argues that the development of creation theology is not simply due to the ancient Near Eastern sources. The concern of the

Old Testament theologian should be to uncover the various forms of the tradition of creation in the Hebrew Bible.

However, Childs does not probe the sapiential texts for their theological understanding and contribution to the task at hand. This represents the greatest weakness of his work, for he simply restates von Rad's major positions articulated in his *Wisdom in Israel*, which is not a theology of the sages. Furthermore, Childs's theology comes under heavy criticism from many circles for his confusing definition of "canon," "canonical approach," and "believing community," and for his failure to include Judaism and history in his theological work.[34] Furthermore, he is not successful, in my judgment, in trying to adjudicate between the three major canons of Catholicism, Judaism, and Protestantism that differ in the collection of books and in the order of their arrangement. In my judgment, these are the major weaknesses of a book that attempts to make canon a theological category of primary importance in divine revelation.[35]

Evaluation

I shall not rehearse the major criticisms of canonical theology, since I have conveniently summarized these in my *Collapse of History*. In spite of the fact that his theologies are beset with several inherent weaknesses, Childs's canonical approach does give an important place to creation theology, especially when looking at the canonical ordering of the Old Testament and the fact that it begins with two rather different creation accounts in Genesis 1–2. However, the rather cursory look at the contribution of the sages to the theme of creation gives this literature only limited value in the consideration of the theology of Israelite and Jewish wisdom literature. Hence the strength of his approach also has become its weakness through turning a deaf ear to the voice of wisdom, which also speaks from the context of the canon.

CREATION AND HISTORY (HISTORY OF RELIGIONS)

Erhard Gerstenberger

In his *Theologies in the Old Testament* Erhard Gerstenberger uses the approach of the history of religions in tracing out the major theological elements in the Old Testament. He makes clear the diversity of theological views that emerge from the changing sociohistorical contexts through which Israel lived. He outlines, then, these developing Old Testament theologies in his understanding of the major sociohistorical periods in Israel: the family and clan, the village and small towns, the tribal alliances, the monarchical state, and finally the confessional and parochial communities.

When he comes to the Second Temple, Gerstenberger examines the faith community of "Israel" following the two exiles. By the fifth century BCE, the Torah was shaped into its final form, followed by the canonization of the prophets approximately at the beginning of the second century BCE. While he does not develop this point, the formation of the Torah led to its identification with wisdom in certain psalms (1, 19, and 119) and in Ben Sira. Now the commandments and the salvific narratives are written down and eventually become the basis for a scribal religion. In addition, monotheism develops in its full form, allowing "Israel" to worship Yahweh in a foreign land and to negate the existence of other deities (cf. the wisdom texts, including Wis. 13–15).

With the exiles in Babylon, the Jews began to encounter mythologies that affected their religion, including those that had to do with creation. Especially important was the Babylonian god Marduk's defeat of Tiamat, the personification of chaos. Following the death of Tiamat, Marduk creates the world, a mythological narrative that is reflected in the Bible (těhôm, תהום, possibly linguistically related to Tiamat; Gen. 1:1ff.; Pss. 18, 77, 104, 114; Isa. 52:7–8). Yahweh, the supreme Deity, created both the cosmos and humanity (Job 38:4–11 and Ps. 8). Images of the defeat of chaos are found in the Yahweh speeches in Job 38:1–42:6. This use of ancient Near Eastern creation images in Job, among other sapiential texts, points to the international character of wisdom theology.

Thus, from Gerstenberger's theologies, one discovers the metaphors of Yahweh as a fertility deity, a storm god, a divine warrior, king, the giver of the law, the conqueror of chaos, and the one God. These metaphors shape the theology of the sages that centers on the creation of the cosmos and humanity and divine providence that establishes and maintains righteousness in the world. While well argued and carefully developed, Gerstenberg's treatment of wisdom is rather limited. One does not learn how he would see the development of wisdom and its theological expressions within this social history.[36]

Evaluation

A number of important scholars have recently combined the history of religions with biblical theology to shape their presentation of the faith of ancient Israel and early Judaism. This revival of the history of religions as an entrée into the religious world of Israel should have allowed a substantial place for the depiction of the social roles of scribes and sages, together with their creation theology in regard to the periods of Israelite religion. However, for whatever reasons, these theologies provide only cursory looks at wisdom theology.

OLD TESTAMENT THEOLOGY AS CREATION THEOLOGY

H.-H. Schmid[37]

Several scholars have argued for the primacy of creation (and providence) in Old Testament theology.[38] In doing so, they provide a striking alternative to the emphasis usually placed on salvation history. Among these is H.-H. Schmid. In 1974 Schmid, using a history-of-religions approach, asserted: "The concept of creation has been a topic rather quietly discussed in the theology of the last ten years."

At the time many scholars held that creation was of secondary rank to soteriology. Whoever wished to give creation theology a higher rank was viewed as attempting to set forth a natural theology, which, since Barth, was not deemed Christian.

Schmid noted that many earlier biblical theologians tended to regard creation as chronologically late and theologically secondary. By contrast, Schmid held that creation faith, derived from the concept of "order" (defined as "righteousness") present in ancient Near Eastern religions, forms the central theme of biblical theology, elevated even above the understanding of saving history. The specific formations of Israelite features of Old Testament theology are seen as "transformations of universal human presuppositions of thought and therefore as solutions—possibly specific solutions—to basic universal problems." For Schmid there is no ancient Near Eastern culture that does not speak in various ways through the medium of several literary forms about creation (myth, hymn, didactic narrative, and saying). But it is especially ancient Near Eastern myth that provides the form and content by which creation theology is expressed. Schmid offers the important insight that myth has to do not only with the continuing empowerment of nature, but also with the foundation and legitimizing empowerment of the state.[39] Schmid notes that these features are present in wisdom literature, although he does not provide a full articulation of its particular views. According to Schmid, "History is understood as the fulfillment of creation and the production of the order of creation."[40] "Creation faith, which means the faith that sustains and has created the world with its various orders, is not a marginal theme of biblical theology, but rather for all intents and purposes its essential theme."[41] For Schmid, then, creation and universal order comprise the horizon of biblical theology, not salvation history.[42]

Evaluation

Schmid's strong points are, first, his recognition of the theological value of creation theology, perhaps as early as the beginning of the united monarchy. Second, his use of the history-of-religions method allows him to position Israel's creation theology in the context of the ancient Near East. Third, his understanding of creation as a just order permeating the cosmos and social life provides an ethical content to the cosmos, and human society is to actualize this order in its institutions and in the conduct of individual behavior. Fourth, he recognizes that the order of creation was used to legitimize and empower the state. Fifth, wisdom theology is thus given an authentic place in Old Testament theology.

CREATION AND THE GRAMMAR OF FAITH

Walter Brueggemann

Walter Brueggemann approaches Old Testament creation theology by a "grammar of faith," with special interest on construing God through important verbs. He goes a step further than von Rad in including creation along with other expressions of divine activity as part of "Israel's core testimony."[43] Even so, he concludes that creation faith "does not arrive at anything like a doctrine of creation."[44] There is no doctrine or system of creation, but rather an interpretation that affirms Yahweh to be the creator. Instead, creation faith is part of the testimony of the believing community to its God who has saved them and entered into covenant with them. Drawing on the theology of imagination, Brueggemann refers to covenant as an "imaginative construal."[45] He understands the two themes of creation and covenant as belonging to what he construes to be a "contractual theology."[46] In creation theology, there is the belief that the world is ordered and governed, whereas in the covenant understanding one discovers a political metaphor for the rule of law, coherence, and order in life. Thus the two elements join together to form the essence of Old Testament theology. This understanding of creation was co-opted by royal dynasties that used it for legitimizing and sustaining their ideology and propaganda.[47] Hence it is a theology that is particularly dangerous, if used inappropriately by tyrants seeking to control the world and human beings by referring to the political system they rule as the embodiment of divine order. Subsequently, a counter-theology was elaborated by prophets and others who demanded justice for all, including especially the marginalized poor.

Overall, Israel understood creation theology as eliciting the power and grace of Yahweh as creator within the context of the covenant. In addition, creation witnessed to Yahweh as creator, an affirmation and praise that occurred most likely in the context of worship. Furthermore, Israel's theology of creation had ethical demands that allow the ongoing existence of the community of faith. For Israel, God was discovered not simply in the mighty acts of salvation history, but also in the processes of creation that continue from the past into the future. God was also the God of fertility whose blessings brought about the fructification of the world, making life possible in all of its dimensions.

Evaluation

Brueggemann's theology provides an important place for creation in the comprehensive scheme of Old Testament theology. He builds on earlier approaches in pointing to the significance this theme possesses, and he shapes a theology that allows for disparate, even contradictory, voices to speak. His metaphors for God are expressed in divine names, roles, and activities, thus allowing for the recognition that God-talk is not literal, either in the Bible or in the present. His metaphorical schematic shaped by the image of the courtroom allows for various "testimonies" and "counter-testimonies" to be expressed, without negating or relegating to the realm of unimportance the diversity of theological views to be expressed and heard.

CONCLUSION AND SUMMARY

By way of summary, it is clear that, even when creation is given an important place in the theology of the canonical writings of the Hebrew Bible, wisdom literature and its teachings are rarely granted any substantial role in expressing the various understandings of this theological theme. The theology of Schmid provides an important basis for understanding wisdom theology, while Brueggemann's grammar of faith (earlier called "word theology") assists in understanding the role of language in theological expression, including that of the sages. Finally, the history-of-religions approach opens many doors to the social world as a major contribution to theological thinking. Overall, then, for voices of the sages to be heard in the articulation of Old Testament theology there must be, first of all, recognition of the important place of creation. Once this view is recognized, the sages of Israel and early Judaism may be offered a place at the table of theological discourse.

WISDOM IN OLD TESTAMENT THEOLOGY: THE FORGING OF A DEFINITION[48]

The meaning of the term "wisdom" (*ḥokmâ*, חכמה)[49] is important to determine before writing a theology of the faith and practice of the sages. If one focuses on the meaning and use of the noun *ḥokmâ* and its verbal, nominative, and plural forms: *ḥākam*, *ḥākām*, and *ḥŏkmôt*, one discovers three general features of this root (*ḥkm*) in sapiential literature.[50] First, wisdom is a body of knowledge, a tradition that sets forth an understanding of God, the world and nature, humanity, and human society. Eventually, in the Second Temple period, wisdom was equated with Torah, in particular laws that deal with human behavior and responsibility. This body of knowledge contained social, theological, and ethical features that, on occasion, were distinctive when compared to other traditions, especially those of the prophets and the priests. Acquiring this knowledge involved not only rote memorization and the copying of ancient texts, but also critical engagement, dialogue, and disputation in which later sages drew upon their own experience and understanding to evaluate what they were being taught in the schools and by the learned tradition of the ancestors. Knowledge was not a passive body of data, but rather an active force that shaped the behavior of the students and enabled them to understand and then live within the cosmic and social order of justice set forth by the creator and sustainer of reality. The sages thought by their actions they participated in the sustaining of social order that was at the basis of communal life.

Second, wisdom is understood as discipline (*mûsār*, מוסר), that is, both a curriculum of study and a structured form of behavior designed to lead to the formation of character. Character was shaped through study, reflection, and the actualization of virtue in both discourse and action. This embodiment of moral virtue led the sage to live in harmony with the cosmos, society, and the Creator. The result of this type of existence was well-being that included both a sense of internal peace and contentment and the external accoutrements of honor, respect, integrity, and dignity. Long life, prosperity, and joy became the possession of the one who was wise.

Third, wisdom was moral discourse and behavior that constructed and legitimated a cosmology in which righteousness, both correct and just behavior as well as proper decorum, ordered the world, society, and individual existence. Through the attainment of wisdom, the sages were able to enter into and dwell within an esthesis of beauty, order, justice, and life. Wisdom was both life giving and life sustaining, not only for the world and society but also for the individual sage. This world construction was to provide the sages insight into the nature and character of God, although a dimension of mystery imposed its constraints on their ability to comprehend the Creator and divine acts. Life, too, continued to have its contingencies, because the fulll and complete knowledge of God and divine behavior could never be fullly grasped and the outcome of actions could never be fully known.

Fourth, the semantic range of wisdom and its derivatives included the terms *bînâ* ("insight," בינה) and *da'at* ("knowledge," דעת) and their derivatives, while its antonyms are *kĕsîl* (כסיל), *ĕwîl* (אויל), *sākāl* (סכל), and *nābāl* (נבל), all of which mean, in essence, "foolish" "fool," or the untutored, thus lacking in sense and the knowledge needed for guidance that led to life. The various types of wisdom included, first of all, court wisdom associated with the monarchy and the royal school that educated scribes for service in the bureaucracy and undertakings of the kingdom or state, especially in their developed abilities to read, write, copy, transmit, and give utterance to the documents, edicts, and traditions of society. In addition, the wisdom of artisans is the required and developed skill in crafting both the artistically pleasing and the pragmatically needed. Next, wisdom, in another stream of sapiential tradition, also was equated with mantic knowledge, that is, instruction in the esoteric teachings of the cult (divination of magicians and pagan priests) or the hidden activities of God (apocalyptic). Finally, wisdom, associated with God, is often a personified and eventually hypostatized attribute seen in the activities of Woman Wisdom, originally a goddess in Israelite religion prior to the development of monotheism, and then a personified metaphor. As a goddess she would have been the divine patron of the sages and the school, praised for the knowledge and life she provided.

APPROACHES TO WISDOM
IN OLD TESTAMENT THEOLOGY[51]

Prelude

In addition to the major theologies examined above for their views of creation and often wisdom, several other scholars have written important works of wisdom in Old Testament theology.

The Pagan Character/Secularity of Wisdom:
Horst Dietrich Preuss

For interpreters who thought salvation history, covenant, and/or election presented the major theological paradigms of Old Testament theology and at the same time gave little attention to the theological legitimacy or importance of creation, it is not surprising that the wisdom literature of the Hebrew canon was largely ignored. In the extreme case of Horst Dietrich Preuss, prior to publishing his Old Testament theology he considered wisdom to be pagan, that is, borrowed from non-Israelite sources and subsequently not contributing to Christian theology. Indeed, Preuss contended that the deity of Wisdom and the God of the Torah and the prophets of the Hebrew Bible are not the same God.[52]

Later in his career, Preuss did find an important place for the ethics of wisdom literature in his Old Testament theology.[53] However, he lessened its value in his remarks that sapiential ethical instructions and admonitions belong neither to the covenant at Sinai nor to the saving acts of Yahweh. For him, this diminished their revelatory and authoritative role.

The International Character of Wisdom: Ronald E. Clements

In his brief theology of wisdom in the Old Testament, Ronald E. Clements largely ignores creation theology.[54] Instead, he concentrates on the international origin of wisdom, so that by the time it entered into Israelite thought, it had already become an ancient and hallowed tradition in the surrounding cultures, several of which extended back into the fourth millennium BCE. He also speaks of the democratization of wisdom as it moved from the royal court to the teachings of the people by rabbis in later centuries. In spite of the subtitle, however, the book offers very little that could be deemed to be theological in nature.

Wisdom, Covenant, and Torah Piety: Bernard W. Anderson

As noted earlier, Bernard W. Anderson sets forth the idea of covenant as central to Old Testament theology. But what of the theology of the sages who, prior to Ben Sira's emphasis on the Torah in the early second century BCE, make no reference to Sinai or to covenant? Anderson's response is less than insightful when he notes the wisdom texts "scarcely mention the characteristic themes of Israel's faith: the choice of Israel, the covenant at Sinai, the coming of the Day of Yahweh, the temple as the place of the divine presence, (and) the messianic king to come."[55]

Anderson begins his explanation of wisdom theology by pointing to the "crisis of covenantal theologies."[56] With the shock of the exile and the collapse of an earlier theological understanding shaping the institutional life of temple and king, Anderson thinks it is Israel's response to these disturbing questions of faith that provides a different recourse than is found in covenantal theologies. First, there is the observance of Torah (Ps. 1:1). Torah, of course, is not simply law but rather testimony to the totality of Israel's "root experiences," including the episodes of salvation and divine commandments that lead to life.[57] Torah became the basis for Judah's existence during the time of Ezra and Nehemiah (c. 400 BCE), was viewed as a divine gift, and incorporated God's discipline for life. Part of this argument, of course, follows the discredited view of placing the Torah in the Second Temple, a position advocated by Julius Wellhausen and many other Protestants, until the 1980s, in their interpretation of the law. Anderson indicates that the Torah was closely linked to wisdom (Deut. 4:6; see Qoheleth and especially Ben Sira, who virtually identified wisdom and Torah). The Torah in written form, argues Anderson, gave impetus to Josiah's reform in the seventh century BCE. This is certainly true of the Deuteronomistic History, but I would ask if this is really history with a strong theological mode of explanation or a revisionist attempt by Deuteronomists to rewrite the past according to their own ideology? Anderson goes on to note that in Torah piety there is a correspondence drawn between the created order and the Torah (see Ps. 19). The lateness explicitly argued for the theological importance of Torah and implicitly suggested for wisdom certainly devalues the role of both in the formulation of Israelite and Judahite faith. Anderson attempts to avoid this pitfall, but does not do so successfully.

Anderson then turns to wisdom theology to address the issues of suffering, the divine relationship to Israel, and the justice of God, all of which are not adequately addressed by his three major covenant theologies. Without any clear explanation, however, Anderson begins to address the theology of Proverbs from the time of the united monarchy many centuries before the crisis that gave rise to these aforementioned issues. Thus he is inconsistent in disregarding his primary premise. Anderson suggests that wisdom originated in the early monarchy when its own theology, which did not make a place for Israel's sacred story, began to develop: "there is no reason to doubt that Solomon took an active interest in the cultivation of wisdom in Israel."[58] This view, I submit, has little historical justification, as many have indicated. Nevertheless, for Anderson wisdom in Proverbs often deals with the social order over which the king was to rule justly in the same way that the order of the cosmos reflected the wisdom and righteousness of Yahweh (cf. Prov. 25:2–3). There is, then, in Anderson's thinking, a view that wisdom theology was based upon the larger witness of creation. However, the sages' moral guidance in Proverbs lacked the sharp indictment of misused power by royalty that one finds in the prophetic corpus. Instead, it has the appearance of a much more socially conservative ethos.

Anderson affirms Roland Murphy's position that "the covenant relationship to the Lord does not figure directly in the wisdom experience; it is bracketed, but not erased."[59] Murphy and Anderson can reach this position only canonically, however, since this theme is absent from Proverbs, Job, and Qoheleth. Anderson's argument begs the question rather than points to any evidence. Instead of moving into creation theology as the basis for sapiential faith, he intimates that covenant theology is assumed by the sages. But, one may ask, on what grounds may this argument be made outside the disputed canonical approach that is decidedly antihistorical?

Anderson notes that the theological dimensions of wisdom included several tenets, beginning with the major affirmation of the sages: the fear of the Lord (Prov. 1:7; 9:10; 15:33; Sir. 1:11–30). This "fear" in Anderson's view is "reverence, or awe . . . toward a supreme power."[60]

A second theme of wisdom literature, in Anderson's view, is "living in harmony with the Divine Order."[61] The sages sought to discover a righteous order that held together the cosmos. The "righteous" person (*saddîq*, צדיק) was the one who lived in concert with this overarching cosmic order and thus experienced life and well-being, whereas the wicked (*rāšāʿ*, רשע) violated this order and experienced destruction. For Anderson, this view was connected to the principle of retribution in which God rewarded the righteous and punished the evildoer.

Third, wisdom theology is similar to royal theology, since they both share a vertical heaven-earth dimension. Wisdom articulates the features of a cosmic order as the basis for its understanding of the social order. This view, according to Anderson, is influenced by Egyptian theology. By maintaining the social and cosmic order, Israel repels the powers of chaos present in infertility, famine, plague, and war.

Fourth, Anderson then turns to a detailed discussion of creation theology in wisdom literature (Prov. 3:19–20). He begins by mentioning Sirach 24, the poem that tells of Wisdom's searching for a resting place (24:3–6) and finally taking up residence in Israel, especially in the sacred tent on Mount Zion in Jerusalem (24:10–12). Anderson contrasts this with Proverbs 8–9, which does not mention Israel's sacred story. Instead, one finds in Proverbs reference to a universal, ecumenical, and cosmic perspective not unlike that in Psalm 104. In Proverbs, then, one discovers the personification of wisdom as a feminine individual and as a prophetess (1:20–33 and 8:1–21) who stands in the marketplace or city gate calling upon people to follow her. She is in 8:22–31 the one who was present when God created the heavens and the earth and assisted him in this effort (cf. Sir. 24 and Wis. 7–9). In the poem in Prov. 8:22–31, so Anderson concludes, she is depicted either as a little child or a craftsperson (v. 30). Wisdom is the best and first of divine works, preexistent, and present with God during creation. In this poem Anderson sees that Wisdom is a "participant in the work of creation" and agrees with Murphy[62] that more is at stake here than mere literary personification. Rather wisdom becomes God's voice in summoning those who would listen to come and learn the path to life.[63] She represents divine presence in the world of everyday experience.

Fifth, Anderson returns to his theme of crisis when he addresses the issue of the "justice of God" and in particular the response of the sages. Anderson begins by mentioning the collection of the "Sayings of Agur," which indicates that God is beyond human perception (Prov. 30:1–4). The variety of responses to this divine mystery includes both the perspective that the knowledge of God resides in the fear of God and in the Torah (Job 28:28 and Qoh. 12:9–14) and the view of skepticism. The issue of theodicy becomes acute in the book of Job. In the speeches of Job the problem becomes a theological one in arguing that something has gone wrong with God. The covenantal response of suffering as a result of those who failed to live up to the requirements of divine commandments no longer rings true in the context of underserved suffering by the innocent. The Yahweh speeches respond by indicating that Job, and thus the sages, do not have the knowledge to understand the secret of divine creation. Anderson concludes that in the Yahweh speeches there is a great chasm between divine and human wisdom, such that it is impossible to understand why the innocent suffer. Finally, in Qoheleth God and divine wisdom become completely inaccessible to human understanding. However, humans may experience joy during the time God allows them to live.

Sixth, Anderson argues that in the postexilic period there is a movement toward Torah piety in which obedience to the Torah becomes the theological and social center of emerging Judaism (Ps. 119). He also notes that Torah became a major source of wisdom (Deut. 4:6; Sir. 24:23). Eventually, in Ben Sira the life that is based upon the Torah corresponds to the existence that is provided by the cosmic order of creation.[64] The correlation of creation and the Torah is set forth especially in Psalm 19.

Anderson's work on the theology of the sages is well done, in spite of its limits. He certainly points to the significant place that creation has in their literature and then to the prominent role this theme has in Israelite theology, in spite of the fact that he, like Eichrodt, privileges the various forms of the covenant for Old Testament theology. He does not provide an incisive analysis of the nuances of wisdom theology in its plurality of expressions. He ignores the differences among books in the internal variations and often opposing views, including, for example, the contrast between the theology of creation in Proverbs 8–9 and that of the "Sayings of Agur" (Prov. 30:1–4), or the opposing views of Job, his adversaries, and Yahweh whose speeches conclude the poetic drama. He does not give due recognition to the movement of the sages from a skepticism about apocalyptic in Qoheleth to an appropriation of these features, beginning as early as the Wisdom of Solomon.

The Unique Character of Wisdom Theology: Jutta Hausmann

While agreeing with Zimmerli that creation is at the heart of wisdom theology, Jutta Hausmann provides an important discussion in an incisive article that serves as a prolegomenon to the shaping of a wisdom theology.[65]

First, one needs to rethink the matter of the relationship between deed and result, including its dogmatic formulation in certain texts. There is an openness even in the older wisdom texts that allows for discontinuity, especially due to divine discretion. There is often no concrete articulation of particular attitudes or insights. Indeed, wisdom often does not set forth specific rules of behavior, but rather recognizes that there may be various responses occasioned by different circumstances.

Second, additional reflection on the relationship of individuals and the community in certain wisdom texts needs to be undertaken. While the Hebrew Bible as a whole has particular interest in the community and the nation, wisdom texts primarily give their attention to individuals and their fortunes. In common with other Old Testament texts, however, wisdom does have an interest in the impact that the individual has on the community.

Third, there is also the question of the place of "individual piety." This question takes on added significance when one takes into consideration the Psalter.

At least in Proverbs and Qoheleth there is no indication of a personal piety in the form of an "I-Thou" relationship. The book of Job is different in that there is this type of close relationship between God and the character Job. Still, there is the fundamental question of how extensive this is in this book.

Fourth, wisdom's situation of everyday activity and experience must be distinguished from other Old Testament emphases on the historical experiences of the nation. Wisdom's issues of everyday life are not related to matters of the salvation or punishment of the people of Israel. While nonwisdom texts may involve experience, unlike wisdom they are connected to the relationship between God and the nation.

Fifth, and finally, the special nature of sapiential texts is dependent upon wisdom's literary forms. Unlike prophetic texts or the Psalter, wisdom is generally not interested in preaching the word of God or in offering up prayers that provide the occasion for describing and addressing the Deity. This means that another type of spirit is involved in wisdom texts that not only presupposes different situations, but also has different functions than nonwisdom literature.

Sapiential thinking sets forth clearly its own accents. These stand in a positive relationship to other theological expressions of the Old Testament. When these are set forth in a clear fashion, the theological features of individual wisdom texts may be more clearly recognized.[66]

Hausmann's contribution to what one may consider a prolegomenon to sapiential theology is well stated. She agrees with Zimmerli that Old Testament wisdom finds its theological basis in the doctrine of creation. She rightly criticizes the extreme position taken by William McKane that wisdom moved from a secular to a theological activity. She has laid important groundwork in moving toward the construction of a theology of the sages. However, she has not addressed major theological questions, including, for example, the relationship of wisdom theology to the theologies of other Old Testament texts, the importance of ancient Near Eastern texts for understanding the theology of Israel's sages, and the historical setting of wisdom texts and their function in Israelite social communities and institutions. Finally, she does not broach the question of the ideology of these texts to determine their use in shaping social worlds in which certain groups, for example, the sages and their patrons, stand to profit.

CONCLUSIONS

Except for Preuss in his earlier work, each of these scholars has sought to find a limited place for wisdom in Old Testament theology. The later Preuss treated Old Testament theology according to the rubric of election and responsibility and positioned the role of wisdom under the function of moral instruction that wields, however, no religious authority. Clements's recognition of the international character of wisdom tends to place this literature alongside similar literature of the ancient Near East and indicates that nothing is specifically Israelite about this theology. However, there is little that is theological about his work. Anderson's theology gives primary emphasis to covenant, which eschews an important place for wisdom. While he notes the importance of creation, he fails to give a nuanced formation of the understandings of this theme in the sages. Hausmann's introductory remarks are suggestive in assaying the current place of wisdom theology, in particular her emphasis that wisdom's focus on the "individual" may be an important avenue to constructing sapiential theology. Finally, Anderson's view of "Torah piety" points clearly to one aspect of the theology of the sages. Yet he is unconvincing in arguing that covenant theology is assumed by the sages, an *argumentum ad silencio*, at least until Ben Sira. As insightful as they often are, these approaches do not provide a comprehensive strategy for identifying and then explicating the major features of wisdom theology. Nor do they intimate how the sages' understandings of creation contribute to the entire theology of the Hebrew Bible.

Chapter 3

The Book of Proverbs[1]

INTRODUCTION[2]

My thesis is that creation, expressed through cultural metaphors, is the central theological theme of the sages.[3] These metaphors originated in mythological traditions of the ancient Near East. These mythological traditions and eventually Greco-Roman literature were available to Israelite and Jewish sages who comprised the court officials; teachers in the royal school; composers of chronicles, narratives, and literature; and archivists of a variety of documents, including laws and court histories in Jerusalem. Indeed, Israel's sages were part of the scribal groups in the cultural regions of the Eastern Mediterranean world and were well acquainted with the literatures of the Fertile Crescent and eventually Greece and Rome. The sages of Israel and early Judaism acknowledged they were part of an international group of intellectuals whose wisdom was accessible to the wise of the various cultures (1 Kgs. 5:9–14). Thus it would be unwise to ignore cultural engagements and appropriations.

ISRAEL'S ENGAGEMENT WITH ANCIENT EGYPT

Historical Prelude

The collections and concluding poem of the book of Proverbs are difficult to date. However, I would suggest that much of the text, including most of the collections, although not the final redaction, originated during the period of the later monarchy of the First Temple. The three empires with which Israel and then Judah interacted were Egypt, Assyria (especially as a subjugated kingdom from 732 BCE to the revolution of Josiah beginning in 627 BCE), and Babylonia (as part of an imperial province 605–539 BCE). Based on literary parallels and material data, it is likely that the greatest cultural impact on Israel and Judah during the period prior to 586 BCE came from Egypt.

The New Kingdom

On the basis of material culture we know that Egyptian military invasions into Syria-Palestine and the establishment of garrisons and trading centers occurred as early as the New Kingdom. These incursions resulted from the ambition to control land for lucrative trade in the Syro-Palestinian region in Mesopotamia and maritime routes in the Eastern Mediterranean region. However, these desires, which never totally disappeared in later dynasties, were severely restricted by the invasion of the Sea Peoples at the end of the Late Bronze Age. It appears that Israel's wisdom tradition originated in the monarchic period, perhaps as early as the time of the Davidic-Solomonic empire, although on a much more limited scale than is represented in 1 Kings 3–11. Indeed, it is far more likely that a full-scale administration largely made up of offices and scribes located throughout the kingdom of Judah did not appear until the reign of Hezekiah. Scribes under the direction of a royal court and priestly hierarchy would have been involved in the administration of these increasingly important and related institutions. Even following the return from Babylonian captivity in the Second Temple period, the scribal ranks would have begun to grow once again in assisting the local governor's administering of the colony of Judah and the temple's functioning as a national institution for a small state. This provided some autonomy for indigenous peoples to deal with local matters and cultic activities under the watchful eye of the empire.

Third Intermediate Period to the Saite Dynasty[4]

The decline of Egypt during the Third Intermediate era (1069–664 BCE) was the result of internal discord. The Nubians overthrew their Egyptian overlords, while a rival dynasty to the one that ruled Lower Egypt at Memphis was set up in Thebes to rule Upper Egypt. A third dynastic center came to power in Tanis, resulting then in the struggle of these three dynasties for power over the entirety of Egypt. The political fragmentation during the Third Intermediate Period resulted from the lack of a central administrative center governed by one dynasty. The "Tale of Wenamon" (ca. 1076 BCE) early on points to the loss of power and stature of the Ramesside Dynasty as it came to its demise, followed by rival dynasties.

The Twenty-first Dynasty (1069–945 BCE) continued Egyptian efforts to establish a military and economic presence in Syria-Palestine (see the political refuge offered to Hadad in 1 Kgs. 11:14–22, following David's conquest of Edom). After the death of David, Siamun (978–959) assisted Hadad to reclaim his kingdom in Transjordan. One reason for this may have been the interests the Egyptians had in using the "King's Highway," which passed through Edom. Siamun also invaded Philistia in order to cash in on the prosperous sea trade in the Mediterranean ports from Egypt north to the southern Levant. He even took the Philistine stronghold of Gezer, until he gave it as a marriage gift to Solomon in securing an important trading partner in the region (1 Kgs. 3:1; 7:8; 9:16, 24; 11:1–2; 2 Chr. 8:11).[5] If this marriage did indeed occur and was not simply part of the Israelite enhancement of the famous king's legendary status, this would suggest an early example of Egyptian influence at the Israelite court in Jerusalem.[6]

The most significant ruler of the Twenty-second Dynasty was Sheshonq I (945–924), a Libyan who established his authority over the former Tainite kingdom and rulers. Having entered into an alliance with Thebes, he came to rule over southern Egypt through his son, Iuput, who was both a military commander and high priest of Amon. The Bubastite Portal of the main temple at Karnak portrays a relief that points to his victory against Israel and Judah (in the fifth year of Rehoboam) and the conquest of the cities of Gaza and Megiddo.[7] He sought to continue to create instability in a divided kingdom (1 Kgs. 14:25–26; 2 Chr. 12:2–9), to increase his empire's resources with Asian booty, and to put an end to the Israelite domination of inland and maritime trade. His ambitions died with him, however, as his successors could no longer continue to enjoy his and his son's military success.

The rulers of Cush broke away from Egypt and then succeeded in establishing the Twenty-fifth Dynasty (747–656). Kashta and Piy (747–716) were able to rule most of Egypt. Piy's successor (Shabaqo, 716–702) brought to dissolution Saite power and then established his new capital at Memphis. While the powerful Libyan families continued to cause internal disturbances, a more ominous threat was raised by the expanding Assyrian Empire that had conquered Mesopotamia and Israel by the latter part of the eighth century, with the subordination of Judah (beginning with Ahaz in 735–715) and the fall of Samaria in 722. Sargon II (722–705) expressed the Assyrian desire to control the sea trade by subduing both Judah and Philistia. Hoshea of Israel in 726 had appealed to a local Egyptian king (a Libyan, Osorkon IV? 2 Kgs. 17:4) for help in repelling the Assyrians, but this support did not materialize. Sargon II struck the final blow against the Israelites in taking the city of Samaria and thereafter soon came into control of the Philistine region. Discord in Egypt was occasioned by the Libyan rulers and the Assyrians entering into an alliance that opposed the Cushites for control of Egypt.

Hezekiah of Judah received military support from the Cushite ruler (most likely Shabitqo, 702–690), who sent an Egyptian army to relieve Jerusalem from the siege of Sennacherib (2 Kgs. 18:13–19:37). The Assyrian Chronicles include a text that boasts of Sennacherib's laying waste to forty-six walled cities in Judah and then settling into a siege of Jerusalem (*ANET*, 287–88). While the Assyrians devasted much of Judah, Jerusalem was besieged but not taken. Egypt and Assyria continued to fight for control of Syria-Palestine for the next half century. Eventually, Esarhaddon (681–669) enforced Assyrian hegemony over the Cushite rulers, but this proved to be of limited value, since the various areas of Egypt continued to engage in revolutionary activity even during the reign of the last strong Assyrian ruler, Assurbanipal.

An Egyptian renaissance of political power occurred with the Twenty-sixth Dynasty (664–525) under Necho I, Psamtik, and Necho II. Egypt entered into an alliance with Assyria that sought to halt the advance of the Babylonian forces and its newly emerging empire. This alliance led to the reunification of Egypt for the first time in four centuries. This cooperation of a stronger Egypt with a declining Assyrian Empire was a potentially powerful force, and Egypt hoped to regain its international prominence during the reign of Necho II (610–595). His goals included not only using Assyria as a buffer between Syria-Palestine and the eastern region of Mesopotamia, but also taking economic control of the Levant. If successful, this Egyptian ruler even hoped to make forays into northwestern Mesopotamia that would culminate in an Egyptian presence deep into the region of western Mesopotamia. However, the death of Assurbanipal in 627 initiated an irreversible decline in Assyria's political and military position. Even with the aid of the powerful Egyptians, the Assyrians could not stop the Babylonian advance that led to their conquest of the entirety of Mesopotamia, Syria-Palestine, and eventually even the area beyond the Sinai into the region of the Nile.

The attempt of Josiah (640–609) to rebuild an empire in Israel and Judah failed when his forces were defeated at Megiddo by Necho II. With Josiah's death in this battle, Judah came under Egyptian control until 605, when Nebuchadrezzar decisively routed the Egyptian forces of Necho II at Carmchemish. Judah fell under Babylonian control. Later, Psamtik II (595–589) and his successor Apries (589–570) aligned with the small nations of Syria-Palestine against Nebuchadrezzar to stop his advance southward, but they failed. Following an initial rebellion led by Jehoiakim that was put down and resulted in increased tribute and a limited exile (597), the Babylonian king decisively defeated Zedekiah during a failed revolution. In 586 Nebuchadrezzar II razed Jerusalem, including the temple, and led its disgraced leaders into exile. Further Egyptian ambitions for an Asian empire were dashed. Aphries' alliance with the Phoenician cities may have been in response to a Babylonian invasion of Egypt in the 580s,[8] but in any event, Ahmose II (570–526) was able to repel a Babylonian invasion of his homeland in the fourth year of his reign. With the rise of the Achaemenids in Persia (550–332), however, a strategic alliance of Egypt with Babylonia, Lydia, and Sparta was formed to stymie this new threat. The Persians eventually defeated this extensive military collaboration, and Psamtik III was defeated by Cambyses (525–522) at the battle of Pelusium in 525. Now Egypt was incorporated into the huge Persian Empire. Egypt's political, economic, and military interaction with Judah largely ceased until the Hellenistic Ptolemaic Empire was established at the end of the fourth century BCE.

ANCIENT EGYPTIAN WISDOM LITERATURE[9]

Perhaps the most important theme in Egyptian wisdom was the affirmation of "world order" (*ma'at*, "truth, justice, and order") that is reflected in the social order. *Ma'at* was on occasion worshiped as a goddess, the sun god Re's daughter, who also was a patron god of the sages to whom they gave expressions of their devotion. Other deities included especially Thoth, who also was honored by the sages for his divine wisdom. Through the incorporation of this order of creation in social laws and sapiential teaching, the Egyptian state was considered to be stable and capable of maintaining itself into the future.

The following points serve as an introductory summary to characterize the religious thought of Egyptian wisdom. First, the sages of Egypt constructed a worldview based on the religious concept of *ma'at*, the principle of a just order that was personified as the divine daughter of Re, the sun god. Ptahhotep, a powerful vizier and one of the earliest known sages, teaches his son:

> Justice[10] is great, and its appropriateness is lasting; it has not been disturbed since the time of him who made it, (whereas) there is punishment for him who passes over its laws. It is the (right) path before him who knows nothing. Wrongdoing has never brought its undertaking into port. (It may be that) it is fraud that gains riches, (but) the strength of justice is that it lasts, and a man may say: "It is the property of my father."[11]

Second, Egyptian wisdom literature may take a step toward monotheism, although this is debated. The literature tends to use *ntr*, the generic term for "god," although its universal character may have allowed the hearers of the instruction to fill in the blank. The sages taught that "god" was involved in the personal lives of those who followed their teachings. And retributive justice was also at work in this relationship.[12] The "deity" is the one who brings personal reward to his devotee and the judge who is concerned with behavior on the earth.[13]

Third, the anthropology of the sages, while adopting the conservative teachings of mortuary religion, which became increasingly democratized, emphasized that one should follow the moral, religious, and social teachings of the wise in order to make a successful transition to the afterlife. Additionally, the ideal sage was the one who was the "silent man," the person in control of his passions, especially his anger, and who avoids loquacious talk. The most important human organ for learning was the "heart," which was identified as the intellect capable of reasoning. Human opposites, in particular the fool ("heated man") and the wise ("cool man"), are the most important category for classifying humanity. Instruction was given in order to stabilize human society and to avoid conflict between human groups.

Fourth, the major purpose, especially articulated in the instruction literature, was to experience the good life, regardless of how it was specifically defined during the various ages. This meant that wisdom was designed to enable the sage to avoid the difficulties and pitfalls of life while pursuing and obtaining the rewards for which one strove: wealth and position, inner peace and well-being, and honor and respect. During critical periods, however, the sages often questioned the ancestors' traditional teachings, ranging from divine justice to mortuary religion.

EGYPTIAN EDUCATION[14] AND SCRIBES[15]

The Israelites held Egyptian wisdom in high regard (1 Kgs. 5:10) and borrowed freely from their sapiential traditions, in particular those of the schools in the court and temples. The literature became more conscious of reaching more lowly placed groups of scribes and officials, and not simply the elite of Egyptian society. In addition, the sages of Egypt offered important comparisons to those of ancient Israel.

EGYPTIAN AND ISRAELITE CULTURAL INTERACTION IN IRON AGE II

Introduction

The administrative structure of the different countries, trade, literature, and architecture point to the interaction of Egyptians and Israelites/Judahites during Iron Age II. Among the literary points of contact, the clearest is the "Teaching of Amenemopet," which was a major source for the collection of sayings found in Prov. 22:17–24:22. Other evidence for possible literary contacts with Syria-Palestine include the presence of demotic fragments of the Aramaic "Tale of Ahiqar"[16] and the similarity of literary forms, including those common to wisdom literature (especially the instruction and its admonitions, prohibitions, and sayings).

The Egyptian Influence on the Israelite Royal Administration[17]

There is some evidence of Egyptian influence on the royal officials and some of the administrative operations.[18] When Wen-Amon, the emissary of the pharaoh, speaks to Zakar-Baal of Byblos, the case is made that he understands and writes in hieroglyphics. This "king" (called a "chief" by the author of Wen-Amon) has a scribe who writes a letter, serves as a messenger, and also is the overseer of food. There are also Egyptians who function at the king's court, for example, a butler named Penaum and a singer, Tanno.

EGYPTIAN INFLUENCE ON ISRAELITE WISDOM TRADITIONS AND LITERATURE

Prelude

Most important for this study is the Egyptian influence on Israelite wisdom. This influence is clear in regard to Amenemopet and likely the case in regard to other instructions handed down in the circles of Egyptian schools. Exactly how the sages of Israel became familiar with Egyptian wisdom is not known, although it is likely through the Phoenicians who had commercial relationships with the Egyptians by means of sea trade. In addition, it may be that a variety of languages and literatures were studied in the school. This knowledge would be necessary for both diplomacy and commerce.

Egyptian Wisdom and the Israelite Wisdom Literature[19]

In addition to the above, there are further indications of the influence on Israelite scribes and Hebrew by their Egyptian counterparts and hieratic script. D. B. Redford has pointed to over forty words in Old Testament Hebrew that he thinks likely derived from Egyptian.[20] Thirteen are architectural, many refer to the cult, three have to do with garments, and others point to scribal instruments (seal, ink, and palette), an interesting observation for my thesis of Egyptian influence on Israelite wisdom.[21] Egyptian idioms, translated into Hebrew, include "eternal home," "wall of bronze," the "tree of life," and the "way of the living" (the first, third, and fourth appear in Israelite wisdom texts: Qoh. 12:5; Prov. 3:18; 5:6; 6:23; 10:17; 15:24). Whether the influence was direct or passed to Israel through the mediating Canaanites and Phoenicians is a question that cannot be answered with precision. More specifically for this volume, Nili Shupak has noted that Hebrew sapiential texts have numerous expressions that are similar to ones in Egyptian wisdom. Terms common to both are "instruction" (*s'b3y.t* = *mûsār*), "beating" (*ḥwi* and *ḫnkn*; *šbd*, "rod, stick" = *nākâ*, *šebeṭ*, i.e., beating an indolent student), "lazy/idle student" (*wsf* = *'as*el*), "ignorant student" (*'iw.ty ḫ3.ty'* = *ḥāsar lēb*), person of "positive character" (*ḳb* = *kar rû'aḥ*), and the "ear" as the organ of learning.[22] She notes that these expressions are limited to wisdom texts in Israel.[23] This suggests that the Israelite/Judahite sages either knew Egyptian directly or indirectly through Phoenician and Canaanite contacts. The knowledge of Egyptian wisdom would have been mediated through the court and the school during the period of the Israelite/Judahite monarchy.[24]

Royal Wisdom in Ancient Israel

Another indication of a connection with Egyptian wisdom occurs in the theme of royal wisdom that is important in the book of Proverbs. Egyptian wisdom was largely associated with the royal court and the temples that enjoyed royal patronage. Texts include the royal instructions (Amenemhet and Merikare) and the "Loyalist Instruction," copies of which were transmitted by scribes in the schools

Proverbs contains three collections that have the appearance of royal sages issuing wisdom to and about kingship: 16:1–22:16; 25:2–27; and 31:1–9. These wisdom texts likely issue from sages serving in the royal court and its administration, although the third, "The Instruction of Lemuel," is an Arabic teaching offered by the queen mother to her son who has just assumed the position of chief. The social status of the teachers and especially their students reflects that of the aristocratic elites with power, position, and wealth. Absent is any criticism of the institution of the monarchy or any indication of misrule. Sages include the wise counselors and officials mentioned in the Succession Narrative and the cabinets of David and Solomon, much like Egyptian sages that included the viziers. In Prov. 16:1–25:27, the king is mentioned twenty-four times (16:10, 12, 13, 14, 15; 17:7; 19:10, 12; 20:2, 8, 26, 28; 21:1; 22:11, 29; 23:1; 24:21; 25:1, 2, 3, 5, 6, 7, 15). Of course, 25:1 is a superscription, but contains perhaps an important historical reference to the "officials of Hezekiah" who copied the sayings of Solomon.

The Theme of Royal Wisdom in the Second Collection (Prov. 16:1–22:16)

The collection in 16:1–22:16 contains a brief section that developed in the royal court or in a school that has in view the court and kingship (16:1–15). One finds here the entwinement of creation theology and the topos of kingship. In terms of the latter are sayings indicating that the king's decisions in judgment are "inspired" (*qesem*, קסם),[25] Yahweh directs human plans, economic justice is established by Yahweh, the "abomination of kings" (*tô'ăbat mĕlākîm*, תועבת מלכים)[26] is to perform evil, the royal "throne is established on [his] justice" (*biṣdāqâ yikkôn kissē'*, כסא יכון בצדקה), righteous speech delights the king who loves those who speak "uprightly" (*yāšār*, ישר), and the light of the king's face brings life while his "favor" (*rāṣôn*, רצון) is like the cloud that brings spring rain. Like the pharaoh, the Israelite king is responsible for maintaining and implementing justice. The sages in both Israel and Egypt are to be loyal servants to the king in his varied activities that establish social and even cosmic order.

The Theme of Royal Wisdom in Proverbs 25:2–27

The superscription, "These are other proverbs of Solomon that officials of King Hezekiah copied" (25:1), has often been dismissed as a redactional invention.[27] However, the content of the first part of the collection in 25:2–27 appears to be what Ray Van Leeuwen calls a "proverb poem" that is addressed to royal courtiers.[28] Hezekiah was king of Judah in the late eighth and early seventh century (715–687 BCE). The Deuteronomistic Historian made him into a "second Solomon" (2 Kgs. 18:1–20:21; 2 Chr. 29:1–32:33; Sir. 48:17–23). While the king in this poem does not possess the divine attributes of the ruler in the "Loy-alist Instruction," he does have the ability (wisdom?) to "search out" (*ḥăqōr*, חקר) the *deus absconditus* and discover his secret plans and activities. God is the one whose "glory" (*kābôd*, כבוד) hides things, while the ruler shares in this "glory" (*kābôd*) to discover what he is doing (cf. Deut. 29:29). Second, the king's mind (*lēb*, לב) is "unsearchable" (*'ên ḥēqer*, אין חקר), comparable to the height of the heavens and the depths of the earth. "Unsearchable" refers elsewhere to seeking out God and determining divine actions (Job 5:9; 9:10; 11:7–10; Ps. 145:3; Isa. 40:28). The most significant saying affirms that the royal throne is established on justice (*biṣdāqâ yikkôn kissē'*, בצדקה יכון כסא, Prov. 16:12) and the wicked are removed from his presence (cf. the Egyptian king's throne).[29] The verb "estab-lished" (*kûn*, כון) is used of the act of divine creation and infers stability for the cosmos (Prov. 3:19; 8:27; 24:3, Pss. 93:1; 119:90; Job 28:25, 27).

The Theme of Kingship in the Instruction of Lemuel (Prov. 31:1–9)

The one instruction that is similar in form to the Egyptian royal instructions of Amenemhet and Merikare is found in Prov. 31:1–9. This text is a royal instruc-tion of a young Arabian ruler or chief (Lemuel) by his queen mother[30] when he is making the transition to the throne.[31] The tribe to which the young king belongs is an Arabian one (Mas'aia), known from Assyrian sources in the late eighth century BCE, whose routes of migration were in Arabia, Edom, Trans-jordan, and beyond Seir (see 1 Kgs. 5:9–14, and Job and his three friends). While he is advised to be on his guard against wayward women and strong drink, he is also responsible for judging righteously and distributing justice to the poor (cf. Ps. 72). Once more, the ruler is responsible for establishing righteousness in soci-ety, a common theme in Egyptian and Israelite wisdom.

Amenemopet and Proverbs 22:17–24:22

The Egyptian wisdom text "The Instruction of Amenemopet" (ca. 1100 BCE) was popular at a time when Egyptian power has waned and Egypt has entered into the upheavals of the Third Intermediate Period. This instruction is known to the editor of the collection in Prov. 22:17–24:22 ("Sayings of the Wise," *dibrê ḥăkāmîm*) who uses it in putting together his teachings.[32] D. C. Simpson has convincingly argued that this Egyptian text precedes the biblical collection.[33] An Egyptian official, the overseer of lands, instructs his son Hor-em-maa-kheru, a priestly scribe, in a text of thirty chapters on proper behavior that will result in honor and success. We are not sure how this Egyptian text came to be known in Israel. However, it was likely used in an Israelite school dating as early as the eighth century BCE. The latest copies of this text that have survived date to the Twenty-sixth Dynasty (sixth century BCE).

The Men of Hezekiah and Proverbs 25–29

This collection is said to derive from the editorial work of Hezekiah's scribes, who copied the wisdom sayings of Solomon (Prov. 25:1). It may not be coincidental that Hezekiah established a pro-Egyptian lobby at court that Isaiah opposed (Isa. 30:1–17).

Conclusion

The indications of Egyptian influence on the wisdom tradition in Israel, in particular Proverbs 1–9 and Proverbs 22:17–24:22, point to an important relationship between Israelite wisdom and the culture of Egypt.

INTERNATIONAL WISDOM IN THE ISRAELITE SCHOOLS IN THE PERIOD OF THE MONARCHY[34]

The direct evidence for the existence of schools in ancient Israel during the First Temple period is sparse. Yet there are some brief indications of royal schools in 1 Kgs. 12:8, 10; 2 Kgs. 10:1, 5–6; 2 Chr. 17:7–9; temple schools in Isa. 28:7–13 and 2 Chr. 22:11 (cf. 2 Kgs. 12:3), wisdom schools (Prov. 5:13; 17:16), and prophetic "schools" in 2 Kgs. 6:1–2; Isa. 8:16; 28:9; 50:4–9.[35] The evidence is comparative (i.e., the existence of scribal schools in Egypt and Mesopotamia) and inductive (i.e., similarities in language, thought, and activity, e.g., formal instruction) and strongly suggests a social group that would have been formed in a school tradition. Shupak concludes her comprehensive study with the following remark about schools and the courts where the schools for elite children would have existed: "It would therefore seem reasonable to assume that the first educational institutions in Israel were inspired by an Egyptian archetype, and that the book of Proverbs—especially its second collection—served as learning material in these institutions."[36] These royal schools provided an important setting for the scribal engagement of Egyptian and other cultures.

THE LITERARY STRUCTURE OF PROVERBS

Seven collections of varying forms of wisdom rhetoric, an introduction (1:2–7), and a concluding poem, "The Woman of Worth" (31:10–31) comprise the book of Proverbs.[37] The plural *mĕšālîm* (משלים), "sayings" (singular *māšāl*, משל, "saying") and the plural construct, *dibrê*, דבר, "words," are the terms used for a collection that is shaped in a variety of ways: similar forms, or common themes, and/or poetic features. The elegance of sapiential rhetoric equates with the sages' literary depiction of the world as one of beauty and balance.[38] The sages invited their hearers to enter with them into this world of sapiential imagination in order to know the righteous order of the cosmos, a just society, and moral behavior. From observation of the world, the sages developed sayings that themselves were minute estheses designed to shape social and behavioral existence and to shape the righteous order of the social group and the community in which they functioned. The elegance of the language strongly supports the view that highly educated and skilled sages produced this volume over the centuries.

Each of the seven collections is introduced by a title or superscription:

1. 1:1 "The Proverbs of Solomon, the son of David, King of Israel" (*mišlê šĕlōmōh*, משלי שלמה)

2. 10:1 "The Proverbs of Solomon" (*mišlê šĕlōmōh*, משלי שלמה)

3. 22:17 "The Words of the Wise" (*dibrê ḥăkāmîm*, דברי חכמים)

4. 24:23 "These also Are (the Words) of the Wise" (*gam-'elleh [dibrê] ḥăkāmîm*, גם אלה [דברי] חכמים)

5. 25:1 "These also Are the Proverbs of Solomon, which the Men of Hezekiah, King of Judah, Edited" (*gam-'elleh mišle šĕlōmōh 'ăšer he'tîqû 'anše ḥizqîyâ melek-yĕhûdâ*, גם אלה משלי שלמה אשר העתיקו אנשי זקיה מלך יהודה)

6. 30:1 "The Words of Agur" (*dibrê 'āgûr*, דברי אגור)

7. 31:1 "The Words of Lemuel, King of Massa, which His Mother Taught Him" (*dibrê lĕmû'ēl melek maśśā' 'ăšer-yissĕrattû 'immô*, דברילמואל מלך משא אשר יסרתו אמא)

Date of the Collections

Based on content, theology, limited references to the scribal profession, parallels with Egyptian wisdom, and the superscriptions, the collections in Proverbs, with the possible exception of the "Sayings of Agur," which originates in a skeptical tradition similar to Qoheleth, may have originated during the period of the later monarchy. The introduction to the book in 1:2–7 and the poem on the "Woman of Worth" in 31:10–31 are redactional additions most likely inserted during the Persian period. The lack of references to the temple tradition and the priestly Torah, so prominent in Ezra–Nehemiah and the book of Ben Sira, would suggest a conclusion prior to the reform of Ezra in the late fifth century. This absence of formative postexilic traditions of temple and Torah could also point to a social location for the final shaping of Proverbs in a school associated with the colonial government, not with the temple.

Thematic Introduction to Proverbs

While most of Proverbs, in my judgment, likely originated in the period of the later Israelite/Judahite monarchy, postexilic scribes were responsible for editing the book of Proverbs as a compendium of sapiential teachings, forms, literary features, professional counsel, and religious teachings during the Persian period to fit on a single scroll. The major themes of the book include: the righteous order that permeates creation and society, divine creation and providence, divine retribution, the role of the king, the importance of the acquisition of wisdom, the contrast between wisdom and foolishness (wise/foolish), choosing the right path, the consequences of doing or not doing certain actions, the power of the word with a particular emphasis on elegance of expression and persuasion, and a preoccupation with female figures (wives, the queen mother, mothers, personified Wisdom and Folly, the prostitute, the adulteress, and the wise woman). Wisdom has a religious orientation (see, e.g., "the fear of Yahweh/God") throughout its history, including the book of Proverbs, and there is not even so much as a hint that that there was a development from secular to religious to theological wisdom. These themes are integrated by a sapiential understanding of creation.

WISDOM AND THEOLOGY IN PROVERBS 1–9[39]

Prelude

The first collection consists of ten instructions, five poems on Woman Wisdom, and an initial protrepsis, that is, an invitation largely to young men to take up the course of wisdom (1:2–7). In its final edited form, this collection serves to introduce a variety of wisdom sayings and teachings found throughout the collection.[40] The ten complete instructions are positioned in 1:8–19; 2:1–22; 3:1–12; 3:21–35; 4:1–9; 4:10–19; 4:20–27; 5:1–23; 6:20–35; and 7:1–27,[41] while the poems on Woman Wisdom occupy a rhetorically significant place at the beginning and the end of the collection (1:20–33; 8:1–11; 8:12–21; 8:22–31; 9:1–18) to form a literary inclusio that underscores the importance and role of Woman Wisdom in creation, providence, and instruction in the moral life.[42] Woman Wisdom gives utterance not only to the voice of the teacher in Proverbs 1–9, but also to that of God, and thus equates wisdom instruction with divine revelation.[43]

By means of the wisdom poems and their metaphors for creation, the teacher stimulates his students' imagination to enter a world of sapiential discourse in which God through wisdom dwells and sustains life.[44] By means of the rhetoric and themes of chapters 1–9, reality becomes an esthesis in which there is the coherence of order and beauty. Through the acts of divine creation, captured in the metaphors of creation and envisioned by the human imagination, reality is shaped and sustained. By entrance into this world of beauty and symmetry, the sages come to know Wisdom and experience her gifts of life.[45] This world is divinely ordered, from its inception in primordial creation to its continuation through the present into the future.[46]

This literature, while on occasion referring to the metaphorical depiction of divine wisdom and the sapiential tradition as Woman Wisdom, originally pointed to a goddess who was the daughter of Yahweh and the patron of the sages. The power of chaos is embodied in Yamm, who engages in combat with the Divine Warrior.

Wisdom Leads to Theological Understanding and Ethical Conduct (1:2–7)

The introduction sets forth both the purpose of Proverbs 1–9, and, following the final redaction of the book, of all of Proverbs. Instruction in the discipline of wisdom (*mûsār*, מוסר) is the purpose of the book. This means that the follower of wisdom throughout life comes to the knowledge of God, the world, society, and human behavior. Through the embodiment of sapiential piety and virtue (i.e., the "fear of God," "fear of Yahweh"), the sage not only receives the blessings of human living but also is active in constructing a world (cosmos and society) for human dwelling.[47] The introduction, then, serves as an invitation[48] to pursue the study of wisdom.

Sapiential teaching is offered to three distinct audiences: humanity in general, the "simple" or unlearned, and the "sage" who seeks to increase his understanding and deepen his embodiment of sapiential virtues. The introduction exhorts humans in general "to know wisdom (*ḥŏkmâ*, חכמה) and discipline (*mûsār*, מוסר)" and "to understand sayings of insight (*bînâ*, בינה)." This points to the universal domain and call of wisdom, although not everyone accepts the invitation. Further, the introduction seeks "to provide the unlearned with shrewdness (*'ormâ*, ערמה)" and "youths with knowledge (*da'at*, דעת) and planning (*mĕzimmâ*, מזמה)," while "the sage will hear and increase in learning (*leqaḥ*, לקח)" and "the person of insight will receive guidance (*taḥbûlôt*, תחבולות)."

Finally, the introduction provides one more emphasis. Study begins with "the fear (*yir'â*, יראה) of Yahweh,"[49] which provides the major inclusio for the entire book of Proverbs (1:7; 31:30). Sapiential understanding and behavior begin with a religious piety that is characterized by faith in God as the creator and sustainer of life (see 9:10; 15:33; 31:30; Job 28:28; Ps. 111:10; Sir. 1:1–20).[50] Meditation on the holy and prayer, to mention two of the more important features of scribal piety, and the study of wisdom are not opposites, but rather are complementary. One enters wisdom's house only through the door of sapiential piety. One is hard-pressed to prove that wisdom was ever secular in nature and content, even in its earliest expressions. To trace the development of wisdom from an early secular tradition to a late religious one is misleading. Therefore, the quest for wisdom begins with a faith in God that seeks understanding.

Wisdom as Goddess and Instrument of Creation: Proverbs 3:13–20[51]

The first text that explicitly sets forth creation theology in Proverbs is 3:13–20, crafted into a wisdom poem of three strophes: the first tells of the joy that comes to the one who finds wisdom; the second portrays wisdom in the guise of an ancient Near Eastern goddess of life; and the third describes wisdom's role in creation.

This didactic poem is an *'ašrê* (אשרי, "happy/blessed"), instructive poem (cf. Pss. 1, 32, 34), introduced by a "happy/blessed" saying (Prov. 3:13–15). The "happy" saying provides the poem's theme and crafts its rhetorical structure (see the occurrence of *'ašrê* in vv. 13 and 18).[52] The praise of Yahweh in this poem is redirected to wisdom, the divine attribute that he uses in his role as the creator and sustainer of the world and as the redeemer who delivers Israel and individuals from their distress (e.g., the creation hymns in Pss. 8, 19A, 104).[53] Redemption of the individual or the nation and creation are the two reasons that Yahweh is praised in the Psalter. Hymns extol the majesty and greatness of God, demonstrated in these mighty, redemptive, and life-giving acts.

The first strophe (vv. 13–17) portrays the well-being and joy that comes to the one who discovers wisdom. Her value is more than silver, gold, and jewels, and indeed beyond any treasure the human heart may desire. She offers to her followers long life (see 3:2; 22:4), riches (14:24), and honor (8:18).

In the second strophe (v. 18), wisdom is personified as a "tree of life" (see Gen. 2:9; 3:22, 24), a major symbol of fertility goddesses in ancient Near Eastern religions.[54] Life is the core value in Proverbs, especially when accompanied by longevity, happiness, wealth, and honor (Prov. 3:2, 8:18; 14:24; 22:4). It is likely that this description of Woman Wisdom both here and in chapters 8–9 borrows from an ancient Near Eastern goddess (possibly Astarte or Ishtar but more likely Ma'at or Isis)[55] who personifies truth, justice, and the order of the world[56] (see chaps. 8–9; Job 28; Sir. 24). It is only in Wisdom 7–9 that she becomes a hypostasis of divine wisdom, still marked by the features of a goddess, quite probably Isis. Like Ma'at, she holds in one hand "life" (cf. the Egyptian *ankh*) and "wealth and honor" (the Egyptian *was*, "scepter") in the other.[57]

These blessings were normally the gift of God (1 Kgs. 3:3–14), but here they are the rewards of Woman Wisdom freely given to the wise. The sages appeal to the imagination when they present wisdom (*ḥŏkmâ*, חכמה; a feminine noun) in the guise of a fertility goddess and a powerful woman (e.g., queen mother) who endows those who love her with the gift of life, riches, and honor. Thus those who discover and "embrace" (see Prov. 5:5) Goddess and Mistress Wisdom are "happy/blessed" (3:13, 18).[58] For a largely male audience, this erotic language is used to depict Woman Wisdom here and in chapters 8–9 as an intellectual love that attracts young men and sages to disciplined study and moral living (*mûsār*, מוסר).

The creation narrative in J (Gen. 2:4b–25) provides some of the imagery for this strophe.[59] The tree of life in Gen. 2:9; 2:16–17; 3:11; 3:22–24 (cf. *1 Enoch* 25:4–5; 4 Ezra 2:12; 8:52; 4 Macc. 18:16; Rev. 2:7; 22:2, 14, 19) is associated on occasion in the Hebrew Bible with wooden poles or sacred trees (*'ăšērôt*, אשרות; Deut. 16:21; 1 Kgs. 15:13; 16:33; 18:19; 2 Kgs. 13:6; 17:16; 21:7, 23, 15; cf. Prov. 11:30; 13:12; 15:4), a common symbol for the fertility goddess Asherah, worshiped in Israel and Canaan.[60] In this proverbial poem, however, the tree of life and the tree of knowledge of good and evil (an expression for wisdom) are merged into Goddess Wisdom. In addition, as Van Leeuwen has demonstrated, the major poems about wisdom in 3:13–20 and 8:1–36 are linked thematically and verbally to the poem about the "Woman of Worth" in chapter 31.[61]

The third strophe (3:19–20; cf. Jer. 10:12 and Ps. 104:24), which rhetorically appears separate originally from verses 13–18, is added to indicate that Yahweh used his wisdom in both the origins of the earth and in supplying the life-giving rain that fertilizes the cosmos. Because of the association with the original *'ašrê* poem, this divine wisdom used by Yahweh in creation is the same one that gives life to those who find her. The wise poet also indicates that this life-giving wisdom is an essential element of the cosmos itself and implies that the obtaining of her allows the sage to understand the nature of creation.[62] This imagery is common in other texts in describing God's use of divine wisdom in creating, ordering, and sustaining the world (cf. Pss. 104:24; 136:5; Jer. 10:12; 51:15).[63] Two verbs of creation are used to speak of God's originating the cosmos, *yāsad* (יסד, "established"; Amos 9:6; Isa. 24:18; 48:13; 51:13; Zech. 12:1; cf. Prov. 8:29); and *kûn* (כון, "secured"; Prov. 24:3; Pss. 93:1; 119:90; Job 28:25, 27; cf. Prov. 8:27). These verbs portray God as the architect or builder who lays down a strong foundation and secures a building's walls and columns (cf. Prov. 9:1; 24:3–4; Job 38:4–7; Ps. 104:5). This image of the divine architect is a metaphor for portraying the skill and knowledge God uses to secure and order the cosmos (mountains, Job 26:11 and Ps. 18:7) and to support the sky with a roof constructed over the cosmic sea.[64] By following wisdom, the sage is given the same wisdom to anchor his/her life in the reality of creation.

The third verb for God's creation of the cosmos is *bāqa'* (בקע, "divide"). Yahweh makes use of his knowledge (= wisdom) to "divide" the primeval sea, Yamm (ים; see Isa. 51:9–11; Job 38:8–11; Prov. 8:29).[65] This verb may have its origins in the mythological image of Marduk "splitting open" the chaos monster to protect the world from being inundated by chaos.[66] *Těhôm* (תהום) or *těhômôt* (תהומות) in Hebrew is the cosmic ocean (Gen. 1:2; 7:11; 49:25; Deut. 33:13; Job 38:16, 30; Pss. 74:12–15; 77:17; Prov. 8:24, 27–28; Hab. 3:8–10) that may be linguistically related to the Akkadian Tiamat, the chaos monster who threatened to devour the gods. After splitting her in half, Marduk used her carcass to create the cosmos (*ANET*, 67). Prince Yamm, the Canaanite god of the sea and the personification of chaos, was identified with the sea that is split in half and then crossed by the liberated exiles in Isa. 51:9–11. This poem echoes the mythological imagery of a *Chaoskampf*.

The sustenance of the cosmos is mentioned in an image in Prov. 3:20—"the skies continue to drip their dew." This life-sustaining moisture (cf. Job 28:25, 26; 36:27–28; 38:28, 37; Ps. 78:23) reflects the first act of J's creation narrative, which speaks of a "mist" arising from the earth to water the dry land (Gen. 2:6).

For this poet, Wisdom, portrayed as a goddess, is the giver of life, happiness, wealth, and honor; possesses great value; and becomes the agent of divine creation in originating and sustaining the cosmos. Dwelling within a poem of elegance and beauty, Goddess Wisdom becomes a literary metaphor for identifying the sapiential tradition with the divine attribute used in creating the cosmos.[67] Through the obtaining of Wisdom in studying and embodying the teachings of the sages, one possesses not only her bounties but also the means by which to understand creation and providence. By means of the artistry of this elegant poem, the poet shapes the order of the cosmos.[68]

Wisdom as Teacher, Goddess, and Divine Offspring: Proverbs 8:1–36

Once more personified wisdom plays the major role in this poem, which consists of some five strophes. The poem is an elegantly crafted text that largely focuses on Woman Wisdom's first-person praise of herself (i.e., aretalogy). This poetic exquisiteness is seen, for example, in that verses 1–11 and 22–31 have twenty-two lines (the Hebrew alphabet has twenty-two characters), while verses 32–36 consist of eleven lines. The poem also is organized in terms of form and theme into five strophes: verses 1–3 ("The Sage's Introduction to Woman Wisdom"), verses 4–11 ("Wisdom's Call"), verses 12–21 ("Wisdom's Providential Rule"), verses 22–31 ("Wisdom's Place in Creation"), and verses 32–36 ("Wisdom's Instruction of Life").[69] Woman Wisdom is portrayed in this poem in several literary guises drawn from the social and mythological worlds, including that of a peripatetic teacher who searches out and invites human beings to learn of her instruction (strophes I and II, vv. 1–11) and then seeks to persuade them to listen to her teaching (strophe V, vv. 32–36). This role of teacher and her invitation provides the inclusio for the entire poem. Other roles include her portrayal of a goddess of life, her presence at creation, and her description as the offspring of Yahweh who mediates between humanity and the creator and providential sustainer of the cosmos (strophes III and IV, vv. 12–21 and 22–31).[70] Taken together, these strophes suggest metaphorically that Woman Wisdom is the divine teacher mediating between God and humanity.

In 8:1–3 the voice of the sage introduces Woman Wisdom as a peripatetic teacher who journeys to a city to find students. In the ancient Near East at times the world is depicted as a city,[71] suggesting that it is a metaphor for the cosmos in this context. Of special importance are those cities dedicated to particular deities, and those that serve as the political capitals of a kingdom or empire. As the god's possession, these cities are understood as the center of the world where the divinely appointed rulers and the temple and its rites are understood as the means of maintaining the order of heaven and earth. Israel depicts Jerusalem in these mythological images, especially in the Zion tradition (see Pss. 46, 48, 76). This would fit the connotation of the parallel term, *těbûnâ* (תבונה), which points to understanding, practical knowledge and skill, and the ability to plan and accomplish an activity. The cosmos is thus "built" like a city. This relates closely to Wisdom's knowledge in "building" creation (Prov. 3:19; 8:27–31; Jer. 10:12; 51:15; Ps. 136:5).

She stands on the street or way (*derek*, דרך)[72] and at the "entrance of the portals" (*bêt nětîbôt*, בית נתיבות)[73] or the gates (literally the "mouth of the city," *pî-qāret*, פיקרת) that led to the temple and palace (*bêt*, בית).[74] The temple and the palace were located normally on the acropolis, not only for defense but also to portray the image of divine transcendence (the quarter of the city located skyward), the dynasty as ruling under divine selection. Jerusalem has the Solomonic temple and palace in close proximity on the highest point of Mount Zion (see 1 Kgs. 3–11, 13). The temple is described as being located on the heights (see Jer. 17:12; 31:12; Ezek. 20:40). David's palace was further down the mountain.[75] In the wise poet's metaphorical world of the city, however, wisdom is found making her way "on the summit of the acropolis" (*ro'š-mĕrômîm*, ראש מרומים), where she utters her teachings of life and rules over the cosmos and its social embodiments among humans.[76]

As a teacher, Wisdom takes her place at the gates of the city (Prov. 8:3; cf. 1:21), a place teeming with public activities, including judgment, prophetic announcements, commerce, and the arrangement of marriages within this legal sphere (e.g., see Deut. 21:9; 2 Sam. 15:2; 18:24; 19:1; Job 29:7; Amos 5:12, 15; Ruth 1:21). Metaphorically speaking, the gate is a threshold to a new way of life, when one leaves behind an earlier stage of existence and moves into a new one.[77] The image offered in this part of the poem is that of the teacher, in this case Woman Wisdom, who offers her discipline to the passersby who are foolish and without discernment.[78] In ancient Israel, Yahweh was often depicted as the divine judge whose just decrees gave creation its beginnings and enabled it to continue.[79] Wisdom's presence at the gate points to her involvement in the everyday life of human beings by issuing moral teachings that lead to life. She then offers up a hymn of self-praise as the queen of heaven who controls history, chooses kings to rule (a common ancient Near Eastern theme), and brings wealth to her followers. The fourth strophe is also a hymn of self-praise (Prov. 8:22–31) in which she describes her origins as the child of God present at creation and her position as the mediator between heaven and earth. She concludes with offering to her students an instruction of life (8:32–36).[80]

Verses 8:4–11 contain a protrepsis in which Wisdom as teacher invites humans to accept her course of study (see 1:21, 24, 28; 9:3). She offers humanity (*'ādām*, אדם) this protrepsis to learn of wisdom, for her words are truthful and right. Her "discipline" (*mûsār*, מוסר) is more valuable than precious metals and rare coral. This invitation and the location in a city, along with Wisdom's role as a teacher, identify the imaginative venue of the poem as a wisdom school in an urban setting. The invitation to the course of study consists of two features: exhortation (often in the form of commandments and prohibitions followed by rewards promised to those who accept the invitation and punishment for those who reject the instruction) and affirmation, that is, the repeated emphasis placed on the veracity of what is taught. Those whom she addresses are all humans, thus indicating the international character of wisdom in Israel, and the "simple ones" (*pĕtā'îm*, פתאים) and "dullards" (*kĕsîlîm*, כסילים), terms that point to those untutored in the education that the wise have to offer. Wisdom's invitation is offered to all humanity who are unlearned. Woman Wisdom raises her voice and offers an exhortation (see Prov. 5:13; Job 34:16; Isa. 28:23), only here she is the "voice" of God (Isa. 40:3, 9) that embodies the wisdom tradition, urges its actualization in human life through discipline, and affirms its validity.[81] In Prov. 8:3 her invitation is described as a "cry" (*rinnâ*, רנה), which is often a shout, sometimes cultic, of exultation (Jer. 31:7; Job 38:7) or a lament of great distress (Lam. 2:19). However, here the "cry" is an exhortation to learn her instruction (in Prov. 1:20) and to warn that catastrophe will overcome the ones who dally in accepting her discipline.

In 8:12–21 Wisdom becomes a royal goddess,[82] clothed in the guise of a mythological queen of heaven (Ma'at or Isis) who possesses both the charms of a fertility goddess and the insight of wisdom. In ancient Egypt the goddess Isis (here Woman Wisdom) offers her lovers and devotees the throne and legitimates their rule. The royal theology in Israel adopts much of the ancient Near Eastern mythical understanding of kingship.[83] The ruler is responsible for enacting *ma'at*, "justice and truth" and the order of the cosmos, in his reign. There are even elements in this theology (Pss. 2:7; 45:7; 110:3) in which the king is addressed as "god" and is the "firstborn" of Yahweh. In these texts, the monarch is given certain features that point to a divine nature. In addition, Yahweh selects and legitimates the dynasty of David (2 Sam. 7 and Ps. 89) and provides Solomon with the wisdom necessary to rule his nation (1 Kgs. 3:1–15).[84] This royal covenant, which becomes important in the Deuteronomic theology in Judah by warning of its excesses, is presented in a narrative rendition of Nathan's prophecy. The focus in the Deuteronomistic History is not on the divine nature of the king, but rather on the covenant that is maintained by Torah. This prophecy contains Yahweh's promise that he shall establish a dynasty ("house") for David, the first offspring being the one who will construct the temple. This throne will be established forever, and the relationship between Yahweh and the royal descendants is described in the kingship language of "father and son." While Yahweh promises that he will punish David's offspring when they sin, he also pledges he will not take from them his "steadfast love" (*ḥesed*, חסד), a theological term used for the bond between covenant partners.[85]

It is important to note that nowhere in Proverbs or in the other two canonical wisdom books is there any reference to the covenant between David and Yahweh. Instead, in this poem and further on in the sayings concerning kingship, the ruler and his house remain unspecified. Wisdom's selection and legitimation of kings is universal and is related to both their divinely given insight and their just rule (see 2 Sam. 14:20; 1 Kgs. 3; 4:29–34; 10:1–10). It is not until Ben Sira (47:1–11) that the Davidic covenant is mentioned in this corpus. In the Wisdom of Solomon the teacher presents a detailed exposition of 1 Kgs. 3:1–15. In Wisdom 7–9 the son of David is chosen by God to rule over his people. Solomon especially prays for and receives wisdom that enables him to rule with justice and according to the dictates of the sages. There is mention of the Lord's command to erect the temple in the city of his "habitation" (i.e., Jerusalem; Wis. 9:7–8). More important to the sages than the dynastic covenant with the house of David is the role of the king as a wise ruler who establishes and maintains justice in his social world.

Israelite and Judahite kings, the recipients of God-given righteousness, are expected to rule and judge the nation and his people with justice, defending the cause of the poor and punishing their oppressors. In so doing, God will provide the nation with prosperity and the ruler with long life, wealth, and honor (see Ps. 72).[86] Woman Wisdom gives to the rulers she chooses counsel necessary for effective governance (*ēṣâ*, עצה). This is a type of political and military wisdom that enables them to carry out their plans successfully.[87] Wise and righteous rulers enable their people to live in harmony with the cosmos and to experience prosperity, while wicked ones and their nations experience calamity (Job 12:18; 36:7).

The key passage that sets forth the theology of this poem, and indeed the entire first collection, is the fourth strophe in Prov. 8:22–31, which presents a description of Woman Wisdom's origins as the divine offspring, her presence at creation, and her role in mediating between Yahweh and the human world.[88] Unlike 3:19–20, Wisdom is not the agent of creation, but rather the firstborn. Thus the strophe concentrates on her status as the offspring of Yahweh. The form of this strophe is a hymn of self-praise in which Woman Wisdom describes herself as the darling child of Yahweh.[89]

One metaphor for the description of Yahweh is that of parent, while Wisdom is metaphorically portrayed as the divine offspring. Yahweh is both father and mother. Yahweh both fathers (*qānâ*, קנה)[90] and gives birth (*ḥûl*, חול)[91] to Wisdom. As the father and mother of Wisdom, Yahweh "procreated" and gave birth to her as the firstborn of creation "before all other things made in primeval times" (*pĕ'ālāyw*, פעליו; "things made"). She was the "first" of his "creative activity" (*derek*, דרך).[92] The term for "firstborn" in 8:22 (*rē'šît*, ראשית) indicates that wisdom is either the best (see "firstfruits," Amos 6:1, 6) or, more likely, the firstborn of creation (see Pss. 78:51; 90:2; 105:36; Job 15:7; 40:19). While there are exceptions, in the social world of ancient Israel, the firstborn son, assuming there are male offspring, is normally regarded as the primary heir of the family household (Gen. 43:33), receiving a double portion (Deut. 21:17) and at his father's death replacing him as the head of the family.[93] In cases where fathers have no sons but only daughters, however, provisions are made for them to be heirs as long as they marry within the father's clan (Num. 27:1–11; 36:1–12). In this strophe Wisdom, a daughter, is the only offspring of God and is therefore the favored child. It is personified Wisdom, a female, who holds this position of privilege.

Wisdom's origins are described in Prov. 8:23 in images of either birth ("poured out") or the inauguration of royal rule ("installed"). The verb *nāsak* (נסך) may mean both. "Poured out" (Gen. 35:14; Exod. 25:29) likely suggests the imagery of procreation, either in the emission of semen or in the breaking of the water in the mother's womb during the birth of her child. "Installed" (Ps. 2:6) would suggest the inauguration of royal rule, but "poured out" better fits the context of procreation and birth.

In a typical formula found in ancient Near Eastern creation texts, each of the lines of the three couplets in Prov. 8:24–26, with one exception (v. 26b), is introduced by "when there were no" (*bĕ'ên*, באין) or its parallels "before" (*bĕṭerem*, בטרם; and '*ad-lō'*, אד-לא). This negative way of describing reality prior to creation, a common formula in ancient Near Eastern creation texts, suggests not *creatio ex nihilo* but rather that the present order of life was fashioned out of an unformed chaos. In verses 24–29 the lines portray reality in the typical tripartite spheres (cf. Exod. 20:4; Ps. 24:1–2): earth, the deep, and the heavens (skies). In Israel and often in other cultures, this three-stage cosmos is held in place by the mountains viewed as great pillars. These pillars, and at times a heavenly vault (Gen. 1:6–8), are stablilizing structures that keep reality from collapsing. The vault also holds back the waters of chaos that, left unrestrained, would inundate the world and return the cosmos to the unformed state prior to divine creation (cf. Gen. 1). This image suggests the metaphorical portrayal of Yahweh as the divine builder or architect who constructs reality into these three parts and secures them. Yahweh is also portrayed in the metaphor of the royal judge who issues two decrees: one restrains Prince Yamm,[94] the embodiment of chaos, from inundating the cosmos; while the other legislates into existence the "foundations of the earth" (Prov. 8:29). Both decrees secure the stability of the cosmos, allowing the new creation to endure.

The most debated part of this strophe is verse 30a, which centers on the proper translation of 'āmôn (אמון).[95] While a number of different translations and subsequent interpretations have been offered, two have more evidence and are more cogent. One is represented by the NRSV: "Then I was beside him, like a master worker." This translation regards Wisdom in the same way she is presented in Wis. 7:22. In the latter text, wisdom is metaphorically portrayed as a preexistent architect (technitēs = 'ûmmān) who designs and builds the cosmos.[96] This is possible, since the imagery in Prov. 8:27–29 presents the metaphor of Yahweh as architect or artisan. However, it is Yahweh who is the fashioner in this poem and not Wisdom.

The other meaning is the one I have suggested in my translation: "I was beside him like a little child." I argue that the noun is the Qal passive participle of the verb 'āman (אמן, 'āmûn = Aquila, tithēnoumenē, τιθηνουμενη), a metaphor appropriate for this context, since Yahweh "fathers" and "gives birth" to Wisdom earlier in the poem. This "little child" is the "delight" (ša'ašu'îm, שעשעים) of Yahweh who is a proud parent receiving pleasure from the play of his offspring.[97] This delight, occasioned by her play and her rejoicing in the world of humanity, provides the intimate link between the Creator and the world of human dwelling.[98] Through their knowledge of her, the sages came to an understanding of creation. This is due to her representation as the only witness to this divine activity.

Finally, in the fifth strophe, Wisdom resumes the role of teacher and offers her protrepsis once again (8:32–36). She exhorts her audience (her "sons," bānîm, בנים) to listen to her, affirming that those that do will find life and obtain Yahweh's favor, while those who do not "love death."[99] This protrepsis returns the listener to the second strophe when Wisdom as a teacher first opens her mouth to offer to humanity an invitation to take up her course of study. Only now, Wisdom as a teacher is both the queen of heaven who provides them with life, honor, and wealth, and the divine offspring who mediates between Yahweh and the world of human habitation. The image of the ones who watch for her at her gates and wait by the portals of her door returns to the imagery of the first strophe, suggesting that Wisdom and her teaching are the means by which humans may enter into the world ("city") of creation and experience the life that is offered.

This closure, where the end returns to the beginning, gives the invitation of Woman Wisdom an aura of divinity that transcends the nature of a human teacher.[100] By taking up her discipline, humans participate in the knowledge and life-giving power of wisdom who, metaphorically, is a personified deity, orders society by the selecting and rewarding of righteous rulers, and entices them as her children to maintain the creation where humans dwell.[101]

It is instructive to observe that on two occasions (8:32, 34) Woman Wisdom uses the term "happy" (*'ašrê*, אשרי), which refers to the well-being that comes to those who engage in the study of wisdom (see 3:13–20). The goal of the protrepsis is the cultivation of wisdom that enables one to become a sage (*ḥăkāmû*, חכמו; "to become wise," v. 33).

Chapter 8 uses several metaphors from cosmological and anthropological traditions in other wisdom texts and in the creation myths of Israel and the ancient Near East in order to provoke the imagination of the hearers of the text, described as humans without knowledge, who are potential students to enter Wisdom's course of study. God is presented in three metaphorical depictions: the master builder who structures a tripartite world, the parent (father and mother) who engenders and gives birth to Wisdom as a divine child, and the judge whose commandment keeps the sea within its assigned boundaries in order to keep its destructive waters from flooding the land of human dwelling. There is no intimation of a primordial struggle with Yamm, who here, while personified to have a will that would choose to submerge the earth with its watery abyss, is prohibited from doing so by the divine commandment.

The poem also makes use of several metaphors to speak of personified Wisdom's several roles. She is the teacher who searches for students to assume her discipline (strophes I, II, and V). She is the queen of heaven who selects, gives life to, honors, and makes wealthy kings who, in ruling justly, enable their society to live in concert with the cosmic order and to experience well-being and prosperity. Indeed, within this well-crafted poem of elegance and beauty, Wisdom, the personification of sapiential tradition, lives and provides order and life. Wisdom is also personified to be the firstborn (and only) child of Yahweh, and in her play she evokes joy from Yahweh in the world of human existence. She provides the linkage between the Creator and his creation. Through the delight Yahweh has for her as his child, Wisdom serves as the mediator between heaven and earth. The divine child, Wisdom, enables the world and its human creatures to continue to live and to experience life in its fullness. Finally, she is the sole witness to God's creation, although in this text she is not involved in that activity. Through understanding her, one comes to the knowledge of God and creation. Gale Yee writes: "Woman Wisdom not only personifies God's own wisdom but also the human wisdom tradition itself. Divine wisdom and human knowledge find their unity in the personification of Woman Wisdom." In addition, Wisdom "represents divine immanence in the created world of human beings."[102]

On the basis of these two poems, it becomes clear that the faith of the sages in Proverbs 1–9 is centered in a theology of creation, in terms of both the origins of the cosmos and its sustenance for human dwelling.[103] The continuation of the forces of life operative in the cosmos is associated on occasion with retribution in which righteous actions by those who take up wisdom and the rulers who oversee their kingdoms lead to blessing, while injustice or the rejection of the call of teacher Wisdom results in not only the destruction of the "fool" but also endangers the continuity of the vital order at work in the cosmos and its social incarnation. The faith of the sages is expressed in terms of key metaphors used to portray Yahweh and wisdom. These metaphors are central to a theology of imagination that stimulates the hearer's mind to meditate on and then express poetically the mysteries of creation, both the origins of the cosmos and its sustenance by Yahweh, and the wisdom tradition that depicted God as the creator of heaven and earth who used wisdom to create and then to continue to sustain the world. Creation was not a once-for-all event locked inescapably in the confines of a primordial past, but rather was viewed to be a continuous action in shaping a world of bounty that the sages assist through their teaching. This cosmic order was to permeate the society of Judah in order that justice and wisdom might result in communal harmony and well-being.[104]

COSMOLOGY AND ANTHROPOLOGY IN PROVERBS 10:1–22:16

Introduction

Proverbs 10:1–22:16 is the second major collection (*měšālîm*, משלים), consisting of 375 sayings, in the book of Proverbs. These proverbs are placed in several wisdom forms and address many topics.[105] This lengthy collection has two parts: chapters 10–15, and 16:1–22:16, which vary in terms of form and content. The first subsection contains largely antithetical sayings that set in opposition the wise (or righteous) and the fool (or wicked). The second subsection (16:1–22:16) consists primarily of synonymous and synthetic sayings. In this subsection, one notes in particular the importance given to speech. Yahweh sayings and court sayings, uttered by those educated in the rhetorical arts, address the topic of wise and foolish speech. For the sages, language possessed the power not only to observe but also to shape the reality of which it speaks as well as the one who utters the speech.[106]

Creation and Justice: Proverbs 14:31

Justice is understood in the wisdom texts as a righteous order established by Yahweh at creation and maintained through divine oversight and actualization of the principle of retribution. Society is to reflect this divine order in its institutions, particularly those of kingship, family, and the legal process. Humans, created by Yahweh, are to take up the discipline wisdom has to offer and to embody its teachings in their character and behavior. In this conservative tradition, the sages speak of order in terms of the "fear of Yahweh" (piety), moral actions within the social order, and obedience to the wise instructions. Sages were taught not to rebel against this social order, since it was grounded in the justice of divine creation. There is no hint of a prophetic outcry opposing injustice done to the poor. Justice, as seen through the eyes of the sages, who were either well-to-do or served those who were, included providing impartial legal decisions for the poor, as well as seeing to it that they received the goods necessary for sustaining life. While one may reconstruct the sages' understanding of a just order, several sayings speak directly of this topic in theological terms by attributing its requirements to Yahweh as the creator of human beings.[107]

The initial theological saying about justice occurs in an antithetical proverb found in the first subsection, 14:31—"He who oppresses a helpless person insults his creator, but he who is kind to the needy honors him." Ancient Israel's social system, designed to provide the essentials for the poor, is described in the legal, historical, and prophetic texts, and less so in the other poetic literature, including that of the sages. The social system operated through two avenues of support for the destitute, who included landless Levites, widows, and orphans. The primary avenue was through the more substantial and extended families of the poor, who received support usually by being absorbed into these households. This social system worked primarily through the household's male members who were the next of kin to the impoverished. The second avenue was that of charity or alms given by the well-to-do, that is, outright gifts and the leaving of gleanings in the field for the poor to gather for food. The social principles that operated in the households and in the larger communities and that provided the system of charity were family solidarity (kinsmanship), the law of the levirate, and the moral responsibility of providing offerings of victuals needed to sustain life.

Family solidarity was the social basis for the household and family members' responsibility for one another. Extending beyond the family were the clan, households largely related by blood and marriage, and the tribe, a consortium of clans that in its folk traditions traced its origins back to a founding ancestor (cf. the twelve tribes of Israel and their eponymous patriarchs, e.g., Gen. 49). This social principle originated during the pre-state period and continued to function in the household well into the Greco-Roman period. One of the traditions that made up the system of social solidarity was the *gōʾēl* (גֹּאֵל, "redeemer"), who ransomed, protected, and defended the weaker members of the extended family.[108] For example, members who, due to misfortune, found themselves forced to sell the household's property and even themselves into slavery to meet their debts were to be redeemed by this redeemer, most often the next of kin to whom this responsibility fell (Lev. 25; Ruth; Jer. 32). Related to the tradition of the *gōʾēl* was the law of the levirate, in which it was incumbent upon the male next of kin to marry the widow of his deceased relative in order to father and raise up for him children, who would not only continue his name but also inherit his property (Deut. 25:5–10).[109] This was one means of maintaining the integrity of the individual family household and at the same time reducing abject poverty. This meant that the inducement to perform the responsibility was based on familial blood relationships. The legal system allowed the next of kin to renounce his obligation, even though there appears to be the stigma of shame attached to him for doing so (cf. Boaz and Ruth in the book of Ruth and her shameless kinsman whom the narrative does not name). This would then shift the responsibility to the second closest kinsman to assume the role of protector and provider.

Elsewhere in the biblical literature, the duties of the next of kin were extended to include everyone who had the means to provide charity to the poor, including even resident aliens (see the Covenant Code in Exod. 20:22–23:33, the book of Deuteronomy, and prophetic literature, e.g., Amos). Legal codes single out especially widows, orphans, and resident aliens without household support to be the recipients of charity from their neighbors (Exod. 22:21–27; Deut. 10:18; 24:17–21; 26:12–13; 27:19). Other social legislation calls for the giving of alms to the poor (Deut. 15:7–11), returning to the needy their property left in pledge when borrowing tools and implements from more affluent neighbors (Exod. 22:25–26; Deut. 24:12–13), the prohibition against the charging of interest to anyone, including especially the poor (Exod. 22:24), and the timely payment of the day laborer on the evening of the day the work was performed (Deut. 24:14–15).[110] In addition to harvest gleanings left in the fields for the poor to enjoy, the tithe of the third year was collected to benefit the destitute (Deut. 14:28–29). While it appears highly impractical and thus was not put into practice, the Sabbatical Year was legally stipulated to leave the harvests of that year in order to provide victuals for the poor and wild animals (Exod. 23:11), to forgive all debts (Deut. 15:1, 4), and to free slaves (Exod. 21:2–6; Deut. 15:12–18). Even more remarkable, but probably never implemented, was the Year of Jubilee (the fiftieth year in a cycle of seven times seven years) that required the returning of ancestral land to its original landowners (Lev. 25:10).

Kings and temples also were responsible to provide for the indigent in society. The kings were to protect legally (see Ps. 72:4) and to provide with food the poor and the weaker members of society (e.g., Ps. 22:26), while the temples took into account the impecunious by allowing them to offer less expensive gifts and sacrifices to Yahweh and to support the temple personnel (Lev. 12:8; 14:21; 27:8) and in the incorporation of laws in the legal codes that assured even the poor food, protection from oppression, and the benefit of God's protective care. Even though they were poor, the indigent were given permission to participate in festival celebrations and to enjoy the benefits of community and gifts of charity (Deut. 16:11–12). The Law and the Prophets condemned oppression of the poor and the ignoring and repression of their needs and legal rights.

On the basis of the above, one of the major social metaphors in the Bible for Yahweh is redeemer (*gōʾēl*, גֹּאֵל) of Israel from Egyptian slavery (Exod. 15:13; Pss. 74:2; 77:16; 78:35). He also is the redeemer of the poor who rescued them from their suffering and oppression by the powerful and wealthy (Exod. 22:21–27; Jer. 50:34). This also became a social principle that required the more affluent to aid the poor in their suffering and not to oppress them unjustly. While not explicitly indicated in the book of Proverbs, it is not inconceivable that this metaphorical rendering of God may have been part of the sages' understanding of their social responsibility.

The related themes of rich and poor or wealth and poverty are present in the wisdom texts, although with different understandings.[111] The sages valued wealth for its many benefits and regarded it as a divine gift for following the discipline of the wisdom tradition (Prov. 10:2, 15; 13:8; 14:20; 18:16, 23; 19:4). In addition, diligence and hard work were believed to result in riches (10:4–5). Thus it is no wonder that the sages tended to deprecate poverty, brought with it many limitations and dreadful consequences (14:20; 18:23; 22:7). Unlike certain religious traditions, for example, Christian monasticism, poverty was not valued for leading to a higher form of spirituality and religious existence, but was a wretched state to be avoided if possible (10:15). Wealth was not considered by the sages to be a hindrance to the wise life, but rather was viewed as a reward for orderly and moral existence. Poverty was at times even thought to result from laziness (6:6–11; 10:4–5; 24:30–34; 26:13–16) as well as from wickedness (12:3; 13:25, 33). Yet there were exceptions, including the fact that the wicked at times did acquire wealth and power through despicable behavior (11:16; 28:15–16; 30:14), and there were righteous people among the poor (15:16–17; 16:8, 16, 19; 17:1; 28:6). As noted previously in 8:19, wisdom was preferred over wealth. Through the capacity of sapiential imagination, some of the sages were able to envision a future world in which the poverty of the indigent would be eliminated and Yahweh would ensure that they would be vindicated and allowed to experience well-being and justice (Job 32–37; Prov. 2:21–22; 10:30; 21:13; 22:16; 24:20; 28:20).[112]

The proverb in 14:31 observes that the oppression of the poor person insults his Creator, while kindness extended to him brings the Creator honor. It is remarkable to note that there is no qualification of the poor that would require one to support them. The only significant characteristic is their poverty, nothing else.

Unlike some of the prophets, Israel's sages did not rail against an unjust social system that oppressed the poor, although they were critical of the powerful and rich whose opprobrious behavior led to their harsh treatment of the indigent. And they did expect those who were God-fearing wise men and women to treat the poor with justice and to sustain them in their degrading destitution. Wealth and poverty were viewed as part of the order of society; thus the sages did not initiate programs that were designed to eliminate pauperism. Poverty was a social fixture that bred injustice. Rather, through commandments to which they alluded and their own exhortations, the sages expected the righteous to care for those who lived in the midst of scarcity and need. For the sages, the poor's rights to exist and to have their needs met were based not on a theology of exodus liberation, but rather on a sapiential understanding of creation and providence: God is the creator of both the rich and the poor as well as the powerful and the weak. Thus all people deserved justice and support even when languishing in poverty.

Although the sages, with the exception of Qoheleth, avoided arguing that individuals were predestined to exist in these classes, they did think that being overwhelmed by destitution was the result of human sin and divine punishment or as divine testing and helpful discipline that would enhance moral character. Even so, Yahweh was believed to act on behalf of the insolvent to punish those who afflicted them and to require the wise to rescue them from the dire straits into which they had fallen (Prov. 22:23; 23:10–11).[113] This was one of the theological affirmations that urged the sage to live in harmony with the cosmos and thus to experience well-being and the many blessings of wisdom. Yahweh, of course, was the one who sustained this righteous order and thus enabled the wise, through his oversight and acts of retribution, to experience the goodness of a full and happy existence.[114]

Two synonymous words refer to the poor in 14:31: *dal* (דל) and *'ebyôn* (אביון, "poor, lowly, weak, and helpless").[115] These words are commonly found in texts that speak of the needy who require the support necessary to live (Lev. 14:21; Deut. 15:7, 9; 24:14; Ruth 3:10; Job 31:16; 34:18; Pss. 82:3; 109:16; Prov. 22:9). These people are contrasted with those who are rich and powerful (Exod. 30:15; Prov. 10:15, 22:16; 28:11). Groups of the destitute include families devastated by various catastrophes (1 Sam. 3:1), orphans (Prov. 22:22), and widows (Job 31:16). They depend on the generosity and justice of the wealthy to have their needs met and their rights upheld (Job 29:16; 30:25; Prov. 29:14; 31:9). Without the support of those with more resources than they need, the poor often will not survive, even though their oppressors will increase their possessions (Ps. 37:14; Prov. 28:8; Amos 2:6; 5:12). Thus this proverb emphasizes that proper support of the poor brings honor to the Creator, while their oppression insults him.

The theological foundation of social responsibility for the poor is clearly a theology of creation, for the Creator is the one who has formed and given life to the poor and continues to provide for them (Job 29:16; 30:25; 31:16–23; Ps. 112:9; Prov. 31:9). Ultimately, charity to the poor resides within the kindness of Yahweh, who created every human being (cf. Exod. 22:27).

In this antithetical proverb, two types of treatment of the poor are contrasted. "Oppress" (*'āšaq*, עשק) is used in the Hebrew Bible to refer to the harsh treatment of the poor in a variety of ways: extortion, exploitation, defrauding them of their goods and rights, unremunerated labor, enslavement for debts, and the general neglect of their needs (Deut. 24:14; Jer. 7:6; Ezek. 22:29; Amos 4:1). The theological rejection of the oppression of the poor is based on creation theology: oppression of the poor "insults" (*ḥērēp*, חרף) the Creator (*'ōśē*, עשה).[116] *Ḥērēp*, an active verb, is used in the Hebrew Bible to refer to insulting language that mocks, derides, or taunts its object (Prov. 17:5; see Judg. 8:15; 1 Sam. 17:10, 25, 26, 36, 45; Isa. 65:7; 2 Kgs. 19:4, 16, 22, 23). This proverb insists that the oppression of the destitute reproaches his (the poor person's) Creator. As often found in the Hebrew Bible, Yahweh is the protector of the poor and strongly aligns himself with them. In this saying, Yahweh is the creator of the poor. Thus to oppress his human creature, even a poor person, insults the Creator. The second part of this antithetical saying contrasts showing "kindness" (*ḥānan*, חנן) to the poor. This term is a reference to an act of charity extended to the poor, regardless of merit (see Pss. 37:21, 26; 112:5; Prov. 19:17; 28:8). In other words, the act of charity is one of grace, freely given. The charity is a gift of goods that the poor person needs in order to endure.

According to this saying, an act of charity consisting of something necessary for sustaining life "honors" (*kābēd*, כבד) the Creator. The word *kābēd* in the Hebrew Bible includes a variety of actions that glorify and show respect to others, including God (1 Sam. 2:30; Isa. 24:15; 25:3; 43:20; Pss. 22:24; 50:15, 23). The word may also mean to "worship" God, including the giving of sacrifices (Isa. 43:23). Thus the saying indicates that an act of charity done on behalf of the poor person "honors" the Creator (cf. Mic. 6:1–8), or is equivalent to an act of devotion extended to God in worship. The verb is used to speak of "honoring the poor" in Prov. 28:8 and Ps. 109:12.

Creation and Theodicy: Proverbs 16:4[117]

The problem of theodicy becomes severe in the wisdom tradition because of two key affirmations: the righteous order of creation[118] and the teaching of providence and divine retribution.

Near the beginning of the second subsection of the collection in 10:1–22:16 (i.e., 16:1–22:16), a synthetic proverb sets forth a very brief explication of the problem of evil:

> Yahweh has made everything for its purpose,
> even the wicked for the day of trouble.
>
> (16:4)

This is the last of four proverbs that broach the topic of the relationship between human plans and divine purposes (16:1–4). This proverb deals with the topic of theodicy.[119] In this saying, the verb that refers to divine creation is *pā'al* (פעל, "has made"). When God is the subject of the verb, the term is employed to refer to divine creation and providence (including retribution; see, e.g., Job 36:3; Ps. 74:12; Isa. 41:4). "Purpose" (*ma'ăneh*, מענה) most often conveys the idea of "answer, response" (Prov. 15:1; 29:19; Job 32:3, 5). In this saying, the noun denotes either the purpose of an activity or a corresponding idea.[120] This proverb explains the reason for the creation of the "day of trouble" (*yôm rā'â*, יום רעה), a time of judgment and punishment that will afflict the "wicked" (*rāšā*, רשע). The proverb does not intimate that Yahweh has created someone evil by nature, but rather that the divine origin of a time of trouble in providential rule has its purpose: to punish the wicked. This is a sapiential explanation of retribution. In traditional wisdom, the sages know the times, that is, when to act so as to be successful and when not to act to avoid failure. The more traditional sages, especially Ben Sira, articulated the view of a bipolar reality in which good and evil were opposites, though each had its place and function in reality. The sages taught that the wise were those who understood the structure of time and thus could act in ways to be successful or to avoid misfortune (see especially Qoh. 3:1–15; 7:14; 9:12; 12:1).[121] In this proverb, the wicked are created for the "day of trouble," a time of judgment and punishment (Prov. 11:4; Qoh. 7:17).

Creation and Economic Justice: Proverbs 16:11

Situated in the midst of sayings about the king, this proverb addresses Yahweh's concern for economic justice in the marketplace. Social institutions were to reflect the righteous order of creation. Social institutions, especially kingship, were created to be just and supportive of life (2 Sam. 14:26).[122] One of the metaphors of royal responsibility for justice is the idea that righteousness establishes the ruler's throne (Prov. 16:12; 25:5; 20:28 [LXX]). Hellmut Brunner has argued that these proverbs reflect the Egyptian view that the pedestal of the royal throne is identified with the primeval hill upon which the Creator stood when he brought reality into existence and established *ma'at* ("justice," "truth") as the order of creation. Brunner bases his argument on the fact that the hieroglyph for the royal pedestal and that for *ma'at* are the same.[123]

> A just balance and scales belong to the LORD,
> all the weights in the bag are his work.
>
> (16:11)

While the king is commissioned to actualize economic justice in Israelite society, Yahweh is still ultimately the one who oversees it. In this saying, the weights and measures used for grain, olive oil, and wine bought and sold in the markets belong to Yahweh, who ensures through retributive justice that accurate measurements are used in dispensing agrarian products. Standard weights and measurements are implied in several biblical texts (Lev. 19:35–36; Ezek. 45:10), and those who cheat and steal by shorting those with whom they do business are to be punished (Deut. 25:13; Prov. 11:1; 20:10, 23; Amos 8:5; Mic. 6:10–11).[124]

Worthy of note is the statement in the second line of the saying: "weights in the bag are his [God's] work (*ma'ăśeh*, מעשה)." "Work" occasionally refers to the creation, to the things that God has created, including the cosmos, and to different things in the created order, including human beings (Job 14:15; 34:19; Pss. 8:4; 19:2; 103:22; 104:24; 111:2, 7).[125] The term also refers to divine activity in history and in human life (Josh. 24:31; Judg. 2:7, 10; Qoh. 8:17). The theology of Prov. 16:11 is creation.

Creation and the Poor: Proverbs 17:5

The second subsection (16:1–22:16) of the larger collection (10:1–22:16) addresses once again the issue of creation and the poor (see 14:31). In this case, what is condemned by the saying is the improper attitude directed against the unfortunate:

> The one who mocks the poor insults his creator;
> he who is glad at (his) calamity will not be held innocent.
>
> (Prov. 17:5a)

The crimes against the poor in this saying include "mocking" (*lōʿēg*, לֹעֵג) him and "being glad" or "rejoicing" (*śāmēaḥ*, שָׂמֵחַ) over his calamity (*ʾēd*, אֵיד). Mocking involves hateful words spoken to the poor and shaming them, when presumably they approach someone to request help. This verbal abuse is directed against the destitute in place of the charity that the law and the sages require (see Job 21:3). Instead of offering aid to the impoverished, the wicked person rejoices over the poor person's calamitous state (cf. Ps. 35:26).

Mockers and deriders, according to this proverb, will not "be held innocent" (*yinnāqeh*, יִנָּקֶה). This verb refers to one who is not found blameless for sins or crimes in a court of law (Num. 5:28, 31). The language is metaphorical, since "mockers" would hardly be brought to trial. In addition, the verb may also suggest the notion of not being absolved from the social, legal, and moral responsibility to give aid to the destitute (Gen. 24:8, 41; Num. 32:22; Deut. 15:7–11; 24:12–15). Shame, not legal punishment, is the sentence.

Echoing the language of Prov. 14:31, the theological foundation for 17:5 is that these actions of mocking and derision of the poor "insult" (*ḥērēp*) their "creator" (*ʿōśēh*). As noted earlier, God strongly identifies with the poor (see Prov. 22:22–23; Sir. 4:1–10; Deut. 10:28; Isa. 3:13–15). The liberation of slaves in the exodus from Egypt is the theological basis in the legal and prophetic texts for divine support of the poor. However, the sages founded their theology of charity on creation.[126] It is the Creator who will not hold guiltless the person who rejoices over the calamity of the destitute, ignores their pleas for help, and exploits them. As both public defender and judge in a legal case, it is the Creator who condemns their mockers and deriders. To "mock" the poor is to "mock" Yahweh (cf. Prov. 14:31).

Organs of Perception and Knowledge: Proverbs 20:12

For the sages, the knowledge of God came through the tradition of the ancestors; observation of the cosmos, society, and human experience; reflection on and remembrance of sapiential teachings and experience; rational analysis that was in part related to the understanding that there were connections between elements in nature; and the activation of the imagination by means of key metaphors.[127] Imagination begins with the perception of the cosmos, society, and individual behavior, which lead, then, to critical reflection and rational analysis. All knowledge, including knowledge of God, is revealed through the order of creation, the tradition of the ancestors, and sapiential imagination that begins with the perception of creation and the memories of tradition, but then moves into other areas: critical reflection, redescription of reality, and the rendering of God and human existence.

Creation theology is the foundation of sapiential epistemology and the understanding of God, since insight came through the organs of perception. Thus in the second subsection of the second collection, the saying in 20:12 reads:

> The hearing ear and the seeing eye,
> the LORD has made them both.

Yahweh's creation of human beings is a significant theme in 14:31, 22:2, and 29:13. The organs of perception that make knowledge possible are created (ʿāśâ, עשׂה) by Yahweh: the "hearing ear" (Prov. 15:31; 25:12) and "the seeing eye." These are the organs that enable wisdom to be learned and assessed (Exod. 4:10; Ps. 94:8–9).[128] Unlike the priests, whose special knowledge of God, time, history, and the world came primarily through the casting of lots, or the prophets, whose ecstatic experiences and visions gave birth to their religious knowledge, the sages speak normally of organs of perception that observe, experience, analyze, reflect, and imagine.

Yahweh as Creator of Rich and Poor: Proverbs 22:2

Once again the second collection approaches the theme of creation as the theological basis for the topic of rich and poor. The proverb in 22:2 reads:

> The rich and the poor meet together;
> Yahweh is the maker of them all.

Wealth and poverty are significant subjects in the list of primarily synthetic and synonymous proverbs positioned in the concluding grouping of the second collection (22:1–16). The verb "meet together" (nipgāšû, נפגשׁו; see 29:13) refers to an intentional, not a chance, meeting between two or more persons (see Gen. 32:18; 33:8; Exod. 4:24, 27; 1 Sam. 25:20; 2 Sam. 2:13). Frequently, the meeting involves either arbitration to avoid litigation, the ending of mistreatment, negotiation, or intercession (Gen. 32:18; 33:8; Ex. 4:24–26). In this case, the rich and poor (ʿāšîr wārāš, עשׁיר ורשׁ) meet intentionally.[129]

The reference to Yahweh's creation of humanity, including both classes, the wealthy and the poor, would then refer to their common origins and providential guidance. The saying intimates neither divine predestination nor the doctrine of merit regarding economic status. Instead, when the poor approach the wealthy for support, they both are to remember that God has created them all. The poor and the wealthy share the same humanity, involving their creation and providential oversight.

By way of summary, one should say that the collection in 10:1–22:16 stresses that human society in general, and its specific institutions of household, social classes, royal court, law court, and avenues of charity, are formed and sustained by the Creator of heaven and earth by means of command and retributive justice. The divine justice of the cosmos is to be embodied by the community's members in order to participate in the sustaining and continuation of society.

CREATION, RICH, AND POOR IN PROVERBS 25–29

Introduction

The fifth collection, consisting of two sections (chaps. 25–27, 28–29), attributes its origins to the literary activity of the "men of Hezekiah," who are said to have "copied" or "collected" (*he'tîqû*, העתיקו)[130] Solomonic proverbs. Hezekiah, a Davidic king of Judah, reigned from 715 to 687/686 BCE and was viewed favorably in the Deuteronomistic History (2 Kgs. 18:1–20:21) in contrast to the kings of Israel and most of the other rulers of Judah, save for David, Solomon, and Josiah. None was without sinful behavior, but each, on the whole, was just and faithful. The superscription (Prov. 25:1) points to the activity of scribes and sages in the royal court of this king during the late eighth and early seventh centuries BCE. The several references to the institution of kingship (see especially 25:2–7, 15) and the emphasis on justice in this collection support the social location of the court, perhaps a royal school for the education of courtiers and royal scribes.[131] The collection's possible location within a royal school is supported also by the fact that it contains six references to Yahweh or Elohim (25:2, 22; 28:5; 29:13, 25, 26). These texts speak of the divine glory (*kābôd*, כבוד) that conceals his providential actions. He combines justice tempered with mercy, is known through the sapiential tradition, creates all of humanity, provides security to those who trust him, and ensures that justice is actualized in human society.[132]

The first section in chapters 25–27 is dominated by comparative proverbs, while the second in chapters 28–29 consists primarily of antithetical sayings that emphasize the contrast between the just and the wicked (cf. chaps. 10–15)[133] and broach the topic of rich and poor.

The Poor and the Oppressor: Proverbs 29:13

The synonymous proverb in the second subsection (29:13) brings up the subject of the intentional encounter between the poor individual (*rāš*, רש) and his "oppressor" (*'îš tĕkākîm*, איש תככים; cf. 14:31 and 22:2).

> The poor person and the oppressor meet together,
> Yahweh gives light to the eyes of both.

"Meet together" (*nipgāšû*, נפגשו), as indicated in the preceding saying (22:2), refers to a meeting that has a purpose, in this case an encounter in everyday dealings or possibly the court. *Tôk* (תוך) refers to one who causes harm to the poor, in this case (see Pss. 10:7; 55:12; 72:14).

The second line (Prov. 29:13b) points to the tradition about the creation of humanity as the theological basis that should inform a planned encounter between the two: Yahweh, as the creator of all humanity, "gives light to the eyes of both." *Mē'îr* (מאיר, "to give light") is a metaphor for Yahweh's giving of life to all human beings, including the poor individual and his potential oppressor (Job 3:16; Pss. 13:4; 38:10; 49:9; Ezra 9:8). The term could also suggest "enlightenment," in the sense of knowing justice.

In the context of an intentional meeting between the poor and those who have the ability to cause them injury, both need to remember their common origins and providential oversight. And both should recall the teaching that Yahweh is the special defender of the poor who are treated uncharitably and is the one who rescues them from their plights.

CREATION AND REBELLION IN THE "WORDS OF AGUR": PROVERBS 30:1–4

Agur is a mantic sage in ancient Israel, thus a model for later ones, including Joseph, Daniel, Enoch, and those who pursued this avenue of wisdom. His "words" may include all of chapter 30, although the extent of this collection is debated.[134] However, every scholar attributes the first four verses to the original collection, and this is the part that broaches the themes of creation, divine power, and human ignorance (cf. Job 28; Pss. 73, 90; Isa. 49:1–4; Bar. 3:29–30). The superscription (Prov. 30:1a) is difficult to translate, but I suggest the following:

> The words of Agur, son of Yakeh, a son of Massa;
> the oracle of the man.

The word *maśśā'* (משא) may be either a geographical location, Massa (cf. Prov. 31:1), or a noun used to designate the collection as a "revelation." There was a place in Arabia (see Gen. 25:14, which refers to the name of a son of Ishmael) that bore this name.[135] This translation would suggest that Agur is a sage from the East, likely speaking out of a mantic wisdom tradition in Arabia.[136] However, the word *maśśā'* ("burden, utterance, revelation") also could refer to prophetic speech given in the state of ecstatic revelation (2 Kgs. 9:25; Isa. 14:28; Ezra 12:10; 2 Chr. 24:27; Jer. 23:33–38; Zech. 9:1; 12:1; cf. the superscription of Habakkuk, 1:1).

The "words"[137] of Agur are called a *něʾūm* (נאם), that is, an "oracle," generally a term that refers to a prophetic word of God ("says the Lord"): Gen. 22:16; Isa. 14:22; 30:1; 31:9; Ezek. 13:6, 7. Occasionally, *něʾūm* refers to the ecstatic speech of a prophet or the song of an inspired psalmist (Num. 24:3, 15; 2 Sam. 23:1).[138] The words of Agur, then, are presented as mantic or charismatic wisdom. This means that, instead of taking up the discipline of wisdom taught in the schools by sages (see Prov. 30:2–3), Agur possesses mantic wisdom[139] given to him in inspired states by God (see Job 4:12–21). This would be the only place in Proverbs that mentions mantic wisdom. It is the omission of this tradition from Proverbs that makes the geographical meaning of the term more likely.

It remains unclear as to whether the entire chapter constitutes the collection of Agur, or only verses 1b–4, to which a response is made and other sapiential materials are added. The chapter comprises the following literary and thematic materials:

Verses	Form(s)	Theme
30:1b-4	rhetorical questions	enigma of creation
30:5–6	saying and admonition	divine truth
30:7–9	numerical saying	deceit and content
30:10	admonition	dangerous speech
30:11–14	four sayings	the wicked
30:15–16	numerical saying	insatiable desire
30:17	saying	dishonoring parents
30:18–19	numerical saying	mystery
30:20	saying	the adulteress
30:21–23	numerical saying	the world upside down
30:24–28	numerical saying	wisdom of little creatures
30:29–31	numerical saying	arrogance
30:32–33	admonition	arrogance

The major theme of this collection is the arrogance that causes one to reject divine sovereignty and to overturn the social order. This prevailing theme is found in 30:1b-4, 7–10, 13, 17, 21–23, 29–31, and 32–33.

Myth and Wisdom

Verses 1b–4 are extremely hard to translate with any certainty. I offer the following translation, which suggests that the verses refer to impossible questions about creation:

> 1b. I am weary, O God,
>   I am weary, O God, and I have become exhausted;[140]
> 2. Because I am more stupid than anyone else,
>   and I lack human insight.
> 3. While I have not studied wisdom,
>   I possess nevertheless the knowledge of the holy ones.[141]
> 4. Who has ascended to heaven and come down?
>   Who has gathered the wind in the fold of his hands?
>   Who has wrapped the waters in a garment?
>   Who has established all the ends of the earth?
>   What is his name and what is his son's name?
>   Surely you know!

If indeed the entire redacted collection of the "Words of Agur" is primarily concerned with the sin of arrogance, then it may be that this first section presents in the form of either impossible or rhetorical questions the theme of rebellion against creation, which is a mythic theme that I have explored in detail in my earlier monograph on Job.[142] In the ancient Near East, rebellion is grounded in hubris (the pride that leads human beings to reject the rule of heaven).[143] Agur's questions are probably not asking for information that is beyond human knowledge, but more likely are rhetorical, with unmistakable answers.[144] Agur concludes that it is God, not human beings, who has the wisdom and power to rule the cosmos, thus repudiating the rebellion of Job, who seeks divine knowledge and ultimately the throne of the ruler of heaven and earth.

In addition, the journey to the heavens and the return would likely refer to the mantic sage or seer. In Mesopotamia there are numerous references to sages prior to and following the cosmic deluge who, possessing divine knowledge, taught the arts of civilization to human beings.[145] The primodial *apkallus* achieved immortality and resided in the heavens with the cosmic gods, while the postdiluvian ones (Gilgamesh and Danel) did not receive this status. Prediluvian sages included Adapa (denied immortality) and Šuruppak in Sumer-Akkad, and Šubeʾawilum in Ugarit. Those who experienced the flood and represented the transition from the primordial *apkallu* to the postdiluvian *apkallu* were Ziusdra, Atra-ḫasis, and Utnapishtim in the Sumero-Akkadian tradition and Zurranku at Ugarit. These did gain divine immortality. Mantic wisdom points to an alternative sapiential tradition in Second Temple Judah, and has as one of its major themes the sage's "journey to the heavens" to obtain esoteric knowledge. In Jewish apocalyptic, Enoch returns with divine revelations that are esoteric, while in Mesopotamian mythology Adapa (the one known for great wisdom) and Utuabzu (another name for Adapa?) descend from heaven with wisdom. In some of the stories, these *apkallus* sought to transmit their special knowledge freely to human beings. Yet the gods denied humans the comprehensiveness of divine wisdom and immortality, attributes they reserved for themselves. This capricious act may reside behind the skepticism of Agur. According to Agur, there were great sages of the primordial past who ascended into heaven, yet none has returned. His son could have been the biological descendant mentioned in these legends. But since no one has descended again, this question also is an impossible one. The small collection of Agur in its early form of the first four verses is the one mantic collection in Proverbs.

A mythic metaphor is that of "ascending" (*ālâ*, עלה) and "descending" (*yārad*, ירד) in the first question in Prov. 30:4. In Gen. 28:12 Jacob dreams that he sees "angels" "ascending and descending" a ladder that reaches into the heavens. When he awakens from his dream, he names the place of revelation Bethel, or "house of God," perhaps reflecting a ziggurat or elevated temple. This metaphor occasions the idea of the revelation of divine knowledge (see Isa. 14:12–21; Ezek. 28). "Ascending" to heaven refers either to the obtaining of mantic wisdom or to human hubris that motivates people to believe they can scale the heavens and rule the cosmos themselves (cf. Gen. 11). "Descending" refers either to the return of the mantic sage with his revelation or to the fall of the arrogant from heaven (Job 20:6; Ps. 73; Isa. 14:14–15; Amos 9:2).[146]

Agur emphasizes in Prov. 30:1b–4 that he has no formal wisdom education and thus is not a traditional sage. Yet he still argues that God has given him mantic wisdom that allows him to recognize the futility of human sages' efforts to understand the Deity and the heavenly world. By echoing the legendary texts of the "Dialogue of Pessimism" and the "Epic of Gilgamesh," as well as the ascent of the Day Star (Isa. 14:12–21) and the fall of the king of Tyre in Ezekiel 28, Agur rejects the possibility that humans, on their own initiative, may ascend into the heavens to acquire either divine wisdom or immortality. Thus the answer to his initial and subsequent rhetorical questions in verse 4 is "no human being," with the implicit understanding that only God has divine wisdom and immortality.[147] The only mythical figures who ascended to heaven and returned were the *apkallu*s, including Adapa, who came close to eating the food of immortality, having been summoned to the world of the gods by Anu. This mythical image is later subsumed into apocalyptic literature involving the heavenly journey of Enoch to obtain esoteric knowledge.[148]

The following three rhetorical questions are similar.

> Who has gathered the wind in the fold of his hands?
> Who has wrapped the waters in a garment?
> Who has established all the ends of the earth?

All three have to do with divine creation and sovereignty over the cosmos. The image of "gathering the wind (אסף רוח, *'āsap-rûaḥ*)" is found also in Job 34:14–15 and Ps. 104:29. These latter two texts use the phrase to speak of the Creator's "taking back" ("gather," אסף, *'āsap*) his "spirit" (רוח, *rûaḥ*) resulting in death (Ps. 104:29–30) or, more likely, the "life-giving" spirit that he gives to animate all life. If God were to "take back" this spirit of life, then everything would perish (Job 34:14–15). Thus, for Agur, only the Creator is the one who gives and takes back his vivifying spirit. The second rhetorical question Agur asks is who has the power to "wrap the waters" (*ṣārar-mayim*) in a garment. This creation metaphor is found also in Job 26:8: "He [God] wraps the waters in his thick clouds." This metaphor suggests God's divine power in maintaining the separation between the dry land and the waters (Gen. 1:9).

The third rhetorical question reads: "Who has established all the ends of the earth?" "To establish" or "to set up" (*hēqîm*, הקים) is a creation metaphor that refers to God's establishing limits, in this case the "ends of the earth," that point to the outer boundaries of the cosmos (Deut. 33:17; Ps. 59:14), including even those regions opposing divine rule (1 Sam. 2:10; Ps. 2:8–9). The obvious answer is God. Thus the entire cosmos is covered in these three rhetorical questions.

The rhetorical questions of Agur concerning creation and divine rule end with his query: "What is his name and what is his son's name?"[149] This interrogative capstone emphasizes that no human being has the wisdom and power to create and rule over the cosmos. It is the epitome of human hubris to think that mortals have the ability to ascend into the heavens and to reign over the cosmos in the place of the Creator or to descend with esoteric knowledge to impart to human beings. This arrogance in which humans do not recognize their limits threatens the cosmic order and leads to the chaotic fall of creation (see 30:21–23). The skepticism of Agur and his assault on the creation theology of the sages derives from his crushing devaluation of human knowledge and its extremely limited areas of certainty.

The Collapse of Order: Proverbs 30:21–23[150]

Another reference to creation and its stability being threatened by humans who do not recognize their mortal limitations occurs in one of the five numerical sayings present in this brief collection. Whether the voice of Agur continues after verse 4 is doubtful. However, in the redaction of the remainder of the collection by one or more traditional sages, the observation is made in 30:21–23.

> Under three things the earth quakes,
> yea, under four it is unable to endure:
> a servant when he becomes a king,
> a fool[151] when he has sufficient bread,
> a spurned woman when she marries,
> and a maid when she supplants her mistress.

Numerical sayings, a common form in sapiential literature, elicit parallels between items or actions that the sages considered to reflect an underlying relationship. Comparisons were drawn between three, four, or even seven things or activities. In 30:21–23 the saying points to four things in human society and relationships that destabilize the created order: a slave becoming a king, a fool who has enough to eat, a spurned woman who marries, and a maid who takes the place of her mistress. What these transformations have in common is that the people who normally suffer from social stigmas and lower standing in society disrupt the social order when they supplant their overlords, have sufficient nourishment, or lose the shame of being rejected, and come to embody destructive arrogance and engage in actions that disrupt the harmony of the community.[152] The social world of traditional wisdom was conservative and resistant to change. Thus a slave, often a foreigner taken in war or an indebted Hebrew, could never become a king. In addition, a fool, according to the sages, often went hungry because of his refusal to work hard or his failure to plan. However, a satiated fool who continued to disregard wisdom's teachings threatened the normal operations of an orderly society. A woman despised or "spurned" by her suitors would ruin or make miserable any man foolish enough to marry her. Finally, if a "maid," usually a lowly servant who carried out only menial tasks (Exod. 11:5; 1 Sam. 25:41; 2 Sam. 17:17), supplants her mistress, then the social order is shaken as is the cosmos, which the social order embodies.

This undoing of the social order results in the "quaking" (*rāgaz*, רגז) of the earth. *Rāgaz* is used in regard to earthquakes in theophanies that visualize the response of creation to the Divine Warrior, who comes to do battle against chaos in mythic form or historical incarnation (Job 9:6; Ps. 77:16–20; Isa. 13:13; Joel 2:10; Amos 8:8–10).[153]

This numerical saying fits the thematic context of this collection: arrogance leads to foolish human actions and to the disruption of the cosmic and social order. Humans and the social groupings to which they belong are to continue in order that creation and society may also endure.

THE HISTORICAL THEOLOGY OF THE BOOK OF PROVERBS: CONCLUSION

Wisdom and Mythic Metaphors

Throughout the history of the development of the collections of the book of Proverbs, from the monarchy until the Second Temple in the Persian period, the sages in Proverbs, including teachers, composers, and redactors, make substantial use of metaphors in their teachings about the two related creation traditions present and often presented together in the Hebrew Bible: cosmology and anthropology. They speak of the world as the creation of God brought into existence by his offspring, Wisdom, and her rule over the earth in maintaining cosmic order. And they indicate that providence continues to sustain the cosmic and social order through obedience of the sages to the wisdom tradition, which includes in particular accepting the social responsibility of the poor and lower social classes that were believed to reflect the order of the cosmos and to result from divine initiative. This language of creation makes frequent use of metaphors that the sages appropriate from the mythic traditions of the ancient Near East, in particular the creation mythology of ancient Egypt: Wisdom is the child of the divine parent who rejoices over the inhabited world and its human population (3:13–18, 19–20; 8:22–31).

Divine Creation and Providence

The sages in Proverbs use a variety of metaphors to stimulate their imagination to portray the cosmos as the creation of a God who established and now oversees the structures of life. Through their rhetoric, the sages develop metaphors of creation that become the major vehicles for conveying their teachings, while the literary structure of sayings, didactic poems, and instructions depicts an esthesis of order and beauty that engages the imagination of the audience. Those who accept their invitation to learn from them enter into and dwell in the imaginary world they construct. God is the creator and sustainer portrayed by a variety of metaphors taken from the social world of the sages. While not specifically named warrior, king, judge, parent, teacher, or architect/artisan, God carries out these roles and functions. The allusion to the chaos myth is found in 3:19–20, where he splits open the deep, while the fertility myths of the origins of the gods are used to speak of God fathering and giving birth to his daughter, Woman Wisdom, who participates with him in the creation of the cosmos (8:22–31). As father he is the progenitor of his daughter, Wisdom, and as mother he gives her birth (8:22–25). Furthermore, he is also the architect who designs and then constructs the cosmos like a builder laying a foundation (3:19). The cosmos is an object of art, a city, a kingdom, and even a household in which Yahweh, Wisdom, and humans dwell in harmony and joy (8:1–11; 9:1–6), under divine providence.

As the creator and sustainer of humanity, God is the divine judge, who often renders his verdicts in rescuing the poor, blessing the righteous, and punishing the wicked (17:5; 22:22–23). Further, he provides both the poor and the oppressor light (a metaphor for both insight and life) and is the creator of organs of understanding that allow humans to know the world and to grasp the wisdom necessary to understand it (20:13). His role as king is implied in the metaphor of his daughter Wisdom, who rules over the earth (Prov. 8).

Creation and Anthropology

In their imagination, the sages categorize humans within a dualistic structure of wise/righteous and foolish/wicked. Traits of both are observed, delineated, and incorporated in the sapiential traditions. It is through the divine gift of wisdom, enhanced by study, reflection, and action, that humans learn to actualize justice in social life. God has given humans the organs of perception that enable them to understand knowledge and to become wise. And God is the one who requires justice for the poor and oppressed. Further, all people, rich and poor, have the same origins as the creatures of God, and all deserve both respect and sustenance. According to the instructions of the sages the poor enjoy the special protection of God. He will rise up in judgment against their oppressors and bring to destitution the wealthy who ignore their pleas. Finally, humans who respond to her invitation are Wisdom's students, lovers, and children who may receive the blessings she offers. Through obedience to wisdom, humans shape their character and make incarnate the wisdom tradition. And through their actions and speech, they shape a reality of history and language that undergirds and actualizes cosmic justice.

Creation and Goddess Wisdom

Permeated by justice, the cosmos is a world of both beauty and life. Wisdom is the first of God's creations who rejoices over the wonders of the inhabited world and its human inhabitants. Woman Wisdom, depicted in images of an ancient Near Eastern fertility goddess (cf. Isis), is incarnate in the instruction of the wisdom tradition, assumes the role of the teacher of humanity, and offers her moral instruction to those who would accept her invitation to learn from her. She is the incarnate voice of God who provides insight into both the Creator and the reality he has made and rules. Woman Wisdom is also the queen of heaven who dispenses wisdom and life to her devotees and chooses kings to rule in justice. The theology of kingship in the book of Proverbs is based on creation. Sitting on a throne based on righteousness, the king is selected by Woman Wisdom to rule over the nation. Through the righteous reign of the divinely elected king, justice, which permeates the cosmos, is actualized in the kingdom and results in social order, harmony, and well-being. The wise are the lovers of Woman Wisdom who, in their passion for knowledge, gain the insight to life filled with goodness and blessing. Finally, while creation and the voice of Wisdom tell of the divine nature of God, he continues to remain largely hidden from human insight.

Sapiential Creation and the Discourse of Power[154]

Ideology plays a substantial role in the shaping of literary texts. Most texts articulate what is considered to be in the best interests of the group that produces them. This is part of the quest for power of every social group seeking to establish its worldview and sociopolitical institutions through which self-interest grounded in the communal ideology is mapped. This means, then, that there are no "innocent" texts that are devoid of ideological concerns. How this plays out in the interpretation of wisdom theology is especially important to recognize. Indeed, the theology of the sages represents the major features of their ideology that undergirded their role within the larger social structure of ancient Israel and early Judaism.

The sages played a significant role in the administrations of the court. This is obvious from the scribes and sages mentioned in the narratives, particularly the Deuteronomistic History. The sages saw themselves as servants to the king, and some of them even achieved high office in the royal court. Lesser scribes served in the various roles of the royal administration, ranging from correspondence, to archiving, to taxation, to diplomacy. To achieve these positions, children of the elite attended wisdom schools that prepared them to acquire the knowledge produced by the culture, to interact with texts and persons from other cultures, and to carry on important social roles. Buttressing these social roles was the shaping of a theology in which the institution they served (i.e., the monarchy) was viewed as the instrument through which social order was effectuated. The theology of creation, in which a divine order regulated both nature and society under the watchful eye of the creator acting through the principle of creation, was socially and politically conservative. God (or wisdom) chooses kings, rules nations, and determines the events that affect their existence. By integrating themselves into the harmony of the cosmos and the social order that reflected it, the sages were destined to achieve well-being and success, measured in terms of social status, honor, respect, accumulation of resources, the household, and longevity. Their embodiment of sapientially prized virtues assisted in maintaining the stability of the social order based on the rule of a wise king, who reigned according to the dictates of justice. The sages of Proverbs had little place for radicals and malcontents who demanded a more just society (e.g., the classical prophets). Of course, Agur, not incidentally an Arabian rather than an Israelite or Judahite, does lampoon the obvious limits of knowledge that constrained the epistemology of the sages. Nevertheless, in Proverbs 30 his skeptical questions in verses 1–4 become a foil for the traditional sages to repudiate.

Chapter 4

Exilic Wisdom and the Babylonian Sapiential Tradition: The Book of Job

INTRODUCTION

Prelude

Following the destruction of Jerusalem, Judah became a Babylonian province under the governorship of Gedaliah, a political appointee by the Babylonian court. His father (Ahikam) and grandfather (Shaphan) had been prominent officials in the court of the Davidic kings, since Josiah and the reform (2 Kgs. 25:22). However, Gedaliah was soon assassinated by Ishmael, a descendant of the Davidic royal house, for collaboration with the Babylonians. The successors to Gedaliah are unknown, although it is likely the Babylonians appointed another Judean governor from the province, a practice that may have continued until the Persian period when Judah was incorporated into the larger Persian province of Abar Nahara ("Beyond the River"), which was overseen by a Persian official. A Judean governor still ruled Judah locally, but the Achaemenids appointed, at least in the early years, a descendant of the house of David (Sheshbazzar and Zerubbabel), and thus an exile, to serve. Not surprisingly the Persians sided with the returning exiles in the struggle to obtain the leadership roles in the colony following the decree of Cyrus in 538 BCE and the initial phase of the return to Jerusalem and Judah from exile. Since the leaders of the Judahite community were taken to exile, the Achaemenid court viewed them as the nucleus for a restored nation that would become a formative part of a larger province (see Ezra and Nehemiah).

The devastation of Judah and Jerusalem by the Babylonians was unparalleled in Judah's history, although its sister nation to the north, Israel, had been obliterated by the Assyrians. The issues of government, religion, and economy became predominant in the efforts to survive in both the *gôlâ* (גולה) and in the decimated homeland. The social, economic, political, and theological issues were interrelated. Economic devastation, exile, the slaughter of many in the war, the end of kingship, the homeland's loss of experienced and educated leadership, and the destruction of Jerusalem and the temple had to be addressed not only in terms of measures necessary to re-create a communal infrastructure, but also theologically. The justice of God and the meaning of election came under serious question. The responses of the exiles and those who remained in the homeland varied from the Deuteronomistic Historian's doctrine of retribution for corporate guilt occasioned by the sinful leadership of kings, to the repudiation of the power and justice of Yahweh (e.g., the wicked in Ps. 73), to debates over theodicy (especially Habakkuk and Job), to the anticipation of new acts of divine salvation and liberation (Second Isaiah).

The sage who composed the Joban dialogues turned once again to myth in Israel and the other nations of the ancient Near East. Many of the earlier conservative themes no longer obtained in a world of national holocaust. Thus myth had to be reexamined for metaphors that would render a new metanarrative for the sages in exile. The result was the poetic dialogues placed in the book of Job. The poet makes substantial use of the two classic Akkadian creation traditions (cosmology and anthropology), *Enuma eliš* and *Atra-ḫasis,* as well as sapiential wisdom texts, in particular disputations (see "The Babylonian Theodicy").[1] The poetic book is a theological investigation by a sage who examines the pressing issue of the justice of God within the context of fundamental social, political, economic, and religious change.

The History of the Neo-Babylonian Empire[2]

The poetic dialogues were written most likely during the period of Babylonian captivity (586–539 BCE), following the devastation of Judah and the sacking of Jerusalem. The Neo-Babylonian Empire (626–539), founded by Nabopolassar (625–605), following the conquest of Assyria, soon became the most powerful political presence in the ancient Near East.[3] His successor, Nebuchadrezzar II (604–562), defeated the Egyptian forces at Carchemish in 605, a stunning loss that led to their withdrawal eventually into the borders of native soil. This battle was followed by the defeat of the smaller kingdoms, and gave the Babylonians control of Syria-Palestine by 601. The city of Ashkelon that had been under Egyptian control was taken, but the Egyptians repelled the Babylonian forces that attempted to invade Egypt in 601. Judah, the small state in the south, came under Babylonian control (605–539).

When Jehoiakim (609–598), who had been placed on the throne by the Egyptians, decided to cease sending tribute to Babylon and joined the coalition of rebellious states in 601, Judah was doomed to defeat. His hope, shared by the other rulers of the region, for Egyptian support never materialized, and he died just prior to the first, limited exile of the leaders to Babylonia that occurred in 598. A later rebellion under the Judahite king Zedekiah met with an even worse and more devastating fate. He too depended on help from Egypt, but this also failed to come to fruition. The city of Jerusalem was destroyed and the major exile occurred (586). Following Nebuchadrezzar's death in 562, the last king of the Neo-Babylonian Empire, Nabonidus (555–539), took the throne after seven years of political turmoil. He moved to Tema in Arabia to secure a more defensible city. His rule ended when Cyrus the Great, the first of the Achaemenid rulers, easily took the city of Babylon in 539. Soon thereafter the Jews in captivity were given the option of returning to their homeland.

THE BABYLONIAN PERIOD IN JUDEAN HISTORY[4]

The Aftermath of the Babylonian Conquest

The widespread devastation of Judah reached its culmination in the fall of the capital in 586. The literary and archaeological evidence for the destruction of Judah demonstrates how massive it was. The razing of Jerusalem was so complete that it was not until Nehemiah in the fifth century that a reconstruction of the city's fortifications began and were then completed. The destruction of the temple and the ending of the monarchy, coupled with the exile of most of the population of the city, including the remaining upper class and artisans being taken to Babylon, was disastrous for the Judean sense of nationalism and its related theology.

The History of the Jews in Judah

In the eyes of the minimalist school, Israel largely created its entire preexilic history ex nihilo from the time of the patriarchs to the beginning of the Persian conquest of Babylon. The minimalists have used the language of Chronicles (2 Chr. 36:17–21) to construct "the myth of the empty land,"[5] that is, there was no exile. This narrative of destruction and exile was fictional. Peter Frei and Klaus Koch have added the twist that "Persian" propaganda, in legitimating Achaemenid rule over Judah, regarded the Torah as the creation of the Persian court.[6] The Jews loyal to Persia who needed a basis for their claim to Judah in the satrapy of Abar Nahara needed this type of propaganda. The exile was thus invented, either by supporters of the Persian Empire for their own ambitions, or by Persians who sought to empower locally loyal supporters. Yet if this thesis in one of its different versions is accurate, then why is there negative criticism of the Persians and their rule?[7] And how does the Persian invention of the Torah itself advance Persian self-interest? Neither theory is convincing.

Although the evidence for an exilic period in Judah is small, what there is cannot be lightly dismissed by ideologues opposed to historical reconstruction. The view that there was an important community both in Judah and in exile is abundantly evident in efforts to write a plausible history of this period.[8] Although there are few biblical references to the exilic community in Judah, enough Persian material culture points to the empire's presence in the region. Even if one disregards the Deuteronomistic History, Chronicles, Jeremiah, and Ezekiel, to name some of the more extensive statements, the book of Lamentations is best understood as emerging from a time of a destroyed Jerusalem and a temple left in ruins. Judah would have been subject to the same destruction of countries carried out by Babylonian armies that was at the center of the major foreign policy of Nebuchadrezzar II.[9] Archaeological evidence indicates that the Jewish community of the sixth century was greatly reduced in size.[10] The political and economic collapse occasioned by conquest and exile would have been devasting for the "people of the land" left to fend for themselves in what would have been wretched circumstances (see Lam. 2:2; 5:2–5, 9–11). While it is difficult to accept as historical the expression in Chronicles that during the exile the land was left completely desolate (2 Chr. 36:17–21; cf. Lev. 26:37–39; 2 Kgs. 24:14; 25:12; Jer. 39:10; 52:15), the country was stripped of its political, physical, and economic infrastructure. Thus some efforts were undertaken by those who remained to establish a communal existence[11] so that, when part of the exiled community began to return and to reclaim land and political authority, they were opposed by this group (Ezra 4:1–5; 10:1–17).[12]

The exile was not simply a debilitating experience, but also became a transforming one for biblical theology.[13] Certainly the anger against the Babylonians was not always subdued, as evidenced by the depictions of the desire for revenge against Nebuchadrezzar and the Babylonians (Jer. 50–51, especially 51:34–35; Ps. 137). These new developments in history led to a transformation of the theology of the sages.

The Jewish Community in Babylonian Captivity[14]

The conditions of the exiles are difficult to reconstruct with any reasonable degree of certainty, due to the lack of substantial evidence. Two extremes have been suggested as operative conditions of the exiles in Babylonia. Peter Ackroyd, while noting the conditions were "uncongenial," still remarks that it would seem that the Judean exiles had a reasonable degree of freedom, lived together in their own communities, served the Babylonians, and yet also were allowed to carry out a normal life of agricultural existence.[15] On the other extreme is the position of Bustenay Oded, who argues that the exiles, while not imperial slaves or subjected to permanent, harsh, physical labor, were still made to engage in forced labor, if and when their captors required it.[16] The latter position would provide a social background to Job's frequent references to forced labor and slave status in his diatribe with Yahweh. He presents himself in these terms, due to his ruthless treatment by Yahweh and the disparagement directed against him by other members of his community (Job 30; see below). However, it does appear that religious ritual and worship were permitted in certain locations (cf. Ezra 8:15–20). Oded's reconstruction does allow for the exiles to have essentially self-administered communities for internal matters, and thus he rejects the notion that they held the legal position of slaves. Yet how does this correlate with the contrary statement of Ezra in Neh. 9:36 that the liberated Jews were slaves? The answer depends on how to define the term "slave." If it refers primarily to people led into exile against their will and governed by a foreign empire that denied them the rights of citizens, then they were, for all intents and purposes, slaves. They were probably pressed into service by their captors for a variety of projects that required their labor and skills. Otherwise, they were allowed to inhabit their own communities and exist under an authoritarian system.

We know very little about the elite of Jewish society and leadership taken into captivity (see Lam. 1:3), although this group would have included not only members of the royal aristocracy, but also other members of the court, highly placed officials, the wealthy, intellectuals who taught in the royal school, and artisans. Thus the poet of Job could be placed among these deportees (see the character's description of wealth, fear of God, and respect in both the older tale in Job 1 and in the poetry, especially chaps. 29–30). They were collectively known, along with the other groups of Judean exiles, as the *'am haggôlâ* (עם הגולה), the people of the exile, and were regarded theologically by the Chronicler, Jer. 24:1–10, and Ezek. 33:23–29 as the legitimate elect community of God. It is evident from the biblical texts dealing with the period that this group was interpreted not only as socially and intellectually superior to "the people of the land" (Jer. 24:29), but also as the chosen vessel of Yahweh who would carry on the election tradition and one day would return to inherit the land, rebuild the temple, and reinstitute the institutions of the Davidic monarchy (Jer. 30–31) and related ones (a royal administration, and likely a school and a library for archives).

Based on what little literary and archaeological evidence we have, it is apparent that the exiles of Judah lived in their own villages, which were ensconced among the settlements of exiles from a variety of conquered peoples, and that they were able to form their own communities and associations. In addition to the substantial growth in the numbers of villages in the central flood plain of the Euphrates during the Neo-Babylonian epoch (from 143 villages in the Middle Babylonian period to 182 during the Neo-Babylonian period) that would have included Jewish communities,[17] there are also the Murashu documents, a later archive from Nippur, which contain many Hebrew names. While these texts date from the reigns of the Persian kings Artaxerxes I and Darius II, they probably reflect developments during the earlier Neo-Babylonian period. Some of the captives, joining other conquered groups, likely were put into forced labor in Babylonia as imperial slaves.[18]

Indeed, even those who settled into their own ethnic communities likely did not possess any rights of citizens. The language of imprisonment and metaphors of slavery are numerous in texts likely dating from this period (Isa. 43:6; 45:14; 52:2; Jer. 34:13; Mic. 6:4; Pss. 105:18; 107:14; as we shall see, they provide the major metaphorical depiction for human existence in Job). Members of the Judean captives became compulsory laborers and royal slaves who served as imperial land tenants, as well as craftsmen and builders of royal projects.[19] This situation likely would have continued throughout the entire period of their captivity under Babylonian hegemony.[20] This social status is reflected in Job's metaphorical description of humanity as living the dreadful lives of slaves.

LITERARY ACTIVITY DURING THE EXILE

Prelude

The exile was a period for prolific composition and editing of texts, especially among the exiled Judean intelligentsia in Babylonia. To preserve the past and to respond to the difficulties of the present, and to shape a hopeful future that encouraged a ravaged people to live into its possibilities, the writing down of past written and oral traditions and their editing became important tasks for the exiled scribes, including the sages whose orientation to social life in the monarchy was under threat. Indeed, the exiles included both a former king, Jehoiachin, and a blinded Zedekiah and their larger Davidic families. How much their authority continued into captivity with them is impossible to say, although one could speculate that their exiled courts, priests, and scribes would have shown them deference. However, the questioning that required the reworking of tradition and a meaningful response had to engage the issues of the destruction of Jerusalem, the exile of the house of David, the loss of the temple and the execution of its higher echelon of priests, and the slaughter of so many, including aged and young inhabitants who could not engage in military defense. The literature, still preserved, provides an inside look at the devastation and the responses to the period's pain and challenges. Among these, the book of Lamentations, with its depiction of the devastation of the city of Jerusalem, provides the insight of the community left behind to attempt to engage in efforts to rebuild both lives and faith. The social and economic effects of the period had to be explained theologically to a severely traumatized population in Judah and in the captivity, before the rebuilding of the nation devastated by war could even be reimagined.

The forced separation between the remnant of those left behind and the captives, who included the former aristocracy and intelligentsia, led to different responses and eventually to conflicting views of life and the building of sociopolitical institutions formed to express their varied existences during the exilic period. Issuing from the experiences of the people left behind in exile were two important texts: Lamentations, with its mournful cries from Jerusalem, and

Habakkuk, who, in asking the question of theodicy, "how can God use a wicked nation to destroy his own elect nation," receives the general and somewhat discomfiting answer that "the just shall live by faith." This would be of small comfort to mothers whose children perished in the holocaust of flames and to exiles who were languishing in a foreign land.

Jewish Literature Written in Babylon

Not only did intellectuals among the Jews in Judah both prior to and during the exile present different responses to the crisis of the exile, but so did leading voices among the exiles. The latter community's views ranged from the assurance of divine deliverance, to a desire for revenge, to portrayals of the new Jerusalem once the captivity was over, to intense questioning of the justice of God and the nature of human existence in the cosmos. These expressions are found in Second Isaiah, part of Ezekiel, the Deuteronomistic History, and, of course, the book of Job. Ezekiel advanced the theology of an elect people whose entire history had been one of wickedness. The small comfort he offers is that of individual responsibility, that the "sins of the fathers" would not continue to "be visited on the heads of their descendants" until the third or fourth generation. Even so, this teaching became a monstrous view of individuals' sins as the basis for their destruction in the face of the suffering of the innocent who were not responsible for the destruction or destitution. Second Isaiah simply announced that the time of punishment was at an end and hoped to raise the eyes of the exiles to a future redemption by adapting the language of the exodus from Egypt to speak of a time of new liberation that will allow the captives to return home. He even introduces the theology of vicarious suffering, indicating that the punishment and death of the righteous had a redemptive effect of removing wickedness from the chosen people. Yet again this indirect explanation of the Babylonian holocaust is built on the sands of corporate sin as the reason for the exile. Finally, the Deuteronomistic Historians offer the theological response of retribution and choice. People are offered the options of choosing life or death, of being faithful to Yahweh through obedience to the commandments and acts of love for the neighbor or remaining defiant in rejecting the law and the commandment of love. Even so, these historians cannot escape the same trap of arguing that wickedness of kings, other leaders, and the people themselves led to the exile. The only text of the period that captures the outrage of the exiles is Psalm 137, which, in response to the captors' taunts about the ineptitude of their Deity, expresses words of vengeful exclamation of mothers bereft of their murdered children: "Happy is he who dashes the heads of your [the captors'] little ones against the stones."

Dating the Poetry of Job

If the poetic dialogues emerge as the calculated theological response to this crisis, then the other segments of the book fall into place chronologically. First, the prose narrative, partially preserved in Job 1–2 and 42:7–17, would likely date from a preexilic period in a wisdom setting that offers a response to undeserved suffering in the form of the faithfulness and patience of Job. Two poetic compositions later in the Persian period would have been added to the dialogues: the poem on Woman Wisdom (chap. 28) and the Elihu speeches (chaps. 32–37).

The book of Job and its various parts provide no direct evidence as to location and historical setting. One reference to the integrity of Job, probably from an older folktale, is found in Ezek. 14:14. Thus it appears that by the time of Ezekiel in the early sixth century BCE the narrative, a didactic tale, had already achieved some notoriety. It is likely that the folktale was told orally and then possibly written down during the First Temple period in order to present a story of edification for young students in wisdom schools.

Several factors point to the location and period of the dialogues being composed during the Babylonian exile. First, if one reviews the wisdom corpus as a whole, the book of Job, including its additions, would have been composed prior to the periods of Ezra in the early fourth and Ben Sira in the early second century BCE when the Torah and the themes of salvation history were combined in shaping the theology of the Second Temple sages. These themes are not present in the dialogues.

A second factor is that of theological crisis with which the poetry struggles, and in particular the theme of theodicy. The poet's rejection of the doctrine of retribution (cf. the affirmation of the teaching in Prov. 10:3, 29; 12:2; 16:3, 7; 17:3; etc.) would enable the people in exile to realize they were not responsible for the tragedies of the destruction of Jerusalem, the devastation of the land, and their consequent removal to Babylon. Rather the fault lay with a Deity who had turned against his own people and indeed against the entire creation. This provided a difficult but possible interpretation of the horrors of the holocaust. It was this period that challenged traditional faith. New theological traditions and the rewriting of older ones were required to provide the basis for the renewal of national life.

The third factor is that this period was the most theologically creative and productive one in the history of ancient Israel and early Judaism, prior to the late Hellenistic period. This outpouring of written texts was intent on preserving the past and formulating a new theological and national identity. It is within this creative flow of composition that the book of Job is likely positioned.

A fourth factor derives from the extraordinary parallels between the themes, language, and forms of Babylonian wisdom and those of the Joban poetry. These would derive only from a direct knowledge of Babylonian wisdom resources and perhaps even an acquaintance with their sages and teachers. After all, Aramaic had become largely the common language of the Near Eastern world, and it would not be surprising to find Judean intellectuals well educated in various languages, including Babylonian cuneiform and Aramaic, having the ability to interact with their conqueror's traditions and intellectuals.[21]

A fifth and final factor is linguistic. It has been recognized for a long time that there is a close affinity between the language of the poetic book of Job and Second Isaiah, with a secure dating of the latter in the exile.[22] Placing Job in the first generation of exiles explains the absence of major traditions of election, salvation history, covenant, and Torah. The poet thus shapes his own theological response to the captivity by including views from the Babylonian tradition, and his own unique perspectives on the suffering of the innocent and the issue of theodicy. It was in Babylonian captivity that the poetic dialogues were written and allowed to reconfigure substantially the meaning of the earlier prose tradition of Job.

Other features include the reference to "the Satan" in Job 1–2 as an office (cf. Zech. 3:1–2) and not a personal name as it became later in the postexilic period (1 Chr. 21:1), the likely dependence of Job 3 on the lament of Jeremiah in 20:14–18, and the literary style that is close to that of the exilic prophet Second Isaiah.

WISDOM IN MESOPOTAMIA AND ITS INFLUENCE ON THE BOOK OF JOB

Introduction[23]

It is noteworthy that in Akkadian the terms for "wisdom" include not only practical advice and ethical decision-making, but also magic, cultic skill, and priestly knowledge. The sage's knowledge derives not only from personal experiences and ancestral teachings, but also from the revelation of divine knowledge given him/her by the gods or transmitted by the priests who possess it due to their mastery of omenology.[24] Of course there were many areas in which the sages lacked knowledge or sufficient insight, for example, the world and activities of the gods. For Sara Denning-Bolle these same terms for "wisdom" and "wise" may often refer to numerous occupations, skills, and bodies of learning. Wisdom also means "knowledge," "craft," "intelligence," "skill," and "clever."[25] She notes that this vocabulary stresses "capability, knowledge required of a craft, skill, and expertise." The words, however, also refer to active knowledge that may include rituals of sacrifice and the reading of omens, something not in the repertoire of Israelite and Judahite sages.[26] The connections between wisdom and cult, and between wisdom and esoteric knowledge and activity, point to a close relationship between these areas.[27]

The Apkallus

An important group of the wise, in addition to sages and scribes, is reflected in the mocking of Job by Eliphaz, who asks his opponent if he thinks he is the first man (15:7–16). This series of satirical questions combines the related traditions of the first man, and especially the *apkallu*, present in Sumero-Akkadian literature and art. Babylonian sages, of whom the literate exiles would have had some knowledge and even contact, were teachers, administrators, and scribes who traced their tradition to the ancient *apkallus*, from whom they believed they were descended. Prior to the great deluge, the *apakallus* received the knowledge of the gods concerning the making of the important institutions of civilization and the shaping of human culture, both needed for humans to exist and continue. Assumed to have begun in the promordial beginnings, the knowledge of these primordial savants continued after the flood through the great sages, the *ummanu*s. One of the *apkallu*s was Utnapishtim, also called Atra-ḫasis, "The Exceeding Wise."[28]

Schools

A social institution in Babylonia that produced the literature and copies of Mesopotamian classics is the school. The schools in the regions of Sumer and Akkad are well documented in the literature and material culture, particularly in the archives of cuneiform tablets that have been excavated and translated. The Sumerians called a school the *edubba* ("tablet house"), and the subsequent Akkadian cultures called it the *bīt ṭuppi*. These schools and the texts that refer to them are well summarized in a variety of modern studies.[29] While Nabû and Marduk were the gods who possessed and acted on the basis of wisdom and Ea was the patron deity of the sages, Nisaba was the protective goddess of the *edubba* who received the teachers' and students' devotion. This may suggest a similar understanding in ancient Israel and Judah, where Yahweh/Elohim is mentioned in the wisdom texts and is the focus of sapiential piety ("the fear of the Lord/God").

WISDOM LITERATURE IN SUMER-AKKAD AND THE BOOK OF JOB[30]

The Babylonian Theodicy[31]

This diputation bears striking resemblances to the Joban dialogues. It surprisingly indicates a strong indifference to injustice and evil. Also appearing in the "dark ages" of the Cassite rule of Babylonia,[32] a time of despair reflected in a number of writings, this dialogue includes a sufferer and his friend.[33] Unlike the later dialogues in Job, these disputants exhibit mutual respect. The sufferer laments his situation of suffering within the context of the eternal decree of death, made even worse by the abandonment of his personal god. The friend exhorts him to persevere in both piety and patience, observing that the wicked will receive their just chastisement. However, a skeptical sufferer retorts with his decision to repudiate both piety and wisdom, since they bring him no respite from his ordeal. Indeed, his experience is common to creatures and humans, meaning that the deity is responsible while humans continue in their indifference. In his final speech, the friend expresses his empathy with the sufferer and supports his argument. Indeed, the gods are responsible for creating humans with a wicked nature inclined toward lying. Finally, the sufferer exhorts his friend to stand by him. Yet he never denies his innocence. He concludes still exhorting the deity, his consort, and the god of justice, Shamash, to redeem him from his unjust suffering.

A Version of the Just Sufferer

Jean Nougayrol has offered a critically reconstructed Old Babylonian text from Ugarit, which he calls a "version of the just sufferer" (AO 4462),[34] that also echoes parts of the arguments of the dialogues of Job, especially the speeches from the whirlwind and Job's responses. Though fragmented, the text appears to present a dialogue between a righteous sufferer and his deity. An omniscient narrator portrays the suffering and distress of the sufferer that he seeks to have his deity redress. The sufferer even repents, although he is at a loss to know what his guilt is. Like Job, he also questions his god as to why he is suffering so intensely. The deity responds that he is redeeming him from suffering, but also admonishes him to remember his god, who is his creator, if he wishes to have a happy conclusion to his difficulties. When he is redeemed, the man tells of his salvation and then praises his deity. Like the book of Job, there is no explanation of his or humanity's unjust suffering. Once delivered, the sufferer speaks of his experiencing well-being and being granted life. He then engages in praise of his god who has redeemed him. The question as to the reason for his suffering is not answered.

"I Will Praise the Lord of Wisdom"[35]

Especially comparable to Job in content and a similar historical setting are a number of poems and dialogues that may have provided the poet a prototype for his disputations. Written during the Cassite period in the Late Bronze Age, "I Will Praise the Lord of Wisdom"[36] is an autobiographical narrative in which the voice of the text assumes a persona of a nobleman who speaks despairingly to Marduk, his personal deity, of his shameful loss of status and personal suffering and degradation. Finally, after his laments and the visit of diviners, the god redeems him. In the conclusion, the nobleman comes to the temple (Esagil) to express his thanksgiving and to offer his sacrifices to Marduk and his consort.

The Dialogue between a Man and His God[37]

The other texts appear to have been written near the end of the Late Bronze Age period when the Cassite reign was beginning to dissipate. "The Dialogue between a Man and His God" is a second text similar to Job.[38] This dialogue includes two speakers.[39] The first is a nobleman who has lost favor with both his lord and his god, leading to his intense suffering. He expresses his innocence, and, like Job and the psalms of accusation, even holds his god responsible. Yet he has no recourse but to continue his lament and express his cry for deliverance (see Job's opponents advising him to do the same, e.g., 5:8–27). At the conclusion, a third-person narrator speaks of the young man's deliverance. Thus the example of this person is clearly upheld: plead to the personal god for deliverance from suffering and restoration may result.

The Dialogue of Pessimism

A third parallel text to the poetic dialogues of Job is "The Dialogue of Pessimism."[40] Originating in the Cassite period, possibly the twelfth century BCE, this Akkadian text is a dialogue, not a contentious disputation. If serious in purpose, the text concludes with the denial of all meaning (cf. Qoheleth). If satirical, the composition lampoons the sagacious effort to discover the way of living that will lead to meaning, possibly even success. What the lord in this text desires is a course of action that gives direction to living, that is, something worth pursuing. Making a choice, his accommodating slave is quick to confirm the decision with obvious advantages that will accrue, but also then supporting the master's decision to abandon that choice, pointing to the disaster that would result. The slave is the true sage, for he recognizes that there is no true course of action to discover meaning, even offering his life to prove his point, confident that the despondent master would not live more than three days after his faithful slave's death. Although there are numerous parallels between this text and Job, the latter has no real consideration of suicide. Instead, Job is driven by his desire to prove his innocence and to uncover the sadistic Deity who destroys what he created.

Conclusion

These literary parallels with the book of Job not only illuminate and enrich the meaning of the text, but also raise the important questions with which the Job of the poetry dwells: theodicy, the relationship between ethics and success, retribution, the abusive deity, human suffering, and even a final judgment (occurring in the Joban narrative and some of the fables). In addition, these texts suggest a context in which the Joban poet was active: the Babylonian captivity in which the sage may have had access to these texts or at least knew of them by oral communication of the sages in the court and temples.

THE NARRATIVE AND SAYINGS TRADITION IN ARAMAIC: THE WISDOM OF AHIQAR[41]

Another popular wisdom text of the same period as the Joban dialogues is "The Wisdom of Ahiqar." Written in Aramaic, this text, likely redacted in its final form in the sixth century BCE,[42] originated in Syria, although it is found in numerous places during its transmission history in the ancient Near East. The papyri at Elephantine contain the narrative and sayings of Ahiqar, thus indicating that the final edition was no later than the fifth century BCE.

As is the case with Job, the narrative and the sayings are composed at different times. The Aramaic of the sayings is more antiquated than the standard Imperial Aramaic of the narrative and contains features of Canaanite. The popularity of the final form of Ahiqar is indicated by its translation into several other languages and the discoveries of copies in a widespread area of the ancient Near East. One very late literary text from Warqa reads, "In the time of King Esarhaddon, *a-ba-^dNINNU*-da-ri whom the Aramaeans call ^m*a-ḫu-u-qa-a-ri*, was *ummanu.*"[43] While this is a tablet dating from the Seleucid period, it does point to a tradition of an Aramaean, Ahiqar, who held the position of a sage in the late Assyrian period. It suggests a widespread literary tradition of Ahiqar, but is not evidence of his historicity. This also correlates to the indications of Aramaic scribes in the court of the Neo-Babylonian Empire, especially as Aramaic became the lingua franca of the Levant.[44]

While the narrative is well preserved and is not difficult to translate, the sayings have numerous lacunae.[45] The narrative is much better preserved. As is the case with the Joban and Joseph legends, the narrative of Ahiqar is a didactic tale that includes a protagonist or hero who, although wise and virtuous, falls into crisis due to the evil machinations of an antagonist. Ahiqar, "a wise and skillful scribe" who is the vizier of the Assyrian king Esarhaddon, is imprisoned due to the deceit of his nephew Nadin. There he composes his sayings, and then is released and restored while Nadin is reprimanded and ultimately dies.

The content of the sayings is noted for the praise of the king and his fearsome power and a poem to Wisdom. The latter is present in saying 13 and parallels Job 28:

> From heaven the peoples are favored;
> Wisdom is of the gods.
> Indeed, she is precious to the gods;
> Her kingdom is *et[er]nal.*
> She has been established by Šamayn;
> Yea, the Holy Lord has exalted her.[46]

The important parallels of this Aramaic text to Job are significant: the combination of a narrative story with wisdom sayings and teachings, the poem about Wisdom, the importance of language, and the theme of the power of the gods, who should not be offended.

THE SOCIAL DEPICTION OF JOB AS LITERARY CHARACTER

The Social Status of the Disputants

The hero of the folktale, Job, is a wealthy aristocrat renowned for his wisdom, piety, and justice, while his three friends with whom he debates are also members of the elite of society. In the transition to the poetry, however, the status of the characters is altered in the case of Job, who has plummeted into the refuse pit, losing all of his wealth and children, while the three opponents continue in their elitist position. Unlike Job, who is willing to question the major tenets of sapiential teaching, including the justice of God, the well-being of the righteous, and the theory of retribution, the three friends (who slowly become his opponents) are the champions of divine justice and the advocates for the validity of retribution. At issue is the justice of God and trust in the goodness of the Creator. Not only are the characters well-to-do and highly educated and thus members of the social elite, but so is the author, an intellectual who writes for others of the same social and intellectual class.

Were Job and His Opponents Professional Sages?[47]

The term "sage" (ḥākām, חכם) occurs in the dialogues and in the speeches of Elihu (5:13; 9:4; 15:2, 18; 17:10; 34:2, 34; 37:24). God is called a sage in 9:4, while two of the other texts use adjectives (34:34; 37:24). Synonyms include ārûm (ערום; "shrewd," 5:13, 15:5), maśkîl (משכיל; skilled, prudent, 22:2), yōdĕ'îm (ידעים; knowing ones), and anšê lēbāb (אנשי לבב; people of understanding, 34:10, 34). Eliphaz regards Job as a sage (15:2–3), and thus instructs him to abandon his hubris and attack on divine justice and incorporate instead the virtues of the wise man, especially the "fear of God."[48] Indeed, Job's use of sapiential language, references to key wisdom themes, and even critical engagement of earlier teachings indicate he is a sage. While Job denies that his opponents are true sages (13:5, 17:10), their advice and behavior suggest they were reared in the wisdom tradition. In the folktale, Job is not called a sage, although his greatness is said to be "greater than all other sons of the East" (1:3; cf. the portrayal of Solomon in the Solomon narrative, 1 Kgs. 3–11, and especially 1 Kgs. 5:9–14). Two features of his character point to his being an aristocratic sage: he "fears God" and he "turns from evil." The wealth and social status of Job in the narrative is picked up in Job 29–31. In addition, Job's sarcastic wit, his articulation of sapiential forms, his critical responses to the wisdom of his opponents, and the numerous inferences that he is a sage, point to his probable identification as a sage. He has the ability not only to write, but to draw up a legal document of accusation against Elohim (31:35). Further, Job regards his experience as a māšal (משל), an "example story," while the comparison is made with tōpet (תפת; a place of refuse, 17:6). Thus Job indicates he is an "example story" of abuse by a God turned cruel.

Job's three opponents, Eliphaz, Bildad, and Zophar, are traditional sages who attempt to grapple with Job's predicament and to instruct him in the proper course of action, that is, repentance and lamentation. Of course, their primary concern is to substantiate the major teachings of the wise: the justice of God, the traditional interpretation of suffering (patient acceptance of divine discipline or punishment for sin), the incontrovertible doctrine of retribution, and teaching based on experience in correlation with the instructions and observations of the ancestors. Some of this echoes the retributive theory of justice found in Deuteronomy, also a book with a longer tradition edited in the exile. Young Elihu, arrogant and boisterous, uttering speeches Job does not hear much less address, also thinks he is a sage in spite of his few years.

Eliphaz asserts that he (and by implication his codefenders of divine justice) is a sage who knows the ancestral wisdom tradition (15:17–19) in which his own teaching is grounded (15:18), thus giving it the impress of authority. He recognizes that the contingencies of life restrict human wisdom, while, in his view, God is the one (and only one) who subverts the wisdom of the sages, leading them to destruction (5:12–13). Eliphaz begins even in his first speech by implying that Job's soliloquy identifies him as one of the proud and rebellious sages whose wisdom subverts morality and religious faith.[49] These sages, full of their own self-worth, join hands in oppressing the poor and in committing acts that do violence to the moral order (Job 20:19; 22:5–9; 24:3, 9; 29:16–17).[50] If indeed, as it seems, these two types of sages, exemplified by Job and Eliphaz, represent different groups of sages in exile, then it is clear this crisis has led to severe strains within the community of sages. The exiles are responding in radically different ways to the loss of kingdom, land, and status.[51] Thus more is at stake than the intellectual or idealistic presentation of religion and concepts. What is contested is who will shape the present and future community of Jews and become their social, political, and intellectual leaders.

THE MEANING OF WISDOM IN JOB

Job and Aphoristic Wisdom

The poetic dialogues of Job are clearly "aphoristic" in the sense used by James Williams.[52] The poetic Job's dialogues are filled with subversive questioning and accusation that undermine and deconstruct the traditional teachings of religious scribes, who regarded all knowledge and insight as beginning with the "fear of God/Yahweh" and who served in the administration of the royal court as loyalists of the ruling monarch. Thus Job questions and on occasion even repudiates the fundamental teachings of the conservative sages who preceded him and were also represented in exile in Babylonia. Falling under his sustained assault are the formerly revered teachings of retribution, the righteous order of cosmos and society, the providence of God, the value and implementation of the divine gift of wisdom, and most importantly the justice of God. Because of his knowledge of the tradition, rhetorical skills, use of sapiential forms, and severely criticized wisdom themes, there is little question that the poet himself is a sage.[53] If he does compose his dialogues in the exile, there is little outlet for his writing, save in a school that would have continued to write, edit, and preserve literary traditions. Like other sages of the period, the poet of Job likely would have known Akkadian and Aramaic, the two successive international languages of the Levant and Mesopotamia since the end of the Late Bronze Age.[54]

Mantic Wisdom

The mantic wisdom so prominent in Mesopotamia appears in the book of Job. Job's opponents refer to esoteric knowledge to substantiate the authority of their

teaching. Thus it is revelation (4:12–21), a theme also present in the Joseph narrative and in apocalyptic (see the Enoch and Daniel literature), that is one of the
sources of their wisdom. Eliphaz describes a spirit appearing to him during a
dream who revealed to him that no human being could be righteous and pure in
the sight of God, or perhaps, translated in another way, more righteous and pure
than the Deity (4:12–21; cf. 15:14–16; 25:2–6; 26:4). The young Elihu expresses
a similar view in 32:8, 18; 33:14–18; and 36:7–12. Further, very untraditional
is the appearance of Yahweh in the whirlwind, from which he speaks to the rebellious Job. Job even notes that, while he previously had heard about Yahweh in
the teachings of the community, he now sees him. This manner of revelation
points to the fact that mantic wisdom, long on the fringes of sapiential teaching,
has taken a major step into the center of the wisdom tradition, paving the way
for the association of seers and sages in the figure of Enoch. The poet of Job may
have developed this view in recognizing that disputation alone, without awareness of divine knowledge and final judgment, cannot hope to lead to the proper
understanding of the most important issues with which the sages grappled: the
related themes of theodicy and retribution. This in itself suggests a severe crisis
in the community in which the poetic dialogues are written. More than argument based on tradition is required to address the questions of the community.

Yahweh as a Sage

Yahweh is also the God of wisdom in the book of Job.[55] This parallels the theology of the sages in the other cultures in the ancient Near East who regarded gods
like Thoth and Nisaba as gods of wisdom and as patrons of the sages, their scribal
craft, and their schools.

THE GENRES AND LITERARY STRUCTURE
OF THE BOOK OF JOB

Introduction

How are we to understand the literary genres of the book of Job in terms of political struggles among exiles themselves and eventually the common foe, the "people of the land"? Several genres have been proposed for the poetic dialogues: a
dramatized lament,[56] a paradigm of the answered lament,[57] litigation,[58] and sapiential disputation.[59] Obvious dimensions of each are present in the poetic book.
But the most extensive is the disputation. It is this form, and this form alone, that
allows competing groups, particularly the traditional and radical sages, to engage
in disputations, that is, speeches of serious contestation. For, after all, more is at
stake than simply the enjoyment of an intellectual debate. What is at issue is nothing less than power, knowledge, and the future leadership of a presently exiled
community. This assumes that some sort of school existed in which literary tra-

ditions and the teaching of youth continued even in exile. The poet competes for what all teachers have sought to have: the loyalty and conversion of their students to their points of view. It is this group of educated elite that would constitute the center of political agency for the radical sages. It is well known that a thriving Jewish community with significant sages continued at a later period. These sages composed, edited, and formulated the Babylonian Talmud within a school tradition. For this school to have had its roots in the exile makes eminently good sense. In addition, the dialogues of Job have important parallels in ancient Near Eastern wisdom literature, in particular works from the Babylonian wisdom tradition, that assist in shaping the literary and intellectual contours of the book.[60]

The task of form criticism applied to the book of Job is to attempt to understand the genres that were used and developed by the poet living in captivity among a people who were forced to shape new institutions and patterns of social interaction within the larger Babylonian context that regarded them as captives and state slaves. While most exiles likely had the opportunity to exist in an internalized community of their own people, they also were subjected to Babylonian state policies regarding their status as state slaves who could be required to perform whatever services the state required of them.

This said, what of the literary form of the book of Job? In recent discussions, literary critics who espouse the theory of new criticism have attempted to read the book of Job as a continuous narrative, ignoring in my judgment the varied and contradictory views expressed, the importation of later texts, and the major linguistic differences among the units, especially the prose didactic legend and the dialogues.[61] I do not find it helpful to ignore the stages of development of the book and the varied historical circumstances that gave rise to them. Some of the variety of literary forms and the different responses to the book's major questions point to the development of the book in redactional stages. This recognition is preferable to understanding the book as lacking generic composition and the unconvincing attempt to force unrelated pieces into a literary whole that ignores conceptual and linguistic variety. Other attempts to assign Job to a single specific literary form also have failed to capture its literary nuances. Seeing the volume only as a lawsuit, a dramatized lament, a paradigm of an answered lament, or a disputation belies the extensive literary and formal diversity. Indeed, elements of each of these are present in the volume. However, the overarching literary character of the book is best viewed as a collection of several genres that were used by sages of many generations in composing and editing the book until it reached its final form in the latter part of the Second Temple period.

Internal to the book of Job, the primary literary forms are the didactic narrative, lament, and disputation. While a continuing school of sages edited the volume many times over a period of centuries, they did not choose to eliminate inconsistencies, as was also true of most biblical books as well as later writings, including the Mishnah and Talmud. Variety was far more valued than consistency, for it allowed to come to expression different interpretations of matters of importance. Subsequently, the tradition history of the book points to a changing

social context interacting with its larger sociopolitical setting that may be theo-
retically postulated with careful analysis. The tradition history of the Book
unfolds as follows: a didactic tale, still largely, although not entirely, preserved in
the prose narrative forming the present prologue and epilogue. This story proposes to students the importance of the virtue of continuing to believe in the justice of God and to remain patient in suffering, hoping that, like the great man of
integrity, Job, redemption will come and those who oppose his steadfastness are
exposed and on occasion even punished. The setting for this book, possibly an
Israelite or Judean wisdom school, is not threatened by significant crisis. Rather
the narrative is limited to the examination of Job's loyalty to his Deity.

The Didactic Narrative

This particular didactic narrative, which portrays the redemption of an unjustly
treated protagonist, is to be dated in a period that would countenance the sim-
plistic affirmation of the virtues of patient suffering by an innocent and morally
upstanding person, who is ultimately redeemed by a formerly suspicious, now
righteous judge. From the unquestioned affirmation of retribution and the sim-
plistic understanding of justice, it is likely that this narrative originated in the
Iron II period prior to the misfortunes resulting from Assyrian, Egyptian, and
Babylonian conquests, beginning in the latter part of the eighth century BCE.
This is likely the oldest part of the literary tradition.[62] Comparable didactic legends include the Joseph story (Gen. 37, 39–50), the Aramaic "Tale of Ahiqar,"
the Egyptian "Protests of the Eloquent Peasant,"[63] the Akkadian "Poor Man of
Nippur,"[64] and the Hittite "Tale of Appu."[65]

The Lament

The Joban poet draws heavily on the lament. The genre is adapted in the two
soliloquies of Job in chapters 3 and 29–31 and is an important feature of the
Joban disputations.[66] This same use and adaptation of the lament were also frequent in some of the wisdom texts of Mesopotamia, including the Sumerian "A
Man and His God,"[67] the Akkadian *Ludlul bēl nēmeqi* ("I will Praise the Lord of
Wisdom"),[68] and two Akkadian texts from Ugarit (R.S. 25.460 and Louvre AO
4462).[69] As was true of the Psalter, the laments in the wisdom texts are from the
first-person point of view in which the one lamenting describes his/her suffering
as a righteous person. The formal features of the lament normally include an
invocation, a complaint or description of suffering, questions of reproach, a petition for help, a condemnation of enemies or imprecations against evil persecutors, an affirmation of confidence, a confession of sins or assertion of innocence,
the acknowledgment of divine response, a vow or pledge, and hymnic praise and
blessings. Job's laments bear a close resemblance to the accusatory laments (e.g.,
chap. 10, 13, and 23) and yet are even more strident in censuring God for

unjustly maltreating a just and innocent individual. Futhermore, in the laments of Job there is no expectation of future redemption, but only the final consequence of eternal death. The political function of laments was to consolidate the nation as a people who depended on divine redemption through the monarchy and to create an outlet for the expression of disappointing defeat and difficulties. In Job, however, the laments become accusations against the justice of God and the effort to overthrow the conceptual framework of the temple's role in effectuating divine salvation. With the repudiation of the justice of God, this priestly theology collapsed. The rebel sages, recognizing the power wielded by the Zadokites, who had controlled the temple, undermined their legitimacy and replaced it with a theology of censuring the Creator and Redeemer.

The Dialogue

The most important literary form in the book of Job is the dialogue, which in this case is a disputation leading to a heated debate. Job's passionate assault on his opponents includes ridicule and the expression of direct accusations of fear and foolish dependence on a disproven hermeneutic of retribution. Job accuses them of continuing their senseless defense of the justice of a God who abuses both his creation and the righteous. The opponents, refusing to bend, counter that it is Job who must have committed some grave offense that has led to his predicament. Of course, we find in the inflexible arguments of the opponents the view that the victim merits whatever suffering he is enduring. While it is not as intense and sharp in its exchanges between the sages, the "Babylonian Theodicy" is the closest form-critically and thematically of the sapiential writings of the ancient Near East to the disputations of Job in the poetic dialogues.[70]

It is true that in the sapiential corpora of the ancient Near East two of these forms are occasionally combined: the Sumerian "A Man and His God" has narrative and lament,[71] the Egyptian "Protests of the Eloquent Peasant" has narrative and disputation,[72] and the Egyptian "Dialogue between a Man and His Ba/Soul" has disputation and lament.[73] Job is the only example of a text in which all three forms are integrated.

The book of Job represents a bold stroke, but if successful in gaining the support of a substantial number of exiles, the way would be prepared for a new sociopolitical reality to come into being. This was no mere theological debate or offer of theoretical explanations of the problem of innocent suffering. By denying the justice and mercy of God, the poet of Job launched a direct assault on the continuing remnants of sociopolitical power in the form of kingship and priesthood, based on a traditional theology. However, the goal of the poet may not have been to convince the exiles to enter into a void of meaningless despair, but to provide them the basis for a new social construction of a future reality in which God or at least past theological conceptions would be repudiated. If God or traditional theology prior to the exile was no longer the center of meaning for people and sages, the only recourse would be to turn to an anthropological understanding in which humans go forth to shape their own reality. This anthropological move provided the beginning for Qoheleth's quest for meaning.

Literary Structure

The many efforts to reconstruct the order and content of the final book have been less than successful in reaching a general consensus. The most troublesome part of the text is the third cycle, when it becomes difficult to know who the speaker is. The redaction of this cycle suggests that Job and the opponents, in chapters 24–27, begin arguing the positions formerly held by the opposition.[74] Even the pattern of alternating speeches breaks down when Zophar has no final speech, while Bildad has only an abbreviated one in 25:1–6. My simple reconstruction removes the difficulties of this third cycle:

21—Job

22—Eliphaz

23—Job

24—Zophar (?)

25:1–6, 26:5–14—Bildad

26:1–4, 27:1–12—Job

27:13–23—Zophar[75]

The poem in chapter 28 is added to the dialogues by a later redactor who rejects the possibility of human discovery of Wisdom, who is present at creation and knows all there is to know about reality (Prov. 1:20–33; 8:1–36; 9:1–6; 13–18; Sir. 24). The Elihu speeches (Job 32–37) appear to me without question to be a later redactional addition. The primary reason this cadre of speeches is added is that the original reading in the introduction had the friends conclude that God was in the wrong.

Other scholars have attempted to combine the two speeches of Yahweh and the two responses of Job into a single speech and one response.[76] The premise of this argument, that much of the lengthy speech concerning Leviathan is not compatible with the language found elsewhere in the poetry, is not particularly compelling. Indeed, their removal results in the elimination of the major inclusio of the book (see chap. 3).

Finally, while a close reading of the book points to major differences between the didactic narrative and the poetic dialogues, some scholars attempt to see these as originally belonging together. In my view, this is the result of an unbending commitment to new criticism that attempts to discover meaning and revelatory insight in even the most significant contradictions of language, style, and theme.

Where are "the satan" and Job's wife in the dialogues? Have they simply appeared at a convenient moment and then exited the stage in a clumsy inexplicable fashion? Can one truly compare the tale's Job, who suffers patiently while clinging to unquestioning piety and acceptance of God's mistreatment, with the dialogues' Job, who engages in a wholesale attack against the justice of God, accusing him of the malicious abuse of creation and creature? How does one explain that the first word out of Job's mouth in the opening soliloquy in chapter 3 is that of curse, in striking contrast to the one who blesses the name of God, who is the unquestioned sovereign of the cosmos? Most revealing is that retribution, nuanced by divine discipline of the just, is supported by the narrative but repudiated in Job's speeches in the dialogues. Does it not seem likely that a wise poet, existing among exiles who have experienced the horrors of holocaust and continue to bear the brunt of ridicule from their rulers, has taken the older narrative, obviously well known in Judah, and transformed it into an angry accusation of the captives who can no longer keep quiet and continue to bless their creator and sustainer?

CREATION IN THE DIALOGUES BETWEEN JOB AND HIS OPPONENTS

Prelude

Traditional sages shaped two theological conventions following the collapse of the nation: the formation of and obedience to the Torah and the universal faith of creation.[77] Both of these were fashioned by the reflection of the sages who rose to the challenge to provide new understandings of God and the Jewish people. Wisdom in the Second Temple period was identified with the Torah and with the new understandings of creation. Job, and later Qoheleth and the Wisdom of Solomon, lean heavily on creation theology to give expression to their theological understandings, while Ben Sira and Baruch coalesce creation and Torah. Indeed, Job uses creation theology to oppose the validity of salvation history and even refers briefly to the exile's devastation of kingship, political counselors, royal judges, administrative officers, and temple priests. In addition, in the same section he tells of the nations that Yahweh, the universal Deity, elevates and then demolishes (12:13–25).

The Prologue: Chapters 1–2

The book begins and concludes with two different scenes, actions, and characters that comprise a didactic narrative known to the early-sixth-century prophet Ezekiel (14:14), who speaks of the righteousness of Job, Daniel (Dan'el, the just Canaanite king), and Noah in reference to even their inability, were they present, to intercede successfully on behalf of a faithless and sinful people about to experience destruction and exile. The genre of the prose narrative, or what remains of it, is to be identified as a didactic legend in which a protagonist embodies virtues for emulation, for they ultimately shape his character in ways that make his deliverance possible.[78] As is the case with its Akkadian parallels, the Joban folktale places the disputation within a mythological context, the judgment of the Creator who determines human fates on the day of the New Year, sets the stage for the disputation, and identifies the issue to be debated: why the righteous suffer. The location of the debate is significant in affecting the character of the disputation. In this case, it is the heavenly judgment scene. Of course, every good tale has one or more antagonists who attempt to effectuate the main character's ruin. These include the satan, Job's wife, and presumably, based on the judgment scene in 42:10–17, the three friends. Even when falsely charged and wrongly treated, sages are to endure patiently their suffering, expectantly waiting for their deliverance by a just Deity.

The prologue is a didactic tale told by an omniscient narrator who knows the conversations in heaven and earth and even the mind of the character Job. The six scenes alternate between heaven and earth, with the hero of the story, Job, unaware of the wager between Yahweh and "the satan." The hero is a legendary sage of great wealth, moral virtue, faithfulness to God, and piety. He embodies the piety and virtue at the heart of traditional wisdom: Job "fears God and turns away from evil" (1:1–5).[79]

The antagonist, introduced in the first heavenly scene (1:6–12), is "the satan," who, as a member of the divine council, has the duty of discovering evil on the face of the earth and reporting to the divine judge.[80] He contends that Job's piety and loyalty to God are the payment Yahweh has purchased by special favor. If disaster strikes him, the satan concludes that Job would curse God. The ruler of the divine council wagers with the satan over Job's response and turns Job over to his nemesis. In two different assaults, Job loses his possessions and his children and then is afflicted with great physical torment. He is left with a wife who attempts to shame her husband into cursing God. Yet Job responds with words of blessing, not cursing, and he maintains his loyalty to God. To drive home the truthfulness and authenticity of his response, the narrator maintains that, in response to the first assault, Job "did not sin or charge God with wrong" (1:22). At the end of the second assault, also acceptingly endured by Job, the narrator adds: "In all this Job did not sin with his lips" (2:10). The prologue ends with the visit of the three friends, who come to console Job but are silenced by the shock of what they see.

The Assault on Creation: Chapter 3[81]

The poetic dialogues begin in chapter 3 with a new Job, who stands in stark contrast to the pious believer in the first two chapters. This second Job revolts against divine injustice, depicted as bordering on sadism. Instead of a compliant acceptance of his destiny, Job engages in wholesale revolt against the creator and ruler of the cosmos, the determiner of fate, and the guide of history. Instead of blessing and praising, the rebel begins by cursing existence, not simply his own, but also that of all creation.

Job begins the poetry (chaps. 3–27) with a soliloquy (chap. 3) that has features of the individual lament.[82] Unlike the laments of the Psalter, however, Job's soliloquy addresses no one, including God or the three opponents, and lacks any indication of hope or expression of thanksgiving for divine deliverance. This dispirited poem emerging from the lips of a despairing Job comprises three separate strophes: verses 3–10—the cursing of conception and birth, verses 11–19—the yearning to have been stillborn, and verses 20–26—the desire to know why the sufferer continues to live. Thus, in the temporal movement, Job's soliloquy proceeds from his past (birth), to his future (death), and back to his present predicament (suffering). Before he enters into the endless void of final darkness, Job seeks to have an answer to his query raised initially in the third strophe of this opening poem of mournful gloom.

What immediately seizes the attention and evokes the imagination of the hearer is the occurrence of the variety of metaphors used for the creation of the cosmos and of humanity. The underlying image is that of the primordial binary pair of light and darkness[83] that occurs as the first act of creation in Gen. 1:3–5. This metaphor conjures up the other binary pairs in the stimulation of human imagination: day and night, life and death, birth and tomb, order and chaos, and knowledge and mystery. What is striking in this poem is not only Job's curse of his own existence whereby he hopes to unleash the power of this potent expression to bring his miserable life to an end, but also his calling up the magicians skilled in the ability to unleash Yamm and Leviathan, the monsters of chaos, who presumably would devour not only Job's night of conception but also the cosmos itself.[84] Thus Job's curse is designed to annihilate not only himself but indeed all of creation.[85] This more comprehensive curse may be the basis for the "rest" (*nûaḥ*, נוח) of death for which Job longs (v. 17). Job's design may be to effectuate the end of all existence, since the poet does not choose the term for divine repose (to rest, *šābat*, שבת) that followed the six days of evenings and mornings of creation in Genesis 1. In Priestly theology, with which the poet would be familiar due to the observation of the Sabbath in exile and to further redactional work on the Priestly source in Babylon, the seventh day was practiced as a temporal institution grounded by God in the foundation of the creation that, when practiced and honored, secured for the community and indeed all of creation the providential forces that renewed life and continued existence (cf. Gen. 2:1–3). The "rest" for which Job longs is also an ironic reversal of that associated with repose (*nûaḥ*, נוח) in the land of promise (Deut. 5:14). Thus Job seeks to subvert all life-providing traditions and the temple in which they are actualized, ranging from creation and providence to salvation in history. This suggests that the poet, while knowing well the complexes of faith centered on election and salvation history, sought to subvert them.

The creation by the word is also reversed (e.g., Gen. 1 and Ps. 33).[86] In the context of creation myth, it is the word of the ruler of the divine assembly that creates and maintains the world (see Gen. 1:26–28; Ps. 82; *Enuma eliš*). In a subversion of this tradition of creation, Job begins with seven curses directed against the "Day" of his birth and the "Night" of his conception. In the ancient Near East, curses are imbued with power that brings destruction to their object.[87] To enhance the efficacy of his power-laden imprecation, Job's curse in verse 8 enlists pagan (Babylonian?) priests skilled in magic to arouse the powers of chaos (Yamm and Leviathan) to destroy not only his own existence, but also the entire temporal order of creation and history.[88] The seven incantations in the first strophe stimulate the imagination to recall the seven days of creation in Gen. 1:1–2:4a, particularly important in the Priestly theology that is being shaped most likely at the same time as Job. "Day" and "Night," the temporal order of creation and history, are assaulted in what can only be described as a blasphemous effort to return to primordial chaos, prior to the time of beginnings.

Another parallel that evokes images of cosmic creation is the use of jussives. The Priestly source uses fifteen jussives in Gen. 1:1–2:4a to accomplish the formation of the cosmos. Job's curses consist of sixteen jussives and prohibitions in his formulation of the seven curses, thereby adding one additional occurrence in order to nullify the creative language of the Priestly tradition in Gen. 1:1–2:4a. Job's curses also evoke the language of the priestly source (Gen. 1:3) in his initial curse, "let that day [the day of his birth] be darkness" (Job 3:4). This curse counteracts the first act of divine creation, "let there be light" (Gen. 1:3).

This soliloquy's second creation image, which becomes the primary one in the entire book, is the contest with the monsters of chaos (Job 3:8; see 7:12; 38:10–11). These powers of nonlife and destruction are common to the mythic traditions of Israel and the ancient Near East.[89] The creator in ancient myth is the divine warrior,[90] who engages in mortal combat with savage monsters of chaos, with the spoils of ruling the cosmos going to the victor.[91] Thus Baal/Hadad, Marduk, Re, and Yahweh are the primary deities of war. Winning this struggle, which is not only primordial but also yearly, even daily, the creator and director of history is proclaimed king, forms the cosmos, creates humanity (or has them made), establishes social order ruled over by human kings, and utters divine edicts to sustain the world by constraining the destructive powers of chaos. The potency of chaos, while subdued, is never completely vanquished, save in eschatological myths of a new age (e.g., Rev. 21:1). Chaos, although defeated by the divine warrior in the primeval battle, continues to be a threat and must constantly be held at bay to keep it from devouring the sun or flooding creation (see Gen. 49:25 = Deut. 33:13).

Once again Job subverts this metaphor by entreating the pagan priests, "the cursers of Yamm,"[92] to use their power to imprecate the night he was conceived and to arouse (*ûr*, עור)[93] Leviathan to destroy both cosmos and history. However, Job's objective is either to awaken the monster to destroy the night during which he was conceived or perhaps, even more ominously, to contend with Yahweh for sovereignty over the earth. Should Leviathan win, then he would return creation to primordial chaos, leading to the collapse of cosmos and history. These pagan priests who practice the black arts, a forbidden craft in "orthodox" Israelite religion (2 Kgs. 23:5; Zeph. 1:4), are exhorted to curse and thus destroy the night of Job's conception.

In the world of myth in which the poet dwelt, the character Job is not simply engaged in a defiant gesture. At the conclusion of the poetic book, in Yahweh's second speech, the Creator gives praise to his mythological nemesis that no human but only he can defeat in battle (Job 40:24–41:26). Deutero-Isaiah calls on Yahweh to rouse himself in order to defeat chaos and its embodiment in fearsome monsters (Rahab, Tannin, Yamm, and Tehom; Isa. 51:9–11). In *Enuma eliš*, Anshar exhorts Marduk prior to engaging in his primordial battle, "calm [Tiamat] with thy holy spell."[94] The stars (Job 3:9) in mythological understanding are divine armies (see Judg. 5:20), the heavenly hosts (*ṣebā'ôt*, צבאות), who fight under the command of the Creator against the powers of chaos. The world of myth, in which the Judahites in exile lived, was a reality of struggle between the powers of life and death seen particularly in the activities of gods. For a person representing a community in exile, to experience the horrors of holocaust, existence should descend back into the "nothingness" of opaque darkness.

The poet also uses the metaphor of birth and nurture to describe both Job's parturition (strophe I; cf. 10:8–11) and his desire to have died prematurely (strophe II). The gift of light in the first line of strophe III could suggest the experience of a newborn at birth, but more likely it is a metaphor for the continuing existence of anyone who suffers. The reference to restraining God from seeking the day (of Job's birth) is a repudiation of the theology of human creation. The affirmation of Yahweh as the Lord of the womb who enables conception to occur, protects and nourishes the fetus, assists as the midwife in the newborn's birth, and then sustains the human being through life is repudiated (see Jer. 1:4–10; Job 10:8–13; Pss. 22:9–11; 139:13–16). Normally, a newborn is a cause for rejoicing (see 1 Sam. 1–2; Luke 1:46–55); but for the language of reversal in Job, his birth is a time not for celebration but rather for lamentation. In contrast to the offering of blessing at the time of birth (see Gen. 1:28) that enhances vitality, Job insists on cursing designed to bring destruction. Day and night, seen as a divine couple in Canaanite myth and here representing the parameters of the cycle of pregnancy, gestation, and birth, are to become, respectively, dark and sterile, incapable of producing and sustaining life. Indeed, in Job's cursing he hopes to remove them from the cycle of the year, and the nocturnal moment of Job's conception is to be cursed by the pagan priests who ordinarily use their magical power to utter an imprecation against Yamm. Job seeks to overwhelm day and night by means of darkness and to have them devoured by Leviathan, the monster of the deep.

The imagery changes to that of questioning in the second strophe (vv. 11–19) when Job engages in an accusatory lament with the serious question of why he was born to suffer. Job agonizes over why he was born and then suckled by his mother's breast instead of dying prematurely (cf. Qoh. 6:4–5). Since all people, rich and poor, had the same origins, the sages taught that the well-to-do had the moral responsibility to provide for the impoverished and indigent (see Prov. 22:2; Job 31:13–15), for Yahweh himself was their defender. In this lament-like soliloquy, Job emphasizes that it is only in the tomb that social differentiations are eliminated. In 3:14–15 Job notes that in Sheol even "kings and counselors of the earth" and "princes" of great wealth are there along with premature fetuses who died as stillborns. There is no privileged class in the land of the dead.

On occasion, the poet presents Job in the images of a former ruler, suggesting perhaps that he had been displaced by a new political order in similar fashion to the sufferer in the Babylonian Theodicy (see chaps. 29–31).[95] However, Job depicts himself throughout the dialogues as a slave[96] who longs for death, even though it eludes him. In the third strophe (3:20–26), Job's questioning of why humans are born to suffer initiates the transformation in his thinking from simply craving death to revolt against the Creator, who gave him life but now misrules the creation.

In the third strophe (vv. 20–26), Job raises two related questions: why are humans born to suffer and why are they enshrouded in the darkness of ignorance, not knowing the way to life? The second question may suggest that humans are not provided with the wisdom or the means to obtain the insight necessary to live a life that embodies sapiential virtues that would lead ultimately to well-being. While expressing these two questions within the framework of defining the meaning of human existence, the poet makes it obvious that Job becomes the test case. In this abbreviated third strophe, Job twice uses the image of light. The first use of the image of light symbolizes mortal life, while the second refers to human knowledge. The two images evoke two questions. Why is "light" (life) given to the one who longs for death? And why is "light" (knowledge) withheld from the one who seeks to understand the path of human existence? This image of light, with its double meaning, serves as an inclusio that reflects the initial language of the first strophe. Now, what Job has most dreaded has come upon him, leading to his deep-seated anxiety. Job dreads most of all a life whose events possess no explanation and an existence in the shadows of ignorance that offers no insight of wisdom into this most pressing of human questions. His former naive trust in a kindly God who provided comfort has been negated by a deity who has turned cruel and provides the tormented no clear explanation.

Eliphaz, Providence, and the Defense of Divine Justice: Chapters 4–5

Eliphaz rejects the content of Job's opening soliloquy by praising God as the sustainer of a just world order upheld by divine retribution, a central Deuteronomic teaching shared by traditional sages. Eliphaz depicts God as the divine judge, whose edicts establish and carry out a retributive system of justice in which the wicked are punished and the righteous are rewarded. Eliphaz also resorts to the understanding of suffering as divine discipline brought upon human beings, all of whom are sinful (4:12–21), in order to prompt sinners to repent, endure their travail patiently, and then await divine deliverance (this teaching too is found in Deuteronomy and in traditional wisdom). Even the righteous may experience the anguish of distress, but this chastisement originating with the hand of God leads to even greater discipline for the sage (4:5–6; 5:8, 17–27). Eliphaz assures Job that the wicked are inevitably punished for their misdeeds at the time of God's own choosing.

In addition, Eliphaz stresses God's care for his creation by sustaining it with the rain needed to revitalize and maintain life through the growing of food in the fields. The same point is emphasized in his doxology uttered in 5:9–16. This type of psalm is a word of praise sung either by one who has been falsely accused of a crime and awaits a declaration of innocence by the judge, or by a guilty person who confesses guilt and declares that the judgment is just.[97] In his doxology, Eliphaz not only praises God for nurturing creation through the sending of the rains to irrigate the fields, but also extols the Divine Judge who acts through retributive justice to rescue the lowly and to castigate the wicked, especially those who misuse their wisdom to plot wickedness. The implication of this doxology is that it is presented to Job as a confession he should utter.

This doxology brings into view three important themes that deal with the three spheres overseen by divine providence: creation (v. 9), nature (v. 10), and society (vv. 11–16). The doxology speaks of divine actions, beginning with the praise of God, who "makes/does great and wonderful things" (*ōśeh gĕdōlôt*, עשה גדלות) "beyond comprehension" (*wĕ'ên ḥēqer*; ואין חקר) and "wonderful things without limits" (*niplā'ôt 'ad-ên mispār*; נפלא ותדרא-אן מספר). These two nouns, "great things" and "wonderful things," allude not only to the defeat of chaos, but also to divine creation and providential rule over nature and history when God is the subject (9:9–10; 37:5, 14; 42:3; cf. Pss. 96:3; 98:1). Most importantly, for Eliphaz retributive justice is grounded in the moral character of God. It is important to note, as one traces the history of wisdom in Israel and Judah, that Eliphaz bases his teachings not only on what have become the sapiential sources for knowledge (experience, analogy from nature, and the appeal to tradition),[98] but also on a visionary or dreamlike revelation that signifies mantic wisdom (4:12–17). Later, Qoheleth takes issue with sages who are beginning to base their teachings on an esoteric knowledge, which occurs in its fully developed form in Jewish apocalyptic (Qoh. 3:9–22).[99] This reference to dream revelation is an indication of the steady development of mantic wisdom that finds its formative expression in apocalyptic.

In the doxology of confession spoken by Eliphaz in Job 5:8–16, the sage's understanding of piety does permit debate and radical questioning of God, as Job has done in Job 3. This assault on divine integrity finally becomes for the "friends" of Job nothing short of blasphemy. It becomes clear in this initial speech of the opponents that retribution and other traditional wisdom teachings, including the justice of God, have hardened into rigid dogmatism that disallows any questioning of their authenticity.

The second theme involves the providential rule of nature: the gift of rain to renew life, including, most importantly, in the fields. The act of creation through the sending of rain to moisten the dry earth and to enrich providentially the fertility of the fields (Gen. 2:4b–6; Deut. 11:14, 17; 28:12; 1 Kgs. 8:35–36; Job 36:27; Ps. 147:8; Isa. 41:18–19; 43:19; 44:3–4; 55:10; Jer. 14:22; Matt. 5:45) draws on the theological theme of divine care for creation (e.g., Ps. 104).

God's providential guidance of the social world occurs in the dividing of humanity into two classes: the shrewd and arrogant mighty who oppress the lowly, and the marginalized poor who will be redeemed and exalted by God through acts of retributive justice (Prov. 26:27; 28:10; Pss. 7:15; 9:16; 35:8; 57:7). This doxology opposes the arrogance and craftiness of counselors who ignore providence in human affairs and oppress the needy to increase their position. Their sense of self-sufficiency and unabashed hubris lead ultimately to their eventual downfall (cf. Gen. 3–11; Ezek. 28).[100] Subsequently, Eliphaz contends that Job should "seek God" (*dāraš 'el-'ēl*; דרש אל אל),[101] abandon his hubris, repent of his sins, wait patiently for deliverance, and, at least by implication, offer to God a doxology.

Eliphaz, like the other opponents of Job, presents a rather stark view of human depravity (Job 4:17–21). The universal human decadence depicted by Eliphaz and, later on, by the other two opponents stands in sharp contrast to the more common Israelite teaching that humans are made in the image of God to rule creation as his earthly surrogate (cf. Gen. 1:26–28; Ps. 8). For Eliphaz, God is the divine builder who, in making humans, constructs them to dwell in "houses of clay" (*batê-ḥōmer*, בתי-חמר) whose foundations are in the dust (*be'āpār yĕsôdām*, בעפר יסודם). Thus in the divine creation of humans they are compared to houses made of perishable materials that have insecure foundations, that is, they are founded upon the dust. Dust is often associated with the tomb. In addition, human beings die quickly like the moth and "without name," that is, without honor and remembrance (Gen. 12:2, 2 Sam. 7:9; Qoh. 7:1).

In Job 5:1–7 Eliphaz utilizes the power of the curse to bring trouble and misery to fools and their households (see Prov. 24:24–25). Using his own powers of observation and experience, Eliphaz mentions that he, having seen fools who had "taken root," uttered a curse against their "habitation" (*nāwēhû*, נוהו), that is, their land and their children. Eliphaz insists that humans, due to the sinfulness of their nature, are born to experience trouble, for being the offspring of Resheph, the god of pestilence and death (Deut. 32:24; Hab. 3:5)[102] who is responsible for disease and plague, they fall victim to his destruction. This wicked nature derives from the substance of human nature. Humans are fashioned from the dust of the earth, fated for the corruption of death (Gen. 2:7; 3:19; 8:21). Furthermore, the fertile earth yields crops, but is also cursed by God and thus also produces thorns, weeds, and disease (Job 7:21; 10:9; Gen. 3:19; Ps. 104:29; Qoh. 3:20).

The Battle with Chaos and Creation by Word: Chapters 6–7

The next significant use of creation theology in Job occurs in his response (chaps. 6–7) to the initial speech of Eliphaz. Job continues to espouse his rather pessimistic view of human existence, first advanced in his opening soliloquy. However, there is agreement between the opponents and Job in their obvious rejections of the positive view of human beings as the surrogates of God in ruling the cosmos and human society. This view continues, but it is added to the cosmic understanding of creation and divine rule. Central to the two acrostic poems that shape the poetic structure of his disputation in these two chapters are the metaphors of the battle with chaos and creation and divine rule by word. In the first two strophes of Job's first poem (6:2–23), he protests the onslaught of the Divine Warrior.

God is portrayed as assaulting Job with a fearsome rage as an opponent in the power struggle to rule over the earth (7:11–21; cf. Pss. 74:13; 88:13–18; 89:11). God uses his weapons to attack Job, who, for a reason unknown to him, has been viewed as the enemy. Especially to be noted is the Divine Warrior's use of arrows to assault his creature (Job 6:4; see Ps. 18:15 = 2 Sam. 22:15; Hab. 3:11; Zech. 9:14; Pss. 77:18; 144:6). The arrows of the Divine Warrior often occur in poetic imagery of the theology of divine justice (Deut. 32:23, 42; Pss. 7:14; 38:3; 58:8; 64:8; 120:4). Theophanic hymns in particular present God as the Divine Warrior who marches forth in battle to slaughter and crush his fearsome enemy.[103] The terrors (*biʿûtê*, בעותי) are the cohorts of divine or supernatural soldiers who follow the Divine Warrior into battle (cf. Hab. 3, which tells of Yahweh's weapons, including "arrows" in v. 14, and his troops in v. 5, "pestilence" and "plague," *deber*, דבר, and *rešep*, רשף). In the third and fourth strophes (6:14–23 and 6:24–30), Job casts indignant, satirical aspersions on the friends for their failure, born of fear, to support him.

The second chapter in this section presents an even more despairing lament and engages in a harsh attack on divine justice. This chapter opens with an accusatory lament (7:1–21).[104] It is clear that Job has not found himself supported by his faithless friends. Consequently, he is alone in his increasingly radical questioning of human suffering and theodicy. He now once again raises his voice to God in a lament-like psalm of accusation and demands to know from the Divine Judge why he afflicts so terribly. What makes the assault so vicious and unbearable is that God does not take into consideration his creature's human frailties and refuses to forgive him of his sins.

In the initial strophe (7:1–6), Job begins his complaint by speaking of the drudgery and misery of human existence.[105] Three nouns depict humanity: *ʿebed* ("slave," עבד), *ṣābā* ("harsh labor," צבא), and *śākîr* ("hired laborer," שכיר). The type of slave to which Job refers is one who is to remain in this intolerable state for life, without the opportunity for freedom, until the release offered by death (Exod. 21:2–11; Deut. 15:12–18). Female Hebrew slaves were forced to be lifelong concubines for their male owners.[106] This lifelong slavery for Hebrew males comes only when they turn down the opportunity for release. Slaves who were foreigners have no recourse but to endure forced servitude until death. This fits the context of Judah in exile, when the Judahites, while perhaps not classified legally as state slaves, were compelled to labor on royal projects at the court's pleasure, and any liberation from exile was considered impossible until the soothing words of hope and comfort came from the lips of the prophet of the exile.

Ṣābā' may refer to military service (Num. 1:3, 20; 1 Chr. 5:18; 7:11), cultic duties of the Levites in the sanctuaries (Num. 4:3, 23, 30, 39, 43), and, in this context, compulsory service imposed by a master on a slave (Isa. 40:2; cf. Job 14:14). The *śākîr* (שכיר), while not a slave, lived a tenuous existence as a hired laborer (Exod. 12:45; Deut. 15:18; 24:24; Lev. 19:13; 22:10; 25:6, 40, 50). These workers, as noted in several texts (Jer. 22:3; Mal. 3:5; Sir. 34:22), were mistreated in spite of protective legislation in Lev. 19:13 and Deut. 24:14–15 that required their employers to pay them on the evening of the day they labored.

In taking on the guise of these socially desperate types of individuals, Job then beseeches God in 7:7–10 to "remember" (*zākar*, זכר) that his life is but breath (*rûaḥ*, רוח), the vital though quickly departing force that enters humans at birth and returns to its divine source at death (Job 10:12; 12:10; 27:3; cf. Gen. 2:7 and Qoh. 12:7).[107] Job reminds God of both the mortality of his human creatures and the transience of their existence (cf. Pss. 78:39; 103:14–18; 144:3–4).

Particularly striking is Job's protest to God in the third (Job 7:11–16) and fourth (vv. 17–21) strophes that supplants the typical plea for deliverance. What Job seeks for himself is the cessation of divine torment and being allowed to die in peace. However, this wish is placed within a direct attack on the justice of God.

The third strophe uses two metaphors important in creation theology. The first is a cluster that refers to the monsters of chaos (Yamm and Tannin, v. 12), while the second metaphor is *hebel* (הבל), expressing the ephemerality of human life. In using the word that later in Qoheleth becomes the dominant thematic term, breath (*hebel*, v. 16), Job notes that life is not only ephemeral but without hope (Pss. 39:6, 12; 62:10; 94:11; 144:4; Qoh. 2:1, 14, 15). Job also uses hyperbole in his questioning of God, asking if he has become the monster of chaos ("Yamm" or "Tannin") that requires he be watched over by a guard.

In 7:12 there is an echo of Marduk's defeat of Tiamat: "Am I Yamm or the Dragon,[108] that you have positioned a guard against me?" God sets up a "guard" (*mišmār*, משמר) as Marduk did following his dividing of Tiamat into two parts to keep the waters of her corpse from escaping into the newly created order to inundate it.[109] This imagery suggests that the poet may be familiar with the Akkadian text *Enuma eliš*.

In 7:17–21 Job issues a parody of Psalm 8 (Ps. 8:5–6 = Ps. 144:3–4). Psalm 8 is a creation hymn that praises God for exalting humanity to kingship over creation and for making humans only a little less than the '*ĕlōhîm* (אלהים),[110] who are the members of the divine council. Using ridicule and reversal to drive home his point, Job states that God has exalted human beings in order to single them out for merciless judgment and destruction. *Pāqad* (פקד, "visit, examine") is among the words that tell of God's gracious deliverance of his people (Exod. 3:16; 4:31; Ps. 80:15). Furthermore, the term is used occasionally in texts that speak of God's searching out the wicked for divine punishment (Ps. 17:3; Jer. 6:15). In Job God's constant surveillance of human behavior is done to bring against people merciless judgment and swift destruction, even for those like the righteous Job who confess their sins and plead for divine mercy.

Divine Tyranny in Providence: Chapters 8–10

Bildad's first speech (chap. 8) repeats the salient points made by Eliphaz in chapters 4–5. What is different in Job's response that follows in chapters 9–10 is that he moves from lament to litigation. While it appears to be an impossible desire, Job hopes to confront God in a trial.

Similar to Eliphaz, who incorporated a doxology (5:9–16) into his initial speech, Job makes use of battle imagery from Akkadian military activity and from the mythological conflict pitting Marduk against Tiamat and Anat against Yamm to utter a doxology that mentions God's trampling of Sea in the contest for rule of the cosmos. As is true elsewhere in his language of subversion, Job intends for his doxology to repudiate the traditional theology of the confession of guilt and articulation of praise.[111] In the larger speech, Job's doxology becomes an indictment of a brutal God who has abused and even turned cruel against his own creation. The doxology portrays the coming of the Divine Warrior to engage in warfare with Prince Yamm (vv. 5–8), God's subsequent creation of constellations and the cosmos with an incomprehensible wisdom (vv. 9–10), and the tyrannical rule of the unjust God (vv. 11–12).

The first two elements are frequently found in doxologies. The upheaval of creation (cf. Judg. 5:4–5; Pss. 68:8–9; 114:3–7; Hag. 2:6, 21), including an earthquake, accompanies the fearsome approach of the Divine Warrior to fight against Yamm (Judg. 5:5; Ps. 77:19; Isa. 41:15; Jer. 4:24; Ezek. 28:20; Joel 2:10; Amos 8:8; Nah. 1:5; Hab. 3:5).[112] The effect of the coming of the Divine Warrior is to produce darkness and not light and to walk upon the back of his defeated nemesis, a common ancient Near Eastern image in scenes of victorious kings trampling their foes (see Pss. 18:8–16; 77:17–20; Hab. 3:15). However, the third element is found in El's commission to Mot to defeat Baal. Even as El, the creator, had sought to subdue the upstart Baal through the divine son, Mot, by directing his offspring to bring Baal into the underworld, signaling the cessation of life-giving rain, so God's wrath is now directed against creation as well as his creature, Job. Yahweh as Divine Warrior has come to destroy, not to redeem, his creation and his human offspring. Two questions by Job underscore the unquestioned sovereignty of God, grounded in unlimited power: "who will restrain him" and "who will say to him, 'What are you doing?'" In the following speech (chap. 11), Zophar uses the first question to point to God's power to enforce his edicts to imprison or to hold court as the Divine Judge (11:10), while Job uses it to refer to the inability to oppose God's will (cf. 23:13). The second is a question whispered by ordinary mortals about their sovereign lords (Qoh. 8:4; Dan. 4:35).

The strophe in Job 9:13–24 continues to combine two recourses for Job: the struggle with the Divine Warrior, in this case Job's own battle, and Job's pondering the pursuit of litigation against God as a corrupt judge who should be issuing judgments to establish and maintain a just order in the universe. It is this latter recourse that Job selects. For Job, Yahweh has abused the standards of justice and should be brought to trial for egregious perversions of justice.

Job decries the fact that not even a deity could "turn back the anger" of God, and that even the helpers of Rahab bowed the knee in submission before him. Thus how could he, a human being, hope to answer the Almighty in a disputation? Now the Divine Warrior attacks him without mercy and without cause, that is, without just reason (see 2:3), and he is not allowed even to catch his breath.

In verse 19 Job once more seeks to engage in legal jousting with the Divine Judge. While Job is convinced that a fair trial based on justice would result in his exoneration and by implication the guilt of God, he fears that the divine power of the unjust judge would so intimidate him that he would be incapable of presenting clearly and cogently his case (9:25–35). Job has come to realize that God has become a wicked, corrupt judge who will not listen to the righteous (see Exod. 18:13–26; 23:8; Deut. 1:9–17; 16:18–26). Convinced of his innocence (9:15, 20; 'eṣdaq, אצדק),[113] he must, however, "appeal for mercy" (9:15; ḥānan, חנן) to obtain justice. The dilemma is that he must make his appeal to a merciless judge who only destroys and does not forgive, but does so "without cause" (9:17, ḥinnām, חנם; cf. 2:3).

In 9:25–35 Job would like to abandon his wretchedness and become festive in spirit. Yet he knows that his pain is unending. In order to bring God to justice, he realizes he must have a fair and just mediator between them who would not be intimidated by the ominous threat of divine power. Thus Job wistfully seeks an "intercessor" or "mediator" (môkîaḥ, מוכיח),[114] most likely a legal official in a courtroom other than the judge.[115] This presence would allow him to enter into arbitration justly and fairly with God (9:33; cf. 16:18–21 and 19:25–27). Job's so-called friends have refused to serve as character witnesses and to acknowledge his innocence, to question divine justice, and to perform the role of mediator due to their fear of alienating God and also becoming victims of his uncontrollable wrath. Job wonders if there might be in the divine council an arbiter who could be authorized by both sides to adjudicate fairly the conflict between them, and who would not be bullied by the threat of divine violence.[116] However, Job finally realizes there is ultimately no one else who would argue his case for him. Unfortunately for Job, God will arbitrate and judge his case in his futile attempts to defend his innocence and to repudiate divine justice. Job protests that if only God would cease from torturing him, then he would speak out plainly in his own defense, and then without fear.

In 10:1–17 Job returns to the accusatory lament in addressing God, not to gain forgiveness and release from harsh suffering, but to present his abiding despair and, most importantly, to question why God seeks to litigate against and ultimately condemn him.[117] In his depiction of Job's outcry the poet draws upon the birth metaphor that presents God once more as the Lord of the womb, responsible for conception, birth, and nurture, but he gives it an astonishing reversal of meaning. The traditional goal of an accusatory lament is to turn God's face toward the sufferer for the purpose of redemption (cf. Ps. 139:13–18), but Job destabilizes this metaphor, which is central for the strophe and thus its tradition, by indicating that the divine intent in his creation is to destroy, not to nurture, his offspring and him.

In the first (10:1–17) and more lengthy strophe of the two that make up the lament, Job is at a loss to know why the Creator would now destroy what he has created in the womb. He also charges that God does not take into consideration the limits of human mortality. This becomes a key consideration in Job's lament.

Job begins with the legal metaphor in the second verse. He makes use of two legal terms: "condemn" (*rāša'*, רשע) and "contend" (*rîb*, ריב). In this context, the term *rāša'* refers to the act of declaring someone guilty (see Exod. 22:8; Deut. 25:1; 1 Kgs. 8:32). Thus the guilty party is condemned by a judge to suffer punishment. *Rîb* means in this context to litigate or "to initiate a lawsuit" (Isa. 3:13; 57:16; Hos. 4:4; Ps. 103:9). The use of these two terms indicates that in Job's thinking God has already tried him and found him guilty. Thus God has sentenced him to suffer for unspecified crimes. But the question for Job is what is the basis for this judgment that has rendered him guilty?

In 10:3–6 God is reminded of Job's origins as the offspring of the Creator, of his human weakness, and of the shortness of life. "Flesh" (*bāśār*, בשר) is a term that often conveys the notions of human mortality and the dependence of the human creature on God, who animates the body with the breath of life (cf. Job 34:14–15 and Ps. 78:38–39).[118] "Eyes of flesh" and "seeing as a human sees" are used to indicate the perception of human beings in their efforts to obtain knowledge. Job, as a human being, knows of his frailty. God, as a divine and immortal being, lacks this perspective. Furthermore, Job refers to his humanness in noting the brevity of human life, comparing it elsewhere to breath, a cloud, or a flower (6:7; 14:2).

What follows in 10:8–11 is a series of contrasts that seek to destabilize the tradition of the creation of humanity. The initial contrast occurs in verse 8. The first line portrays God metaphorically as potter, cheese maker, and maker of cloth who, with artistic skill, has shaped Job in the womb and bestowed upon him both life and steadfast love.[119] Yet instead of continuing with the teaching of divine nurture, as one would expect from this tradition, Job describes God initially as Prince Death (Mot) who devours human beings, and then as the hunter and warrior who assails him. Hunting among the kings was a royal sport demonstrating the prowess of the ruler. The sport was even given a religious understanding in the related senses of the royal rule over the empire and imitating the actions of the gods in maintaining the empire's control over the conquered nations and in bringing new colonies under its hegemony. The mythic character of hunting is seen in the symbolism of achieving order through the killing of a lion (a symbol of strength and the threat of chaos) by the king. In verse 9 God is the potter working with the clay (*ḥōmer*, חמר) to create a human vessel, and one naturally would expect the gift of divine breath to follow (Gen. 2:7). Instead, Job is returned to the dust (*'āpār*, עפר; Gen. 3:19; Qoh. 12:7; Ps. 104:29) from which he was made.

The third and final contrast is found in Job 10:12–17. Job now speaks of the gift of life and providential care, in this instance rooted in "steadfast love" (*ḥesed*, חסד),[120] that includes the preserving of his "spirit" (*rûaḥ*, רוח). However, Job now accuses God of refusing to acquit him of charges and, instead, of renewing a host of witnesses to testify against him. God has hidden within himself his true intent of bringing upon Job suffering and death. While convinced of his "innocence," Job still knows he will regain his honor, given the chance in a fair adjudication of his grievance. Indeed, even in his attempt to defend himself, the Divine Warrior hunts him down and sends his armies to destroy him. One can well imagine the terror this image would evoke for a people whose nation had been devastated by the Babylonian conquest of Judah and the sacking of Jerusalem. This military imagery becomes all the more trenchant for those who had experienced the horrors of the Babylonian holocaust and forced exile. The remark about God "working his wonders against him" (v. 16) is a parody on the divine acts of creating the world, maintaining the order of the cosmos (cf. Gen. 37:14), and redeeming people from distress (Judg. 5:20–21; 6:13).

Finally, in the abbreviated strophe in Job 10:18–22, Job concludes this speech by returning to the language of Job 3. Instead of creating them for providential care, God brings forth human creatures in order to torment them until they perish.[121] The description of death makes use of a variety of images that emphasize two points. First, death is a "land of darkness" ('ereṣ ḥōšek, ארץ חשך), "shadow of death" (ṣalmāwet, צלמות), "a land of turbid gloom" ('ēpātâ, עיפתה), a land "without order" (sĕdārîm, סדרים), and a land where light is like "shades of night" ('ōpel; אפל). Second, the land to which Job is going is the land of "no return" (lō šûb, לא שוב), the underworld. Thus Job accuses God of misruling the cosmos and human history, while Job's faithless friends refuse to support his appeal to God for a fair trial in which he would portray through example and description the hopelessness of humans, who are the scourge of divine, brutal mistreatment.

Divine Misrule of Creation and History: Chapters 12–14[122]

These chapters comprise a disputation that incorporates sections that imitate both a hymn (12:13–25) and a lament (chap. 14). The hymnlike text and the preceding strophe (12:7–12) include important features of creation theology.

Chapter 12 takes the form of a disputation uttered against the three faithless friends. In the second strophe Job refers to creation, whose voice, in this case, through the animals, speaks of God and divine sovereignty over nature (cf. Ps. 19A). For the sages, to experience and understand the world was in some measure a means of achieving the knowledge of God. The sages usually admitted that divine mystery and the contingencies of life denied them the ability to know God exactly and completely. Still, because of their trust in the Creator, they affirmed that he had the well-being of the cosmos and its human creatures in mind.

As has become his pattern, Job tries to subvert this understanding of sapiential revelation issuing forth as instruction from the creatures and the earth. Even the creatures agree with Job that God is the one who brings peace and security to the wicked, while a pious, blameless, and just man like Job is undone by the Creator. Thus Job exhorts his opponents to inquire of creation to learn the meaning of the true nature of God (see Ps. 104:29–30).[123] The image of being in the "hand [=

power] of God" is not an image of security to Job, but rather one of abuse (see Job 10:3, 7, 8, 13; 19:21; 27:11).

Once more Job continues to destabilize sapiential creation theology by using the language of doxology to describe the destructive power of divine providence in directing human history (12:13–25). While Job grants that God has "wisdom" (ḥokmâ, חכמה), "counsel" ('ēṣâ, עצה), "insight" (tĕbûnâ, תבונה), and "power" (gĕbûrâ, גבורה), he rejects the sapiential teaching of providential care for human nations and nature: "if he tears down (yaharôs, יהרוס), there is no rebuilding (yibbāneh, יבנה)."[124] For Job, God utilizes his wisdom and power not to create and sustain life and rule well the nations, but to destroy them. In his divine caprice, he withholds life-giving rain, resulting in famine and death, or he sends floods to inundate the land. He denies to human leaders wisdom and brings mighty nations to their end.

In traditional wisdom, God imparts insight and understanding to human leaders, scribes, and sages (cf. 1 Kgs. 3—"Solomon's Wisdom"; cf. Wis. 7–9). However, Job argues that God is capricious and denies to them the counsel ('ēṣâ, עצה) necessary to lead their nations with justice and success (Job 12:21a, 24b = Ps. 107:40).[125] These social categories are those of the rulers, chief ministers, and priests of Judahite society, as well as those considered sages, including among the chief ministers professional counselors. This text provides a comprehensive summary of those leaders in social positions who were considered to carry out their tasks with wisdom, insight, and knowledge. God removes the insight of leadership from "counselors" (yô'ăṣîm, יועצים), "judges" (šōpĕṭîm, שפטים), "kings" (mĕlākîm, מלכים), and "elders" (zĕqānîm, זקנים); brings to ruin "priests" (kōhănîm, כהנים); humiliates "members of renowned families" ('ētānîm, אתנים)[126] and "trusted ones" (ne'ĕmānîm, נאמנים);[127] pours contempt upon "nobles" (nĕdîbîm, נדיבים), and looses the girdles of "mighty ones" ('ăpîqîm, אפיקים).[128] In addition, he unleashes the powers of chaos ("the depths," 'ămûqîm, עמוקים) and the "shadow of death" (ṣalmāwet, צלמות)[129] that bring destruction to the earth. He exalts and destroys nations, removing reason from their leaders. The result is historical chaos.

As noted earlier, wisdom literature does not mention any of the themes of salvation history until Ben Sira at the beginning of the second century BCE. However, this does not mean that the sages ignore history. Normally in the wisdom tradition, God (or divine Wisdom) is the one who chooses human leaders (cf. Prov. 8:15–16), whose righteous reigns enable their peoples to live in concert with divine order. This is wisdom's understanding of providential history, an alternative to the salvation history in many nonsapiential texts. Job goes a step further than other sages in noting that God directs human history. For Job, however, God does not providentially guide the lives of human communities (Prov. 10:3, 29; 15:3, 29) by bestowing upon leaders divine wisdom (e.g., Prov. 8:15–16), but rather disrupts their existence by exalting and then destroying nations for no stated purpose. Divine destruction is solely a matter of caprice, and wisdom is denied even to kings who rule their peoples and their other leaders (cf. 1 Kgs. 3:3–14). This became one significant explanation of the Babylonian conquest and exile. Instead of pointing to the weakness of Yahweh and the greater strength of Marduk (Pss. 115:3; 137:4), or placing blame on the sinfulness of Judah and/or its leaders (Deuteronomistic History), or questioning the delay of God in bringing redemption to his people while the wicked prosper in their evil machinations and deeds (Hab. 1:1–4), or choosing to hide in the darkness of enigma, Job places the blame entirely on the caprice of a malevolent God.

In this speech, the sovereign rule of reality unfolds according to the edict of the Divine Judge whose decree is without appeal, while the hopeless and futile wish for immortality is presented by the symbolism of the tree. The first strophe concludes that God has decreed (*ḥôq*, חֹק) for humans lifelong slavery from which there is no reprieve.[130] Life for a mortal like Job, who is born of woman, quickly passes. God should not add to human misery by bringing people, doomed to suffer this fate, into judgment for capricious reasons. Job's assessment of human nature even compares to the dark view of the three opponents, for he asserts that no one can make clean what is unclean (*ṭāhôr*, טהור/*ṭāmē*, טמא). Realizing that slavery is inescapable, Job hopes only for the cessation of God's attack so that he may at least enjoy the lot of the hired laborer (*śākîr*, שכיר), until the release of death comes.

In the second strophe, Job addresses the subject of immortality. Trees and water are common symbols of fertility, longevity, death and rebirth, and immortality.[131] The narrative of the Sumerian myth of Dumuzi (Akkadian Tammuz), the shepherd king, and the goddess Inanna (Ishtar in Akkadian mythology)[132] presents the human ruler as the mortal consort of the goddess. Dumuzi dies, but comes back to life in the form of tree sap. The tree of life in Genesis 2–3, planted in the garden watered by the four rivers, symbolizes the immortality offered to Adam and Eve that they lost when they were driven out of the garden due to their violation of the divine commandment not to eat of the tree of the knowledge of good and evil (or, so it seems, wisdom). Had they remained with access to the two trees and partaken of wisdom, the food of the Creator, the boundary between Creator and human mortals would have disappeared. In Sumero-Assyrological mythology and in the Hebrew Bible, the first man is a king who tends the garden and guards the tree of life.[133] The sages of Israel incorporate this mythical imagery into the sapiential tradition in the form of Wisdom as a fertility goddess, who is presented in the metaphor of the tree of life (Ishtar; cf. Asherah in Canaanite religion) and dispenses well-being and insight to the wise (Prov. 3:18; cf. 11:30; 13:12; 15:4, where the deeds and virtues of the wise are a "tree of life").[134] Psalm 1 compares the wise and righteous person to a fruitful tree planted by an ever-flowing stream. Later, in his speech directed against God, Job describes his former life in the image of a well-watered tree (Job 29:19). Even so, in both Mesopotamia and Israel, immortality and resurrection were typically denied mortals, including kings.

The metaphor of the tree, the roots of which may revive its life after its trunk has been cut down, incorporates some of these images in the second strophe, although in Job's own mind death is the fate of all human beings, from which there is no reprieve. Dumuzi (Tammuz) and Baal may wait expectantly for resurrection from the dead that is to be occasioned by their deliverance from the underworld by their divine consorts, but for mortal Job, like all human beings, there is no return from the grave.

In the third strophe, Job announces that the many days of imprisonment in Sheol could be endured, if only God would one day long for the "work of his hands" (10:3, 8–12) and eventually release his slave from death. Yet this momentary illusion of expectant hope is dashed by Job's realization that there is ultimately no deliverance from the shadowy tomb. The illusion of this creation tradition vanishes as quickly and as suddenly as it appeared.

Finally, in the fourth strophe, Job compares the hopelessness placed by God upon a dying human to the steady but time-consuming changes of formations of the cosmos. Eventually, even this hope wanes. Death robs one even of the knowledge of descendants and their fate.

The Fall of the Primeval King: 15:2–16

Eliphaz uses the myth of the primal man, likely borrowed from Akkadian literature, to warn Job of the fate of those who rebel against God. In this new cycle of debate, the friends cast diplomacy to the winds as they enter into a direct indictment of Job. Images of words dominate this speech.

In the first strophe, Eliphaz recognizes the power of language to call into existence, but also to annihilate, as he compares Job's words to the force of chaos (cf. the "mighty wind" in Gen. 1:2, and the desiccating desert storm in Gen. 41:6, 23, 27). According to the observation of Eliphaz, Job has converted himself from the wise man to the fool whose language brings destruction and undermines the traditions of faith and piety that support the orders of society and the cosmos. For exilic and postexilic sapiential piety, meditation focuses its attention on two objects: creation and Torah (see Pss. 1; 19; 119). But Job's speech is a gale that threatens to collapse the structure of reality.

Eliphaz then speaks in the second strophe of the divine council ruled by God and the first man, who was present at creation (cf. Gen. 1–2). In Job's context, his opponents make use of the myth of the primal man, a royal figure who has divine wisdom and guards the tree of life in paradise. This figure is common to Akkadian mythology, especially when depicting the origins of kingship. However, there is a subtle but important shift in the meaning of this image in the Hebrew Bible (see J in Gen. 3–11, and Ezek. 28). This tradition refers primarily to the hubris of the human creature who desires to become a god and rule over the divine council. In J the desire for wisdom was predicated on the serpent's deceitful promise that the human pair would "become like gods, knowing good and evil." This grasping for divinity through the appropriation of wisdom ("knowledge of good and evil") coupled with the immortality that they have been granted is interpreted as revolt against divine rule, a rebellion that spreads throughout the primeval history in J, leading to the call of Abraham in Genesis 12. The curse that results from the rebellion of the first human pair is expulsion from the garden and from the presence of Yahweh, and death (they no longer have access to the tree of life). Ezekiel also portrays the first man as the possessor of divine wisdom; only in this case he is identified with the king of Tyre who in his hubris desired to sit on the throne of El, the head of the Canaanite assembly. The end of this king, according to the prophet, is similar to that of the first human pair in Genesis: he will be expelled from the sacred mountain of El and cast into the Pit.

In Job 15 Eliphaz draws on the Israelite version of the creation myth of the primal man to warn Job of the fate of those who rebel against God.[135] Now moving to indict Job directly, the friends discard all measures of decorum and dutiful respect when they underscore their own glaring belief that Job has become a man of great wickedness who deserves divine punishment. In the first strophe (vv. 2–6), Eliphaz recognizes the power of language to create but also to destroy, as he compares Job's words to the power of chaos. This tradition of primeval rebellion is behind the question of Eliphaz directed to what he perceives to be a Job filled with arrogance: "Were you born (yālad, ילד) the primal man (rî'šôn 'ādām, ראישון אדם) and were you brought forth (ḥûl, חול) before the hills?" In Mesopotamian mythology, the first human, representing collective humanity, is fathered or given birth by the gods, while kings normally trace their origins back to divine parents.[136] In addition, it is important to note that Eliphaz quotes Prov. 8:25—"I was brought forth before the hills."[137] In this poem Wisdom is the first-born of creation.

Eliphaz also asks Job if he has stood in the divine council, another Mesopotamian as well as a Canaanite metaphor. It is the heavenly court where God sits on his throne in the midst of the lower deities where he rules and issues edicts that govern the divine world (see Job 1–2; Ps. 82). The prophets during the Assyro-Babylonian period refer to the heavenly assembly as the place to which they are called to receive divine judgments for human destiny, either redemption or destruction (see 1 Kgs. 22; Isa. 6; Jer. 23:18). Obviously, the question is satirical in order to emphasize the point that, for Eliphaz, the ancestral tradition of wisdom does not belong only to Job. This opponent of Job claims that this tradition supports his own views of divine retribution.

Eliphaz uses these references to creation tradition not only to warn Job of the fate that awaits those who in mythic tradition rebelled against the divine world (see 15:17–35), but also to humble him by disputing that he has the wisdom to know the workings of providence (chap. 12)[138] and to remind him as well of the corruption of human nature. Even the divine council ("holy ones," qĕdōšîm, קדשים, v. 15) God does not trust, presumably because of their rebellion (see the myth of the marriage of the gods with human daughters, Gen. 6:1–4) or misrule (see Ps. 82 and the judgment against the gods for their unjust reign over the nations they had been given to govern); how much less could he trust sinful humans, who are completely depraved? In other words, God is well aware of human hubris and the innate propensity toward rebellion. The last part of the speech depicts a battle in which a wicked man, portrayed as a foolish king, attempts to assault God in war, only to meet with destruction.

The Attack of the Divine Warrior and the Appeal
for a Redeemer: Chapters 16–17, 19

Chapters 16–17 comprise two additional speeches of Job that contain several metaphors for creation and providence. The first is the juridical appeal to the earth and to a heavenly witness to give their testimony to vindicate him by interceding with the divine judge (16:18–22). This is placed within the larger protest against God's assault against him (16:6–17:16).

Once again in Job's disputation, God has become the Divine Warrior attacking without mercy a weak and defenseless Job. Taken prisoner, Job is held in derision and beaten by his captors (cf. Ps. 3:8; Mic. 4:14). Job also is depicted in a common biblical image as a personified city under siege by God and his soldiers (cf. 1 Kgs. 11:27; Neh. 6:1; Ps. 144:14; Amos 4:3; Job 19:11–12) that has no recourse but to put on sackcloth and offer up cries of lament for divine intervention and to plead for mercy from a cruel invader (cf. Jer. 4:14; 6:4, 6; etc.). His defenses gone and without any hope of repulsing the enemy, Job forebodingly anticipates the final assault. Perhaps alluding to his own engagement in mourning rites, Job had hoped to receive mercy from God, much like a king who appeals to the attacking enemy for compassion (cf. the lamentations of Jerusalem, Jer. 9:17–22 and 14:19–22). One cannot help but see in this description of a king and city awaiting their annihilation a reference to the Babylonian siege and final conquest of Jerusalem. There is no invincible Zion, ruled over by an immanent God present in the temple and issuing decrees through the royal house that protects the city from all dangers (Pss. 46, 48, 72). Here Job echoes the language of Psalm 79 that speaks of the ruin of Jerusalem and the defiling of the temple, although unlike this psalmist, he does not offer a lament that contains the hope for divine deliverance in some undetermined future.

Job's only recourse to escape the divine assault is to engage in a mourning rite to seek aid from three sources to help him obtain mercy and justice. He first uses the language of the murdered brother whose blood cries out for vengeance, thus echoing the story of Cain slaying Abel (Gen. 4:10). In addition, Job asks the earth, personified as a witness, to testify on his behalf (Deut. 32:1; Isa. 1:2; Jer. 6:19; 22:29; Mic. 1:2). Third, Job once again expresses his desire that a heavenly intercessor will argue his case before the divine assembly in order to gain his redemption. Yet Job ultimately recognizes the futility of these actions.

In referring to the battle imagery of the second strophe of Job 16:6–17, Job again launches an assault on God in 19:2–12. He becomes both a king who is under attack by his opponent, in this case God, and the city besieged. The language is rather similar to that used by Jeremiah in his "oracles concerning the foe from the north" in Jeremiah 4–10. It may be that the poet has in mind a reversal of the David-Zion (= Jerusalem) tradition that became the central theological expression of the kingdom of Judah (e.g., 1 Kgs. 8; Jer. 21:11–23:8; Amos 1:3–2:5). Witnessing the destruction of his country and the assault against his city, this Job cries out "Violence!" (ḥāmas, חמס), a term that connotes a massacre wrought by a ruthless army (Judg. 9:24; 2 Sam. 22:3; Hab. 2:8, 17; Obad. 10) and the shedding of blood that pollutes the earth (Gen. 6:11). Even the lamentation rituals he performs on behalf of his people do not lead to a reprieve. There is thus no opportunity for the inhabitants of the city to escape.

This strophe may refer to rituals of degradation that were part of Akkadian royal tradition in the annual Akitu Festival.[139] However, missing is the subsequent investiture and the resumption of rule by the king. Both the royal city and the ruler have no hope for redemption. This was true, of course, in the destruction of Jerusalem and the ensuing captivity.

The Sovereignty of God and the Folly of Revolt: Chapters 25–26

The third cycle of debate in chapters 21–27, once correctly edited to indicate who is speaking, points to the increasing crescendo of the three opponents' accusations brought against Job. They have moved from polite innuendo to direct indictment of Job as a wicked sinner. Important is Bildad's metaphorical description of God in the three strophes found in 25:2–6; 26:5–10, 11–14.

Bildad's final speech offers a comprehensive summary of the views of the three opponents of Job articulated throughout their earlier speeches. God is a powerful king ruling over a cosmic reality that he conquered in primeval times. While secretive and not available to human understanding, God has the ability to observe and thus to know everything that happens in the cosmos, including even the behavior of a human being like Job. Bildad argues that only a fool would dare to challenge divine rule or assume that God's knowledge of affairs is limited. The important metaphor in this speech is that of conflict. God has gained and continues to maintain his kingship by the real and threatened use of fear-evoking power. The opening line is the theme for the entire speech: "Dominion and fear are his." Divine rule is based on fear, not justice.

In the first strophe (25:2–6), Bildad begins his speech by restricting kingship to God, and thus contravenes the traditional portrayal of humans as the surrogate of the divine king's rule over creation. He directly challenges Job as the first man who rebels against God and seeks the throne of cosmic rule (Gen. 1:26–28; Pss. 8; 89:20–38). Bildad understands "fear" in the sense of "terror" regarding the great power of God (Exod. 15:16; Isa. 2:10, 19, 21).

In the next two strophes (Job 26:5–10, 11–14), Bildad tells of God's primordial defeat of his rivals: Sheol and Abaddon, the rulers of the underworld; and Yamm, Rahab, and Nahash, who are the monsters of the Deep.[140] For Bildad, even Sheol and Abaddon have been brought into submission by God, along with their inhabitants collectively called the Rephaim.[141] Sheol and Abaddon,[142] personified as both the spheres and rulers of the dead, stand naked before God's sight, a sign of their weakness and humiliation before the Creator. This fearsome God of war also defeats the primordial ocean, the realm of chaos.

After describing the establishment through force of divine sovereignty over the heavens, the underworld, and the cosmic ocean, Bildad then speaks of God creating the world, setting up his sacred canopy over the abyss, thus signifying his control over the power of chaos, assuming his royal throne, and issuing decrees that govern the cosmos.[143]

Images of light suggest the sun deity who journeys across the heavens (cf. Babylonian Shamash and Ugaritic Shapash) and watches over his creation, not to establish and maintain justice, but rather to observe all events. Bildad is warning Job that this God would be aware of any revolutionary plot that a fool might plan.

Once again the rhetorical question is asked, "How shall a human creature be righteous before God, and how shall one born of woman be pure?" Obviously expecting no for an answer, Bildad sets forth once more the friends' view of human nature (cf. 4:17): humans are corrupt. He also parodies Psalm 8, especially verse 5, when he notes in 25:5–6 that even if the moon and stars are not pure in God's sight, how much less are humans, who are maggots and worms, creatures who feed off the dead (see Job 7:5; 17:14; 21:26; 24:20; Isa. 14:11).

Conclusion: The End of the Disputations

Job's redescription of reality is consistently portrayed throughout his speeches by means of the common image of an unjust and powerful empire ruled over by a tyrannical despot who sends his armies to conquer or keep in control all subjects (vassal kings and nations, humanity, and the divine powers of the heavens and underworld) by means of intimidation, restraint, and even ruthless slaughter.

In his discourses with his three opponents, Job has undermined the traditional language of sapiential faith by subverting the metaphorical clusters that serve as linguistic foundations for creation (word, artistry, fertility, and struggle). He argues that the divine tyrant is corrupt and brings destruction to his own creation. Humanity is not the one chosen to rule over a life-sustaining creation, but rather is a maltreated slave who is predestined to a life of drudgery and ultimately death. In view of this misrule of the cosmos, Job has assumed the role of the first man, who seeks to remove God from the throne and to rule the world in justice. What we experience in Job is a clash between two major creation traditions that have their origins in Akkadian literature, *Enuma eliš* and *Atra-ḥasis*.[144] Job, the tragic hero, is engaged in an assault on God to remove him from heaven's throne, while God's attack on Job is occasioned by identifying him with the dark forces of chaos challenging divine rule.

CREATION IN THE WHIRLWIND SPEECHES AND JOB'S RESPONSES: 38:1–42:6

Introduction

The lament and the oath of innocence in Job 29–31 provide the transition between the debates with the opponents to the disputation speeches of Yahweh. What Job demands from God is a bill of particulars in setting a trial. In the context of a just trial, Job is convinced that he can prove that God has misruled the cosmos and should be replaced as the sovereign, presumably by humanity. Job's last resort is to indict God and to remove him from the throne in a court where justice would prevail. Undoubtedly, he considers this action to be a spear thrust into the heart of the Creator. If God responds, he will have to admit to misrule. If he does not respond, his silence will prove his guilt. In either case, Job will prevail. Even so, will Yahweh abdicate the throne? The conflict is intensified by the shift to the covenantal name for God: Yahweh.

Unique for wisdom literature are the theophanic appearance of Yahweh in the whirlwind and the uttering of his own words. The whirlwind (se'ārâ, סערה) may refer to either a violent storm (Ps. 107:29; Ezek. 13:11) or a theophany (Ezek. 1:4). Yahweh is the storm-cloud Deity (cf. Judg. 5:4–5; Nah. 1:3–5; Hab. 3:3–15), who has come to do battle both with Job, his human nemesis who has dared to challenge his rule, and the two monsters incarnating chaos: Behemoth and Leviathan (cf. Marduk and Tiamat). Indeed, these forces, Job included, have joined together to remove Yahweh from his throne. Elsewhere in wisdom literature, the revelation of God comes through the observation of the cosmos and human experience, formulated into teachings that make their way into the tradition of the sages.[145] The divine speeches of Yahweh, who directs two disputations against Job, make use of two primary metaphors: word and battle. If we connect the speeches with the annual period of the beginning of the New Year (see Job 1–2), it would appear that Yahweh, the creator and ruler of the heavens and the earth, has come to defeat once again the powers of chaos. This would suggest, as we shall see, that chaos still bides its time and threatens to destroy creation. Thus Yahweh must continually exert dominion through his never-ending conflict with the forces of chaos. This annual struggle, dramatically performed at the Akitu Festival during the New Year's celebration, is the mythic structure that provides the intellectual and literary context for the two speeches. However, included among the supporters of Yamm is Job, who has used the sacred language of curse and the sapiential discourse of disputation to try to overthrow the Creator.

In addition, the poet's construction of these speeches from the whirlwind destabilizes the paradigm of the first man, symbolic of all human creatures, who is to rule over creation. In this mythic structure, humanity, as is true in Akkadian mythology, is a lowly creature totally subject to divine sovereignty and who dares not challenge this supremacy. The theme of the revolt of the primordial man and humankind (e.g., Gen. 3; Ezek. 28; Atra-ḫasis) comes to symbolize Job's efforts at assaulting the justice of God. For Yahweh, humanity's place is that of acknowledging submission to the Creator of heaven and earth.

The First Yahweh Speech: 38:1–40:2

Yahweh's initial speech has two major sections, thematically speaking. The first has to do with the tripartite cosmos: heaven, earth, and underworld, while the second focuses on the creatures and the monsters of chaos.

Opening with questions of challenge and imperatives to the rebel Job, Yahweh's introduction uses the two metaphors that provide the controlling images for the disputation with his human opponent: word and struggle. The form of the speeches is that of disputation, appropriate both for these two metaphors and the continuation of the earlier debate between Job and his friends turned accusers. The introduction to the first speech occurs in 38:1–3. In Old Testament theophanies, Yahweh comes as the storm god to do battle, now with a human rebel who has dared to oppose divine rule.[146] Yahweh challenges Job to a battle of words and while doing so holds his opponent in contempt (Exod. 5:2; Judg. 9:28, 38; 1 Sam. 17:26; 25:10; Isa. 28:9; Job 26:4). "Counsel" in this context would best be understood as referring to Yahweh's plan in creating and ruling the world (cf. Job 12:13; Ps. 33:11; Prov. 8:14). By contrast, Job's word (curse, challenge, disputation, and indictment) "darkens" Yahweh's life-giving plan, a metaphor that not only suggests the obscuring of knowledge but also the returning of the world to primordial chaos by subverting the structures of social life and creation (cf. Job 3). By use of the imagery of battle and disputation, Yahweh challenges Job to a war of words and implicit struggle (Ps. 45:4; Isa. 5:27; 8:9; Jer. 1:17).

One of the primary forms in the two Yahweh speeches is the rhetorical question. His questions have an obvious answer, "Yahweh," or they at least imply that Yahweh knows the answer and Job does not. The first speech is sapiential pedagogy that makes use of onomastica or lists involving creation, especially the different regions and features of the cosmos, including allusions to the Titans opposed to the gods and the mentioning of the untamable animals that resist human rule. The questions in the divine speeches have the purpose of demonstrating to Job that only Yahweh, not an ordinary mortal, has the knowledge and power to rule the cosmos.[147] Their purpose is to humble Job into uttering words of contrite doxology, that is, to praise the justice and goodness of the creator and provider of heaven and earth, and to admit his own guilt in questioning God.

Moving directly into the first major section of his initial speech, Yahweh combines a hymnic description of creation with questions of disputation. This initial section of the first speech focuses on the cosmos, which includes four spheres: chaos, the earth, heaven, and the underworld (38:4–11). In uttering these rhetorical questions, Yahweh uses four primary metaphors to describe his activity in creating and ruling creation: artistry, birth, fertility, and word. Yahweh is first described as the divine builder who constructs the cosmos much like a house.

The poet employs images of house building, including Yahweh "establishing" (yāsad, יסד)[148] the foundations of the earth, the setting of "measurements" (memaddêhā, ממדיה),[149] the stretching out (nāṭaʿ, נטה)[150] of a measuring line (qāw, קו),[151] the sinking (hoṭbeḥāʾû, הטבעו)[152] of pillars or capitals (ʾădānêhā, אדנוה)[153] of the dwelling, and the laying (yārâ, ירה)[154] of a cornerstone (ʾeben pinnātāh, אבן פנתה).[155] In addition, his artistry created a world that leads to the expression of exultation (rān, רן)[156] and the shouting of praise (yārîʿû, יריעו)[157] by the heavenly choir of the divine council and the stars of heaven (38:7). Of course, in hymns praise and cries of exultation are expressed by worshipers engaged in celebration of Yahweh's divine acts in creation and history. Only here it is the heavenly choir, not an earthly one in the temple, that glorifies the creator of heaven and earth and the providential guide of human history.

In the second strophe (38:8–11), the birth of Yamm is depicted in metaphorical language that describes him as "bursting forth, issuing from the womb" (*gîaḥ reḥem*, גיח רחם[158]). Yahweh is described as the midwife who wraps the newborn in swaddling clothes (*ḥatullātô*, חתלתו[159]), and yet also as the one who places bars around Yamm's abode to keep him from inundating the created earth. This bar mirrors the image in *Enuma eliš* when Marduk, having slain Tiamat, set up a "bar and posted guards. He bade them to allow not her waters to escape."[160] Yahweh holds back Yamm's fierce waves by means of setting up a bolt and bars to keep it restrained within its house. Thus it is neither wisdom nor humanity that is mentioned as the infant nurtured by Yahweh, but rather their nemesis. Another metaphor is used in Yahweh's issuance of a divine imperative (*ḥōq*, חק)[161] to Yamm: "Thus far you may come, but no farther; and here must your arrogant waves be stayed?" Thus at the time of creation and in the continuance of the earth, the word as commandment has imbued within it a divine power that both creates and restricts the forces of reality. This imagery represents only a short step away from the view of the Torah as instruction that produces order in the community, a view that finds its first expression in the Torah psalms of the sages.

In the third strophe (38:12–15), the light of morning and dawn not only discovers wickedness through the rays of their illumination, but also is withheld from those who defy the rule of God (cf. Ps. 19A). One of the typical presentations of creation and providence in Akkadian mythology was Shamash, who moved across the heavens and below the earth in the underworld, symbolizing both the cycle of rebirth at sunrise in the east and death during its western entrance into the netherworld or cosmic sea in the evening. "Every sunrise was a repetition of the 'first occasion,' the creation of the world in the beginning."[162] The purpose of this myth and ritual enactment was to sustain the order of creation. Each day Yahweh issues a command that brings into existence a new creation operating according to the norms of justice. Yet in the cultural world of Job in Babylon, it is the Akkadian deity, Shamash, who discovers through its penetrating rays the deeds of humans, including those who are wicked and subversive of divine and legitimate human rule.[163] In the final strophe (38:19–21) of this first section of the first speech, the mystery of the abyss and the city of death ("death's gate[s]," Pss. 9:14; 107:18)[164] remain hidden, for humans cannot enter their domain and then return to the world of the living. In adapting the mythical metaphor of Akkadian religion, the poet points to Yahweh's indictment of the wicked that does not allow them to participate in any regeneration or to experience well-being in life.

The second section of Yahweh's initial speech consists of some six strophes that direct questions to Job concerning the heavenly region: light and darkness, weather, precipitation, the constellations, and the clouds (38:19–38). The cosmological metaphors for Yahweh are varied: builder, giver of fertility, judge, king, sage,

and warrior. First of all, Yahweh builds a cosmic irrigation canal to water a waste-
land uninhabited by humans, suggesting the canals of the city of Babylon that redirected the waters of the Tigris and Euphrates rivers (vv. 25–27; see Gen. 2:4b–7).[165]
However, these cosmic canals are for the channeling of water to thirsty deserts
where *no humans live*. A clearer statement repudiating anthropocentricity in the
cosmos could not be made (contra Ps. 8). Yahweh, in addition, presents himself as
both the father and the mother of moisture necessary for life (Job 38:28–30), while
his voice of thunder commands the waters of the clouds and the gift of his wisdom
enables the ibis and cock to announce that a storm is drawing nigh.[166] The depiction of a high god as the provider of rain is common in the rich lore of the mythologies of the ancient Near East from which Job draws.[167] God's wisdom and decree
tilt the waterskins of the heavens to saturate creation (v. 37). Like the Divine Warrior in theophanic hymns, Yahweh stores up snow and hail to use as weapons during "a time of trouble" and "the day of battle and war" (see Judg. 5:20–21; Pss.
18:3–4; 29:1–2; Isa. 30:30; Amos 5:8–9; 9:6) and binds the constellations of the
Pleiades, Orion, the Mazzaroth, and the Bear and her cubs. These are the ancient
Titans,[168] who challenged divine rule, and, once defeated, were transformed by the
Creator into stellar constellations (cf. Job 9:9; 25:2–3). The speech concludes with
a reference to the wisdom and insight of the ibis and the cock (38:36) in the midst
of a final strophe on the phenomena of the heavens that provide life-giving rain
for the earth and its creatures (clouds, lightning, and the waterskins of heaven, a
metaphorical reference to clouds filled with moisture that bring rain to the earth).

The second major section of this first speech from the whirlwind presents Yahweh as the one who providentially cares for animals, especially the wild beasts
untamed by human beings (38:39–39:30; see Ps. 104). This section of Yahweh's
speech pictures six pairs of animals who share similar features and are nurtured by
Yahweh, providing them with various things necessary for survival, from instinct,
to food, to the capacity to reproduce: the ibis and the cock already mentioned at
the end of the first speech, the lion and the raven, the ibex and the hind, the wild
ass and wild ox, the ostrich and the lion, and the hawk and the vulture. Important to notice is that each of these creatures, with the exception of the horse, are
wild beasts that dwell in regions uninhabited by human beings and that are uncontrolled by human efforts. Even human mastery of the horse is difficult. In the
Priestly document of Gen. 9:1–17, when God establishes a covenant with Noah
and the cosmos, creatures tremble in fear before human beings. In P humans are
ordained to reign as God's surrogate in the world (cf. Ps. 8). This is not the case
in this speech, for these are wild animals, most of whom are inimical to human
life and are certainly outside humanity's control. In addition, there may be an
implicit reference to the hunting of several of these beasts by ancient Near Eastern kings in demonstrating their great courage and skill and as ritual acts designed
to secure order in society and the cosmos.[169] This was especially an activity of both
the Egyptian pharaohs of the New Kingdom and of the Assyrian rulers. Yet Yahweh subverts this tradition of anthropology in which humans are kings ruling the
world as his divinely commissioned surrogates (see Ps. 8). Yahweh now speaks of

sustaining an environment hostile to human life (see Isa. 13:9–22; 32:12–14; 34:8–15; Jer. 50:39–40). The anthropological tradition frequently depicted in the metaphor of humanity exalted by God to rule the cosmos as king is undone. Dwelling in this reality, Job, unlike humanity in the Priestly source in Genesis 1–11, receives no divine commission to go forth and subdue the cosmos. This region and its creatures lie beyond the capacity of humans to control.

The inclusio at the end of this first speech resumes Yahweh's challenge to the one who has revolted against divine rule (Job 40:1–2). If Job wishes to engage in litigation against Yahweh, he will have to serve as his own intercessor. In mocking language, Yahweh asks Job if he can answer the questions posed to him. If he does, he must admit that Yahweh is the powerful and wise creator and lord of history, in contrast to his weak and ignorant interlocutor.

Job's First Response: 40:3–5

One begins by asking: How legitimate is it for Yahweh to ignore the questions of justice and divine misrule of the cosmos, theological and ethical in nature, by giving Job a lesson in divine power exerted in controlling the cosmos? Would the sages who heard and read this narrative not object to Yahweh's failure to respond to the issues in this first speech? Job's response to Yahweh's challenge is to refuse to answer. The translation of verse 4 is critical to the interpretation at this point. Many suggestions have been offered, but perhaps the most frequently encountered is exemplified by the NRSV: "See, I am of small account." This suggests that Job has been moved by the initial speech at least to admit his own insignificance. However, a more likely meaning appears to be: "since I am held in contempt by you," a meaning that indicates Job's dismay to learn how little he (and the rest of humanity) is valued in Yahweh's world. The Hebrew particle ḥēn (הֵן) usually means "since," or "seeing that this is so," while qallōtî (קַלֹּתִי, a Qal verb) clearly means "to be held in contempt" by another (Gen. 16:4, 5; 2 Sam. 1:23; Jer. 4:13; Hab. 1:8; Nah. 1:4). It is not a confession of his weakness that Job is acknowledging. What he has recognized is that in the world that Yahweh has fashioned humans are not important or cherished. Indeed, for Job the divine speech proves that retributive justice is a false teaching. God even cares for a part of the world that is hostile to and damages human life. Refusing to answer is Job's only recourse of defiance.

The Second Yahweh Speech: 40:6–41:26

Having not cowed Job into submission, which would normally be acknowledged in the expected proper response of doxology in which he admits his sin of hubris, Yahweh utters a second speech that challenges his human adversary in an even more confrontational fashion. In this second speech, beginning in 40:6, the controlling metaphor is battle.

In the introduction to the second speech (strophe I, 40:1–8), Yahweh asks his challenger if he is attempting to prove his innocence by "negating" (pārar, פרר)

that of the Divine Judge. This verb is the same one used to describe the "splitting in half" of Prince Yamm in the battle preceding creation (Ps. 74:13), an act also of Marduk, who, after cutting Tiamat in half, uses her body as the substance from which he creates the cosmos. The Joban poet is alluding to the mythical struggle in primordial beginnings. Further, the "strong arm" (zĕrô'a, זרוע) and "thunder" (qôl, קול) are images also associated with the storm god (cf. Baal) who comes to do battle with chaos or the enemies of Israel (Judah).[170] The poet draws from both the mythology of the high god, El, the creator, the father of the gods, and the *deus otiosus*, who has withdrawn into transcendent mystery, and the *theologoumena* of Baal, who defeats Yamm (Lotan) and engages in mortal combat with Mot.[171] These mythological images identify Yahweh with Marduk, the divine warrior and creator, El, the supreme god and creator, and Baal, the ruler of the cosmos.

In verse 10 Yahweh commands Job to don the royal vestments of "greatness" (gā'ôn, גאון), "exaltation" (gôbâ, גובה), "majesty" (hôd, הוד), and "splendor" (hādar, הדר).[172] These terms are references to Yahweh as the ruler of creation and the one who providentially guides human history to destroy the wicked and exalt the righteous (Pss. 21:6; 45:4; 104:1; 111:3). Yahweh commands Job that, once he assumes the position of divine ruler and judge, he is expected to "humble" the arrogant, "subdue" the proud, "tread" them under foot, and bring them ultimately to their grave. These are military images of the warrior king. The "arrogant" in verse 11 (gē'eh, גאה) refers in wisdom texts to those who depend upon their own resources and abilities and repudiate the rulership of Yahweh (see Prov. 15:25; 16:19). In a mocking statement, Yahweh announces to Job that if he is successful in removing the wicked from the land of the living, then he will "praise" ('ôdĕkā, אודך)[173] him as ruler of creation (see Pss. 18:50; 30:13; 35:18; 43:4; 44:9; 54:8; 99:3). What appears to be implied throughout this speech is that Yahweh opposes and subdues chaos and the wicked, but even he cannot eliminate them.

The following strophes describe the fearsome power of two monsters of chaos: Behemoth and Leviathan.[174] The praise of the opponents in war and a description of their strength and prowess are found elsewhere in the Hebrew Bible (e.g., Jer. 4–10). If Job is so bold as to think he is able to rule in justice the creation, then he must defeat the enemies of chaos that Yahweh, like Baal in his battles with Yamm and Mot, must hold at bay to keep them from destroying creation. The first ferocious beast of chaos who is the nemesis of Yahweh is Behemoth (40:15–24).[175]

Behemoth (bĕhēmôt, בהמות) is a plural of majesty in Hebrew, intimating "great beast," likely a large and powerful animal (hippopotamus[176] or water buffalo[177]) that symbolizes chaos.[178] Yahweh describes Behemoth as a creature that he "made like you" (i.e., Job). It is neither humanity that is the first among creatures nor Woman Wisdom who is the first and the best of those elements made by God. Rather it is Behemoth who is the "first of El's works" (rē'šît darkê-'ēl, דרכי אל ראשית). This language reflects that used to refer to Woman Wisdom in Prov. 8:22 and the first man in Gen. 2:4b–7. Behemoth is the first and presumably the most important creature of creation. Behemoth, not Wisdom or humanity, reigns as king over the domain of wild beasts and accepts tribute (*bûl*, בול) from the mountains (*hārîm*, הרים), the supporting pillars of the earth. This mighty beast dwells in marshes and streams and knows no fear. Only Yahweh, his creator, is the one who can bring forth his sword and do battle with him.

Behemoth is but one primeval monster with whom the ruler of creation must contend for sovereignty over the cosmos. Yamm has already been mentioned, and Leviathan is to follow. In Assyro-Babylonian art the king or a deity (e.g., Ninurta) is often depicted as defeating in battle and killing a dreadful monster who embodies chaos, thus establishing order in creation and society. The monster is often portrayed with snakelike features and as a ferocious beast such as a lion or a dragon.[179] As early as the First Dynasty of Egypt, the king, in the role of the god Horus, hunted the red hippopotamus, who symbolized Seth, the god of chaos who killed Osiris, the father of Horus.[180] Horus defeated Seth and ascended the throne of Egypt, leading to order and stability in creation and society. This allusion in Job to ancient Near Eastern art and mythology, most likely Akkadian, suggests that Yahweh has come to do battle with Behemoth, the embodiment of chaos, who opposes divine rule. Job, if indeed he is the royal primal man, must defeat and then control Behemoth in order to replace Yahweh as ruler of the cosmos (see 40:8–14). Thus Yahweh does not directly state that he originated evil, personified by Behemoth, but the implication of this chaos monster as the "first of the works of El" suggests that the Creator, Yahweh, who now serves in the capacity of the Canaanite high god, is the author of evil. In addition, the fearsome qualities of the strength and power of Behemoth are stressed so as to contrast them with the weakness of humans. Allowing Job to rule the cosmos means that he first must defeat the powers of chaos on a daily and annual basis in order to secure the continuation of life.

The last section of Yahweh's second speech turns to the praise of the ruler of the seas, Leviathan (40:25–41:26). Leviathan (Lotan) is far more fearsome than Behemoth. In Ugaritic mythology, Baal and Yamm, the son of El, vie for mastery of the earth, with Baal emerging victorious. As the mythical monster of the seas representing chaos, Leviathan, an incarnation of Yamm, existed prior to creation and must continue to be held in check by the Creator if life is to continue on the earth. He is identified in two other exilic texts with the waters "above the earth" and "below the earth" and the preexistent Tehom ("Deep") in the demythologized Priestly document of Genesis 1, and with Rahab and Yamm, who represent the wilderness, in Isa. 52:9–11. Should Job wish to ascend Yahweh's throne, he must face this awesome foe in mortal combat. Can Job use hooks and ropes to capture this terrible monster and make him beg for his life? Can Job force Leviathan to cut a "covenant" with him (Gen. 9:1–17)[181] that would make this monster his servant forever? If mortals tremble in fear at even the suggestion of "awakening" the powerful Leviathan (see Job 3:8), would they dare "to stand before," that is, oppose, Yahweh (see 2 Sam. 22:6, 19 [= Ps. 18:6, 19]; Job 30:7; Ps. 17:13)? This praise of the invincible Leviathan, whom only Yahweh can restrain, concludes with the statement: "no one upon earth can rule over him." He "is king over all the proud beasts," most probably those fierce animals in the first speech who are untamed by human creatures (cf. Job 28:8).[182] Unlike the animals who fear humans in the Priestly narrative (Gen. 9:2), Leviathan and his animal cohorts know no fear. Thus no human could vanquish them, even if he summoned his courage and took on these terrible opponents. Yahweh alone is able to subdue them, but even he cannot eliminate them and the threats they present.

Job's Second Response: 42:1–6

The second response contains at least features of the doxology in which he acknowledges that Yahweh has the power and wisdom to create and sustain the world. Whether this response is praise, parody, or rejection depends on the translation and meaning of 42:6.

1. Then Job answered the LORD:
2. "I know that you are capable of all things, and that no plan you propose will be impossible for you.
3. 'Who is this who conceals counsel without knowledge?'
   Therefore I have acknowledged I do not understand,
   there are divine acts too wonderful for me, which I do not know.
4. 'Listen now, and I will speak,
   I will question you and you inform me.'
5. I have heard you with my own ears,
   even now my eye beholds you.
6. I protest,[183] but feel sorry for dust and ashes." (42:1–6)

In 42:2 Job's words reflect Yahweh's language of judgment in Gen. 11:6, bringing to mind the story of the Tower of Babel, an image that reflects the ziggurats in Mesopotamian religion and the futility of human arrogance (Gen. 11:1–9). Job's statement is close to a quotation of this text, thus acknowledging that only Yahweh is the sovereign ruler of the divine kingdom whose word of judgment determines the destiny of the world. This is appropriate for understanding at least the view that Yahweh controls human history and the forces of chaos and even directs their movements. In Job's context of the Neo-Babylonian Empire and Judah's languishing in exile, this confession would mean Yahweh is responsible for what has transpired. However, Job's issues are not the sovereignty of Yahweh, but rather theological and ethical in scope. Is Yahweh a deity of justice? Has he misruled the universe? Should he abandon his cosmic throne? Should he continue to be worshiped, and if so, on what basis?

Job quotes in verse 3 Yahweh's earlier words introducing his first speech (38:2). The clear implication is that Yahweh is the one who conceals counsel without knowledge, in this case without revealing what he does. Indeed, Job confesses that he does not possess the knowledge to understand divine acts in creation and history, "wondrous things" (*niplā'ōt*, נִפְלָאוֹת) that redeem and bring life. In these two revelatory speeches about the nature of creation and the challenges of divine rule, Job has finally heard the voice of Yahweh with his own ears and he has seen him with his own eyes. Yet what does this direct revelation teach Job about Yahweh that is new? He has already acknowledged his great power and wisdom. Is he actually now engaged in a doxology in which he admits his guilt for accusing Yahweh of misrule?

I suggest that Job, having "heard" these speeches and "seen" Yahweh in this theophany, has confirmed what he has already stated: Yahweh is unjust and has governed the world without compassion. Now, by quoting Yahweh's own question, "Who is this who conceals counsel without knowledge," Job accuses the Creator of deceitfully hiding the truth about his misrule.

In verse 6 a defiant Job expresses his opposition to a cruel Yahweh and feels compassion for humans who are forced to live under the tyranny of an abusive lord: I protest ['em'as; אמעס], but feel sorry for [niḥamtî; נחמתי] dust and ashes ['āpār wā'ēper; עפר ואפר][184]).

That Job is not offering a "confession" of arrogance or blasphemous accusation is obvious from the larger context of the Yahweh speeches. Not once did Yahweh say, through the continuing roll of strophes and elegant language, that he is just. To suggest that Yahweh is saying that "my ways are not your ways" or that "my knowledge and activity" cannot be comprehended does violence to the meaning of the larger text. It should be noted that 'em'as (אמעס) is an active verb and does not mean "I despise myself." Rather, in Job it means "to protest" (Job 7:16; 34:33; 36:5). This compares with other uses of this active verb in the Hebrew Bible: "despise," "reject," or "protest" (1 Sam. 15:23, 26; Jer. 7:29; Hos. 4:6; 9:17; Amos 5:21; Job 19:18; Prov. 15:32). Further, the Niphal niḥam (נחם) followed by 'al (על) means "comforted over" (2 Sam. 13:39; Jer. 16:17; Ezek. 14:22) or to "have compassion for"/"feel sorry for" (Ps. 90:13). This construction means "repent of" only when followed by the word "evil" (Jer. 8:6; 18:18; Joel 2:13). Job is not "repenting in" dust and ashes, but rather he expresses his despondency over human fate. He feels sorrow for human beings (i.e., "dust and ashes"), a compassion absent from the nature of God. Job refuses to be intimidated, for he remains defiant. It is Yahweh who has been judged guilty, not the mortal Job, for the voice from the whirlwind has been condemned by his own words.

THE RESTORATION OF JOB AND THE REDEMPTION OF GOD: THE EPILOGUE (42:7–17)

In Job 42:7–17 the book returns to its older didactic narrative and tells of Yahweh's judgment. The return to this world, however, no longer elicits first, but rather second naiveté, for with the retelling of the tale by the insertion of the poetic dialogues and speeches from the whirlwind, it becomes impossible to reaffirm the teachings of retribution, the discipline of undeserved suffering, and divine temptation by "the satan." Even the justice of God cannot be confessed.

The retelling of the tale leads to the condemnation of the staunch defenders of retribution, the rejection of the unquestioned justice of Yahweh, the restoration of Job, and perhaps even more importantly the redemption of God.

The epilogue ends the book with two interrelated scenes: judgment (42:7–9) and restoration (42:10–17). It is not clear what the original didactic tale had expressed in the central part of the story. This has been replaced by the poetic disputations. In any case, Eliphaz as the leading voice of the opponents is condemned and commanded along with Bildad and Zophar to offer sacrifices (seven bulls and seven rams) and then to have Job offer intercession in order that they may avoid condemnation, since they had not spoken correctly (*nākôn*, נכון) about their creator as has Yahweh's servant Job. Job's restoration consists of receiving a double portion of possessions he had lost and the birth of ten new children, even though he apparently has the same wife. This is likely an attempt at sexist humor. Although she had urged her husband in 2:9 to curse God and die, there is no reference to her in the conclusion. As a wisdom narrative, the old tale presented the embodiment of the sapiential virtue of unquestioned faith in spite of horrible suffering. Of course, the story concludes with the normal redemption of the protagonist and the humiliation of his opponents.

Finally, not only is Job's integrity upheld by the divine verdict, but Yahweh is also vindicated. His allowing "the satan" to arouse his suspicion about Job's real intentions in pious obedience and faithful living led to the unjust and brutal affliction of his loyal servant, not only in losing his possessions and health but also in the deaths of his ten children. Such a theological portrait of a divine tyrant willing to destroy even those who are rumored to be disloyal cannot stand in the face of the overwhelming crisis faced in the Babylonian conquest and exile. Yahweh must act to set things right, which, after all, is the responsibility of the Divine Judge. Subsequently, in the restoration of Job there is the redemption of God. Only then can a just God legitimately rule the cosmos and direct human history.

REDACTIONAL ADDITIONS

The Search for Woman Wisdom: Chapter 28

The elegant poem on personified Wisdom in Job 28 is similar in numerous respects to other sapiential hymns: Prov. 8:22–31 and Sirach 24. However, both of these poems speak of the instruction of humans and their ability to understand wisdom and therefore Yahweh, while the poem under consideration (Job 28) declares the humans do not have the capacity to discover and understand divine wisdom.

Consisting of four strophes (vv. 1–6, 7–12, 13–20, and 21–28), this poem contains a refrain that twice asks the thematic question: "Where shall wisdom be found, and where is the place of insight?" (vv. 12, 20).

In this hymn, creation consists primarily of the earth and its treasures, although there are brief mentions of Yamm, the heavens, Abaddon, and death.

As for human beings, revelation of ultimate matters, held by an unfathomable Woman Wisdom, is denied them. Instead of seeking out answers to questions that deal with the nature of reality and divine character, they are to "fear God and turn from evil," as did the unreflecting and naive Job of the prologue. There is no reference to the dominant metaphors of creation through struggle and insurrection by the primeval man that had been present in the other portions of the book. In addition, if Job had reached this conclusion, then both his preceding arguments and Yahweh's following disputations would be senseless.

The hymn to Wisdom presents God in the guise of two major metaphors: as the builder who measured and weighed the wind and the showers, and as the judge who has established an "edict" for the rain. God alone knows the location of cosmic wisdom, knowledge denied to human beings. Only he knows the place of Woman Wisdom who is hidden in mystery. God is the one who "established (i.e., created; see Jer. 10:12; Ps. 65:7; Prov. 8:27) her and searched her out (ḥāqar, חקר), that is, knows her intimately (Job 5:27; Prov. 25:2; Ps. 139:1). Instead of seeking out answers to questions that deal with the nature of reality and divine character, humans are to "fear God and turn from evil," as did the unreflecting and naive Job of the prologue.

Finally, following creation, Yahweh, the cosmic judge and incomparable sage, instructed the first human and all who followed him: "Behold, the fear of the LORD is wisdom, and to turn from evil is insight." Humans, in compliance with divine teaching, are to live as unquestioning, pious, and righteous slaves, obedient to God. The rebel of the prologue is, in the view of this later sage, engaged in acts of hubris in both pursuing the impossible quest of knowing the secrets of divine rule and the nature of the cosmos and thinking that he could demand of God sovereign justice. This allusion to J's primeval narrative involving Adam is important in that it evokes the myth of divine origins. For the traditional sages, wisdom was created first, followed by other elements, including humanity (cf. Gen. 2:4b–3:24 and the theme of hubris leading to the punishment of alienation from God and ultimately death).

The Speeches of the Intruder, Elihu: Chapters 32–37

The four speeches of Elihu also engage in a second, redactional rejection of the earlier poet's rewriting of the Joban narrative. These speeches are found in 32:6–33:33; 34:1–37; 35:1–16; 36:1–37:24. The redactor sets the stage for his entrance by allowing Elihu a self-introduction to his speeches: he, although a young sage, feels constrained to enter into the debate to defend God, because the three friends had declared God (not Job!) to be in the wrong.[185] Creation language figures prominently in the first, second, and especially fourth speech. The anthropological tradition is used in the first two speeches, while the last speech includes an important reference to cosmology.

Elihu argues that both his knowledge and the authority of his teaching were based on inspiration. For example, he teaches that the spirit dwells in a person and the breath of God enables him to understand. It is the "breath" (*nĕšāmâ*, נשמה) of life (Gen. 2:7; 7:22; Job 27:3; 33:4; 34:14) or the divine "spirit" (*rûaḥ*, רוח), which animates the human person (Gen. 6:17; 7:15, 22; Isa. 42:5; Zech. 12:1; Ezek. 37:5, 6, 8, 10, 14; Qoh. 3:19), that is the source of inspiration (cf. Num. 11:26–30).[186] He understands this "breath of Shaddai" to be like that of prophetic charisma that becomes the basis for his insight. Elihu argues that since Job and he both are created as mortals of clay and endowed with the gift of the divine breath, even Job's age and experience, valued as important for obtaining wisdom and acting according to its dictates, provide him with no advantage. Elihu regards the inability of Job and his friends to find convincing answers and to present persuasive arguments to address the problem of theodicy to result in the failure of both traditional and radical wisdom.

In 32:21–22 Elihu argues that retribution is the basis for this understanding of inspiration. Rejecting flattery and respect of persons as vices, Elihu indicates that his Creator would bring him to destruction, if he engaged in the same improper speech and behavior that the elder Job has pursued. God not only breathes into a person the inspired and animating breath, he also destroys those who misuse language. Likewise, this same inspiration is at work in God's warning humans of their iniquity by means of visions in the night (cf. 4:12–21) so that they may turn from evil and save their lives from death (33:12–18).

Elihu uses the same image associated with creation when he refers to the breath of God as the animating principle of all life (34:14–15). The text echoes others in the Bible that speak of God's animating breath, including especially Psalm 104 (see also Gen. 2:7; 3:19; 7:21–23). According to Elihu, the divine breath that gives life to all creation also dwells within human beings, providing insight and understanding to those who would listen to divine instruction. The "returning to the dust" echoes the J narrative's verdict of Yahweh directed against the disobedient Adam (Gen. 3:19).

In comparison to Prov. 22:2, Elihu also emphasizes that the mighty and wealthy enjoy no special favor with God, for their origins are the same as the poor (Job 34:17–20). God, the Creator who forms both rich and poor, lowly and mighty, in the womb, is no respecter of persons, for they all are the work of his hands (cf. Job 10:3; Prov. 14:31; 17:5; 22:2). When humans are sinful, God brings quick and unexpected destruction upon them, regardless of their social status. Even so, Elihu especially emphasizes that divine retribution will punish the powerful aristocracy (Job 34:17–30).

In 36:5–12 Elihu speaks of the exaltation of the righteous, using royal language in doing so. Drawing heavily on images associated with the enthronement of kings (cf. 1 Kgs. 1:32–40; Job 40:10–14; Pss. 2; 8; 110), Elihu speaks of God's eventual exaltation of the oppressed righteous to sit on royal thrones forever. Contrasting images of slavery are used to describe those weighed down by sin, especially the arrogance of hubris (cf. Isa. 14 and Ezek. 28). According to Elihu, rebels—and these include Job—may hope for deliverance only through obedient service to God.

In the last speech, Elihu utters a doxology in praise of Yahweh and asks Job questions no mortal can answer: like those of Yahweh in the following "speeches from the whirlwind," they deal with the "wonderful works of God" (Job 36:24–37:24). Unlike the interrogation of Job by Yahweh, Elihu's questions are not designed to intimidate Job to move from silence to praise. Rather his examination is designed both to humiliate Job and to contrast the power, justice, and mystery of the Almighty with the weakness and dark ignorance of his mortal antagonist. The desire is not to evoke praise, but to intimidate the mortal Job with a description of the awesomeness of God.

Traditional metaphors are reused in these two additions in the attempt to return to the theology prior to the holocaust of Babylonian destruction and exile. They issue deadening and lifeless metaphors that evoke a hollow and sterile understanding that is not capable of reshaping the traditions of sapiential faith.

THE HISTORICAL THEOLOGY OF THE BOOK OF JOB

Divine Creation and Providence

As has been noted, the dominant metaphors for creation and providence in Job are word and struggle. These two metaphors emerge from Babylonian and Canaanite myths as well as the theological language of the earlier traditions of ancient Israel and Judah. The Babylonian myth of creation (*Enuma eliš*) tells of the creation of the world by Marduk, following his slaughter of Tiamat. Marduk then takes the throne and rules over the divine council. Following the creation of humanity, fate is dictated by this cosmic judge. The poet, who appears to know this myth, appropriates it by telling of God's vanquishing of Leviathan and then taking his throne where he rules over the divine council and decides human fate, both in general (to serve as slaves to the gods) and in particular (the annual destiny of humans, including even the righteous like Job). The poet began the story of Job with the usual introductory narrative (chaps. 1–2), which has the mythic images of the divine council and predestination of human beings, but then makes an abrupt change in the presentation of Job's opening soliloquy (chap. 3). This speech no longer serves as an attestation of the acceptance of one's plight at the hands of God, but rather issues a series of curses that ironically repudiates the didactic prose character's refusal to yield to both his wife's and the satan's testing. The poet does so by replacing the friends' former speeches, which likely urged him to maintain unquestioningly his loyalty to God, with increasingly passionate dialogues over divine justice and the revelatory theophany of the whirlwind speeches.

In the poetic speeches of Job, the transformed sage attacks the justice of God, comparing the creator and sustainer of the cosmos to an oppressive despot who seeks to destroy the work of his own hand. Psalm 8, a creation hymn that describes the divine exaltation of humans, who are made only a little less than the gods, being crowned with glory and honor, is satirically repudiated in Job

7:17–21. Likewise, the divine warrior of Canaanite and Israelite hymnology depicts the theophanic coming to defeat the powers of chaos. Only in the poet's theology of reversal, the enemy who suffers from the brutal assault of God is Job, the righteous sage. The friends continue to uphold the righteousness of God, concluding that Job must be an appalling sinner to merit such loathsome punishment. With Job's oath of innocence that concludes the dialogue with the friends (chap. 31), there is no final resolution of the disputation.

The "voice from the whirlwind" (38:1–42:6) and Job's two responses are intriguing in that the divine speeches point in a new direction. While Yahweh, the God of election, is the creator who restrains Yamm with his edict, he must continue to do battle with the two monsters of chaos: Behemoth and Leviathan (40:15–41:34). Furthermore, he appears to imply to Job that neither of them is capable of defeating the proud and wicked and bringing them into the underworld. Consequently, Yahweh is not all-powerful, but rather he must continue to battle evil in the forms of chaos and wickedness. In Babylonian ritual, the annual Akitu Festival included the battle with Marduk and Tiamat for supremacy over the earth. With Marduk's victory, the fates are determined for the coming year. This language of myth appears to be well known by the poet as seen in the prologue and the annual meeting of the divine council when Yahweh's judgment leads to the establishment of the destinies of the nations and people. It is also important to note that Yahweh ignores the two critical questions raised by Job in the earlier dialogues with his opponents: the explanation of why humans, especially the righteous, suffer and the questioning of the justice of God. In the speeches from the whirlwind, Yahweh does not defend his justice or explain why retribution is a false teaching. Instead, Yahweh proclaims his profound wisdom and his commanding power to be superior to those of his would-be human rival. However, Job had already acceded to these points he considered to be unquestionably the case and simply reiterates them in his second response (42:1–6).

The poet has allowed the conclusion of the old didactic narrative, now appearing again in the form of the conclusion of 42:7–17, to be endowed with new meaning: Job has his integrity upheld by the ruler of the divine assembly, who now renders judgment. The friends, who had unflaggingly held to the inviolable righteousness of God, defended him without daring to question, are condemned by the Divine Judge as having spoken "incorrectly" about God, while Job's portrayal of an opprobrious and destructive deity who has vitiated the standards of justice is said to be "correct." Retribution and the refusal to question divine justice are rebuffed as false.

This rereading not only allows Job's integrity to be endorsed by the verdict of the Cosmic Judge, but in addition allows God to be vindicated, although in a different way than was perhaps intended originally by the tale. In the prologue, the suspicious nature of the Divine Judge as to the intention behind Job's moral and faithful devotion is aroused by the satan. This evokes in the Divine Judge the cruel mistreatment of Job and the death of his ten children. This depiction of a divine tyrant who is without pity arouses among the captives in Babylon the refusal to accede to this violence. Thus, with the poetic insertions, now the didactive narrative allows God to set things right, which, after all, is the responsibility of the *šopēṭ*, the judge. This verdict results not only in the restoration of Job but also in the redemption of God. Only a God of justice merits praise.

Creation and Anthropology

One of the poets literary contacts with the didactic narrative is the continued use of the term *'ebed*. However, the term in the tale is used to refer to a faithful and loyal servant, while the poet uses the term metaphorically to mean "slave." In the dialogues, Job becomes much like the slave in Babylonian mythology in which humanity is created to carry out the onerous tasks of slaves to the gods (see Atraḥasis and Job 7). However, Job, God's slave, now questions divine justice. While he is not a king who rules over the cosmos, Job still engages in an assault on the divine tyrant whose anarchy brings destruction against even the righteous slave who serves him loyally. Job engages in an accusation uttered through the power of language (the metaphor of word) to challenge God's supremacy over the earth. Yet, in view of his mistreatment, symbolizing that of the nation in the Babylonian holocaust, in the poetry Job asserts his own righteousness, although not his perfection, for he recognizes that he has committed less than egregious sins and rejects the contention that unknown sins have led to his present torment. By contrast the friends set forth the innate wickedness of humans, compared by Bildad to a worm. Humans, they assert, must be in the wrong, and the friends are horrified by Job's attack on the righteousness of God.

In the epilogue a new reading is facilitated by the insertion of the poetic dialogues and speeches. The poet causes the slave Job to reenter the narrative world of the divine assembly ruled over by Yahweh. Once again it is the New Year and God's decrees determine the destinies of the cosmos and its inhabitants. This time, it is a righteous edict and not a questioning suspicion that issues forth in judgment. Yahweh affirms Job's righteousness and rectifies the earlier injustice of the prologue. Yahweh's edict "sets things right" by declaring Job's arguments to be correct and the friends, who had defended divine justice and advised Job to repent of his sins, to be in the wrong. Ironically, this judgment of Job's innocence results in Yahweh's self-condemnation.

Creation and Goddess Wisdom

Traditional sages were not pleased with the poet's retelling of the Joban tale. Subsequently, in the final editorial formation of the book they incorporated two additions: the hymn on the inaccessibility of wisdom (chap. 28) and the speeches of Elihu (chaps. 32–37). Each of these attempts a new reading that varies from that of the poet and likely originates in a time when the captivity was over and traditional wisdom in the form of Ezra and Ben Sira had reemerged as the dominant expression of the sages' understanding of knowledge, retribution, and belief.

These redactors reused the older metaphors in order to reclaim the faith that no longer is disturbed by the crisis of the Babylonian destruction of Jerusalem and the subsequent captivity. Assuming the final verse of 28:1–28 was added to the poem prior to its insertion in the poetic dialogues, the didactic composition on wisdom is an expression of Second Temple piety in which wisdom is identified with the fear of God. This poem speaks of the failure of humans to locate and understand divine wisdom. The refrain, placed in the form of a question, expresses the theme: "Where shall wisdom be found, and where is the place of insight?" (vv. 12, 20). While humans lack both the power and the knowledge to discover wisdom, God is both the sage and the judge who alone knows the dwelling of wisdom in the structure of his world and creates and issues decrees that regulate this order. Thus he oversees providentially all that exists in earth and heaven and creates both wind and rain, which produce the richness of the soil. Thus what the poetic Job had sought to know, that is, the essence of reality, the nature and activity of God, and the answers to perplexing questions are to be set aside. Instead of seeking this knowledge, humans are to "fear God and turn from evil" in the same way that the unquestioning Job of the prologue did.

As for Wisdom, this poet presents her as coming to expression in the imagination of God, who pictured her in his mind, spoke her into existence, permeated creation with her, and came to know the intricacies of her nature (Job 5:27; Prov. 25:2; Ps. 139:1). Thus Wisdom is the anchor by which the Creator secured the foundations of the world (Jer. 10:12), the mountains (Ps. 65:7), and the heavens (Prov. 8:27). God alone knows her location and her being. Following creation, God, like a sage, instructed the first human and all who came later: "Behold, the fear of the LORD is wisdom, and to turn from evil is insight" (v. 28). Humans are to follow divine teaching and live an unquestioning, pious, and righteous life.

Creation and the Speeches of Elihu

The speeches of Elihu (Job 32–37) derive from a marginalized community that is on the periphery of political and religious power. He becomes the voice for their protests against the leadership of Second Temple society, most likely the aristocracy and the priestly hierarchy of the Zadokites. The sage who composes these four speeches (32:6–33:33; 34:1–37, 35:1–16; 36:1–37:24) is dissatisfied with the earlier poetic dialogues. Indeed, the introduction to the speeches indicates that he is "angry at Job because he justified himself rather than God" (an accurate reading of Job's speeches) and "at the three friends of Job because they had found no answer, though they declared God (not Job) guilty." The sage who composes these speeches is critical of both traditional and radical wisdom to discover answers to major theological questions, including those treating theodicy and retribution. Thus he claims inspiration for himself (32:8) in order to combat the typical view that wisdom came with age and experience. The spirit (*rûaḥ*) of the Almighty dwells within humans in conferring divine revelation, which is the source of knowledge. He also notes that God sends visions in the night to warn people to turn from their wickedness and to gain salvation from death (cf. Elihu's poem in 4:12–21). Finally, according to Elihu, the Creator does not countenance the one who flatters, indicating the one who engages in uttering wise speech. Thus it is the divine spirit, which also is used on occasion to speak of creation or acts of creation, that resides in the sage and enables him to speak with insight. In the second speech, Elihu once more speaks of the life-giving spirit of God that animates all that exists (34:14–15; cf. Ps. 104:29–30). Consequently, the divine spirit is the source of both life and inspiration.

In the final speech, Elihu, who utters the voice of the oppressed, speaks of the exaltation of the afflicted righteous who will sit forever on royal thrones. In doing so he borrows the language of the enthronement of kings (cf. Gen. 1; 1 Kgs. 1:32–40; Job 40:10–14; Pss. 2; 8; 110) and the striking differences found in Isaiah 14 and Ezekiel 28 that speak of gods and kings filled with hubris meeting their destruction. It is important to note in this anthropological language that the poet of the Elihu speeches is well aware of the mythological depiction of the rebellious kings who seek to reign in the place of God.

Knowledge and Power in the Book of Job[187]

If the old narrative of Job is redacted in the exile by the addition and insertion of the dialogues, how does this reflect the social setting of the community? And to ask Foucault's question, how does the relationship between knowledge and power come to expression among the various groups of exiles in Babylon who are articulate and propagate views that support their own interests? Through historical imagination that works with fragments of evidence, one may suppose there coexisted in exile a variety of groups who struggled to find their own identity through the avenues of various fields of knowledge and discourse, including, of course, wisdom. The objective of each was not only the reshaping of group identity, but also the desire to achieve a position of power in relationship to others outside their social and epistemological boundaries.

We have one strong indication of this in Deutero-Isaiah, the prophetic voice of at least some exiles, who sought to return home and reestablish things much the way they had been prior to 586 BCE. However, for this group, represented by an articulated text, the demise of the monarchy allowed no political resurrection for the house of David and its members, especially two exiled kings, possibly dead, whose families wished to reassert their position of power, once a return to the homeland was realized. For Deutero-Isaiah, there is no future monarchy, but rather a reconstituted people of God who would live as loyal supporters of the new Achaemenid Empire. In addition to these two groups, a peace party and a nationalistic party of those seeking to regain power that had been lost, there was the priestly group of Zadokites still hoping to maintain their power over the Levites and to regain the control of a rebuilt temple and its liturgy. They would make their peace with whatever political group, foreign or internal, came to power. Finally, the rivalry among the sages was especially intense. The traditional sages had held important positions of leadership in the former administration and were second only to the kingship in authority. Even if the monarchy was not reestablished, this group, through its advantage of knowledge, and therefore substantial power, would have much to say about the construction of new institutions, legitimizing these through redacted texts, and power. They might not wield power, but they stood next to it and enjoyed its benefits. Their alliance with the priesthood would present a formidable power bloc. Thus a traditional theology and common sapiential forms were a part of their repertoire. For the poet of Job, however, his group strongly contested the traditionalists for authenticity and the power and wealth associated with their achievement. A repudiation of former institutions and a discredited religion would sweep away all rivalries, leading then to a new way of existing in the world in which leadership and therefore power and its accoutrements would be accessible to the new and radical sages. This later group gambled the most, and had the most to lose, if their ambitions were not realized. But they also had much to gain. The one thing that united these competing groups would be their contention for leadership against a common enemy: the "people of the land," who, joined by non-Israelites and non-Judahites, had been left to rebuild a nation in which they had the say. This conflict between the former exiles and the population of the land was destined to be intense, and indeed did not cease until the total destruction of Jerusalem and the temple in 70 CE.

Chapter 5

Scribalism and the Torah in the Wisdom Tradition

HISTORY OF THE PERSIAN PERIOD

Scribalism and Torah

The Persian period witnessed the development of what would become in later Babylon and Eretz Israel an extremely important scribal and scholarly tradition in two geographical locations, shaping and then writing down the Mishnah, the midrashim, the Babylonian Talmud, the haggadah, and the halakah. The most important sage of the period was Ezra, "the scribe of the law of God Most High" in the mid- to late fifth century BCE, who became the model of the interpreter of the Torah under the Zadokite priests in the Second Temple. Other sages included in particular the school of the Deuteronomic scribes, originating as a group as early as the eighth century BCE, a rival scribal group that eventually edited the final forms of Deuteronomy, the Deuteronomistic History, and the Deuteronomic redaction of several books that would become part of the canon. The Deuteronomic school differed in numerous ways from the school typified by Ezra, particularly in the former's emphasis on the shaping of a different Torah, the themes of salvation history and retribution, and the important institution of

137

the limited Davidic kingship. Since two rival priesthoods (the Zadokites and the Deuteronomists) continued into the Babylonian exile and the Second Temple that followed, it is not surprising that each had its own scribes who composed and redacted their literature, until finally in the fifth century BCE the Zadokites gained control of the high priesthood and the Deuteronomists were no longer permitted to serve in priestly functions. Instead, they continued their work as scribes and served in minor cultic roles, but the dominant Zadokite group assumed and maintained control of the major priestly functions and was in charge of the temple in Jerusalem. Without a Davidic king to assume the role of leader of the Second Temple community, the high priest of the Zadokites appropriated a higher degree of authority and worked with the provincial administrator in managing local affairs under the watchful eye of the Persian satrap of Abar Nahara.

The Chronicler's History, consisting of the books of Ezra, Nehemiah, and 1 and 2 Chronicles, and the Torah Psalms (1, 19B, and 119) are the primary sources for attempting to understand the scribal tradition of those who served the Zadokites in the Second Temple. Texts mentioning their roles and functions are found in the books of Ezra and Nehemiah and the Torah Psalms (1, 19B, and 119), which were composed in the Persian period, and in 1 and 2 Chronicles, written in the Hellenistic period. One discovers in each of these texts information about the social roles of scribes and their religious piety. For our purposes, Ezra's prayer in Nehemiah 9 includes the emphasis on God's creation and providential direction of the world (see v. 6). This parallels with Psalm 19, which combines Torah with cosmology. Ezra's prayer is placed within the ceremony of the reading of the Torah that is central to the first day of Tishri, later known as Rosh Hashanah, and the subsequent seven-day Festival of Booths. Theologically understood as equated with wisdom, the Torah was believed to be grounded in the order of creation that sustained life and provided direction to faithful Jews.

Cyrus II and the Foreign Policy of the Achaemenid Empire[1]

Cyrus II, the Achaemenid King of Persia (559–530 BCE), entered the city of Babylon in 539, where he was proclaimed the new ruler of the once mighty empire. With the taking of Babylon, Persia became the empire that ruled the ancient Near East and even Egypt for some two centuries. The road of Cyrus to this status was a long and winding one. Defeating the Medes by 550, he then took control of Lydia in 546. For six years (546–540) he extended his empire in the east. The Behistun inscription, dating from 520, indicates that Parthia, Drangiana, Aria, Chorasmia, Bactria, Sogdiana, Gandara, Scythis, Sattagydia, Arachosia, and Maka were taken and absorbed into the Persian Empire. It is likely that Cyrus defeated most of these nations.

His policies for ruling his empire included propaganda in which he presented himself as the worshiper of the gods of the nations he conquered. Cyrus referred to himself as the devotee of the local gods and supporter of local temples. This removed the requirement, repugnant to many nations, of being forced to worship the gods of the conqueror. Due to religious tolerance, Judaism was allowed to develop during the first half of the Second Temple without interference from Persian authorities.[2] In addition Cyrus ended the policy of exile and allowed nations to continue with the infrastructure of their leaders intact.[3] In the Cyrus Cylinder, Cyrus blamed the Babylonian king Nabonidus for being an oppressive ruler, while he himself was "king of the world, great king, legitimate king, king of Babylon, king of Sumer and Akkad, and king of the four rims (of the earth)," whose rule was loved by Bel (Marduk) and Nebo. In return for the support of Marduk, he became his devotee. He also claimed to have abolished forced labor from the various locales in Mesopotamia, returned the images to their pillaged temples and sanctuaries that had been taken as booty by the Babylonians, and established new sanctuaries and rebuilt old ones among the conquered people. Finally, he allowed their captives the choice to return to their native lands or to stay in Babylon. One expects that this same type of propaganda was issued in Judah to present the Persian king as an enlightened ruler. In addition to promoting local law codes as the basis for social and civil life, Persian rulers allowed continuity with the former Davidic dynasty and the governors of the Jews in Judah. Yet the Persians were harsh in their treatment of disloyal nations.[4] Those nations that dared to create disturbances were brutally treated. It is also doubtful that Cyrus was actually supportive of local religious cults. He and the later Achaemenids may not have suppressed local religions as long as they did not foment and advance revolutionary activities. The support of local temples, if actually carried out, would have allowed this system to be used for the collection and payment of taxes and tribute.

For the satrapy of Abar Nahara, the system of propaganda that gave limited local authority to indigenous governors of the province of Judah was part of an overall imperial policy intended to create a stable empire. So was the codification of local laws, a policy that likely accelerated the development of the Priestly document and its use by Ezra in regulating Jewish life.[5] While not denying that P was largely a religious document, Peter Frei and Klaus Koch set forth the highly questionable thesis that the source was authorized by the Persian government and at least indirectly would have supported Achaemenid rule.[6] Yet if this is a legitimate insight into the origins of P, one would need to explain why the negative criticism of Persian rule would have appeared in the Chronicler. Furthermore, this would have been in contrast to the evident nationalism found in Haggai and Zechariah, who suggest revolution should occur in order that autonomy may return to Judah.

Although it is difficult to imagine that P was officially sanctioned by the new rulers and that prophetic nationalism was not disturbing to the empire, many Jews appear to have been loyal to the Achaemenid dynasty at least until the coming of Alexander some two centuries later. In the middle of the sixth century BCE, Second Isaiah, preaching in Babylon, proclaimed Cyrus to be Yahweh's messiah. This message is thought to capture the positive support of the Persians by at least some of the Judahites in exile.

Even local rule by native administrators could serve as a stabilizing force in preventing disturbances to the tranquility of the empire.[7] In addition, peaceful and cooperative nations could be quite useful in providing for military support against rivals, including the Egyptians to the south and the Greek states to the west.[8] Social, political, and economic policies favorable to Persian interests were made part of official policy.

From Cyrus to Alexander

The entire reign of Cyrus was marked by military activities in the building of the Persian Empire. He died near his seventieth year of age in battle against the nomads, the Massagetae (Herodotus 1.201–4). Biblical references to Cyrus occur first in the written prophecy of Second Isaiah (44:28; 45:1)[9] in the middle of the sixth century BCE, followed by the Chronicler (2 Chr. 36:22–23; Ezra 1:1–4; 6:3–5) in the fifth and fourth centuries, and the book of Daniel in the first part of the second century (1:21; 6:28; 10:2).

Cambyses II (530–522 BCE), who followed his father, was successful in conquering Egypt. Among his military successes was the conquest of Egypt in 525. However, he died in his trip from Egypt back to Persia to quell a local revolt. The struggle for the throne that followed culminated in the accession of Darius I (522–486), a member of the Achaemenid royal house. Elam, Babylon, and Egypt rebelled, with the most troublesome revolt that led by Nebuchadrezzar III, the son of Nabonidus, and then Neuchadrezzar IV. Indeed, it may have been due to the revolt in Babylon that Zerubbabel, the Davidic descendant and governor of this part of the satrapy, became implicated, at least as implicitly suggested by Haggai. But the defeat of this rebellion led to the desire of Darius to spread the Persian presence eastward into Eastern Europe against the states in Anatolia and Greece and westward into India. He even subdued Thrace in 512 and engaged the Scythians at the mouth of the river Danube. When allied with the states in Anatolia and Cyprus, however, the Greek states proved to be a significant power to resist aggressively the Persians. Hostilities between Athens and other Greek nations led to the defeat of the Persian forces at Marathon in 490. The revolution that was also initiated in Egypt required a response from Darius, although he died during his preparations to launch an invasion. Darius was given the major credit for the development of a massive imperial bureaucracy resulting in twenty satrapies administered by governors appointed by the court. Local laws were reformed and codified to allow for the administration of each satrapy and to provide a conduit for taxation and tribute. This likely propelled Judah's efforts at codification in the Priestly document, giving increased significance to the Torah, temple, and Zadokite priesthood.

When Xerxes I (486–465) assumed the throne, he was immediately confronted with another Egyptian rebellion that ultimately was put down by 483. The letter of accusation against Judah and Jerusalem in Ezra 4:6–16 suggests Jewish participation in this rebellion. The ruler then faced another revolution in Babylon that, while defeated, led to Babylon's removal from the satrapy of Abar Nahara, leading then to a reorganization that involved Judah. Xerxes' efforts against the Greeks met with catastrophe. He was defeated in the important battles at Salamis and Mycale, while his entire fleet was destroyed at Eurymedon.

Darius II gained the throne in 423 and ruled until 404. Facing rebellions in Media, Anatolia, and Syria, the satrap of Egypt left to help defeat these revolts. This led to scattered resistance in Egypt. Two letters from the military colony of Elephantine sent to the governor of Judah and the two sons of Sanballat, governor of Samaria, complain of the destruction of the Yahweh temple in the colony by Egyptian rebels. This led to an increased role of the high priest of Jerusalem's temple, since the Persians, ending this pogrom, required that only he could preside at the offering of sacrifices. This in effect ended the prominence of this Egyptian Jewish temple.

Another major impact on Jews in Judah came during the reign of Artaxerxes II Memnon (404–358). It was during his reign that the long and slow descent of Persian hegemony and power irreversibly began, climaxed by Alexander's final defeat of Darius III. Artaxerxes II's sending of Ezra to Jerusalem to lead a reform that required obedience to the Torah again increased its importance. When Alexander defeated the forces of Darius III (336–330) at Issus, the Greek Empire soon replaced that of the Persians in the East. When resistance continued at Tyre, Gaza, and Samaria, Alexander defeated them as well. While our sources do not allow us to reconstruct the history of the Jews during this early transition to Greek rule, the new empire and its successive kingdoms resulted in significant change for the colony.

JUDAISM IN THE PERSIAN EMPIRE

Historical Overiew

The lack of extensive literary sources and archaeological data make it very difficult to reconstruct this period of Jewish history. The Priestly document's final redaction, the completion of the composition and redaction of Deuteronomy and the Deuteronomistic History, Chronicles, Ezra–Nehemiah, several prophetic texts (Joel, Second and Third Isaiah, parts of Ezekiel and Jeremiah, Haggai, Zechariah, and Malachi), and some of the writings, in particular the Psalter and the book of Proverbs, provide some suggestive indications of the social and religious life of this period of the Second Temple. The biblical materials, including especially Ezra–Nehemiah, point only to Jerusalem and two time periods: 538–515 BCE and 458–432 BCE.[10] However, these texts of Ezra and Nehemiah have an ideological agenda in placing into prominence Jerusalem, the high priesthood, the Torah, and scribalism. These texts themselves are plagued by contradictions. The books of Ezra and Nehemiah offer at times different scenarios and dates, leading to the difficulty faced in reconstructing even the major events of the Persian period. We are limited to generalizations that represent Jewish life in Persia, the significant returns from exile in the late sixth century, and the commissioning of

Ezra and Nehemiah. Yet there are some cultural materials in the forms of Persian inscriptions, papyri (especially from Elephantine), and coins that, when combined with the writings of Ezra, Nehemiah, and a few other biblical texts, allow a provisional picture to emerge.[11]

The Province of Judah in the Political Organization of the Persian Empire[12]

During the administrative overhaul of the empire, orchestrated by Darius II (Herodotus 3:88–95), Judah was situated within the satrapy of Abar Nahara (Ezra 4:10–11, 16–17, 20; 8:36; Neh. 2:7, 9), directly governed by a Persian official. These larger administrative changes had important implications for the social history of Judah. The states of Judah, Gaza, Ashdod, Samaria, and Arabia were the provinces (*mĕdînôt*, מדינות) of the satrapy along with their smaller national divisions (*pĕlākîm*, פלכים) throughout the history of the later Persian Empire.[13] Local governors of the districts and nations were supported by officials called *sĕgānîm* (סגנים, Neh. 5:17 = the Daliyeh papyri). Within the administrations Jewish scribes would have served these three tiers of governored satrapies (satrapy, province, and district) and had multiple administrative responsibilities, including codification of laws, regulating the judicial system, rasing taxes and tribute, overseeing the economic engine, writing official correspondence, and archiving records. Due to revolutionary activities in Babylonia, the nation was soon separated from this province. The Persian court allowed Jewish governors (at first descendants of the royal house of David) to administer the internal operations of Judah as part of the larger satrapy, which was then directly under the oversight and authority of a Persian governor backed by a military unit stationed near the capital. In addition to the Jewish governor who officiated locally in exchange for Judah's loyalty to the empire, the high priest also had an enviable position in both shaping internal legal matters through the interpretation of the Torah and in the economic power of the temple generated through gifts, sacrifices, tithes, and festivals. The ongoing work on the temple in the period of the Second Temple was a major economic stimulus for Judah and especially the sacred city of Jerusalem. Indeed, the temple seems eventually to have become something of a national bank and treasury, evidenced by foreign rulers occasionally looting it.

The unity of Judaism, save for foreign intrusions into the religion, was stressed in a highly idealized fashion in the period of Ezra and Nehemiah. Historically there was likely fierce internal competition for power among a variety of Jewish groups during this period. Zealots, inspired perhaps by Haggai and Zechariah as well as other nationalistic prophets, may have attempted to foment rebellion in order to return to establish an independent state under the dynasty of David. Zerubbabel was the original "signet ring," and the zealots would have seized their opportunity during the internal power struggle following the demise of Cambyses. The push to complete the temple, beginning in 520, was important, since this was a sign that independence was soon to be achieved. What happened to this governor and the assumed revolt can only be imagined, but the Persians dealt harshly with disloyal subject nations.[14]

The Persians supported the governorships of local leaders (including those descended from the dynasty of David) as long as they were loyal, the Zadokites and their control of religious affairs especially associated with the temple, and the codification of P as the basis for the reform of Ezra. Thus a conservative religious tradition of Torah, the Zadokite priesthood, the Jerusalem temple, and indigenous leadership on a local level were the pillars of Second Temple Judah. Save for the zealots, the Jews who gave allegiance to the Persians were content to accept foreign rule in exchange for economic, social, and political stability. If the conservative and compliant party of Ezra and Nehemiah in the late fifth century and following achieved the upper hand and garnered the support of most of the populace of the province, then their alliance with the existing power would prove far too strong to be disturbed seriously among the radicals. Indeed, Ezra brought together the offices of priest and sage, but it is interesting that he did outrank the priesthood, politically speaking, and even made major religious decisions and assumed the key priestly role in presiding at the major religious festivals. If this presentation is historical, it would demonstrate that the conservative sages who identified wisdom with religion (the "fear of God" and temple worship) and the Torah gained the upper hand in the Second Temple.

A number of papyri suggest that several Jews were Persian citizens who worked in the Persian administration in a variety of satrapies, including not only in Abar Nahara, but also in the cities of Elephantine, Nippur, Sippar, and Babylon. The documents of the Murashu family of Nippur (455–403 BCE) contain some typically theomorphic "Jewish names," suggesting they were descendants of the exiles. The occurrence of theomorphic names including not only Yahweh but other deities in the same family may suggest that loyalty to Yahweh was declining, although it may have become stronger after the rebuilding of the temple, the refortification of Jerusalem, and the reforms of Ezra.[15] The book of Ezra does suggest that the Persian court admired Jewish monotheism, likely due to its similarities to their own Zoroastrian religion.[16]

Still, it is the case that most of our information about Jewish life depends on the canonical texts. There were religious disputes, as serious as the practice of several different religions (e.g., Marduk and Nabu in Isa. 62:4; Jer. 33:24; Ezek. 37:11, 14). Some even chose to worship a variety of gods (Jer. 5:12; 16:13; 17:13), while continuing to consider themselves loyal to Yahwistic religion. In the growing and substantial community in Babylonia, there may even have been the plan to construct a Yahweh sanctuary (cf. Ezek. 20:39), although clear evidence is lacking.[17]

The Returns from Exile

The Edict of Cyrus (Ezra 1:1–4) in its Hebrew form differs in important ways from the Aramaic version (Ezra 6:2–5). In the unlikely event that one or both of these are historical proclamations from the Persian court, the differences between the two could be explained by reference to the different audiences addressed: a Hebrew version written for a Jewish audience and an Aramaic one being the more official proclamation of the court.[18] In the Hebrew version, Cyrus issued a proclamation that claimed, since "the LORD, the God of heaven," was responsible for his empire, he was now commanded to show his respect and thanksgiving by building him a temple in Jerusalem. The Aramaic version is intended to provide the specifications for the building of the foundation and to effect the return of the temple treasures stolen by Nebuchadrezzar. The second, "official" version is less theological and more administrative. In either case, propaganda would have provided the major tendenz in the issuance of the edict in either version.

The *gôlâ* community returned to Judah from captivity in several groups over a twenty-year period in large enough numbers to begin the arduous task of rebuilding Jewish society and the infrastructure of Jerusalem and its environs. The first return, which began in 538, continued intermittently for the first twenty years of Persian rule. The rebuilding of the temple (Ezra 3) began by 536, although the major work was carried out during the time of Zerubbabel the governor and Jeshua (or Joshua) the high priest (the first priest in the Hebrew Bible to bear the title of "high priest"). The first phase of reconstruction, lasting some seven months, culminated in the building of the altar of the temple. Offerings were instigated and a few weeks later the Festival of Tabernacles was observed (Ezra 3:1–5). Resistance to this first effort came from local inhabitants (Jews remaining during the exile and/or foreigners opposed the work). In 520 the work of the temple renovation was resumed, after difficulties had interrupted the initial efforts. The building of the temple was completed in 515 (Ezra 6:15), which was greeted by the joy of the new generation of Jews. From Persian sources we know that the codification of local law codes also was undertaken during the reign of Darius in order to achieve civil stability in the provinces.

The Reforms of Ezra and Nehemiah

Artaxerxes II commissioned the priestly scribe Ezra to travel to Jerusalem to instigate a wide-ranging social and religious reform. He was followed shortly thereafter by Nehemiah, who was commissioned to rebuild the city walls and to provide a military installation to withstand Egyptian and Philistine incursions into the area.[19]

According to the book of Ezra, the scribe and priest was commissioned by Artaxerxes II in the seventh year of his rule, circa 398, to travel to Jerusalem and to lead a major reform of Judaism especially in the city (Ezra 7:7). Given extensive powers over all Jews living in Abar Nahara, Ezra was sent to establish the laws of the Torah and to see that they were instituted in social and religious life. Religiously conservative, he sought to remove foreign influence on Jewish life by ordering the divorce of Jews intermarried with non-Jews and to prohibit any worship of other gods. Any other social ordinances or religious practices not legitimated by the Priestly document are eliminated. It was especially his authority to establish the Torah as the basis for Jewish life. While he had received substantial authority to accomplish his mission, including judicial powers to enforce the law's basis for Jewish life in the province, there is no evidence in the Chronicler's History that he used it to carry out his mission. Emerging apocalypticism and nationalistic ambitions of certain prophets were also countered by Ezra's mission, supported by Persian interests. Stability meant an uninterrupted flow of taxes and tribute from Judah to the Achaemenid court and a stronger military site in the south to protect against any Egyptian incursions.

The two objectives of Ezra's reform, the restoration of the temple cultus and the codification of the law, both designed to achieve internal stability, were the same as those of the Egyptian scribe and priest Udjahorresnet, commissioned by Darius I. This Egyptian official oversaw the restoration of the cult at Sais and the codification of Egyptian law into Aramaic and demotic.[20] On the reverse side of the Demotic Chronicle, the text reads that Darius ordered "the wise men be assembled . . . from among the warriors, the priests and the scribes of Egypt so that they may set down in writing the ancient Laws of Egypt."[21] The similarities between the two missions suggest they were part of a Persian strategy designed to produce social order throughout the satrapies and provinces.

Ezra required the ending of marriages between Jews and non-Jews in order to avoid the impurity of "holy seed" (Ezra 9:1–2; cf. Deut. 7:6). A Jew came to be defined both by Jewish ancestry and by obedience to the Torah (Ezra 9:2; 10:9–12).[22] Ezra's positions on marriage and obedience to the Torah were stringent compared to other, more moderate views.[23] The moderates included even members of the high priestly family, for four of its members had non-Jewish wives (Ezra 10:18). Some of the prophets encouraged the acceptance of non-Jews into the community, if they followed the major stipulations of Judaism (Isa. 56:6; cf. Zech. 8:20–23). Only ninety Jewish men put away their non-Jewish wives, suggesting that a relatively small number were willing to enter into divorce proceedings. According to the scribes who composed Ezra, whatever good transpired in the period was attributed to Yahweh and not the Persian sovereign (Ezra 7:27–28). Indeed, in his great prayer of repentance in Nehemiah 9 presented before the assembled Jews on the twenty-fourth day of the seventh month (perhaps Yom Kippur), he is presented as protesting to Yahweh, "Here we are, slaves to this day—slaves in the land you gave to our ancestors" (v. 36). This indicates that the composers and editors of the Chronicler's History considered the Persians to be oppressive rulers.

The book of Nehemiah follows and presents a legendary autobiography[24] of the Jewish official in the Persian court who received the commission to rebuild the fortifications, especially the surrounding city wall, of Jerusalem. As governor of the province, he also engaged in some religious reforms. Presented as the cupbearer of Artaxerxes II (Neh. 1:11; cf. Gen. 40:1, 2, 5, 9, 13, 20, 21, 23; 41:9; 2 Kgs. 10:5; 2 Chr. 9:4), he has similarities to the legendary Ahiqar, a sage who also was the cupbearer, the keeper of the signet ring, and the financial secretary, for Tob. 1:2 notes he was second in authority only to the king himself. Thus his duties likely far exceeded tasting the wine of the king to ensure it was not poisoned, to include those of a counselor who possessed significant official authority. In seeking the king's permission to undertake the mission to Jerusalem to rebuild its fortifications (Neh. 2:5), he demonstrated due reverence in the royal presence (2:2).

Having received royal authorization, he came to Jerusalem as governor in the twentieth year of the reign of Artaxerxes (ca. 384 BCE), in my view also Artaxerxes II (Neh. 1:1; 2:1), to erect fortifications by rebuilding walls and gates (Neh. 1:3), necessary for both Jewish security and the strengthening of a Persian stronghold to guard the southern reaches of the empire as it extended into Egypt. He continued to base Jewish society on the Torah. The efforts at refortification were opposed by Judah's neighbors, including Sanballat, the governor of Samaria, Tobias of Ammon, Geshem, an Arab sheik from southern Judea or the Negev, and a Jewish landowner east of the Jordan River (Neh. 3:33–4:17; 6:1–19). Since both Sanballat and Tobias had intermarried with Jewish women of Jerusalem, they feared the danger that a strong Jewish city would pose for them economically and politically with the Persians. These adversaries attacked the builders to halt the work on the walls, leading to the necessity of the Jewish inhabitants to divide into workers and an armed guard (Neh. 4:15). Failing this, these opponents incited local prophets to preach against Nehemiah. Finally, they even tried to have him assassinated.[25] But each scheme failed (Neh. 6).

Nehemiah was concerned not only with dictates of the Torah and continuing Ezra's reform, but also with handling the socioeconomic burdens of Jerusalem's citizens (see Neh. 5). The wealthy, who included aristocratic families, highly placed local officials, and the compliant high priestly families, were remiss in their social responsibilities for caring for the small landowners, tenant farmers, and day workers. The poor property owners often faced mortgaging and eventually losing their land, were required to pay high interest rates for borrowed goods and victuals, and at times even had to sell their children into slavery in order to exist (Neh. 5:2–5). The additional Persian taxation, when added to their local destitution, often resulted in the breakup of households and in family members having to sell themselves into slavery. Meanwhile, vast accumulations of wealth, especially in the Persian court but also among the wealthy in the local satrapies, were an economic reality in Persia.[26] Nehemiah's reform proved radical in attempting to confront these injustices. He required that lands be returned to the original owners who had been forced to sell and that large debts were to be canceled. The Priestly Code would have been extended to include laws prohibiting these injustices.

Finally, Nehemiah was also adamant about following scrupulously the laws governing the Sabbath. He may have initiated his religious reforms with the public reading of the Torah, probably the Priestly Code.[27] This public reading occurred on the first day of Tishri in a ceremony that lasted from early dawn to noon. Ezra read the Torah in Hebrew, while the Levites interpreted and translated it into Aramaic for those in the assembly who did not understand Hebrew. This explanation may have been a precursor to the later targumic traditions. This day of festivity was devoted to feasting, expressing acts of joy and celebration, and distributing food to the poor (Neh. 8:1–12). The following day the priests, Levites, and lay heads of the clans assembled while Ezra read to them the requirements for Sukkot, whereupon the people went to gather branches and leaves to construct their booths. These are the places where they dwelt and sat to read the Torah daily throughout the holiday. Then the people reassembled on the twenty-fourth of Tishri in order to fast and mourn (an early form of Yom Kippur?) while they read the Torah, confessed their sins, and vowed to follow the commandments of the law of Moses (Neh. 10:30). This oath was then sealed with a covenant requiring the prohibition of intermarriage, the strict observance of the Sabbath and the Sabbatical Year, the annual temple contribution of a third of a shekel, and the giving of firstfruits and other contributions to the temple for the sustenance of the priests and Levites (Neh. 10:31–40).

After twelve years as governor, however, the official of the Persian ruler went back to Persia. When he later returned to Judah, he discovered that the situation had once more deteriorated with intermarriage, the allowing of Tobias the Ammonite once again to have a room in the temple, the ignoring of the tithes to support the Levites, the casting aside of many of the temple obligations, and the violation of the Sabbath. Nehemiah's return and renewal of efforts at reformation are mentioned in Neh. 13:4–31, but not commented on as to their success or failure.

Unity and Diversity in Judaism in the Persian Period[28]

Judaism in the Persian period was heterogeneous. Thriving communities, separated by geography and culture, were found throughout the ancient Near East: Babylon, Egypt (especially Elephantine), and Samaria were substantial. The relationship to Judaism in Judah was often only tangential. Efforts at unity were made in terms of the shaping of a canon of authoritative literature, especially the Torah, the temple, the city of Jerusalem, and monotheism. Obviously, not everyone viewed these three elements in exactly the same way: they were important to many Jews but not to others. For example, monotheism was clearly affirmed in the literature of the period and yet did not lead to the eradication among Jews of polytheism or at least tolerance of other religions.[29] Even the religion of Yahweh took on many forms. For example, the solar shrine at Lachish, a Yahweh sanctuary, was erected during the Persian period.[30]

The devotion to the temple in Jerusalem did not eliminate the construction and operation of other temples in Lachish, Samaria, Leontopolis, Elephantine, and Qasr el-Abd of Hyrcanus at Araq el-Emir in Transjordan. It is clear that there were many high places, including Dan, where the *bāmâ* (במה) continued until the Hellenistic period. Other outdoor shrines that carried on their rituals and worship included those found in Carmel, Hermon, Tabor, and others.

Prophecy and the development of apocalyptic added to the mix. One would expect that a similar diversity existed among the scribes and sages of Judah. Those who supported the priesthood, perhaps even working directly under them, and the foreign dominion of the Persians engaged in helping to shape the unity needed for a definable Judaism.

THE EMERGENCE OF SCRIBALISM DURING THE SECOND TEMPLE PERIOD

Scribes in Judah: Introduction

Professional scribes in the Second Temple received the common titles of *sōpēr* (ספר), *siprā'* (ספרא), and *liblār* (לבלר), while their Greek titles in the Hellenistic period were *grammateus* (γραμματεύς), and *liblarios* (λιβλάριος). Scribes continued to serve in a variety of roles in the administrations of the government and temple, in private practice, and in the schools as teachers.[31] The most prominent ones would have enjoyed significant positions in the government. Thus the legendary Ezra, receiving the commission of the Persian court, likely served also in this role.

The Development of Jewish Scribalism in the Persian Period[32]

While wandering charismatic and institutional prophets and apocalyptic seers were common in the Second Temple, the significance they enjoyed among the public in earlier times dissipated. Far more importance was placed on the high priest and the leading sages. Indeed, within the sapiential tradition, the claim was made that now the sages, at least certain select ones, were the beneficiaries of divine inspiration (so claimed Ben Sira). During the Second Temple, a new type of scribe emerged who served as the interpreter of Torah and eventually of other parts of Scripture.[33] This role is likely one held earlier by sages involved in the legal sphere as jurists; only now with the importance placed on the Torah, its interpreters assumed positions of even greater esteem.[34]

Jewish Scribes as Redactors in the Second Temple Period

Scribes edited and redacted the Torah and eventually other texts in the Tanakh, including the Psalms. The number of the books of Torah shaped the compilation of five collections of the Psalter. Three psalms (Pss. 1, 19B, and 119) engage in praise or lament and moral guidance provided by the Torah and were written by sages. The Torah Psalms in particular combine creation, the glories and guidance of the Torah, and wisdom, which taken together represent a major theological development in the Second Temple.[35] Indeed, the frequent presence of sapiential literary forms, expressions, and themes in much of the Hebrew Bible is strong evidence that the scribes and sages were those who shaped the canon in its final form.

Ezra, the Scribe and Priest of God Most High

Ezra became the legendary priest-sage who incorporated within his literary persona the key dimensions of the Second Temple sage, priest, and prophet. Later, he was even presented as an apocalyptic seer.[36] Commissioned by the Persian court, he bears the Aramaic title of "the priest, the scribe of the law of the God of heaven" (*kāhănā' sāpar dātā' dî-'ĕlâ*, כהנא ספר דתא דיאלה, Ezra 7:21). He makes his legal decisions by proceeding "to inquire of" the Torah of Yahweh (*lidrōš*, לדרש), a former prophetic expression that describes the obtaining of an oracle (1 Kgs. 22:8). Another prophetic image is used in the language of "the hand of Yahweh" coming upon him (7:6, 9 = Ezek. 1:3). Yet he is also the one who teaches the Torah to the people. Ezra in the Chronicler combines the roles of priest, sage, and prophet, interpreting the Torah by means of inspiration and Torah (Josephus, *C. Ap.* 1:40–41; *Ant.* 11:120–158), as well as officiating at important temple festivals, including in particular the dedication of the new temple.[37] Later apocalyptic writers selected him as the ideal seer whose journeys to heaven provided him the esoteric understanding of the hidden secrets of the cosmos and history.[38]

The narrative of the person of Ezra may be little more than a literary personification of the period of early Judaism. The stories, acts, and speeches of Ezra are on the whole literary fiction to support some of the major themes of the Chronicler's History and the ambitions and purposes of those who shaped these books. While filling a variety of roles, Ezra is presented particularly as engaged in a religious reform, following the pattern set by Josiah (king), Hilkiah (priest), and Shemaiah (wise official) in the latter part of the seventh century BCE. Ezra's roles correspond to the ideological concerns of the Chronicler: the importance of the Levites, the Torah, and the temple. As a historical figure shrouded in legendary accounts, Ezra likely preceded the Jewish governor Nehemiah.[39]

In the decrees of Artaxerxes in 7:12–26, written in Aramaic,[40] Ezra is called "the priest" (*kāhānā'*, כהנא), and is portrayed in the biblical account as a descendant of the chief priest Zadok.[41] He is also "the scribe of the law of the God of heaven" (*sāpar dātā' dî-'ĕlâ šĕmayyā'*, ספר דתא דיאלה שמיא, Ezra 7:12, 21). In 7:6 he is described as a "scribe skilled in the law of Moses" (*sōpēr māhîr bĕtôrat mōšeh*, ספר מהיר בתורת משה), thus able to read, write, and interpret, in this case, the "Torah of Moses."[42] His title as a *sōpēr māhîr* is found in the royal marriage hymn of Ps. 45:2, indicating it may have been known in the preexilic period (i.e., if the superscription is as old as the hymn). In the Aramaic legend of Ahiqar, this esteemed official is also called a ספר חכים ומהיר (*sāpar ḥakkîm ûmāhîr*) who gave "advice/counsel" (עטה). In Ezra 7:11 the king also refers to him as "the priest, the scribe of the book of the words of the commandments of Yahweh and his statutes for Israel" (*hakkōhēn hassōpēr sōpēr dibrê miṣwōt-YHWH wĕḥuqqāyw 'al-yiśrā'el*, הכהן הספר ספר דברי מצות יהוה וחקיו על-ישראל).

In Ezra–Nehemiah, Ezra reads the Torah, observes (or composes, עשה, *'āśâ*, a more likely meaning in this context) it, and teaches Israel its laws and ordinances

(Ezra 7:10). In these texts, then, a *sōpēr* is one who not only reads, writes, and transmits the Torah, but also interprets it and even passes judgment on the basis of this law as his legal code. Ezra was granted the power by the Persian court to appoint judges and magistrates "according to the God-given wisdom" (*kĕḥokmat ʾělāhāk*, אלהך כחכמת) that he possesses, and to pass sentence on offenders, punishments that could include death, for violations of the Torah (7:25–26). He also was given the vessels of the temple to return, supposedly along with the financial support he needed for the success of his reform. In addition, the temples were an important institution for collecting revenue to be sent to the Persian court, which grew enormously wealthy.

Ezra's activity of reading occurs during the first day of the seventh month, the day of the new moon that introduces the most important month of festival ("this day" refers to Tishri 1, which was later known as New Year's Day, Rosh Hashanah). The festival occurred two months after Ezra arrived in Jerusalem (Ezra 7:9; 8:2). Upon the conclusion of the reading, the Levites went among the assembled crowd reading from the law of God, "with interpretation" (*mĕpōrāš*, מפרש, Neh. 8:7–8). "And they explained [the reading] so that they [the people] understood" (*wĕśôm śekel wayyābînû bammiqrāʾ*, ושום שכל ויבינו במקרא). The ability to read, speak, and clarify the meaning of the Torah likely followed a tradition of interpretation that these scribal Levites must have learned in a temple school. Ones mentioned who "interpreted" (*mĕbînîm*, מבינים) the Torah were listed by name, likely scribes and Levites. The scribes were Jeshua, Bani, Sherebiah, Jamin, Akkub, Shabbethai, Hodiah, Maaseiah, Kelita, Azariah, Jozabad, Hanan, and Pelaiah.

The Sages and Torah Piety

The sources that depict the piety of the sages of the Second Temple indicate that it developed extensively in this period. All we know of the First Temple sages and scribes is their common affirmation that the "beginning of wisdom is the fear of God." This piety embraced related features: God (monotheism), the temple (in Jerusalem), and Torah.[43] While intimated in the reform and speeches of Ezra (cf. Neh. 9), the three Torah psalms appear to be firsthand expressions of the objects of religious allegiance and dedication. This piety in particular looked at the Torah as divine teaching, grounded in creation and providence (see Job 33:26; Qoh. 4:17; 8:10; Sir. 24:10–11; 36:13–14; 45:9, 24; 47:10, 13; 49:6, 12; 50:1–2, 7, 11; 51:13; Wis. 9:8–9). Torah was identified with the wisdom of the sages.

Conclusion: The Jewish Scribes of the Achaemenid Empire

The scribe in the literature of the Chronicler's History served in many roles in the Second Temple, ranging from private service to public administration. As one might expect, however, the heaviest concentration was given to the associations of the scribe with the temple and administration of the province of Judah. These scribes continued the traditional functions of reading, writing, speaking, transmitting and editing tradition, copying texts, and producing records. Similar scribal roles were assumed by Jewish sages in other regions and temples, as indicated by the Elephantine papyri. In the books of the Chronicler the work of the scribe on occasion is related to the work of the Levites in public reading and teaching of the law to laypeople. Scribes, modeled after Ezra, would have engaged in temple service, governmental adminstration, and teaching in schools. Most important is that the scribe became the interpreter par excellence of the Torah who combined secular laws with religious duties.

WISDOM LITERATURE AND THE SCRIBE IN ACHAEMENID PERSIA

Jewish Wisdom Literature in the Persian Period

The canonical literature of the Second Temple focuses primarily on the themes of moral, spiritual, and physical reformation of Judah and the formation of Judaism, the rebuilding of the temple and the return of Yahweh to take up residence there, the completion of the Torah, the editing of numerous canonical books, the eschatological proclamation of prophets who speak of the inauguration of the kingdom of God with its center in Jerusalem, the reestablishment of the house of David, and the emergence of apocalyptic. The glowing predictions of Second Isaiah and the glorious temple of Ezekiel 40–48 lost their luster in the face of continued hardship. The priests and sages, who emphasized the worship of the reconstructed temple and the actualization of the Torah, formed one major party that pointed to collusion with the Persian Empire, until its demise at the hands of the troops of Alexander, while the prophets and apocalyptic seers formed a second party that looked to a new messianic age in which the Persian Empire would fall into disarray and a restored Jerusalem would become the center of the new, divine reign.

Sapiential Composition of Wisdom Psalms

One of the important expressions of sapiential piety was composition of sacred literature. This included the wisdom psalms, which are comparable to sapiential psalms found in Qumran and Ben Sira. Even the disputations of Job, in particular the laments (e.g., Job 3) and theophanic hymns (5:9–16 and 9:5–10), the hymns of Ben Sira to the creation and the Torah (e.g., Sir. 1:1–10), and the poems inserted into the collections of Proverbs (3:19–20; 8:22–31; 9:1–6, 13–18) and the Wisdom of Solomon (7:22–8:1) reflect this general genre of literature.

The sages sought through their behavior, artistic work, and piety to shape and maintain the righteous and beneficent order of creation. The wisdom psalms may be identified by the presence of typical sapiential forms, the use of particular sapiential saying to provide the structure of the psalm, the syntax of expressions found often also in the books of wisdom, the occasional occurrence of the alphabet acrostic (cf. Pss. 25, 34, and 119), and typical themes.[44]

Wisdom Psalms in School and Temple[45]

It seems clear from a careful reading and analysis of the Psalter that the sages wrote a number of sapiential psalms for use in praise and instruction. While the particular psalms belonging to this category are disputed, they most likely include 1, 19, 32, 34, 37, 49, 73, 111, 112, 119, 127, and perhaps 104. The wisdom psalms were used to praise Yahweh as the God of creation (Pss. 19, 104), to provide youth (students in wisdom schools) with moral instruction, to reflect on the theological issues of theodicy and the suffering of the righteous (Pss. 49, 73), and to give thanks to Yahweh for the Torah as the guide for the moral life (Pss. 1, 19, 119). These psalms find parallels not only in the wisdom literatures of Israel and Judah, but also in the other countries of the ancient Near East. Particularly suited for the postexilic period of Judaism in the Persian Empire are the three that deal with the Torah. Their emphasis on the law in this period corresponds to the role of the scribe who reflects on and interprets it.

THE PSALMS OF TORAH

Introduction

The *tôrâ* (תורה) in wisdom literature normally has the meaning of "teaching" or "instruction" of the sages (Prov. 7:2; 13:14), of the "father" (Prov. 4:1–2), and of the "mother" (Prov. 1:8; 6:20), which is significantly different from the priestly and prophetic torah. It is in the Priestly narrative, the Deuteronomistic History,[46] and the books of Chronicles, Ezra, and Nehemiah that one finds the association of Moses with the Torah. Moses is the lawgiver, and the Torah consists primarily of laws and commandments of social and cultic obligations said to be given at Sinai. Much later, the rabbis even argued that the oral law also had the same origins.

The Torah psalms point to the scribal praise of Yahweh for the gift of the law that provides the pathway for wise and moral living. The codification of P coincides with the high esteem given to the Torah in the later wisdom literature (e.g., Sir. 24), including these psalms. Theologically conceived, the Torah was viewed as the divine teaching of the Jewish community for the purpose of shaping and continuing the righteous order of the cosmos and the Jewish community.

Psalm 1: The Two Ways[47]

The scribal redactors of the Psalter have positioned the first psalm to intimate that it is through the Torah that the worshiper is to understand the psalms that follow.[48] These redactors, who probably completed their work during the third century BCE, are scribal *Schriftgelehrteren* (authorities on Scripture) whose activities occur within the auspices of the temple hierarchy, in particular the sacred site's archival library and its probable school, which likely served to educate future scribes, who would enter into a variety of professions in the social world of Jerusalem and its environs during the Persian and Hellenistic periods. A school of scribes also was active in providing a sapiential edition of much of the Hebrew Bible that was an important dimension of the canonical process that led to the final shape of the canon of Scripture toward the end of the first century CE. This initial psalm is found also in another redactional text, Jer. 17:5–8, indicating that it was among the repertoire of texts from which scribal redactors drew in pursuing their literary editing of biblical texts.

This psalm has a number of terms frequently found in wisdom literature. They include עצה (*ʿēṣâ*), רשעים (*rĕšāʿîm*), לצים (*lēṣîm*), דרך (*derek*), חפץ (*ḥēpeṣ*), ידע (*yādaʿ*), and צדקים (*ṣĕdāqîm*). In addition, several common wisdom themes are found in sapiential literature: the contrast between the righteous and the wicked (cf. especially Prov. 10–15), retribution, and the meditation on the Torah (common in the Second Temple), which is Yahweh's divine instruction.

Psalm 1 consists of two strophes (vv. 1–3, 4–5) arranged in a chiastic structure and concludes with a proverb that summarizes them both. The first strophe depicts the righteous person with three verbs pointing to different positions of the human body: "walking" (*hālak*, הלך), "standing" (*ʿāmad*, עמד), and "sitting" (*yāšab*, ישׁב). The righteous person is to keep his distance from the wicked. The ungodly are also described with three terms: "wicked" (*rĕšāʿîm*, רשעים), "sinners" (*ḥaṭṭāʾîm*, חטאים), and "scoffers" (*lēṣîm*, לצים). The first term, רשעים, in wisdom texts[49] connotes "the wicked," in particular those who either do not follow the dictates of wisdom or who transgress the teachings of sapiential instruction and thus subvert the social order, while חטאים ("sinners") is a parallel term for those who violate the teachings of the wise.[50] לצים ("Scoffers") in wisdom literature[51] refers to the arrogant, who are incapable of receiving or resistant to sapiential moral instruction. There are also three terms for referring to the advice, path, and assembly of the wicked: עצה (*ʿēṣâ*), דרך (*derek*), and מושב (*môšab*). The metaphor of the fruitful tree is found elsewhere (Amenemopet IV; Jer. 17:5–8; Ezek. 29:1–5) and refers to the thriving of a righteous person. Form-critically, the poem begins with an *ʾašrê* (אשרי, "happy") saying, a typical wisdom form, and concludes (v. 6) with an antithetical or contrastive proverb that provides a summary for the entire psalm: "Yahweh knows the way of the righteous, but the way of the wicked will perish."

The one theme in the first strophe that is not contrasted in the second is the "delight" (*ḥēpeṣ*, חפץ) in and "meditating" (*hāgâ*, הגה; v. 2) on the Torah, acts of piety for the Second Temple sage.[52] This literary device heightens the importance of meditation on the law. There is no indication it served as a cultic psalm to be sung in worship. Rather, it has more the appearance of a sapiential poem that contrasts the behavior of the righteous and the wicked that would have been produced by a sage in the context of a sapiential school. This emphasis on meditation on the

Torah fits very well the sapiential piety developing in the Persian period that will eventually reach its high point in the work of the sage Ben Sira. This psalm also suggests that the Psalter was used not only as a songbook for Second Temple Judaism but also as a collection of texts for private meditation and reflection.

Psalm 19: The Revelation of the Creator (A) and the Guidance of Torah (B)

The creation hymn in Psalm 19A consists of two strophes. The first one (vv. 2–5b) draws on mythological imagery associated with two gods of Canaan involved in creation and judgment: El and Shamash.[53] It reveals the heavens praising El, even though their words are not audible. By means of their order and beauty, the heavens and the firmament still raise their voices in praise of the glory of the Creator. This same description occurs in Job 38:7, in which Yahweh is praised by the heavenly hosts. The theme in these two sapiential texts is that God's glory is revealed in the works of his creation.

In the second strophe (vv. 5c–7) the sun is personified as a bridegroom emerging from his marriage tent located in the sea and making his way across the heavens.[54] Once the sun's circuit across the heavens during the day is complete, this heavenly body, depicted as a bridegroom, then enters again into his nocturnal tent, until the journey begins the next day. Shamash in Canaanite (šps) and Akkadian religions is the god of justice who oversees and distributes justice on the earth. In 19:7 the sun god's heat and light (חמה, ḥammâ) are compared to the passion of a virile and sexually active bridegroom.

With the shift from creation to the Torah in the second psalm (Ps. 19B), the divine teachings of God are now revealed in words, and not simply indirectly in the design and beauty of the creation. The earlier sages had understood Wisdom as the goddess or a personified divine attribute to be the instrument through which the world was created and ordered with justice as the centrifugal, cohesive force holding together the cosmos and prohibiting chaos from overwhelming it (Prov. 3:19–20; 8:22–31). This was coupled with the revelatory character of wisdom, which contains both the will of God and the responsibilities of humans. In the Second Temple period, it was only a short step to the equating of wisdom and Torah. Thus borrowing from the mythological imagery of creation and revelation in Psalm 19A, this sage also describes the revelation of God taking written form in the Torah. As the light and heat of the sun warm the earth and provide the means to see, so the Torah "enlightens" (מאירת, mĕ'îrat) the eyes of the wise in their lives and behavior.

It appears that Psalm 19 consists of two originally different pieces: Psalm 19A, a hymn in praise of the Creator, and a thanksgiving psalm to Yahweh in gratitude for the gift of the Torah, which instructs the obedient in moral and religious living and enables them to detect hidden sins (Ps. 19B). Presumably the composer of the second psalm or perhaps a later redactor brought the two poems together to portray two types of revelation: natural revelation through creation and the revealed will of Yahweh contained in the Torah. The language reflects Second Temple wisdom language and points to the identity of this redacted psalm as a wisdom composition. Key terms include: תורה (*tôrâ*), בין (*bîn*), תם (*tām*), רצון (*rāṣôn*), חכם (*ḥākām*), פתי (*pĕtî*), ישר (*yāšār*), לב (*lēb*), מאיר (*mēʾîr*), יראת יהוה (*yirʾat YHWH*), and צדק (*ṣedeq*). The overarching theme is revelation: the Creator has revealed himself in both the cosmos and the Torah, both of which testify to his glory and righteousness and at the same time provide insight into how to live wisely and in order with both the cosmos and the community. Thus one finds the tripartite theological synthesis of creation of the cosmos (particularly in this case the heavens, the temporal polarity of day and night, and the sun, which gives light and warmth), the law of Yahweh (which is perfect and contains the divine commandments that "rejoice the heart" and "enlighten the eyes"), and the pious sage (anthropology) who finds in the Torah the means by which he is instructed and kept from the dominion of sin. This structure indicates that cosmology and human behavior are brought into concert by means of the divine revelation of the Torah, which is grounded in the order of creation. The association of the revealed law with the divine creation in wisdom, including this psalm, provides an important insight into the faith of the Jewish community in Jerusalem during the Persian period: the Torah has become one of the central theological themes in early Judaism. The poem on the Torah and the heavenly praise of creation are combined through scribal redaction to form a psalm that is the literary and artistic expression of the meditation and words of sapiential reflection that rejoices the heart and is dedicated to Yahweh, the rock and savior of the psalmist. The Torah not only "enlightens" the pious as divine instruction, it also "rejoices" the heart (משמחי-לב, *mĕśammĕḥê-lēb*), another feature of sapiential piety.

One of the strongest features of Jewish spirituality is its connection to joy. Joy is seen as a feature of worship that results from participation in divine service and is the proper attitude of the worshiper (cf. Ps. 100:2). In addition, two particular elements occasion joy: the reverence for the law shown by its observance and study (Ps. 19:9; cf. Ps. 119) and the culmination of personal piety (see Ps. 16, especially v. 11) when the worshiper knows he/she exists within the presence and concern of God.[55]

In this hymn in praise of the Torah, its status as a divinely inspired teaching that is given by God to the sage to illuminate his sins and to guide his life is foremost in the scribal author's composition, which is a text to be read and studied as well as to be sung in joyous thanksgiving. The incomparable worth of the Torah (19:10) echoes that of wisdom in Proverbs (3:13–17; 8:18–21). The Torah is perfect, pure, and the source of righteous teaching in enabling the pious sage to identify his sins, which include presumptuous pride (cf. Prov. 5:23; 19:27), and especially those that are hidden. It is also noteworthy that the petition of the wise psalmist in the concluding verse (Ps. 19:15) compares to colophons written by scribes in the ancient Near East, including Israel, to serve either as summaries or to indicate the role of the creator of the literary text, if not both. From this concluding verse, it is clear that the psalmist (or the community that sings this psalm) is strongly attached to the Torah, and attributes to it its great value for teaching about his sin.

Psalm 119: The Praise of Torah and a Wisdom Lament[56]

It is obvious that a scribal interpreter of Torah composed this didactic psalm, which contains elements of both thanksgiving and lamentation. The Torah becomes the basis not only for moral instruction but also for the lament and thanksgiving in that it is understood as the means by which to escape the wicked and evil and to gain forgiveness for sins. It fits very well the period of the Second Temple when the Torah, especially during and following the reformation of Ezra, became central for the scribes and priests. Only someone well educated in sapiential rhetoric could have composed this lengthy psalm, which uses a variety of synonyms for the law as many times as possible within the context of an alphabetic acrostic. Thus it is likely that a scribe of the Torah, educated in a scribal school in Jerusalem, is its author. The psalm may be classified topically as a Torah psalm. In terms of form, it reflects a mixed genre. On the one hand, the psalm is one of thanksgiving to Yahweh for the gift of the Torah. On the other hand, it is a lament containing the plea that the psalmist follow the commandments, the attestation of contrite repentance, the request for protection from both private sins and the wicked, and the appeal to God for forgiveness. The thematic focus is on the praise of the Torah, its guidance in life, and contrite repentance for a sinner who, while having committed errors, is still committed to obeying the Torah. The eight synonyms for "law" are אמרה (ʾimrâ), דבר (dābār), מצוה (miṣwâ), חק (ḥōq), עדות (ʿēdût), תורה (tôrâ), משפט (mišpāṭ), and פקודים (pĕqûdîm). Each of the twenty-two strophes contains from six to nine of these terms. Only three lines (vv. 3, 90, and 122) do not contain a term for "law."

One gains from this psalm indications of the role of its composer. In 119:18 the psalmist prays: "Open my eyes that I may observe miracles from your law (tôrâ)." This expression of eye opening likely refers to the scribe's desire for divine inspiration, especially in view of the fact that he repeatedly asks for instruction in the Torah (vv. 12, 27, 33, 64, 66, 68, 73, 108, 124). Indeed, he even echoes the Priestly benediction of Num. 6:25 in verse 135, suggesting that he knew the Torah intimately and granted its keeping to the priests, whom the scribes served in shaping the ongoing tradition and in preserving the traditio.[57] Other sapiential features include the hidden and mysterious character of both sin and wisdom (cf. Ps. 139:6; Prov. 30:18; Job 42:3). Verse 18 also reflects the prophetic inspiration found in Ezra 7:6, a subject found also in Ben Sira (39:6).[58]

This psalm is partially construed as a lament. The sage, enduring great difficulties that have yet to be divinely addressed, repeatedly asks God to deliver him from both his persecutors and his suffering, something he expects due to his faithful adherence to the teachings of the Torah. He urges God to act on his behalf and to rescue him from distress. Verse 154 makes this clear. He calls upon God to serve in the role of the redeemer to exact retribution for the shedding of his blood, if it comes to that.[59] By contrast, the wicked persecutors have flouted the law and thus deserve to be punished.

It is important to recognize that this Torah hymn is directed to God as the giver of the commandments that lead to life. Trusting in the revelation of the Torah, the psalmist tells of the deepening of the religious experience of God that derives from the study of Torah.[60] In addition, the psalmist proclaims that he has been created by God (v. 73), leading to divine instruction that requires obedience to the law. The psalm expresses the belief that the law is given by God to his followers to direct their lives in accordance with divine instruction. The association between wisdom and Torah is found in sapiential language throughout the psalm, particularly in meditation on the Torah, the creation of humanity, the prayer for wisdom, and moral instruction. It is important to note that in strophe XII the psalmist speaks of the cosmic foundation of Torah, thus placing it within the order of creation.

SAPIENTIAL THEOLOGY: WISDOM, TORAH, AND CREATION IN THE PERSIAN PERIOD

Divine Creation and Providence

On the first day of the seventh month (Tishri), later known as the Day of Atonement, Ezra summons the people to Jerusalem, to the square before the Water Gate, and reads from the Torah. He reads standing on a wooden platform from early morning until midday. Thirteen levitical scribes translate what he reads (the Hebrew text) into Aramaic and interpret the Torah in order that the audience may understand what is read (Neh. 8). The following day, the heads of the families begin to celebrate the Festival of Tabernacles, beginning with studying the words of the Torah. The booths are constructed and the festival is celebrated for a week, followed on the eighth day by a "solemn assembly." Then, on the twenty-fourth day of Tishri, the people of Israel assemble in Jerusalem once again and participate in rites of penitence. The liturgy includes in sequence the reading from the book of the Torah for a fourth of the day and confession and worship for another fourth of the day. During this time of penitence, Ezra utters a prayer (Neh. 9:6–37) that includes the major features of salvation history, beginning with the creation of heaven, the earth, and the seas and all that dwells within them (9:6), and then focusing especially on disobedience to the Torah leading to punishments, particularly in the form of the conquest and rule by other nations. This prayer points to the combination of creation and Torah, the primary theological emphases in the wisdom psalms.

Psalm 19 is consistent with this emphasis in Ezra's prayer. In the first strophe of Psalm 19A (vv. 1–5b), the wondrous beauty and the power of fashioning creation are revealed to the community of worshipers in their observation of the cosmos and in the imagination stimulated by their collective praise. In the second strophe (vv. 5c–7), Shamash, the god of judgment in Canaanite and Akkadian religion, is the one who, in his journey across the heavens, is able both to revitalize the creation and to engage in judgment of nations and persons on the earth. This twin function of revitalization and judgment is captured by the word "heat." The sun god provides *ḥammâ* (חמה), which intimates both heat and light. Thus Shamash is the creator and sustainer of the cosmos who distributes justice to those upon the earth. This early example of natural religion underscores the theology of revelation that issues forth in praise of creation and justice that are continually renewed.

The second part, Psalm 19B, makes the transition from the creation and guidance of the cosmos and revelation through nature to the roles and functions of the Torah in the Second Temple community. Sages often regarded wisdom metaphorically as both a transcendent instrument of God's acts of creation and an immanent power operative in guiding the world through destiny, revitalization of life, and instruction of the sages (Prov. 3:19–20; 8:22–31). This psalm brings together these various functions of wisdom and equates them now with the Torah. It is the Torah that is the source of divine revelation, "enlightening" (מאירת, *mĕ'îrat*) the eyes of the sages so that they may know God, the divine will, and proper behavior. Indeed, through the observation of the Torah, the world is sustained and life is revitalized. Only now it is sin that has replaced chaos as the opponent of life that is to be restrained. Obedience to the Torah brings this about.

It is through the two parts of Psalm 19, as it is edited in its canonical form, that the sage teaches that the Creator has revealed himself in both the cosmos and the Torah. These provide the righteous sage the means by which to live faithfully and to promote the forces of life in the cosmos. This text indicates that cosmology and human behavior are integrated by divine revelation in creation and Torah.

Creation and Anthropology

These psalms of Torah also speak to the topic of creation and anthropology. In Psalm 1 the one who is "blessed" keeps himself apart from the company of the wicked. Part of this strategy of avoidance is the meditation on the Torah. Meditation is understood as studied reflection. Careful and astute observation of the Torah results in God's protection as the one who directs human events, while the pathway of those who are wicked is sure to lead them to judgment and consequent destruction.

Especially important in the category of creation and anthropology is Psalm 119 and the sage's affirmation in the initial line of the tenth strophe (vv. 73–80) that God has created and enlightened him in order that he may be resolute in his obedience to the law (v. 73; cf. Ps. 8 and Job 10). This writer points to the divine purpose of the creation of human beings: "Your hands made me (*'āśâ*, עשה) and fashioned me (*kûn*, כון),[61] enlighten me so that I may learn your commandments (*miṣwôt*, מצוה)." Through the life lived in commitment to the Torah, others will observe him and rejoice over his faithfulness. Even when he suffers, God's steadfast love embraces him, while the wicked and the proud who have persecuted him will be shamed. The psalmist expresses the belief that the law is given by God to his followers to direct their lives in accordance with divine instruction. This connection between wisdom and Torah is present throughout the psalm. This emphasis on the tradition of the creation of humanity and the cosmos (cf. strophe XII) derives from the features of the lament, which are strongly present in this psalm, since the lament is seedbed for the tradition of the creation of the human individual (see, e.g., Ps. 139; Job 10).[62]

Creation and Goddess Wisdom

In these three psalms, composed by sages during the Second Temple, the Torah now assumes the earlier role of goddess Wisdom and becomes the divine instruction offered to faithful scribes. Psalm 19 unites together a song in praise of the creator and sustainer (originally El and Shamash) with a lament in which the Torah is also extolled and God is petitioned to keep the psalmist from transgression. Together these two originally separate hymns become a meditation that the editor offers to God in praise of his creation and his gift of the Torah. The value of the Torah (19:10) reminds the audience of the incomparable worth of wisdom in Prov. 3:13–17 and 8:18–21. Psalm 119 has features of both thanksgiving and lamentation. Using eight different terms for "law," the psalmist argues that the Torah provides religious instruction. In addition, the lament into which the Torah and its synonyms are inserted expresses the psalmist's request of God to escape the wicked and to gain forgiveness for his own sins. Likewise, the thanksgiving provides the scribe's joy at the gift of the Torah to guide the wise in their efforts to be obedient to divine teaching encompassed in both the law and the sapiential instructions.

Power, Ideology, and Torah Piety in Early Judaism

The sages in the Second Temple were engaged in activities that would place them at the center of Jewish life and make them second in power and influence only to the Zadokite priests who controlled the temple cult, and with the help of their scribes and the legitimation of the Persian court established the Torah as the constitution of Second Temple Judaism. In addition, the scribes' administrative service to governors also would have allowed them to wield considerable political power, especially by those who ascended to the roles of advisors to these governing officials. Finally, as the interpreters of Torah they became jurists and teachers who sought to place their own stamp on the social order.

Noting the variety of expressions of Judaism in various locations in Eretz Israel, Transjordan, and Egypt, it is clear there was no standard form. The Zadokites and their scribes were in competition for the temple tax and cultic loyalty with other temples, including the ones in Elephantine in Egypt, the Samaritan cultic site at Gerizim that was transformed into a Greek-styled temple in the

Hellenistic period, and the sanctuary at Lachish. Of course, there were numerous high places throughout Eretz Israel that competed for the loyalty of local Jews. How many different gods were worshiped in the Second Temple period even in the province of Judah is difficult to say, based on the present lack of evidence. It is likely, however, that the reform of Ezra, like those of Hezekiah and Josiah before him, sought to shut down the sanctuaries of other gods and to forbid the integration of Yahwism and a variety of pagan religions. The proclamation of divorce of foreign wives was the extreme measure to try to eliminate foreign worship and practices considered tainted. However, this decree of divorce seemed to have had little effect.

Conclusion

The sages in the postexilic period who were composers and interpreters of texts belonged to an important social profession in Judah and understood Judaism to consist primarily of four major features: God (monotheism, creation, and providence), Jerusalem, the temple (the place of divine immanence), and Torah. The three Torah psalms indicate that the theological emphases of the sages added these elements to their theology of creation and providence. Now the Torah, grounded in creation and providence, and the temple and its rituals are key to the renewal of life, especially during the temple Festival of the New Year in which the creation is renewed by means of the temple liturgy and the reading and teaching of the Torah. The Torah and the temple take on significant cosmological and moral characteristics that actualize divine creation, providence, and human righteousness.

During the Persian period the Torah became the theological center of traditional Jewish wisdom. This became the means for associating creation theology with sapiential ethics. The metaphor that dominated the Torah psalms was that of the word, revealed by God in the law and actualized in obedience and human actualization. In the Second Temple, Yahweh is the lawgiver who gives to his loyal servants divine instruction through the Torah that brings life and salvation from both personal evil and arrogant transgressors. The Torah is now identified with the order of creation that sustains the cosmos and with wisdom that instructs the sages in ways to live in harmony with God and society. Indeed, the tradition of the creation of the individual is appropriated to speak not only of God's creation of the psalmist, but also to enlighten him with the knowledge necessary to live a righteous existence. Through this life of obedience to the Torah, the sage participates in the sustaining of creation and in serving as an example to others, both the wicked and those who would take up the path to wisdom. By the time Ben Sira's text is composed, the Torah's assimilation into creation's cosmological and anthropological spheres is at the heart of sapiential understanding.

Chapter 6

Wisdom and Egyptian and Hellenistic Skepticism: The Book of Qoheleth

HISTORICAL AND SOCIAL INTRODUCTION

Prelude

Qoheleth engages two important traditions developing in the period in which he lived and taught: late Egyptian wisdom and Hellenistic culture, which extended its influence into Judah especially in the third century BCE during the reign of the Ptolemies. Both of these cultural and religious expressions provide a background to understanding the book of Qoheleth, and indeed play a role in shaping both the somber mood of this sage and the content of his teachings. Perhaps the most arresting features of Qoheleth are its omission of many traditional features of Jewish faith and culture, and its denial of others. This Jewish sage, thinking that Judaism has failed to achieve a credible vision and commanding presence in the lives of people, particularly the intellectuals, sets about to reorient Judaism to a philosophical quest to determine the good in human existence, and, upon its discovery, to shape a new wisdom, grounded in humanism, that enables people through their conduct and thinking to experience that good. The central issues of human living are no longer to be answered theologically by divine revelation or by determining the nature and activity of God, but rather by human experience and reflection.

History of the Ptolemaic Empire[1]

In the latter half of the fourth century BCE, Alexander the Great marched his army of Greek warriors into Asia and conquered the Persian Empire. For Judah this would mean a transition of significant consequence, not only in terms of political change but also in regard to cultural and religious adjustment. While hellenization made an important impact on the variety of cultures and peoples in the East, there was no governmental policy of an enforced imposition of Greek culture and religion. At the same time, the rise of the Greek ruler cult, especially in Alexandria, and the growing popularity of the mystery religions in the West contributed to the mélange of religious cults in the eastern Mediterranean world. Acts of the Greek rulers and the increasing variety of religious and cultural responses to Hellenism eventually solidified into various rival sects. For example, Alexander's permitting the Samaritans to build a temple on Mount Gerizim that rivaled the one in Jerusalem led to serious conflict between Samaria and Judah for four centuries (Josephus, *Ant.* 11.8.4, 321–24).

Once Alexander's empire came to be divided among his greatest generals, Egypt fell under the domination of the Ptolemies, who ruled without dynastic interruption until the conquest by Rome. Ptolemy I Soter (305–285) became the founder of the Ptolemaic Empire (305–30) that blended Greek culture and Egyptian religion in a state that possessed and developed significant resources, power, and intellectual faculties. Located near the old northern capital of Thebes, Alexandria, which was a new city that attracted scholars from the western and eastern worlds, became a city rich in culture and productive in intellectual attainments. Indeed, Jews congregated there in significant numbers and developed a rich Hellenistic Jewish tradition.

Hellenization was a multifaceted ethos that led indigenous cultures and religions to blend with those of Greece, thus providing a substantial unity among the Greek kingdoms of the east and the states in the older Greek world. Judaism responded to hellenization in different ways. Of course, the two extreme responses were a complete rejection of Greek culture and intellectual knowledge due to its pagan character on one side, and assimilation on the other. The first response issued in a position to which the most reactionary Jewish groups held, including the rural priestly family of the Maccabees, at least in its first generation, when it led a revolt against Antiochus IV Epiphanes in 167 BCE. However, this extreme position was held by enthusiastically orthodox Jews who were often sympathetic to the revolutionary zealots throughout the remainder of Greek and Roman subjugation of Judah leading to the destruction of Jerusalem in 70 CE. The other of the two radical positions was taken by those Jews who were attracted to the culture and religions of the East and abandoned their own native traditions in order to merge into the new civilization. One hope, of course, was to obtain citizenship in a Greek polis and its associated status and privileges. However, most Jews dealt with Hellenism in more moderate and varied ways and positioned themselves between the two opposing responses.[2] Greeks tended to consider ethnic groups who came under the umbrella of their hegemony to be "barbarians" who were not on the same plane as the Greeks themselves. This elitism was the result of both Greek feelings of superiority and political policies that favored them over the indigenous peoples.

While culturally united through language, art, and philosophical teachings, the Greek kingdoms were political rivals who sought to enhance their territorial holdings through conflict among themselves. There was a lengthy struggle between the Ptolemies and the Seleucids, which proved to have important consequences for Judah. The Ptolemies did not force the Jews, even those living in Egypt, to abandon their traditions and to adopt Greek ones. Rather they allowed Judaism to develop in its own ways. Even with the development of the ruler cult in Ptolemaic Egypt, Jews were not forced to participate. Neither the rulers nor the Greek deities, especially the mystery god Dionysus, who achieved prominent notoriety in the reign of Ptolemy IV, had images to which the Jews were forced to pay homage. While the Ptolemies controlled Judah for more than a century, the victory of Antiochus III at Panium in 200 BCE led to the change that had significant influence on the fortunes of Judea. The most important consequence was the later conflict with Antiochus IV Epiphanes, who interfered in Jewish religion by selling the high priesthood, finally forbidding the practice of Judaism, attempting to force Jews to worship other gods, and launching a major pogrom. This led to the outbreak of hostilities from 167 to 164 BCE that culminated in the victory of the Maccabees and the establishment of native rule under the Hasmoneans.

The Ptolemaic Empire began to lose its international prominence, beginning with the final years of the reign of Ptolemy III Euergetes I (246–221) and continuing with the reign of Ptolemy IV Philopator (221–205). By the reign of Ptolemy V Epiphanes (194–181), the Ptolemies had lost their territories in the East, outside Egypt. This decline climaxed in the enforced patronage to Rome and the final conquest of Egypt by Augustus (31 BCE) in his defeat of Mark Antony and Cleopatra.

Qoheleth is generally dated to either the late Persian or Ptolemaic period. While evidence is only inferential, my preference is to place this book during the final quarter of the third century BCE.[3] He may have taught during the precipitous decline of Ptolemaic power and status in Asia.[4] Normally, the end of a period of lengthy rule is accompanied by the onset of a despondency that is reflected in its literature composed at the time. This is true of Qoheleth and his assessment of human governments in general.

According to Polybius, the decline set in due to the poor administration of the kingdom and the accumulation of ostentatious wealth.[5] The degree of the indigenous people's resentment is captured by the Demotic Chronicle,[6] which points to a future native king of Heracleopolis who would bring an end to Greek political dominance and rule. In spite of these difficulties, Ptolemy IV still launched a major buildup of his naval forces and an extensive building program that included the enhancements and renovations of sanctuaries. When Ptolemy IV died, the decline in Ptolemaic status and power began to occur, and with the Syrian victory in the Fifth Syrian War (202–197), Ptolemaic Egypt had been pushed back within its own borders. With the victory of Antiochus III at Panium in 200, the Egyptians had lost their assets in Asia.

The Egyptian Sage in Ptolemaic Egypt

The long tradition of wisdom compositions, beginning in the first half of the third millennium, continued into the early Roman Empire. With the Hellenistic period, however, sapiential texts were now being composed in demotic and Greek. Several writings point to an interaction with Hellenistic culture, including in particular "The Sayings Collection of 'Ankhsheshonq," "The Teaching of Pordjel," and "The Teaching of Papyrus Insinger." It is possible that Qoheleth would have known of these instructions and been influenced by their ideas. One of these texts, Papyrus Insinger, shared Qoheleth's views on moderation, fate, and divine inscrutability. In any event, this same cultural interaction is reflected in Qoheleth.

The Egyptian text that is especially similar to the biblical book of Proverbs is "The Sayings Collection of 'Ankhsheshonq."[7] Composed in the demotic script perhaps in the third century BCE,[8] this text contains an assortment of proverbs and sayings that are of different length and placed together with no apparent order. While the majority are one-line sayings, there is occasionally some thematic connection of adjacent sayings. The major difference from the book of Proverbs is the collection's insertion within the middle of a narrative that speaks of the imprisonment of 'Ankhsheshonq for scheming to murder the king. This is a literary topos common in wisdom literatures of the ancient Near East, including especially the Joseph narrative and the legend of Ahiqar. The fiction presented in this Egyptian text is that of a famous teacher and scribe, currently in prison, who instructs his son preparing to join his father's profession.[9] Indeed, the closest literary and thematic parallel to the instruction is the "Instruction of Ahiqar."[10] The noteworthy themes include the contrast between the wise and the foolish, good and evil women, and wealth and poverty. Other common wisdom topics include family, friends, landlords, neighbors, religious obligations, management of one's affairs, the relationship between cause and effect, retribution, and two formulations of the Golden Rule. Retribution is the instrument of divine judgment and maintenance of order. The text has the purpose of providing a son with the admonition to serve the god, act justly, give attention to family relationships, and practice wisdom in everyday life.

"The Teaching of Pordjel" is a second Hellenistic Egyptian collection of sayings directed to the scribe's "beloved son."[11] While formally not an instruction, this text nevertheless contains proverbs, admonitions, and prohibitions rendered in one-line sayings. Themes are typical sapiential ones: giving to the god what is due him/her, keeping one's distance from the robber and the stupid man, avoiding illicit sexual relationships with married women, controlling passions (i.e., not becoming a "heated man"), refusing to curse or withhold what one is obligated to give to the master, and giving proper attention to instructing one's son.

Papyrus Insinger is a third collection of sayings that perhaps was produced as early as the beginning of Hellenistic rule of Egypt.[12] That fragments of copies of this text from the early Roman period have been discovered indicate that this collection entered into the stream of Egyptian tradition.[13] The most complete text, dating from the first century CE, contains thirty-four columns of numbered teachings (twenty-five) arranged according to subject matter. The central and organizing concept for this teaching is the understanding of balance, which was necessary for maintaining order in the cosmos and in society. Like Qoheleth, this sage teaches that the deity is inscrutable, but unlike Qoheleth justice is never questioned, much less denied. Other important themes include moderation (cf. Qoheleth), the contrast between the wise and the foolish, and a thoroughly Greek notion of personified Fate and Fortune.[14] Qoheleth has a variation of this theme in his view that the fate of each person has been determined by the inscrutable God, an unknown fortune that is determined in a completely capricious manner. This Egyptian sage may have had access to the moral philosophy taught by paid teachers who were sophists, to public lectures, and, if he knew Greek, to some of the important philosophical writings of the day. This text is closest thematically to those of popular Greek philosophy, including Stoicism and Epicureanism. This writing is further evidence that the sages of the eastern Mediterranean world engaged the traditions of their own and other cultures (Greece, Egypt, and Eretz Israel).

The Sage (Sophos) in Greek Philosophy

The circles of higher education in Greek culture, beginning in the fifth century BCE, included a number of different schools: the academy, the lyceum, and those of rhetoric. Sophists, who generally sought a basic knowledge of many philosophies and other areas of culture, nevertheless still tended to gravitate toward one particular school and its leading philosophers, especially in the basic area of epistemology. Honored teachers and philosophers became the models for students they taught to emulate in their behavior, thinking, and decorum.[15] In addition, there were major philosophies and their representatives in the third century BCE: Stoicism, Epicureanism, Skepticism, and Neo-Pythagoreanism.

Education in the Hellenistic World[16]

Paideia and especially its practical cultivation in the major types of schools in Greece and the larger Hellenistic world became the defining feature of Greek culture and the consequent hellenization that began in the aftermath of the wars of Alexander. "Paideia" refers to both the process of education that enabled a child eventually to take his place in society, and the cultured state of the educated person.[17] The view of paideia as the state of the "cultivated mind" enables a person to become virtuous and civilized, whereas its lack makes one a "barbarian." It is a lifelong quest that does not end once education in the gymnasium has come to an end. Philosophy and a culture grounded in philosophy are based on paideia. The most prominent educational institution was the gymnasium, which served the children of the elite who possessed Greek citizenship and had the wealth to support their sons through this process. The gymnasium's course of study broke down into three main parts: primary, secondary, and tertiary.[18] Students raised in a Hellenistic family had an advantage over those who were not, but that does not mean that non-Greeks, who held citizenship, could not easily learn Greek and therefore have access to Greek culture.[19] Without citizenship, however, they were normally excluded from attending the gymnasium. The families of non-Greeks were forced to hire tutors for their children and to seek an education in a less prestigious school, for example, a school of rhetoric that stressed proper speech and composition by references to famous texts and writers, culture heroes, and the gods in order to present compelling cases. Those seeking to become lawyers attended one of the schools of rhetoric if they were unable to gain entrance into a gymnasium. At the age of seven, students of the gymnasium learned the basics of reading and writing, moving from letters to syllables to sentences to short poetic passages. At the age of ten or eleven, students entered into a secondary school in order to master the reading, understanding, and emulation of more complex texts, to compose more complicated writings, and to become proficient in grammar. In addition, they learned the content of some of the Greek culture heroes and used their writings to enhance their own rhetorical and compositional skills. The third stage of education was designed to shape the ideal man, who was schooled in a variety of disciplines, made physically fit from the intense training in sports, and learned to embody the major virtues of paideia. This last stage began at the age of fifteen and was carried out under either the auspices of the teachers of the school or an employed tutor. One of the key areas of education was exercises in the arts of *progymnasmata*, rhetorical and literary style and argumentation.[20] These exercises became more and more complex until the students became rhetoricians.

Education in the *ephēbion* was reserved for graduates of the gymnasium who had excelled in their studies and training and sought a specialization in a particular career. In this context students received more specific education in one of the important professions: military leadership, teaching, and positions of note in the administration. Schoolbooks of these advanced institutes of learning included selections from the literary masters to foster a greater skill in perfecting an elegant Greek style. The writings of great philosophers were studied to learn metaphysics, ethics, the arts, the sciences, geography, mathematics, and rhetoric, while classics were read and emulated to cultivate an elegant style and content. This education effectively ended the students' devotion to traditional Greek religion, in particular the Olympian gods, and mythology and its explanatory and magical means of achieving order and balance in the cosmos. Strongly contested were the ideas of divine retribution and the nature of the gods. The common portrayals of the gods were often roundly criticized, and their behavior, including caprice, lust, and injustice, were ridiculed.[21] While all Greeks, including the

highly educated, participated in the great festivals and especially the games associated with the festivals, this did not mean that the intellectually sophisticated
bought into the mythos of state religion. Intellectuals did not necessarily deny
the existence of the gods, but their traditional portrayals were often criticized and
rejected. Even Epicurus, a materialist, believed in the gods, but saw them as far
removed from participation in the world in which humans lived. For many
Greeks, the mystery gods from the East became increasingly attractive.

Alexandria soon became the center of Hellenistic education and knowledge as
well as commerce and art for the entire eastern Mediterranean world, until this
coveted position was taken by Rome in the late first century BCE. It was in
Alexandria that some Jewish youth, who came from well-connected and wealthy
families in Alexandria, attended gymnasia. Philo participated in sports and held
them as activities of honor, and likely held in Roman times the coveted status of
citizen of the polis.

Lists of names of *ephēboi* from the early Roman period included some that were
Jewish, indicating that some Jews even pursued specializations in the advanced
school.[22] Greek cultural life, which included the games[23] and the theater, engaged
Jews of Alexandria with a stimulating and vibrant refinement of elegance, and a
captivating comprehension of art and knowledge opened Hellenistic Jews to a new
and wondrously appealing world, one that could be exercised in a way conducive
to the practice and articulation of their religion. The concreteness of the grammar
of Greek and its vivid array of expressions led Jews to adopt this more familiar language in composing their literary works. Indeed, first the Torah and then the entire
Hebrew Bible were translated into Greek. Even the intermeshing of Jewish religion with Greek philosophy, metaphysics, epistemology, and religion transpired
to reshape the character of Judaism, while keeping its central affirmations inherent in its tradition alive and making them more appealing. This reconfiguration
ranged from the equation of the God of Israel with Zeus, to the identification of
Moses with the founder of the animal cult in Egypt, to Jacob and his sons as the
builders of pagan temples. There was also the threat of assimilation of Jews completely into the cultural environments in which they lived.

Jewish Education in the Hellenistic Period[24]

What of schools in Eretz Israel? As for Jerusalem, 2 Maccabees mentions and then
strongly condemns the design of Jason to build a Greek-style gymnasium in
Jerusalem as a major piece of his plan to transform the old eastern city into a magnificent Greek polis (2 Macc. 4:7–22). Due to the Maccabean rebellion that broke
out, however, this effort seems to have had little effect on Jewish education.

We may assume that teachers and students of different Jewish schools would
have also studied the languages and traditions of other ethnic communities in the
region and the cultural products of Hellenism. The location of the school would
have included the household, the manse of the teacher, the marketplace in a city,
and a building either attached to a synagogue or located in the vicinity of the

temple. Lectures, classes, practicums, and tutorials would have been the instruments of instruction.

Unfortunately, we know nothing specifically about Qoheleth's education, although his writing betrays a familiarity with popular Greek philosophy, indicates he knew Greek, and was likely familiar with the Hellenistic villa, which could have been either his own residence or that of the father of one of his aristocratic students (2:4–8). He is himself the embodiment of what might be called Jewish paideia, since his thought is radically opposed to most Jewish compositions. His text indicates that the educated sage embodies certain virtues and follows their lead in behavior.

JUDAISM IN THE PTOLEMAIC EMPIRE[25]

Jews in the Ptolemaic Empire[26]

We are well informed about the Jews in Egypt. During the Hellenistic and early Roman periods, Jews in Alexandria were the third largest population group, second only to Hellenists and Egyptians. Relations with the Ptolemaic rulers were generally very positive, for they gave significant privileges to the Jewish *politeuma*, even though conditions deteriorated with the inclusion of Egypt within the Roman Empire in 31 BCE. In addition to the primary sources of papyri and inscriptions,[27] important texts written by Jewish literati that interpret Judaism in the period include the works of Josephus; 1, 2, and 3 Maccabees; the Third *Sibylline Oracle*; and the *Letter of Aristeas*.

While many Jews did not enjoy citizenship of the *poleis* of the Ptolemaic Empire, some did, probably because of wealth and/or service. Among the prominent Jews were Dositheus, the son of Drimylos (in the Ptolemaic court), who abandoned Judaism; and Onias IV during the second century BCE. Josephus asserts that these two Jews commanded the army of Ptolemy VI Philometor. This Ptolemy even had a Jewish philosopher named Aristobulus as his private tutor (2 Macc. 1:10). The nephew of Philo, Tiberius Julius Alexander, an apostate, even ascended to the position of governor of Egypt and opposed internal terrorist attacks against Rome initiated in Egypt during the first century CE. Cleopatra II, toward the middle of the second century BCE, named two Jews, Helkias and Ananias, to serve as the commanders-in-chief of her army. Their loyalty to their own people was demonstrated when they advised her against invading Judea during the reign of Alexander Jannaeus (*Ant.* 13.354). The cost of this advance in status for some involved the abandonment of Judaism. For example, the above-mentioned Dositheus, who held several positions of importance, eventually entered the Alexandrian priesthood of the deified Ptolemies (see *CPJ* 1:127; 3 Macc. 1:3). The choice to leave Judaism during the reign of the Ptolemies was due to personal ambition and not political pressure, for these rulers did not force or require their subjects to convert to or engage in another religion. The apostasy of Jews was roundly condemned, as 3 Maccabees demonstrates. This writer argued that apostates should be executed.

With one possible exception, Jews living in both Egypt and Judah experienced excellent relations with the Ptolemies during the third century BCE. No local revolt is reported or even any minor dispute recorded, save for 3 Maccabees, and its credibility appears rather dubious. Jews in Judea and Egypt celebrated the victory achieved by the forces of Ptolemy IV against those of Antiochus III in the battle at Raphia. However, the writer of 3 Maccabees, whose text may be dated to the early Roman period, joined several other historians, non-Jewish, in criticizing this ruler. This Jewish text is a legendary romance that narrates the attempt of Ptolemy IV to enter the sacred temple of Jerusalem when he stopped there on his way home following his great victory.[28] He was prevented from doing so when he was miraculously strickened with paralysis. Humiliated, he returned to Egypt to have his revenge and to punish the Jews who resisted the worship of Dionysus. His scheme was to gather together Jews in the great coliseum in Alexandria and have them crushed by a stampede of five hundred elephants, a plan that caused great joy among the native Egyptians. This plan backfired, however, when two angels intervened, and instead of rushing forward to trample the Jews the animals went berserk and retreated, killing many Egyptians. The fabulous and at times comedic character of the story, coupled with the lack of any corroboration, makes these events highly unlikely. This Jewish writer may have confused Ptolemy VI Philometor with Ptolemy IV. Then too, this later Ptolemy was a strong devotee of the god Dionysus.[29] If there is any historical thread in the story, it is likely to be found in the reign of Ptolemy VI, who was angry that the Jews refused to worship his god.

In spite of this crisis, at least fictionalized in Jewish storytelling, the Jewish writer of 3 Maccabees was at pains to point to the loyal support of the Jews for the Ptolemaic dynasty, and this loyalty was rewarded. One such case in point is Philometor's resettlement of Jews in the "district of Onias," near Leontopolis, in order to bolster the defenses of Egypt against further attempts of the Seleucids to invade Egypt. Jewish loyalty was strong, and Philometor knew he could depend upon his Jewish troops to fight well against the rival Seleucid kingdom. The most one may deduce from this story of persecution is that it represented anti-Jewish sentiment during the time of the early Caesars, possibly during the reign of Caligula and the Roman prefect of Egypt, Flaccus. This writer also was a strong advocate of obedience to the law, including kashrut, admonished the killing of some three hundred apostate Jews, and rejected Greek citizenship, since it would require the worship of false gods. However, this text gives no indication of the importance of the temple to Egyptian Jews.

Palestinian Judaism in the Ptolemaic Empire[30]

The urban culture of the eastern Mediterranean world that preceded Alexander possessed a variety of cultural traditions, many of which had been in existence centuries, even millennia, before the upstart Macedonian young warrior entered into this ancient world.[31] Even Greek settlements in Eretz Israel, chiefly in the former Phoenician and Philistine cities on the coastal plain, existed long before his wars of conquest. Tel Dor, for example, gives significant testimony to a pre-Alexandrian city in which Greek culture thrived.[32] This means that Alexander and his successors did not normally build new cities (Alexandria was an exception), but rather ancient ones were reshaped by Greek officials according to the model of the Greek polis. Even so, this did not lead to the eradication of older, entrenched cultures or to the extermination of indigenous populations. Indeed, the ethnic groups who peopled these cities and the surrounding regions were vastly superior in number. Subsequently, the Hellenistic rulers established a cultural system of status involving citizenship that showed preference to Greeks living in these cities, tried to impress the indigenous populations with the presentation of civilization in the Hellenic mode, which was translated into the notion of superiority, and attempted through paideia to inculcate Greek virtues, values, art, literature, sciences, and, above all, language into non-Greek populations. Greek governments and laws, the use of Greek both officially and commercially, cultural life, customs, and religious cults were dominant, but there was no concerted effort at the cultural genocide that imperialists of later epochs would practice.

Save for Gaza and later on Samaria, all the cities of Eretz Israel accepted without significant resistance Alexander's rule.[33] Gaza's resistance, stimulated by its continuing loyalty to the Achaemenids, resulted in its wholesale destruction, the enslavement of its population, and the resettlement in the city of people from the nearby countryside. When Alexander visited Egypt in 331 BCE, the city of Samaria chose to rebel, resulting in its defeat, the execution of its leaders, and its resettlement with Macedonian troops. Yet these were the exceptions.

In the effort to ensure Greek control of the area, incentives, including especially land grants and favorable taxation, were offered to Greeks who would immigrate to these new lands. Greek leaders also sought to attract the loyalty of the wealthy and powerful class of indigenous populations by offering local rule to the leaders, supporting the important temples of their gods, and giving them some significant involvement in commercial ventures. Yet to maintain what was familiar along with their Greek identity, these immigrants brought with them their culture, religions, gods, mythologies, and other traditions. Even so, fascination with Eastern religions led to accommodation on the part of some Greeks, as, for example, the hybrid Greek and Persian mystery religion, Mithraism, demonstrates. Even the gods of the local nations were supported, for, it was imagined, they had power in their own local spheres of rule and needed to be both placated and used for sustaining Greek rule over lands and peoples.

The term "Judaism" (*Ioudaismos*, Ιουδαίσμος) appears first in 2 Macc. 1:1 (see 2:21; 8:1; 14:38). The same book (2 Macc. 4:13–14) mentions the first known occurrence of "hellenization" (*Hellēnismos*, Ἑλληνίσμος), meaning "Greek culture." Efforts to contrast dramatically Hellenistic Judaism in the Diaspora with an inward-looking Judaism of the province of Judah have been discontinued. Martin Hengel has argued that by the middle to the end of the third century BCE, thus about the time period for Qoheleth, Judaism in Eretz Israel, including even the Holy City, had become as thoroughly hellenized as Judaism in the Diaspora.[34] This does not mean there was a monolithic Hellenistic Judaism both in Judah and the Diaspora, for the hybrid character of Hellenism developing among different, older cultures led to many forms of expression.[35] These differences in hellenization were also expressed in the variety of beliefs, practices, and orientations of Judaism.

Many earlier scholars concluded that indigenous cultures, not matching the apogee of Greek civilization, were submerged into the dominant culture or transformed into something totally different than the traditions formerly created to define social and political life. This colonial perspective uncritically appropriated the Greeks' own views of their superiority, not realizing the arrogant falsehood this view embodied. Postcolonialism in the present will no longer allow this metanarrative invested by the West to go unchallenged. Indeed, the Greeks and Romans expressed their cultural hubris in extensive literary outpourings, artistic achievements, and structures of governance. Today it is clear that local traditions remained vital and impervious to cultural genocide. The reactions to Hellenism by local populations ranged from adoption to repudiation. More often a transforming process integrated the two cultures into something new and vibrant.[36] After all, many of the so-called transformations were largely superficial. Most Greek regions in the empire were not monolinguistic nor did they reject indigenous languages' influence on the Greek tongue; rather they were multilingual with Greek and local languages influencing one another.

Hellenization and Judean Urban Centers[37]

Hellenistic cities in Israel, built on earlier urban sites, were initially situated along the coast of the Mediterranean Sea, from Egypt to Tyre. With the advance of Alexander's armies, however, Greeks began to move inland, setting up Hellenic governments and domination in the interior, including Tiberius and Samaria. These Greek cities, whether or not officially proclaimed as such, became the centers for Hellenic domination of government, culture, commerce, language, and wealth. Those Greeks who came to Judea from the period of Alexander and later were largely without means in the world from which they originated, and came in pursuit of wealth and status in the new lands, now incorporated into Hellenistic empires. Of course, the cities of Judea, including Jerusalem, could not begin to compare to the commercial and cultural attainments of Alexandria and other prominent cities in Asia such as Pergamum, but they were hellenized.

There is no doubt, based on literary narratives and material cultures, that Hellenistic influence on Jewish life was extensive. Even the center of Judaism, the sacred city of Jerusalem with the temple and its traditions of law and religious practice, experienced the dramatic impact of this imported culture.[38] To mention only one example, a Greek *agoranomos* involving an overseer of the markets was established in Jerusalem prior to the Maccabean revolt (2 Macc. 3:4).[39] Applebaum points to Qoheleth's description of economic wealth in 2:4–9, resulting from commerical activities made possible by hellenization that included agricultural estates and a system of slavery. His own wealth, if he is describing himself in this section, would have derived from his commerical involvement in the "provinces" (*mĕdînôt*, מדינות, 5:7; 2:8) and the coastal cities (*mĕdînôt hayyām*, מדינות הים).[40] Although Qoheleth uses hyperbole to portray himself as wealthier than anyone who lived before him in Jerusalem, he represents "the growth of a new class of landlords who derive their wealth from agricultural production combined with commerce, but who reside principally in Jerusalem."[41] A class of patricians whose wealth derived from land ownership, agriculture, commerce, slavery, and advances in technology appeared in the region.[42] Based on his mastering of Hebrew, his implicit knowledge of the larger Hellenstic world, and his assuming the character of the long dead, famous ruler Solomon, the teacher himself may have belonged to the aristocratic elite of Jerusalem. Either that or he was a sage employed by them to teach their students. Unless this text is his valedictory address, however, it is doubtful any aristocrat of power, wealth, and influence would choose to expose his son or sons to this dark despair that repudiates the very values that drive their existence. This text, if we assume it was a public teaching, could have come only from a man of wealth and prominence himself. Would the status and influence of this unknown sage place him on the same footing as the family of the Tobiads (see Josephus, *Ant.* 11.4; 12.160; cf. *CPJ* 1:115–30), the opponents of Nehemiah (Neh. 2:10, 19: 4:3, 7; 6:1–19; 13:4–8), who lived originally in Ammon? From what we know of this family, its members were strongly influenced by Hellenism, were wealthy landowners, possessed high political office extending back into the Persian period, were close associates of the high priests, and gave loyal support to the Ptolemies (1 Macc. 5:9–13).[43]

According to Josephus, Joseph (the son of Tobias) was the nephew of the high priest Onias II and received the tax contract for Judean agriculture from his uncle. Thus people of substance were favored by the Ptolemies in their distribution of royal contracts, regardless of their standing in their local communities. Since the Tobiads were not supporters of conventional Judaism, including the strict adherence to the Torah, and cultivated positive and beneficial relations with their Greek masters, they were often either held in contempt or at least placed under suspicion. These Jews, on the periphery of their own culture and religious identity, illustrate that there were people who did not share the more conservative views of the traditionalists like Ezra in an earlier time. Other wealthy landowners possessed estates, as indicated by the complaint to Antiochus V, mentioned in 1 Macc. 6:24, that rebels had appropriated their estates.[44] At the same time, it would be difficult to imagine that many aristocratic families would have subscribed to the extremely skeptical views of Qoheleth that rejected the values the wealthy held dear. Even so, skepticism was not unique to Qoheleth, but was found throughout the eastern Mediterranean world and took root among intellectuals who were obviously either self-sustaining or employed by the wealthy.

Greek Epigraphy in Hellenistic Palestine[45]

Another area that points to the widespread presence of Greek culture in Eretz Israel during the Hellenistic and early Roman periods are Greek names, Hellenic architecture, and the discovery of Greek papyri, coins, epitaphs, and inscriptions. Many Jews of Eretz Israel had Greek names, including some of the later Hasmonean rulers (Hyrcanus, Aristobulus, Alexander, and Antigonum).[46] There were approximately thirty Hellenistic cities in Palestine whose material remains point to the presence of Greek architecture, coinage, and cultural and domestic artifacts.[47] Greek was a culture influencing not simply the upper class, but also many who belonged to the more common groups of people.[48] Most of the epigraphic materials from this period are Greek, although some are in Hebrew and Aramaic.[49] Coins, as early as the time of Alexander Jannaeus, were embossed with both Hebrew and Greek letters. Even synagogues in Israel had Greek inscriptions, indicating that the worshipers could read and speak Greek.[50] Greek documents found at Masada and in the Qumran archives indicate that some scribes read and wrote Greek. Rabbinic literature contains literally thousands of Greek loanwords.[51] On the basis of the epigraphic evidence, it is clear that the population of Palestine during the Hellenistic and early Roman periods was bilingual (Greek and Aramaic) and in some cases even trilingual (Greek, Aramaic, and Hebrew). This hellenization of culture was already developing extensively by the time Qoheleth lived and wrote in the latter part of the third century BCE.

Hellenistic Jewish Literature in Eretz Israel

The Hellenistic period was an especially prolific period for Jewish literati in Palestine and Egypt, and represents the zenith of Jewish literature prior to the composition of the Talmud and other texts during the Middle Ages. Indeed, many of the issues reflected in Qoheleth and later in Ben Sira and the Wisdom of Solomon are found in both Jewish literature and pagan texts of the period. Qoheleth's criticisms of traditional Jewish orthodoxy and orthopraxy would have been directed not simply against the traditional wisdom of the past, represented by the book of Proverbs, as has often been argued, but also toward sapiential, priestly, and apocalyptic contemporaries who wrote and taught during the same cultural and political climate. Indeed, the opponents of Qoheleth with whom he does battle are not the Jewish traditionalists of the past, but groups contending for power and status in the Hellenistic period.

Other Hellenistic writers in Eretz Israel close to the time that Qoheleth lived included Theodotus,[52] Philo the Poet,[53] and Eupolemos.[54] Their texts, along with the later 3 Maccabees (composed in Greek, though anti-Hellenistic), demonstrate an intellectual tradition of Hellenistic scholars, who composed largely in Greek, that was present in Eretz Israel in the third and second centuries BCE.[55] Thus for Qoheleth to have lived and breathed the air of third-century Jerusalem, he would have had ample opportunity to become knowledgeable of the Greek language and to have had at least some acquaintance with Greek literature and philosophy.

Jerusalem as a Hellenistic City[56]

Greek culture was not limited to the coastal cities or those inland urban sites that welcomed the new civilization because of its many benefits. It also filtered into all dimensions of life in Jerusalem. During the five "Syrian Wars" (274–271, 260–253, 246–241, 221–217, and 202–198 BCE) leading to the development of competing Jewish groups who supported one or the other of the two Greek empires, garrisons of Greek groups were stationed in and near the city. Indeed, Jerusalem was a key city in the highlands that was important as a military stronghold. And it is clear that there were powerful Hellenistic Jews in the city, at least by the time of Antiochus IV, as evidenced in the struggle for the high priesthood that led to a bidding war. The author of 2 Maccabees could even say that the temple in Jerusalem was the most famous sanctuary in the entire world (2:2), suggesting his awareness of others in the eastern Mediterranean region.[57]

Hecataeus, a Greek historian who wrote at the beginning of the third century BCE,[58] described Jerusalem as a city under the hierocracy of Sadducean priests who controlled the temple, which not only provided them with enormous prestige and social status through the teaching of the Torah and the operations of the cultic sacrifices, festivals, and Sabbath worship, but also with access to a steady stream of revenue. The powerful Sadducean families became wealthy as well as politically influential. In addition to the hierocracy of priestly families, the lay aristocracy also possessed economic and political power in the province and particularly in Jerusalem. They were represented by a council (*gerousia*, γερουσία; see 2 Macc. 11:27; 3 Macc. 1:8; Josephus, *Ant.* 12.3.3, 138, 142), although the precise authority and power of this group remains unclear.

Material Culture in Hellenistic Jerusalem[59]

Hecataeus writes: "as a result of their mingling with men of other nations (both under Persian rule and under that of the Macedonians who overthrew the Persians), many of their traditional practices were disturbed."[60] This "disturbance" caused division and dissension among the Jewish population of the province. Greek names were used among the aristocracy at the end of the third century BCE, while the Tobiads, some of whom moved to Jerusalem, had a Greek secretary and employed Greek teachers for their children. There appear to have been Greek teachers even in the house of Simeon II.[61] In all likelihood, Jerusalem would have had sages and scribes who knew several languages, including Greek, Aramaic, and Hebrew. Even Jerusalem coins were minted with the images of Ptolemy I and Bernice I as well as of Ptolemy II and Arsinoe II, and had embossed on them an eagle, the symbol of Ptolemaic rule.[62] Other material remains from the third and second centuries BCE include a thousand stamped jar handles of amphorae, containing wine that originated in Rhodes, that have been excavated in Jerusalem. These jar handles are engraved with official Rhodian stamps and are dated by the names of local priests.[63] These give evidence of commerical activities between Jerusalem and the Greek world. The Zenon papyri also point to the involvement of the Ptolemies in commerce in Judah and even mention Jerusalem several times.[64] First Maccabees 12:20–23 (see Josephus, *Ant.* 12.4, 10, 225–27) reproduces in part a letter that indicates correspondence took place between the high priest Onias II and Areus, king of Sparta. More than a century later, Jonathan the Hasmonean sent a letter to Sparta that renewed the association between the two countries (1 Macc. 12:1–18). Jason, defrocked from his position as high priest, fled to Sparta, for they were a "kindred people" (2 Macc. 5:9). *The Letter of Aristeas* (v. 38) refers to Jewish scribes who knew well both Hebrew and Greek and therefore could produce a Greek translation of the Hebrew Bible.

The social composition of Jews in Jerusalem during the period of the Ptolemies is difficult to reconstruct from the limited written sources we have. It is clear, however, that the high priest and the Sadducees had a substantial position of power and wealth due to the Torah, the temple, and both the Temple and the priestly taxes. There was considerable involvement in the commercial activity in the Greek world so that Aramaic, Hebrew, and Greek had to be known and spoken by most residents, including even laborers, and there would have to have been multilingual scribes who were able to speak, read, and write these three languages. This commerce points to the existence of a wealthy merchant class and also lower-stationed businessmen who were involved in the transport and selling of goods. The training of scribes necessary for economic, priestly, and governmental administrative tasks would likely have been in different schools, ranging from one attached to the temple, to private ones attended by aristocratic youths, to family guilds, and to private tutors.

The Struggle with Hellenism in Jerusalem[65]

When Zeno visited Jerusalem circa 259 BCE, he presented it as a provincial temple city that was rather insignificant politically and economically. The wealthiest Jew of the period, Tobias, was the brother-in-law of the high priest Onias II, but it was his son Joseph who took up residence in Jerusalem, serving as a financial banker, thus indicating the cosmopolitan character of some of its Jewish citizens. Since there was no gymnasium in Jerusalem until after the assumption of the high priesthood by Jason, people like Qoheleth and the Tobiad family were not hostile to the new civilization, but rather were inquisitive and open-minded regarding its culture and ideas, even adopting a number of them.[66] Even the prohibition against images did not obtain when it came to the minting and use of Greek coins that had images of rulers, while the zeal for following the commandments of the Torah is not present in the texts concerning Tobias and Qoheleth. These are suggestive of a Jerusalem with a rather diverse Jewish and non-Jewish population. While hostilities lay beneath the surface of Jewish factionalism, however, open conflict between Hellenistic Jews and the traditionalists did not materialize until the Maccabean revolt.

HELLENISM AND THE BOOK OF QOHELETH

Hellenism, Hellenization, and Qoheleth

Debates about the meaning of "hellenization" have continued for a century, but I have chosen the definition of Martin Hengel: It is "a complex phenomenon which cannot be limited to purely political, socio-economic, cultural or religious aspects, but embraces them all."[67] Thus it includes paideia, philosophy, rhetoric, traditional religion, the newly emerging mystery religions, the Greek language, art and architecture, and a variety of political and social features. While the rapid expansion of hellenization was due to the military conquests of Alexander, this does not mean there was negligible Greek influence in the ancient Near East, including Israel, prior to this time. Even if one does not consider the invasion of the "Sea Peoples" into coastlands of Egypt and the western Levant, archaeological evidence attests to significant Greek presence on the coasts of Syria and Egypt from the early eighth century BCE. Even early classical prophets recognized this fact (Amos 9:7; Jer. 47:4; also see Gen. 10:14; Deut. 2:23; 1 Chr. 1:12). The Chronicler in the fourth and third centuries BCE (Hellenistic period) knew a good deal about Greek warfare, money, and economics.[68] Prior to Alexander, some local mints produced coins similar to Greek ones, and imported Attic pottery contributed to the luxury items obtained through trade. Greek mercenaries and merchants were present during the later monarchy of Judah. Eretz Israel was no homogenous culture when Alexander the Great entered Syria-Palestine.[69]

The influence of hellenization on Judea must have been substantial during the period of the Ptolemies, the Seleucids, and finally Rome, especially in the cities.[70] It was not only the more liberal Jews of the aristocracy who embraced Hellenism. Common merchants and the lower class must have known some Greek, since it was the language for international commerce and diplomacy. Grave inscriptions of both the wealthy and the poor included ones written in Greek. Although there was no Greek gymnasium or *ephēbeion* until the time of Jason the high priest under the reign of Antiochus IV Epiphanes, the sentiment must have been building among some of the aristocracy of Jerusalem.

The Hellenistic rulers tended to be benign in their treatment of the nations they conquered, perhaps a necessary policy, since the Greeks were overwhelmingly in the minority. These rulers were also tolerant of local religions. They also gave their support to indigenous families to govern internally. One new policy originated by Alexander was the founding of new Greek cities throughout the Greek empire, especially built for Greeks who were veterans or functionaries in administration and commerce for carrying on city life. Other, ancient ones were on occasion rebuilt in a Greek style and given this status.

The fundamental question for aristocratic Jews among the literati was how to maintain Jewish tradition in the context of a Hellenistic world: cultural assimilation and complete rejection of all things Greek were the two extremes, with most people more likely in the middle. However, the most telling difference between Jews and Greeks was that the former had learned to differentiate more between religion and culture, while the latter integrated the two, at least when it came to state religions and politics.[71] While paganism embraced polytheism and tended toward tolerance, even respect, of other religions, the rub came when Jews denied the authenticity of the other gods.

Qoheleth in the Hellenistic World

Like many well-to-do Jews in Jerusalem, Qoheleth[72] would have had ample opportunity to become acquainted with Hellenism.[73] He could have traveled outside the environs of Jerusalem and had firsthand contact with Egyptian and Greek cultures. He also would have found Jerusalem a thriving city imbued with Hellenism in his own native context. The conduits to Hellenism were through the mediation of literature, commerce, and governmental administration.[74] The Zeno papyri are direct evidence that Greek was well known among the Judean Jews as early as 250 BCE. Hellenism and indigenous cultures existed side by side, and there were various approaches to their integration. This integration was true of Judaism.

Where would we place Qoheleth in the Hellenistic world? I place him in the cultural and philosophical tradition that comprised a mixture of things old and new that was appealing especially to the educated aristocracy in upper-class Jerusalem. Aristobulus and Ben Sira were similar, although the latter tended toward a more reactionary position. If Qoheleth is positioned in the latter part of the third century in Jerusalem, then this would explain why the spirit of his text exudes that of Hellenistic culture and philosophy of the period.[75] Hengel contends that Qoheleth was "a skeptical sage in the Ptolemaic period with international experience [who] spoke only about the one universal God." He calls the Jewish God, "the God," emphasizing distance, and not YHWH, and speaks like a Greek who adheres to fatalism in speaking about an unknowable and "inexplicable fate."[76] Several features of Hellenistic ideas, including especially features of Greek philosophy, compare with some of those found in Qoheleth.[77] While no words in Qoheleth possess a Greek derivation (i.e., Graecisms), Qoheleth's vocabulary does contain several parallels to Hellenistic Greek words and their meanings. Hengel points to several Greek expressions in Qoheleth: the frequent use of the terms *miqreh* (מקרה) and *ḥēleq* (חלק) as reflecting the Greek terms *moira* (μοιρα) and *tychē* (τυκή) that refer to fate and fortune/portion. "Under the sun" (תחת השמש, *taḥat haššemeš*; = ὑπὸ τὸν ἥλιον, hypo ton hēlion) appears often in Greek literature, while *hebel* (הבל, "nothingness/ephemerality") suggests the Greek term *typhos* (τύπος). In addition, *laʿăśôt ṭôb* (לעשות טוב; 3:12) parallels *eu prattein* (εὖ πραττεῖν) or *eu dran* (εὖ δρᾶν), and *ṭôb ʾăšer yāpeh* (טוב אשר יפה, 5:17) reflects the common Greek expression *kalos agathos* (καλός ἀγαθός) or *kalon philon* (καλόν φίλος).[78] Antoon Schoors also thinks that Qoheleth came under the influence of Greek thought.[79] Among the possible Greek expressions he finds are "to see the sun" (lir'ôt 'et-haššāmeš, לראות את-השמש, 6:5; 7:11; 11:7; this takes on the meaning of "live," e.g., οὐδέ νύ μοι κῆρ ἤθελ' ἔτι ζώει καὶ ὀρᾶν φάος ἠελίοιο; "nor had my heart any longer desire to live and to behold the light of the sun"; cf. Homer, Od. 4.540). The expression 'āśâ yammîm (עשה ימים, "spend the days"; 6:12) equals Greek poiein chronon (ποιεῖν χρόνον). The word 'ōlām (עלם) assumes the meaning of Greek aiōn (αἰών) in 1:10; mālē' (מלא, 8:11; 9:3) means "to make full, satiate, impregnate" in the sense of Greek plēroō (πλερόω), and tûr (תור) is influenced by the Greek term skeptomai (σκέπτομαι) in 1:13; 2:3; and 7:25, where the term means "mental exploration."

Braun also argues that certain terms and expressions in Qoheleth have some strong similitarity to Greek ones.[80] He adds: הבל (hebel) and τύφος (typhos), "wind," "smoke," "dampness," "darkness," "blindness," and "vanity"; יתרון (yitrôn), "what remains," and ὀφέελος (ophelos), "excess"; עמל ('āmāl), "laborious activity," and πόνος (ponos); טוב לפני האלהים (ṭôb lipnê hā'ĕlōhîm), "good/pleasing before God," and θεόφιλία (theophilia), "friends of God"; and טוב אשר יפה (ṭôb 'ăšer yāpâ) and καλόν φίλον (kalon philon), "the divine gift of the good and beauty." Qoheleth would have undoubtedly known Greek philosophy in a popular form, even though there is no explicit evidence he could read Greek. Thus he may have gained some familiarity with Hellenism through oral culture. However, can we imagine a sage living in Jerusalem at the end of the third century BCE without knowing how to speak and read Greek?

Further, Qoheleth has numerous teachings that match Hellenistic philosophical understanding, including the one of fate and determinism: humans are born, are predestined to live a certain period of time, and then die at an appointed time.[81] The joy or happiness that comprises the central teaching of this book is often found in Greek philosophy. The cautious and unrestrained attitude toward cultic piety is perhaps influenced by Greek philosophical views critical of religion. The fact that salvation history, the chosenness of Israel, the covenant, and the Torah are absent allows Qoheleth an unrestrained entrance into the Hellenistic world. If Qoheleth was familiar with popular Greek philosophy and features of Hellenistic culture, it is clear that he is eclectic in what he transmits in his own instruction.

The iron wall built around Judaism by the reactionary Jews was due to a variety of observances they considered to be critical to their identity: kashrut and other social practices, recognizing the dangers of improper contact with non-Jews in a variety of ways, including especially marriage, strict adherence to the Torah, and observance of temple ritual. They offer comfort, meaning, and purpose to Judaism. Yet these restrictions have no place in the despair of the sage Qoheleth. Instead, he warns students to be careful when "approaching the temple," tells them not to offer the "sacrifice of fools," and advises them to be circumspect in offering vows (4:17–5:6). Even so, parallels with Hellenism should not obscure that Qoheleth remained a Jewish sage who combined his sapiential tradition, at least the elements to which he wished to adhere, with Hellenistic philosophies.

He does break significantly with his tradition when he questions the justice of God and rejects the doctrine of retribution, but he was not alone in doing so.

The Anthropological Approach of Qoheleth

What then is the ideology of a sage like Qoheleth, who had an aristocratic background and placed himself in opposition to the several groups vying for power and influence in the third century? For Qoheleth, wisdom's traditional creation theology, conveyed through important metaphors examined earlier in Proverbs and in the speeches of Job's opponents, was not capable of answering in a satisfactory way the questions he raised about determining what was good in human existence. This sage attempted to shape vital metaphors into compelling articulations of creation faith and the moral life, but ultimately failed in his quest. Tradition no longer provided a reservoir for cosmological images of faith and appropriate assessments of human nature and function in the world due to Qoheleth's critical engagement of experience and observation. Further, Qoheleth could not discover any evidence of divine action or presence in a reality in which justice and well-being for the wise and the righteous did not prevail.

The cosmological rendering of a world of goodness in which moral action led to desired consequences could no longer sustain itself in an enigmatic and fearful reality that gave no appearance of responding at all to human behavior.[82] "The God" was hidden in darkness and could not be known. There was no evidence of divine retribution, and what occurred seemed to be the result of mere divine caprice.[83] Thus a very different way of looking at human existence in the world needed to emerge. With the elements of the religion of Torah set forth by the priests and traditional sages of the Second Temple no longer central to human faith and action, he begins his quest to discover the answer to the essential question of human life: "What is the good for humans to do under heaven during the few days of their life?" (2:3). The answer for Qoheleth lay not in theology, but rather in a philosophical understanding of human experience. It is a human question that he seeks to answer, and it resides in the activities and experiences of the engaged mind of the reflective sage.

EGYPTIAN AND HELLENISTIC SKEPTICISM IN THE THIRD CENTURY BCE

Introduction

The Ptolemaic rule of Judah occurred during an age of great cultural and, at times, even military achievement, but it also was a time of considerable unease for intellectuals. The rule of the Ptolemies over Palestine (301–198 BCE) was not only peaceful, but also apparently popular among the contemporary Jews.[84] However, it was also a time of growing skepticism in Greek philosophy and some elements of Egyptian wisdom that contributed to the context for the emergence of the skeptical worldview of Qoheleth.

Egyptian Grave Autobiographies[85]

One of the examples of integration of Hellenistic Egyptian writing and thought with Qoheleth is the close parallel between Egyptian grave autobiographies and Qoheleth's deep sense of skepticism about the ability to know anything for certain and to his preoccupation with death.[86] While there are no third-person biographies in ancient Egypt, many texts pose as autobiographies. This fiction persisted for three thousand years, and, perhaps due to Hellenistic influence, became especially frequent in the Late Egyptian Period. Many of these texts are presented as the address of the dead to those who visit their tombs. These grave autobiographies represent a long and carefully cultivated tradition that changes in response to the fluctuating, irresolute movement of history and culture. These fictional narratives are carved, embossed, or painted and placed in tombs of the necropolises. Not all of the tomb dwellers who address the visitors are men; some are women. The somber mood of these fictional accounts from the dead is pervasive. The desire most commonly expressed is that proper behavior while alive will allow the tomb inhabitant to continue to exist beyond the pale of death by entering into the afterlife. These tomb autobiographies speak of the accomplishments of the deceased and the integrity of their behavior.

These autobiographies assume one of two forms: a sequence of epithets and expressions that portray the dead person's traits and biographical information, and a narrative that presents the major events of his/her life. The autobiographies beseech visitors of future generations to provide them with the victuals necessary for survival in the future life and to pronounce offering formulae, while warning them against tomb desecration. These actions, if heeded, would preserve the tomb occupant in the future life. The narrator of the text is the deceased person who inhabits the grave, thus giving the impression that the autobiography was a posthumous speech directed to the visitors of the deceased that sought to admonish them to pursue a righteous existence, which would allow them entrance into the future life.

Listed among the common traits of the deceased are his/her intelligence and wisdom, faithfulness to the personal deity, and performance of deeds of virtue and charity. The expectation is that the gods rewarded the "god-fearers" with health, goods, long life, children, a proper burial, and life beyond the grave. Expressions that teach the joy in living include: "follow the heart" (*sms ib*),[87] which points to the fulfillment of one's desires, while "happiness" (*ndm ib*)[88] suggests satisfaction with life, a type of contemplative joy and contentment that envelops one prior to death. The specific purposes of these autobiographies are twofold: to demonstrate that the deceased have lived life in accordance with the principles of *ma'at* and to make a strong case for his/her admission to the afterlife. These texts, due to their formal features that emulate the instruction and the values and virtues articulated, have much in common with wisdom literature.[89]

These intimate that scribes of lower ranks earned their living through these compositions that likely were written and sold to the relatives of the deceased attending to his/her interment. Artists were then employed to engrave or paint them on the tombs. This is due to the probability that the authors of the inscriptions were scribes of lower ranks who studied in the wisdom schools.

Autobiographies assumed a more pessimistic mood that began to appear with some frequency in the sixteenth century BCE, and grew in number and intensity in the Hellenistic and early Roman periods. The gods had become more tyrannical, capricious, and unjust.[90] Death was viewed as a time of sorrow and loss and as an entrance into darkness. In addition to survival beyond the tomb, other more tangible forms of immortality came to be coveted: the continuance of a good name, the corporate remembrance of virtuous deeds, and the producing of numerous progeny.[91]

Egyptian tomb autobiographies have much in common with the testament of Qoheleth, ranging from the somber mood evoked by the text, to a first-person narrator, to a high degree of skepticism about values once thought achievable, and to the emphasis on joie de vivre.[92] The epilogue even reads like an obituary for the teacher, summarizing his life in terms of the activities of a sage who taught people wisdom, wrote words of truth, and collected and arranged sayings (12:9–10).[93] Like some of the pessimistic tomb autobiographies, Qoheleth accentuates the repeated conclusion that inescapable darkness and sorrows of the grave may be countered only by the short-lived experience of joy while alive (2:24–26; 5:18–20; etc.).[94] While these texts are largely fictional, they do provide important insight into the virtues, culture, and history of ancient Egypt.

Greek Skepticism[95]

If Qoheleth lived in the third century BCE, he would have had the opportunity to encounter Greek culture and philosophy firsthand. Along with Greek inhabitants, commerce, and culture in the region, Hellenistic views of the world were expressed in philosophical schools and extended their reach far into the Near East. These reached Jerusalem and exerted their influence until the destruction of the city by the Romans in 70 CE. Greek literature and mendicant sophists would have been present in Judea in the third century BCE. Ben Sira also noted that sages traveled to other lands (39:4), and this may have been true of Qoheleth. We can only conjecture the level and degree of Qoheleth's knowledge of Greek philosophy and the Greek language, but certain phrases and themes in Qoheleth point to parallels with skeptical literature. It is also difficult to imagine that a sage teaching in a wisdom school, especially in the cultural amalgam during the Hellenistic period, would not have known Greek and the Hellenistic literary tradition.

Pessimism had been a feature of the classical tradition from its earliest days.[96] Greek drama exposed human weakness of even great heroes and the consequences of failure. In Homer (eighth century BCE) gods and the cosmos were eternal; humans were fated to live only brief and ultimately tragic lives that ended in the darkness of the underworld. Zeus, the one who established the fates of humans, was capricious and consigned even heroes to the shadow world of Hades. Indeed, part of the nobility of humans was their courage to face death in war and acts of adventure and to rejoice over their lives.[97] Hesiod (ca. 700 BCE) was also known for the pessimism that found its way into his compositions, due in part to the gods who fixed the fates and pursued desultory decisions that even led to their support of evil, the existence for which they were responsible, even over the good.[98] Only human activities, carefully pursued, gave humans the ability to find sense in the world. Theognis (fifth century BCE) composed elegies that negated the hopes of humans in life and the future and exposed their untrustworthiness and wickedness.[99] Sophocles and Euripides (contemporaries in the fifth century BCE) also depicted the tragic in human life.[100] Sophocles described humans as ignorant fools afflicted by some fateful error that drove the story until its final end in misfortune. The gods determined the fortunes of humans, and yet were incapable of being known. Ironically, it was only through the experience of the tragic that one encountered the universal nature of reality and became truly human. For Euripides the myths are nothing more than exposés of the gods, who were irrational, unjust, and capricious. The gods were indifferent to human strivings, while chance, disorder, and irrationality characterized the tragic fates of humans. Their final destinies were impacted by their own uncontrolled passions and innate flaws.

In addition to pessimism, skepticism was also an important feature in Greek intellectual ruminations, and was present especially in the musings of the post-Socratic schools of the Cynics, the philosophical school of Cyrene, the Stoics, and the Epicureans.[101] However, it was especially philosophical Skepticism and the extreme limits it placed on epistemology that had a major impact on the intellectual world of the Hellenistic period. The Skeptics were quick to reject any abstract system of thought that could not be subjected to empirical analysis.

"Skeptic" (derived from *skeptikos*, σκεπτικός) refers to an "inquirer," who, not satisfied that current knowledge was verifiable, continued to search for what was true. Eventually, the quest resulted in the doubt that anything could be affirmed as undeniable. Sextus Empiricus, writing at the end of the second and the beginning of the third century CE, sets forth in his *Pyrrhoniae hypotyposes* the goal of Skepticism to be "the hope of attaining freedom from disturbance" (*Pyr.* 1.8, 12).[102] Yet the passageway to this end was to discover a criterion by which to establish what was true and then to differentiate it from "falsity." Since this defining criterion lay beyond reach, it was necessary to suspend judgment on determining what was true. Practical wisdom that dealt with the obvious was to be followed when it came to everyday decisions, for these were simply commonsense judgments (*Pyr.* 1.29).

The important Skeptics included Parmenides, Heraclitus, Protagoras (who was an opponent of Socrates), Gorgias, and above all Pyrrho of Elis (ca. 365–272 BCE). Pyrrho contended and sought to demonstrate that equally substantive arguments could be made for or against a proposition. Thus humans must suspend judgment on the reliability of data derived from the senses and live in reality as it appears, not necessarily as it is. The external world, and more specifically things as they are cannot be known by either reason or the senses. While common-sense decisions are necessary, achieving any certainty about the world, moral values, or the existence of God is beyond human ability. His views greatly influenced the thought of the Middle and New Academies of Athens.

This philosophical orientation of the New Academy flourished for approximately two centuries (ca. 269–early to mid-first century BCE).[103] They contended that even Plato could be properly understood only through the lens of Skepticism. The major philosopher of the New Academy who shaped it into a major philosophical system was Arcesilaus, scholarch from about 265 to 240 BCE. Using the Socratic method, he required the suspending of judgment (*epochē*, ἐποχή) about the truth of everything unless it could be unquestionably proven. Of course, nothing could be, meaning then that absolute truth was impossible to obtain (*akatalepsia*, ἀκαταληψία). Since both sides of a position could be argued effectively, nothing could be affirmed to be resolutely true.[104] He was especially critical of the Stoic and Epicurean understanding of epistemology, since both schools held that sense perception provided the basis for affirmations that are certainly true. Other noteworthy Skeptics included Carneades and Clitomachus. Carneades refined Skepticism by setting forth the theory of plausibility (*pithanon*, πιθανόν), meaning that while a proposition could be affirmed, it was still contested. No sense impression could ensure that it corresponded to a fact. Thus the "plausible" was not a certain guide to what was true.

HELLENISTIC SKEPTICISM IN QOHELETH

Qoheleth in the Hellenistic World[105]

How influential would Hellenism, especially the teachings of Skepticism, have been on Qoheleth, who taught and wrote in the latter half of the third century BCE? Would this sage have been so sheltered that he was unaware of the larger zeitgeist of the period in which he lived? And what of his students who came to him from aristocratic families engaged in political and commercial ventures? Does this wise man simply stay within the walls of his own inherited tradition, blind and impervious to the Sturm und Drang of the eastern Mediterranean world? When intellectual contests, searchings for meaning in new and exotic religions, military ventures involving the struggles of kings for land, power, and wealth, and internal political and religious wranglings grew to levels of unmatched intensity, can we imagine a sage impervious to all of these upheavals, boarding himself up within a private world of inner thoughts and isolated reflection? Yet these are often the assumptions residing behind many of the efforts to interpret the teachings of this unknown sage.

In my judgment, placing Qoheleth within its social world is critical to understanding its teachings, purpose, and relationship to Judaism as a whole. From the

data I have summarized, it is clear that Jerusalem in the late third century BCE
was enduring an intellectual, cultural, and historical ferment of competing religious and philosophical understandings, languages, military activities of warring
states, and Jewish religious and political groups competing for power, status, and
wealth. To regard Jerusalem as a cultural backwater isolated from these stirrings is
to deny the material evidence, inscriptions, and texts that appear in the late fourth,
third, and second centuries BCE in this urban setting. This means, then, that the
interpretation of Qoheleth and the articulation of its teachings for life could occur
legitimately only by taking note of the pluralistic world in which it took shape.

The philosophical tradition most akin to Qoheleth's worldview was that of
Greek Skepticism developed and transmitted at the time in which he lived and
wrote by philosophers of the New Academy. He certainly did not draw on any
previously existing text within his own native tradition that would have prepared
him to take his journey into skepticism. Even the "Instruction of Agur" (Prov.
30:1–4) focuses only on the inability of humans to scale the heavens (a metaphor
for obtaining immortality and divine knowledge for the benefit of humanity).
This brief instruction, filled with questions that even the sage does not attempt
to answer, leaves one totally unprepared for the incredulous skepticism of the "son
of David."

There were also pieces of literature containing in poetic and narrative form the
same topics and very similar points of view. Rainer Braun's analysis, while claiming too much in the area of influence, is still useful in pointing to themes of con-
gruence between Greek philosophy and writings and the book of Qoheleth: (1)
justice avails nothing, either for the practitioner or for the world; (2) truth cannot
be obtained; (3) both sides of a case concerning the veracity of an argument may
be equally argued to the point that it is impossible to differentiate what is true
from what is less true or even false; (4) it is impossible to know beforehand the
outcome of an action; (5) the divine is far removed from human perception or
experience and cannot be known; and (6) the human quest to determine the good
is doomed, epistemologically speaking, from the beginning.[106]

Qoheleth moves from theological affirmations, which are not self-evident and
based on experience and rational reflection, to humanism, in which human qualities, activities, and experiences provide reasonable answers verified empirically to
important philosophical questions. Central to Qoheleth is his quest to determine
"what is the good in human living" (*mah-ṭôb lā'ādām baḥayyîm,* מה טוב לאדם בחים).
In discovering this "good," it would be possible to construct a reflective life that
would enable one to build upon this central feature a way of thinking and behav-
ing that would prove both meaningful and successful. Thus moral behavior
required a "good" or a criterion for assessing what was good or evil as well as an
absolute ground for knowledge and behavior. Qoheleth searched for this "good"
in a variety of activities, accomplishment, honor, or teaching that would endure
the critical scrutiny of his own penetrating criticism. Yet he was unable to discover
it in anything that he tried. Thus it was impossible to construct a consistent moral
system, for there was no absolute ground. Even justice and wisdom, two major

sapiential virtues, could not assure one of the advantages to living a moral life based upon them, because human experience could not demonstrate that justice existed, and wisdom, severely limited by the constrictions imposed by the hidden God, offered no advantage to the sage. Unlike his ancestors, whom he disputed, Qoheleth was unable to shape a worldview reflective of perceived reality that then could be used to evaluate and judge human society and individual behavior. Tradition was nothing more than the vaguely remembered musings of dead sages that provided no insight into the reality of present existence. Their views were but mere opinions that bore no substantive weight.

In a way, Qoheleth's quest bears the hallmarks of the tragic, for he is undone by the impossibility of success based on an identified virtue. Yet, unlike Homer's heroes, humans who are remembered for great deeds, Qoheleth speaks of the failures of collective memory to preserve the accomplishments of even the most significant people of the past. Even Qoheleth's own name is not preserved, although his writing and his title have been transmitted for many centuries. Nonassertion, central to Skepticism, did lead ultimately to tranquility and the cessation of anxiety. Deeply distraught over the failure of his quest and the meaningless of life he was forced to declare, Qoheleth still is able finally to accept nonassertion, and to turn then to the joy that may be obtained in human living. Tranquility based on nonassertion is the state of life to be achieved, according to the Skeptics, while both the Egyptian tomb autobiographies and Qoheleth find in the joie de vivre the goal to which people are to aspire. The one caveat for Qoheleth is that "joy" is the "gift" of the capricious God, who imparted it only to those who pleased him. Yet how to please him is never stated.

Unlike many of the Skeptics, however, Qoheleth did not, of course, deny the existence of "the God." Since the sixth century BCE, most Greek philosophers rejected, strongly criticized, or lampooned the mythic depictions of the Olympian deities, although many continued to have some conception of the Divine. Qoheleth does not explicitly deny "the God," but his views about the hidden God are clearly meant to deconstruct the portraits of various tradents and composers in Israel's and Judah's literary and religious past. Qoheleth's acceptance of the reality of "the Deity" was an opinion without certainty; but, not doubting the existence of God, he still viewed this being in terms of a divine power concealed in a canopy of divine mystery that emitted only the characteristic of capriciousness. "The God" determined the movements of human history, decided human fate, aribtrarily chose those who would receive his gift of "joy," and was a frightening power who could bring destruction at any moment of his own choosing. Indeed, the inability of human beings to develop a cosmology or course of history based on their observations was due to the restrictions imposed by God. Humans could not penetrate the veil of mystery covering time and event, and thus they were left in the darkness of their own bewilderment. This made it impossible for even a sage to imagine a world of sacred dwelling in which divine presence and action shaped a beneficent sphere of justice. Indeed, Qoheleth saw a world filled with corruption and oppression, based on authoritarian power, and not a cosmos in which retribution operated to secure righteousness and well-being. This is the world that God has made.

Epicurus has often been misinterpreted and maligned in supposedly teaching the unrestricted pursuit of pleasure. This is a caricature of a great philosopher. Epicurus did teach that "pleasure is the beginning and end of living happily" (*Men.* 128), but also that its opposite, pain, was to be avoided. The highest degree of pain is unsatisfied desire; but, at the same time, the lust that drives humans to satiate their passions normally resulted in pain, not pleasure. Thus Epicurus taught that more important than pleasure was *ataraxia*, "freedom from disturbance."[107] This was the state the philosopher should seek to attain. Qoheleth did taste of the variety of pleasures of the senses, but discovered that they too were not lasting, the fundamental criterion of his quest. Thus he taught a medium ground between the desire for wisdom and pleasure that would be the proper state for the sage to seek to achieve. Joy, if experienced, was the one experience that made life livable.

THE BOOK OF QOHELETH

Scribes in the Hellenistic Period: The Ptolemaic and Seleucid Empires

With Judah's entrance into the Hellenistic world of the Ptolemies and Seleucids and beyond into the larger eastern Mediterranean world, Jewish sages and their compositions increased dramatically in number, and, added to the material culture and the epigraphy of the period, provide a clear look into the profession of the sage and the lives, fictionalized as well as historical, of leading intellectuals. By far the most important literary creation was the Septuagint (LXX), which provides literary and hermeneutical information about the scribes in what would become canonical, deuterocanonical, and pseudepigraphical literature composed in Greek. The Hebrew terms for scribes, *sōpēr* (ספר) and *šōtēr* (שטר),[108] were translated by *grammateus* (γραμματεύς), meaning in the LXX those scribes who, in various occupations, possessed the still rare ability to read and write. In the LXX and other Jewish Greek literature of the period, these roles included royal officials, administrators, financial accountants, army scribes, clerks, teachers, lawyers, and officials. In the LXX Pentateuch, judges and lawyers were given the title *grammatoeisagōgeus* (γραμματοεισαγωγεύς), meaning a magistrate or official of letters.

Another document that provides some insight into the nature and activity of the Jewish scribes during the Hellenistic period is the "Seleucid Charter," recorded by Josephus (*Ant.* 12.138–44). Josephus explains that Antiochus III sent letters to his governors to inform them of the privileges he had granted the Jews. While Josephus quotes three of these letters, one is especially important for understanding the Jewish scribe (*Ant.* 12.142). In speaking of the right of the Jews to practice their own religion, exemption from taxation was enjoyed by the personnel of the Jerusalem temple, which included the priests, the "scribes of the temple" (*grammateis tou hierou*, γραμματεῖς τοῦ ἱεροῦ), and the temple singers. If Josephus is accurate, then this document refers to a group of scribes functioning in the temple shortly after the time of Qoheleth and during or just before the activity of Ben Sira. We can only guess what their duties associated with the temple would have involved, but certainly they would have included composing and interpreting commandments and the Torah, writing compositions for the liturgical services, maintaining the archive, keeping financial records of gifts, and administering the various operations. While they would have been under the authority of the high priest and the priestly hierarchy, they still would have possessed considerable power in the most important and influential Jewish institution in Judah during the Hellenistic period.

Qoheleth and the Scribe in the Ptolemaic Period

The scribal profession expanded rapidly during the Ptolemaic period, as demonstrated by references to them in contemporary literature, including numerous compositions and extensive examples of epigraphy. Scribes served in professions requiring their services in all areas of the empire, from the administration of the royal court to the local towns. The large number of Greek epigraphic materials, in addition to those in Aramaic and Hebrew, demonstrates that Greek was well known and used in Judea as well as in other provinces. The conducting of business required scribes who were skilled in the reading and writing of documents. Demotic Egyptian may have been known by at least some well-educated Jewish scribes in Judah and Egypt. It would be hard to imagine that Qoheleth and the students he taught were not familiar with the languages and some of the texts of this broader cultural world.

The Social Status of the Teacher in the Epilogue[108]

The testament of Qoheleth is written in Hebrew by a wealthy Jewish sage, a teacher, who likely taught in a wisdom school in or near Jerusalem in the final quarter of the third century BCE.[109] The epilogue (12:9–14), composed by a traditional scribe who was the second voice occasionally heard in the text (11:9b)[110] and who edited the book, writes what Fishbane describes as a colophon similar to others found at the end of numerous ancient Near Eastern texts.[111] Indeed, the epilogue reads like an obituary. This traditional scribe taught the "fear (*yir'â*, יראה) of God," moral discernment and action, obedience to the Torah, and retributive justice. This suggests he would have been a sage similar to the traditional *ḥākām* (חכם) represented by Ben Sira, Theodotus, and Philo the Poet.[112] He warns the audience against the skepticism of Qoheleth and notes that too much study and composing is dangerous. Instead, one should "fear God and keep his commandments," the major emphases of Second Temple wisdom.

In the epilogue this editor writes that Qoheleth was a sage (*ḥākām*, חכם) who "taught" (*limmad*, למד)[113] the "people" (*'am*, עם)[114] "knowledge" (*da'at*, דעת,

12:9).[115] The traditional epilogist notes that Qoheleth also engaged in several other scribal activities. He composed "collections" (*mĕšālîm*, משלים; cf. Proverbs) and redacted sayings (*dĕbārîm*, דברים, v. 11) of various sapiential forms, described as "ordering" (*ʾizzēn*, אזן), "examining" (*ḥiqqēr*, חקר), and "editing" (*tiqqēn*, תקן). The "sayings" in verse 11 are the "sayings of the wise" (*dibrê ḥăkāmîm*, דברי חכמים, i.e., the sayings of the ancestral sages). These words provide guidance in wise and righteous behavior and in providing order in life. *Mĕšālîm* (משלים), "collections," the plural of Hebrew *māšāl* (משל, "saying"), are assemblings of wisdom forms on the basis of formal and/or thematic features.

Qoheleth as a Sage

Placing Qoheleth in the last quarter of the third century,[116] I suggest that the teacher used the fiction of a Solomonic (royal) testament (12:9–14) that is similar to two Egyptian forms: the autobiography found on tombs and Egyptian sapiential royal testaments.[117] He taught in a cosmopolitan Jewish Ptolemaic school (intimated in the epilogue in 12:9–14 especially in the comment that he "taught the people [or 'students'] knowledge," 12:9b) in Jerusalem. He may have been a man of considerable means (2:4–9), or at least represents himself so fictionally, donning the guise of Solomon. The elegance and learned character of his writing indicate that his family would have had to expend considerable funds in order for him to achieve this level of education, learning in a school and perhaps from paid tutors. The accurate description of the estate in chapter 2 indicates a familiarity with this type of expansive household and suggests that he himself may have lived in this type of social and economic environment.

In additon to the epilogue, the variety of sapiential forms also identifies him as a learned and wise composer: the testament, different types of proverbs, rhetorical questions, instructions, admonitions, prohibitions, didactic poems, and lists. In addition, the term *hākām* (חכם) is frequently found, and the vocabulary reflects the language present in other wisdom books.[118] Wisdom topics he addresses include creation, retribution (or justice), epistemology, cosmology, anthropology, morality, joy, greed, family, the contrast between the righteous and the wicked, the king, women, speech, hard work, and the brevity of human life. Yet he is distinctive in articulating a deeply ingrained skepticism about sapiential themes. He also leaves unmentioned a theology of salvation history centering on the ancestors, exodus, wilderness, and conquest (or entrance into the land), although it would be inappropriate to regard him as ahistorical. Indeed, what causes him considerable consternation is the conclusion that God has denied to humans a comprehensive understanding of time and history. He mentions King David, the royal institution, and the temple, but no Zion theology belies his comments. In addition, his own distinctive themes include the mystery and caprice of "the God"; the use of the distancing term to describe the separation of God in heaven and humans on earth, the impersonal expression "the God"; and especially the pivotal terms *hebel* (הבל), probably best translated as "ephemerality," and a "chasing after wind," likely the inability of humans to retain the life-giving spirit.[119]

THE GENRE AND LITERARY STRUCTURE OF QOHELETH

The Genre of Qoheleth

The issue of the genre of the book has been much debated over the years, with little that is fresh added to the discussion.[120] The book of Qoheleth has typically been considered as one of the following: sayings collections, first-person testaments, and internal disputations between a radical sage and his conservative opponent.[121] In regard to literary criticism, the book has been seen to reflect either unity or variation pointing to a composite text. If regarded to be a sayings collection,[122] similar to those in Proverbs, it also contains didactic poems. Viewed in this way, the book of Qoheleth is a collection of sayings of a wise teacher on a variety of topics that assume the individual forms of proverbs, instructions, poems, and first-person observations (cf. 12:9–12), held together by a loose rhetorical structure.

A second understanding regards the brief text to be a wisdom testament or autobiography, occasionally fictional, written in the first person (see 1:12–2:26; 3:10–4:16; 5:12–6:6; 7:15–10:7). The person speaking tells of his/her personal experience, relates it to one or more sapiential virtues, and offers general instruction in a variety of matters.[123]

A third view is that Qoheleth is a philosophical essay, known in Hellenistic Greece, that included private reflections on the efforts to discover meaning and used *chreia* and the diatribe, especially common for Cynics and Stoics.[124] These essays consist of a reflection containing a statement of purpose or theme and a subsequent discussion and evaluation, an instruction containing a warning, and a diatribe in which an imaginary opponent is debated.[125] Qoheleth also contains other Greek parallels. These include the fiction of the philosopher king, for example, "The Cynic Hero and Cynic King," the latter being both a ruler and a teacher of students.[126] In addition the pessimism about the advantages of wealth and wisdom in Qoheleth is paralleled by similar pessimism in Greek popular philosophies.

Comparative studies have usually pointed to three literary types found in Egypt that provide important form-critical and thematic comparisons to Qoheleth: "The Songs of the Harper," grave inscriptions, and royal testaments of deceased kings.[127] I would suggest that the literary form of Qoheleth combines the tomb autobiography with the fiction of a royal Egyptian testament issued from the grave. Other canonical and pseudepigraphical Jewish texts provide evidence of the substantial presence of this literary form in Israelite and Jewish literature: the testament of David (1 Kgs. 2:1–12), the *Testament of the Twelve Patriarchs*, and the *Testament of Job*.[128] The fictional setting given for each of these is the approaching death of the patriarch or ruler, who wishes to instruct his descendants on how to live the moral life.

The sage who composed the book of Qoheleth chose the literary convention of a deceased king, in this case Solomon, to address a school of wisdom students on what he has learned from his many experiences. Pseudonymity is common in sapiential writings as well as most of the Tanakh (e.g., Proverbs, the *Testament of the Twelve Patriarchs*, the *Testament of Job*, *Pirke Abot*, the "Instruction of Ptah-hotep," the "Instruction of Amenemhet," and the "Instruction of Ahiqar").[129] The second narrator's voice, who also was likely the editor, ignores this convention and identifies Qoheleth with the author of the book.[130]

Royal testaments and grave autobiographies present the fiction of a dead person who, speaking from the tomb, undertakes to instruct the living in the wisdom of life.[131] This fiction of the royal voice fits well the tradition of the ruler's wisdom used in governing his/her kingdom.[132]

The Literary Structure of the Book

The literary structure of Qoheleth is built on the central theme of the book: *carpe diem* ("seize the day"), which is repeated seven times in strategic parts.[133]

Frame 1:1–11 and 11:9–12:14

Introduction		*Conclusion*	
1:1	Title	12:9–14	Epilogue
1:2	Theme: "Breath of breaths," says Qoheleth. "Breath of breaths. All is breath."	12:8	Theme: "Breath of breaths," says Qoheleth. "All is breath."
1:3	Central Question: "What remains to a person from all the labor at which one toils under the sun?"		
1:4–11	Two-Stanza Poem Cosmology (vv. 4–7) Anthropology (toil; vv. 8–11)	11:7–12:7	Two-Stanza Poem Anthropology: *Carpe Diem* (11:7–10) Cosmology and Death (12:1–8)

Internal Structure: 1:12–11:6

I. 1:12–5:19 Cosmology, Anthropology, and the Moral Order: Human Action
    Key Refrain: "Breath (and a striving after life's spirit)"

    1:12–18   Twofold Introduction to Sections I and II
    A. 1:12–2:26   Solomon's Accomplishments
        Carpe Diem: Conclusion (2:24–26)
    B. 3:1–15   Time (human toil and divine action)
        Carpe Diem: Interlude (3:12–13)
    C. 3:16–22   Judgment and Human Nature
        Carpe Diem: Conclusion (3:22)
    D. 4:1–5:19   Royal Rule and the Cult
        Carpe Diem: Conclusion (5:17–19)

THE THEOLOGY OF THE BOOK OF QOHELETH

Introduction

The form and artistry of the testament are such that to divide the materials into themes, without considering how these intertwine with the literary shaping of the text, would violate the meaning of the text. Of course, this is true of all literature, but it is especially true of this text in the wisdom corpus of the Tanakh. The testament is enclosed within two poems that form a remarkable inclusio that establishes the parameters for the quest for the "good": creation and anthropology. The repetitive expression of the testament first occurs in 1:2 and serves as an inclusio in 12:8, with numerous occurrences within the two framing locations:

hăbēl hăbālîm (הבל הבלים), says Qoheleth,
hăbēl hăbālîm (הבל הבלים), all is *hābel* (הבל).

Occurring thirty-eight times, *hebel* is the leitmotif in the testament and contains in this text a restricted semantic range of meaning.[134] Scholars have most frequently defined *hebel* as meaning:

1. "vanity," in the sense of meaninglessness, emptiness.[135]
2. "absurdity," that is, a disparity between what is reasonably expected and what occurs, or the irrational that negates "human actions of significance and undermines morality."[136]
3. "absurdity," that is, the inconsistent, unpredictable, and mysterious.[137]
4. "ephemerality," meaning everything associated with humans quickly passes.[138]

To determine which of these contains the root meaning of the term, one should also consider its relationship to the metaphorical phrase *rĕ'ût* (*ra'yôn*) *rûaḥ*, רוח (רעיון) רעות, which occurs seven times (1:14; 2:11, 17, 26; 4:4, 16; 6:9) and is used to point to the result of the effort to find meaning in human existence.

The literal meaning of *hebel* (הבל), of course, is "breath" (see Job 7:16; 9:29; Pss. 39:6–7, 12; 62:10; 94:11; 144:4). In my judgment, Qoheleth uses this metaphor to evoke the imagination to visualize and recognize the experience of ephemerality or evanescence. For example, in 6:12 Qoheleth writes, "For who knows what is good for one while living the few days of one's brief (*hebel*, הבל) life, for he [God] has made them like a shadow?" Thus human life and individual days are viewed through the metaphorical lens of breath, that which is quickly fleeting. This root meaning does not negate the expansive connotations of absurdity, futility, and vanity, but these take a secondary place to evanescence. I suggest the repeated expression *hakkol hebel ûrĕ'ût rûaḥ* (הכל הבל ורעות רוח) in 1:14; 2:11, 17, 16; 4:4, 16; and 6:9 should be translated: "all is ephemeral and a desire for [life's] vital spirit." Human existence and accomplishments are ephemeral. Even so this does not negate the fact that humans still possess the desire to retain the life-giving breath given them by the Creator (Qoh. 12:7; Ps. 104:30).[139] I take the word *rĕ'ût* to be equated with Aramaic *rĕ'a'* (רעא), meaning "to take pleasure in, to desire."[140] The latter term is also frequent in late Hebrew.[141] Thus the internal consternation of humans is that they are ephemeral creatures desiring the impossible: to retain the divine spirit that animates human life. Thus a more elegant translation would be: "all is breath quickly passing and a desire to retain life's animating spirit."

The leitmotif of *hebel* ("ephemerality") is followed by the central question of the first section.

> What is the *yitrôn* (יתרון) to a person in all his labor,
> at which one labors under the sun?
>
> (1:3)

Translating *yitrôn* as "profit," this question is a rhetorical one with an expected negative answer: life's actions are without profit. This rhetorical question underscores Qoheleth's view that life is ultimately meaningless. *Yitrôn* is found only in Qoheleth and is usually translated "profit" or "advantage."[142] However, the verb *yātar* (יתר) means "to remain" in 1 Sam. 25:34. Qoheleth desires to find something that endures beyond the limited lifespan of a human being, something that would enable one to live beyond the grave, at least in human memory. Thus *yitrôn* in Qoheleth intimates "continuation" or "endurance." This question prompts him, in the role of the famous and wealthy King Solomon, to initiate his quest to find an answer, a quest that breaks down into the two major parts in the structure of his testament: doing and finding.

The other important word in this programmatic question (1:3) is *'āmāl* (עמל), meaning "toil," "labor," and "activity." Qoheleth has in mind onerous toil. This term occurs thirty-five times in Qoheleth. C.-L. Seow submits that the word "refers to the routine struggle of humanity to achieve some end or other. Toil is the tiresome effort expended over an enterprise of dubious result."[143]

A Poem on Cosmology and Anthropology: 1:4–11

Following the introduction is a poem on cosmology and anthropology. The two strophes of this introductory poem (1:4–11) establish the parameters of the entire testament:[144] the cosmos endures, while human individuals do not.[145] For Qoheleth, two things endure forever. The first is the cosmos, and the second is the grave (12:5—humanity's "eternal home"). Everything else is ephemeral. It is within these two frames of eternity (the cosmos—1:4, and the grave—12:5) that historical time occurs (1:12–11:8). Diachronically the movement of the literary structure of the testament is from creation, to history, to death,[146] which cycle is paralleled by human life (birth, existence, death).

While each generation of humanity quickly passes, it is followed by the unending succession of others. The nature of the cosmos is characterized by endless motion, the blowing of the wind, the rising and setting of the sun, and the running waters of streams into the sea that never fills. This eternal sameness offers for Qoheleth no inspiration, or hope, or stimulus for theological imagination. Instead, this consistency represents the utter tedium experienced by observing these movements of the entities of the cosmos. Likewise, each generation of humanity quickly passes so that there is no memory of former times.[147]

This poem rejects the traditional understanding of creation and providence.[148] Indeed, these are absent from the entire testament. The activity in the world lacks any observable evidence of divine providence or purpose. God is absent not only from the poem but also from the cosmos.[149] This contrasts with the majestic portrayal of the Creator in Ps. 104:29–30 in which the Creator continues to breathe life into existence and to send life-giving water in the form of rain. The constant movement of the elements fails to evoke human praise, but rather only wearies the human spirit.[150]

The second strophe on anthropology correlates with the two major parts of the larger testament: knowing and doing. In traditional wisdom, the three major faculties (speech, sight, and hearing) are the gifts of God that allow humans to discover and create knowledge. These three human faculties equal the number of the three active agents of the cosmos in the first strophe. For Qoheleth, the faculties and rational analysis of experience do not lead to the discovery of the meaning of human existence or the nature and character of "the God."

Even Qoheleth's Deity, "the God," is not present in this poem, either directing nature or acting providentially in history. God cannot be observed to be active in the processes of nature. Even the observation of the movement of the forces in nature, coupled with the awareness of the succession of the generations, provides no opportunity for the sages to discover insight for living. Qoheleth's skepticism about the obtaining of knowledge begins with his failure to discover in providence, cosmology, and anthropology any basis for wisdom's underpinning and cultivation.[151]

Verses 9–10 note humanity's innate desire to accomplish something lasting that will enable them to be remembered and later honored by the successive generations. However, all that humans effectuate already has been done before them. Thus there is nothing new. Even the comings and goings of generations, along with their deeds, is a continuing process that leads to weary observations.[152]

The phrase "under the sun" occurs twenty-nine times in Qoheleth (1:3, 9, 14; 2:3, 11, 17, 18, 19, 20, 22; 3:1, 16; 4:1, 3, 7, 15; 5:12, 17; 6:1, 12; 8:9, 15, 17; 9:3, 6, 9, 11, 13; 10:5), while "under the heavens" is found three times (1:13; 2:3; 3:1). These related metaphors in this poem and indeed in the entire book have the effect of distancing humanity from God. Humans are limited to the earth, while "the God" dwells in the heavens (5:1).[153] Since this sage regards the divine world as closed to human perception, "the God" is mysterious and remote.

The implications of Qoheleth's understanding of human life occurring within the framework of a world that experiences motion but no change and the inability of humans to influence this reality are stunning.[154] Social oppression, whether dictated by the mysterious, unknowable Deity or caused by the injustice of the powerful, knows no constraints. Humans without power have no ability or divine ally to defend themselves against the wicked. One unavoidable consequence of this skepticism is that it supports the status quo of a corrupt social world.[155]

The Twofold Introduction: 1:13–15, 16–18

Following this poetic beginning, Qoheleth begins to search for something in human character or an action that produces something that endures (1:12–5:19). The larger literary structure for this quest comprises the two sections of cosmology and anthropology. The body of the two-part testament has a double introduction, each concluding with "a desire for the spirit" (vv. 14, 17). The sage follows Hellenistic tradition by referring to his own ancestry (1:1, 12), being a "son of David" and king over Jerusalem. The establishment of a noble lineage is a way to capture social status (see Plutarch, *Lives,* and Tacitus, *Agr.* 4.1). This same tradition is found in early rabbinic and Christian texts (cf., e.g., *Gen. Rab.* 33; Matt. 1:2–17; Luke 3:23–38), while even Josephus claimed royal descent from the Hasmoneans (*Life* 2, 4).

Qoheleth announces it is his intention to use wisdom to investigate (*lidrôs*, לדרש) and to search (*lātûr*, לתור)[156] everything "which is done under heaven," that is, all cosmic movements and human actions. In anticipating what he concludes at the end of his quest, Qoheleth observes that it is "an evil task (*'inyan rā'*, ענין רע)[157] that God has given humans to occupy themselves (לענות, *la'ănôt*)."[158] Then he states what becomes his standard conclusion: "all which is done under the sun" is *hebel* (הבל, "ephemeral"), and yet is motivated by the desire to retain the *rûaḥ* (רוח, life-giving "breath"). The teacher sets forth his reflective observation about human activities by using the word *rā'â* (ראה) to speak not only of his perception but also of his experience of something.[159] He concludes on the basis of his observation that all human efforts are *hebel*, since humans seek to create something that either endures, lengthens life, or at the very least will be remembered. Yet only "the

God" decides success and failure, sets the life spans of humans, and incarcerates them in forgetfulness. Humans seek what God denies them.

The Quest for the Good: 2:1–26

What is a sage to do, if cosmology and theology provide no basis for determining what is "the good" in human living? Piety that focuses on the Torah, mysticism that moves into the realm of apocalyptic, and nationalism that seeks independence from political oppression are three possible responses. Qoheleth, however, turns to anthropology, beginning with human activity, seeking to discover something, associated with human beings, that endures. In 2:1–26 of the first section, which concentrates on human undertakings, "Solomon" carries out and then describes his wonderful accomplishments, in a text that is based on 1 Kings 3–10. These are royal projects: the building of houses (palace and temple?—1 Kgs. 5–10), the excavation of pools (Neh. 2:14; 3:15), the planting of vineyards (Jer. 52:7; Cant. 6:2; 8:11), the cultivation of gardens and parks, and the growing of every kind of fruit tree (Gen. 2:8–9, 15–17; 2 Kgs. 25:4; Jer. 39:4; 52:7; Neh. 3:15). These images likely refer to Solomon's building activity, especially the Greek villa, replete with private and sacred landscaping, groves of trees, and pools of waters (cf. 1 Kgs. 5–10). This construction is followed by a listing of what the king possesses: flocks, silver and gold, provinces, and singers and concubines (cf. 1 Kgs. 5:2–8; 10:1–11:3). He sums up these descriptions of deeds and wealth, obtained by wisdom (cf. 1 Kgs 3:28; 5:15–26; 10:7–9), by concluding he thus surpassed all who had preceded him in Jerusalem (e.g., David and the Canaanite kings of Jerusalem; see 1 Kgs. 10:23–25).

This mentioning of the great accomplishments also occurs in the grave biographies and royal instructions of Egypt. These were normally self-testimonies that spoke of the deceased person's virtuous actions that placed him/her within the harmonious order of cosmos and society, thus meriting not only continuation in human memory but also entrance into the afterlife.

It is not a coincidence that "the great works" of Solomon are placed in seven sections (cf. the sevenfold occurrence of the *carpe diem*). Each of the seven sections consists of a poetic couplet. In all of the things Solomon achieved and acquired, the single benefit from his toil was the pleasure (*śimḥâ*, שמחה)[160] derived from his labor. This was his "portion" (*ḥēleq*, חלק),[161] that is, the divine fate set forth by "the God." Yet, as death and the passage of centuries unfailingly demonstrated, both magnificent works and individual joy soon faded and disappeared. Recognizing the ephemerality of all things, Solomon concludes with the startling announcement that he hates life. Even wisdom offers to the sage no advantage over folly. Death is inescapable even for a wise king who has done great things. Disturbing is the realization that what has been accomplished is left to a successor who may be wise or foolish. In spite of the fact that he has not labored for what he inherits, he still will rule (שלט, *šālaṭ*)[162] over what his dead predecessor, the former king, has built and acquired. This reality causes Qoheleth to hate all his toil (2:18–23). He concludes with the first occurrence of the *carpe diem*: "there is nothing better for mortals than to eat and drink and to find joy in their toil" (2:24–26). The experience of joy belongs to the "hand" (or "power") of "the Deity" (see 9:1), who gives it only to those who please (*ṭôb*, טוב) him. Even joy is fleeting, however, for it is *hebel* (הבל), an ephemeral experience that quickly fades.

The Meaning of Time: 3:1–13

Also important to Qoheleth's search for meaning in anthropology is the understanding of time. Sages sought to unravel the complexity of time in order to achieve successful outcomes (Wis. 7:15–22; cf. Prov. 27:23–27; Qoh. 3:12; Sir. 4:20).[163] In the wisdom tradition, event and time were inseparable. For actions to achieve a successful outcome, sages had to know when they were to be undertaken.[164] According to Qoheleth's poem in 3:1–13, there are episodic times for every event and its opposite that together comprise the integrative polarities of life.[165] Yet knowledge of the larger structure of time was essential for penetrating into the meaning of human existence and from there to construct a temporal reality that led to the moral life.

Qoheleth's well-known poem in 3:1–13 places episodic times for specific events within the larger context of cosmic and historical time: "there is a temporal order (זמן, *zĕmān*)[166] for all reality (הכל, *hakkol*), and an occasion (עת, *'ēt*) for every event (חפץ, *ḥēpeṣ*) under the heavens" (3:1).[167] Some fourteen pairs of opposites make up the major events of human life, ranging from birth and death to war and peace, polarities that define the place of human existence and action. The teacher expresses a view of fate in which God is ultimately responsible for all significant events within the larger structure of cosmological and historical time. This includes the birth and death of human beings. While the times for the beginning and ending of life are determined by God, the other activities may be pursued to some extent by individual choice.[168] What limits this notion of freedom is the action of the unknown God, who decides to do whatever he will when he so chooses.

For Qoheleth, humans live within the interstices of polarities, until they meet their final destiny in the tomb. He views creation within the realm of the aesthetic, if not the moral. The goodness of creation is seen in the יפה, *yāpeh*, literally "beautiful," which blossoms at its height, but only for a brief time, quickly passing. This may echo the divine evaluation of creation in Gen. 1:31 ("everything that he had made . . . was very good"), but in Genesis the expression is *ṭôb* (טוב, "good"), that is, appropriate, orderly, and complete. The problem that engages Qoheleth is the assertion that God denies even to sages any comprehension of the larger temporal order of the cosmos: God "has put eternity" (*ōlām*, עלם)[169] into humanity's mind (see 1:4, 10; 2:16; 9:6; 12:5; and especially 3:14) within which these events occur (cf. 8:17 and 11:5), but does not reveal how they fit together in the larger temporal structure.

Consequently, the correlation of episodic, human action with divinely determined times is impossible within the larger temporal order of 'ōlām. Thus humans are enclosed within a mysterious present not knowing what may happen. They are at the mercy of either fate or chance. Humans pursue actions, but they cannot know their outcome. One may only rejoice in the "day of prosperity" and learn from the "day of adversity" that God is the one who structures time and determines the course of significant occurrences (7:14).[170] Thus all actions are accompanied by unlimited risk.[171]

The inability to discern divine activity and time contradicts the theologies of salvation history and cultic ritual that reactualized them in sacred drama and festive times. The individual and the community come to self-understanding through the narrative worlds they construct and in which they live. Thus individual life is a constituent dimension of the community's past experience, present existence, and anticipated future. The crisis for Qoheleth is the inevitable loss of collective (1:8–11) and individual (5:20) memory. With the loss of memory, experience does not achieve unity through time. Rather experience fragments into disconnected pieces of isolated perceptions. All that remains is the isolation of the present moment.[172]

Divine Actions and Time: 3:14–22

In 3:14–22 Qoheleth argues that humans, unlike "the God," do not possess the ability to "search out what already has transpired" (יבקש את-נרדף, yĕbaqqēš 'et-nirdāp), that is, the past that humans forget and the future that they cannot anticipate, and to transform time and experience (past, present, and future) into a coherent whole. The tragedy for humans is that "the God" does not reveal to them the direction or movement of history. Nevertheless, the mystery and power of "the God" at work in directing the course of events within a temporal framework forms the basis for human piety. Here "piety" is not respectful worship, but rather the angst created by fearful foreboding of the unknown.

In 3:14–22 Qoheleth begins by remarking that, in contrast to the actions of humans, whatever "the God" does endures forever. He further notes in an enigmatic statement: "God searches out what already has transpired (yĕbaqqēš 'et-nirdāp)," meaning that only divine memory recalls past actions and may lead to their repetition. The teacher then refers to his observation of the injustice that characterizes human actions in the "place of judgment" (the court; 3:16), a remark made all the more poignant by the fact that kings bear responsibility for justice (Ps. 73) and serve as supreme judges (cf. 1 Kgs. 3). While Qoheleth appears to affirm there is a time that God establishes for eschatological judgment (Qoh. 3:17), he quickly reverses himself.[173] The judgment of "the God" serves only to demonstrate that humans and animals share the same nature and fate—death.

Qoheleth alludes to the tradition of the creation of humanity (Gen. 2 and elsewhere) when he concludes that humans and animals have the same animating "spirit" (רוח, rûaḥ; see Ps. 104:29–30; Job 27:3; Isa. 42:5) and at death return to the same place: the "dust" (עפר, *ʿāpār*) of the earth (Gen. 3:19; Pss. 104:29; 146:4; Job 10:9; 34:15).[174] The apocalyptic teaching that at death the spirit (*rûaḥ*) of humans returns to God, while that of animals goes down to the earth (*ʾereṣ*),[175] thus suggesting some sort of heavenly afterlife, is for Qoheleth impossible to know. Elsewhere, Qoheleth notes that death is oblivion (e.g., 8:10). He does indicate in 12:7 that at death "the dust returns to the earth and the spirit (*rûaḥ*) returns to the God who gave it." However, this occurs in the context of the grave as the eternal home of humankind (12:1–8). For Qoheleth, at death the divine breath that animates human life returns to its source. Qoheleth's view in chapter 3 opposes the apocalyptic sages, who say there is an afterlife.[176] There is in this sage's text no reference to the tradition of human beings who rule over the creatures as God's surrogate (Gen. 1:26–28; Ps. 8). Qoheleth has no reference to sacred time (contrast Ben Sira), thus offering no possible cultic reactualization of salvific events of divine creation and redemption.

Kingship and Temple: 4:1–5:19

Qoheleth then approaches the related topics of kingship and temple, related since kings were responsible for maintaining royal religion and the operation of the state sanctuary (4:1–5:19; cf. 1 Kgs. 5:15–8:56). Kingship is a common topic in wisdom literature, in large measure due to the fact that rulers, at least prior to the fall of Jerusalem in 587 BCE, were patrons of wisdom. However, the specific royal theology centering on the house of David is not articulated (contrast 2 Sam. 7 and Ps. 89). The traditional sages respected and feared kings and taught prudence and discretion in their presence (Prov. 16:1–8, 14–15). The sages thought that kingship was based on the cosmic order and that rulers were responsible for sustaining a just and prosperous society in line with the divine structure and justice of creation. The best example of this is the statement that the throne is *biṣdāqâ yikkôn* (בצדקה יכון): "established in/by means of righteousness" (Prov. 16:12).[177] "Established" (*kûn*, כון) is a common term for divine creation and maintaining the order of the cosmos (Prov. 3:19–20; 8:27). If the preposition *bĕ* (ב) is taken to be a locative ("in"), the saying indicates that the institution of monarchy is grounded "in" the cosmic order. If the preposition *bĕ* (ב) is given an instrumental meaning, then the saying teaches that the stability of the throne (and subsequently the entire social order) is secured "by means of" the king's righteous rule (cf. Prov. 20:29 [LXX]; 25:5). Furthermore, the traditional sages believed that God chose kings to rule, endowed them with wisdom and righteousness, and required justice from them (Prov. 8:15–16). The gifts of God offered to kings through Woman Wisdom are riches, honor, and life (Prov. 8:17–21, 32–36). The traditional sages did not openly criticize kings and kingship, since rulers were their patrons, and their own ideology was based on cosmic and social order that legitmated the monarchy.

Solomon, however, considered in sapiential tradition to be both the patron of the sages and wisest of all kings (1 Kgs. 3–10), criticizes royal rule, undermining the theological basis for the legitimation of the monarchy. Qoheleth, speaking as Solomon, observes "oppression" (ʿāšaq, עשׁק) in society, a term usually associated with the abuse of lowly placed people: slaves, corvée workers, day laborers, the poor, widows, and orphans (Jer. 22:13–19; Ezek. 22:6–12, 29). The prophets censured rulers for two reasons: many denied justice to the poor and often defenseless persons that was guaranteed to them by God, and rulers refused to extend the poor mercy (Amos 2:6–8; 4:1–3). God was often depicted in the prophetic traditions as the special protector of the poor, who would see to it that their rights and necessary support were maintained (Jer. 22:2–5). Isaiah even notes that God was the one who would wipe away the "tears of the oppressed" (Isa. 25:8). An important feature of sapiential ethics was to provide for the needs of the poor (Prov. 14:31; 22:16; 28:27), but the traditional sages avoided any criticism of monarchs or the institution of kingship.

When Solomon speaks in chapters 4–5, it is to articulate his observation that the powerful "oppress" (ʿāšaq, עשׁק) victims. There is no expression of divine championing of the poor, condemnation of rulers for social injustice, or any reference to corrupt leaders facing divine retribution. The monarchy for Qoheleth is grounded in "power" (kôaḥ, כֹּח), which includes oppressive rule. Standing behind this abuse is God himself. Seeing this is true, Qoheleth then opposes the tradition of the creation of humanity by declaring not only that the dead are better off than the living, but that more fortunate than the living or the dead is the "one who has not been, and has not experienced the evil deeds that are done under the sun" (4:3). This strongly pessimistic conclusion is similar to Job's opening soliloquy (chap. 3) and Jeremiah's lament (20:14–18) in which both curse their conception and birth.[178]

Qoheleth presents a brief discourse and set of instructions that broach the topic of priestly religion and the temple cult (4:17–5:6), which are under the oversight of the house of David.[179] The Solomonic tradition, shaped by Deuteronomistic editors, pays significant attention to the building of the temple and to the inauguration of the royal cult (1 Kgs. 5:15–8:65). In his lengthy prayer in 1 Kings 8, Solomon emphasizes in a Deuteronomistic speech that God's all-encompassing presence could not be contained even by heaven and earth, much less the temple (8:27–30), and that social justice is an important responsibility of kings, for God responds to the pleas of the afflicted (8:22–61). Solomon then sets forth the various situations in which prayers, especially laments and oaths, will be offered, asking God to hear these prayers and respond in justice and mercy. After the royal blessing upon God and Israel (8:54–61), peace offerings (22,000 oxen and 120,000 sheep), a burnt offering, a cereal offering, and a great feast ensue. In the Deuteronomistic formulation of Solomon's speech, the temple and its cultic activities are necessary for maintaining the covenant relationship with God, especially when Israel has sinned. Sin violates the integrity of the covenant, causes a breach in the relationship with God, and leads to punishment. By means of the cultic activities of prayer, blessing, and sacrifice, however, the breach may be repaired and the well-being of both nation and repentant sinners restored.

The renewed emphasis on the temple and the "prince" (nāśîʾ, נשׂיא) in the blueprint for restoration in Ezekiel 40–48, the rebuilding of the temple as reflected in

Ezra and Nehemiah, and the major themes of the prophetic books of Haggai and Zechariah were extensions of this tradition in the Second Temple. The temple ritual was to secure divine blessings for the king (on occasion directed to the foreign ruler), the nation, and the worshipers. Even after the end of the monarchy, messianic hope was kept alive for its restoration. Yahweh was understood as the "king" of all nations and the creator of both the cosmos and humanity. Because of the presence of Yahweh in the temple, Jerusalem came to be understood as the center of the earth (Pss. 46, 48, and 87) from where shalom radiated throughout the earth.

This temple tradition, renewed and augmented in the postexilic period, especially in the final redaction of the Priestly source, is absent from Qoheleth. It is interesting that the teacher, speaking as King Solomon, makes no mention whatsoever of the Zion tradition in this instruction offered about the temple and cultic worship. He also does not draw on the theology of the Davidic covenant. Jerusalem is mentioned only in the prologue as the dwelling place of the royal teacher (1:1). Eventually, Zion theology is integrated into the conservative wisdom tradition, as evidenced in the book of Ben Sira, but not so in Qoheleth.

The teacher's instruction about priestly religion and cultic activity in the temple, however, is quite different from Zion theology. He offers five admonitions that handle the following topics: sacrifice, prayer, vows, willful sin, and piety. In the first admonition, Qoheleth sets the mood for the entire instruction: "Be on your guard when you approach the house of God" (4:17). This caution should characterize one's activity in the cultic realm, since it is possible to experience destruction in the performance of religious duties. This admonition is supported by a "better" saying: "to draw near to listen is better than the sacrifice of fools, who do not know that they are practicing evil." Qoheleth characterizes foolish behavior as including the offering of sacrifices, and prefers silence to the utterance of cultic prayers (which would have included hymns, thanksgivings, and laments).

Prayer (להוצי דבר, *lĕhôṣî' dābār*) is addressed in the second prohibition. One should be careful not to speak to God in haste, for "God is in heaven and you are upon the earth; therefore let your words be few" (5:1). In Deut. 4:39, to which Qoheleth alludes, God is in heaven and on the earth, but Qoheleth makes no mention of divine presence on the earth, and that would include the temple. God and humanity dwell in different spheres of reality. The Deuteronomistic History makes the point in Solomon's temple dedication that God's presence could not be limited to the sacred precincts of the temple (1 Kgs. 8:27–30). Solomon, speaking in Qoheleth, underlines the distance between the transcendent and mysterious Deity and the human world, leading to God's hiddenness. Cultic action could have no positive influence in leading to divine blessing, thereby directly contradicting priestly theology and the central emphasis on prayer in 1 Kings 8. Qoheleth stresses that the worshiper should exhibit a quiet demeanor when approaching the temple and avoid ostentatious display. The wisdom of the sages emerges in Qoheleth's remark that "a dream comes on account of much activity, and the voice of a fool with many words." Dreams, at times regarded as signs from the Deity, were interpreted by cultic officials (and later apocalyptic seers). For Qoheleth, dreams are not the means of divine revelation, but rather are the result of burdensome labor. Hence only fools (priestly interpreters and worshipers) speak often and long in the temple.

Vows and willful sins of the tongue (lying, false oaths) are also examples of foolish talk that Qoheleth advises his students to avoid in the third and fourth prohibitions (5:3–5). While Qoheleth intimates that it is foolish to make a vow to God, once made there is the obligation to fulfill it in good time. Qoheleth stands in agreement with Priestly and Deuteronomic teaching that it is better not to vow than to vow and then fail to pay (Deut. 23:22–24; Num. 30). In addition, Qoheleth warns against misrepresentation of a falsehood to an official of the temple, a priest to whom one was required to offer a sin offering, suggesting that the lie was only an "unconscious or inadvertent sin" (Qoh. 5:5; cf. Num. 15:22–31; Lev. 4:2, 22, 27–30). This untruth only compounds one's guilt, leading to God's destroying the "labors of one's hands."

Qoheleth's last admonition to his audience in regard to cultic religion is that they should "fear God" (5:6). Unlike the meaning of the phrase in Proverbs, Qoheleth understands that "fear of God" is dread, even terror, evoked by the unfathomable sovereign of human history. This expression does not suggest the belief that "the God" is the creator and beneficent, just ruler of the cosmos. Rather, the phrase "to fear the God" is the anxiety and terror of humans who recognize that he directs all life at his capricious discretion.[180] For Qoheleth discreet, guarded speech, not sacrifices and prayers uttered by the loquacious priests and worshipers, is the recommended behavior for temple assemblies.

It is ironic that Qoheleth as Solomon, the one in tradition who constructed the temple and served as the high priest who dedicated it with a great festival fanfare, questions the value of cultic religion. In contrast to priestly religion and traditional wisdom, Qoheleth teaches that cultic acts do not order the cosmos, do not procure divine blessing, and do not bring society into harmony with God and the world. Instead, they are primarily foolish acts that may bring destruction, if the worshiper is not careful. God is far removed from the world of human dwelling, and it is best not to draw divine attention to oneself by a misdeed or foolish act within the sacred precincts. True piety consists of fearing the mysterious God who has ultimate power over each and every life. The grand theological vision of priests and temple prophets, centered in the sacred temple and its efficacious ritual, is not present in the reflections of this sage.

There is a hierarchy of officials who oppress the poor, with each level of officials being corrupt (5:7). Unlike Proverbs, Qoheleth has no indication of God creating both the wealthy and the poor, meaning that this shared humanity is the ethical basis for charity. Qoheleth teaches that the appeal to higher officials does not aid the poor in obtaining justice.

The following verse is extremely difficult to translate and interpret. Perhaps Qoheleth has witnessed the corruption that results in the ruler's illicit possession of a cultivated field (see Ahab's means of obtaining ownership of Naboth's vineyard, 1 Kgs. 21). Yet Qoheleth does warn corrupt kings and officials that their love of money does not lead to satisfaction, that the procurement of wealth produces little more than observing one's possessions, not their use, and that wealth is easily lost so that there is nothing to leave to one's heir (vv. 9–15). Qoheleth concludes that it is senseless to labor so hard for riches and to experience only anger, sickness, and resentment instead of the joy or well-being that is the one boon in human living (see 5:17–19).

Conclusion to Section One

The first major section addresses human labor, with Solomon on occasion alluding to his own impressive accomplishments: the building of major structures, the accumulation of wealth, the enjoyment of physical pleasures, the power of royal rule, the making of legal decisions, the typical human activities that have their opposites, the success story of the poor wise son coming to the throne, and the practice of cultic activities. In every case the king concludes: each human activity and its results are ephemeral. Every action is grounded in the elusive desire to master and perpetuate life and to gain a lasting remembrance. Even activities guided by wisdom cannot guarantee success, which without joy lacks any real value. Thus even Solomon, Israel's most honored ruler and patron of wisdom, could neither master life nor endure forever in human memory. Labor and accomplishments devoid of joy are without value. The desire to retain the life-giving spirit is not fulfilled. Nothing remains of self and accomplishments. All is breath, ephemeral.

The Interlude: 6:1–9

Between the two major sections on doing and knowing, Qoheleth inserts a brief interlude. He begins this brief pause by speaking of the absence of joy (6:1–6). The most valued "good" in human existence, according to Qoheleth in the initial section, is the divine gift of joy that one may experience from what one does. All of life's accomplishments are ephemeral, even as existence is portrayed as breath that quickly vanishes. Subsequently, the experience of joy, while also fleeting, is the single value that one may or, for that matter, may not experience, since "the God" determines who receives this gift and when. Qoheleth continues to remind his audience that even this ephemeral value is a gift, completely dependent on the caprice of divine will.

Qoheleth, speaking as Solomon, reflects on the tragedy of the absence of joy. Two examples are given. The first (6:2) is that of humans to whom God gives great wealth, possessions, honor, and all that they desire, and yet does not grant them the capacity to enjoy them (cf. 2:24–26).[181] Instead, a stranger (*nokrî*, נכרי), not even a family member or a descendant, enjoys them (cf. 5:12–14; 6:2). The second tragic example is that of the person who begets a hundred children and lives many years and yet does not enjoy or find satisfaction in the good things of life. Thus a stillborn child, who does not experience even a brief moment of life and receive a proper burial but goes immediately into the darkness, is better off (see Job 3). To have many children and to live a long life, two sapiential values, do not lead to joy. Using hyperbole, Qoheleth emphasizes that even if this person who does not experience the good in living should endure twice a thousand years, the stillborn child who has never lived nor seen the sun is still better off. But, all in all, the same ultimate fate awaits them both: death.

The second part of the interlude deals with a variety of matters: an insatiable appetite, the lack of advantage of possessing wisdom, the lack of profit to being a wise yet poor person, and the folly of limitless desire (6:7–9). These verses indicate that joy is not to be identified with the satiation of appetites and the fulfillment of desires. God alone provides this gift that resides beyond human striving.

The Creation of Humanity: 6:10–8:15

In the second section, Qoheleth investigates human knowing (6:10–11:8). This analysis of sapiential epistemology also is stimulated by the question: "What is good to humanity in living?" Or, less literally, "What gives meaning to human life?" The topics studied are the limits of wisdom, the advantages of wisdom over folly, and the use of wisdom in mastering life. All of these topics have in common Qoheleth's affirmation of the sovereignty of the unknown God.[182] Wright has noted that the key refrains for this section are "cannot find out/who can find out?" and "do not know/no knowledge."

The first part of the second section is 6:10–8:15. In the introduction (6:10–12), Qoheleth begins with a statement about the creation of humans that originates in the Yahwist's narrative of creation in Genesis 2: what exists is that which has been "named" (*niqrā' šĕmô*, נקרא שמו, 6:10). To name something may refer to its creation in both the Bible and the ancient Near East (e.g., Isa. 40:26), to shape the object's character, and to have sovereignty over it. The name embodies the character and nature of what is created. God has named humanity (*'ādām*, אדם), says Qoheleth, that is, created them and determined their nature (Gen. 1:5, 8, 10, etc.). Thus sages, including Qoheleth, through their powers of observation come to their views of anthropology. However, the characteristic feature that Qoheleth chooses to emphasize is human weakness, especially when compared to God. Humans (*'ādām*) cannot argue with one who is stronger than they, that is, God. This view is not unlike the one expressed in Job (e.g., 9:13–19).[183]

Job's presentation of human nature, emphasizing the weakness of humanity and the inability to defeat God with sapiential disputation, may well have influenced Qoheleth's examination of epistemology. Unlike Job, however, Qoheleth does not make use of the discourse of disputation to defy God's sovereignty over the world. Rather, Qoheleth begins with an affirmation of the sovereignty of God in his quest to determine what is good in human existence. He begins this pursuit of knowledge with two questions that shape the direction and content of the entire second section: "Who knows what is good for humanity in living the few days of their ephemeral life?" "Who can tell humans what will follow them under the sun?"

The second section begins with a collection of *mĕšālîm* (7:1–14): proverbs, "better" sayings, and admonitions, as one would expect of Solomon from reading the book of Proverbs. The key emphasis in this section is placed on the term "good" (*ṭôb*, טוב), sometimes used in the construction of "better" sayings; this is "better" than or has an advantage over something else.

Ironically, the initial four sayings unexpectedly value death over life: the day of death over the day of birth, visiting the "house of mourning" (i.e., lamenting the deceased) over visiting the "house of feasting," sorrow over laughter, and taking to heart the fact of death as the end of human life. These sayings appear to be subversive aphorisms, sayings that seek to overturn the conventional worldview and its undergirding by the social knowledge of the wisdom tradition.[184] These aphorisms inform Qoheleth's audience that the world is not a place of just order ruled over by a beneficent creator, but rather a place of injustice overseen by a mysterious, capricious deity. Consequently, sapiential behavior is not capable of shaping a just world and does not lead to well-being. These aphorisms subvert the remainder of the collection, which is taken from traditional wisdom and which provides legitimation and authority to the teachings of conservative sages, for example, the rebuke of the wise is preferable to the laughter of fools.

The remaining two sayings in the collection (vv. 13–14) invoke once again the theme of divine tyranny: humans cannot alter divine works, while God creates both the good and the evil day. The good day is the day to rejoice, while the evil day is a time to reflect on the fact that "the God" is the creator of both, that he alone determines the course of events and their times in order to prevent humans from finding out anything that will occur after them.

The first-person narration begins again in 7:15. Here "Solomon" issues a first-person narrative about a righteous person he has seen who perishes in his righteousness, and a wicked person who continues to lengthen his life by evil deeds.

Once again several traditional sayings are inserted into the collection in 7:19–22, with the first emphasizing wisdom's value over many rulers. Yet Qoheleth returns to his first-person stance to engage in a subversion of traditional wisdom. Qoheleth even reports of his failures in coming to understand reality (both good and evil) in a comprehensive way through experience and knowledge. Futile were his efforts to discover wisdom, while reality ("that which is") is incapable of being understood. His experience with the seductress is probably explained in terms of the general Near Eastern metaphorical model for folly. Dame Folly leads to destruction and premature death (cf. Prov. 9:13–18).[185] Only the one whom God has favored escapes the destruction she brings, while she ensnares the one not divinely favored. Yet it is divine caprice that delivers one from folly, not one's wisdom that helps to make life-giving decisions. Qoheleth remarks that he has found only one righteous man in a thousand, but he has never found among these a righteous woman.[186] This number may allude to Solomon's seven hundred wives and three hundred concubines. Males could take little solace in the assumed superiority of their sex. Qoheleth did validate the observation that "God made humans upright, but they have sought out various devices."[187] "The

God" is not responsible for creating humans corrupt, and thus is not culpable for their wicked deeds.

Qoheleth returns again to traditional wisdom sayings, this time stressing the importance of the knowledge and the interpretive skill of the sage as well as obedience to the sovereign ruler (8:1–5). Qoheleth rejects the teaching that the sage knows how to act successfully in the presence of the king by noting that evil so clouds the mind that one is not capable of knowing how to act so as to secure the royal blessing and to avoid the king's destruction. No one is able to know the outcome of a course of action, to control the life-giving spirit, or to rule over (i.e., to determine) the day of one's death. "The God" alone has the power to give and take life, and to this power all must yield. Qoheleth does not contradict the sovereignty of the king, although his power over human beings is to their detriment. But even kings must recognize that God reigns over them as their sovereign.

Qoheleth then looks at the perplexing problem posed by the delay of the punishment of the wicked. Through means of his own investigation, he examines the issue of the burial of the wicked who repeatedly entered the holy place (the temple?) and were praised in the city (Jerusalem?) for their piety. While punishment may be delayed, eventually their day of retribution will come. They eventually die and are buried. By contrast, contends Qoheleth, the God-fearer will experience well-being, while the wicked, lacking in true piety, will not continue to lengthen their days. Is this a traditional affirmation by Qoheleth, who refuses at this point to deny that retributive justice is operative in the world? More likely it is a traditional belief that he casts aside in the next verse (v. 14): just retribution does not bring punishment to the wicked and reward to the righteous. Indeed, often the very opposite occurs. Divine sovereignty is not characterized by the Deity's governing of the world by retributive justice.

Providence and Divine Rule: 8:16–9:10

Qoheleth begins this second investigation of divine sovereignty and human wisdom by referring once again to his efforts to understand God's providential governance of the world. Yet in spite of his best efforts, Qoheleth admits he has failed. And once more he anticipates his later conclusion. From his own failure, he decides that no one may find out the principles of divine governance, not even a sage (an apocalyptic seer), who may pretend to know.

Qoheleth then states his belief that the righteous and the wise are in the "hand" (יד, *yad*) of God (9:1).[188] God's "hand" in Hebrew may suggest the idea of protection, an image often associated with divine providence. More likely in Qoheleth, however, the term assumes another common meaning, that of "power," meaning that humans, including the righteous and the wise, find themselves subject to the power of "the God," which may be protective or hostile. This is a point Qoheleth has already made. Due to divine mystery, Qoheleth remarks that one cannot be sure that coming under the power of "the God" is a result of divine hatred or divine love. In any case, all humans share the same fate: death.

Qoheleth places humanity within a series of polar oppositions, concluding that the people within the opposing categories share the same fate (cf. the opposites in the poem on time, chap. 3). This is due to the lack of retributive justice and the conclusion that "the hearts of humans are full of evil" (9:3; cf. Gen. 6:5). Restating the integrative theme of the lack of knowledge, Qoheleth contends that the dead know absolutely nothing at all. At least the living, by contrast, know they will die. This is the one thing in life that humans "know." But knowledge of the manner and time of death's occurrence is denied them.

Qoheleth then develops the third part of this second section when he reexamines the theme of divine sovereignty and the limitation of human knowledge (9:11–11:8). In 9:11–16 Qoheleth builds upon his theme that in exerting the providential direction of reality, "the God" rules the world with uncontested power. For this sage, however, the contingencies that have always haunted the efforts of the wise in securing divine knowledge and the understanding of creation have been even more accentuated to the point that any human skill or ability cannot escape the reality of chance. The teacher recognizes that wisdom is of little use to combat contingencies that may dramatically affect one's life. Qoheleth denies that humans have the capacity to know "their time," that is, the temporal structure within which occur the events of their lives and those affecting their existence. Hidden from their awareness is the occasion of their demise. Human beings, like the fish and the birds, are subject to entrapment at an evil time. Turning to a parable, Qoheleth examines another illusion that severely restricts the value of human knowing, the caprice of fame. Under assault by a mighty king, a city is saved from conquest by a poor sage, but tragically no one remembers his name. Nevertheless, Qoheleth does not abandon his human wisdom. He still affirms the intrinsic value of wisdom over might, even when the words of the sage are rejected.

The Sage and the Fool: 9:17–11:8

Here Qoheleth assembles a collection of sayings, most of which teach the insights of traditional wisdom, especially in contrasting the sage's and the fool's speech and decorum. Returning to the fiction of speaking as Solomon, Qoheleth inserts several sayings that take up the matter of kingship. Within this discourse of traditional wisdom, Qoheleth's own voice twice intrudes in order to destabilize this world of reason and moral causality: "There is an evil I have seen under the sun. It is like an error that proceeds from the ruler. The fools are placed in many exalted positions, while the wealthy sit in a humble place. I have seen slaves upon horses, and princes walking like slaves upon the ground" (10:5–7). This classic depiction of a world upside down, in which the normal social order has become topsy-turvy (see Prov. 30:21–23), subverts the social order of the traditional sages, who teach that the wise succeed and prosper and the fools fail because of their own stupidity. The absurdity of the present social order demonstrates the impotency of wisdom to steer a rational course toward certainty and well-being.

Qoheleth's voice is heard a second time in the conclusion (11:1–8). It is not incidental that the theme of "not knowing" occurs in these verses four different times. The first occurrence is found in an admonition that exhorts the distribution of charity to many, thereby establishing a social network that may protect the community's members, including the giver, from future disturbing contingencies ("you do not know what evil may happen on the earth," 11:1–2). The fourth occurrence also deals with contingencies and the inability to know what will succeed or fail (11:6). This should not lead to paralysis, but rather the sage should proceed with a life based on wisdom.[189] More significantly, in the second and third occurrences, Qoheleth subverts the tradition of the creation of the human being that affirms that God shapes and forms individuals in the womb, breathes into them the breath of life, and protects them in daily living (Job 10:8–12; Ps. 139:13–16). By contrast, Qoheleth depersonalizes the tradition with the remark: "Even as you do not know what is the way of the breath in[190] the bones in a womb that is with child, so you do not know the work of God who does everything" (11:5).

It is clear in these concluding verses that the repetition of "do not know" points to Qoheleth's emphasis on human ignorance and the inability to penetrate behind the veil of divine mystery. Yet, by omitting any reference to divine activity in the shaping of life in the womb, the teacher disassembles one of the central tenets of creation theology in the Hebrew Bible and the wisdom corpus. The second part of the comparison underlines once more Qoheleth's conclusion that, while God determines the events of reality, divine action cannot be understood, predicted, or known by even the wisest of sages.

The sages were concerned to come to an understanding of the temporal order of cosmology and history, for this comprehensive structure provided the context in which individual actions could be guided to successful outcomes (Wis. 7:15–22). Distinctive in biblical understanding is the sapiential teaching of the "correct" or "appropriate" time for the acts of individuals within the larger framework of divine providence (Prov. 27:23–27; Qoh. 3:12; Sir. 4:20).[191] In the wisdom tradition, event and time were inseparable. Actions were meaningful and successful only if a judicious, moral event occurred at the proper time.[192] To be wise entailed not only righteous behavior, but also knowing the appropriate time for prudent action. Knowing when to undertake a particular course of action was the key to its successful outcome. But for Qoheleth this knowledge of time and action is impossible, especially since the activities of providence and their temporal framework are not open to human beings, including even the sages.

A Poem on Anthropology and Cosmology: 11:9–12:7

The concluding poem brings the royal testament of Qoheleth to a close, balancing the anthropology and cosmology of the two strophes of the introductory poem (11:9–12:7).[193] The two themes of the poem are "rejoice" or "take pleasure" (śāmaḥ, שׂמח) in strophe I and "remember" (zākar, זכר)[194] in strophe II. In the first strophe (11:9–10) there is the seventh and final occurrence of the *carpe diem*, in which Qoheleth, in using the creation image of light and darkness, admonishes the students to rejoice in the sweetness of youth, for "childhood and youth are *hebel* (הבל, "ephemeral"). In spite of the caution of a second voice in 11:9c, that of a redactor who intrudes to warn the young against consummating their joy in unlicensed frivolity ("but know that God will bring you into judgment for all these things"), Qoheleth's counsel remains clear: enjoy life while the physical capacities for celebration are at their height.

The meaning of the allegory in the second strophe has often been debated. In general, however, interpreters have seen it in one of two ways: an allegory of old age and growing decrepitude or the metaphorical description of the decline and final eclipse of either a large estate or a city.[195] The allegorical interpretation of the approach of old age is often strained, leaving much to the interpreter's imagination. The interpretation of the decline of a large estate or city follows a more literal and obvious translation. However, this decline becomes a metaphor for the decline and death of human beings and the end of the cosmos.[196] This strophe represents the end of the world that is described as the decline and death of civilization and nature.

The second strophe, found in 12:1–7, begins with a continuation of the *carpe diem*, but quickly changes in mood and substance. "Remember your creator [or 'tomb'] in the days of your youth," the sage instructs, adding the sobering remark: "before the evil days come, and the years draw near in which you say, 'I have no pleasure in them.'" The opening line contains a long recognized *crux interpretum* (*bôrĕʾêkā*, בוראיך), most frequently translated as "your creator." This translation is questionable due to the plural form of the noun ("creators"). In the oldest surviving interpretation of this text, preserved in the tractate *Abot* 3:1 in the Mishnah and attributed to Rabbi Akabia ben Mahalalel, one reads:

> Aqabiah b. Mehallallel says, "Reflect upon three things and you will not fall into the clutches of transgression: Know from whence you come, wither you are going, and before whom you are going to have to give a full account (of yourself). From whence do you come? From a putrid drop. Whither are you going? To a place of dust, worms, and maggots. And before whom are you going to give a full account of yourself? Before the King of kings of kings, the Holy One, blessed be he."[197]

According to *y. Soṭah* (II, 18a), Rabbi Akabia is reflecting on Qoh. 12:1a in this teaching and has in mind three similar terms: "your well" (*bĕʾêrekā*, בארך), "your pit" (*bôrekā*, בורך), and "your creator" (*bôrĕʾêkā*, בוראיך). "Well" and "pit" are metaphors, respectively, for the mother's womb and the grave.

Qoheleth has selected a word that, through similarity in sound and spelling, would stimulate the imagination to think of all three possible objects. This is the understanding of the mishnaic and talmudic interpretations and is a common feature of Hebrew rhetoric. If so, the resultant meanings for the poem would be as follows. First, in regard to "your well" (*bĕʾêrekā*, בארך; i.e., womb; cf. Prov.

5:15, 18, where the wife is called the "well" or "cistern"), conventional wisdom presents God as the one who both fathers the child and conceives and bears to term the fetus in her womb (cf. Prov. 8:22–31). At birth God serves as the midwife and then the caring parent who nurtures the child through life. This parent is the one upon whom the one born may call for protection from distress. According to Qoheleth, God is not the divine parent who redeems his/her children from trouble. In recalling the remark in 11:5, which mentions the breath of life entering into the embryo of a pregnant woman, there is no mention of the tradition of divine creation of the individual. Even the idea of divine nurture of the new life is alien to Qoheleth's theology. To "remember" one's origins in the womb, for Qoheleth, would be simply to remember one's mortality.

The second translation, "your pit" (bôrekā, בורך, "grave"), plays upon a major theme in Qoheleth. For this sage, death is the final end of the human creature. To remember one's grave reflects a traditional wisdom teaching: one is to provide for parents and oneself a proper burial (2 Kgs. 9:33–34; Isa. 14:19; 22:16–17; Job 21:32; cf. the Egyptian "Instruction of Hordjedef"). In Israel it is a moral and customary responsibility to provide for the family tomb. Yet Qoheleth's use of the traditional teaching is unsettling. For this sage, the visit to the ancestral tomb should give one pause, for it is here that one sees the eternal home to which one is called.

The third meaning, "your creator" (bôrĕ'ĕkā, בואריך), is also given a subversive content by Qoheleth. In the traditional creation theology of wisdom and especially the psalms of lament, "remember your creator" involves the human and divine response to suffering. The congregation is to recall the mighty deeds and salvific acts of God, including the slaying of the chaos monster and the creation of the world, in order to establish the basis for hope in present redemption and to remind God to act to redeem his people (cf. Pss. 74 and 77). For God to "remember" his people means to deliver them (Ps. 74:3–4). For Qoheleth, God is indeed the powerful tyrant whose power directs the world and determines the fates of human beings, but he is not the redeemer who enters into life to save the human creature. Thus while the students are instructed to remember God, they should not expect God to remember them.

Following this opening exhortation, Qoheleth crafts a third strophe that divides into four subdivisions, all introduced by temporal adverbs or adverbial phrases common to creation texts: 'ad 'ăser lō' (עד אשר לא, vv. 1b, 2a, 6) and bayyôm (ביום, v. 3a). In creation contexts these temporal phrases normally provide a prolegomenon to divine creation by describing primordial time prior to creating the cosmos (cf. Gen 1:1–2; 2:4b–5; Prov. 8:22–26; and Enuma eliš).

These and similar temporal phrases introduce the four divisions of Qoheleth's second strophe: the approach of old age when joy is negated (v. 1b–c), the cataclysmic end of the cosmos signified by the darkening of light and the return of the primeval deep (v. 2), the end of civilization and the fertility of nature (vv. 3–5), and the final expiration of human life (vv. 6–7). Thus the poem captures the same movement of the larger testament: from cosmos to history to death.

These temporal phases in Qoheleth do not introduce descriptions of chaos prior to creation, but rather the state of nonexistence following the end of creation. Here one finds the inextricable entwining of anthropology and cosmology in Qoheleth: the decline of human vitality and death compares to the decline and death of the cosmos. Indeed, creation is reversed: the movement is from life to death, from cosmos to chaos.

The steady approach of death (v. 1b–c) is the context for the meaning of the conclusion of the second section. Thus the students are exhorted to remember their creator (or grave) when they are young, "Before ('ad 'ăšer lō', עד אשר לא) the evil days come, and the years draw near in which you say: I find no joy in them." For Qoheleth joy is the one gift of God to humans, an experience that derives from eating and drinking, sexual intimacy, and labor. Old age and eventually death ("the evil days") negate the capacity for joy.

With this introduction, the poem then begins to depict the termination of the cosmos (v. 2): "Before ('ad 'ăšer lō', עד אשר לא) the sun darkens, the light, the moon, and the stars, and the clouds return after the rain." The darkening of light is the first act that negates the cosmos, thus alluding to the creation of light by its separation from darkness on the first day in Genesis 1 (vv. 3–5), while the creation of the stars of the heaven and "the greater and lesser lights," the sun and the moon, occurs later on the fourth day (vv. 14–19). The darkening of light, signaling the end of the world, is a common motif in cosmological myths of reversal, prophetic eschatology, and apocalyptic (e.g., Job 9:7; Jer. 4:23; Amos 5:8; Hab. 3:11). Even the reference to the "clouds returning after the rain (gešem, גשם)" may echo the flood tradition in which God unlooses the waters of the deep to inundate the inhabited world bringing all life to an end (e.g., Gen. 6–9; Amos 5:8).[198]

In Qoh. 12:3–5 the major clauses are introduced by the temporal phrase bayyôm (ביום; cf. Gen. 2:4b), and indicate the approaching end of civilization and of creation. This collapse depicted in these verses indicates the final end is total and complete. The watchmen who guard the city against surprise assault quake in terror, and even virile warriors bow their backs in submission before the unnamed foe. Several images point to the end of fertility: women cease grinding grain (a metaphor for a sexual position), and those who "look through the windows" (an image for fertility priestesses or prostitutes) are encased in darkness.[199] The birds of heaven are frightened away by noise (qôl, קול), which signals the trumpet's blast announcing the approach of the enemy (see Exod. 9:16; 20:18; Amos 2:2), and the city no longer hears the sweet melodies of songbirds—that points to the obliteration of the city by the conqueror. The vegetation of the land is devoured by grasshoppers (cf. Joel 2) who fatten themselves on the blossoms of almond trees, the first tree to bloom in spring, while the berries of the caper-bush, gathered in the fall harvest and thought to be an aphrodisiac, fail to produce (the population of the city has been wiped out). This decline and end of civilization and nature is occasioned by humanity (האדם, hā'ādām) marching toward the "eternal home" (bêt 'ôlām, בית עולם), a common metaphor in Egyptian and postbiblical Hebrew for the grave.[200] Women mourners who survive the holocaust take to the streets to perform their dirges of death. Providence does not secure the continuation of civilization, humanity, and creation.

Verses 6–7 bring to conclusion the second strophe and the poem. Introduced by the same temporal phrase (עַד אֲשֶׁר לֹא, *'ad 'ăšer lō'*, "before"; see Prov. 8:26), four images are used to depict metaphorically the end of existence: "Before the silver cord is taken, and the golden bowl is broken, and the pitcher is shattered against the fountain, and the wheel is broken at the cistern." These four images for life and its conclusion in death are followed by a line that is taken from the creation-of-humanity tradition (see Gen. 2:7; 3:19; Job 10:9; Ps. 104:29–30); "and the dust returns unto the earth from which it came, and the breath returns to the God who gave it." With this climactic conclusion, Qoheleth portrays a poetic reversal of cosmic creation that is compared to the end of civilization and the death of the human creature. The end of civilization, of light and life, and the onset of eternal oblivion is metaphorically described as the obliteration of a city and by the death of human beings. Death negates all traditional theologies of cosmic creation, providential guidance, and divine redemption. At death "the dust returns to the earth from which it came, while the breath returns to the God" (cf. Ps. 104:29–30; Job 34:14–15; Isa. 42:5; Ezek. 37:5).

In Qoh. 12:8 Qoheleth returns to the theme of the book: "breath of breath," says Qoheleth, "all is breath," thereby presenting his final closure (cf. 1:2). For Qoheleth, speaking as Solomon, human life, its experiences and its accomplishments, are ephemeral. Nothing human endures, including even the memory of who has existed or what he or she has accomplished.

The Epilogue: 12:9–14

The epilogue, consisting of three parts, is attached by a narrator-redactor who speaks in the third person. This third-person voice begins by listing the major activities of Qoheleth: "teaching the people knowledge," reflecting on the meaning and value of proverbs, and editing them into a collection, "the sayings of the sages."

The narrator (= redactor) then turns to his or her own understanding of the nature and purpose of collections of wisdom sayings by using two metaphors: "goads" that prod one to action and "firmly fixed nails" that provide stability and structure in life. The narrator next warns against speculative teachings that move beyond the guidance and constancy of sayings collections. Indeed, while there is no end to the writing of books, the narrator concludes that too much study is without profit, producing not enlightened understanding and proper behavior, but rather weariness of spirit. This becomes a warning to those who listen too closely to the teachings of Qoheleth.

The narrator, a traditional sage, concludes with his admonition that summarizes his or her own understanding of wisdom: piety ("fear God") and obedience to the law ("commandments"). These two elements, common in Second Temple wisdom, combine to form the framework of the duty of the faithful sage. The motivation clause for piety and obedience contains a warning to the would-be followers of Qoheleth: God will bring every action to judgment, including even that which is done in secret, both good and evil (cf. 11:9).

THE HISTORICAL THEOLOGY
OF THE BOOK OF QOHELETH

Creation and Providence

For this sage, cosmology is deemed critical in attempting to understand the nature and activity of God. Yet, to his chagrin, there is no insight into divine nature derived from the observation of nature. Thus "the God" is a *deus abscon-ditus*, incapable of being known.[201] The teacher's estrangement from his religious world and the instruction of the ancestors led to his skepticism, which is based on his fundamental theological assertion: "the God" is a divine despot whose actions are autocratic, terrifying, and lacking in righteousness. Humans exist in a world where the *deus otiosus*, while in an unapproachable heavenly world and absent from our world, predestines human beings to their future and dictates the course of events. Unlike the sages who went before, Qoheleth acquiesces to the skeptical view that "the God" possesses an unlimited power that cannot be constrained even by righteous standards. This means that there is no righteous order permeating the cosmos. In addition, for Qoheleth, there is an unbridgeable chasm between the Deity, who dwells in heaven, and humanity, who live upon the earth (5:1). Even human wisdom cannot mediate between the two spheres of heaven and earth. While the cosmos is viewed as beautiful, it is not permeated by justice and wisdom. Thus there is lacking any cosmological grounding to human virtue, while even the sage is incapable of understanding God and goodness through the observation of the world.

In Qoheleth's understanding of time, only the cosmos and the tomb are eternal (1:4; 12:5), not humans (3:11). Humans go in quest of living or producing something for eternity, but this goal is denied them. For this sage, human actions occur according to a divine structure of time, and yet the tragedy for humans is their inability to understand this chronology and to know when something will occur. Without the ability to know the larger chronology of events, humans, even sages, cannot achieve a favorable outcome. Subsequently, they are incapable of accomplishing the "good" in human existence, especially defined as actions and virtues that lead to a long, happy, and productive life.

Creation and Wisdom

Unlike his peers in the sapiential corpus, Qoheleth lacks any reference to Woman Wisdom, whether a goddess or a personification of a divine attribute. This is due in part to the role she plays in Proverbs in mediating between heaven and earth. This means that the embodiment of the teachings of the sages provides the means by which humans, among other things, may come to a knowledge of the creator and sustainer of the cosmos. The figure of Woman Wisdom also is used by other sages to speak of both the creation and the providence of God. On occasion she is the instrument of divine creation, thus symbolizing the means by which humans may come to an understanding of God and moral action through the study and practice of sapiential instruction. At other times, she is the manifestation of the providential rule of creation, society, and human existence. Through the study of wisdom, the sages come to exist in harmony with an order of justice leading to life. In his quest to discover the "good" in human life, Qoheleth does not abandon wisdom, but he does recognize its severe limitations. While people may obtain wisdom, even its possession does not mean that they will necessarily be righteous. Indeed, for this sage, very few are just. Further, the value of wisdom is seriously diminished in that it does not provide a means to observe the dictates of justice and to live accordingly. Even sages are sentenced to the unalterable decree that all must die. In realizing this, Qoheleth denies to wisdom any utilitarian value. Even the sages cannot be sure that existing under the "hand" (i.e., power) of God is for their benefit. In Qoheleth's experience, the increase in wisdom leads to the recognition of both the injustice that afflicts human beings and the powerlessness to achieve a fair and equitable society. Fate and circumstance come to all. Qoheleth's dilemma is a crisis of the imagination. Entrance into the future by the shaping of new and powerful metaphors that actualize life and justice is denied even to those possessing wisdom.

Creation and Anthropology

Finding no basis for moral action and value in either the nature and activity of God or in the observable cosmos, Qoheleth turns to anthropology to determine the "good" in human living. He examines a variety of accomplishments, experiences, and possessions, but ultimately discovers that all is "ephemeral and a desire for the spirit." The central metaphor for Qoheleth's understanding of human existence is *hebel*, often translated as "breath," yet meaning evanescence. A comparable metaphorical expression is the "desire for the life-giving spirit," the vain hope of humans to retain the life-giving breath of the Creator given them at birth. The one thing of which humans may be certain is that death comes to all. And in the eternal tomb, people are oblivious to what happens in the world of the living. Humans are sinful, impotent, and mortal who may not escape the fate of death. Yet this wickedness is not the result of God's doing, but rather is due to humans following their own inclinations: "God created humanity upright (*yāšār*, ישר), but they follow their own contrivances." For Qoheleth evil is not part of the essence of human nature, but rather is created by human behavior.

Qoheleth mentions the mystery of conception, but he does not draw on the typical sapiential metaphors of the divine parent or midwife who provides humans life and nurture (11:5). Indeed, conception is as mysterious as the hidden God. The teacher mentions the tradition of the creation of humanity, but only to emphasize that death eventually comes to all. While humans are born only to return to the dust (*'āpār*, עפר) from which they were made, it is impossible to know whether the animating soul (*rûaḥ*, רוח) "ascends upward," that is, returns to God. It may be that humans, like other creatures, simply die and decay. Qoheleth ends his teaching by indicating that the "spirit" returns to the Creator (12:7), but he is suggesting nothing more than the return of the life-giving breath, not an immortal soul, to the God who gave it.

Even so, Qoheleth does not end his quest for "the good" in resignation. True, he does emphasize moderation, even in regard to righteousness and wisdom, for neither has any reward. He also counsels his students in 5:6 to "fear God," emphasizing that they should submit to the reality of divine sovereignty. God, while acting in secret, is the ruler of the cosmos, while humans do not possess the ability to manage their own affairs and determine their destinies. God, not humanity, rules over creation and directs history, although in complete secrecy. Indeed, the refusal to acknowledge God's sovereignty and to recognize human limitations could result in the loss of the one divine gift that is the "good in human existence": joy. Qoheleth associates well-being with the human capacity to experience "joy" or "satisfaction," which may result from eating and drinking (the symposium),[202] the intimacy experienced with one's beloved, and the labor that one pursues. While life itself is odious or an evil business (ענין רע, *'inyan rā'*) due to "the God's" own doing (1:13), he still bequeaths moments of joy to those who "please" him. Thus this one gift is contingent on the caprice of "the God," for one never learns how to gain his favor. Even when this experience comes, it is quickly gone.

To emphasize the value of joy, the literary structure of Qoheleth is organized around the sevenfold occurrence of the *carpe diem* ("enjoy the day"): 2:24–26; 3:12–13; 3:22, 5:17–19; 8:15; 9:7–10; and 11:7–10. In the first five occurrences, the expression takes the form of a declaration that is based on Qoheleth's own experiences. The final two, however, are expressed as third-person admonitions, demonstrating that Qoheleth now transmits to his students what he himself has learned. The two admonitions are significant in that this form is rare in Qoheleth, occurring only in a few places: the instruction concerning the cult in 4:17–5:6, the collection of sayings in 7:1–2 and Qoheleth's instruction that follows in 7:13–18, the warning in 7:21, and the teaching in 11:1–6. The interlude in 6:1–9 judges life without joy to lack value. Negating once more the creation-of-humanity tradition, Qoheleth affirms that it is better to be an aborted fetus than a person who has wealth, possessions, honor, one hundred children, and long life, but all without joy. Consequently, while joy is a limited good, it is the only good in human living.

Wisdom, Power, and Wealth in Qoheleth

Qoheleth's ideology, shaped in part by Greek Skepticism and Egyptian grave autobiographies, presents a disconcerting view of status and power in human society. It is difficult to imagine that the primary voice of the sage who speaks through the mouth of the long dead Solomon is engaged in a quest to enhance his own and his students' power and wealth. Indeed, just the opposite occurs. Enmeshed in a regional skepticism that claimed the adherence of many of the intellectuals who lived in the eastern Mediterranean world in the third century and following, this sage deconstructs the entire paradigm of supremacy and wealth. Indeed, the voice of the wise king repudiates this ruthless quest for position and influence by examining it through critical analysis and weighing it on the scales of human experience. He concludes this quest is "*hebel* (ephemerality) and a pursuit after wind." Power and wealth, like all other desires of the human heart, do not endure, and even the memory of the great kings do not continue after they descend into the darkened slumbers of human forgetfulness. Kingdoms rise and fall, wealth is gained only to be lost or wasted on the fool, glory is a vain illusion, and status leads to nothing but consternation of the human spirit. Only the moments of joy, quickly passing, gained from eating and drinking (conviviality), labor that satisfies but produces nothing that would endure, and the solace of the embrace of a woman loved, are the experiences that transcend the darkness of the brevity of a life destined to end in the eternal home of an unremembered tomb. Only the unknown God has power to control the world and establish the fates, and the outcomes of these decisions lay beyond the ken of mortal comprehension. No priest, no seer, and no ruler could escape the fate that has been determined for him, any more than he could escape the final darkness into which all in due course would unavoidably enter.

Conclusion: Creation and the Quest for the Good in Qoheleth

Qoheleth's anthropology is pivotal in understanding his theology in general and in particular his formulation of the creation of humanity and the related deliberations over providence. The root metaphor of creation in Qoheleth is "ephemerality" (*hebel*) and its synonymous expression, the "desire for the life-giving spirit." Try as they will, even the sages are incapable of retaining the living spirit used by the Creator in animating their life. Even their actions are incapable of producing something that endures, whether lasting honor, an upright and noble family of descendants, or a product, be it something made or a noteworthy teaching. This ephemeral nature of human existence that ends inevitably in the darkness of the tomb contrasts with the eternity of the cosmos and the tomb, about which he speaks in graphic metaphors (the constant movement of the forces of creation as contrasted with the enduring, unchanging cosmos, and the slow deterioration of the city and the body that ends in the constancy of death).

One by one, the major tenets of traditional wisdom are deconstructed by a sage who reflects the skepticism of his age, especially documented in the Skepticism of Plato's Academy beginning in the later part of the third century and the tradition of Egyptian grave autobiographies continuing into the Ptolemaic period: the teaching of retribution, which values wise and virtuous actions that lead to divine blessing and admonishes against wicked behavior that results in punishment; the revelation of the justice of God that is expressed through the righteous order of creation; the divine gift of conception, birth, and oversight; and the value of wisdom, which leads to happiness and success expressed through the gifts of longevity, honor, a respectful family, and wealth. In their place is the possibility of experiencing moments of joy, which, even if they come, quickly pass. These occasions of joy, as brief as they are, depend on the capricious decision of the unknown God who determines the destiny of each person, unknown to all, and then sentences each human, regardless of moral living or social status, to the unending, opaque darkness of the tomb. The creator and determiner of destinies is an all-powerful tyrant and a capricious despot who rules without opposition. Thus even the theology of creation and the kingship of God provide no comfort to the one "who fears the God" and seeks to live a wise and moral life of pious rectitude. While he flirts with the apocalyptic teaching of life beyond death, he ultimately rejects it as unproven. Death, for Qoheleth, is a dark and inescapable void in which there is no remembrance of the past, no awareness of the present, and no evidence of a future. Based on the certainty of the experience and the criterion of what is self-evident, the one "good" in human life, contingent on the whimsy of divine decree, is the fleeting moment of joy that may come on occasion to those who "please" the unknown God.

Chapter 7

Hellenistic Wisdom in Judah: The Book of Ben Sira[1]

THE SELEUCID EMPIRE

The History of the Seleucid Empire

The victory of Seleucus I at Ipsus (301 BCE) paved the way for Seleucid control of the northern part of the previous Achaemenid Empire (Persia, Media, Elam, eastern Lydia, and northern Syria).[2] This empire, ruled over by a succession of powerful rulers, eventually came to control the regions between Lydia to the Iranian plateau and even beyond, and Coele-Syria, which included the tiny province of Judah. Unlike the Ptolemies, who essentially maintained the political structure of the countries they ruled, the Seleucids established political satrapies, together with a new imperial administrative system. This system operated an efficient administration for the collection of tribute and taxes.[3] Furthermore, numerous new cities and military colonies sprang up in their territories due to the encouragement of other peoples, especially from Greece and Greek cities elsewhere, to come and settle. While Sardis in western Turkey and Seleucia on the Tigris served as the political capitals of the empire, Antioch became a major regional center in northern Syria that was to exert considerable power over and influence of Judah during the time this province fell under its sway (200 BCE). Conquest and control of the various *ethnoi* within their empire was maintained by a strong military and navy, and the kings themselves assumed direct leadership over the armed forces and joined them in their expeditions.

Antiochus III (223–187) began his expansion by bringing Parthia, Armenia, and Batria into his empire (212–205). When he won the victory at Panium (200) in the fifth Syrian war against the forces of his Ptolemaic rival (Ptolemy V Epiphanes, 205–180), thus reversing his earlier defeat at Raphia at the hands of the army of Ptolemy IV in 217, Judah was brought into the new empire. The response of the Jews was to welcome the new king to Jerusalem and even to assist his taking of the Holy City. He took all of Palestine, including the coastal cities, and as a result of his gratitude for Jewish support in this war he exempted the city of Jerusalem from taxes and even granted financial backing to the temple. Finally, he met his defeat at the hands of the Romans when he invaded Thrace, losing to them the key battle at Magnesia in 190. His territory in Asia Minor was reduced, and turning eastward he died in battle at Susa in 187. His eldest son and successor, Seleucus Philopator (187–176), was praised in 2 Macc. 3:3 for his generosity toward the Jerusalem temple. It was only when Antiochus IV Epiphanes ascended the throne (175–164) that the war with the Ptolemies finally came to an end. Antiochus IV tried to invade Egypt but was turned back by the threat of the Romans. The Seleucid Empire came to its demise in 64 BCE in its defeat at the hands of the Roman general Pompey. Rome took Jerusalem the following year. These regions, including Judah, then became Roman provinces.

The Historical Location of Ben Sira: The Seleucid Empire

It was not until Antiochus IV Epiphanes (175–164 BCE) assumed the Seleucid throne that conditions became grave for the Jews. After selling the Jewish high priesthood to two successive competitors in order to raise needed money to support his military expeditions and deposing Onias III, the legitimate high priest, the monarch resorted to force to coerce the Jews into abandoning their native religion and customs in favor of Hellenistic culture. While Ben Sira lived and collected the sections of his book prior to this reign, there are a few internal indications of tensions, including the prayer of Ben Sira (36:1–22), which, if not a later insertion, calls upon God to bring judgment and retribution against the foreign people. The encomium in chapters 44–50 that ends with Simeon II (219–196; see the panegyric in 50:1–21) implies that the high priest had only recently died. Thus while Ben Sira may have hoped for the culmination of Jewish history with political independence, there is no real indication of this outside the suspect prayer in chapter 36. He certainly expresses no strong degree of nationalism, centered in the expectation of a future messiah and an independent kingdom.

During the life of Ben Sira, it may have been that the Jewish *gerousia* (γερο-σία) or council of elders (*'ĕdat śibʿîm*, עדת שבעים) was allowed to deal with internal matters according to their own laws and customs. Perhaps the high priest presided over the council, likely composed of aristocratic leaders of the city.[4] However, each satrapy was governed by a Syrian *stratēgos* who assumed full authority, including military control. The city in which Ben Sira resided was growing in wealth and culture, indicated by the move of Joseph and his sons, members of the powerful Tobiad family (Josephus, *Ant.* 12.160ff.), by architectural achievements in western Jerusalem by the Temple Mount, and by multilingual inscriptions.[5]

JUDAISM IN THE SELEUCID EMPIRE

Palestinian Judaism and Hellenization

Hellenization penetrated not only the prominent, wealthy, and politically important cities in the east, but also the more remote and less prestigious ones. While the lingua franca and political systems brought about a highly organized cultural and commercial enterprise, it was no small matter to obtain citizenship in the Greek *polis*. In addition, the cultural process was one of fusion in which the indigenous cultures integrated into overarching Hellenism, considered by the Greeks to be superior to native ones.

Hellenism has been described as a "civilization of *paideia*,"[6] since schools were established throughout the empire and the consequent kingdoms. One of the important literary products that has some parallel with Ben Sira's collection is the writing of florilegia made up of summaries of Greek literature, including especially the poets and philosophers, to provide ready access for youth to become well rounded in their knowledge, even though superficial, of Greek intellectuals and poets. Education was the primary means by which hellenization took root in the East, but only Greeks and those of Greek descent were permitted to attend gymnasia and then the more advanced schools of specialization known as the *ephebia*. Ben Sira's knowledge of the Greek language and Greek literary texts, especially noted in several of his themes, knowledge of Greek virtues, and his use of Greek rhetorical forms, indicate he had studied not in a gymnasium, since the first one in Jerusalem would have been built after 175 BCE, but under one or more Greek tutors.[7] It is wrong to consider him a conservative opposed to any form of Hellenism. Instead, he should be placed between the two worlds of older Judaism and newer Hellenism and understood as one who sought to work out something of an accommodation between the two. However, the book does not present so much a contrast between a conservative Ben Sira and a liberal Hellenistic Jewish aristocracy, as it does a developing sapiential tradition that assists in forging a teaching that has deep roots in the Jewish past and still makes use of current Greek and Jewish culture.[8] Even so, his strong allegiance to the Torah, not Greek philosophy, is the chosen path to the knowledge of God, piety, and the moral life.[9]

Wisdom in the Sect of the Dead Sea[10]

The establishment of the Qumran community center may have occurred as early as the last quarter of the third century and as late as the early first century BCE.[11] This group of sectarians, whether an Essene community[12] or not, was strongly opposed to the priesthood in Jerusalem and the Jerusalem temple and became even more disaffected by the growing hellenization of Jerusalem and the larger region of Judah, the persecution of Jews by Antiochus IV Epiphanes, the selling of the office of the high priest by Antiochus IV Epiphanes to Jason and then to Menelaus, and the upper-class status of the Sadducees who collaborated with the Ptolemies and then the Seleucids to enhance their economic and political status.[13] The issues thus were not simply religious and theological, but also clearly social, economic, and political.

Among the many writings discovered in the caves adjacent to the Qumran community center was a series of fragments that point to the existence of an important sapiential text: 4QInstruction (*mûsār lĕmēbîn*, MLM, IQ26, 4Q415–418, and 4Q423), composed in a Herodian script, and, save for a few fragments, 4Q416, 4Q417, and 4Q418, badly damaged.[14] 4QInstruction's identification as a sapiential text with elements of apocalyptic is based on forms, themes, and vocabularly. Common sapiential forms include admonitions, sayings, and instructions with parenetic features.

The three important themes are the identification of the Torah with the sapiential primeval order, the "Vision of Knowledge" in 4Q417 1 116–117 similar to the revelation obtained by Enoch, and the "mystery that has come/is/is to come." The first two themes, the Torah and the vision of knowledge, point to the sapiential and apocalyptic primeval order with cosmological and eschatological features and provide the basis for the way of life.[15] And the moral dualism of earlier wisdom (e.g., wisdom and folly) becomes the eschatological drama of the ages that culminates in the final judgment (4Q416 1 and 4Q418 69 II).

The third theme is encapsulated in the expression *rāz nihyeh* (רז נהיה), which means "a mystery that has come," "a mystery that is coming," and a "mystery that is to come."[16] One of the meanings of wisdom, then, is the knowledge of this "mystery" (רז, *rāz*).[17] This "mystery" is "a body of teaching that involves creation, ethical activity, and eschatology" (e.g., 4Q417 2 i 8–9).[18] Creation and cosmology are not only eschatological,[19] but also comprise the divinely determined order of the cosmos and the events of human history.[20]

A second complex of wisdom manuscripts, the "Mysteries," (1Q27; 4Q299–301) that tells of "God's foreknowledge and predestination of all events and plans in history."[21] Since humans do not innately know this wisdom that God used in creation and that contains the knowledge for life and salvation, it is not only bestowed upon ones selected by God, but also searched out by humans who have the gift of insight. This wisdom comes as the result of both gift and quest. Even so, wisdom's foundation is located in creation from its inception and offers moral counsel for life.

Thus wisdom texts[22] found among the Dead Sea Scrolls not only examine and teach the features of the moral life, but also project a theological worldview based on the creation of the cosmos viewed through an apocalyptic lens. The integration of wisdom and apocalyptic is a distinctive development in early Judaism, for it led to the creation of an important worldview that distinguished it from the Zadokites and their scribes and many other Jewish sects emerging in the middle of the Hellenistic period. From their writings, it is likely their community was both an oppressed and marginalized one, with the expectation of a final reckoning in the end time when the wicked would be destroyed and the righteous and faithful would be preserved. 4QInstruction and other wisdom texts not only teach the community's members how to exist in this time of "twixt and between," but also to see this righteous behavior as a means for ushering in the final judgment. The zeitgeist of the sectarians includes the opposition between evil and suffering, on one hand, and preparation for the end time on the other. With the new reign of God, the Torah would be scrupulously preserved and followed, the evil conquerors destroyed along with their collaborators, and the exaltation of the righteous would be realized.

The scribes who composed and copied the scrolls are disaffected sectarians who turned their backs on the priesthood and temple of Jerusalem, withdrew to the desert, and awaited the coming day of restoration when the wicked priest and his followers would be removed and the temple cleansed and presided over by the true priests and their leader. This view of making things right through the establishment of justice that would lead to the exaltation of the righteous was the social background for understanding the apocalyptic of the Dead Sea Sectarians and God's eventual redemption of a polluted creation and people from wicked priests and oppressive, foreign lords.[23]

The Scribes and the Institution of Schools

It is evident from both the prologue and the internal witness of his collections and poems that Ben Sira was a scholar of Scripture as it had developed during his time (the third part of the canon was still unsettled) and knew some of the Greek literature in at least a superficial way, possibly through the circulation of florilegia.[24] It is likely that he was a sage who taught and wrote in a school under the jurisdiction of the temple.[25] The location of this school could have been his home or a synagogue. His students included residential youth studying to become Torah scribes and perhaps laity on the Sabbath.[26] His school is mentioned in his invitation in 51:23—"Turn to me, O unlearned ones, and take up residence in my house of study (*bēt midrāš*, בית מדרש).[27]

Based on what occurred in Qumran, Ben Sira's school could also have been a center for copying, archiving, studying, and interpreting biblical books. That his writings were known beyond the city boundaries of Jerusalem is indicated by the discovery of a partial manuscript of his work at Masada and the fragments in the literature of Qumran.[28] To develop this type of reputation, he may have been associated in some official manner with the temple. This is underlined by his high regard for the Jerusalem priesthood, Simeon II, and the temple. It is conceivable that his school would have been located in or adjacent to the temple compound.

Another institution with which Ben Sira's school would have been associated is the synagogue. The initial purpose of the synagogue ("assembly of the congregation," *synagōgē*, συναγωγή) may have been originally not a place to worship but rather a location for public gatherings for a variety of social and religious activities, including study and learning. It is only after the destruction of the temple by the Romans in 70 CE that the synagogue also became primarily a "place of prayer" (*proseuchē*, προσευχή).[29] Textual and archaeological evidence for the earliest known synagogues points to the third century BCE in Hellenistic Egypt. Several synagogue dedications occur in this century in Egypt,[30] and a papyrus letter dating from 218 BCE in the town of Anexandrou-Nesos refers to a synagogue. Other archaeological evidence for synagogues in the Diaspora prior to 70 CE includes Delos (second–first century BCE), Ostia (reign of Claudius in 41–54 CE), and Rome.[31] The archaeological evidence in Eretz Israel is as early as the second century BCE. Qumran is one place where one or more synagogues existed. The other synagogues included the ones at Gamla, Masada, 'Ein-Ged; Na Caran, Herodium, and Capernaum. Recently, the oldest synagogue in Israel has been discovered in Hasmonean Jericho. Philo notes that the Essenes had halls of assembly called *synagōgai*, although all of these were not necessarily places for worship. Lee Levine notes that the evidence for schools in synagogues prior to 70 CE is limited. However, he mentions the rabbinic tradition (*y. Megillah* 3, I, 73d; *Ketubot* 13, 35c; *b. Ketubot* 105a) that tells of 480 synagogues in pre–70 CE Jerusalem, each with a primary school (*bēt sēper*, בית ספר) and a more advanced school (*bēt talmûd*, בית תלמוד).[32] While this number is exaggerated, it is not unlikely that Jewish children and future scribes and teachers studied in this type of educational setting. Josephus indicates that Jewish youths received formal instruction, indicating a practice that would have been true, at the latest, in the first century CE when he wrote (*C. Ap.* 2.204). This would likely have occurred in the synagogues of Eretz Israel. The inscription of Theodotus (a Greek inscription that was found on the wall of a presumably pre–70 CE synagogue in Jerusalem that identified the donor responsible for its construction) may also refer at least indirectly to a school, since it mentions the study of the commandments: "Theodotus . . . built the synagogue for reading of the law and for teaching of the commandments, also the stranger's lodging and the chambers and the conveniences of waters for an inn for them that need it from abroad."[33]

It is difficult to pinpoint any evidence to suggest that the schools in Ben Sira's day were influenced in any way by the Hellenistic gymnasium. His school would have focused in its curriculum on Jewish tradition, wisdom, and the Torah. It is likely that, with the strong presence of Hellenistic culture, the study of Greek and the reading of a florilegium may well have been included. The curriculum would likely have included reading, writing, composing, mathematics, literature, the sciences, music and the arts, and the study of languages used in the cultural and political environment.

THE INTERNATIONAL SETTING OF WISDOM IN THE HELLENISTIC PERIOD

Wisdom Texts in Hellenistic Egypt

Wisdom from Egypt during the Hellenistic period was available to the larger world, although it is difficult to know if Ben Sira would have had exposure to Egyptian literature. There is little creditable support for the notion that he could read demotic and was influenced by demotic wisdom texts.[34] Many of the literary forms of Hellenistic Egyptian wisdom are parallel to those in Ben Sira: the hymns to the Creator (cf. Papyrus Insinger), instructions, and sayings. And there are some parallel themes. The most one can plausibly argue is that Egyptian wisdom texts provide some insight into the international context in which Ben Sira taught and wrote.

Egyptian demotic texts testify that the sages of the eastern Mediterranean world, ranging from Greece into western Asia and northern Africa, "worked in a medium which they recognized as being an international one. And they were all the more ready to spread and trade their wares as their subject matter was designed for teaching, persuasion, and the widest possible consumption."[35] An important example of this international context for wisdom is provided by ostraca from the temples to the healing gods (two deified sages, Imhotep and Amenhotep, son of Hapu) at Deir al-Bahri. These ostraca of votive inscriptions and graffiti in demotic script and Greek provide interesting information about the wide sweep of cultural contact. Perhaps the most interesting is "The Counsels of Amenotes," written in Greek and attributed to Amenhotep, son of Hapu. This text consists of eighteen fragmentary lines in which virtue is taught through the sayings of a variety of Greek sources, including the "Sayings of the Seven Sages." This writing was composed by a Hellenistic Egyptian sage using Greek wisdom to enhance his native tradition.[36]

The Teachings of Hellenistic Egyptian Sages[37]

Four important Egyptian collections date from this period and show a remarkable degree of parallelism with Jewish wisdom, in particular Proverbs and Ben Sira. Texts of demotic wisdom literature have been discovered that date as late as the second century CE.

Written, engraved, or embossed on the walls of the family burial chamber of Petosiris, dating from the early years of the Ptolemaic dynasty, are texts from the classical period down to the time of the construction of this tomb. One of these texts has been found in the family tomb of Petosiris.[38] A high priest of Thoth in the temple at Hermopolis, Petosiris assumes the role of teacher, offering instructions to those who visited his tomb. In his autobiography, he boasts of his divine service and accomplishments in following the "way of life." This text is similar in form and content to other traditional literature in Egypt and Eretz Israel of the Hellenistic period, including especially the instructions of Ben Sira and several Egyptian tomb biographies mentioned below.[39]

One of the important traditional Egyptian wisdom texts from the Hellenistic period is the "Sayings Collection of 'Ankhsheshonq,"[40] found on a papyrus scroll dating from the late first century BCE. The beginnings of the top lines of all twenty-eight columns have been lost. Two papyri from the second century BCE cite the text, suggesting that the original dates from the early Ptolemaic period. The text is a loose collection of proverbs and sayings. However, what is different for a sayings collection is the introduction of a later narrative. 'Ankhsheshonq's discovery of a plot by his friend and patron to assassinate the king and his failure to disclose the impending action to the proper officials leads to his implication and subsequent incarceration. In prison, he asks his captors to provide him pen and paper to allow him to submit to his son in writing words of wisdom for directing life. While the end of the narrative has not been preserved, based on the standard form of this type of comedic story (cf. Joseph and Ahiqar), one may conjecture that the wronged sage is liberated and restored to his position of honor.

What is particularly remarkable is the presence of a number of themes drawn from Hellenistic literature that include the wide gamut of Aramaic and Greek wisdom. Close parallels are found in the "Instruction of Ahiqar" and Greek *gnōmologia* (γνωμολογία) of poets and sages (e.g., "The Sentences of Sextus" [first century BCE], the content of which is similar to Ben Sira). There are also echoes of traits of Hellenistic moral treatises that also include quotations and the wise sayings known or written by the composer (see, e.g., Pseudo-Isocrates, *Ad Demonicum*). Important themes include the contrast between the wise and the foolish, the wealthy and the poor, and women of nobility and those of seductive character. Also present are the themes of fulfilling one's responsibilities to the Divine, proper conduct in managing affairs, the relationship between cause and effect, two expressions of the so-called Golden Rule, and retribution. The teaching is offered by a father to his son to prepare him to replace him in his position.

Another wisdom text from Hellenistic Egypt is the "Teaching of Pordjel,"[41] which quotes 'Ankhsheshonq several times. It consists of aphorisms without any obvious thematic arrangement. The teaching's oldest manuscript is a papyrus dating from the second century BCE,[42] suggesting the text likely originated some time earlier.[43] A scribe named Harmais writes this text to his "beloved son." It is possible that the author was a learned priest, pointing to a parallel with levitical scribes. Important themes include paying the god his due, avoiding the thief and the stupid man, refraining from a sexual liaison with a married woman, controlling passions, avoiding cursing of the master and paying him his due, and the proper instruction of a son. Thus the instruction focuses on moral behavior as a parent, husband, and servant.

I have briefly discussed the fourth example of an Egyptian wisdom text, Papyrus Insinger, in the chapter on Qoheleth.[44] Containing some thirty-four columns, this largely preserved teaching originated prior to the first century CE, since one manuscript dates from this time. Fragmentary papyri of the early Roman period point to its continued popularity. The sayings collection consists of twenty-five numbered teachings arranged according to subject matter. The theme of equilibrium that resides at the basis of the understanding of cosmic and social order is the major topic. The Deity is inscrutable, but his justice is never questioned.[45] Other important themes are fate and fortune, the activities of the deity, the importance of work, the practice of moderation and the avoidance of vices like gluttony and lechery, honoring parents, avoiding fools and thieves, generosity, self-control, dispensing with worry, patience, abstaining from vengeance, shunning violence, and, most importantly, the fear of God, divine omniscience, and retribution found in a hymn to the creator.

This Egyptian sage had access to Hellenistic philosophy and culture. His writings demonstrate a general knowledge of Stoicism and Epicureanism, which indicates intercultural activity by this and other Egyptian sages. For this text, the god is the one who provides the sage care and the capacity to search out, find, and practice what is good. The hymn to the creator (32.1–18) is especially important for comparison to Ben Sira (cf. especially Sir. 33:10–15). In 33.6 he notes: "The fate and the fortune that come, it is the god who sends them." The creator is the one who creates and orders the cosmos and human beings, as well as the one who distributes retributive justice. Furthermore, Papyrus Insinger emphasizes, as do the Stoics and Ben Sira (see, e.g., Sir. 33:10–15; 37:11–17), the teaching of opposites. The deity is the one who creates opposites, which constitute the structure of creation.

Jewish Literary Sources Produced in Seleucid and Hasmonean Times

There is a substantial number of Jewish texts from Egypt and Judah, beginning in the final quarter of the third century BCE, written in either Greek or Hebrew. Some have important similarities to Ben Sira. These include Demetrius, Baruch, and 1 and 2 Maccabees, which represent a variety of different responses to Greek culture.

Demetrius, a Jewish historian in Alexandria, composed his history during the last quarter of the third century BCE.[46] He wrote to convince Ptolemy IV Philometor (222–205) of the ancient and noteworthy history of the Jewish people. Since the Greeks placed exceptional value on a people's antiquity, this history would serve to enhance the status of Jews in this part of the Hellenistic world. The history of Demetrius, from the fragments that are quoted, parallels several elements of Ben Sira's "Praise of the Pious" in chapters 44–50. Both Demetrius and Ben Sira placed significant emphasis on the Torah, regarding it as history and moral instruction on the continuation of the ancestral religion and the Jewish community.

In examining the dramatis personae of Hellenistic Jewish legends, it is clear that Baruch[47] the scribe was among those who continued to enjoy a position of prestige.[48] He provides a paradigm for the Second Temple sage in Hellenistic Judaism who is wise, virtuous, and devoted to the Torah. The different sections of the apocryphal book of Baruch were probably originally written in Hebrew,[49] although the book in its final form is extremely difficult to date.[50] The final form may have taken shape just following the Seleucid takeover of Palestine, making it a contemporary piece to the text of Ben Sira (ca. 190 BCE). The major version exists in Greek, since no Hebrew text has survived.[51] This text contains important parallels to Ben Sira, but perhaps the most noteworthy is the hymn in praise of wisdom (3:9–4:4), which compares to the wisdom hymn in Sirach 28.[52] Divine wisdom is integrated into the teachings of the Torah (3:9). This accords with the didactic narrative that, also like Ben Sira, emphasizes the law, which is identified with wisdom.

First Maccabees,[53] written originally in Hebrew, likely dates from the last half of the second century BCE, possibly early in the reign of John Hyrcanus (134–104; cf. 16:23–24).[54] The last verse of the book suggesting that John Hyrcanus had died was likely added later. Written in Jerusalem, this anonymous historian seeks to accomplish two purposes: to indicate how Jewish identity could be maintained and to glorify the Hasmonean dynasty. In opposing assimilation, 1 Maccabees points to a Jewish community that will develop a national culture and historical consciousness to oppose the attraction of hellenization.[55] This effort does not exclude the use of Hellenistic thought and literary expressions, but it does underscore the strong opposition to absorption into pagan culture and religion in reactionary Jewish circles.

A second Jewish history, this one written originally in Greek, narrates the internal Jewish struggles between the high priest Onias III, overseer of the Jerusalem temple, and Simon, a Benjaminite.[56] Second Maccabees admonishes the Jews of Egypt to celebrate the Festival of Hanukkah in honor of the defeat of Antiochus IV Epiphanes and the rededication of the temple in 165 BCE. The narrative describes Judas Maccabeus's heroic victory over the enemies of Judah, who engaged in three different attacks on Jerusalem (2:19–15:39). Jason of Cyrene, whose five books of history the epitomator abridged into one narrative (2:23), may have written in Jerusalem during the first or second year of the rule of Judas (166–161), as an eyewitness to the events he describes. The epitomator would have abridged the text a generation or two later. The original language of both 2 Maccabees and Jason of Cyrene was Greek.[57] The epitomator likely concluded his work sometime between 124 BCE and 50 CE, although it would have had several redactions.[58] Philo (*Prob.* 13.89) and 3 Maccabees are familiar with 2 Maccabees 7–9, and the book is the basis for 4 Maccabees in the first century CE. However, it is not mentioned by Josephus.

The author of 2 Maccabees brings together two traditions: Jewish religion and Greek historiography. He shapes his text by using Greek literary canons, including the dimension of pathos, in nuancing the narration of history. Retribution, creation, the resurrection of the righteous, the divine presence in the temple, and the temple ritual are important theological emphases. Further, divine providence continues to operate in redeeming God's people and punishing their enemies. Thus it is important to celebrate the Festival of Hanukkah, for it praises God's victory over the Syrian Greeks. If Judean in origin, as its eyewitness stance appears to make it, this text indicates that Greek literary forms, language, and culture significantly influenced Jewish writers in Judea as well as in Alexandria.

Major Themes of Jewish Literature in the Seleucid Rule of Judah

Jewish literature in Judah and Egypt, following the victory of Antiochus III at Panium and the incorporation of Judah within the Syrian Empire, reflected different views of Hellenism and the response Jews should make. Radicals on the left who immersed Judaism totally into Greek culture and thought opposed the reactionaries who rejected en toto anything Greek. However, most of the literature adheres to positions between these two opposites. Written in Hebrew, 1 Maccabees followed the path of maintaining Jewish identity by rejecting Hellenism, while the community of Qumran, also strongly anti-Hellenic, stressed Jewish wisdom, obedience to the Torah, and apocalyptic to speak of the imminent future. Composed in Greek, 2 Maccabees sought to blend Jewish tradition and Greek historiography. The Jews of Egypt were exhorted to practice the Festival of Hanukkah, for it celebrated God's providential defeat of the great enemy of the Jews, Antiochus IV. Ben Sira was a conservative in maintaining a strong allegiance to Judaism and its institutions of temple and priesthood, and yet still used a number of Hellenistic forms and concepts to present its teachings. Torah is identified with wisdom, while the temple is central to Jewish religion. Creation and providence in nature and history are affirmed as central to the writings of these Jewish intellectuals.

INTRODUCTION TO THE BOOK OF BEN SIRA

The Sociopolitical World of Ben Sira

When Judah came under Seleucid rule, one of the important consequences for Jerusalem was the new policy to establish military alliances in the form of royal charters. This type of charter provided Jerusalem a degree of political and fiscal independence in exchange for military support (Josephus, *Ant.* 12.138–46). Furthermore, while Jerusalem was classified as one of the temple cities and was required to pay additional taxes to the Seleucid court, the city also stood to profit in receiving royal bequests of money and land.[59] The early Seleucids, prior to Aniochus IV Epiphanes, allowed local priesthoods to be hereditary and practiced a policy of noninterference. A high degree of status accompanied the office of the high priest, who also enjoyed power, wealth, and above all influence in local affairs. The priests and the temple were allowed to receive the temple tax from the Jews in Judah and in the Diaspora.

The paramount purpose of Ben Sira is to articulate a worldview from the standpoint of a temple sage, living in Jerusalem, who wished to extol his native traditions in the multifaceted reality of the Hellenistic Empire of the Ptolemies and the Seleucids. The book is a collection of a lifetime of teachings and insights that the sage committed to writing. The sociopolitical world is essentially one of peace with the final culmination of history, God's kingdom and its center in Jerusalem, only a step away. While not explicitly speaking of the dissolution of the Seleucid Empire, its collapse was necessary in order for the final conclusion of history and creation to reach their fulfillment: the reign of God through the immanent dwelling of wisdom in the temple on Mount Zion that radiates throughout the world. The book is not shaped by an underlying hope for the restoration of a Davidic monarchy. Rather, the sociopolitical understanding in evidence is that of a theocracy in which Yahweh will reign through wisdom from Jerusalem and rule over all the earth. This is the reason, therefore, for the panegyric to Simeon II at the conclusion of the body of the text, before the addition of the concluding signature or colophon. This high priest will have successors who, in line with the covenant made with Phinehas (50:24; 45:24–25; see 1 Macc. 2:54 and especially Num. 25:1–15) will inherit this office forever.

Ben Sira sought to walk a narrow line between the political rule of the Seleucids, under whom the Jews enjoyed a relative degree of freedom and prosperity, and the final culmination in history when God through wisdom and the temple would rule over all the earth. Certainly Ben Sira did not wish to upset either the Seleucid rulers or the Zadokites, who enjoyed their favor. Thus he remained politically and religiously conservative, believing that God would ultimately work out the final stage of the future according to divine decree. This conservatism, in line with the social and political views of the Zadokites, penetrated into his teachings regarding all areas of life. Thus the text is heavily patriarchal, as is the priestly Torah, elitist in supporting the Zadokite aristocracy, supportive of the political order, and traditional in supporting both religious rites and festivals of the temple and the themes of salvation history. Yet it is careful in its embrace of Hellenistic ideas and rhetoric so as not to accept anything that would undermine Zadokite Judaism.

The Social Status of Ben Sira and the Roles of the Scribes[60]

The book of Ben Sira is the first to identify the author by name, "Jesus, son of Eleazar, son of Sira of Jerusalem" (50:27). His grandson calls his grandfather "Yeshua." The prologue depicts Ben Sira as one who combined *paideia* (παιδεία, "education, teaching," "the state of being educated," and a "cultured mind") with *sophia* (σοφία, "wisdom"). Ben Sira bears the name of Simeon, ben Yeshua, ben Eleazar, ben Sira in 50:27. However, Simeon is likely Simeon II and should be placed at the end of verse 24. It is likely that Yeshua's father was Eleazar and his grandfather Sira.

Although Ben Sira was the first mentioned scribal interpreter of Scripture since Ezra, it is plausible that this role of interpreter of Torah and the expanding canon would have been continuous for sages in Second Temple Judah. Ben Sira's canon of Scripture now includes the Torah, the Prophets, and other Writings, a third division of the Tanakh not yet finalized. His grandson indicates that Ben Sira devoted his life to both the study of books of Scripture placed into these three categories and the writing of instruction and wisdom so that those who "love learning" should be better prepared to follow the Torah. The epilogue or colophon (50:27–29) describes the book as containing the sayings and wisdom teachings of Ben Sira that would become a source of teaching for anyone who wished to become wise. The prologue, epilogue, and contents of the book indicate that Ben Sira was a scribe or sage, likely a Zadokite sage under the direction of the high priest, and in 51:23–25 a teacher operating a boarding school for students.[61] He may have been the rector of a temple or synagogue school in the vicinity of the temple. As a composer he wrote instructions, sayings, poems, hymns, and an encomium, nuanced by an apologetic character. His book underwent some later redaction, although the extent is difficult to identify precisely. In his poem on the roles of the sages, which may have been autobiographical, Ben Sira compares his profession favorably to many others (38:24–39:11).[62] He gives the appearance of wealth and social elitism, knowing how to write and serving in close proximity to the high priest (see 23:14; 39:4) whose audience consisted of students who came from the Jewish aristocracy.[63] His excellent education would have been expensive, and he owned land (7:3, 15, 22) and slaves (7:20–21; 33:25–33; 42:5). These are two indications of his affluence. Yet like the sages before him he exhorted his students to show charity to the poor and warned about the dangers of wealth (5:1, 8; 9:13; 11:14; 12:9; 13:3–7, 21–24; 14:3–10; 21:5; 31:1–7, 23–24; 40:13–14). Joseph Blenkinsopp suggests that he may have had access to the royal court of the Ptolemies, although this seems implausible.[64] Ben Sira implied that he traveled extensively (31:9ff. and 39:4), and he pointed to the necessity of leisure time to engage in reading and writing (38:24ff.). These too suggest he was a man of considerable means.

Ben Sira fully expected to gain entrance to the Hebrew canon, for he considered his teachings to be inspired (24:30–34).[65] While his book did enter into the Alexandrian canon that eventually is reflected in the LXX, he failed to be included in the Hebrew canon, perhaps due to the later tradition that limited inspiration to the period from Moses to Ezra. Martin Hengel surmises that Ben Sira may have held an important position as a judge or political counselor and perhaps was even a member of the *gerousia* or council of elders.[66] These are possible, but not provable. Because of his devotion to the temple and loyalty to the high priesthood, some scholars have suggested that Ben Sira may even have been a temple scribe mentioned in one of the royal decrees of Antiochus III (Josephus, *Ant.* 12.138–139).[67]

Surprisingly, the term "scribe" occurs only once in the surviving Hebrew manuscripts (38:24) and once more in the Greek of Sir. 10:5. In 38:24 he writes: "The wisdom of the sage (ספר) increases wisdom, and the absence of business pursuits allows one (time) to become wise." The Greek translation reads: "The wisdom of the scribe is in the opportunity of leisure, and the one who lacks business will become wise." There is a second occurrence in the Greek translation of Sir. 10:5: "in the hand of the Lord is the success of a man, and he will place his glory upon the face of a scribe (προσώπῳ γραμματέως)." Finally, the term usually translated "commander," occurring only once in Ben Sira (10:5), is likely a term for a scribe who records or enacts a law: "In the hand of God is the rule of every man, and before a commander (מחוקק) he will place his majesty." This is the one place in Ben Sira where the term מחוקק (*mĕḥôqēq*, "commander") is present. In the Greek text it is translated "scribe" (*grammateus*, γραμματεύς). The term *mĕḥôqēq* occurs several times in the Hebrew Bible and means "ruler," "commander," and "a leader in war and peace" (see Gen. 49:10; Num. 21:8; Judg. 5:9, 14; Isa. 33:22 = Sir. 10:5). The Hebrew verbal root of the term, *ḥāqaq* (חקק), means "to engrave/to enact laws," while the noun *ḥôq* (חוק) means "law." Thus the Greek translator probably had in mind a scribe in a legal role, or possibly a military scribe attached to the army who recorded and distributed provisions and materiel (see Philo *Flacc. 3; Agr.* 148; Josephus, *Ant.* 7.319).

Ben Sira: The Traditional Sage

Ben Sira is a sage who is part of the religious and political establishment in Jerusalem. He is likely an opponent of Qoheleth, who preceded him by no more than a little over a generation,[68] and is under the hierarchy of the Zadokite priests whom he supports, in particular the office of high priest (cf. the eulogy to Simeon II in chap. 50). He also points to the temple as the central institution of Jewish life, identifies the Torah with wisdom, and seeks to place the present theocracy within the framework of both creation and salvation history. The temple in particular is grounded in the beneficent order of creation, while Judah in his day is the climax of salvation history, perhaps waiting only for the final liberation from the Syrian Greeks who occupy the land with their troops and rule over the elect.

Ben Sira's ideal sage, described in 38:24–39:11, has features extolled and mentioned elsewhere in the book. He is pious and prayerful (Sir. 14:20a; 15:1; 18:27 = Prov. 14:35; 25:15), engaged in the study of rhetoric (perhaps including not only the Hebrew language and its classics but also the great compositions of Greek literature; Sir. 39:1–2 LXX), knows the teachings of past sages (6:35), engages in the composition of wisdom (18:27–29; 24:31–34), is able to conceal both his thoughts and the secrets of others (8:19; 9:18 = Prov. 10:19; 12:23), avoids improper relations with women (Sir. 42:12–14 = Prov. 23:26–28), can control his appetites (Sir. 31:12–21 = Prov. 20:25–26), is generous to the needy (Sir. 4:1–10 = Prov. 11:17, 24–25), and reflects on and implements the Torah and other wisdom traditions in his behavior (Sir. 38:34 LXX). God is both creator and sustainer, acting through the principle of retribution (7:1–3; 29:11–13; 40:12–27 = Prov. 10:25, 30). In addition, the primary virtue of the wise man is the "fear of Yahweh" (cf. Proverbs), which is expressed in piety, faith, trust, and obedience (Sir. 1:10–20; 19:20; 32:24–33:1; 34:13–14).

Ben Sira: The Scribal Interpreter of Scripture

The responsibility of interpreting the Torah, and indeed the larger expanding canon, and then teaching the content and the interpretive process to his students, is the central feature of Ben Sira's activity. He may have descended from a priestly family (50:27 indicates he was a "son of Eleazar," and his teachings indicate he is devoted to the priestly office and the temple), although there is no evidence he served as a priest.[69] He notes that the priests taught the Torah (45:17) and the scribes the larger collection of books (38:34b–39:1–11). This probably means the priests interpreted the ritual law of the Torah while the Levites and scribes provided instruction in its social and moral commandments. Josephus refers to scribes of the temple (*Ant.* 12.42 = γραμματεῖς τοῦ ἱεροῦ), a possible social identification for Ben Sira.[70]

The portrait of the ideal sage in 38:24–39:11 may be autobiographical. He begins by speaking of the importance of the possession of the "fear of God" and the study of the Law of the Most High God. Ben Sira then extols the scribal profession by placing it above all others and details the activities pursued by contemporary sages: the study of Scripture (law, wisdom, and prophecies), wisdom texts, sapiential language (proverbs and parables as well as thanksgivings), familiarity with the lives and discourses of the ancestors, participation in public councils and assemblies, serving in the role of judges, engagement in expressions of piety, including prayer and supplication, attending to great people, appearance before rulers, diplomatic service in foreign countries, and providing instruction in schools.[71] Based on features inherent in his book, the texts studied by the sage would also have included summaries of Hellenistic and demotic literature. Ben Sira is a cosmopolitan man of the world who is receptive to non-Jews, except for two texts the authorship of which is questionable (36:1–11 and 50:25–26). Ben Sira makes no mention of kashrut or separation from non-Jews. He does emphasize that the life of the sage requires leisure time unencumbered by the constraints inherent in other occupations. He makes no distinction between sages and scribes. They appear to be synonyms.

Ben Sira describes his quest to discover wisdom and to embody it in his teachings and life in the autobiographical text 51:13–30. This quest and obtainment provide the basis for his invitation to take up residence in his house of learning. What he offers is moral and religious instruction to those who study in his school. Ben Sira even likens this teaching to special revelation in a prophetic mode.[72] Thus Ben Sira is an elitist whose wealth, education, literary prowess, and profession of teaching provide him the status and opportunity to teach male students of aristocratic Jewish families.[73]

The scribal interpreter of Scripture is now divinely inspired (see 38:24–39:12) and replaces the prophets in the knowledge of the will of God. Ben Sira even appropriates prophetic ideas and literary forms, for example, the threat in 35:11–24, in order to reinforce this view.[74] Together the Torah, the Prophets, and the other books are the source of divine wisdom, the knowledge of which comes to the inspired sage God has chosen. The construction of the Second Temple by Zerubbabel and Joshua, mentioned in the "Praise of the Pious," and echoed once again in the activities of Simeon II in chapter 50, points to the eschatological redemption of God that is nearing fulfillment. All that is left is the ending of foreign domination of

Judea. In his biblical interpretation, Ben Sira shapes an approach that still allows for the judicious engagement of Judaism with Hellenism in a period prior to political tensions that first emerged during the reign of Antiochus IV Epiphanes.[75]

The Sage as Teacher[76]

Ben Sira taught in a school located in Jerusalem. This is clear from both the literary forms and content of the collections he wrote and organized into his book. The autobiographical poem in 51:13–30 tells of his quest to find wisdom and then to actualize its teachings and insight in his behavior. His obvious success leads to his protrepsis to young men to take up residence in his house of learning. Thus he states in 51:23: "Turn to me, O unlearned ones, and take up residence in my house of study" (*bêt midrāš*, בת מדרש).[77]

Later he concludes his book with a parenetic exhortation and speaks of the many who listened to the knowledge taught to him in his youth: *rabbîm šāmĕʿû lĕmûdî nĕʿārôtî*, רבבים שמעו למדי נערותי (51:28). His grandson, who edited and translated into Greek his grandfather's teachings, indicates that Ben Sira was among those who "were eager for knowledge" (*philomathountas*, φιλο-μαθοῦντας, prol. 5), occupied himself with both *paideia* (παιδεία) and *sophia* (σοφία), and devoted himself to read the Law and the Prophets and the other books of the ancestors. This he did in order that one might "make progress" in living according to the law. Professional teachers were older sages to whom youth came for instruction at their private homes or in their schools (3:29; 6:34, 35; 8:8, 9). Sages are the ones who spoke to youth seeking instruction (9:14), while the "righteous" were sought out to be their hosts (9:16).[78] However, among his students were not only young men but also leaders in the community (33:19; 37:19–26). Indeed, he even engaged in the teaching of the people (*hāʿām*, העם), unless the term refers to a particular group.[79] This likely refers to the instruction in the Law on the Sabbath and during public assemblies in festival periods offered to the gathered assembly. Moses and Aaron in the "Praise of the Pious" were also teachers who instruct (*lāmad*, למד) the people in the law (*ḥôq*, חוק; 45:1–5; 45:6–22). However, they are not called sages or scribes. Education included instruction on behavior and decorum as well as the areas requisite for a profession. The "fool" (*sākāl*, סכל) was the uneducated and the person incapable of learning (cf. 19:23). He fails to "fear God," obey the Torah, practice self-control, speak properly, develop his intelligence, and receive an education.

The Sage as Prophet[80]

As one of the aftermaths of the Babylonian destruction of Jerusalem and the failure of both the glowing predictions of a new Israel by Second Isaiah and the emergence of an independent state, driven by nationalistic predictions made by Haggai and Zechariah, prophecy began a downward spiral, which was difficult to conclude. Indeed, penetrating antiprophetic assessments were voiced in the later Persian period (see, e.g., Zech. 13:2–6). In addition to the development of apocalyptic, in which the seers replaced the prophets as the leading voices of some communities and groups, sages also began to assimilate features of the prophetic persona and role. This is noted by Ben Sira, who sees certain sages (especially himself) elected to receive the divine spirit that inspires didactic writings (see chap. 39). This adaptation of the sage to incorporate the prophetic role was limited to call (election) and inspiration, and did not include prediction and social criticism.

Summary: The Scribe in the Seleucid Period

During the period of Seleucid rule in Judah, important changes in the office of scribe occurred. The increase in literary activity, required by the expanding influence of Greek culture throughout the eastern Mediterranean world, led to the substantial growth in scribal ranks.[81] In addition, the evidence for the origins of the synagogue in Egypt and the eventual appearance of similar houses of assembly in Judah in the late second century BCE point to the likely association of schools for the education of youth and scribes in cities and towns throughout the Hellenistic world. Some scribes became important officials while others were teachers and private amanuenses performing a variety of duties requiring the production and preservation of different types of records. Not all scribes were necessarily conservative supporters of the status quo, although they had a propensity for social conservatism. During the later revolts against Rome, we find scribes who were active in the efforts to overthrow foreign rule.[82] Ben Sira was likely a teacher in a school related to the temple and carried out his activity as a scribe under the direction of the Zadokite hierarchy.

Genres and Literary Structure

Ben Sira taught his students a variety of literary forms, including sayings, poems, and seven from Greek literature: the florilegium, *gnōmologia* = *paroimia*, apostrophe, aretology, protreptic, parenesis, panegyric, and encomium.[83] The last one was, of course, a major type of rhetoric used by Greek writers.[84] The florilegium was a summary of Greek philosophy, while the *gnōmologia* = *paroimia* was a list of sayings. The apostrophe involves a reference to imaginary opponents and was indicated by modulating the voice in speaking the words of the adversaries, since works were read aloud.[85] The aretology was a text of various types listing the virtues of gods. The protreptic was the exhortation, usually issued by a teacher to youth, to enter the course of instruction under his tutelage (51:23–30), while parenesis was an instruction consisting of moral teachings.[86] The panegyric, originating in the funeral eulogy, came to be used in the praise of gods and humans, exemplified in the self-praise of Wisdom as Isis in chapter 24.[87] The encomium was a narrative of characters praised for their virtues. There are also sapiential forms found in the wisdom literature of Israel and Judah. These forms include sayings (the *māšāl*, a variety found throughout the book), the instruction, the hymn of praise similar to those in the Psalter (1:1–10; 18:1–7; 39:12–35; 42:15–43:33; 50:22–24; 51:1–12), the didactic poem (e.g., chap. 24, Woman Wisdom), the prayer of petition (22:7–23:6; 36:1–22) similar to those in the Psalter, the autobiographical narrative (33:16–18; 51:13–15), onomastica (43:32–33), and the didactic narrative (7:22–23, 24–27; 41:1–15).

The Literary Structure of Ben Sira

While the present book of Ben Sira came together over several generations and was edited by later hands, the structure of the composition consists of three well-integrated and coordinated parts: chapters 1–24, 25–43, and 44–51.[88] Each part concludes with a poem or psalm: chapter 24 (a hymn of wisdom's self-praise), 42:15–43:33 (a hymn on creation), and 51:13–30 (a poem describing Ben Sira's search for wisdom). The concluding chapter (chap. 51) also includes an overview of the entire book, uniting the three sections: Ben Sira's prayer of thanksgiving for Yahweh's deliverance (vv. 1–12), the invitation (in Hebrew, not in the Greek recensions) to his audience to give thanks to Yahweh for his redemptive deeds that issue forth from his mercy that "endures forever," and a description of his own successful quest to find wisdom that becomes the basis for his invitation to youth (vv. 13–30).

Following the prologue, the introduction to Ben Sira consists of a poem on wisdom and creation (preserved only in Greek) that focuses on the key theme of the first literary section (cf. the poems on personified Wisdom: 4:11–19; 6:18–37; 14:20–15:10; 24:1–34). This initial poem compares to the one on Woman Wisdom in its conclusion (chap. 24) and to the one on creation in 42:15–43:33 that ends the second part of the book.[89] Taken together these poems provide a literary frame or inclusio for the two parts that set forth the common themes of wisdom and creation. The third section, chapters 44–50, shifts to a history of the ancestral heroes who were pious and performed great deeds on Israel's behalf.

Major Theological Topics and Purpose

Wisdom, Torah, creation, and salvation history are the principal, related themes of the book. However, there are others that remind us that the book is a sapiential text: for example, proper speech, friendship, the decorum of women, sexual comportment, and etiquette. The book is not only an instruction in purpose, but also an apology that seeks to convince students of the origins of wisdom in their own tradition, which is now imparted to them. This contrasts with the attraction of the philosophies of the Greeks.[90]

The Dating of Ben Sira

The grandson writes in the prologue that he arrived in Egypt in the thirty-eighth year of the reign of Euergetes (most probably Ptolemy VIII Euergetes II, 170–164, 145–117 BCE). This would be 132, thus indicating that the date of Ben Sira's book is likely written by the sage sometime between 200 and 175 BCE. Plausibly the ruler would have been Ptolemy VIII Euergetes II Physcon (145–117), who ruled as a co-regent with Cleopatra II (170–164) and as king in his own right in 164–163. But due to the decision of Rome, he became king of Cyrene in 163. In 145 he returned to Egypt and claimed the Alexandrian throne, having his nephew murdered. He ruled as king or shared the throne with Cleopatra II and Cleopatra III, his two rival wives until his death in 117.

The book was more than likely published close to 175 when Ben Sira would have been around sixty. This would allow his grandson, likely an infant when the book appeared in Hebrew, the time to grow up and travel to Egypt when he was in his forties (132 BCE) and then to translate into Greek and publish the volume in his sixties (ca. 117).[91] John Collins, among others, suggests that his translation was completed just after the death of Ptolemy VIII in 117.[92] Toward the end of the book, a concluding colophon in 50:27–29 (obscured somewhat by the addition of an appendix in chap. 51) is written in the first person. The author and collector of this "book" identifies himself as Jesus, the son of Eleazar, the son of Sirach, of Jerusalem.

The Hebrew and Greek Texts of Ben Sira[93]

The poor state of the Hebrew text seriously complicates the interpretation of the book. Approximately two-thirds of the Hebrew text has survived in the original language in a variety of textual recensions.[94] The Greek translation (LXX) is better preserved, since it contains the entire book, but even it exists in two major recensions: a short text (GI) and a longer expanded one (GII).[95] The Hebrew text is preserved in part in six different, medieval, Cairo Genizah[96] manuscripts (A, B, C, D, E, and possibly F), fragments from Qumran (2Q18; 11QPs^a), and twenty-six fragments including a lengthy section (39:27–44:71) and much smaller ones found at Masada (M). The fragments found in Qumran and Masada are the oldest, and both, on paleographic grounds, may be dated to the first century BCE. However, it is generally conceded that the Genizah manuscripts still represent an ancient literary tradition. These Hebrew texts also point to two different recensions: a short text (HTI), representing the closest text we have to the original of Ben Sira, and a longer, expanded text (HTII) that is lengthened by the addition of verses by later editors. The translations and interpretations of passages below will essentially follow ms. B., the best preserved among the surviving Hebrew texts, and the critical Greek text of the Göttingen LXX, established by Joseph Ziegler, for those places where no Hebrew ms. survives.[97] The primary critical texts are those of Pancratius Cornelis Beentjes for the Hebrew, which will be followed when extant and not corrupt, and Ziegler for the LXX.[98]

TEXTS OF CREATION THEOLOGY
IN THE BOOK OF BEN SIRA[99]

Introduction

Creation theology is the theme of Ben Sira that unites the book into a well-constructed literary composition. Others include: wisdom,[100] the fear of God,[101] Torah, and the history of salvation. Yahweh is the creator and sustainer who determines fates and acts to reward the faithful and punish the wicked. This matrix is the theological construct of wisdom literature from its very inception, and the teachings of Ben Sira continue this emphasis.

The theology of Ben Sira is not significantly different from that of Proverbs when it comes to creation or morality for that matter. However, this sage does make three major additions to the earlier traditional teachers' extant writings. First, he chooses to identify wisdom with Torah, viewing the law especially through the understanding of the book of Deuteronomy (e.g., see Deut. 4:5–6).[102] The order of creation ("wisdom") is now equated with the order of the Torah[103] that embodies the teachings of God for wise behavior that characterizes all faithful Jews. Ben Sira's view is cosmological,[104] since wisdom may be found not only in the Torah but also in the order intrinsic to the world of creation. Second, not only is wisdom present in the Torah and revealed in the cosmos, it also takes up residence in Israel and is exemplified in the lives of great men from Jewish history. Thus Ben Sira was a theologian who, like Second Isaiah before him, combined creation theology with salvation history (cf. Wis. 10–19). This is the first known example of the combination of creation with salvation in a sapiential text. Third, Ben Sira approaches the issue of theodicy through the lens of creation theology.[105] The sage uses this theme to respond in two related ways to this most pressing problem: to portray the character and design of divine activity in the beginning and to explain that all things act according to the purpose for which they were made.

The combination of wisdom and Torah within the larger framework of creation helps us understand both the theology of the sage and his sociohistorical milieu.[106] Proverbs and Job use the term *tôrâ* in reference to sapiential teaching. However, the Torah Psalms (1, 19, and 119) and, in particular, Ben Sira equate the wisdom with Torah, the teachings of the commandments. The language in Sirach 24 that praises personified Wisdom uses images that refer to the Torah, thus identifying the two. In speaking of her origins, Wisdom's self-praise in the form of an Isis panegyric indicates that she proclaims to the community of Israel, "the assembly of the Most High," "I came forth from the mouth of the Most High" (24:3). At the conclusion of the hymn in chapter 24 (vv. 23–34), Ben Sira identifies wisdom with the Torah: "All this is the book of the covenant of the Most

High God, the law that Moses commanded us as an inheritance for the assembly of Jacob" (for the expression "book of the covenant," see Exod. 24:7; for the "law that Moses commanded," cf. Deut. 33:4).

This identification of Torah and wisdom continues in later Jewish texts and becomes a central theological view of rabbinic Judaism. For example, in Baruch 3:9–38 and 4:1–4, which likely are dependent upon Sirach 24, one discovers a similar identification of wisdom with the Torah. The theme of Torah is an important one in this period when the Pentateuch has been completed and regarded as Scripture and when the sociopolitical character of Judaism has become, at least to the traditional wise and to the Zadokite priests, a theocracy that is the culmination of history. The Torah becomes the localized constitution of this community.

The Origins of Wisdom and Creation: 1:1–10

The opening poem introduces several themes about wisdom and creation that recur throughout the composition: Wisdom (cf. Prov. 8–9) traces her origins to God, who created her before all other things. While cosmic Wisdom is identified with both the revelatory word of God and the divine commandments of the Torah, only God comprehends its mystery and expanse (cf. Job 28). The ability to comprehend Wisdom, which shapes and then is revealed in creation, is a divine gift to those who love God.[107] Divine revelation of the Creator is made possible only by means of this gift bestowed upon those whom he has chosen (i.e., the elect and especially their leaders).[108]

If one includes the additions from the expanded GII, the literary structure of this poem is based on four questions found in verses 2, 3, 6, and 7, the first two asking about the incomprehensible and vast nature of creation and the last two about the knowledge of Wisdom, in particular her origins and activities. This structure underscores the emphasis on Wisdom as the key to understanding the cosmos. The answers to these questions are found in verses 8–10 with the caveat that only Yahweh knows Wisdom in her totality. This denies to other religions, to apocalyptic seers, and to Hellenistic philosophers the ability to know Yahweh. He is the one who is "wise" (sophos, σοφός) sitting on the divine throne. This cosmic ruler is the creator ("he created her," ektisen autēn,[109] ἔκτισεν αὐτήν) and designer of Wisdom ("he saw and apportioned her"; eiden kai exērithmēsen autēn, εἶδεν καὶ ἐχηρίθμησεν αὐτὴν; cf. Job 28:27) who pours her out over all creation and offers her as a divine gift. The metaphor of "seeing and recounting" is similar to the description of Ptah's creation in which something is formed in the mind and then created by speaking. Her "root" (rhiza, ῥίζα) refers to both her origins and essential vitality known only by the Lord. Human beings do not know her. "Her wonderful feats" (panourgeumata, πανουργεύματα) are the mysterious actions of Wisdom in bringing redemption and life. She was "created before all other things." Yet this divine, cosmic Wisdom, who was poured out over all the earth at the time of creation and who continues to be the instrument of divine providence, is imparted as a divine gift only to those who love God, making known at least some of the secrets of creation and divine activity to those who possess her. Like the gift of the divine spirit of which the charismatic prophets had spoken, she is poured out over all creation (1:9; cf. Num. 11:29; Ezek. 39:29; Joel 3:1–5)[110] and dwells among "all flesh." This means, then, that heavenly Wisdom, the first act of creation and the one who reveals the Creator, is present throughout all creation and resides among human beings. However, she is available only to those who love (*agapaō*, ἀγαπάω) him. Cosmology and anthropology are combined in this opening poem by personified Wisdom in order to shape a politically and socially conservative worldview (see Prov. 8:22–31 and Job 28). Unlike humans, who are limited in their knowledge of the cosmos, the Lord knows all things, including Wisdom.

Wisdom's Role in Creation and Providence: 16:24–18:14[111]

This lengthy section on creation and providence is one of several extended compositions on this subject (see 39:12–35 and 42:15–43:35). One finds five poems linked together: the creation of the cosmos (16:24–30), the creation of humanity (17:1–10), law and judgment that includes retribution (17:11–24), a call to repentance (17:25–32), and divine mercy (18:1–14). This composition, along with the first poem in 1:1–10, are what one might best regard as reflective meditations on creation and providence in the Hebrew Bible, particularly in Genesis 1–3.[112]

The initial poem begins with an introduction to the instruction (Sir. 16:24–25). Then follow two strophes (vv. 26–28 and 29–30) that use different images to present God as creator. First, by means of the spoken word, God assigns every natural element of creation to its place and enables each of his works to accomplish its particular task or function forever (vv. 26–28). These "works" likely include the heavens and the earth, along with the natural elements that comprise each sphere: the heavenly bodies of sun, moon, and stars, as well as the wind, rivers, plants, and trees. Elaborating on the first creation account in Gen. 1:1–2:4a (the power and ordering of the divine word), Ben Sira states that this continuous regularity and order in the operations of the heavens and the earth is achieved because the works of creation are obedient to the divine imperative (see Isa. 40:26). The works of creation are personified not as divine powers possessing their own will, but rather as obedient forces following the directives of the sovereign God for their own operations. All things are created to exist in harmony and are obedient to the divine will in following what God has determined for them to be and to do.

In the initial strophe, Ben Sira speaks of the Lord as having "created" his works from the "beginning," "making them," and "assigning" to them their tasks. These works he "ordered" forever and established their "domains" for their generations. The various works have never been "abandoned" and they have never "disobeyed" "his word." This strophe serves as the major point for the entire section (16:24–18:14): obedience to God's commandments, whether by the elements of creation or by the human creature, and acting according to their divinely instituted tasks lead to harmony, order, and well-being. God has not chosen to create and then ignore his works. He rules over them in providence.

The second strophe (16:29–30) elaborates on the creation of living beings in Gen. 1:20–25 and 2:19 (cf. Ps. 104, especially vv. 24–30) by presenting God as the beneficent Lord who, having looked upon the earth, fills it with good things and covers its surface with every kind of living being. The poem suggests that "every living creature" is taken from the earth and at death returns to it (see Gen. 2:19; 3:19; Ps. 104:24–30; Qoh. 12:7). The world is filled with "good" (*agathōn*, ἀγαθῶν) things, echoing Gen. 1:1–2:4a, which describes each element of reality as "good" (*ṭôb*, טוב) and the entire creation as "very good" (*ṭôb mĕʾōd*, טוב מאד). This poem thus expresses the general Israelite view that creation is "good," that is, orderly, beautiful, and life-enhancing and -sustaining.

The creation of the cosmos is followed by the creation of humanity in the second poem (Sir. 17:1–10; cf. especially Gen. 1:26–28; 2:7; 3:19; Job 10; Pss. 8 and 139).[113] This second poem has two strophes: the creation and role of humanity in the cosmos (vv. 1–4), and the gifts of wisdom and piety (vv. 6–10). While humans are made in the divine "image" (*eikona*, εἰκόνα), they also, like all other living creatures, are "created" (*ektisev*, ἔκτισεν) from the same earth to which they eventually return (Gen. 3:19; Ps. 146:4; Qoh. 3:20–21; 12:7).[114] In spite of human mortality, God has given humans authority over the earth (cf. Gen. 1:26–28 and Ps. 8), puts the fear of them in all living creatures (Gen. 9:2), provides them a place to inhabit (i.e., the earth; cf. Gen. 1:28 and Prov. 8:30–31), and sets a predetermined time for their existence (i.e., the human life span; cf. Job 14:1–2; Ps. 90:10; Isa. 65:20). The divine image, possessed by all humans, points to their role in ruling the earth as the surrogate of God, and not to their nature. To facilitate this human rule, God "clothes them with strength that is appropriate for them." This "strength" most likely refers to the appropriate power humans possess to carry out the divine imperative of ruling over the earth (contrast Job 10:4–9, which describes the frailty of human existence).[115] The terror that animals have of humanity assists humans to have authority over the earth and its creatures (cf. Gen. 9:2). As the cosmos is obedient to divine rule, so the animal kingdom is obedient to human sovereignty.

The second strophe describes humans as possessing two important gifts from God: wisdom (here the ability to deliberate and reason by means of the organs of perception; cf. 1 Kgs. 3:9; Prov. 20:12) and piety (i.e., "the fear of the Lord"; cf. Prov. 1:7). The divine wisdom operative in the cosmos becomes the pattern for human understanding and moral behavior.[116] Unlike the negative implications of "knowledge of good and evil" in the J story of creation (Gen. 2:17; 3:5, 22), wisdom is freely given and does not bear the onus of rebellion against divine rule. In this strophe, however, wisdom enables humanity to know and then to choose between "good and evil" (*agatha*, ἀγαθά, and *kaka*, κακά; see Gen. 2:9, 16–17). Humans are endowed with wisdom that empowers them to rule beneficently and well God's good creation, a point drawing on ancient Near Eastern royal ideology.[117] Humans, through God's gift of wisdom, have the capacity to reason and to choose the "good" that will enhance and extend life and well-being. Later, the teacher ascribes to humans the responsibility to engage in labor that is a "heavy yoke" (Sir. 40:1), although this toil is not a punishment for human sin.[118]

Ben Sira offers the most detailed definition of the "fear of God" in wisdom literature, for this expression serves as one of his most prominent themes. In this second strophe, he professes that God places in the human heart the "fear of him" (Sir. 17:8) so that people may praise the Creator for his marvelous deeds (cf. 1:11–20).[119] As noted earlier in the discussion of the "fear of God" in Prov. 1:7, the phrase is the acknowledgment that God is the divine creator and sovereign of the world, an attestation that leads to faithful praise. The "fear of God" is also a charismatic endowment of the wise ruler who is therefore able to rule the kingdom with justice (see, e.g., Solomon's prayer for wisdom in 1 Kgs. 3 and the gifts of the spirit given to the ideal king in Isa. 11:1–9).

The third poem (Sir. 17:11–24) moves from the creation of the cosmos and the dominion of human beings over the earth to Jewish election (first strophe, vv. 11–17) and divine judgment (second strophe, vv. 18–24). Ben Sira is the first sage to combine sapiential teaching about creation with the normative traditions of Israelite faith that focus on salvation history associated especially with the exodus and the temple. In this poem, the election traditions of covenant and law are grounded in the theological formulations of the creation of the world (16:24–30) and of humanity (17:1–10).

This legal instruction, which encompasses the teachings of wisdom, is a "law of life." The reference to the "law of life" undoubtedly points to the Torah (cf. 45:5) and is a description borrowed from Deuteronomy (Deut. 30:11–20; 32:46–47). Sirach 17:13 echoes the Sinaitic tradition's reference to the Israelites beholding the theophany that accompanies the giving of the commandments (Exod. 19:16–24; cf. Exod. 19:9), only in Ben Sira the people see this divine glory, while in P they are limited to hearing the voice of Yahweh speaking from the "thick cloud on the mountain." The connection of wisdom (= Torah for Ben Sira) with life is a frequent concept in sapiential teachings (Sir. 19:20; cf. Deut. 4:6; Prov. 1:32–33; 8:32–36). To obtain wisdom, the student is to study the Torah and its teachings (Sir. 15:1), and it is a primary source of meditation (6:37). Those who are wise will adhere to its commandments (24:24).

For Ben Sira God gave Israel the Torah as an "inheritance" (eklērodotēsen, ἐκληροδότησεν) and becomes God's special revelation to them. This Torah is placed within an "eternal covenant" (διαθήκην, diathēkēn; αἰῶνός, aiōnos) that God has established with his chosen people. In the Hebrew Bible the expression "eternal covenant" is used of several covenants: the covenant between God and all living creatures in which God promises not to destroy again the creation (Gen. 9:16); the covenant between God, Abraham, and his descendants (Gen. 17:7, 13, 19); and the covenant between God and Moses (Exod. 31:16; Lev. 24:8; Num. 18:19). Ben Sira's remarks about Israel's seeing the glory of God and hearing his voice (Sir. 17:13) make it apparent that the "eternal covenant" is the Mosaic covenant established at Mount Sinai (Exod. 19:16–19; 24:15–17; see Sir. 24).[120] God's revelation at Sinai is summarized in two parts in this strophe: "avoiding all unrighteousness," and the commandments concerning the neighbor. The avoidance of evil is a summary of the Law's and wisdom's comprehensive teaching about moral conduct. It is God himself who has chosen Israel to be his special "portion" (*meris*, μερίς) to nurture and sustain (see Exod. 19:5; Deut. 7:6; 14:2). This association of election and the Mosaic covenant with wisdom and creation, actualized in the ritual celebrations and festivals of the temple cult and the high priesthood of the chosen Zadokites, provides the authoritative grounding of the sociopolitical reality of Ben Sira. The sage has drawn on every conceivable theological tradition to authenticate his vision of the theocracy in which he now lives and the irreversible movement toward the exaltation of Israel over not only the nations but also the cosmos itself.

In the second strophe (Sir. 17:18–24), the emphasis then shifts to divine judgment, where God, the Creator, is aware of human behavior and requites the wicked and the righteous with their just deserts. This points to what happens to those who abrogate the teachings of Torah and wisdom with their evil behavior. Retribution is based on disobedience to the revelation of the Torah to Israel, a Deuteronomic teaching. Thus it is not the nations but the elect who are the subject of the poem's emphasis on divine judgment. With election comes additional responsibility. God will redeem his people who are good or those who repent of their wickedness, but also will requite the wicked.

The fourth poem in this section (17:25–32) is a summons to repentance that recalls several prophetic and sapiential texts (see, e.g., Jer. 3:11–4:2; Prov. 1:20–33). In speaking of repentance and the mercy of God, the poem moves back to creation. God's mercy is given to humans, for they are but "dust and ashes" (see Job 42:6). Thus the inherent limitations of human existence (mortality and weakness) are recognized by a merciful God who is sure to forgive those who repent and turn to him.

The fifth and last poem (18:1–14) in this section consists of three strophes (vv. 1–6, 7–10, and 11–14), each of which returns to one of the three main themes of the earlier poems: the creation of the cosmos, the creation and roles of humanity, and the compassionate mercy of God. The first strophe speaks of God's wondrous deeds, mighty power, and unlimited mercy that transcend all human descriptions and understanding. God is portrayed as the eternal and just judge who rules in majestic glory and great power over his creation. The insignificance of humanity is expressed in the second strophe to provide a major contrast. Verse 8a echoes Ps. 8:4 (cf. Job 7:17) with the question: "What is a human being, and what worth is he?"

This strophe emphasizes humanity's brief life span, little worth, minor accomplishments, and inability to comprehend the wonders and glory of God and his works (cf. Job's defense made to God). In view of the greatness of God and the insignificance of humanity, even human good and evil are worth little consideration.[121] This contrast between the sovereignty and greatness of God and the insignificance of human beings is the poem's basis for the mercy of Yahweh expressed toward humans that is mentioned in the third strophe (Sir. 17:11–14). The divine judge is patient with mortals for their weaknesses and is forgiving of their sins. Indeed, like the wise teacher, God reproves, admonishes, teaches, and shepherds (see Pss. 2; 23; 80; Isa. 40:11; Ezek. 34:11–16) his human creatures. Subsequently, those who are obedient to the teachings of God are especially the beneficiaries of divine forgiveness.

In this lengthy composition (Sir. 16:24–18:14) five wisdom poems examine the themes of creation, law, and election. For Ben Sira the order and regularity of the cosmos results not only from the wisdom and governance of the Creator, but also from the obedience of the creation to the rules governing its existence established by God at creation. Humans, too, made in the divine image and given dominion over the other creatures, are endowed by the Creator with wisdom and the "fear of God" that form the basis of and potentiality for obedience. Thus obedience to God, the foundation for order and regularity in nature and human society, is grounded in creation theology. It is effectuated through behavior governed according to the Torah, that is, wisdom, which permeates the cosmos and makes it possible to live a life in concert with the divine will. Abrogation of any of these features (law, wisdom, election, covenant, and creation) is not tolerated by this socially conservative sage.

Wisdom's Search for a Dwelling Place: 24:1–34[122]

In chapter 24 Wisdom once again is personified as a heavenly goddess who engages in a hymn of self-praise (see Prov. 8 and Greek aretologies of the goddess Isis). Unlike Job 28, this hymn is mainly spoken in the first person (Sir. 24:3–22; see Prov. 8:1–9:6), so that Wisdom is the one who praises and describes herself. There are examples of hymns in which gods and goddesses of the ancient Near East and Greece sang hymns of praise (or panegyrics)[123] in honor of themselves.[124] Ben Sira borrows this genre in composing his literary hymn in which this personified metaphor, Woman Wisdom, praises herself in the midst of two audiences: her own people (i.e., the Jews) and the divine council in heaven.[125] This hymn describes the divine origins and cosmic rule of Wisdom (cf. 1:1), her "covering the earth like a mist" (cf. Gen. 1:2), her taking up residence in Israel and Jerusalem, her identification with the temple cult and the Law, her description as the tree and waters of life, and her invitation to participate in a banquet of life that offers her fruit to her followers.[126] She is identified with both the transcendent realm of divine dwelling and the immanent presence of God on the earth and particularly among the chosen people.

This hymn of self-praise contains the following literary structure: a third-person introit (Sir. 24:1–2), the origins and rule of Wisdom (strophe I, vv. 3–6), Wisdom's residence in Israel and Jerusalem (strophe II, vv. 7–11), Wisdom and the tree of life (strophe III, vv. 12–17), Wisdom's invitation to the banquet of life (strophe IV, vv. 19–22), Wisdom's identification with the Law and comparison to the rivers of life (strophe V, vv. 23–29), and the life-giving waters of Wisdom's teaching (strophe VI, 30–34). The thematic movement of the poem points to the actualization of heavenly wisdom in Second Temple Judaism. Ben Sira makes significant use of the Wisdom poems in three earlier texts: Prov. 1:20–33; 8:1–36; and Job 28 (see Wis. 7–9), as well as the Isis hymns offered in praise of this popular Egyptian deity who, with Serapis her consort, became the most honored divine pair of the mystery religions. The social force of this and other passages where the sage speaks in similar ways is to entrench firmly the office of the sage in all theological traditions that make up his view of reality. The authority of the sage in teaching Torah and wisdom cannot be ignored, for to do so is to experience divine punishment and destruction. This theology provides the authoritative basis for the office of the sage, the teaching of wisdom, and the interpretation of the Law. Wisdom from the sage is not something that one may choose to accept or reject, but rather is an instruction that is incontestable. Any idea of argument and debate, so common in wisdom circles before and after Ben Sira, is disallowed. To reject this teaching is to reject life.

Chapter 24, due to its location in the literary structure of the book and content, provides the theme and high point of the entire book.[127] The other themes and key terms that occur in the remainder of the book are used by Ben Sira to flesh out the present poem: covenant, law, wisdom, history, creation, and temple. The structure of the poem unites the major sections of the book. Structurally and cosmologically, wisdom is the center of reality, both the symbolic universe depicted by Ben Sira in his literary formulation and the mythic, theological world of the sages.[128]

The introit (vv. 1–2) places Woman Wisdom in the divine "assembly of the Most High" and indicates that she opens her mouth to praise herself and her virtues. The assembly is a mythic image that points to the council of the gods presided over by the creator and sovereign of the heaven and earth. The title for God, "Most High (hypsistou, ὑψίστου)," is one of exaltation, originating in Canaanite religion, where the creator god, El, was the ruler of the council of gods. The "assembly of the Most High" is the divine council (see Isa. 6; Ps. 82; and Job 1–2) that by Ben Sira's time has become a heavenly court consisting of God and the "host" of heaven, the latter demoted to demythologized deities who now are heavenly creatures possessing a variety of functions.[129] Among them is Wisdom, a goddess created by God and the all-encompassing presence who is found throughout the earth and rules over the nations. This personified metaphor is an example of Ben Sira using the language of myth to narrate divine creation and providential rule (see Sir. 1:1–10; Prov. 8:22–31; Wis. 7–9).[130]

In the first strophe (Sir. 24:3–6) cosmic Wisdom describes her origins in the mouth of the Most High, evoking the metaphor of God's speaking reality into existence (see Gen. 1:1–2:4a; Ps. 33).[131] Wisdom then is compared to a "mist" (homixla, ὁμίξλη) that covers the earth, poetically identifying this ordering principle of creation with the "mist that arises from earth that waters the entire face of the ground" in the second creation narrative in Genesis. In Gen. 2:6 the first act of creation was the watering of the land. Ben Sira appropriates this image from the J creation story to identify Wisdom as the water that permeates and brings life to the cosmos (see Sir. 24:23–29 and 30–31).

Ben Sira goes on to describe Wisdom's dwelling place in the heights or mountains, a typical location in ancient Near Eastern and Israelite mythology for the dwelling of deities. This is likely due to the majesty and awe-inspiring view of mountain peaks extending into the heavens that are covered with clouds: for example, Mount Sinai/Horeb (Exod. 3; 19; and 24) and Mount Zion (Pss. 48:2; 68:16; 84:5). The "pillar of the cloud" is another dwelling place of Wisdom and echoes the "pillar of the cloud" in Exod. 13:21–22 that, along with the "pillar of fire," points to the guiding presence of God in the Sinai. The "pillar of the cloud" also is used of a theophany associated with the tent of meeting in Exod. 33:7–11, the place where Moses received the oracle of God, thus recalling the Sinai tradition. In the poetic imagination of Ben Sira, Wisdom's dwellings express both the transcendence and immanence of God and their association with creation, redemption, and revelation. He speaks of three spheres of the cosmos: heaven (or "the heights," *hypsalois*, ὑψηλοῖς), the abyss, and the earth (cf. Yahweh in Job 38–41). The "vault of the heaven" (*gyron ouranou*, γῦρον οὐρανοῦ) refers to the firmament (*rāqîaʿ*, רָקִיעַ) that in Genesis 1 separates the waters into two regions: the waters above and the waters below (see Sir. 43:12; Job 22:14; Prov. 8:27). In the Priestly creation story, this vault is called heaven and contains the lights that separate night from day and determine the festivals, seasons, and years (see Gen. 1:6–8, 14–19). The "depth of the abyss" (*babei abyssōn*, βάβει ἀβύσσων) refers to the lower regions, especially the cosmic ocean or chaos that existed in P prior to creation (Gen. 1:1–2). In Ugaritic myth Leviathan inhabits the deep. Prince Yamm, the antagonist of Baal, the god of fertility, ruled over this region and contended with him for sovereignty over the earth. Yahweh also fought with monsters of the deep and Prince Yamm in gaining and maintaining sovereignty over the earth (see Job 38:8–11; Ps. 74:12–17). In Ben Sira, however, it is Wisdom who proclaims that she "rules over the waves of the sea and over all the earth." Wisdom now assumes the role of God's surrogate in expressing divine sovereignty over the cosmos (heavens, earth, and sea). It is especially important to note that features and language usually associated with God are now applied to Woman Wisdom.

The second strophe (Sir. 24:7–11) combines divine creation and sovereignty in which Wisdom has a substantial role in the election of Israel and in the study and embodiment of her tradition by the sages. Cosmic Wisdom, fashioned (*ktizō*, κατίζω) by God, goes in search of a people among whom to take up a place of rest ("rest," *anapausis*, ἀνάπαυσις) and is commanded by her Creator to "set up her tent" (*skēnē*, σκηνή) in Jacob and to "make her inheritance" in Israel.[132] Wisdom's seeking of "rest" in v. 7, imitating Israel's own desire during her journey in the Sinai wilderness after the exodus and prior to settlement in Canaan, uses the same Greek word for resting from labors on the seventh day in the Septuagint's translation of Exod. 23:12. Similarly, in Exod. 23:11 the land is to lay fallow in the seventh year so that the poor and the wild animals may eat. Wisdom's resting place in the "beloved city" (Sir. 24:11) mirrors the rest on the Sabbath that not only reinvigorates the weary but also liberates people from the oppression of hard labor, an interpretation present in the exodus theology of Deuteronomic law (Deut. 5:15). It is the same invigorating, renewing, life-giving rest promised to those who respond to the sage's invitation (*protrepsis*) to take up the study of wisdom (LXX Sir. 6:28; 51:27). Election language dominates this strophe. "Tent" is a metaphor for Israel, and reflects the "tent of meeting" in which the wilderness community placed the ark of the covenant and Moses encountered the divine presence and received his divine revelation. The tent was the visible sign of divine dwelling among the tribes and was even a portable shrine, located in sacred cities in Israel prior to Solomon's building of the temple in Jerusalem. "Inheritance" (*klēronomia*, κατακληρόω ἀλτηουγή; v. 8 uses the verbal form) is a common election term that denotes Israel as the special possession of God (Deut. 4:20; 1 Sam. 10:1; 1 Kgs. 8:53; etc.). In Sir. 24:8 Israel is the inheritance of Wisdom. Thus the sage, well versed in Scripture, combines the creation theology of P with the exodus liberation of D.

"Lodging" (*aulizomai*, αὐλίζομαι) in Ben Sira's "house of interpretation" (LXX Sir. 51:23) to pursue his course of study reflects Wisdom's dwelling (*aulizomai*, αὐλίζομαι) and flourishing in Israel in 24:7. The reference to the tent or tabernacle reflects the wilderness tradition and its celebration in the pilgrimage festival of Tabernacles. In this tradition and its reactualization in worship and sacred memory, God's providential guidance of Israel through the Sinai, symbolized by the dwelling in tents of pilgrims who come to Jerusalem for the festival, is celebrated. Israel's transient existence in the wilderness time is reflected in living in tents or tabernacles. Yet Ben Sira also has in mind the sacred tent or tabernacle as a place of revelation, now provided by Wisdom. In verse 8 of this psalm, Yahweh is asked to enter into the sanctuary and to come to his "place of rest" (*aulizomai*, αὐλίζομαι; LXX Ps. 131:8), an action symbolized by the procession of the ark into the temple. Now it is Wisdom, the symbol of divine presence, who finds her resting place in the temple, where she ministers unto God.

The election of Zion (= Jerusalem) as the dwelling place of Yahweh and the site of the Solomonic temple, which is rebuilt in the late sixth century BCE (2 Sam. 7; Pss. 46, 48, 76) is another significant sacred tradition, in this case that of Zion, used by Ben Sira in this second strophe (24:10–11). It is Wisdom who is present in and ministers, like a Zadokite priest, before God in the temple[133] in Jerusalem, the "beloved (*ēgapēmenē*, ἠγαπημένη) city." Now Wisdom is identified with the priesthood that "ministers" or "provides divine service" (*leitourgeō*, λειτουργέω) to the Creator first in the tabernacle in the wilderness and later in the temple (Exod. 28–29; Lev. 6–9) located in the "beloved city," Jerusalem (cf. Pss. 87:2; 132:14). Ben Sira partakes of the Second Temple traditions of Jerusalem, especially the temple, which takes on cosmic significance as the center of the earth where God as creator and lord of history dwells and defeats the forces of chaos (both mythical and historical) that threaten his sovereignty and the order of creation and history (e.g., Pss. 46; 48; 76; Ezek. 40–48).

Ben Sira combines this election tradition with creation theology in the second strophe in several ways: God, the "creator (*ktistēs*, κτίσας) of all," "fashioned" eternal Wisdom and "commanded" her to dwell among the Israelites. Ben Sira's use of the term "rest" (*anapausis*, ἀνάπαυσις) echoes not only the sacred traditions of wilderness and settlement, but also suggests the Priestly understanding of the Sabbath and creation: God "rested" (*katapauō*, κατάπαύω) on the seventh day, following creation (LXX Gen. 2:1–4a) and commanded Israel to sanctify the Sabbath by resting (*katapauō*, κατάπαύω) from their labors (LXX Exod. 20:8–11). Subsequently, Wisdom's "resting" among the Israelites points to their election as the people of God, the exodus and tabernacle, the creation and renewal of the earth through Sabbath rest and worship, and the invigoration of life that comes through sapiential discipline (piety and study = *mûsār*, מוסר).

In this second strophe it is cosmic Wisdom, created by God, who goes in search of a resting place and pitches her sacred tent in Israel following a time of wandering and searching. It is Wisdom who, taking up residence in her tabernacle, represents the divine presence among Jacob. And it is Wisdom who engages in sacred service in the tent, identifying the liturgical rituals of the priestly service with the study and devotion of the sage. Through the worship of God that recalls and then reactualizes the salvific force of God's redemptive history and the sages' quest for wisdom, life in its abundance is experienced and renewed. This does not mean that God is simply the God of Israel, for he is a universal Deity. Rather, he has elected Israel to be his chosen people, signified here by Wisdom's taking up residence among the people of Israel in the temple in Jerusalem. Wisdom's dwelling among the people of Israel is done in obedience to the divine commandment. Eventually, through cosmic wisdom and the elect people, God comes to be known by and to bless the peoples of the earth.

The third strophe (vv. 12–17) of this poem presents two important images: paradise and cultic service. Wisdom speaks of her "taking root (*rhizoō*, ῥιζόω) among an honored people" and becoming a flourishing tree that sends out its branches in arable soil for nourishment. Israel, the elect people, nourishes Wisdom and enables her to grow (cf. Ps. 1:3). Wisdom is compared to six different types of luxuriant, graceful, and mighty trees (cedar, cypress, date palm, olive, plane, and terebinth), to rose bushes in Jericho, and to a fruitful vine. Ben Sira may have in mind a comparison of Wisdom with the sacred garden of myth found in the garden of Eden in Genesis 2 and in Mesopotamian mythology, where trees are planted in the sacred garden of the temple (cf. Gen. 2:8–9, 15–17). In Mesopotamian mythology the royal king guarded the "tree of life" that was denied human beings. This is reflected in Gen. 2:9, and Wisdom was identified with the tree of life in sapiential imagination (cf. Prov. 3:18). Adam is the one who tends to and guards the sacred garden.

In Sir. 24:15 Ben Sira mentions the fragrances and aromas identified with cultic service, including incense used in tabernacle worship. The perfumes in v. 15a were mixed with olive oil to produce holy oil used to anoint the tent, the ark, other sacred equipment, and the priests (Exod. 30:23–30), while various resins (galbanum and mastic) and the oil of mollusks (onycha) were blended with frankincense to manufacture incense for sacred service in the holy tabernacle (Exod.

30:34–38). Thus Wisdom's identification with the sacred nature of the temple service points to the important relationship of these two paths to God, blessing, and life. Wisdom, like the priesthood and the cultus, functions as an intermediary between God and the world. As is the case with the temple worship, Wisdom becomes a means by which to approach God and to obtain life. Finally, like the cultic service, Sabbath, and festivals, Wisdom revitalizes and continues the cosmos.

The conclusion of this strophe depicts Wisdom as a luxuriant tree (here a terebinth) whose branches are characterized by "glory and grace" (*doxa*, δόξα, and *charis*, χάρις; cf. *Sib. Or.* 5.427). Its vine produces "graciousness" or "grace" (*charis*, χάρις), that is, divine mercy delivers from destruction and opens the door to life (LXX Gen. 6:8; Exod. 33:12; Qoh. 9:11; 10:12) and offers the gift of "fruit of honor and wealth" (*ploutos*, πλοῦτος). Honor and wealth are the coveted gifts bestowed upon the wise (Prov. 3:16).

The fourth strophe contains Wisdom's invitation (protrepsis; Sir. 24:19–22; cf. Prov. 8:32–36; Isa. 55:1–3; Matt. 11:28–30) to eat and drink of her. In Prov. 9:1–6 eating and drinking the victuals of the banquet to which Wisdom invites the "unlearned" occur after having built her spacious house or palace to celebrate the inauguration of her reign of life (cf. Prov. 9:1–6). These victuals also reflect those of a sacred meal of communion between God and worshipers (e.g., Exod. 24), only now it is the eating and drinking of Wisdom that bring life and well-being. It is important to note that the appetite and thirst for wisdom are never satiated and quenched. This suggests that the pursuit and study of wisdom is a lifelong task (see Prov. 1:2–7).[134]

The fifth strophe (Sir. 24:23–29) identifies Wisdom with the Torah (see Deut. 4:6; 33:4; Ezra 7:15, 25), which later becomes personified and preexistent in rabbinic Judaism.[135] Education came to focus on the Torah in the Second Temple period, as noted by the authors who speak of the scribes and Levites as teachers of the Torah to the Jewish people in Neh. 8:9. It is clear that Ben Sira regards the Torah as the central subject of the curriculum of his school. This theme of the Torah or commandments is found over fifty times in Ben Sira.[136]

In the same strophe, the poet returns to the images of paradise and election to stress both Wisdom's life-giving powers to creation and sovereignty over the nations. Paradise is suggested by the four rivers (Pishon, Gihon, Tigris, and Euphrates), which form from the cosmic life-giving river watering the garden of Eden once it leaves the garden, to flow throughout the earth (Gen. 2:10–14). Ben Sira also identifies Wisdom's instruction with the fertility of the land made possible by two rivers: the Nile and the Gihon. The inundation of the Nile Valley by the Nile River enriched the soil and made agriculture in Egypt extremely productive, while in Israel the Gihon's flowing waters brought life to nearby vineyards and the city of Jerusalem. The abundant waters of these rivers that bring fertility to the land illustrate the life-giving powers of Wisdom.

Ben Sira's poem then speaks of the association of Wisdom with the primeval man (24:28). He argues that the first man (Adam) did not come to a full knowledge of Wisdom, even as the last will not. However, he does not insert the negative associations with the "tree of knowledge of good and evil" present in the J narrative (Gen. 2–3). His assertions are more likely associated with the wisdom of the primeval man, who in ancient mythology was a royal king who possessed wisdom and guarded the tree of life.[137] Ben Sira's emphasis on the inability to comprehend the vastness of Wisdom (24:29) does not mean he endorses the skepticism of the poem on the inaccessibility of Wisdom in Job 28. Rather, Ben Sira stresses that the totality of Wisdom cannot be grasped by any human being, a point common in wisdom literature.

The final strophe (Sir. 24:30–34) highlights the image of Wisdom as life-giving waters, only now she is compared to a canal or aqueduct built by humans that channels water from a river to nourish a garden. The comparison of wisdom to life-giving water is common in wisdom (cf. Ps. 1, where the righteous person who studies Torah is like a tree planted by a stream).

In the latter part of the strophe (Sir. 24:32–34; cf. 16:24–25), Ben Sira speaks once more as an inspired teacher whose instruction is compared to the light of the dawn and whose teaching is "poured out like prophecy" (cf. Joel 2:28).[138] His inspired teachings, so he claims, are to benefit future generations of those who seek Wisdom. Again, he draws on inspiration to emphasize both his authority and that of his teachings.

In this chapter, then, Wisdom is personified as a heavenly goddess who engages in a hymn of self-praise (see Prov. 8 and the Isis hymns of self-praise). This hymn describes the origins and cosmic rule of Wisdom, her taking up residence in Israel and Jerusalem, her identification with the temple cult and the Law, her description as the tree of and waters of life, and her invitation to participate in a banquet of life that offers her fruit to her followers.[139] Ben Sira identifies her with both the transcendent realm of divine dwelling and the immanent presence of God on the earth, particularly among the chosen people. Resting behind all of these affirmations and metaphorical depictions is Ben Sira's theme of creation. Wisdom's origins and rule over all the nations go back to the time of creation. The Wisdom present in the sages' tradition and in creation is also the Wisdom that is equated with the Torah. This theological representation of Wisdom provides the basis for the role and authority of the sage, who, inspired by God, is the interpreter of the Torah and the teacher of wisdom. This theology emphasizes the conservative sociopolitical view of Ben Sira, a view that presents the community of Judah as a theocracy.

Creation and the Providence of God: 33:7–15[140]

The poem on the creation of opposites consists of three strophes that address the general theme of the providence of God (cf. 39:12–35).[141] Once again, this theological tradition provides the legitimation of the office and role of the sage by dealing especially with providence and the challenge of theodicy.[142] Ben Sira proclaims that God has separated the components of reality into contrasting opposites. In this poem, the two categories of opposites are time (sacred and profane) and humans (the good and the wicked).

The initial strophe of the poem on the bipolar order of creation begins with a question that asks why one day is separated from and then regarded as superior to another day, when the sun produces the same light for each day. Verses 8–9 answer this temporal question with the interpretation of divine purpose and predestination.

The answer given to the question in verse 7 is based upon divine sovereignty: on one hand, all days are the same (the sun provides daylight for them all), and yet on the other, God providentially designated certain days to be set apart (i.e., "sanctified" or "made holy," *hiqdîšû*, הקדישו) to be sacred seasons or festival times. In the Second Temple period these "seasons and feasts" distinct from ordinary times would have included the Sabbath (the seventh day), the major pilgrimage festivals of Passover and Unleavened Bread (a festival in the first month, beginning on the eve of Nisan 14 and concluding on Nisan 21), Weeks (a one-day festival early in the third month, on the fiftieth day after the offering of the barley sheaf during the Festival of Unleavened Bread), and Tabernacles (a seven-day festival beginning on the fifteenth day of the seventh month). Also included were the Feast of the New Moon, the Day of Atonement (a communal fast on the tenth day of the seventh month), and perhaps the seventh (sabbatical) year and the Year of Jubilee (the fiftieth year). These holy periods are the times for the Yahweh worshiper to participate in observances and rituals designed not only to worship God but also to revitalize the cosmos and the sacred community, whose teacher par excellence is the sage.

Ben Sira's depiction of the divine division of time into profane and sacred periods leads him to a second consideration: humans who are separated into the two categories of the righteous and the wicked. Thus he moves from cosmology, in particular the bipolar structure of time, to anthropology, where he posits the same dualistic system of opposites and uses the same argument of divine predestination. This was a common bifurcation in Proverbs, especially chapters 10–15.

In wisdom literature the antithesis of good and evil is a common motif, being found in particular in Proverbs, Qoheleth, and Ben Sira. In Ben Sira the good and the evil comprise a variety of features. First, they are fundamental categories of human beings, identified as the pious and the impious (33:14; 39:27), those who are wise and foolish, those who are obedient to the Torah and those who are not, and those who are blessed and those who are cursed (33:12). Good and evil are also elements of human nature (18:8; 39:4). Second, they are the bipolar opposites of the divine works: things that bring blessing and reward and others that produce cursing and punishment. Third, the opposites of times are used to explain that some days are auspicious for good deeds and others are the days when wicked acts occur (33:9). Fourth, these two categories of humanity have to do with epistemology and moral philosophy: the knowledge of good and the understanding of evil (17:7). Fifth, they are the antithetical groupings of human actions.[143] In this poem all humans have the same origins as their primordial ancestor, Adam: God creates them from the soil (cf. Gen. 2:7; 3:19; Qoh. 12:7). Nevertheless, God elected some to be blessed, exalted, sanctified, and brought them near to himself and others to be cursed, a strong endorsement of predestination, occurring in wisdom literature for the first time in Ben Sira's teaching. Ben Sira uses cultic language to speak of two entities: Israel and its ancestors, elected to be a holy nation, set apart for divine service to mediate between God and the world (Gen. 9:1, 26; 12:3; Lev. 19:2); and the priesthood, sanctified to mediate between God and the rest of Israel (Num. 16:5; Ezek. 40:46; 42:13; 45:4). "Blessed" (*eulogeō*, εὐλογέω) in a context of creation refers to the enhancement of life and the powers of procreation (Gen. 1:22, 28), while "exalted" (*anypsoō*, ἀνυψόω; cf. LXX Ps. 112:7) points to God's "raising up" or election of some to exist in a special relationship with him. To be "sanctified" refers to the act of God's separating out someone or something for divine service. "To bring near/before"[144] refers to the presenting of a person or sacrifice to the holy in sacred worship, an action used of both the common worshiper and the priests. Ben Sira appears to use election language to enlarge the boundaries of the chosen to include all those who are righteous. Nevertheless, they still belong to the category of the elect by reason of divine determination, not human choice.

In setting up his major contrast, Ben Sira argues that God has determined others among humanity to be "cursed" (*katarasatō*, κατηράσατω, "afflicted with destruction") and "brought low" or "degraded," probably a social designation for those who are subservient to others (e.g., Gen. 9:25). These would have included those whose wickedness led to divine rejection. In addition, the sage echoes the election of Israel with its exaltation among the nations and the disfavor shown toward other groups, especially the Canaanites of old. The crux not solved by Ben Sira is that he holds to the notion of predestination and yet cannot escape the view that the wickedness of perpetrators is responsible for their punishment.

Ben Sira uses the common metaphor of humans as clay molded by the potter into the desired shape (see Gen. 2:7; Job 10:8–9; Jer. 18:1–6; Isa. 29:16). This metaphor conveys the belief that God predestines some humans to be blessed and others to be cursed. The image of the clay in the potter's hand underscores Ben Sira's contention that the radical sovereignty of God extends to the divine determination of human destiny. Thus God places humans into one of two groups: the blessed and the cursed. Ben Sira likely has in mind the election of Israel from among the nations, a status that is based on the predestination of God, not on Israel's own merit.

The third and final strophe (vv. 14–15) sets forth the general principle of the bipolar division of reality. The general contrasts of opposites in Ben Sira's poem are evil and good, death and life, and sinners and the pious. This "doctrine of opposites" is Ben Sira's attempt to address the problem of the existence of evil that is central to the theological issue of theodicy, the justice of God (cf. 11:14).[145] God is responsible for all opposites that, together, constitute the fundamental structure of reality, including good and evil. It is the radical sovereignty of God that Ben Sira articulates. It is God who has shaped reality into contrasting opposites that exist within a cosmological and anthropological duality (cf.

42:24–25). Consequently, theodicy is answered in part by divine discretion in expressing sovereignty over reality.

Creation and the Defense of Divine Justice: 39:12–35[146]

Here Ben Sira takes a sapiential instruction and crafts it into an elegant wisdom hymn[147] that praises God as creator and sustainer of reality, and at the same time gives voice to a stirring defense of divine justice. In terms of genre, the text is a didactic hymn.[148] Through his praise of God, Ben Sira offers the opportunity for his students to acquire the *doxa* (δόξα) that infuses the God-fearing sage. The theme is the confession of verse 16 that initiates the hymn, contains key repetitive words for the entire poem, and is repeated at the end in v. 33 to form an inclusio:

> All the works created by God are good,
> for he will provide for every need at the appropriate time.

The poetic structure of 39:12–35 breaks down into the following five parts: the introit—the invitation to praise (vv. 12–15); strophe I—concerning creation and providence (vv. 16–21); strophe II—the creation of good (vv. 22–27); strophe III—the creation of evil (vv. 28–31); and a double conclusion—the goodness of divine rule solicits praise (vv. 32–35).

In this lengthy poem on creation, Ben Sira considers the just nature of divine rule and then breaks forth in unrestrained praise of the Creator by shaping a poem of three strophes around the form and content of three wisdom sayings. The first two sayings are disputations found in verse 21:

> Let no one say, "What is the purpose of this?"
> because everything is selected to meet a need.
> Let no one say, "This is worse than that,"
> because everything will come to fruition in its time.

The second disputation is repeated in verse 34: "Let no one say, 'This is worse than that,' because everything will come to fruition in its time." Disputations set forth the arguments of those who disagree and then answer them with a reasoned response. The questions in verse 21 bring to conclusion the first strophe, which addresses the goodness of both creation and providence. The repetition of the second question in verse 34 emphasizes at the conclusion of the hymn that even things that may appear evil are indeed good, if one recognizes their function: the punishment of the wicked.

The second wisdom form is a proverbial confession that occurs in verse 16 and then is repeated in verse 33:

> All the works created by God are good,
> for he will provide for every need at the appropriate time.

This saying occurs in two strategic places within the rhetorical structure of the hymn. Its first occurrence, verse 16, initiates the first strophe (vv. 16–21), which praises as good the works of God in both creation and history. The saying recurs at the end of the poem (v. 33), providing a conclusion to what Ben Sira has learned through his reflection on reality that he expresses in this poem. The saying thus serves as a confession that is expressed in the poetic form of hymnic praise.

The wisdom poem begins with a double introduction: the typical call to listen (addressed in this case to the "pious sons," *hyioi hosioi*, υἱοὶ ὅσιοι) to the wisdom instruction (vv. 12–14a; cf. Prov. 4:1) and the call to praise, common to hymns used in worship (Sir. 39:14b–15; cf. Pss. 47:1 and 66:1–2). The double introduction is paralleled by the twofold conclusion: the proverb in verse 33 and the disputation in verse 34, followed by the reissuing of the call to praise in verse 35.

In the first strophe, Ben Sira affirms the goodness of the work of divine creation and salvific action in ruling the earth (v. 16). He then describes God's omnipotence ("nothing limits his salvation" or "saving deeds," *těšûʿātô*, תשועתו; v. 18) and omniscience ("nothing is hidden from his eyes," v. 19). Even the waters of chaos are ordered by the power of the word of the Creator (cf. Ps. 33; Job 38:8–11). All things are subject to the will of God. This emphasis on the sovereignty of God is strengthened by the affirmation that he is able to see and know all that happens throughout the ages of the earth. The sage then approaches once more the issue of theodicy. He affirms the goodness of God's creation by means of differentiating between the good, who are pious, and the wicked, who are sinful. In using a rhetorical disputation, he states and then opposes the hypothetical arguments of opponents who question the purpose or usefulness of a divine action or an object of creation or who question why some things seem worse than others, that is, inherently evil.

Ben Sira makes his case for the goodness of creation and divine rule by using once again the "science of opposites" (cf. 33:7–15) to argue that good things in creation (see the list in v. 26) are created for the well-being of the righteous, while the same things become harmful to the wicked (see the second and third strophes). Even things that are evil are good in terms of their function: the destruction of the wicked. Ben Sira also makes use of the sapiential understanding of time to reinforce his case for theodicy by submitting that the worth of an object of divine creation is proven at the appropriate time. Thus even something considered evil in itself (e.g., a viper) is good when divine judgment uses its poison to effectuate retribution against the wicked.

Ben Sira does not intimate that there is some mechanically operating system of reward and punishment that is a part of the structure of reality. And he does not claim that the mysteries of reality, including divine actions, may be open to human perception. God is still the one who makes judgments and issues decrees that bless the righteous and punish the wicked, even though his actions may remain concealed. Therefore, the affirmation of God as the just ruler of creation and history breaks forth into spontaneous praise from the lips of the pious sage.

The double conclusion (vv. 32–35) summarizes the entire poem. First, he affirms the goodness of all divine works (v. 33); and second, he rejects the argument that some things are better than others (v. 34). Finally, he returns to the introit by issuing once again the call to praise and bless the name of God (v. 35).

In his poetic description of divine creation and providence, Ben Sira approaches the problem of theodicy that threatens the believer's faith: the acknowledgment of God as the creator of the world who rules over the earth in justice. Particularly disturbing to the pious is the presence of things that have the appearance of evil. Ben Sira does not deny that God created these things, but he does argue that they are good in terms of their purpose: the punishment of the wicked at the appropriate time. This approach to the problem of theodicy is expressed, therefore, in a hymn of praise to the creator and sustainer of the world who rules over the earth in justice. Critical reflection, following sapiential imagination, leads to the faithful affirmation of the justice of God. These two poems (33:7–15 and 39:12–35) address the general theme of the providence of God by focusing on contrasting opposites. The poems serve well Ben Sira's concern to articulate his version of theodicy, for they provide the essential structure of his formulation of a response to the questioning of the justice of God. Ben Sira proclaims that God has separated the components of reality into contrasting opposites. In these poems the two categories of opposites are time (sacred and profane) and humans (the good and the evil). These categories possess as their purpose the reward of the righteous and the punishment of the wicked.

God, the Sage and Creator: 42:15–43:33

Ben Sira composes a hymn praising God as sage and creator that forms the concluding element of the tripartite literary structure of the first forty-three chapters of the book.[149] The "Praise of the Pious" is attached to this text, probably by Ben Sira himself, and is a self-contained entity to which he later adds chapter 51. A scribal redactor finishes the shaping of the book with the addition of chapter 52.

This hymn is a cosmological canticle that depicts God as the sage whose wisdom shapes a reality of beauty, coherence, justice, and life. The rhetorical structure of this hymn includes the announcement of the sage's intent to praise (42:15–17), the unfathomable wisdom of God (42:18–21), the beauty and purpose of divine works (42:22–25), the wonder of sky and moisture (43:1–22), the teeming life of the expansive deep (43:23–26), and the concluding call to praise (43:27–33), which forms the inclusio. Poised at the center of this hymn is the metaphor of divine wisdom that orders and sustains a world of elegance evoking wonderment. This hymn also serves as an introduction to the "Praise of the Pious" in 44:1–50:24 (see v. 33: ḥasîdîm, הסידים; = 'anšê ḥesed, אנשי חסד, 44:1).

The praise of God as the sage who uses his wisdom to create the cosmos is the central theme for this hymn. The vocabulary of God as creator is found in the following texts in Ben Sira: bôrē' (בורא, 3:16), 'ôśeh (עשה, 7:30; 10:12; 35/32:13; 36/33:13; 38:15; 43:5, 11; 46:13; 47:8), yôṣēr (יוצר, 51:12), ktistēs (κτίσης, 24:8), and poiēsas (ποιήσας, 4:6; 39:5, 28; 47:8).[150] In the first strophe ("The Intent to Praise," 42:15–17), the deeds of divine activity are recalled by memory, declared, and then praised. Yet the memory of sacred tradition, transmitted by sapiential and worshiping communities, and reflection correlate the teachings of the past with the results of the present. In this hymn the teacher praises the Creator for his mighty works of beauty and life.

Ben Sira remembers (*'ezkōr*, אזכר, "brings to mind") divine deeds about which he has learned through study of the past traditions and personal observation of creation and providence that provide the basis for the praise of God. These deeds of God include not only world origins by the utterance of his creative word (see Gen. 1; Ps. 33; Wis. 9:1), but also providence, that is, the continuing governance of reality. Yet those who are to praise God by recounting in song his great deeds extend beyond the sage himself to the "holy ones of God" (*qědōšê 'ēl*, קדשי אל), those members of the heavenly council who dwell in the presence of the Lord (see Job 15:15), and his divine "hosts" (*sěbā'āyw*, צבאיו), in this case the personified heavenly bodies of the cosmos who respond obediently by carrying out the commands of the sovereign Lord. The prevailing metaphor for providence in this poem is the divine word that sustains life and establishes justice by means of God's decree (42:14, 26). The imagery, then, is that of the divine sovereign whose edicts create and rule his cosmic kingdom.

Ben Sira once again takes an important image from Priestly language in this second strophe and connects it to the metaphor of word: the "glory" of the Lord. This divine "glory" (*kābôd*, כבוד) refers especially to the "manifestation" of divine presence for the purpose of revelation. Here Ben Sira makes use of Priestly tradition in which the "glory" of the Lord is depicted either as a cloud or in a cloud that guides Israel through the wilderness (Exod. 16:10), covers Mount Sinai at the giving of the Law (Exod. 24:15–18b), and fills the tabernacle and the temple (Exod. 40:34; Num. 20:6; Pss. 24:7–10; 78:60–61). Yet he gives this imagery a sapiential twist. While this way of speaking about divine manifestation connotes mystery and otherness, it also indicates that the purpose of theophany is revelation: God manifests himself in order to issue divine teaching. The sage uses this imagery to speak of the revelation of the works of creation that point to the power, majesty, and benevolence of God. Thus God's glory, like the rays of the sun, is present in all of his works, and they in turn reveal his greatness (see Ps. 19A). For Ben Sira the glory of the Lord points to revelation: creation testifies to the majesty and sovereignty of the Creator. Yet at the same time, this creation that manifests the Lord is the means of divine instruction. Creation not only reveals the Creator, but also becomes the instrument of his teaching given to those who seek wisdom.

In the second strophe of this poem (Sir. 42:18–21), Ben Sira moves to the praise of God and focuses especially on God's unfathomable wisdom. Through wisdom, the ruler of heaven and earth knows the hidden secrets even of the Deep (*těhôm*, תהום), that region of chaos that defies divine order and rule (see Pss. 33:7; 89:10–11; Job 26:12–13), and of the human heart (or "mind"), the part of human nature where decisions are made, conceptions are shaped, and secret thoughts are harbored (see Prov. 15:11). Even the secret plots of chaos and the wicked do not escape the notice of the cosmic sovereign, for his wisdom discovers them all. Due to his wisdom, the Most High is omniscient, knowing all that happens in the past, the present, and even the future. Indeed, in declaring what will be, he brings the future into reality. In other words, God, who does not himself change, has been and continues to be in charge of the permutations of human events.[151] The stable continuity of reality is guaranteed by the immutable God. Unlike human kings, who need counselors to advise them in the setting of royal policy and its implementation (see 2 Sam. 16:15–17:23), God requires no instruction by either teacher or advisor. It is his wisdom that enables him to rule the earth, discover evil, bring its perpetrators to justice, and direct the course of world events. Ben Sira then praises in the third strophe the beauty of the works of God, noting that the divine language of judgment and wisdom also possesses within itself both beauty and the capacity to craft like a skilled artist the words of wonder and elegance (Sir. 42:22–25). The sage recognizes that some things in creation may be more beautiful than others, and yet all of them have a degree of elegance that evokes human appreciation. Thus all the works of God are beautiful and good, not simply in regard to their appearance but also in their appropriateness for their function. Ben Sira portrays the world as an esthesis, that is, an order that is both elegant and purposeful. Thus God's works (both the activities and the objects of divine creation) are beautiful and good. Nothing is created "in vain," that is, without purpose. Each object of divine creation meets a specific need. This synthesis of reality points to an order that is both beautiful and good and continues the same from the beginning of the world throughout all eternity.

Continuing the cosmology of the earlier poem, Ben Sira in the fourth and longest strophe (43:1–22) praises the Creator for the wonders of sky and moisture that also are objects of both beauty and purpose. Ben Sira extols the artistry and order of the heavens and the glistening attraction and life-giving vitality of the various forms of moisture (see Job 38:4–38). In the fashion of an interpreter of Scripture, he begins with a poetic commentary on Gen. 1:14–19 that describes the creation not only of the sun and moon but also of the heavenly host. The sun shines its light and radiates heat, which not only are necessary for existence, but also, if too intense, may desiccate the inhabited earth. Yet the radiance of this heavenly body reveals the power of the Lord who made it. The beauty of the moon, which evokes the awe of the observer, is complemented by its purpose of marking and distinguishing among the times and the seasons. The Jewish calendar, to which Ben Sira refers, is a lunar one that designates sacred times among the days and months of the year by reference to the phases of the moon. Thus again the sage points to the elegance and purpose of the elements of creation.

These two great lights (see Gen. 1:16–19) are among the stars and other heavenly phenomena that possess a glory that originates in the majesty of God and follows the decrees of the Creator. They include the rainbow, lightning, thunder, winds, and clouds. Even the variety of the forms of moisture (rain, snow, hail, and dew) brings both life and destruction as instruments of divine judgment. These elements are quite similar to theophanic hymns (see Judg. 5; Hab. 3; Pss.

18; 68; 104) that describe the coming of Yahweh to do battle against chaos in order to establish justice and continue life. These cosmic elements are the instruments of God's power in ruling over the earth to punish the wicked and to establish order and life in the cosmos.

The fifth strophe (Sir. 43:23–26) describes God's rule over the third part of reality: the Deep (*těhôm*) or the waters of chaos that oppose divine sovereignty. For Ben Sira it is divine wisdom or "thought" that controls the chaos monster Rahab, while God places the islands in the Deep and fills its cosmic waters with a great variety of life, including the "mighty ones," most likely a reference to the great sea monsters of Gen. 1:20–23 (see Behemoth and Leviathan in Job 40–41). For Ben Sira the Deep does not pose a threat to divine rule, for God's wisdom keeps both the chaos monster and the mighty waters in check. Ben Sira ends this hymn with the enigmatic statement concerning what appears to be the "messenger" or word of God. This verse refers to the notion that each element of creation functions according to its purpose, even as the Creator's words bring about and then regulate what he decrees. Each element of creation serves as the messenger of God that carries out the divine order with purpose and success.

In the conclusion (43:27–33), Ben Sira then states the central theological emphasis of the entire book and exhorts his audience to engage in praise of this God of greatness, power, and mystery whose works of creation are only slightly known.[152] In 43:27 he concludes:

> More things like these we shall not add.
> The last word is: "He is the all" (*hû' hakuol*, הוא הכל).

This is the final, all-conclusive affirmation that Ben Sira is able to make. It forms the confession that the Creator's wondrous mystery and majesty extend beyond the greatness and awesomeness of his works. Ben Sira affirms that God "is the all," that is, the one not only whose nature and glory are revealed in his works, but who also is present in the objects of his creation. Indeed, he is the creator of all things (see 18:1; 24:8; 51:12). God is the one who alone is truly wise and fearful. Ben Sira is not a pantheist, but the expression does suggest that divine wisdom dwells within the cosmos, an idea that is indebted to the Stoics' teaching of the universal law or reason that permeates reality. Yet even those few works the sage can observe and then describe are but an indication of greater, more magnificent things that remain hidden to human perception, even as the majesty of the Creator is far greater than his divine works reveal. Yet while the sage has glimpsed only a small part of the esthesis of symmetry and beauty, it is enough to provide the basis for praise. Finally, he affirms in a concluding saying (v. 33) that God has given to those "pious ones" (εὐσεβέω, *eusebeō*) who praise him the same divine wisdom that orders and sustains the world. These "pious ones" (*'anšê ḥesed*, אנשי חסד) are the heroes of the faith, praised in chapters 44–50. They are the ones who, by means of wisdom, embody Israel's salvific history and experience the redemption intended for cosmos and history.

THE PRAISE OF THE PIOUS: CHAPTERS 44–50

Introduction

Ben Sira was the first known sage to combine the theology of creation with the saving history.[153] His theological prototype for this combination was Second Isaiah's exodus typology and mythological portrayal of cosmic creation. Indeed, creation was even added to the "confession of faith" in Ezra's prayer of contrition found in Neh. 9:6–37. Ben Sira's history, while taking a Greek form (the *encomium*) instead of earlier biblical narrative historiography, is a continuation of the development of Jewish history writing: the Deuteronomistic History, Ezra and Nehemiah, Chronicles, 1 Esdras, and 1 and 2 Maccabees. What is unusual about Ben Sira's recounting of salvation history is that it is portrayed through the piety and righteous deeds of Israel's ancestors (*'anšê ḥesed*, אנשי חסד, 44:10). This glorification of human beings belongs to the literary and cultural world of ancient Greece and is expressed particularly in a genre called the *encomium*. Ben Sira's history of the famous "Men of Piety" was influenced by Greek historiography in which the antiquity of national origins is combined with praise, in particular, of human beings. In addition, the slander of the Jews by Egyptian and Greek authors demanded a response that led to this eulogy of famous heroes of the Jewish people.

These men of piety (*ḥesed*, הסד) and glory (*kābôd*, כבוד) were individuals of greatness, that is, they worshiped the Most High, to whom they were loyal; they radiated the divine aura (vv. 2, 13) and performed renowned deeds for which they were remembered. They were predestined by the Lord, performed noteworthy feats (vv. 3–6), were honored and remembered by the people in contrast to others who have been forgotten (vv. 7–9, 14), were godly and righteous, and had descendants who were to prosper (vv. 10–13).

Sirach 44–50 as a Greek Encomium[154]

There were four major types of Jewish historiography during the Hellenistic period: chronicles (Demetrius), historical romances (Artapanus), epic poets (Philo and Theodotus),[155] and the encomium (Ben Sira and the Wisdom of Solomon).[156] The object of praise in this great "hymn" is not Yahweh, but rather "Men of Piety" (*'anšê ḥesed*, אנשי חסד). In doing so, Ben Sira appropriates from Greek literary canons the encomium, a literary form that was originally a eulogy spoken in the context of a funeral.[157] There were biblical antecedents for this narrative, but nothing that comes as close to Sirach 44–50 as does the Greek encomium. These antecedents in biblical literature include the Joseph narrative (Gen. 37, 39–50), Deuteronomy 32, sections of 1 Kings 3–11, and Psalm 78. The encomium later became synonymous with the panegyric of human saints and heroes in the context of celebrations and festivals. Thus three terms—eulogy, encomium, and panegyric—identify distinct categories of literary forms. While the encomium is the overarching form of the "Praise of the Fathers," the other two forms echo throughout the text.[158]

Epideictic (*epideixis*, ἐπίδειξις) literature in Greek rhetoric is usually understood as a general literary genre that encompassed several more specific forms.[159] Epideictic refers to a "kind, genre" (*genos*, γένος) of Greek rhetoric. According to Aristotle, there are three kinds of rhetorical speeches: deliberative (*symbouleutikon*, συμβουλευτικόν), forensic (*dikanikon*, δικανικόν), and epideictic (*epideiktion*, ἐπιδεικτιόν) (*Rhet.* 1.3.3). Each one addresses a different type of audience: legislative assembly, the *dikastas* (i.e., a judge of "things to come"), and the ordinary spectator, who is interested only in the skill of the orator (*Rhet.* 1.3.2). The three differ in purpose: the first two seek to persuade, while the third is to entertain. Thus the word *epideictic* means "display." This type of speech may offer "praise" (*epainos*, ἔπαινος) or "blame" (*psogos*, ψόγος) (*Rhet.* 1.3.3). According to Thomas Lee, "epideictic" appears to be the term used to designate that class of oratory with a *Sitz im Leben* that was in neither the assembly nor the law court. It was applied to those speeches through which the rhetor sought to impress his audience rather than to persuade them.[160] I would modify this remark by noting that the sage's listing of the deeds of the great heroes of the past is done in order to exalt Jewish history and to encourage contemporary Jews that God throughout their history has continued to deliver them. Indeed, listing the deeds of famous heroes is a key feature of the encomium in proving the validity of what is argued. Within this category there were a variety of possible forms through which this goal could be accomplished: the rhetor might offer an oration in praise of someone or something, or he could choose to compose a vituperative piece.

Several related forms were sometimes subcategories of epideictic: the eulogy (*eulogia*, εὐλογία), offered in honor of the deceased; the funeral speech (*epitaphios*, ἐπιτάφιος), which became understood as an encomium of the dead to which a lament was attached; and the panegyric (*panēgyrikos*, πανηγυρικός), a public speech of praise of a person or group composed for and delivered to an assembled public. However, the one form of epideictic that relates to all three of these is the encomium (ἐγκώμιον).[161] It is the single form that includes the variety of features of epideictic literature.[162] This is the form that is most consistently used in Greek rhetoric and is delivered to praise an individual. It is undoubtedly the genre that provides the literary character for Ben Sira's "Praise of the Pious."[163] In addition, Ben Sira also makes use of "example stories" (*paradeigmata*, παραδείγματα)[164] or "series of examples" in 44:15–49:16.[165]

In noting the important features of Ben Sira's encomium, the sage follows the essential characteristic of amplification, that is, eliminating or suppressing any demeaning factors and adding qualities that enhance the person's character and prestige.[166] Indeed, Ben Sira often engages in revisionist, romanticized history, not unlike that of 1 and 2 Chronicles, in which he selects, omits, rewrites, and praises the great heroes of the past who were pious, righteous, faithful, honored, and therefore to be remembered. Through their prodigious deeds and remarkable embodiment of preeminent virtues, their descendants will continue for all times. Part of his literary approach is highly selective, both in his choice of heroes and in the amount of space he gives to those who are considered. It is striking that he makes no mention of Saul and Ezra, while the priestly figures Aaron, Phinehas, and above all Simeon II receive his greatest attention and most glowing accolades. Joseph, understood as the father of the two large northern tribes, Ephraim and Manasseh (Gen. 48) is not mentioned until the end, in 49:14–15, possibly because of Ben Sira's understandable dislike of the Samaritans (northern Israel) and their continuing opposition, supported by the Transjordanian Tobiads, to Judah that took the form of seeking to subvert the policies of Simeon (50:26). Saul's omission is understandable due to his failures and sins, but not Ezra's. Even Nehemiah is briefly mentioned (Sir. 49:13). Not only is Ben Sira a noted sage like Ezra, but in addition he utters a praise of the scribal office in 38:24–39:11 and holds the law in high esteem (17:11–12; 23:23; 24:23; 41:18; 42:2; 45:5; 49:4), as did Ezra. These facts points to the close relationship of the sage to the priesthood and the Torah. He mentions Enoch and Noah in the beginning (44:16–18), but not Adam until the very end in a brief remark (49:15). He omits any reference to women, and he describes only four southern kings who were of significance in the Deuteronomistic History and Chronicles (David, Solomon, Hezekiah, and Josiah).[167] Ben Sira takes no notice of any northern ruler, gives scant attention to Jeremiah and Ezekiel in contrast to a more lengthy discussion of Isaiah, and refers to the Twelve Minor Prophets only as a group. He tells more about Aaron than Moses. There are no references to the sins of any of the heroes, except in a very general way (thus David's sins and those of Solomon are taken away by the Lord). Thus while he mentions that Noah was perfect and righteous, he does not refer to his drunkenness or to the sin of Ham. The creation of humanity is mentioned briefly, only at the end in reference to Adam: "above every other created living being was Adam" (49:16).

The "Praise of the Pious," in assuming the form of the Greek encomium, may have been a literary text for reading in the school where young students would learn their history and the embodiment of virtue by righteous men and a cultic panegyric that praised Israel's heroes. This account of Israel's salvation history served as the outgrowth of the progressive realization of the redemptive purpose of creation. That it concludes with the praise of Simeon II, which especially describes his cultic performance on the Day of Atonement, also may suggest that this encomium was composed for reading (50:1–24) either during this day of remembrance and purification of the sanctuary or during the pilgrimage festival of Booths/Ingathering that followed. It is quite likely, therefore, that this encomium was written to be read in the school and in a cultic setting when Judah's ancestors were remembered and praised.

Literary Structure[168]

The literary structure of the "Praise of the Pious" is composed, first of all, to trace the redemptive history of Israel brought about by the righteous and virtuous acts of its ancestral heroes, and second, to highlight in particular the importance of the office of the high priest in general and the heroic accomplishments of Simeon II. This latter purpose is obvious in that the final and longest of the sections contains the praise of this high priest and is placed at the grand culmination of the composition (50:1–21). One should not forget that this encomium, with its list of heroes, is introduced by a majestic hymn on creation that contains the works of creation in a list (42:14–43:33). Thus there is a close relationship between creation and salvation history effectuated through the acts of pious heroes. The poetic encomium opens with the call to worship by the sage (v. 1), followed by a proem (vv. 2–14). Then occurs a series of heroes who performed righteous and noble deeds in Israel's history. Thus, structurally, we have the movement from creation to history that is fulfilled in the work of Simeon and the temple service. The glory of God that is bestowed upon and then reflected by the virtuous men and their noble deeds in the hymn of the "Praise of the Pious" is the same divine glory that permeates creation (42:16).[169]

Following the introductory proem that sets the stage of redemptive history through the manifestation of divine glory in the pious acts of righteousness and virtue (1:1–15) is a list of ancestral heroes who are characterized by similar features: Enoch, Noah, Abraham, Isaac and Jacob, Moses, Aaron, Phinehas, Joshua, Caleb, the judges, Samuel, Nathan, David, Solomon, Rehoboam, Jeroboam, Elijah, Elisha, Hezekiah, Isaiah, Josiah, Jeremiah, Ezekiel, Job, the Twelve Prophets, Zerubbabel, Jeshua, Nehemiah, Joseph, Shem, Seth, Enosh, Adam, and Simeon.

Based on the comparison of each of these units and their characters, it is clear that a certain profile of the hero emerges.[170] Burton Mack points to seven features of this profile and five subtypes of hero that are set forth, although there are later additions that do not conform to the profile: Enoch in 44:16, Elijah in 48:9–11, and Enoch (mentioned a second time), Joseph, Shem, Seth, Enosh, and Adam in 49:14–16.[171]

In examining the general pattern of characterization, there is no single profile of an individual that contains all of the features that are highlighted. The precursor, presumably the biblical tradition, provides the larger background for the reader in examining and reflecting on each person. However, the seven components of the general pattern for these individuals consist of the following: a designation of an office, the mention of divine approbation or election, a reference to covenant, a mention of the person's character and/or piety, an account of the person's deeds, a reference to the historical situation, and the mention of reward. According to Mack's analysis, the determining factor that unites these components is the office. Five separate offices are mentioned: priests, prophets, kings, multiple offices (Moses as teacher, prophet, and ruler; Phineas as priest and prophet; Samuel as prophet, judge, and priest; David as king and warrior; Simeon as priest and king), and judges.[172] This central role of the office upon which Ben Sira reflects points to his view of the social structure of the new and reconstituted Israel: "The greatness of these heroes is directly related to the great significance of these offices."[173] An ancestor's greatness lay in his holding of an office, which the Creator has made glorious. Of special emphasis is the activity or set of deeds the person has performed. What is stressed is not the great skill, knowledge, or strength of the person, but rather the deeds that are associated with his office. Of course, the greatest puzzle is why the office of the sage/scribe is omitted, especially by one who sees himself as the epitome of the wise man. The purpose of the hymn is to serve as "a mythic charter for Second Temple Judaism."[174] It concludes with Simeon II and his activity during the Festival of Tabernacles, thus pointing to the final realization of human history through the reconstitution of the people of God, the power of the cult, and the celebration of the giving of the Torah to restore the order of both the cosmos and history. There are seven characteristics, seven kings, and seven prophets, pointing to the "perfection" of the redemptive quality of creation and history. To participate in the Festival of Tabernacles is to participate in the final actualization of the salvific order of creation and history, not just of Israel, but also of all peoples. Thus the preceding creation hymn and this recounting of the praise of the pious ancestors are integrally connected into one grand mythic scheme of creation, history, and fulfillment in the celebration of Tabernacles in the temple. It is not insignificant that the concluding praise of Simeon II includes cosmic features associated with his glorious robes worn during the festival (50:5–11). "The glory to be seen is just that this correlation has been achieved—the glory of God's works in the order of creation reflected in the glory of his purposes actualized in the order of human history."[175]

The concluding chapter of the encomium serves as a eulogy in praise of Simeon II (50:1–24). The positioning of this chapter in the literary structure of the book serves to associate the works of God in creation (42:15–43:33), the activities of the individual ancestors (chaps. 44–50) in the history of Israel, and the temple.[176] Thus through this artistic rendering creation and history are knitted together as the fundamental themes of Israelite and Jewish theology as set forth by this sage. The major themes of the encomium of Simeon II include his care for the sanctuary and the city of Jerusalem, his glory, liturgy as the revitalization of Israel, the cosmic significance of the cult and of wisdom, and the reality of the covenant.[177] Particularly important for creation theology is the renewal of the cosmos through the celebration of Tabernacles. The festival celebrated the past salvific actions of God on behalf of the Jews and anticipated the future glories that they would receive. Simeon's glorious appearance in the liturgy of the Day of Atonement is compared to the rainbow (50:7), the sign of God's promise to Noah that the earth never again will be destroyed by water (Gen. 9:13, 14, 16; cf. Sir. 43:11). In 50:22 there is the blessing of God, who "everywhere works great works" and nurtures humans from birth. The description of Simeon's glorious appearance in 50:6–12 is similar to that of Wisdom in 24:13–17. The priest's liturgical service in 50:14 and 19 compares to that of Wisdom in the sacred tent in 24:10. This indicates that the priestly work of Simeon II, especially in the temple, reflects the activity of wisdom, which is the divine order of the cosmos (cf. 4:11–19).[178]

THE HISTORICAL THEOLOGY OF BEN SIRA

Creation and Providence

Ben Sira makes use of numerous metaphors to speak of God, many of which have to do with creation of the cosmos and providence, and have their roots in earlier books of the Tanakh. For example, his reflections on creation theology in the earlier biblical traditions, especially Genesis 1–3, are found in Sir. 16:24–17:14, where God created both the cosmos and human beings. The dominant metaphor is the divine word and its correlative expressions of wisdom, commandment, and mouth. Wisdom originates from the mouth of God and covers the earth like a mist (cf. Gen. 2:5), while God's word orders and sustains the creation. Through his word, God establishes a bipolar structure of creation designed to punish the wicked and reward the righteous. This is detailed in the poem in 33:7–15. Here Ben Sira associates two major themes: first, God preordained certain days to be holy and others to be common and ordinary, thus selecting times for worship and festivals necessary for the creation of the vital forces of life; and second, related to this is the view that human beings, created from the dust and thus possessing the same origins (cf. Gen. 2:7), are predestined either to be blessed or cursed. Similarly, the hymn that praises God in Sir. 39:12–35 also broaches the theme of theodicy and the nature of divine works. He utters a confession in verse 16 that is repeated in verse 33: "All the works of the Lord are very good, and whatever he commands will be done at the appointed time." Like Second Isaiah, Ben Sira also integrates creation and salvation history into one comprehensive statement.

This theme of creation, expressed through a variety of metaphors, shapes the literary structure of the book. The first act of the creation of the cosmos is the fashioning of Sophia (1:4), thus making Yahweh the God of Wisdom. In turn, he gives wisdom, which permeates reality, to those who worship and love him (1:9–10). In 24:8 Yahweh is the "creator of all things." When Wisdom, who originated from the mouth of God, goes in search of a habitation on the earth, he commands her to take up residence among the people of Israel, to dwell in the temple in Jerusalem, and to be present in its cultic worship (chap. 24). Thus Wisdom and Torah take on both a universal meaning in creation theology and a particular one in describing Wisdom's election of Israel, and especially the temple in Jerusalem, as her dwelling place. In the conclusion of the book, prior to the addition of the encomium (chaps. 44–50), Ben Sira speaks in hymnic praise of the splendors of creation (42:22–43:33).

The sages actualize and then constitute the cosmic order by following both the Torah and sapiential instructions. Ben Sira gives a mythic identity to the Torah, identifying its five books with the five streams of paradise that flowed from the garden throughout creation (Sir. 24). Wisdom comes from the mouth of the Creator, searches for a home, and takes up residence on Mount Zion in the temple in the midst of Israel. The "book of the covenant of the Most High God" was the Law given to Moses that now is read to Jewish assemblies and in Torah schools associated with the temple and the synagogues. From Ben Sira it is only a short step to what the rabbis later taught about the Torah as the instrument of divine creation and the source of knowledge for understanding everything in the heavens and on the earth. While believing that wisdom and Torah are equated, Ben Sira still acknowledges that he has witnessed only a slight trace of the God who is hidden in mystery. God's glory and greatness far exceed the sage's own ability to recognize and to fathom him.

Creation and Anthropology

Ben Sira gives substantial play to the tradition of the creation of humanity, and in doing so makes significant use of important metaphors that are prominent in the Bible. Especially conspicuous are the formulations rendered by the creation of humans by the divine craftsman (cf. Gen. 2 and Job 10:8–12). As was the case in Proverbs, Ben Sira affirms that the poor enjoy the protection of the artistic craftsman who "formed" them. God is the divine potter who shapes the nature and destiny of human beings. Like Adam, God made all human beings from the earth. When Ben Sira describes conception, he points to God's forming of humans in the womb and bestowing upon those who are faithful to him the gifts of wisdom and piety. In describing humanity's role and function in the cosmos, Ben Sira portrays humans as kings ruling over creation (cf. Ps. 8). They are created in the divine image, rule over the other creatures who fear them (Sir. 17:4; see Gen. 9:2), and are feared by the lesser creatures. God gives humans wisdom that they may rule the world in justice (see 1 Kgs. 3:3–14). In addition, Ben Sira teaches that humans are created with free will (Sir. 15:11–20), and that they obtain their knowledge of the Creator through their "fear of God" (i.e., piety and obedience) that is equated with reflection on and living according to the Torah.

Creation and Goddess Wisdom

One of the major theological themes in Ben Sira in which the tradition of creation is couched is that of the roles and functions of wisdom. For Ben Sira, Wisdom is the personification of a characteristic feature of God that originated in the time of creation and served as an implement for the shaping of the cosmos. In addition, divine wisdom revealed in creation, the Torah, and the providential guiding of the ancestors becomes the order of justice that permeates and sustains reality. Further, wisdom becomes a teaching that, identified with sapiential instruction and the Torah, may be studied, learned, and incorporated in both the character and behavior of the sages. Wisdom is the divine inspiration that enables the chosen sage to sing the praises of the Creator and to live according to divine dictate. Finally, Wisdom becomes the way of expressing divine immanence. Through her, God acts to reconstitute and sustain creation, to provide the means for knowing his divine will, and to guide the ancestors through Jewish history. The term "wisdom" (ḥokmâ, חכמה; sophia, σοφία) points to a body of specialized knowledge or skill (38:1–3) that originates with God, who then enables the sages to learn it. Wisdom is especially praised in chapter 24, which depicts her as deriving from the mouth of God, dwelling in Israel among the chosen people, taking up residence in the temple where she becomes identified with its liturgy, and being equated with the covenant of Moses. In the first poem (1:1–10), Wisdom originates with God who alone is wise and to be feared (1:8). In this hymn she is said to be preexistent, originating before all else (1:4). While God makes her available to all those who love him, he alone knows her intimately, for he created (*ektisen*, ἔκτισεν) her. God himself poured her out upon all his works (1:9), making her the divine principle that orders all of creation.

Conclusion: The Wisdom of Ben Sira and Its Theological Metaphors

By means of his imagination, which issues forth in productive metaphors, Ben Sira constructs a synthesis that unites creation and redemption into a compelling theological vision. He returns to the formulations of the traditional sages and biblical texts to shape his own imaginative rendering of God, the cosmos, humanity, wisdom, and for the first time among the sapiential teachers Israel's election and salvation history. Thus he is a conveyor of the wisdom tradition, an interpreter of a growing canon, and a creative hermeneut who sets forth a poetic and narrative theology that resonates within the culture of the Hellenistic period in Jewish history as it unfolds in the city of Jerusalem.

In the activation of cultural memory, Ben Sira draws on the texts, traditions, and institutions of his own time. For example, the earlier Jewish presentations of Woman Wisdom (Prov. 1:20–33; 8–9; Job 28) are enriched by mythic images of the Isis cult that had sunk deep roots among the Jews not only in the Diaspora but also in Judah. A key example of the activation of memory is his appropriation of the stories of the Jewish heroes of the faith to demonstrate that through these ancestors God has led the elect people to the culmination of history in his own day. Yet to present this narrative, Ben Sira adopts the popular encomium from Greek historiography, demonstrating that his audience and fellow sages made use of Greek literary forms and thought to recast their faith and tradition. The transparency of his general response to Hellenism is demonstrated by his use of Greek literary forms and his adoption of a number of philosophical views, in particular several that are at home in Stoic morality and cosmology. Even the mystery religions do not escape his compliance to cultural features, as is noted in particular by his portrayal of Woman Wisdom in the guise of both the Old Testament formulations that preceded him and the popular goddess Isis. The enmity evoked by conservative Judaism against Hellenism that came to full expression during the later reign of Antiochus IV Epiphanes is not evidenced by his own conceptualization of Judaism. His composition intimates that his students and colleagues would have known at least to a minimal extent the thoughts, forms, and compositions current in the Hellenistic culture of the eastern Mediterranean world.

Ben Sira's devotion to the traditional Zadokite priesthood and in particular its high priesthood is evidenced in part by his instructions to support them and the temple cult in which they are active and by which they are sustained. But paramount among his teachings about the priesthood are the references in the encomium to the high priests Aaron, Phinehas, and especially Simeon II. Indeed, the history of humanity and the election of Israel reach their culmination in the office and virtuous life of Simeon II. The narrative of vignettes of the lives of famous men in human and ultimately Jewish history points to the direction of providence that culminates in the establishment of the temple community in Jerusalem ruled over by the high priest Simeon II. Indeed, Ben Sira understands that he himself lives in the end time that requires only one additional episode for final completion: the removal of the Ptolemaic Empire and the concurrent renewal of self-rule through a priestly theocracy serving the divine king.

Creation theology provides the metaphors for rendering this new theological synthesis. Through the metaphor of Woman Wisdom, the first act of creation, God becomes present in the world of human nations and Judah in particular, permeates the order of creation making possible the providential continuation of the world, and enters into sapiential instruction and priestly Torah to direct the behavior of the faithful. By entering into the temple and becoming identified with the acts and materials of cultic liturgy, the ongoing existence of both the cosmos and the elect is made to endure. Even so, divine transcendence plays a substantial role in this theological synthesis, for heaven is the dwelling place of the creator and sustainer who judges the world through actions of blessing and punishment. Indeed God has created a bipolar structure to encompass all things, including the differentiations of time, events, and retribution. While Wisdom, Torah, and creation reveal in part the nature of God, Ben Sira recognizes that he is incapable of penetrating completely divine mystery. He knows God and divine action only to a limited degree.

The Quest for Power, Wealth, and Status

Different groups in Judah during the period of the lifetime of Ben Sira engaged in strong competition for the highest possible social status, which, if achieved, would make them, and particularly their leaders, rich and powerful. The major groups who engaged in the struggle for supremacy within the colony of Judah were the Zadokite priests, the apocalyptic seers, the revolutionaries, and the different groups of scribes. Each of the scribal groups would have been aligned either with one of these major Jewish social groups or with the foreign governments that ruled Judah and extracted taxes, produced and kept official records, and attended to the military requirements of the nation to whom they were in subjection.

Ben Sira was clearly a teacher and scribe who was loyal to and served the priestly families of the Zadokites and their current high priest. The Zadokites were loyal to the ruling government, which gave them special privileges regarding exclusion from taxes and the right to govern internally the Jewish people on the basis of their Torah. Subsequently they opposed nationalists, who sought through armed conflict to gain Jewish independence, and apocalyptic groups like the Essenes, who claimed esoteric knowledge and taught erroneous doctrines that included resurrection of the righteous from the dead. Ben Sira's conservative political stance is noted not only in his instructions and eulogy in praise of Simeon II, but also in his view that creation was the grounding of the Torah that in turn taught its followers how to behave morally and faithfully. Indeed, cosmic Wisdom took up her abode in the temple on Mount Zion and became identified with the waters flowing from the garden that fructifies nature, with the spices of the liturgical celebrations, and with the covenant of Moses. What is more, the movement of history has now culminated in the theocracy of Judah and awaits its final realization in the elimination of foreign groups from the sacred homeland. With this theology, Ben Sira gives himself a substantial role in Jewish society, for he is the interpreter of the books of the Tanakh and assumes a place of honor in his envisioned world of God's making.

Chapter 8

Wisdom and Alexandrian Hellenism: The Wisdom of Solomon

HISTORICAL PRELUDE

The End of the Ptolemaic Empire and the Rule of Imperial Rome[1]

The high point of Ptolemaic Egypt had been achieved during the third century BCE. This international prestige was resurrected for a short time during the reign of Ptolemy IV Philopator, who defeated Antiochus III at Raphia in 217. But this glory faded in a relatively brief time. Following the defeat of Egypt by Antiochus III at Panium in 200, Ptolemaic power continued to wane and, subsequent to the defeat of their navy at the great sea battle of Actium of Mark Antony and Cleopatra in 31 BCE, the Roman Empire absorbed Egypt into its growing number of subjugated kingdoms.

Alexandrian Jews in Imperial Rome

Alexandria was made the new capital of Egypt by Ptolemy I Soter. The polis quickly became the major cultural center of the Mediterranean world, containing, among other things, the *Mouseion* and the unparalleled library in the ancient

Western world (Diodorus 17.52.5). Serving as the seat of the Ptolemaic government also gave the polis extraordinary political prestige, military power, and cultural significance unrivaled in the eastern Mediterranean world of the Hellenistic Empire. After Alexander's death and the eventual partition of the empire among his generals, the Ptolemies ruled Egypt (and Judea until 200 BCE) until the Roman conquest of 31 BCE that led to the absorption of the city's immense wealth and cultural attainments.[2] Jews began to take up residence in the city in large numbers, beginning as early as its origins. They had lived in Egypt for several centuries before this time. One well-known site is the military colony in Elephantine founded as early as 650 BCE.[3] Numerous Jews had already immigrated to and settled in Egypt at the end of the eighth century BCE, as a consequence of the Assyrian conquest of Israel in 722, and then again in the early sixth century following the sacking of Jerusalem by Nebuchadrezzar II (586). While most seemed to have settled in one of the larger cities (πόλις, *polis*), others lived in the villages in the countryside (χώρα, *chōra*), especially those who had served in the Greek armies and their descendants and were rewarded with land grants as compensation.[4] A large number of Greek inscriptions[5] and a number of manuscripts from Elephantine provide important social and religious information about the Jews in the cities and the countryside.[6]

The first Roman Caesar to rule over Egypt was Octavian (Augustus; 27 BCE–14 CE). Under his reign, the Jews of the empire were the recipients of royal favor, although this status dissipated significantly in the reigns of the emperors who followed him. His wife Livia contributed golden utensils to the temple in Jerusalem, and Philo reports that the emperor himself paid for a daily burnt offering, a practice that was continued through the reign of Claudius. Augustus even permitted Jews to assemble, uninhibited by any restraints, in their synagogues. When Sejanus, an advisor to Tiberius (14–37 CE), was given a free hand by the increasingly isolated emperor to make many internal Roman decisions, he began to persecute the Jews of Italy who were loyal supporters of the ruler whom he hoped to undo. Finally, Tiberius, made aware of the intrigues of his advisor, had him executed in 31 and then offered comfort to the offended Jews in the empire, disallowing anyone to oppose the Jewish practice of their traditions. In 32, however, Flaccus was granted the post of prefect of Egypt and conditions ripened for Jewish persecution. He eventually authorized a pogrom against the Jews, only to be stopped by Caligula, who executed him for causing disturbances to the social order.

Philo paid two visits to Rome as the leading envoy of a Jewish Alexandrian delegation, the first rebuffed by an emperor, Gaius Caligula, filled with his own self-importance and desire to be worshiped as a god, and the second culminating in Claudius deciding against forcing his subjects to honor him as a god as long as he was alive. Claudius denied the rival Greek Alexandrian delegation's request for its own internal senate, questioned whether education in the *ephēbeion* would lead one automatically to Alexandrian citizenship but did allow contemporary ephebes to be citizens, and brought to an end all hostilities against the Jews, requiring that tolerance be extended to them. However, Jews were not to be granted the coveted citizenship of the polis of Alexandria. In words that would later have ominous repercussions, he warned the Jews against engaging in treacherous acts of disloyalty that would be countered by resolute retaliation.

Philo made the highly exaggerated claim that two of the five quarters in Alexandria were Jewish and that a million Jews lived in Alexandria by the first century CE (*Flacc.* 43).[7] Even though these are greatly inflated numbers, cultural and literary evidence points to the large number of Jewish inhabitants in this major city of the Diaspora. While Jews during the Ptolemaic period were identified as an *ethnos* (ἔθνος), they were never considered to be full citizens of Alexandria. Nevertheless, the Ptolemies allowed them their own communal structure and many rights, including that of self-regulation of their internal social life and the freedom to practice their native religion.[8] Thus they were a recognized community, self-governing, and in charge of many of their own affairs, and had at their head an ethnarch (ἐθνάρχης), even though they did not comprise an actual *politeuma* (πολίτευμα) in the sense of a self-sufficient political entity of citizens. Rather, they were constituted as an ethnic and cultic group.[9]

The meaning of *politeuma*, especially as it relates to Jews of Alexandria, is disputed. The term could be used in three ways: the political makeup of a Greek polis; the inhabitants of an area, including a city; and a community of aliens within a Greek city. This term, in referring to the Jews of the Greco-Roman period, would be appropriate in the third sense only.[10] The legal powers of Jews in administering punishment for the violation of their own laws was limited. For example, they were not allowed to exact the death penalty. Obviously, no Greek city in Egypt possessed independence of any kind, but was under the control of the hierarchical bureaucracy of the dynasty, first of the Ptolemies and then of the Caesars. Any city and any ethnic group within a πόλις (*polis*) had to have a charter, granted by the ruler, to be constituted and to exist. Jews presumably had this charter and were granted the right to follow their ancestral laws, thus having the right of internal autonomy, as long as their ancestral laws did not impinge on the political and legal laws of the larger city and then the kingdom. Jews were allowed to build and attend synagogues, to have their own courts of justice to arbitrate disputes and make legal decisions, to educate youth in the Torah, and to elect their own officials for operating and overseeing the mechanics of their community. At the head of a Jewish community was the ethnarch, who "ruled the people, judged its cases and supervised the implementation of contract and orders, like the ruler of an independent state" (Strabo as quoted by Josephus, *Ant.* 14.117). Augustus replaced the ethnarch with a *gerousia* (γερουσία; Philo, *Flacc.* 74), a group that numbered seventy-one (*Tos. Sukk.* 4.6; *b. Sukk.* 51b). Philo refers to the members as *archōns* (ἄρχων), although this may have been a term reserved for the most highly placed and regarded ones (cf. Josephus, *J. W.* 7.47). Josephus calls these important members "the heads of the *gerousia*" (*J. W.* 7.412). Decisions affecting the community appear to have been made by the *archōns* and the *gerousia*. Other important positions in the Jewish community included the head of the *gerousia* (the *gerousiarchēs*, γερουσιάρξης) and several officials of the synagogue: the head (*archisynagōgos*, ἀρξισυνάγωγος), the overseer (*phōnētēs*, φωνητής), and the secretary (*grammateus*, γραμματεύς). There were also Jewish courts (Josephus, *Ant.* 14.235), although individual Jews possessed the right to appeal to the secular city court. Jews also enjoyed certain privileges that included freedom from having to offer sacrifices to other deities, the right to observe the Sabbath and other religious holidays without having to work or schedule events, freedom from military service largely because of Sabbath observance, and the collection and sending of money to Jerusalem for the temple. Yet no Jewish community in any city possessed any political power. During the reign of the Ptolemies Jews were classified among "other Hellenes," while the Egyptians were initially excluded entirely. This Jewish status was to change with the Romans, who denied them citizenship of a polis.

The Schools in Greece and the Egyptian Greek Diaspora[11]

As discussed under Qoheleth, Hellenistic schools provided the major conduit for disseminating Greek language and culture throughout the ancient world. Those Jews who possessed Greek citizenship were allowed entrance into these Greek centers of education, first the primary and secondary schools, then the gymnasia. The "ephebate" who attended an ephebion or graduate school was one who specialized in a career. Prior to the Hellenistic period, the *ephēbeia* was a military school in which young men would train for a two-year period for the civil military. By the Hellenistic period (third century, BCE), the *ephēbeia* had become something like graduate or postgraduate centers of education for specialization and were found in major Greek cities (the *poleis*).

Hellenistic philosophers (e.g., Arstippus, Theophrastus, Cleanthes, Zeno, Chrysippus, and Clearchus) wrote numerous treatises on education. Education was private, meaning that fees were charged that were normally paid by aristocratic parents, although private patrons financially assisted some teachers out of their own funds. There were also students who came to the great centers of learning seeking the instruction of famous rhetors and philosophers who took up residence there.

Judaism and Hellenism in Alexandrian Egypt[12]

The new Alexandrian Empire and its successors in the dynasties of Alexander's generals (the *Diadochoi*) began a thorough reorganization of existing cities, the establishment of new "Greek cities" for Greeks who had served the empire during its wars of conquest, the constitution of the laws of the local cities, the establishment of an educational system, and the operation of the different political systems of the Greek kingdoms.[13] For several centuries (from 331 BCE to 66 CE), then, a significant period of cultural adaptation and literary productivity emerged in Hellenistic Egypt when Jews, especially in Alexandria, placed their native traditions into new Hellenistic forms, language, and cultural norms.[14] Shaye Cohen calls this period the first "Golden Age" in Judaism.[15] There were, of course, no rabbis and no rabbinic tradition in Egypt. A rich literary tradition, however, emerged among Jewish intellectuals who likely served as teachers in Jewish schools that may have been influenced by the composition of Greek gymnasia. This literary activity, not incidentally, began with the translation of the Torah into Greek, later to be followed by the translation of the entire Hebrew Bible. The Jews in Alexandria and the rest of Egypt increasingly lost their knowledge of Hebrew. Greek soon replaced Aramaic as the lingua franca of the new empire forged by Alexander, and became the primary spoken and literary language of the Ptolemaic kingdom, including the Jews of Egypt. While traditional native languages continued to be spoken among indigenous communities and were often used in religious rituals, Greek entered into the domain of native education and religion. This is one reason the Torah, and later the remainder of the Hebrew Bible, were translated into Greek. Jewish intellectuals in Alexandria learned to read and write in Greek and became knowledgeable of the Greek literary tradition, ranging from mythology, to philosophy, to grammar, to history, to law.

JEWS IN THE ROMAN EMPIRE[16]

When Octavian incorporated Egypt into the expanding Roman Empire, Alexander's former empire in Egypt and thus Ptolematic rule came to a final end. Even so, Alexandria, after Rome, was the second most important city in the eastern Mediterranean and was enormously prosperous due to commerce, trade, and grain. The Ptolemaic army was replaced by Roman legions, and Egypt was ruled by a succession of prefects appointed by and answerable only to Rome. Anti-Roman sentiment in Egypt was extremely pronounced, even as Greek rule was often resisted in the centuries before. The Egyptians found that their privileged status in their native country, which had continued for most of the reign of Augustus, was eventually stripped away.[17]

Initially, the Jews of Egypt and the Romans appeared to enjoy good relations.[18] Augustus issued to the Jews of Alexandria his thanks and underscored their ethnic and political rights, inscribed on an official stele (Josephus, *C. Ap.* 2.37) that Josephus erroneously attributes to Julius Caesar and wrongly claims that this was evidence of their full citizenship. For the first two generations of Roman rule, as noted above, the Jews were allowed to have their own ethnarch, although Augustus ended this official office in about 11 CE, while the Greeks themselves had neither king nor council (*boulē*, βουλή). The Jewish support of Roman interests created a good deal of resentment in the former Ptolemaic capital. The Jews of Alexandria had supported the effort of Gabinius to reestablish Ptolemy XII Auletes in 55 BCE as well as Caesar's backing of Cleopatra in 47 BCE. Jews did enjoy a large degree of self-regulation in the Roman Empire and were allowed to live according to their ancestral laws. The *Letter of Aristeas* 310 mentions that the Jewish community was allowed to organize itself in Alexandria as a *politeuma* (πολίτευμα, an ethnic community or cult society), although they did not possess the status of a political organization essentially involved in self-rule. Jewish law could be used as civil law when internal disputes arose between Jews, and there were numerous synagogues scattered throughout the city.

However, the first sign of a shift in the political status of Jews in Egypt occurred during the reign of Augustus, who imposed a poll tax on the Egyptians and the Jews, both of whom were classified as noncitizens. The Romans had delineated people into different ethnic classes, including native Egyptians, other populations, and those of Greek descent. Only those of Greek descent were allowed to participate in the *ephēbeia* or to enjoy education in the gymnasium, a major requirement for any who would become Roman citizens and sought involvement in political affairs. The Roman poll tax (*laographia*, λαογραφία) was based on social differentiations: Romans, citizens of Greek cities, and *peregrini* ("foreigners"). Roman policy allowed the first two classes, considered to be full citizens, either complete release from certain taxes or at least assessment at a reduced rate, while the latter, who did not possess citizenship, had to pay them in full. Most Egyptians and Jews were classified in the third category. This represented not only an additional financial burden, but was also personally degrading to the social status of both ethnicities. Jewish activists considered this demeaning social definition to be insulting and sought to have their grievance redressed by the Roman authorities. The matter is a subject found in several Greek papyri of the time. This effort to obtain the status of Greek citizenship led to serious clashes between Greeks and Jews on one hand, and Jews and Egyptians on the other. There were exceptions to the general rules for possessing Greek citizenship when individuals could prove that their ancestors were citizens, but only a few Egyptians and Jews could claim this status.[19] It is likely that the door was open to citizenship for a very few Jews who had significant wealth and political influence, but in general it was not open to most. Josephus claimed that Jews possessed equality of rights with Greeks, but this inaccurate assessment likely derived from his apologetic concerns. Third Maccabees (1:3) suggests that Jews lacked citizenship, although they might obtain it by completely giving up their Judaism. The Jewish community was loyal to Rome, for its members recognized the serious consequences of the loss of Roman favor (see Philo, *Somn.* 2.123–32). Anti-Jewish sentiment entered the Roman court beginning first with Germanicus (see Josephus, *C. Ap.* 2.63–64) and becoming especially pronounced during the reign of his son, Gaius Caligula (37–41 CE). The eventual end of this prominent Jewish community came with its destruction by Trajan in 115–117 CE, due to a Jewish revolt.

ANTI-JUDAISM AMONG GREEK AND ROMAN LITERATI[20]

Historical Overview

Several factors led to the composition of the Wisdom of Solomon, written by a well-to-do Jewish teacher who may have achieved prominence in the Jewish community. One was anti-Judaism, evidenced by the sometimes virulent polemics of certain Greek and Egyptian Alexandrians. Some Greeks and Egyptians vilified the Jews' ancestors as lowly, leprous, and diseased slaves, who ate animals that represented the gods and thus angered them, factors leading their ancestors to drive them out of Egypt. They returned centuries later as unwelcome settlers. They were depicted not only as carriers of disease and lepers but also as physically inferior.[21] While this anti-Jewish sentiment was present for several centuries in Egypt, the climate did not become especially hostile to Jews until the Roman period. While a variety of reasons explain the tensions among Greeks, Egyptians, and Jews, the major factor was the issue of privileges, some of which the Jews possessed, others that they desired but were denied. The most virulent animosity developed between the indigenous Egyptians and the Jews (Josephus, *C. Ap.* 2.69).[22] This enmity well explains the strong condemnation of the Egyptians in the Wisdom of Solomon (chaps. 11–19). In 38 CE the Jews of Egypt were beset with ethnic and urban violence directed against them. Anti-Judaism eventually culminated in the extermination of the Jewish community in Egypt. This anti-Judaism provides a background to three Jewish wisdom texts written in the Greco-Roman period from the third century BCE into the first century CE (Qoheleth, Ben Sira, and the Wisdom of Solomon).

Among the earliest anti-Jewish writers, Manetho was one of the most celebrated scholars in Greco-Egyptian circles of his day.[23] Born at Sebennytos in the Delta, which was the capital of the thirtieth Egyptian dynasty, Manetho (ca. 300 BCE) became an Egyptian priest at Heliopolis. During the Greek rule of Egypt, he received from Ptolemy I Soter I and Ptolemy II Philadelphus the patronage of the Ptolemaic court.[24] He may have helped to establish a cult of Serapis during the reign of Ptolemy I (305–285 BCE). During the reign of Ptolemy II Philadelphus (286–246), the king purchased enslaved Jews from their owners and set them free (*Let. Aris.* 22–24). All the Jews in Egypt, both those who had come to Egypt before Alexander and those who came later, were released as freedmen. This event most likely was understood theologically by the Jews as a "new exodus," while anti-Jewish Egyptians like Manetho, displeased with this new freedom, began their literary assault on Judaism in general and the Jewish recounting of the exodus in particular.

Apollonius Molon

According to Josephus, Apollonius Molon, a rhetor of the first century BCE, was a virulent anti-Jewish writer. His two most famous pupils were Cicero and Julius Caesar. At Rhodes he encountered the anti-Jewish ideas of Posidonius (135–51 BCE) and thus propagated similar charges.[25] In his anti-Jewish polemic, he wrote a separate book on the Jews and disparaged them throughout this writing. This treatise was a συσκευή (*syskeuē*, i.e., a polemical treatise; Eusebius, *Praep. ev.* 9.19) and most likely a history of Jewish origins. Apollonius argued that the Jews were expelled from Egypt due to a terrible disease that afflicted them. He belittled Moses by calling him a sorcerer and disparaged his work as lacking in any moral worth. Apollonius regarded the Jews as haters of human beings (*misanthrōpoi*, μισανθρώποι) because of kashrut and strong bonds of community. He castigated the Jews for not worshiping the same gods as other nations, thus making them, in his view, atheists (*atheos*, ἄθεος; Josephus, *C. Ap.* 2.148), for refusing to admit to their community those who held different ideas of God, for rejecting any association with those who followed a different custom of life, for disallowing any kindness toward any Gentile due to their misanthropy (Josephus, *C. Ap.* 2.258), and for offering a fattened Gentile as a yearly sacrifice (Josephus, *C. Ap.* 2.79).[26] The Jews were depicted as cowards, fanatics, and the least talented among all the barbarians (Josephus, *C. Ap.* 2.148).

Apion

Apion, who wrote in the first half of the first century CE, was a Hellenistic Egyptian, hailed as a prominent writer and politician of his day.[27] He obtained Alexandrian citizenship, a notable achievement for Egyptians, and was the chief representative of the envoy of Greeks and Hellenistic Egyptians of Alexandria in obtaining an audience with Gaius Caligula in opposing Philo, the leader of the Jewish delegation, who failed in the attempt to restore Jewish privileges enjoyed by the Jews of Alexandria during the period of the Ptolemies and continued by Julius Caesar and Augustus (Josephus, *Ant.* 18.257–60). Granted an audience with Caligula, Apion argued that the Jews were disloyal subjects of Rome for not paying homage to the emperor. Caligula scorned the Jewish delegation for not worshiping him and dismissed them without addressing their grievance. His slandering of the Jews occurs in the third and fourth volumes of his Egyptian history (*Aegyptiaca*; see Clement of Alexandria, *Strom.* 1.21). In his attack he uses the standard rhetorical pattern for reviling nations and cities that were neither Greek nor Roman.[28]

The summary of Apion's anti-Judaism by Josephus occurs in three parts: the exodus (cf. Wisdom of Solomon), the attack on the rights of the Alexandrian Jews, and the belittling of the temple and Jewish religion. Apion joins other Hellenistic Egyptians in their disparagement of the Jews in Egypt and gives similar reasons for the exodus.[29] He presents Moses as an Egyptian and the Jews in Egypt, themselves Egyptians, as suffering from diverse diseases and afflictions that led to their being driven out of the country, and he was especially harsh in his criticism of Jews in Alexandria (Josephus, *C. Ap.* 2.21). In following the frequent charge of Jewish misanthropy, Apion added, according to Josephus (*C. Ap.* 2.258), that they took an oath that forbade goodwill to be expressed to any pagan, especially Greeks. The most damaging of his charges against the Jews was his assertion that they engaged in acts of sedition against the empire (*C. Ap.* 2.68). Apion represented a significant threat to the Jews because of his political stature and the popularity of his *Aegyptiaca*, which became a standard portrayal of Egyptian history.[30] Other pagan writers who slandered the Jews included Posidonius, Cicero, Horace, Chaeremon, Lysimachus, and Tacitus.[31]

GREEK AND LATIN WRITERS SYMPATHETIC TO JUDAISM

Not all pagan writers engaged in harsh polemics against the Jews of Judea and the Diaspora. Strabo of Amaseia (ca. 64/63 BCE–23 CE) was a Greek historian and geographer whose *Geography* (*Geographica*) covered all of the nations known to Greeks and Romans during the rule of Augustus Caesar (27 BCE–14 CE). In Rome he composed his *Historical Sketches* (*Historica Hypomnemata*), consisting of forty-seven books that covered the history of the world from the conquest of Greece by the Romans in 145 BCE to the beginning of the principate of Augustus in 27 BCE. His history has been lost, save for some fragments preserved by Josephus in his *Antiquities*.[32]

It is from the quoted sections of his *Geographica* that we may determine his views of the Jews and Judaism. Strabo expressed the common view that the Jews of his day descended from the Egyptians. Moses came from Egypt, founded a religion based on a deity without images, and portrayed God pantheistically as not only encompassing humanity, land, and sea, but also as identical with heaven, the universe, and nature (16.2.36.761).[33] Strabo expressed the common view among Greek intellectuals that the rejection of images is based on reason, for no sensible person would consider an image to resemble God or to be divine. Further, Strabo narrates that Moses founded Jerusalem and set up a government for the people, attracted the attention of other nations for his ethical and religious teachings, and established a manner of transmitting his righteous teachings to his successors. His sympathetic depiction of Moses is particularly noteworthy (16.2.36–37.761).[34] He considered him a lawgiver who also laid claim to divine inspiration (e.g., Minos, Lycurgus, and Tiresias; cf. Diodorus 1.94.1–2). Moses is also depicted as a prophet ("mantic") who belonged to a noble list of mantics that also included Teiresias, Amphiaraus, and Trophonius.[35]

Strabo blamed the later introduction of superstition on the priests. Thus, in his view, Judaism had declined into a superstitious religion of laws concerning diet and became a militant group that sought to destroy the centers of Hellenistic civilization (16.2.39.762).[36] Clearly, Strabo did not share in the anti-Jewish views found in some of the non-Jewish writers mentioned above.[37]

JEWISH LITERATI SYMPATHETIC TO HELLENISTIC CULTURE

Introduction

Presenting varying responses to Hellenistic culture, numerous Jewish literati, including historians, sages, philosophers, and apologists, explained and defended Judaism from pagan criticism.

Pseudo-Hecataeus[38]

Josephus attributed two works, *On Abraham* and *On the Jews*, to Hecataeus of Abdera (Josephus, *Ant.* 1.159; *C. Ap.* 1.183–204; cf. Eusebius, *Praep. ev.* 13.13.40), although these were written by the unknown Jewish author, Pseudo-Hecataeus.[39] Pseudo-Hecataeus, in his text *On the Jews*, mentions that Jews immigrated to Egypt following the Ptolemaic sacking of Gaza in 312 BCE. Especially emphasized are the high priest Ezekias, who spoke of the benefits that accrue to emigration, loyalty to Jewish laws and ancestral faith, the land of Judea, and the Jerusalem temple. Josephus implies that this work was a comprehensive depiction of Jewish history and social practices. Bar-Kochva places the writing during the height of the Hasmonean period, and, similarly, Holladay proposes that *On the Jews* may be as early as the middle of the second century BCE.[40] This text was written for a conservative Jewish community in order to preserve their traditional practices and beliefs in the Diaspora.

Artapanus

The little that remains from the Jewish historian and writer of romance Artapanus (who produced a work named *Judaica* in the first fragment and *Concerning the Jews* in the second and third fragments) consists of three fragments that are preserved in Eusebius (*Praep. ev.* 9.18.1; 9.23.1–4; 9.27.1–37), who quoted them from Alexander Polyhistor.[41] The fragments, heavily dependent on the Septuagint and Jewish Egyptian legends, have features of romantic history, the encomium, and apologia.[42] They focus on the relationship that Abraham, Joseph, and Moses had with Egypt. Most likely Jewish himself, Artapanus composed a romantic encomium that praises these three heroes of Jewish history and implicitly functions as an apology. Artapanus considers these three figures of Jewish antiquity to be the founders of culture and benevolent in their support and treatment of the Egyptians. Thus the apologetic aspect of this text is not polemical but rather amicable, seeking to curry the favor of the Hellenistic Egyptians. The historian is considered to be an extremely liberal Hellenistic Jew who was not threatened by other Hellenistic traditions, while continuing to remain loyal to his own faith.[43] While God is present in working through these ancestors, their deeds and virtues are singled out for praise. The date and exact provenance of Artapanus are difficult to ascertain, for he is not mentioned in any pagan or Jewish writings. In broad terms, he lived and wrote between 250 and 100 BCE in Egypt.[44] Due to his apologetic efforts to respond to the anti-Jewish polemics of Greek Egyptian writers like Manetho and to the presupposition that the Jewish temple in Leontopolis is in existence, Holladay dates his career more specifically to the reign of Ptolemy VI Philometor (180–145 BCE).[45] His references to Egyptian traditions indicate that he likely writes in this part of Africa. And, of course, Jewish apologists were especially found in Alexandria, making this city the probable location for the origin both of this writer and his composition.

In the first fragment, Abraham is presented as coming to Egypt, where he taught the Egyptians astrology before returning twenty years later to Syria. Joseph's career is detailed in the second fragment that condenses the Joseph narrative in Genesis 37 and 39–47. He is hailed not only as the "lord of Egypt" but also as the one who benefited culturally the Egyptians. The third fragment is an Egyptianized account of Moses, who was the grand cultural benefactor of Egypt, a military strategist for the Egyptians engaging in battle against Ethiopia that resulted in this country's defeat and the building of a city in his honor (Hermopolis),[46] and the founder of Egyptian cults, even being revered himself as divine (Hermes = Egyptian Thoth). Artapanus narrates the death of Pharaoh Chenephres for blaspheming the Jewish Deity, yet states that Moses brought him back to life. The account of the plagues markedly omits the Passover, presenting rather a summary of the exodus and offering rational accounts of the crossing of the Red Sea. Missing are any references to Moses as lawgiver. He is said to have invented for the Egyptians boats, architectural devices, military equipment, waterworks, and, most importantly, philosophy. In founding the Egyptian cults, he taught hieroglyphics to the various Egyptian priesthoods. He maintained the position that the Jewish Deity is the "master of the universe," while the Egyptian gods and animals they worshiped were explained euhemeristically as useful inventions.[47] Artapanus places a significant emphasis not on fidelity to the Mosaic Law but on the affirmation of the Jews' superiority (especially because of their one God and their heroes) to other peoples (including their religion and culture). Jews are to relate to their tradition not through the requirements of religion, but rather through the virtuous character and heroic deeds of their ancestors, who treated the Egyptians well in founding their culture and in supporting their existence.

Ezekiel the Tragedian

One of the responses to the Egyptian criticism of the Jewish exodus from Egypt is that written by Ezekiel the Tragedian, a Hellenistic Jew who most likely lived in Alexandria. His book, the *Exagōgē* ("Leading Out"; seventeen fragments are preserved in Eusebius, *Praep. ev.* 9.28.1; and several by Clement of Alexandria, *Strom.* 1.23),[48] dates from the first half of the second century BCE, when the relations between the Jews and Egyptians had greatly deteriorated. The drama begins with Moses' birth and continues with Moses and the Israelites journeying into the wilderness (Exod. 1–15). Ezekiel's story is replete with a combination of biblical and fictional features and characters. While he makes significant use of the Septuagint, he writes elegant Greek in iambic trimeter, the literary form of Greek tragic drama, and makes good use of Greek writers (cf. Homer, Aeschylus, Sophocles, Euripides, and Herodotus). This indicates he is well familiar with and even educated in the Greek literary tradition. He writes in order to glorify Moses and to set forth the most important event in Jewish history, the exodus from Egypt, as under the direction of God (Wis. 11–19). Yet he also omits features that would prove embarrassing when read by a pagan audience.

The Letter of Aristeas[49]

The so-called *Letter of Aristeas*,[50] written by an unknown Jewish author, praises the Jews and Judaism. While largely fictional, this letter still provides the most important witness to the Septuagint, although it is neither written by Aristeas nor a letter in form.[51] Rather its form is that of an apology.[52] The text was written as an admonition to Jews to accept Hellenistic culture and to live without contention in Greek society.[53] The letter also emphasizes the important qualities of Judaism in order to cultivate respect and tolerance for Jews.[54] Jews are to honor their own identity, and yet accommodate themselves to the virtuous aspects of Hellenism. A pseudo-Aristeas, possibly implied as a fictional participant in this translation, wrote the "letter" to his brother, Philocrates, to provide an account of the origins of the Septuagint. An encomium (vv. 121–22) praises the Jewish translators for their excellent paideia, their distinguished parentages, their mastery of Jewish literature, and their knowledge of Greek literature.[55] Jews and Greeks are presented as sharing a common paideia that places reason above emotions among the common values (see also especially clemency and generosity). Indeed, the text speaks of the mutual respect that Jews and Greeks had for one another.[56] According to this text, Jews and Greeks theologically share the view of God as the creator and providential provider of care for humanity, affirmations that are at the center of piety (vv. 2, 24, 37, 42, 131, 215 speak of piety, while vv. 16–17, 132–33, 201 refer to creation and providence). Aristeas even articulated the view that Jews and Greeks worship the same deity, only with different names (Zeus or Jove for the Greeks, v. 16). Kashrut is explained as the ethical means to avoid evil associations and is given an allegorical interpretation. Nevertheless, Jewish religion is superior to all others. Polytheism is described in euhemeristic terms and is dismissed, as is the Egyptian worship of wild animals and other creatures, living or dead (vv. 135–38). The anti-idolatrous polemic is designed to point to the primacy of Jewish monotheism. Most of these themes parallel the Wisdom of Solomon and point to a common understanding of the salient features of Hellenistic Judaism.

Several digressions provide important insights into the practice of Hellenistic Judaism in Judea and especially in Alexandria. One major digression occurs in verses 83–120, which tell of the Jerusalem temple, the vestments of the high priest Eleazar, and an explanation and glorification of the Jewish law. He speaks of Jerusalem and the splendor of the temple placed on its highest hill, while he describes its architecture and cultic implements. Eleazar is described as adorned with glorious vestments containing twelve stones set in gold, a girdle woven in stunning colors, an "oracle" worn on his breast, tassels adorned with flowers, golden bells surrounding the hem of the garment, and a stunning tiara on which is a golden leaf with the name of God (cf. Ben Sira's portrayal of Simeon II in chap. 50).

The date of the writing is extremely difficult to determine,[57] although the question of how Jews are to treat and interact with non-Jews points to a period of some tension, if not crisis. The earliest date is the mid-second century BCE, although tension and on occasion friction between Jews and Egyptians occurred through-out the periods of Persian and Ptolemaic rule. The middle ground appears to be the desire of pseudo-Aristeas for mutual tolerance between Jews and Gentiles.[58]

Aristobulus

Five fragments of Aristobulus[59] have been preserved by Eusebius (*Hist. eccl.* 7.32.16–18; *Praep. ev.* 8.10; 13.12),[60] and they underscore the intent to relate Hellenistic culture to Judaism. Most Christian writers consider him to be a Peri-patetic, although he appears to be more eclectic than that.[61] Among the topics he discusses are the Passover; the nature of God (the problem of anthropomor-phism and the similarity of the views of Moses with those of some of the Greek writers); the dependence of certain Greek writers, including Socrates, Plato, and Pythagoras, on the law of Moses; the similarities of the ideas of Orpheus and Ara-tus to those of Moses; and the Sabbath, which was supposed to have some par-allels to the Greek idea of cosmic order found in Homer and Hesiod. In arguing the last point, he uses allegory and Pythagorean reflections on the number seven.

The writing of Aristobulus was dedicated to Ptolemy, most likely Ptolemy VI Philometor (180–145 BCE), although Ptolemy IV Philometor (221–204) is a possibility.[62] He was an Alexandrian Jew whose composition possessed features of both the encomium and the apologia, and he achieved notoriety as the earli-est known Jewish philosopher whose teachings were eclectic. He sought not only to explain certain features of Judaism that an educated Hellenistic audience might consider offensive, for example, a deity who possessed human features, but also to extol the greatness and even superiority of Moses and the Jewish law. As a theologian, he argued that there cannot be a contradiction between the Bible and philosophy. This was one reason he gave the Torah an allegorical interpreta-tion.[63] He emphasized the unity of all truth and stressed that Judaism is a "philo-sophical school," indeed the most significant one of all. The Deity of the Jews and the God of the Gentiles are one and the same.

Philo Judaeus of Alexandria[64]

The presentation of Judaism by Philo Judaeus (ca. 10 BCE–45 CE) may be char-acterized as a philosophical articulation shaped by Middle Platonism, Stoicism, mysticism, and Pythagorean numerology.[65] Yet his writings, while using allegory as his hermeneutical tool for interpretation, were traditional, since Philo affirmed what was considered to be central to the faith and practice of the Jewish religion. As a loyal Jew he sought to present the major features of ancestral Jewish beliefs and practices in Hellenistic dress, appropriating from his religious tradition what he deemed most important to maintain and to represent this information in ways understandable to a larger Hellenistic audience. He conducted his life according to the teachings of Judaism and yet was cultured in Hellenism, enabling him to bring the two together in a compelling fashion. He was every bit the Alexandrian as well as the Jew. This "cultural convergence," as John Barclay prefers to call it, includes also other Hellenistic Jewish writings open to compatible features of Hellenism.[66]

Josephus indicates that Philo came from one the most prominent families in Alexandria. He likely was born around 10 BCE, and died shortly after the decree of Claudius that prohibited a blanket Jewish citizenship of Alexandria (38–41 CE). Due to the prominence of his family, his command of elegant Greek, and his seemingly firsthand knowledge of the hippodrome, the theater, the palaestra, the gymnasium, and the clubs, he more than likely was a Greek citizen of Alexandria.[67] Yet philosophically, through meditation and mystical experiences, he was also a citizen of the universe, or *cosmopolitos*.

Philo's education was both Jewish and Greek (he likely attended a Hellenistic Jewish Torah school), although the nature of the education that he pursued is enigmatic and may only be inferred from his writings. It is not clear that he knew Hebrew (see *Mos.* 2.37–41) or knew it very well, since his knowledge and allegorical interpretation of the Bible was most likely based on the Septuagint, which he considered to be an inspired translation. In addition to the Bible, he was evidently familiar with Palestinian Judaism's haggadah and halakah.[68] In his essay *On the Preliminary Studies* (*De congressu eruditionis gratia*), he describes in detail Greek paideia carried out in the Greek schools. He mentions that the curriculum consisted of philosophy, grammar, geometry, and music. Philosophy he calls the "lawful wife" (*Congr.* 74–76), since all other areas of study were the "handmaidens" who served what held the most elite position among the intellectual ideals, philosophy. Philosophy was divided into the areas of logic, ethics, and physics (especially cosmology), likely a curricular structure that reflects the curricular disciplines of Hellenistic schools. His religious beliefs are stated in a creed of five affirmations, the first four of which are biblical: God exists from eternity, God is one, the world had a beginning, the world is one, and God exercises divine forethought for the cosmos and its inhabitants.[69]

Philo speaks of education ("encyclical training") of wealthy families in *Spec.* 2.230, *Prov.* 2.44–46, and *Congr.* 74–76.[70] Of course, participation in the gymnasium was possible only for the male elite who were citizens of a polis in Greco-Roman society. Philo's writings demonstrate he was himself well educated in philosophy, grammar, rhetoric, dialectic, literature, mathematics, astronomy, music, and physical activity. He may even have studied in an *ephēbeion*, since he was a highly skilled rhetorician. After all, he led Jewish embassies to Rome to press both for the recognition of Jewish rights and for citizenship in the polis of Alexandria for Jews whose ancestry included citizens of the city in previous times. It also is clear, however, that Philo enjoyed an excellent education in a Hellenistic Jewish school or at least was tutored by Jewish teachers. Having been raised in a Jewish family, he was taught by "divinely gifted men" (*Spec.* 1.314) and thereby became well versed in Scripture and oral traditions passed down by the "elders of the nation" (*Mos.* 1.4).[71] He became an exegete trained especially in allegorical interpretation. Both of these types of education were apparently available to those Jews who were citizens.

Philo also mentions "Sabbath schools," where the population was taught a variety of virtues: good sense, temperance, courage, justice, and so on (*Spec.* 2.62). He notes that Sabbath schools are in the thousands in every city (*Mos.* 2.216). In *Opif.* 128 he remarks that God requires people to dedicate their Sabbaths to philosophy "with a view to the improvement of character and submission to the scrutiny of conscience," and in *Spec.* 2.63–64 he adds that the faithful on the Sabbath focus on duty to God and to others. These lead to the "knowledge and perfection of the mind." The curricula of the Sabbath schools for Jewish youth would have been theological, ethical, and exegetical.

Philo wrote glowingly of Moses as the greatest among the sages, and as the one from whom the Greek philosophers plagiarized their best ideas (*Mos.* 1.1–3). This noted ancestor's intellect and virtue made him the noblest of kings, the holiest of high priests, the wisest among the prophets, and the most excellent of lawgivers in whom the divine laws were incarnate (*Mos.* 2.1–7). Philo even placed himself in the "school of Moses" (*Mut.* 223). His understanding of God (*ho ōn*, ὁ ὤν) is that of the uncreated and eternal Deity, the creator and king who, being invisible spirit, is not to be worshiped by means of an image. The Creator serves as the providential director of reality, and oversees the cosmos and its inhabitants as the divine judge rewarding the righteous and punishing the wicked. His view of the Creator and creation makes use of the metaphor of the architect or artisan who, through the divine *logos* (λόγος), constructs the cosmos according to the design of a city (*Spec.* 1.80–81; cf. Wisd. 7:21).[72] Philo's cosmology is hierarchical, in which reality in its purest form ("the One" = God) descends to lower (earth and creatures) and lower (inanimate) forms. Men are superior to women, for the male has the ability to use the mind and is less connected to the corporeal than is the female. The highest creature, below God, is the male, who is rational, free, and released from captivity to the body and passions.

Philo reflects the Stoic understanding of the world soul when he asserts that the cosmos is in harmony with the Jewish Torah, while the Torah reflects the order of nature in the world. The person who is obedient to the Torah is therefore in harmony with the cosmos. The Logos is central to his philosophy. Since God is unknowable by human beings and could be described only in terms of what he is not, this emanation of the Creator makes the world rational, and, since it dwells within the human capacity to reason, humans are able to understand the world and through it the God who made it. But it is only through a type of intuitive illumination of the soul that this unknowable Deity is capable of being known.[73] The Logos refers to a variety of things, including the divine mind, the idea of ideas, the firstborn son of the Uncreated Father, the shadow of God, the pattern of creation, Scripture, Mosaic laws, human and heavenly beings, the archetype of divine order effectuated through reason, and the human ability to think. It is even a divinely immanent principle that holds all creation together. For Philo the world consists of both the intelligible world, comparable to Plato's world of ideas or forms, and the sensible world, that is, things that are knowable by means of the senses. Thus the world is dualistic, as are humans, who consist of both soul (the higher, immortal part of humanity) and body (the lower, mortal element). Evil comes from matter. The goal of life should therefore be to deny carnal pleasures and other experiences of the senses and to obtain a beatific vision of God.

Philo's anthropology is dualistic, for humans bring together both the spiritual and material elements. The body serves as the prison of the soul, or the mind, that links humans to God. Freeing oneself from the corporeal and passions is the task of the true sage, who then is able to come to God, released from all things material. Philo also speaks of the perfection of the body and soul of the Levitical priests who are made in the image of God (*Somn.* 1.215). The high priest is the symbol of the perfect human being and has the cosmic role of separating the clean from the unclean. His vestments are the symbol of the entire cosmos. The Jews themselves serve the significant role of intercessor for humanity, for they are the priests of all peoples who intercede between humanity and God.[74] Philo extols the Jews' virtue and piety, while vilifying the Egyptians as irrational, hedonistic, and irreligious. In speaking about the plagues he uses the present tense to tell of God's wrath against the Egyptians. They represent corporeal existence and are burdened with passions. Allegorically speaking, every person must escape from Egypt who wishes to see God.

Philo took on the role of apologist in his disputes with pagans and apostates who used a misapplied literal interpretation of Scripture and a misrepresentation of Jewish customs and beliefs to vilify them (see, e.g., *Names*, *Confusion*, and *Migration*). He did not submerge Judaism into the deepest waters of Hellenism, but rather regarded his ancestral tradition as superior to Greek culture. Philo combined allegory with a literal understanding, using the former as a hermeneutical tool, likely borrowed from the Stoics, to explain difficult passages and to obtain knowledge for the soul, while the literal was appropriated for understanding Jewish practices and beliefs that did not require circumspection and were for the body (see *Allegorical Interpretation*). Only intellectuals have the rational souls that are capable of discerning these deeper meanings of the soul. At the same time, he followed on occasion a haggadic practice of inserting explanatory comments in his interpretation of Scripture.

While he much preferred seclusion that allowed him to think and write, political realities could not be ignored that called upon him to defend his own community (*Spec.* 3.1–6). Two treatises focus on the Alexandrian crisis of the Jewish community during the time of the prefect Flaccus, Gaius Caligula, and Claudius. In his treatise *In Flaccum*, Philo explains that several elements of Judaism are so intrinsic to Jewish identity that faithful Jews are willing to give up their lives to maintain them: temple worship, worship in synagogues, the Sabbath, and observing the law of Moses. While he is devoted to the temple in Jerusalem, arguing that the oneness of God should translate into a single temple, he also speaks of the importance of the inner altar of the soul in which God delights. In *De Legatione ad Gaium* he stresses that the deliverance of the Jews from the Alexandrian and Jerusalem crises are proof of God's providential care for both the Jews and all of humanity. What happens to the Jews ("those who see God") is emblematic of God's care for all those human beings who lead spiritual lives.[75]

Philo was involved in Jewish politics in Alexandria. He headed the Alexandrian Jewish embassy to Rome to seek an audience with Gaius Caligula (39–40 CE) to obtain a favorable dispensation from the Caesar to restore their ancestral rights granted by Augustus. Philo believed, wrongly it seems, that the earlier royal decree had included full citizenship in the Greek polis of Alexandria for Jews, at least those who were born in the city. Part of this request was to heighten Jewish prestige in Egypt, and the other part had to do with taxation. The poll tax levied by the empire exempted Greek citizens and allowed Hellenes in the provinces to pay a reduced tax, but Egyptians and Jews were required to pay the full levy. This quarrel over citizenship was one of the reasons for an Egyptian-inspired pogrom against the Jews of Alexandria during the governorship of Flaccus. In addition, one would think that the Jewish celebration of the Passover and the ridiculing of Egyptian religion, especially the mummification of animals, would have added fuel to the flames of anti-Judaism.

Philo lived and wrote in an Alexandria that was experiencing significant tension among Greeks, Egyptians, and Jews. Behind this perturbation were the Jewish enjoyment of privileges and their quest to obtain citizenship. Philo's political actions were given a theological grounding when he contended in *Legatio ad Gaium* that the cause of the difficulties between the Romans and the Jews were largely due to Caligula's self-deification and his demand that the Jews honor him as a god. He contended that Flaccus and Gaius Caligula were enemies not only of the Jews but also of God himself. At least according to Philo's literary license, the arrogance of Flaccus induced him to confess shortly before dying that his persecution of the Jews had led to his downfall. While the ending of his historical essay on the embassy to Caligula has not survived, and thus his interpretation of this Caesar's death is missing, Philo severely criticized him for making himself a god.

The Greeks who lived in Philo's world are depicted by him to be wicked, gluttonous, and licentious. The evil nature of Greek character is especially evidenced, in Philo's thinking, by the gymnasium, which discriminated against the Jews and even became a social center for anti-Judaism.[76] Philo shared the Jewish nationalistic hopes and dreams of dominion.[77] Although this nationalism was not at the center of his philosophical writings, Philo still envisioned the gathering of the exiles and the defeat of the enemies of Israel. The Diaspora would end one day when all righteous Jews would return to Israel, and yet this was still in the distant future. Philo seemed far more concerned with establishing the rights of the Jews in his own world. The Jerusalem temple is significant in Philo, and he gives it a symbolic role as the center of cosmic worship. Following a Platonic understanding of typology, he sees the temple and the buildings of the earthly Jerusalem as representing both the cosmos and their heavenly archetypes. Especially important for the practice of Judaism was worship in the temple of Jerusalem, payment of the temple tax, devotion to the Torah and its interpretation, and worship in the synagogue that was not defiled with images. He was unusually disdainful of idolatry and other religions. His major difference with the deity of the philoso-phers was that the Jewish God was a personal Deity who loves, protects, and shows mercy to his people.[78] This one supreme and only God was to be worshiped. Where many Greeks erred was not in believing in one Supreme Being, but rather in worshiping lower deities. The maintenance of Jewish identity, not the eschato-logical exaltation of a reunited Judaism, was uppermost in his thinking.

Pseudo-Phocylides

A Hellenistic Jewish poet, Pseudo-Phocylides, wrote a text that contains impor-tant features of Jewish sapiential poetry and Greek gnomology and consists of some 230 lines composed in rough dactylic hexameters in the Ionic dialect. These monostichs are sayings dealing with ethics and decision making. The extant materials consist of five manuscripts.[79] The composition, difficult to date pre-cisely, was put together between the later part of the third century BCE and 40 CE.[80] The poem was written in the name of Phocylides, a well-known Ionic poet of Miletus in Ionia during the sixth century BCE who composed sayings that offered advice for life. It would have been written during the times of tensions especially with Greek Egyptians, or just before or following the reign of the Roman emperor Caligula (37–41 CE). In addition, the text gives the appearance of summarizing the moral teachings of the Torah, suggesting then that this was a compendium for Hellenistic Jews living in the Diaspora and attempting to maintain their allegiance to their heritage at the same time they found themselves in a Hellenistic setting outside Palestine, possibly Alexandria. The social setting was likely a Hellenistic Jewish school that educated students in both pagan and Jewish traditions.[81] The poem may have represented an effort to encourage Hel-lenistic Jews to maintain their allegiance to their ancestral values while embrac-ing much of Hellenistic culture deemed compatible to Jewish life. It is possible that the writer also sought to gain sympathy from Greek pagans, at least indi-rectly, for Jews and their religion.

One of the interesting observations about his references to the Ten Command-ments is that there is no mention of the prohibition against images. This omission, along with the absence of any reference to idolatry in the entire book, was most likely due to the author's purposes of appealing to Hellenists who criticized the Jews for their refusal to worship images and to place them at the entrance of the syna-gogues. At the same time, wealthy Jews in Alexandria would have typically had Greco-Roman mythological scenes painted on the walls of their homes. Taken as a whole, the interpretation of the Ten Commandments reformulates Jewish ethics in a manner and content that would be acceptable to a Gentile audience.[82]

The Wise Menander[83]

These sayings, preserved in Syriac, provide an anthology of wisdom designed to teach students the path to successful living. It is probable that the collection is a translation of a Greek Jewish collection that has not survived. Its original location is not known, although several interpreters have pointed to Egypt. This anthology may have been a florilegium in which sayings were collected for teaching both sapiential morality and rhetoric to students in the schools. The most important themes are that God is the creator of all that exists, the fashioner of destiny and history, and to be both praised and feared. He is not removed from human life, but rather may be the one to whom prayers are offered and who can be expected to act in just ways. The author's affirmation of polytheism raises the question of Jewish authorship, although it is not impossible that he was an ecumenist who affirmed many religions and their gods.

ANTI-JUDAISM AND JEWISH DEFENDERS IN THE DIASPORA: A SUMMARY

Alexandria was the center of anti-Judaism for several centuries.[84] Jewish opponents attacked the religious and social teachings of Judaism that were especially opposed to the syncretistic[85] character of Hellenism. Critics were repulsed by animal sacrifice and charged Jews with atheism, since they rejected idolatry and polytheism in favor of an iconoclastic deity whose teachings denied the existence of other gods. Charges of the annual ritual murder of a Greek, philosophical irrationality, and barbarism were other accusations leveled against this significant ethnic minority in Egypt. Especially frequent was the charge that the Jews, largely because of their ritual and cultic laws, were antisocial, and even misanthropic. Hellenistic Egyptians, drawing on centuries of conflict with Israelites and Jews, engaged in a direct criticism of the exodus story, narrated by Alexandrian Jews in the context of their celebration of the Passover.[86] Thus, as the Egyptians told it, the exodus was the result of the expulsion of diseased, leprous, and afflicted people by the ruling pharaoh in order to appease the wrath of the gods. Perhaps the most dangerous charge, uttered for example by the Alexandrian Greek Isodorus and by Cicero, was that Jews sought to increase their own power and caused political instability by seeking to separate themselves from the Roman Empire.

Jewish scholars and teachers responded to these attacks in a body of literature that made use of Greek literary forms, extolled the virtues and exploits of Jewish heroes, praised the glories of Judaism, defended Judaism against its despisers, sought to convert its opponents to an appreciation of or at least a tolerance for Jews and their religion and culture, and attempted to bring apostates back into the fold. Among this literature was the Wisdom of Solomon. There even may have been some effort to proselytize the non-Jews who were sympathetic listeners, especially in an age when enthusiasm for the worship of the Olympian gods had radically declined and people looked to Egypt and the East for new religious meaning.[87] Furthermore, while Caesar Augustus continued to grant many civil and religious rights to the Jews, in following the policy of the Ptolemies, the question of the poll tax led to the larger issue of their citizenship.[88] Denied citizenship of the Greek polis, Jews nevertheless were given important political rights.[89] In 38 CE during the reign of Caligula, the pogrom that Flaccus initiated against the Jewish population in Alexandria desecrated their synagogues and physically abused them. The Jews, under the leadership of Philo, assembled an embassy that went to Rome to appeal to Caligula for their rights, but his death left the issue unsettled. Finally, in reaction to the requests of a second Jewish embassy, Claudius granted the Jews their historical rights, but continued to deny them Alexandrian citizenship. Their sociopolitical status began to decline dramatically due to the failed Jewish revolt against Rome initiated in 66 CE. The rebellion in 115–117 was quelled brutally by Trajan, who annihilated the Jews of Alexandria.

THE ATTRACTION OF HELLENISM

The factors that led to the writing of the Wisdom of Solomon included the attraction of Hellenistic culture and the related desire for Greek citizenship, which led many Jews either to abandon their faith or to accommodate their tradition to Hellenistic culture and religion. In extreme cases, some Jews lost much of their distinctiveness and assimilated into the Greek world. The lure of Greek culture was especially powerful in those areas of the East where hellenization sank deep roots into ancient nations like Egypt. Related to this attraction of the dominant culture is that citizenship in a Greek polis offered full rights to its possessors in all political, economic, and cultural spheres.

A final factor that led to the composition of the Wisdom of Solomon was what may best be described as an internal crisis of the religious spirit in Hellenism, leading to a growing disenchantment with Greek state religion, centered on the Olympian gods, and with the military control imposed by Imperial Rome. Wisdom, the *Letter of Aristeas,* and Philo join with Greek intellectuals in ridiculing Greek myths (*Philo,* Praem. 8), polytheism (*Spec.* 2.164), and the adoration of beauty (*Abr.* 267–68). Thus the wisdom of the East (including Judaism), mystery religions, and the philosophical schools taught their adherents how to conduct their lives in a Hellenistic environment. In cultures that faced the crisis of religious disintegration and social and political upheaval in the period of the empire, beginning with Julius Caesar, the question of a reflective, directed life became uppermost for many intellectuals, including those among the Jews.

INTRODUCTION TO THE WISDOM OF SOLOMON

Prelude

Based on his knowledge of Jewish history and Hellenistic culture, the author appears to have been a rhetor and teacher who received his education in both Greek and Jewish schools in Alexandria. It was likely in a school of rhetoric that he learned the grammar and rhetorical features of Greek, a requirement especially for those who entered into the learned professions. One of the key elements of rhetorical education was to study summaries of the classics and leading philosophies. Thus an acquaintance with what modern scholars sometimes call Middle Platonism would have been part of his studies.[90] It is doubtful this rhetor enjoyed citizenship that would have gained him entrance to one of the gymnasia of the city. The large number of prosperous Jews in Alexandria would have sought out teachers, such as our rhetor, to instruct their male children in the rudiments of Hellenistic education and Jewish tradition. This Jewish sage lived and wrote in the early Roman Empire when, due to hellenization, there was enormous diversity of philosophies, languages, and religions, loosely bound together by Greek culture.

The Social Status of the Author

Unfortunately, we know little that is concrete about the writer. We know nothing of his family and social standing. From the text, which serves as our only primary source, one would surmise that this author was wealthy, schooled in both Greek and Jewish education, and wrote good, if not elegant, Greek. He may have taught either in a Jewish Torah school that was both Hellenistic and Jewish in its curriculum or as a tutor to Alexandrian Jewish youth. Similar to Philo, he likely lived in the prosperous and cosmopolitan city of Alexandria, would have resided in the more wealthy residential area of one of the two Jewish districts of this city, and would have had the opportunity to visit the palaestra, to attend the theater, and to watch the games in the hippodrome. He presumably would have had the freedom to study in the *Mouseion* that housed the great library. He was an intellectual, in any event, but certainly not on the level of Philo (what Jewish intellectual was?). He possibly served at the Alexandrian court during the Roman occupation, for this would explain the addressing of his parenetic text to the "kings of the earth," although this may have been a literary fiction designed to impress a Jewish audience. Due to the encouragement of the expression of cultural views in Alexandria, it is not impossible that he was given an audience to present a rhetorical address to the court. Unlike Philo, he did not serve as an ambassador, but he may have had a leadership position in the community and would have been highly regarded.

The *Mouseion* of Alexandria, built by Alexander, was the major location for the intellectuals of Ptolemaic Egypt, and indeed served as one of the most elite centers for scholars in the eastern Mediterranean world. Like their Greek ancestors before them in Athens, the rulers of Ptolemaic Alexandria attempted to attract to their highly cultured city the brightest of minds to think, study, teach, and write. This they did in the *Mouseion*, which housed the collection of one of the best libraries in the ancient world of the period. Historians, philosophers, artists, scientists, physicians, and mathematicians came to this intellectual and cultural center and tutored the sons of the aristocracy.[91] Even after the great fire that burned the city during the occupation of Julius Caesar, the marvelous library, which was housed in the *Mouseion* during Augustus's conquest of the city in 30 BCE, went unscathed. Only a warehouse with some manuscripts was destroyed.

Philosophers in Greek culture, especially active in the courts of kings and officials as well as in the schools, bore the title "sage" or "wise person" (*sophos*, σόφος). Three schools had representatives in Hellenistic courts, both Seleucid and Ptolemaic: the Peripatetics, Stoics, and Epicureans.

The Sage in the Wisdom of Solomon[92]

The portrait drawn of the sage takes on Hellenistic features in the Wisdom of Solomon. The sage is one who trusts in God (Wis. 1:2, 10–11); longs for Wisdom and prefers her to all other things (7:8–12; 8:2); receives from her the four cardinal virtues of self-control, intelligence, justice, and courage (8:7 = Plato, *Phaed.* 69C; *Resp.* 427E; *Leg.* 631C);[93] acquires knowledge of past and future, nature, and logic, gains the ability to solve riddles (Wis. 7:17–22); is honored by the people (8:10); governs peoples and nations (8:11–12, 14; 10:14); and is given wealth and fame, courage, and rhetorical skill (8:5, 12, 15, 18). The sage will share wisdom with other people, is the stability of the nation, and aids in the salvation of the world (6:23–24; 7:13; 9:18). The sage receives not only contentment and joy but ultimately immortality (7:14; 8:16). He is a leader at home and participates in governing the world with righteousness and holiness (9:3; 12:19).

In the Wisdom of Solomon the sage is particularly the one who aspires to obtain Wisdom (8:2–3, 9), for through her comes the ultimate gift: immortality and intimacy with God (6:12–21).[94] He engages in a hymnic description of her, mentioning her many characteristics, in 7:25–26, 29–30 (see Philo, *Sacr.* 21–29; and Xenophon, *Mem.* 2.1.21–33). In Wis. 9:1–6, 9–10 Solomon beseeches God to send him divine Wisdom, the one who is beside his throne, in order that she may be his companion. It is only through her that one is able to come to a knowledge of God and the divine plan at work in the origin and continuation of the cosmos (9:13–18). Yet this gift of wisdom is possible only by becoming holy through obedience to the divine ordinances.[95]

Hellenistic Culture in the Wisdom of Solomon

The Wisdom of Solomon makes significant use of Hellenistic cultural forms of expression: composition in Koine Greek; interaction with Hellenistic philosophy, including especially Middle Platonism, Stoicism, and Pythagoreanism; and appropriation of Greek literary genres, including various kinds of epideictic literature, parenesis, aretology, and apology. Important terms are *sophia* (σοφία) and *sophos* (σόφος), which mean "wisdom" and "wise," respectively. This wisdom could be the knowledge of many things, ranging from the arts of architecture, building, cleverness, music, medicine, statesmanship, and divination to the practical knowledge issuing from intelligence, good judgment, and common sense.[96] Another term was *deinotes* (δεινότες), which means "clever, skillful" in craftsmanship or in speech. For the writer of this Jewish text, Greek culture becomes the major conduit for the expression of a newly emerging Judaism. Thus his anthropology; emphasis on wisdom's universal availability; the contrast, not between Jews and pagans, but between the righteous and the unrighteous; the universal providence of God; and belief in immortality are strongly Hellenistic. Yet there is such an intrinsic criticism of both a number of Hellenistic religious beliefs and practices[97] and the Hellenistic Egyptians with whom the Jews of the Egyptian Diaspora had so much conflict that the writer of this text warned against any wholesale adoption of Hellenism. The non-Jews, both Greeks and Egyptians, against whom he directs his criticisms are understood to be both enemies and fools.[98]

However, caught in the midst of the conflict between Egyptians and Jews, possibly during the pogrom of Flaccus, the rhetor engages in both an apology that defends Judaism and in an overt assault against the Egyptians. This assault was not intended to be viewed as anti-Roman, but rather as the attempt of a group struggling for citizenship, self-identity within the polis, and hope, not only for the present difficult period but also for the future, when the immortal righteous would sit in judgment of their persecutors.

Wisdom's Defense of Judaism

The rhetor's composition did involve criticism of Greek and Roman religion, but he studiously avoided any overt criticism of the Roman state and the official religion of Rome. Thus his strong assault on idolatry, nature religion, and animal worship is central to his defense of his people's distinct identity in Alexandria. The only implicit criticism of the Caesars came in the portrayal of the wise king, Solomon, who is given the same nature as any other human being. Caligula, of course, contended he was divine and should be worshiped, and the Jewish refusal likely would have had dire consequences had it not been for his timely assassination. While Claudius played the part of a divine ruler, even assuming the dress of Jupiter, thus identifying the Caesars and himself with the great deity of the empire, he was far less enamored with the idea and was rather circumspect in his views. However, while not forcing Jews to worship him or any pagan God, he did warn Philo's second embassy that punishment would be swift and forceful should the Jews of Alexandria cause disturbances that would threaten to undermine the empire. The rhetor's most anti-Egyptian expressions appear in chapters 10–19, which focus especially on the exodus and the cause behind this liberation, the plagues that harmed only Egyptians.

Thus the Jews of Alexandria were an inclusive group, for the most part, in maintaining their own separate identity. Their antagonists were the Egyptians, especially the Egyptian Hellenes. This conflict was shaped by the ideology of power, with neither side finally winning. The sad conclusion of the defeat of the Jewish revolution in Egypt against Rome, during the reign of Trajan, led to the extermination of a highly sophisticated and vital community of Jews who could trace their history in Egypt not only back to their support of Alexander, but, at least in the culture myth of the exodus, to the divine liberation from the harshness of Egyptian slavery.

RELIGION IN ROMAN ALEXANDRIA[99]

Introduction

It is clear from the rhetor's descriptions of various religions that he would have been familiar with the major facets of Greco-Roman, Egyptian, and mystery religions during the first century CE. These are in competition with Judaism for the loyalty of Alexandrians, including Jews.

Greco-Roman State Religion

While the Greeks and Romans celebrated their own religions, they both allowed the different ethnic communities of Egypt and thus the various peoples of Alexandria to practice their own religions. Even in Roman times, Alexandria remained a Greek city. This would mean that the writer would have been familiar with Greek civic festivals that involved parades, feasts, sports, music, and drama, all performed without official priesthoods, but still sanctioned by the gods.[100] The Olympian gods of Greece were taken over by the Romans and made central to their imperial state religion. This religion was coupled with the Caesar cult in which the divine nature of the Caesar was to be recognized throughout the empire. Offerings to idols of the Caesars demonstrated loyalty to the empire. Jews were able to avoid the erection of idols to Caesars in their synagogues, and they usually pacified the emperors by prayers and offerings on their behalf. The author of the Wisdom of Solomon is careful not to attack the worship of the Caesars, but he does strongly emphasize the human origins and nature of rulers and criticize idolatry, offering a euhemeristic explanation for its origins (14:11–31).

Native Egyptian Religions

Native Egyptians had ancient religions of many gods with their temples, priests, and festivals. The antiquity of the religions, the magnificence of the temples, and the education of the priests were held in admiration by the Greeks and Romans. However, the high regard for certain animals that served as the vehicles for the deities was largely misunderstood by Greeks, Romans, and Jews as the veneration of animals. Both Philo and the author of the Wisdom of Solomon criticized the Egyptians for their worship of animals. Thus Egyptian religion was ridiculed, as were the Egyptians. The Egyptians in Alexandria, for the most part, were poor, uneducated, and not skilled in speaking grammatical Greek.

Mystery Religions[101]

In addition to state religion and the Caesar cult in Imperial Rome, new religions emerged that gained large followings of devotees. These included especially the mystery religions of Dionysus, Isis, and Serapis. Dionysus (the "twice-born"), with whom Alexander the Great had identified, became the patron deity of the royal religion of the Hellenistic kings. Dionysus was the son of Zeus and a mortal mother named Semele. Having been taken by Zeus from the womb of his dying mother, he was born from the thigh of his father. Dionysus was a dichotomous deity who was both young and old, male and effeminate, and human and divine. His cult name was Bacchus, and his worshipers entered into states of ecstasy. In the Hellenistic period, Alexandria became a major location for this half-god, half-man. It was here that a great festival in the god's honor was held. Women called maenads worshiped him in the form of the wine god Bacchus[102] and entered into frenzied ecstasy during their celebrations. Male devotees engaged in ritual imbibing of wine. While celebrating the protection of the god in the afterlife, worshipers on occasion had ritualistic orgies. However, these were not central to the religion; rather the purpose was to praise Dionysus as the giver of renewed fertility during the spring and the god who created a bountiful vineyard harvest. Social barriers were broken down in the practice of this religion, since slaves, freedmen, and Roman citizens participated in the cult, as well as males and females.

The veneration of Isis in Greco-Roman religion resulted from the transformation of an Egyptian goddess into a Greek one who became the central deity of one of the most popular mystery religions in Alexandria.[103] The savior of her murdered brother, Osiris, she became identified with Hathor in Egyptian religion. In Greco-Roman religion, however, she was transmuted into the features of Hera and Aphrodite, the two goddesses of love and benevolence toward humanity. Isis became important in that she provided a background for Wisdom in the Wisdom of Solomon and also became her chief opponent in the quest to gain the devotion of Hellenistic Jews in Alexandria. Isis was not only a goddess of love, but also served as a symbol of the enhancement of women's status in Greco-Roman society.[104] Egyptian women had the most elevated social position of women in the Greco-Roman world.[105] Isis raised their social level to that of men, at least in Egypt, requiring that children respect both parents and that both husbands and wives be faithful to each other. The Isis festival was extremely significant and celebrated the discovery and revival of Osiris from the dead. Rituals in her honor at her temples also may have included fertility rites. She offered to her celebrants immortality, morality, and care.

The veneration of Serapis was the third major mystery cult known and practiced in Alexandria, where it was an important religion. It may have been characterized in part by the practice of contemplation. Serapis was honored by the Ptolemies and consisted of a variety of deities and divine characteristics. The Egyptian god Apis, in the form of a bull, and elements of Dionysus and Osiris combined to form this god. His temple, built in the southwestern part of Alexandria, was the Serapeum. While located in an Egyptian section of the city, it is likely that his temple would have been known to the author of the Wisdom of Solomon. He was the consort of the popular goddess Isis.

Jewish Religion

Jewish religion was practiced increasingly in the synagogues, and material culture makes clear that these houses of prayer and assembly were present in the Hellenistic period in Egypt. In the midst of a city filled with temples of many different gods, Jews in Alexandria continued to send their offerings and temple taxes to Jerusalem as long as the temple still stood. The Torah and the festivals were important in the Diaspora, and the Festival of Passover was continued as a family tradition. Indeed, this celebration of liberation from Egyptian tyranny and slavery led to increased friction between Jews and native Egyptians.

Hellenistic Jewish writers, including the sage who wrote the Wisdom of Solomon, set forth a Judaism that was more attuned to Greek cultural ideals, and yet that also praised Jewish history and religion, underscoring the superiority of Jewish religion to the other religions practiced in Alexandria. Thus the author combines the traditions of his Jewish ancestors with philosophical features that primarily stem from Middle Platonism.[106] Middle Platonism rejected the Skepticism of the New Academy of Plato (269 BCE to mid-first century) that was represented by a variety of writers, including especially Arcesilaus, who argued against the ability to obtain knowledge and thus to make any informed judgment. Middle Platonism lacked a good deal of uniformity and drew from other schools (especially Aristotelianism, Stoicism, and Pythagoreanism). Major figures included Albinus, Alcinous, Apuleius, Atticus, Eudorus, Numenius, Plutarch, and, of course, Philo in Judaism, and Clement of Alexandria and Origen in early Egyptian Christianity. While there were major variations among these writers regarding logic and ethics, the most important and consistent contribution was in the area of metaphysics. Middle Platonism emphasized the supreme principle or God and the existence of a nonmaterial, intelligible world that exists beyond and provides the paradigm for this one. These philosophers set forth the opposition of Monad and Dyad, although how the two are related is a matter of disagreement. Antiochus accepted the Stoic view of both an active and a passive principle, and Albinus taught that God is dominant, while matter is passive. A more extreme dualism was espoused by Numenius. In addition to the supreme principle is the idea of the World Soul, a mediating figure responsible for directing all of creation in its multiple forms. In Philo the figure of Sophia is used for the Dyad. Some of the Middle Platonists adopted the Stoic notion of the Logos as the active force of God in the world. Several writers spoke of two deities, a transcendent God turned in upon itself and an active demiurge. Jewish monotheism forbade the possibility of two deities. Thus Philo, for example, spoke of the contrast between God and his Logos.[107]

THE LITERARY FEATURES
OF THE WISDOM OF SOLOMON[108]

Greek Forms

The author of the Wisdom of Solomon, whose writing expressed a Hellenistic form of popular Jewish philosophy with a tinge of mysticism,[109] generated a synthesis of epideictic literature (especially the encomium), aretology, and apologia with the important teachings of Middle Platonism and Judaism in a literary fashion that would maintain the integrity of Jewish faith even though it was dressed in a decidedly Hellenistic guise. As an artist, skilled in the craft of literary composition, he adapted a Jewish literary style and presented his teachings to the dominant cultural and intellectual forms of the period.[110] While he speaks unabashedly of the superiority of Jewish religion to the pagan religions of the Hellenists, he nonetheless appropriates Hellenistic Greek rhetoric to fuse together two different worlds, Jewish and Greek.[111]

The overarching literary shape of the Wisdom of Solomon results from the adroit blending of two common genres in Greek rhetoric: protreptic and epideictic discourse.[112] Other elements of Greek literary rhetoric expressed in this text include the diptych, syncrisis, apostrophe, *prosōpopoiia* (προσωποποιία), and eulogy.[113] In the main, Wisdom is an exhortatory speech or homily of persuasion (*logos protreptikos*, λόγος προτρεπτικός = protreptic)[114] that seeks to convince an audience to pursue a particular course of study, path of life, or way of action (e.g., Wis. 6:12).[115] The thrust of protrepsis is persuasion that urges its hearers to take up a new way of life, in his case the exhortation to demonstrate an even greater allegiance of the ancestral faith required by the circumstances of persecution. Several different groups composed the audience the rhetor addressed. One group consisted of Jews who continued to remain true to their religious heritage and appreciated a compelling exposition of Judaism, but required greater confirmation of the integrity of their struggle. Thus protrepsis is used to present a strong argument in defense of Judaism. A second group on the whole consisted of faithful Jews who were wavering in their commitments to the ancestral traditions due to social stigmas and overt persecution. Exhortatory speech, like that in the Wisdom of Solomon, provided confirmation and encouragement. A third group was composed of apostate Jews[116] who had forsaken their faith, been admonished to return, and been warned of the dire consequences if they refuse (the loss of immortality). For this group, protrepsis became a call to return to a former way of life presently abandoned.[117] Fourth, while the teacher who issued this protrepsis may have hoped to attract on occasion non-Jews to take up the practice of Judaism, he primarily wished to provide an explanation of Jewish faith to Greek intellectuals so they would become sympathetic to Alexandrian Jews and their practices. The composition gives no clear evidence of attempting to proselytize non-Jews. Some of these Hellenists may have been "God-fearers" in a general sense, that is, sympathetic to Judaism, although the meaning of this expression has been much debated.[118] Finally, the fifth group would have been the persecutors of Judaism who tried to belittle its faith and practice as well as slander the character and actions of its members. Thus the text is also a defense of Judaism to its cultured despisers. Whether this last group would have heard this speech that is now committed to writing is an unresolved matter. Indeed, if the rhetor had a public occasion to present his case, then it is conceivable that the opponents of Judaism would have heard it. Whether faithful Jews, apostates, or pagans, the path to wisdom, both divine and immortal, was the goal toward which the audience was exhorted to strive, for in the obtaining of wisdom, revealed to and possessed most fully by the righteous in general and faithful Jews in particular, there was the promise of immortality.[119]

Literary Structure

The genre of the Wisdom of Solomon is the *logos protreptikos*, common in Greek literary circles, particularly among schools and sophists who sought to recruit students to undertake the path of the reflective life that they offered. This genre is combined with a variety of other forms, including in particular the encomium (10:1–11:1) and the apology. The Jewish shaping of the literary character of this text is found particularly in the use of parallelism. Indeed, parallelism is the dominant characteristic of Hebrew.[120] One would expect a well-crafted piece to have a structure that combines elegance with content, and this is certainly true of this Jewish text. A number of similar, though varying, rhetorical reconstructions have been suggested, though the one I find most convincing is that by Addison Wright. He has argued that the book is arranged into two major sections, each consisting of 251 verses of poetry: 1:1–11:1 (560 stichoi), and 11:2–19:22 (561 stichoi).[121] His rhetorical structure for the book, which I largely follow, albeit with some modification, includes the following:[122]

    I. The praises of wisdom (1:1–11:1)
        A. Immortality is the reward of wisdom (1:1–6:21—"The Book of Eschatology")
            1. Exhortation to justice (1:1–15)
            2. The wicked invite death (1:16–2:24)
            3. The hidden counsels of God (3:1–4:20)
            2'. The final judgment (5:1–23)
            1'. Exhortation to seek wisdom (6:1–21)
        B. The nature of wisdom and Solomon's quest to obtain her (6:22–9:18—"The Book of Wisdom")
            1. Introduction (6:22–25)
            2. Solomon's speech (7:1–8:21)
            3. Solomon's prayer for wisdom (9:1–18)
   II. God's fidelity to his people in the exodus (11:2–19:22—"The Book of History")
        A. Transitional section: wisdom saves her own (10:1–11:1)

B. Introductory narrative (11:2–4)
C. Theme: Israel is benefited by the very things that punish Egypt
    (11:5)
D. Illustration of the theme in five antithetical diptychs (11:6–19:22)
    1. Water from the rock instead of the plague of the Nile (11:6–14)
    2. Quail instead of the plague of little animals (11:15–16:15)
        (Digression: critique of pagan religions, 13:1–15:19)
    3. A rain of manna instead of the plague of storms (16:15–29)
    4. The plague of darkness and the pillar of fire (17:1–18:4)
    5. The tenth plague and the exodus (18:5–19:22)

In combining form and content, the rhetor has constructed a progressive
movement from creation and cosmology ("The Book of Eschatology"), to cosmic Wisdom's interaction with Solomon ("The Book of Wisdom"), to cosmic
Wisdom's guidance of Israel out of slavery in Egypt and the defeat of the Egyptians by the transformation of creation ("The Book of History"). This structure
provides a rhetorical depiction of the theme of the text: cosmic Wisdom's active
participation in creation and cosmology, the lives of the faithful, and the movement of history to its future culmination.

THE WISDOM OF SOLOMON IN ESCHATOLOGY, WISDOM, AND HISTORY

Preliminary Considerations

Unfortunately, we cannot be certain about the date, authorship, or social background of the Wisdom of Solomon. However, there is considerable convergence
of opinion about the following matters. Composed in Greek[123] by an unknown
Jewish wisdom teacher who likely lived in Alexandria of Egypt and even may have
had access to the Egyptian court of the Roman appointed prefect,[124] the book
appears to date between the late first century BCE and 40 CE, either near the end
of the Roman Republic or the early years of Imperial Rome.[125] The Wisdom of
Solomon may have been written during a Greek and Egyptian pogrom unleashed
against the Jews in 38 BCE as a response to this unfolding tragedy.[126] The purpose of the book is to present an apology for Diaspora Judaism and to offer both
solace and hope to Jews enduring persecution. To do so, the sage drew from his
own history, colored with Hellenistic features, to tell of the divine salvation of the
ancestors from Egyptian slavery, promising his contemporaries that God would
once again act on behalf of his people to save them from current persecution.

While a variety of dates have been suggested, the one most appealing is the
time of the pogrom of Flaccus in 38 BCE. This conclusion is based on literary
and historical features. The Greek terminology fits especially well the early part
of the first century BCE.[127] The depiction of the persecution of the righteous and

the promise of immortality to those who remain faithful even unto death is appropriate for a pogrom against the Jews. The only known pogrom during the early period of the Roman Empire until the extermination of the Jews at the order of Trajan (115–117 CE) is that occuring during the prefecture of Flaccus when Egyptians and some Hellenes gave vent to the anti-Jewish feelings they harbored.

The Theme of Cosmic Wisdom

Cosmic Wisdom's active participation in creation, in the renewal of life through the order of fertility, in the lives of the faithful sages and Jews, and in the history of Israel, particularly the time of the exodus and the contemporary period, is the defining theme of the book. In the rhetor's cosmology, Woman Wisdom becomes the cosmic principle that "holds all things together," and the link between God and the world (cf. Prov. 8–9; Job 28; Sir. 24).[128] As the actualization of the transcendent Deity on the earth, she is interlaced with creation as the cosmic soul, and she is the fire (or first active, creative energy) that permeated and gave life to all reality. At the same time, cosmic Wisdom is identified with the divine spirit that inhabits the souls of the righteous (1:4–7). In her relationship to humans, she is envisioned by the rhetor as a spirit who loves humans (*philanthrōpon pneuma*, φιλανθρώπον πνεῦμα; 1:6; 7:23). Avoiding the pantheism of Stoicism, the rhetor keeps separate the transcendent Creator who "created the world out of formless matter" (11:17) and the immanent indwelling of a divine spirit, that is, Wisdom (the key feature of God's nature), in the cosmos, in the righteous and wise, and in the acts of salvation typified especially in the earlier deliverance of Israel out of Egyptian slavery, an event that promised God would guide faithful Jews throughout history, including especially the future. Thus this text clearly differentiates between God and the world, making it more Platonic than Stoic, for it is Wisdom who fills the cosmos, not the Creator.

Wisdom's divine character in the texts of Proverbs and Job is metaphorically portrayed as a goddess of insight and life in similar fashion to ancient Near Eastern goddesses, including Anat and Isis. In the Wisdom of Solomon, she becomes the personified attribute of God who dwells on the earth. The rhetor takes this additional step in the representation of Wisdom in order to avoid the problematic polytheism that earlier Wisdom entertained. As the personified attribute of God she is both an emanation and a reflective mirror of God (7:25–26; 9:1–2). Being the emanation (*apaugasma*, ἀπαυγάσμα) of eternal light, she becomes the spirit or mind of the universe, although her subordination to the Creator remains clear (cf. Philo's comparable presentation of the Logos, *Leg.* 1.65; *Fug.* 97; *Somn.* 2.242).[129] Sophia participated in the reality of God and incorporated the divine presence active in the world. This text shapes Wisdom to resemble at times the *pneuma* and *logos* of Stoic philosophy, but her portrait contains also some of the features of Isis mythology.[130]

It is through study, reflection, and Wisdom's indwelling that humans obtain the knowledge of God (Wis. 9:13–18). Occasionally using apocalyptic themes, the rhetor's advancement over revelation in Proverbs and differences from Job (visions and dreams) and Ben Sira (prophetic inspiration) is the teaching that Wisdom dwells within the righteous sage providing knowledge and insight leading to a knowledge of God (cf. Jer. 10; Isa. 41:6–7, 44:9–20; Ps. 115:3–8).

THE BOOK OF ESCHATOLOGY: 1:1–6:21[131]

Introduction

The first subdivision of the initial major section of the book occurs in 1:1–6:21, which, while addressed to the "rulers of the earth," is concerned with the plight of the righteous who are subject to persecution by their wicked opponents, quite likely the Egyptians of Alexandria. This subsection is heavily eschatological and has as its major affirmation the belief that immortality is the reward of wisdom that comes to the righteous and morally pure. It divides into the following chiastic parts: an exhortation to justice (1:1–15), the wicked invite death (1:16–2:24), the hidden counsels of God (3:1–4:20), the final judgment (5:1–23), and an exhortation to seek wisdom (6:1–21).[132] Within the Jewish wisdom tradition, this section is especially a response to the pessimism of Job in his speeches directed toward his opponents, and of Qoheleth and the issue of theodicy (Job 9:25–26; 10:18–22; 14:1–2; 24:11; Qoh. 8:10; 9:5, 14–15).[133] But more importantly it serves as a response to the persecution of the righteous Jews in Alexandria by their Egyptian opponents. The writer promises the gift of immortality to the righteous and wise Jews, while their enemies face divine wrath, punishment, condemnation by the righteous at judgment, dishonorable death, and the extinction of their memory.

The Exhortation to Justice: 1:1–15

This begining part contains an eschatological nuance that is dependent on Jewish apocalyptic literature,[134] and begins with an exhortation to practice justice. This exhortation, similar to the royal testament that assumes the form of an instruction and is addressed to the kings in Israelite and ancient Near Eastern wisdom literatures,[135] is the standard introduction of a *logos protreptikos* and seeks to persuade the rulers of the nations to practice justice. The literary structure and content of this initial part of the rhetorical address are shaped in part by the word "righteousness" (*dikaiosyne*, δικαιοσύνη), occurring in the first (v. 1) and last lines (v. 15). Righteousness is the moral order of both the cosmos and society, an order that kings are to observe in their rule and their subjects are to embody in their behavior and speech. Indeed, righteousness is the fundamental characteristic of both the Lord, presented primarily as the divine judge in this instruction, and personified Wisdom, who in this text permeates the cosmos, fashions human creatures, dwells in pure and honest souls, and indicts the wicked for their evil thoughts and wicked speech. Wisdom in this *logos protreptikos* is the hypostasis of a divine characteristic. She serves as a life-giving and providential force that actualizes divine retribution on the earth and provides the righteous with knowledge. Finally, righteousness is immortal and through its embodiment humans come to possess wisdom and thus eternal life.

In strophe I (1:1–3) of this rhetorical address, the speaker assumes the voice of Solomon, who addresses the "rulers of the earth" with a moral discourse that calls upon them to love righteousness, noting at the conclusion in strophe III that it is eternal and leads to immortality (cf. Pss. 45:8; 72; 1 Kgs. 3:9). One rhetorical device is for the speaker to assume the role of the character who utters the speech (*prosōpopoiia*). Thus this speech assumes the exhortation of the great king of Jewish history renowned for his wisdom. Accordingly, only those who search out, find, and then trust the Lord may possess wisdom and gain immortality. While using different language, this Jewish philosopher stands in continuity with the earlier sages who, to use their wording, affirm that the "beginning of wisdom is the fear of God."

The knowledge of God in whom the righteous trust leads to the understanding and practice of justice and the avoidance of "dishonest thoughts" (cf. LXX Prov. 6:18), a theme that is developed in detail in the second strophe. Wisdom (*sophia*, σοφία), the divine power and holy spirit (*pneuma*, πνεῦμα), embodies righteousness, teaches paideia (παιδεία) or moral discipline, loves humanity (*philanthrōpon*, φιλανθρώπον),[136] and convicts the wicked. She serves in the capacity of divine providence that rules and directs the creation. She enters only a righteous, pure thinking soul (*psychē*, ψυχή) and a body (*sōma*, σῶμα) not "indebted to sin" (1:4).[137] The anthropology expressed in this text speaks of humans being made up of body and soul.[138] Some Middle Platonists also speak of reality containing a third element, the spirit or *pneuma*. This "spirit," with whom Wisdom is identified, is the "spirit of the Lord" (1:7; cf. Isa. 11:2; *1 Enoch* 49:3), and thus is immortal. Humans were not created evil by nature (see Wis. 8:20), but they may become so by wicked behavior and thoughts. Further, Wisdom, who enters the souls of the righteous, is related to both the reason and the moral conscience of humanity. Human nature includes a rational intellect, but the enlightenment of Wisdom that reveals God, teaches righteousness, and leads to immortality[139] is not intrinsic to anthropology (1:15; 3:4; 4:1; 5:15–16; 8:17; 15:3). Rather, the teacher's understanding of immortality is connected with righteousness (3:1–9) and the indwelling of divine Wisdom. At death their "souls . . . are in the hand of God," resting in peace, and possessing the hope for immortality (3:1–9). This contrasts with the wicked, who are punished for unrighteousness, rebellion against God, and the rejection of wisdom. Consequently, their hope is in vain, while their wives are fools, their children wicked, and their descendants cursed (3:10–13).[140] Humans possess a corruptible body in which the immortal spirit may enter, but only if they are righteous. However, for the gift of Wisdom that leads to immortality the teacher indicates that humans must desire Wisdom in order for her to dwell within them. She is a lover of human beings, but being a holy spirit, she is repulsed by sinfulness, deceit, all kinds of wicked language, and illogical reasoning. She dwells only with those who are righteous and think pure thoughts. Although "rulers" are addressed, all humans are to take this instruction to heart, for they, if righteous, are to reign over creation.[141] Those humans who trust in God and are pure in soul and body may find God, embody the spirit of righteousness that provides immortality, and participate with her in ruling over creation.

Wisdom in the second strophe (1:4–11) is described as the "spirit of the Lord" who has "filled the inhabited earth" (1:7–11) and "holds together all things" (*to synechon ta panta*, τὸ συνέχον τὰ πάντα). The Jewish teacher's basic familiarity with Hellenistic philosophy, in particular the notion of the "World Soul" in Stoicism, is indicated in the portrayal of Wisdom (spirit, reason, providence, destiny, and universal law).[142] While the teacher in this strophe moves from anthropology (Wisdom's indwelling) to cosmology (Wisdom as the pervasive presence and unifying power in the cosmos), the purpose is to address the moral virtue of proper speech and to underscore that Wisdom hears all things and ensures that unrighteous talk will be brought to justice. This understanding continues Jewish wisdom's emphasis on proper speech and retribution. In the statement that Wisdom "holds together all things," the teacher contends that she is the binding force that keeps creation from returning to chaos. She is the omnipresent cosmic spirit who is cognizant of all human language and even secret machinations, and issues a report of what humans think and say to the Lord so that he may pronounce divine judgment. Later, the author speaks of the gift of Wisdom to Solomon and her "unerring knowledge of what exists," her awareness of "the structure of the world," and her acquaintance with other elements of the cosmos, including time, the constellations of the stars, the nature of animals, the varieties of plants, the virtues of roots, and all things open to human perception (7:18–22). Solomon, the righteous ruler, received this knowledge, for "Wisdom, the one who fashions all things," is the one who instructed him.

The third strophe is a theodicy that provides an explanation of the origins of Death's incursion into the world (1:12–15).[143] Death is personified as a ruler opposed to life. While exhorting his audience to avoid Death, which threatens them through their deceitful behavior, the rhetor explains that God "did not make Death," thus absolving the charge of divine duplicity in the creating of humanity's greatest enemy. Instead, the divine purpose in bringing reality into existence is emphasized when the teacher argues that God "created all things to exist" (v. 14), that is, all living things were made to live and not to face the terrible fate of death. He adds that God takes no pleasure in the destruction of living things, but rather created "generative powers"[144] to preserve and sustain life. Indeed, Death is not inherent to existing things (i.e., they do not contain within themselves "deadly poison"). However powerful Death (= Hades) may be, it has no control over God's creation. Rather it is the God of life who rules over the kingdom of the living.[145] For the teacher, Death's sovereignty is limited to his own kingdom of the underworld and does not include the kingdom of the earth.

Returning to the language of myth, the teacher implies that Death existed prior to creation and continues to hold sway over his own kingdom. Death is not only mortality, but also becomes the instrument of divine judgment against those who are not just. Death entered the world because of human sinfulness (cf. Prov. 8:32–36; Qoh. 7:29; *1 Enoch* 98:4). In the following section, the wicked are those who by their evil "summoned Death" to take up residence in the world (Wis. 1:16–2:24). Human sinfulness, not God, is the reason for Death's noxious grip on life (cf. Gen. 2–3). It is righteousness, embodied in the behavior of human beings, that becomes the means by which they may become immortal (Wis. 3:4; or "incorruptible," *aphtharsia*, αφθαρσία; 2:23; cf. 6:18–19).[146] The teacher argues that through the possession of righteousness, the human soul and body become the dwelling place of Wisdom, who brings immortality.[147]

The Wicked Invite Death: 1:16–2:24

In the second part of the first subsection, the sage broaches the topic of immorality by articulating two contrasting perspectives: the wicked's view of human existence and destiny, and the teacher's presentation of God's purposes in making human life. He also continues to develop the theme of theodicy addressed in 1:12–15 by adding to his explanation of how Death entered into the world.

This subsection contains an introduction, "The Covenant with Death" (1:16), followed by four strophes: "The Wicked's Assessment of Human Existence" (2:1–5), "The Commitment to Sensuality" (2:6–9), "The Oppression of the Righteous Man" (2:10–20), and "The Purposes of God" (2:21–24).

The teacher condemns the wicked for calling forth Death and then entering into a covenant with him (Isa. 28:15). Consistent with a "speech-in-character" or *prosōpopoiia*,[148] the teacher constructs the discourse of the wicked, who, in this imaginary representation, speak for themselves (1:16–2:24). In this feature of Greek rhetoric, the teacher says that the purpose of this covenant with Death is the wicked's hope that they may avoid their own demise for a time, although they realize that there is no final escape (cf. Isa. 28). Thus they aspire to have at least a temporary reprieve before they too join the world of the dead.

In the third strophe (Wis. 2:6–20), the wicked view human life in pessimistic, materialistic terms. For them, the duration of life is brief and the mode of human existence is sorrowful. When it ends, there is only nonexistence (see Job 7:1–10; 10:20; 14:1–2; Ps. 144:4; Qoh. 2:23; 3:2, 19, 21; 5:17; 12:5). Once they have entered into the underworld, there is no hope for a return (see Job 7:7–10). Death is nonbeing, likened to the state of nothingness prior to birth. In the wicked's view, once they die even their name and memory will be forgotten (cf. Job 18:17; Qoh. 1:11; 2:16; 4:16; 9:5, 15; contrast Isa. 56:5; Prov. 10:7; Sir. 37:26; 41:13; 44:8; Wis. 8:13).

The wicked also deny that there is any divine design in the creation of human life. Human life is but a result of chance, lacking any plan or design. Instead of God breathing into their nostrils the breath of life (Gen. 2:7; 7:22; Job 27:3; Isa.

2:22), the wicked liken their breath to smoke. And reason, the human faculty that for the teacher partakes of cosmic wisdom, is attributed not to the divine shaping of organs of perception and thought (Prov. 20:12), but rather to a spark generated by the beating of the heart. The heart, in their view, is the beating organ that generates fire, the essential element of the material world. This in turn produces thoughts from the smoke that become breath, once combustion has occurred. When the burning spark is extinguished, the body turns to ashes and the breath of life or spirit, equated with smoke, simply evaporates into the empty air.[149] For the wicked, there is no immortal spirit that inhabits the human body and is liberated at death.

Seeing no purpose to their creation and recognizing that death is the final end of human life, the wicked decide on a course of action that combines the pursuit of pleasure, considered by them to be their common fate, with the oppression of the righteous, whose lives and teachings are a reproach to the wicked's way of life. They wish to prove that the faithful, moral existence of the righteous is but an illusion. The identity of the wicked in this section, if referring to a specific group, has been the subject of considerable debate.[150] The wicked have been thought to be followers of either Qoheleth or Epicurus, who misuse their teachings to legitimate hedonism and the persecution of the righteous.[151] Given the setting of first-century Alexandria, however, they are more likely Greek Egyptians and especially those of Alexandria with whom there was a long history of conflict (cf. 12:23–27).[152] Thus the conflict is between Jews and non-Jews in general and Jews and Hellenistic Egyptians in particular.[153] That the Egyptians were the enemies who oppressed the Jewish righteous is strongly suggested also by two statements in 19:13–16. The Egyptians were the ones who both were hostile to strangers (*misoxenia*, μισοσκενία) they had received with great celebration and were their benefactors (see Artapanus), and "afflicted with terrible sufferings those who had already shared the same rights" (19:16). This reference to "rights" (*dikaioi*, δίκαιοι) indicates that the Jews and Egyptians of Alexandria did not hold a different sociopolitical status.

In the last strophe of this part of the first major subsection, the teacher contends that faulty reasoning and the lack of knowledge of God's purposes for the creation of humanity have led the wicked astray. The teacher argues that they have no knowledge of the divine mystery concerning the afterlife and the destiny for which God has created humans (cf. *1 Enoch* 103:2). They do not know that God has created humanity in the image (see Gen. 1:26–28 and 5:1) of his very own being, meaning for the teacher that divine immortality, while not an intrinsic feature of human nature, was nevertheless what God originally intended for humans to receive (thus his understanding of Gen. 2–3). Now, extrinsic to human ontology, immortality has become the reward of the righteous, who pursue moral virtue like athletes in the games striving to obtain the "honored prize" of immortality.

Death's entrance into the world is explained in two ways. First, it was due to the devil's envy (cf. *Life of Adam* 12–17; *2 Enoch* 31:3–6) that was the precursor to human sin (Wis. 2:24). God is not responsible for creating death (1:13). This argument alludes to the fall in Genesis 3 when the serpent tempted the woman and the man to eat of the "tree of knowledge of good and evil."[154] This reference in the Wisdom of Solomon would imply an early identification of the devil with the serpent in the garden.[155] The teacher argues that the devil is envious of humanity, for they were created to possess incorruptibility, given dominion over the earth to rule as God's surrogates, and were worthy of adoration. Thus through the devil's (= serpent's?) envy of humanity's role as rulers in God's creation (cf. Gen. 1 and Ps. 8), Death eventually entered into the world of God's creation to disrupt the original divine plan for human immortality. Yet only they who belong to the devil's party experience the finality of death. Second, Death entered the world at the invitation of the wicked, who entered into covenant with him (Wis. 1:16). This invitation was issued from the recognition of the brevity of life and the denial of any divine design operating in the origins and continuation of creation. This connotes the sage's understanding that humans do not possess an eternal "soul," but rather receive the gift of immortality from the indwelling of Sophia in righteous souls.

The Hidden Counsels of God: 3:1–4:20

The next two parts of the first major section of this *logos protreptikos* address wisdom's leading to immortality, present the fate of the righteous in the hand of God (3:1–4:20), and tell of the final judgment when the immortal righteous pronounce judgment against the wicked (5:1–23). The teacher contends that the souls of the righteous dead are at peace in God's hand, since they were filled with the hope of immortality made possible by the indwelling spirit of Wisdom (cf. 4:1; 5:15). Then, at "the time of their visitation," their hope is actualized in eternal life and in holding judgment over all the earth, even as the Lord will be their king forever (3:8). Thus the teacher has two explanations of immortality, neither of which has to do with human nature. The first is that immortality comes from the indwelling of the divine spirit, Wisdom, in the souls of the righteous. The second is more in agreement with apocalyptic's theme of a final judgment that leads to the distribution of the reward of immortality to those who were righteous in life. While on earth, some have suffered, been tested, and died a sacrificial death for their embodiment of virtue and faith. Indeed, life may be brief for the righteous. Long life, much desired in traditional wisdom, is now replaced with the affirmation that the brevity of existence is even preferable (4:11), since the chances of becoming sinful and thus corruptible are lessened by an attenuated life. After the death of the righteous, they will begin a new, immortal life. Divine judgment may immediately follow death, but the teacher conceives of an eschatological reckoning for which the dead wait.

The Final Judgment: 5:1–23

The teacher then speaks of the eternal life that comes to the righteous, who will one day receive from God a "beautiful crown" (5:15–16). It is the righteous who at the final judgment will judge peoples and nations rather than the wicked, who have persecuted men and women of virtue. When God removes the righteous at their death from the power of the wicked, it should be considered a blessing, for they are safe in the care of God until the final judgment. The metaphor of royalty in traditional creation theology that awakens the imagination to think of humanity's role in the world is now transferred to the future life when the righteous dead "will receive a glorious royalty and a beautiful crown." This depiction of the righteous who will receive a crown and reign as kings after the eschatological judgment is an important theme in Jewish apocalyptic and derives from Greek athletic games in which the victor receives a golden wreath.

While the eschatological judgment will settle the issue of the oppression of the righteous by the wicked, this writer asserts that God has not abandoned creation to the misrule of the devil and his conspirators. The rhetor once more sets forth a theodicy for defending providence and asserts that the Divine Warrior, dressed in battle gear, will be joined by creation to battle against and ultimately defeat the wicked (5:17–23). This hymnic description of divine and cosmic battle is divided into the two parts of the strophe's introductory verse and twofold structure: the Lord's armor (vv. 18–20a) and the retributive weapons of creation (vv. 20b–23).

The divine armor is composed of zeal, righteousness, justice, and holiness, while the forces of creation (lightning, hailstones, the waters of the sea and rivers, and wind) metaphorically become God's weapons to defeat the wicked (see 18:14–16; 19:13–17; Isa. 59:16–18). Because of the eschatological movement of Wisdom 11–19, it could be that this defeat of the wicked is an apocalyptic event still residing in the future. Yet it may also have a more imminent point of reference in the defeat of Flaccus and the Egyptian opponents. The language of chapters 11–19 indicates that the elements of creation are able to transform themselves into the means of the redemption of the righteous and of the punishment for the wicked. In any case, whether eschatological or historical, the teacher wishes to assure his audience that this eventual defeat of the wicked is certain. The wicked will not only experience divine retribution in this life, but they will die without the hope of immortality. In the time of judgment, the righteous will stand up to condemn the wicked, who will recognize too late the folly of their false reasoning and their persecution of the righteous. Indeed, their hope of immortality is "dispersed before the wind like smoke" (5:14).

This section on eschatology contains several themes from apocalyptic literature, something that demonstrates the increasing convergence of the two genres that surmounts, at least in some literature, their substantial disparity. Little wonder then that the teachers of apocalyptic were portrayed as wise seers whose wisdom, however, was insight into the mysteries of time and creation, and not a practical wisdom for directing life in the present. Yet it would be wrong to interpret apocalyptic as referring only to some distant eschatological future. It is coded language that also is used to depict contemporary history, in this case, the struggles between Jews and Egyptians in early Roman Alexandria. The origins of evil, the eschatological judgment, the punishment of the wicked and the immortality of the righteous, divine revelation, and a new creation are traditional apocalyptic themes. But they also ring true for contemporary history in speaking of the imminent downfall of the oppressive governorship of Flaccus and the Egyptians. Thus apocalyptic literature was written in response to historical crises in which its literati looked beyond the present age of suffering to a new period of divine redemption.

Exhortation to Seek Justice: 6:1–21

The teacher now warns the kings and judges of the earth of the eschatological judgment of God, who, having given them sovereignty over the earth, will punish them when they are unjust. It is only by learning wisdom that they may escape from punishment and receive the gift of immortality. God's providential reign (*pronoei peri pantōn*, προνοεῖ περὶ πάντων) over the earth will lead ultimately to the vindication of the righteous. While the author emphasizes the universal nature of wisdom, providence, and righteousness as the key to immortality, he still has in mind primarily the Jews who are the current victims. It is primarily they who, in spite of persecution, observe the teacher's word and thereby learn to become righteous. And they are the ones who are holy through their observance of sacred things (6:9–11). It is through paideia, the discipline enhanced by the desire for immortality and including the gift of sovereignty (6:17–21), that kings who wish to continue to reign may do so by pursuing wisdom.

THE BOOK OF WISDOM: 6:22–9:18

Prelude

The second major subsection of section one is found in 6:22–11:1, "The Book of Wisdom." This segment of the composition consists of the following parts: (1) Introduction (6:22–25), (2) Solomon's speech (7:1–8:21), and (3) Solomon's prayer for wisdom (9:1–18). This discourse, consisting of a variety of literary genres, primarily combines elements of the encomium with Jewish prayer. Creation and salvation become linked in the second major section of part I, "The Book of Wisdom" (6:22–11:1). This linkage occurs in two places: the prayer of Solomon (9:1–3, 9, 18), and the works of cosmic Wisdom in redeeming Israel's early ancestors, from Adam to Moses (10:1–11:1).

Introduction: 6:22–25

In the second major subsection of the first half of the book, the teacher, continuing to speak through the voice of Solomon, sets out to describe the nature of Woman Wisdom, from her origins at the time of creation (cf. Prov. 8:22–31; Job 28:23–28; Sir. 1:4; 24:9) to the point when he came into her possession (cf. 1 Kgs. 3:1–15). This is followed by the part that describes the redemption of the ancestors from Adam to Moses. The introduction to the "Book of Wisdom" (6:22–25) sets forth the teacher's declaration that he will tell his audience about the origins of Wisdom with whom envy will not associate (*phthonō tetēkoti*, φθόνωι τετηκότι).

Solomon's Speech: 7:1–8:21

Now the rhetor assumes the posture of the great, wise, but still mortal Solomon. Solomon begins with a description of his origins (7:1–6), narrating his conception, formation in the womb, gestation period, and birth.[156] These are important references to the tradition of God's creation of humanity, especially the one that speaks of the formation of "the first formed (*prōtoplastou*, πρωτοπλάστου) child of the earth" (7:1; 10:1) and the other that describes Solomon's being "fashioned into flesh" (*eglyphēn sarx*, ἐγλύφεν σάρχ) in his mother's womb, a passive verb that grammatically refers obliquely to divine activity (see Job 10:8–12; Ps. 139:13–16; Qoh. 11:5), coupled with the use of the metaphor of "fashioning, forming" humanity like that of an artist. Solomon descends from Adam, who was formed by God from the earth in imagery alluding to the activity of a potter who shapes the clay into a vessel (Gen. 2:7; cf. Sir. 17:1).[157]

Solomon especially emphasizes the common origins that he shares with all human beings, contrasting himself with Egyptian, Greek, and Roman kings who were deified either before or after death. Even he, a great monarch, had no special birth. He, like all people, is a mortal, a descendant of Adam, and not a divine king who is the offspring of gods.[158] For Solomon, all people share the same beginning and the same departure from life (Wis. 7:6; see Job 1:21; Qoh. 3:19–20; 9:3; Sir. 40:1–2). Wisdom, therefore, may be possessed by anyone, regardless of status. Solomon asserts that wisdom comes through prayer, not because of a claimed divine nature or royal status.

Telling of his prayer for Wisdom (cf. 1 Kgs. 3:5–15) and the good things that accompanied God's gift of her, Solomon describes her inestimable worth and then indicates that his own renowned wisdom was due to God's endowment (Wis. 7:7–14; cf. Ps. 19B; Prov. 3:13–18; 8:15–21; Job 28:15–19). Through this gift, Solomon says that he came to know the structure of the cosmos (cosmology) and what exists on earth (Wis. 7:17–22a). Through Wisdom he received a comprehensive, unerring knowledge of all that exists as well as of the structure of the cosmos (cosmology) and the activity of its elements (physics),[159] the temporal order (calendar) and its association with the heavens (astronomy), animals (zoology), the powers of spirits (either demonology or more likely the impulses associated with human passions),[160] humans (anthropology, philosophy, and psychology), and plants (botany and pharmacy). Solomon becomes the scientist and philosopher who knows the whole of reality and all that exists within it. These topics made up the curriculum of the Greek schools.

The twenty-one attributes of Wisdom are listed in 7:22–23. In verse 21 Wisdom is described as the *technitis* (τεχνῖτις), or artificer, who fashioned all things (cf. 8:6 and Prov. 8:30). This role of Wisdom in creation, shaping and forming what exists (Wis. 8:6), provides her with an intimate knowledge of reality. Subsequently, she is able from her involvement in its construction and design to teach her knowledge of the cosmos to Solomon.[161] In 9:1–2 Solomon recounts that God created all that exists through his word, and by his wisdom he formed humanity to have dominion over the earth. Here Wisdom is active in the creating of human beings, who are made in order to rule as God's surrogates over the world. Subsequently, Wisdom as artisan is linked to traditions of creation, cosmology, and anthropology.

Solomon then proceeds to describe the character and nature of Wisdom (7:22b–8:1). In his description of the nature and activity of Wisdom, he points to some twenty-one qualities she possesses, a number produced by multiplying three and seven. Both are sacred numbers that point to completion and perfection.[162] Solomon presents Wisdom as an attribute of God, who, partaking of his essence, becomes not a divine being like Isis but rather a hypostasis that gives shape and character to a divine virtue.[163] Thus cosmic Wisdom is transcendent and participates in the nature and activity of God. While a transcendent virtue of God's character, Wisdom's ability to "permeate all things" describes divine immanence while avoiding the troublesome problem of pantheism.

Of particular interest are Wisdom's presentation as the breath of God, her ability to renew all things (v. 27), and her entrance into holy souls in each generation. Wisdom's origin as the "breath of the power of God" (v. 25) picks up an image from Ben Sira (Sir. 24:3). She is identified with the creative breath or spirit of God active in creation (cf. Gen. 1:2 and Ps. 104:29–30). Solomon describes the nature, character, and activity of Wisdom primarily in relationship to the features of God. She is a "pure emanation" of divine glory as well as an "effulgence of eternal light," images that point to Wisdom's reflection of the light that radiates from God's presence. She reflects not only the holiness and glory of God's presence, but also his character, being in the "image of his goodness." Her creative power enables the generations of the cosmos to be renewed and to continue (cf. Ps. 104:30). And her dwelling among holy souls enables them to become "friends of God" (a designation of Abraham in Isa. 41:8 and 2 Chr. 20:7) and prophets. "Friends" are those who are loved by God, while "prophets" are those who are inspired by Wisdom to know the will of God (cf. Sir. 39:6). The "holy souls" are the righteous, who through paideia seek instruction and embody it in their character and actions. Indeed, in a graphic metaphor of sexual activity, Solomon asserts that God especially loves those who cohabit with Wisdom. Fertility imagery is used by the teacher to describe both the well-being experienced by those who pursue wisdom and the bonds of love between the wise and Woman Wisdom, who is metaphorically depicted as a fertility goddess and lover. Finally, Wisdom extends over all creation and "orders (*dioikei*, διοικεῖ) all things well," giving all that exists a structure, a pattern of activity, a time, and a place to exist, and providentially directing reality in the fashion of one who administers and governs an idealized house or city.[164] Thus the cosmos is a well-ordered household or polis under the management of Woman Wisdom.

Solomon then speaks of his passion for Wisdom and his desire to take her as his bride (Wis. 8:2–21; cf. Prov. 8:12–21). Solomon, the passionate lover of many women, now seeks to embrace the most desirable woman of all: Woman Wisdom. Wisdom, desired by Solomon to be his bride (cf. Prov. 7:4 and Sir. 15:2), is already God's own lover.[165] Images of royal passion for fertility goddesses are used to describe Solomon's desire for Woman Wisdom, God's consort. As God's intimate companion, Wisdom "glorifies her noble birth," reflected in her hymn of self-praise in Prov. 8:22–31. These images of birth point to the sage's use of the fertility metaphor to reflect the beauty and sexual activity of Isis/Wisdom. Intimacy with God becomes the source of Wisdom's divine knowledge and the basis for her role in creation. She chooses the things that are to be created and becomes both the instrument of his divine activity and the artisan of what is formed. The possession of her is more valuable than wealth and the objects of riches (cf. Ps. 19B; Prov. 3:13–18; 8:10–11, 18–19). Possessed by those who seek her, she becomes their lover and teacher, instructing them in the knowledge of what exists in every temporal mode, from past, to present, to future. Most important of all, her possession, made possible only by God's gift, leads to immortality (Wis. 8:13, 17).

Solomon's Prayer for Wisdom: 9:1–18

Solomon's desire for Wisdom leads then to his prayer to possess her, since she may come only as God's gift (7:7–10). The prayer exhibits the following structure: the address of God and request for Wisdom (9:1–4), the basis for the request (vv. 5–8), the advantage of having Wisdom (vv. 9–12), and the inability to understand God's will without Wisdom (vv. 13–18). In the opening of the prayer, God is addressed as the creator of both the cosmos and human beings, the two traditions of creation theology.

The prayer begins with God's creation of all things by the spoken word (cf. Gen. 1:1–2:4a; Ps. 33; Sir. 24; 42:15). Building on Solomon's petition for Wisdom in 1 Kgs. 3:3–15,[166] the prayer combines a royal petition for Woman Wisdom, the divine lover, to enable the king to rule and judge successfully the people and thus execute humanity's commission to have "dominion over the creatures" (1 Kgs. 3 and Ps. 8) and to "manage the cosmos in holiness and righteousness." Wisdom, the mistress of God and located beside the divine throne (cf. Prov. 8:12–21), is portrayed as the skill and knowledge of the divine builder in the construction (*kataskeuasas*, κατασκευάσας) of human beings (Wis. 9:2; cf. Gen. 2:7; Job 10; Ps. 139).[167] Drawing from the tradition of humanity as king over the earth (Gen. 1 and Ps. 8), Solomon states that humans are created to reign over God's creatures and to rule the cosmos in "holiness" and "righteousness," that is, they are to recognize divine sovereignty and rule according to the dictates of divine teaching embodied in Torah and wisdom.[168] God has given to humans the responsibility to be the surrogates of divine rule and the stewards of creation. The prayer acknowledges that, due to human weakness, mortals are unable to carry out this commission of ruling and managing the cosmos without the gift of Mistress Wisdom.

Later in the same prayer, Solomon speaks of Wisdom's presence at the beginning of creation (Wis. 9:9–11). Solomon asks that he be given cosmic Wisdom, since she was present with God at the time of creation and thus knows his work (cf. Prov. 8:22–31). Wisdom also knows the will of God expressed in the Torah, and thus is able to guide one in behavior that will be acceptable to God. Following in the steps of Ben Sira, the rhetor teaches that the Torah embodies the order and life-giving power of Wisdom in creation. Without this gift of Wisdom, no mortal has the ability to actualize God's will and to behave and speak in ways that are pleasing to him, for the rational capacity is limited by a mortal body that restricts the mind's ability to think and to learn.[169] Here Wisdom is the one who knows the will of God and enables humans to obey the commandments (Wis. 9:13–18; cf. Prov. 30:1–4).

THE BOOK OF HISTORY: 10:1–19:22

Introduction

The second major section of this protreptic speech includes the insertion of the encomium (cf. Sir. 44–50) that recounts the temporal sequence of salvation history, from creation to Moses, from Moses to the entrance into Canaan, to the eschatological realization of redemption in the present (the victory over the Egyptians) and the future (the final judgment).[170] This section has three major subsections: Wisdom's redemption of her own people through the individuals active in the course of salvation history down to the time of Moses (not named, but easily identified) (10:1–11:1), the exodus from Egypt that leads to the establishment of God's people in the land (11:2–18:4), and the eschatological defeat of the enemies of Israel (first the Egyptians in the sage's own time and then the wicked at the end of history) (18:5–19:22). Inserted into the second section is a digression, 13:1–15:19.

Wisdom Saves Her Own: 10:1–11:1[171]

This poem is a transitional one that marks the movement from Solomon as the wise king to God's deliverance of his people. It is divided into seven parts (thus symbolizing perfection), each of which speaks of Wisdom's redemption of a person. Following the form and nature of a Greek encomium, the rhetor focuses now on individuals, from Adam to Moses, who because of their righteousness were saved by Wisdom. The two individuals who are not specifically called a "righteous man" are, oddly enough, Adam and Moses. Wisdom delivers "the first-formed father of the world" (easily identified by the audience as Adam), while, in the last example, Wisdom "enters into the soul of a servant of the Lord" (obviously Moses) and saves the Israelites, who are designated as "the righteous" (v. 20), from their "enemies" (i.e., the Egyptians). Adam's transgression, narrated in the fall in Genesis 3, more than likely precludes his being listed as a "righteous man," in spite of the fact that a tradition (*The Life of Adam and Eve*), which the sage may have known, speaks of his repentance and restoration. However, Wisdom's entering into the soul of Moses is another way of expressing the righteousness or just character of this leader (see Wis. 1:4). Human examples (*paradeigma;* παράδειγμα) of moral behavior are common in Greek literature.[172] Their character and actions embody the virtues of moral instruction and thus are noble examples not only to remember but also to emulate. The rhetor also refers to the wicked, who were embodiments of vices and thus examples of what not to be.

Now Wisdom, a personified attribute of God who was involved in the creation of the cosmos and humanity, becomes the redeemer engaged in acts of deliverance of Israel and the righteous, who, although not named, are easily identifiable through the teacher's descriptions.[173] This role of Woman Wisdom in redeeming the righteous underscores the teacher's affirmation that those who are faithful and righteous may hope for their deliverance and for salvation, both now and in the eschaton (19:22).[174] Wisdom's redemptive activity is not limited to the past, but continues through the present into the future. Important is the change in emphasis from God's performing mighty acts of redemption on Israel's behalf (i.e., the exodus, wilderness wandering, gift of Canaan; cf. Pss. 78, 105, 106, 135, and 136) to Wisdom's redemption of Israel's ancestors: Adam, Noah, Abraham, Lot, Jacob, Joseph, and Moses, who number seven (see Enoch in Wis. 4:10 = Gen. 5:21–24, and the apocalyptic literature associated with him). This parallels Ben Sira's litany of ancestors, "pious men," in the epic poem in Sirach 44–50. In Wisdom 10 the ancestors are saved because of their righteousness and following of Wisdom, while others who were wicked and spurned Wisdom perished: Cain, the foreign nations in Abraham's time (Gen. 11:1–9), the inhabitants of the five cities in the Lot narrative (Gen. 19), Lot's wife, the oppressors of Jacob including Esau, the false accusers of Joseph, and the Egyptians in conflict with Moses and Israel. The emphasis on the virtuous character of the heroes of the past is a strong reflection of the humanistic tradition among the Greco-Roman moralists and philosophers.[175]

The chapter begins with a description of Wisdom's salvation of Adam, the "first-formed father of the world." Referring to the Yahwist tradition in Genesis 2–3, the teacher speaks of the creation and fall. The "first-formed father of the world" is Adam (Wis. 7:1 and Gen. 2:7),[176] who "alone had been created," since Eve was formed from his rib and all other humans were born. His transgression is mentioned in general but not specified. It is interesting that, in contrast to Ben Sira, only his sin, and not Eve's complicity, is touched on. The repentance and restoration of Adam is found in postbiblical literature (cf. *The Life of Adam and Eve*), and this is likely the tradition that allows the teacher to begin with him in listing the ancestors who were saved. Also mentioned is the commission to rule ("have mastery") over creation, an example of the royal metaphor to describe sustaining the order of creation.

Wisdom's task is to enable human beings to realize the original nature of creation, to see that God made the world in righteousness and that humankind was created to rule in dominion over all the divinely created beings (cf. Ps. 8). God uses Wisdom in the creation of the cosmos and humanity, and she is given to the righteous in order that they may understand the divine commandments and act in ways that would please God. Indeed, when humans behave according to Wisdom's dictates, they are saved by her. If they are wicked or oppress the righteous, then they are punished. This is illustrated in chapter 10 by reference to Wisdom's salvation or punishment of the people of Israel's traditional past, including deliverance of the slaves from Egypt and the devastation of the Egyptians. Subsequently, Wisdom becomes the instrument of providence, being active in Israel's redemptive history, serving as the savior of the righteous and acting to punish their enemies. Also important theologically for this teacher is his contention that each time salvation is experienced it becomes a re-creation. Since Wisdom was present at creation, she knows how to bring about salvation for the just. The Jewish rhetor teaches that the exodus becomes the saving event par excellence, but it is also a new creation that is salvific in character (chaps. 11–12). Creation fights against chaos and injustice. Even the final judgment is seen through the lens of creation.[177]

This part of the speech focuses primarily on the theme of the exodus, although it is entwined with features of creation theology and a related criticism of Egyptian critics.[178] Among the pagan writers, especially those who were Hellenistic Egyptians, the forcing of the ancestors of the Jews of Alexandria to leave Egypt, because they were angering the gods over their pollution of the land, transforms the tradition of the exodus into one of punishment and not salvation. For the rhetor, this teaching of the exodus was not only a theological tradition in the Jewish celebration of the Passover as a family festival, but also was used to engage in both an apologetic defense of Judaism and a polemical rejection of the interpretation of contemporary Egyptians.

The narrative is interrupted by a major excursus on the foolishness of non-Jewish religions (13:1–15:19), likely because false worship, particularly idolatry, which characterize Egyptian religion, is viewed as the source for all wickedness. The writer makes use of the literary and rational technique of *syncrisis* (comparison) in order to contrast the misfortunes of the ancient Egyptians with the salvation of the ancestors.[179] The implication is that this same force within creation will punish contemporary Egyptians and deliver the Jews of Alexandria currently enduring persecution. While the Canaanites (who represent the excesses of Dionysian religion) and Hellenistic philosophers come under criticism, the major assault is leveled against the despised Egyptians of the exodus, now representing the community in Alexandria contemporary with the teacher.[180] The primary literary elements consist of an introductory narrative that articulates the theme: Israel is benefited by the very things that punish Egypt (11:2–5), and the illustration of the theme in five antithetical diptychs (11:6–19:22). These antithetical diptychs are water from the rock contrasted with the plague of the Nile (11:6–14), quail contrasted with the plague of little animals (11:15–16:15), a rain of manna contrasted with the plague of storms (16:16–29), the pillar of fire contrasted with the plague of darkness (17:1–18:4), and the death plague by which God punished the Egyptians contrasted with the glorification and redemption of Israel from captivity (18:5–19:22).[181]

Introduction and Theme: 11:2–5

The lengthy narrative on the exodus and wilderness (11:2–19:22) points to the continuing providence of God, who acted to redeem his own people in the past. But the narrative looks not simply to the past but also to the present and future, as the redemptive acts of God continue to save the chosen (19:22).[182] Now the emphasis is no longer on Wisdom as redeemer, who saves righteous ancestors of the past, but rather on God and the chosen in the present. Metaphorically liberation in the exodus is followed by trial in the wilderness prior to entrance into Canaan. Alexandrian Jews may currently be in the wilderness, but will soon experience the new Canaan through redemption and immortality. The introduction, describing Israel's wilderness experience, expresses in verse 5 the theme that unites the entire narrative: "For the things by which their enemies were punished, they themselves, being in need, were benefited."[183] This is the point of the *syncrisis*: that which punishes the enemies of Israel becomes for Israel a blessing. A variation of this theme that shapes this sage's understanding of divine retribution is the point that one is punished by "the very things by which one sins" (11:16).[184]

This theme ties together and shapes the narrative structure of 11:2–19:22, a *syncrisis* that comprises the five major sections (11:6–14; 11:15–16:15; 16:16–29; 17:1–18:4; 18:5–19:22) with each dividing into two contrasting parts (antitheses).[185] This linkage of multiple parts is a rhetorical technique in shaping an argument in classical literature and philosophy by uniting a series of contrasts by means of a common theme. The objective is to determine what is "equal, better, or worse."[186] In each contrast, the elements of creation that God uses to punish Israel's opponents (here the Egyptians during the time of the exodus) become at the same time the means of blessing for the Israelites. The five contrasts are between things that benefit Israel's well-being and the entities that punish the Egyptians. What is important to note is that the teacher combines redemption history with a theology of creation: creation is not a dormant or static entity, but rather a dynamic force continually moving within an order of blessing and punishment through which God through Wisdom works to bring deliverance. At the same time, this uniting of creation and redemption presents a compelling theodicy that demonstrates that divine justice is operative in the cosmos and history even now (19:22). Yet the afflictions of the Egyptians are not only to punish but also to help them come to a conscious understanding of the reality and power of the Lord. Through their reflections on this narrative of salvation history, the wicked learn not only to attribute their own punishment to the Lord, but also to recognize that it was he who afflicted them with the very same instruments that he used to bless the righteous. Subsequently, they should learn that the Lord is both the creator of the cosmos and the ruler of history. In addition, the Egyptians who persecute God's people should also learn that they are punished by the very things by which they sin. Yet they should learn of the love of God, who does not create anything that he would loathe, but seeks always to bring redemption to all. Even so, God's patience is not unending, and after a time of testing and waiting, he will bring destruction to the unjust Egyptians. Here the teacher speaks of an imminent eschatology in which divine justice will soon be meted out.[187]

Water from the Rock as Contrasted to the Plague of Blood: 11:6–14

The first syncrisis compares Israel's divine gift of abundant water in the wilderness with the Nile turning to blood in Egypt. This plague, narrated in Exod. 7:14–25, is interpreted by the rhetor as punishment for the "slaughter of the innocents" at Pharaoh's command to cast the male infants into the Nile in Exod. 1:22. Thus the rhetor establishes a retributive connection to illustrate in striking fashion the contrast between life-giving water in the desert with the deadly waters of the Nile used to murder Jewish male children. In addition, he picks up the theme of testing the Israelites in Deut. 8:2–5 to demonstrate that even their thirst had a divine purpose to demonstrate how the ungodly are tormented. Finally, the Egyptians suffered from the punishment of the drowning of their army in the Red Sea.

The Gift of Quail and the Plague of Little Animals: 11:15–16:15

The second contrast is a lengthy one, interrupted by a diversion that addresses the origin and folly of idolatry (13:1–15:17). Once more the theme of being punished by means of the sins committed is articulated as the unifying theme for this contrast (11:15–16).

In the opening (11:15–20) of the larger section, the teacher addresses God and speaks of his divine mercy in not afflicting the Egyptians with newly created, even more ferocious beasts. The rhetor refers to creation: God's "all-powerful hand created the cosmos out of formless matter" (11:17). For the teacher, creation is not ex nihilo, but rather a process of shaping preexistent matter. The eternal existence of matter was a common Greek idea. In the Hebrew Bible, chaos (*tōhû wābōhû*, ובהו והו, "formless waste," Gen. 1:2) existed prior to creation. So it is that God will not unnecessarily intrude into the natural order, although he has the power to do so. Rather, God arranges the universe according to certain laws of measure and number[188] that govern its existence, so that divine activity does not arbitrarily intrude into the workings of the cosmos (11:20–22).

The rhetor then praises God for loving all that he has created, for this is the ground of his act of creation and the basis for his providential care. Nothing exists or endures save by the love of God. Indeed, because of this divine love, God's imperishable spirit resides within all life, making the beginning and continuation of existence possible. The rhetor uses two specific metaphors of creation and providence at this juncture. The first is the divine artisan (11:24). The second is creation by the word: God "calls forth" things that exist. And there is an allusion to Wisdom in the statement that the divine, "imperishable spirit" resides within all life (Ps. 104).

The Evils of the Canaanites: 12:3–18

The wickedness of the Canaanites is set forth initially to legitimate the conquest of Canaan and the slaughter of its inhabitants. This apologetic for the conquest of Canaan is a topic broached in other pieces of Jewish literature from the Greco-Roman period, including the book of *Jubilees* (second century BCE, 8:8–11; 9:14–15; 10:29–34) and Philo (*Hypoth.* 6.5 and *Spec.* 2.170). Among the "detestable" (*echthista*, ἔχθιστα) practices of the Canaanites were sorcery (*pharmakeiōn*, φαρμακειῶν), abominable rituals (*teletas anosious,* τελετὰς ἀνοσίους), the merciless slaughter of children, and sacrificial cannibalism (the last a retort to Egyptian critics who accused the Jews of annually sacrificing and eating a Gentile). In spite of their terrible acts, God gave them time to repent. However, they were born with an evil nature and were an "accursed" (*katēramenon*, κατηραμένον) race from the beginning who could not change. The religion described is actually that of the Dionysian mystery cult that was popular throughout the eastern Mediterranean world. The Ptolemaic Dynasty adopted Dionysus as their primary deity. Included in this criticism is the religious excess of the contemporary Dionysian revel (*thiasos*, θίασος) and the myth of the tearing apart of Pentheus by the maenads, the female votaries of Dionysus, and the subsequent devouring of his flesh in a festival in the city of Thebes.[189] The banquet celebration of the mystery included the symbolic eating of the flesh of the god.

Egyptian Religion and the Worship of Animals: 12:23–37

The animosity of the Egyptians of the rhetor's day also led to his critical response that concentrates on regarding as irrational the worship of animals (cf. Philo, *Decal.* 52–81; *Spec.* 1.13–31). Ironic is the teacher's view that the animals the Egyptians were accused of worshiping for their protection were the very ones who brought punishment to them. The foolishness of this act of adoration was due to their childlike naiveté.

The Folly of Pagan Religions: 13:1–15:19

Leaving aside temporarily his discourse on the opposites in creation, the teacher engages in a more developed polemic against pagan religion. Four different pagan religions are criticized: nature religion, the worship of animals,[190] fertility cults (especially the Dionysian mystery), and idolatry. Each one has to do with a failure to understand that the one God, who is the creator of heaven and earth and who directs human history with justice, cannot be represented by images or creatures. This digression contains the following seven-part structure:

The Religion of Nature (13:1–9)

The Idolatrous Woodcutter (13:10–19)

The Idolatrous Seafarer (14:1–10)

The Invention of Idols and the Origin of Immorality (14:11–31)

The Faithfulness of Israel (15:1–6)

The Idolatrous Potter (15:7–13)

The Religion of Egypt (15:14–19)[191]

In this section, which forms a chiasm that highlights the fourth element ("The Invention of Idols and the Origin of Immorality"), the rhetor draws on creation to speak of the superiority of Jewish religion and its one true God. What is stressed by the literary structure is that the making of idols is the cause for the origin and spread of immorality. In the chiasm, the religion of nature parallels, structurally, that of Egypt; the idolatrous woodcutter that of the idolatrous potter, and the contrast of the idolatrous seafarer's journey through the seas and the faithfulness of Israel, which understands God's power to be the "root of immortality."

The teacher begins by returning to his view that humans are not born with a knowledge of God; rather this knowledge must be learned or given by the spirit of Wisdom. Humans by nature are "foolish" (*mataioi*, μάταιοι), a word used in the Septuagint to refer to idols (e.g., Jer. 2:5; 8:19; 10:15) as well as idol makers (Isa. 44:9; Ps. 62:10). It simply means "without intelligence" or knowledge, which is gained by study, reflection, and the gift of Wisdom. God is "the one who is" (*ton onta*, τὸν ὄντα; cf. the LXX's translation of the meaning of the name Yahweh: "I am the one who is," *egō eimi ho ōn*, ἐγώ εἰμί ὁ ὤν).[192] The issue for the teacher is coming to a knowledge of this "one who is" apart from special revelation (i.e., Scripture). Is it possible to come to this knowledge through a revelation of nature? For the teacher, the answer is a surprising yes.[193]

The teacher uses the metaphor of God as artisan (*technitēs*, τεκνιτης)[194] to argue that, since they are to be known by and yet differentiated from and superior to what they make, those who worship nature or elements of nature have failed to use their reason to conclude that God is known through his works (cf. Job 38–41; Ps. 19:1; Sir. 43:9–12). Indeed, they should have realized that the divine craftsman is not to be identified with his works, but rather exists in distinction from them. Like the artisan he too is greater than what he has created. It may be that the rhetor is criticizing the tendency of some philosophers to identify the cosmos with the Creator himself. Others have simply identified various cosmic forces (fire, wind, air, constellations, and heavenly lights, i.e., sun, moon, and stars) as gods who "rule the world": for example, Hephaestus (fire), Hera (air), Demeter (earth), Poseidon (sea), Apollo (sun), and Artemis (moon). Even the philosophers associated creative power with certain elements: for example, fire (Heraclitus), water (Thales), air (Anaximenes), and heat (Pythagoras).[195]

Another argument, one based on analogy, is used to suggest that philosophers should have made the correlation between the "goodness" and "greatness and beauty of created things" and the one who created them. This act of analogical reason would have enabled them to know the nature and character of the Creator and his superiority to the wondrous things he has made. While the teacher argues that humans are ignorant by nature, including lacking knowledge of God, they should be able to use their powers of reason to deduce the existence and, to some extent, the divine nature and character from the existence and qualities of creation. Even so, nature worshipers are "little to be blamed," especially in comparison to those who practice other pagan religions like idolatry, animal worship, and fertility cults, for those who worship nature continue to search for God.

In this section on pagan religions, the teacher directs considerable criticism toward idolatry (13:10–15:17),[196] and in so doing draws upon idol satires found in Jeremiah and especially Second Isaiah (Jer. 10:1–6; Isa. 40:18–20; 41:6–7; 44:9–20; cf. Pss. 115:3–8; 135:15–18). Indeed, idolatry, argues the teacher, is responsible for the origins of immorality and the deification and worship of humans, especially kings (Wis. 14:12–21). Important is the teacher's argument that idolatry is both an aberration of creation theology and a failure to understand and recognize the power and knowledge of God in matters of providence.[197] However, he especially emphasizes the folly of idolatry. Part of the occasion for this attack on idolatry was the practice of erecting idols of "divine" emperors before which offerings were made. This matter was not a concern of the Jews in Alexandria during the Hellenistic period, since they were exempted from this requirement. However, idolatry and the ruler cult came to a head in Alexandria when the Roman prefect Flaccus erected statues of the emperor in the synagogues (Philo, *Flacc.* 41–44, 51; *Leg.* 132, 134, 346) along with idols of Dionysus, the patron god of the earlier Ptolemaic rulers, before whom Jews were to make an offering prior to entrance into the synagogue. The ensuing pogrom led to the deaths, rape, despoliation, abuse, and humiliation of Alexandrian Jews. Of course, the Jews were often labeled atheists for refusing to acknowledge other gods and for rejecting idol worship.

In the teacher's discussion of the idolatry of the sailor (14:1–10), he contrasts divine providence with the inability of idols attached to ships to steer them through the perilous waves of sea voyages. The competition for the rich trade of the eastern Mediterranean world was intense among nations who engaged in commercial shipping and established ports from Phoenicia south to North Africa. The quest for divine protection in traveling the seas led to placing carved idols on the masts of ships to keep sailors safe. The teacher develops his argument against this practice of idolatry in several ways. First, the sailor prays to a piece of wood that is more fragile than the ship that carries him. Second, the teacher contrasts the wisdom (*sophia*, σοφία) of the shipbuilder (the *technitēs*, τεκνίτις "artisan/artificer")[198] who constructs the vessel with the folly of the person who makes idols. The idol maker is not an "artisan" who uses wisdom to create images made with human hands. Third, the rhetor contrasts divine providence (*pronoia*, πρόνοια; 14:3; cf. 17:2) that pilots the ship and provides "safe pathways" through the sea with idols that lack the knowledge of nature and the capacity to guide a ship safely to port (cf. Isa. 43:16; Ps. 77:19).

The Origins of Idolatry: 14:12–31

The sage talks of the twofold origins of idolatry: human lust that led to the shaping of beautiful idols, and euhemeristic worship of a dead child made a god by a grieving father. The latter is described as a mystery religion in which the devotees of the dead child, now divine, undergo "secret rites and initiation" (*mystēria*, μυστήρια; and *telitē*, τελίτή).[199] The religious vocabulary of mystery religions is appropriated by the teacher in criticizing false religion.

Idolatry is also an aberration of the creation of humanity, because human idol makers attempt to give life and traits of existence to lifeless objects like stone and wood. In the constructing of an idol, humans are not only attempting to play God, but ironically are trying to create a god in a human image and to make perishable material into a deity. Here the teacher contrasts the folly and hubris of the human idol maker with God's work in making humanity in the divine image (cf. Gen. 1:26–28). In another sense, idolatry is an aberration, because it denigrates the creation-of-humanity tradition in which humans are made in the divine image and rule creation as the surrogates of God. This line of argument winds along several paths. One path leads to the conclusion that idolatry is an act of irrationality. Humans, rational creatures made by God, are the divine image, not idols made to resemble things that are created.

Idolatry: 15:1–19

Another path points to the supreme irony of using the same clay from which humans, including the idol maker, are made to fashion a worthless god (9:2; Gen. 2:7; Job 10:9). This is argued in Wis. 15:7–11. This section is replete with allusions to the tradition of the creation of humanity in the Hebrew Bible, including especially Psalm 104. The teacher observes that the clay from which the idol maker gathers his materials to construct his image is the same clay to which he will one day return when his soul at death must depart to the God who gave it (Qoh. 3:19–20; 12:7). God is the one who breathed the living breath within humanity to provide life (Gen. 2:7). More is at stake than a theological position. Idol makers were part of a major industry in the economy of the empires of Greece and Rome. To attack idolatry damages a prosperous business that was good for a city's economic well-being.

A Rain of Manna instead of the Plague of Storms: 16:15–29

The third contrast in the *syncrisis* opposes the plague of storms that brought destruction to the Egyptians with the manna from heaven. The burning fire and lightning consumed the ungodly, and the flames continued to burn even in spite of water. By contrast, manna, metaphorically described as snow and ice and called the "food of angels," is not destroyed by the fire, that is, sunlight. Once again, in the world of retributive justice, fire "forgets its own power" in order that the righteous might eat what is not totally consumed (v. 23). The teacher then moves to his key argument: creation is directed by God to distribute retributive justice, bringing punishment to the wicked and kindness to the children of Israel who trust in him (16:24–25).

The Plague of Darkness and the Pillar of Fire: 17:1–18:4

The fourth antithesis, which contrasts the plague that afflicts the Egyptians and the pillar of fire that guides the Israelites, moves between the physical description of darkness and light and the moral categories of evil and goodness. The psychological terror occasioned by this plague is graphically described. But the physical act becomes allegorically understood as a spiritual one. Thus darkness becomes the metaphor for evil and the encasement of the unenlightened in darkness, even as light symbolizes goodness. This goodness, represented by the pillar of fire, is metaphorically the imperishable light of the Torah that Israel teaches to the nations.

The Tenth Plague and the Exodus: 18:5–19:22

The fifth antithesis is that of the death of the firstborn of Egypt that leads to the liberation of Israel. In continuing his unifying theme, the teacher argues that these very events by which the Egyptians are punished bring blessing upon the Israelites. In describing God's judgment against Egypt at the Red Sea and Israel's deliverance, the rhetor explains that the transformation of nature occurs not by the miraculous intervention into the orderly process of natural law, but rather by means of the principle of the interchangeability of the basic physical elements in order that the righteous might be saved.[200] The Creator possesses this power of transformation in reshaping nature, but it is a transformation in line with the nature of the physical constitution of creation directed by God.

In his conclusion to the plagues and the salvation at the Red Sea (19:18–21), the teacher explains that the elements that comprise the forces and creatures of nature changed places with one another, in the same fashion as notes on a musical score may be adjusted to alter the rhythm (cf. 16:24–25; this reflects the study of music that was part of the curriculum in the schools). Thus land animals became water creatures and vice versa. Fire was not quenched by water, yet its flames failed to consume or melt. This argument once again allows the teacher to avoid the notion of divine miracles interrupting natural processes that contravene the laws of nature.[201] It is at this point that the teacher abruptly concludes his homily of persuasion by praising the Lord of creation and history who continues to redeem his people. This explanation of the exodus and the events leading up to it and the salvation at the Red Sea is a major part of the teacher's ambition to defend one of the central tenets of Judaism, and to castigate the ancestors of the hostile Egyptians.

This *logos protreptikos* concludes with a doxology in 19:22, a form that was frequently used in late texts (Ps. 150; Sir. 51:30; 3 Macc. 7:23; 4 Macc. 18:24; Tob. 14:15) and especially in Tannaitic literature at the end of a homily (*Sifre Deut.* 342).[202] Thus for this speech, later written down and made into a literary text, the teacher notes that God exalts his people in all things and offers the concluding assurance to his people that God will not neglect to come to their rescue. Thus the concluding doxology offers praise to the one who is sure to deliver the current generation, undergoing persecution and suffering, and to glorify them once again even as he has done in the past.

Summary

In the second major section, "The Book of History" (11:2–19:22), the rhetor moves into a discourse that recounts the events of the exodus from Egypt. These are "God's people" (12:19; 16:2, 20; 18:7) and the "holy nation" (17:2). Within this section, there is a major digression (13:1–15:19) that contrasts the true worship of the Creator (in particular 15:1–3) that leads to immortality (15:3) with a variety of debased religions (with the exception of the worship of nature): Canaanite religion and the slaughter of children and the eating of human flesh and blood (the Dionysian mystery), Egyptian religion and animal worship, nature worship, idolatry, and the worship of dead children. These religions do not lead to the immortality sought by humans who, in the Hellenistic world, turned to the East to seek religious systems that promised eternal life. Indeed, it is from Judaism that, through the power of the Creator and the embodiment of righteousness, redemption from persecution and an immortal soul may be had.

THE HISTORICAL THEOLOGY OF THE WISDOM OF SOLOMON

Creation and Providence[203]

Similar to Ben Sira, this sage also brings together the universal theology of creation with the particular theology of the redemption of the Jews. However, he opens the door to the participation in salvation by all those who are righteous and in whom Wisdom dwells. Indeed, the history of election is interpreted by reference to universal justice.[204] The twin features of universal salvation, inherent within creation theology, and salvation history, which are framed by the theology of election, are showcased in the literary structure of this protreptic discourse that consists of three parts. The initial part is the "Book of Eschatology" (1:1–6:21) in which God creates the world that is filled with goodness and life (1:14), the righteous souls that are receptive to the indwelling spirit of wisdom, the persecution of the just and faithful, and the immortality of the souls of the righteous. The third section, the "Book of History" (11:2–19:22), focuses more on redemption history in general and the early events of salvation that culminate in the exodus.[205] This section, particularly in the excursus on pagan religions, assumes a largely polemical role, most likely due to the conflict with the Egyptians over the issues of Jewish citizenship in the polis of Alexandria and the special privileges granted them by Augustus. However, the polemical criticism takes a wider sweep to include the idolatry of the Greeks (13:1–9), the Dionysian rites of the "Canaanites," and the detestable animal worship of the Egyptians (chaps. 13–15). The interaction of salvation history and creation is demonstrated in the five antithetical diptychs in which the element of creation that serves to punish the Egyptians becomes the means by which the Israelites are blessed.

The teacher uses the general term "to create" (*ktizō*, κτίζω), which means in Greek literature not simply the execution of the act, but also the resolve of founding, establishing, and building especially a city, a kingdom, and a temple, although it also had a wider role in the establishing of other types of human structures (1:14; see 2:6).[206] Since the time of Alexander, the verb assumed a royal resolve and its execution, since the major references of the verb are royal actions. Now God has resolved to create and then rule over the cosmos (cf. Philo, *Opif.* 17). Consequently, God is the one who rules over the cosmos he has shaped and providentially guides the course of Israel's history from the time of creation to the time in which the rhetor and his audience are witnessing a period of intense persecution. He encourages them by teaching that God has not abandoned them to suffer alone, but that the same God who engaged in acts of salvation in the past will do so in the present. Finally, those who continue in their acts of loyalty and faithfulness have the guarantee of immortality and are assured that one day they will rule over all nations under the sovereign dominion of the Creator.

Creation and Goddess Wisdom

Woman Wisdom receives a principal position in the teacher's theology in terms of her roles both in creation and in salvation history. The second book, "The Book of Wisdom" (6:22–11:1), focuses on Wisdom's dual roles in the creation of the cosmos and of humanity and in the salvation of the righteous in Jewish history. She becomes more than a literary personification, for now she is equated with the divine spirit who mediates between heaven and earth (thus hypostatization through metaphor and imagination).[207] Making use of earlier formulations of a personified Wisdom (Prov. 1:20–33; 8; 9; Job 28; Sir. 24) and combining them with images drawn from the panegyric hymns devoted to the goddess Isis, the teacher gives divine characteristics to Woman Wisdom. In his praise of and prayer for Woman Wisdom (Wis. 7–9), Solomon describes the nature, character, and activity of Wisdom primarily in relationship to major features of the character of God (7:22b–24). Thus she is a "pure emanation" of divine glory as well as an "efful-gence of eternal light," metaphors that capture Wisdom's reflection of the light that radiates from God's being. She reflects not only the holiness and glory of God but also his character, for she is the "image of his goodness" at work in the sustaining of the cosmos, in dwelling in the souls of the righteous, and in redeeming the Jews from persecution, thus endowing them with new life and immortality.

The consort of God, Wisdom sits adjacent to his heavenly throne and reflects his glory and attributes in creation, providence, and redemptive history. Wisdom becomes a defining characteristic of God who partakes of his essence. She is both the transcendent participant in the divine nature and activity of God and the spirit that permeates creation in the cosmos. Her presence in the cosmos and in history demonstrates that she is also immanent in the world. Subsequently, Wis-dom becomes the means by which the transcendence and immanence of God are actualized. By means of the nature and activity of Wisdom, this sage seeks to rec-oncile the antithesis between the universalism of creation theology and the speci-ficity of salvation history. Thus not only is Wisdom active in the shaping and direction of the cosmos, she also dwells within the righteous, granting all people the means to become the "friends of God and the prophets" (7:27) and thereby to obtain immortality.

Wisdom's place in the cosmology of "The Book of Wisdom" is to serve as both the instrument of divine activity in creation and the artificer (7:22 and 8:6; cf. 13:1, where God is the artificer) of what is formed. Woman Wisdom serves as the divine fashioner of creation (7:21a), permeating it with her life-giving and regenerative spirit (v. 25; cf. Sir. 24:3) and enabling its various dimensions to cohere in the divine order. Wisdom permeates the cosmos, is the divine spirit (cf. Stoicism's views of "spirit," *pneuma*, πνεῦμα) and the "word" (*logos*, λόγος). Wis-dom is the creative breath or spirit of God active in creation. Lastly, Wisdom extends over all creation and "orders all things well," providing a structure, a pat-tern of activity, a time, and a place for all things to exist within the cosmos. The teacher appropriates the image of Wisdom as a manager who oversees and admin-isters an ideal house or city (cf. the "woman of virtue" in Prov. 31:10–31).[208]

Wisdom also becomes the divine spirit that enters into the souls of the right-eous and blesses them with the munificence of her gifts (cf. Prov. 3:13–18). In the "Book of Wisdom," she becomes a lover, not only as the consort of God but also as the much desired object of human passion. By means of their love for Wis-dom that succeeds in taking her into their embrace, humans come to possess her and through her to experience the gift of immortality (Wis. 8:13). Inserted into his hymn to Wisdom is Solomon's first prayer (7:15–22), in which he asks God for the gift of speech and the moral character that makes him worthy of what he receives, for God is the guide of both wisdom and the sages. In this prayer he lists a variety of areas of knowledge, which reflect the disciplines of a Greek gymnasium and rhetorical school. Wisdom, who is responsible for shaping and creating the cosmos and human beings as the divine artisan and craftsman, becomes Solomon's learned tutor (7:22b). This intimates that the rhetor had studied in one of these schools or under private tutors. In his description of the knowledge he seeks, Wisdom becomes the most important attribute of God, partaking of his essence and assuming the characteristics of a divine being.[209]

Wisdom also renews the human generations, enabling them to endure. Her dwelling among "holy souls" enables them to become "friends of God" (a designation of Abraham in Isa. 41:8 and 2 Chr. 20:7) and "prophets." "Friends" are those who are loved by God, while "prophets" are those who are inspired by Wisdom to know the will of God. The "holy souls" are sages who through paideia seek instruction and embody it in their character and actions. Indeed, in a graphic metaphor of fertility, Solomon asserts that God especially loves those who cohabit with Wisdom. Fertility imagery is used by the teacher to describe both the well-being experienced by those who pursue wisdom and the bonds of love between the wise and Woman Wisdom, who is portrayed as a fertility goddess and lover (cf. Prov. 3:13–18; 9:1–6).

Solomon describes his passion for Wisdom and his desire to take her as his bride (Wis. 8:2–21; cf. Prov. 8:12–21). Solomon, who in tradition (1 Kgs. 3–11) is the passionate lover of many women (cf. Canticles), now seeks to embrace the most desirable woman of all: Woman Wisdom. Wisdom, whom Solomon desires for his bride (cf. Prov. 7:4; Sir. 15:2), is already God's lover and consort. Assuming the images of royal passion for fertility goddesses, the teacher describes Solomon's desire for Woman Wisdom, who takes on the features of goddesses like Isis. Wisdom "takes glory in her noble birth," thereby reflecting her hymn of self-praise in Prov. 8:22–31. Now the child has become the intimate lover of God. Solomon asks that God send him Wisdom, since she was present with him at the time of creation and thus knows his work (Wis. 9:9; cf. Prov. 8:22–31). Without this gift of Wisdom, no mortal has the ability to know God's will and to act in ways that are pleasing to him, for the rational capacity is limited by a mortal body that restricts the mind's ability to think and to learn.[210] Thus Wisdom is the revelation of the will of God (Wis. 9:13–18; cf. Prov. 30:1–4) and becomes the instructor of the righteous, who seek to know her. Adapting Solomon's petition for wisdom in 1 Kgs. 3:3–15,[211] the prayer of Solomon in Wis. 9:1–18 combines a royal petition for Wisdom to enable the king to rule and judge a people with the general human need not only to be successful in executing the commission to have dominion over the creatures (Gen. 1:26–28), but also to rule the cosmos with holiness and righteousness. God has given to humans the responsibility to be the surrogates of divine rule and the stewards of creation. However, Solomon acknowledges that, due to human weakness, mortals are unable to carry out this divine commission without the gift of Wisdom.

Last of all, the rhetor also draws on earlier texts to formulate his own articulation of redemptive history (cf. Pss. 78, 105, 106, 135, 136; Sir. 44–50). He passes in review those saved by Wisdom and then later in the third book, "The

Book of History," describes God's deliverance of the Israelites from the Egyptians. The cosmos is shaped in such a way that the same way of bringing destruction to the wicked Egyptians becomes the source of blessing for the righteous ancestors of Israel during the exodus. At the end of "The Book of Wisdom" (10:1–11:2), Wisdom is at work from the time of Adam in the beginning to that of Moses during the exodus in delivering the righteous during periods of persecution. This brings to mind the present pogrom afflicting righteous Jews.

Creation and Anthropology

The Wisdom of Solomon gives expression to an anthropology that also centers in creation. The major thesis is that God created humanity to be incorruptible, but due to the entrance of the devil and the pervasive spread of human wickedness, death has become the verdict of the Divine Judge. Salvation from death comes only by means of human righteousness and the indwelling of the spirit of Wisdom. While the righteous may suffer and even die, their immortality is guaranteed by Wisdom's dwelling within them. The righteous one day will rule nations and peoples, while the divine king reigns over them all.

In 1:14 the rhetor describes God as the creator who forms "all things" to exist and argues that righteousness is immortal. He denies, then, that God is the one who originated death, but rather created life that would enjoy immortality. In 10:1 Wisdom (literally "she") protected the "first-formed" (*prōtoplaston*, πρωτό-πλαστον) who alone was created among all of humanity. The noun for "formed" is the metaphor taken from the artist, the potter who fashions from clay an object to fire and then, once made, to use. In Greek literature the expression does occur sparingly to refer to the divine act of creating (e.g., Hephaistos's forming of Pandora; Hesiod, *Work and Days* 70–71). Thus God's "forming" of the first man like a potter molds clay and a smith smelts a purified metal are artistic metaphors that describe God's creation of humanity and awareness of their behavior.

The righteous serve as kings over the nations and God's creation. In his prayer for Wisdom, Solomon addresses God as the one who formed humanity to rule over creation and to actualize justice in overseeing the cosmos (9:1–2). Yet even kings have the same common origins as other humans. Appropriating the creation-of-humanity tradition present in Psalm 8 and reflected in Job 10, King Solomon speaks of his own ordinary conception, formation in the womb, gestation, and birth. This contrasts with the royal cults of the pharaohs, the Ptolemies, and the Caesars. While humans are created for immortality, made accessible again through the gift of Wisdom's indwelling in the human soul, the wicked, by contrast, point to chance, not purposeful creation, as the reason for human existence. In their view, human thought and the rational capacity are not the gifts of God's creation, but rather the results that derive from the physical beating of the heart. This beating heart generates fire, which becomes thought, and smoke, which becomes the breath of life. When this fire is extinguished the body turns to ashes and breath is exhaled into the common vapors of the air. Divine reason, in their view, is not part of human nature, while there is no enduring memory of who they are and what they do. At death their memory disappears together with their bodies and their breath. The wicked have entered into a pact with the devil, not in the hope of escaping their ultimate end, but rather to continue their lives for a little longer.

In contrast to the creation of humanity, some wicked humans foolishly engage in the making of gods in the form of idols. The folly of idolatry is that it is an aberration of the theology of God as the creator. In language similar to Second Isaiah (45:20–46:13), the rhetor criticizes humans trying to fashion a god who is greatly inferior to themselves. They are either unwilling or unable, due to distorted reasoning, to recognize that God is their creator who fashioned them, gave them a soul, and breathed into them the spirit of life, offering through his gift of Wisdom the regaining of immortality that had been lost due to the incursion and wickedness of the devil.

The Wisdom of Solomon and an Ideology of Power

The rhetor who composed the Wisdom of Solomon represented Hellenistic Jews living in Alexandria. Their rivalry with the Egyptians over special privileges and the desire for citizenship grew intense. This is noted especially in the outbreak of an Egyptian pogrom undertaken by the mob in the effort to exterminate the Jewish community not only in Alexandria, the center of the conflict, but also in the entire province of Egypt. The contention over citizenship was the catalyst for this pogrom, as noted in Philo's two treatises examined earlier. However, this was but the external expression of a deep-seated antagonism between Jews and Egyptians that had existed for many centuries.

The enmity between Egyptians and Jews well explains the strong condemnation of the Egyptians in Wisdom 11–19. The major issue was not anti-Judaism, a term grounded in theories of race and appropriate since the nineteenth century, but as Peter Schäfer has suggested, "Judeophobia," that is, fear and hatred born of xenophobia that is directed against the Jews.[212] He argues that Greco-Roman hostility, found among the intellectuals and used in opposition to and even persecution of Jews by the mob, is marked by a hatred of Jews because of their exclusive efforts to maintain separateness in social and religious identity. Some Greeks and Romans feared that Jews would impose their values and religion on the Greek and later the Roman Empire, eliminate traditional religion that was integrated into the ideals of political culture and used to legitimate the state, and thus subvert the empire. Indeed, limited proselytism of non-Jews substantiated these fears for a number of intellectuals, officials, and commoners. In addition, the ethnocentrism of Greeks, Romans, and Egyptians played a role in the perspectives held about the Jews and was among the reasons for social tension that occasionally led to militant actions. Indeed, the Jewish refusal to blend into the common culture and religions of these groups and the desire to maintain an identity based on religious and cultural values were taken as obstinate and even dangerous behavior.

Conclusion: Metaphors of Creation and Redemption

In a period of persecution, the sage who composes the Wisdom of Solomon shapes a world of imagination that through the activation of memory coupled with knowledge lays claim to the theological traditions of the past and reshapes them with contemporary Hellenistic forms, rhetoric, and thought to construct a new theological synthesis.[213] Because of God's love for creation and all his creatures, he offers even to pagans and apostates the opportunity to pursue righteousness and to come to a knowledge of the Creator of the cosmos and humanity and thus to regain the immortality for which they, the descendants of Adam, were originally created. Not only kings and rulers of the nations, but all mortals everywhere may shape within themselves a righteous character that allows them to receive Wisdom and through her to obtain the gift of eternal life. The teacher emphasizes that only the righteous receive the gift of Woman Wisdom. While persecuted Jews may suffer, even die, in the present, they will experience immortality and, following the final judgment, will reign over the new world under the sovereignty of God.

For the teacher, God is in control of creation and human history especially through his consort, Woman Wisdom. The righteous, possessing and being led by Wisdom, may wait in confident hope for justice. Because of faithful living, they may rest assured that, even in death, they may expect to reign forever. Creation is shaped so that the same means of destruction become the ways in which Jews are blessed. The same is true of history. Thus the suffering of the present will eventually turn to joy even as the persecutors of the Alexandrian Jews will be punished, while the righteous will experience redemption.

The presentation of Wisdom in this discourse indicates that she has become a divine attribute who has the vital responsibility to link heaven and earth through mediation. Woman Wisdom, who is the heavenly consort of God, at the same time permeates creation, holds it together, provides it with a structure and order, and renews all life. This same cosmic Wisdom also enters into and dwells in the righteous souls in each generation, making them friends of God and prophets, all the while indicting and bringing punishment to the wicked. She provides the greatest gift of God, the possession of immortality, which gives eternal life even to those who suffer and die at the hands of the wicked. Through the love for Wisdom, righteous humans come into her possession. Consequently, for this teacher, Wisdom is the means of the actualization of eternal life for the righteous.

Chapter 9

The Historical Theology of Wisdom Literature: Conclusions

A HISTORICAL OVERVIEW OF THE THEOLOGY OF WISDOM

The Engagement with History

The history of wisdom is difficult to reconstruct, although I am publishing elsewhere a temporal framework that is based on a variety of arguments: allusions to historical events and people, language, and comparisons to other sapiential literature of Judaism, the ancient Near East, and Greece and Rome.[1] It is obvious that the literature, understandings of the sage, and theology in the social world in which they lived and taught possessed a fundamental center, the role of teaching and its transmission in tradition, but also reflected numerous variations that indicate that wisdom interacted with the historical and social changes experienced by Israel and early Judaism. Thus the office of the sage and the teachings of the wise continue to change in response to the external permutations of history and its impact on the course of nations and their sociopolitical and religious institutions.

In addition to changes that occurred internally in response to the modulations of national history and internal social developments, transmutations occurred due to the sages' interaction with a variety of different cultures and their literary and sociopolitical traditions in the eastern Mediterranean world. For the purposes of this investigation, the relation of social role, history, and theology interlinks so that social and political variations over the centuries lead to the transformation of faith and ethics. It is clear that the influence on the office of the sage and the literary compositions of wisdom were open to different cultural influences at different times. It is also true that the theological understanding of the sages, in particular their articulation of creation theology, was transformed in response to a variety of historical and social developments. Sapiential theology and Israelite religion, social roles of sages, and Jewish history were entwined so that different nuances of wisdom theology appear. Indeed, it is the case that creation continues as the center of the matrix of sapiential theologies produced over eight centuries, but the variety of its expression changed in response to the historical events of successive periods, the cultures with which the sages of Israel and early Judaism interacted, and the variety of social roles these sages and scribes pursued.

Power, Wealth, and Status: Theology and Ideology in Wisdom

It has become a commonplace in intellectual circles engaged in the writing of history, theology, and sociology that particular social groups construct worldviews that express their own self-interests. This does not mean that groups always greedily pursued power and its benefits only for themselves, thus negating any possibility of altruism. But it does mean that interpreters should be attuned to the fabric of the social groups that wrote and transmitted texts that reflected what they considered to be of value. The sages of Israel and Judah were as concerned as any social group with the investiture of power and its concomitant premiums of status and privilege. Thus the ambition for power, status, and wealth was a compelling force among some sages who sought to become political counselors and among those they served. Others were already aristocratic owners of property and slaves. Thus it should not be surprising that some privileged sages may have been motivated by maintaining the status quo. The quest for knowledge, honor, and increased piety led others to seek the religious expertise necessary in shaping and interpreting traditions of law and instruction. Finally, all sages were driven by the innate desire to take up residence in corporate memory, which provided existence beyond the limitations of personal mortality, until finally immortality was embraced in the Greco-Roman period.

This quest for power and its compensations did not proceed without opposition, especially from marginalized prophets. Some conflict also occurred among groups internal to the wisdom tradition. Thus the Joban poet's assault on a Deuteronomic theory of justice to portray an acceptable theodicy represents the antagonism between reactionaries and radicals, both contending for sway to be held over kings and people. The traditional sage's response to the mutinous teaching of Agur of Massa is another example of intense debates occurring within the tradition, not simply in order to prove one has the better of the argument, but to obtain a position of honor within the scribal community and the larger society of Judah. Of course, this contention is obvious in Qoheleth.

The clash between sages, both reactionary and radical, and other social groups is also in evidence in the competition for followers who looked for leadership in shaping their own views of the world and providing the basis upon which to construct a daily pursuit of life and its activities. Thus one finds, for example, Qoheleth's contention with apocalyptic sages on their way to a fully developed apocalyptic about a final judgment and an afterlife (cf. 3:16–17), Ben Sira's obituary to prophecy by claiming their inspiration for divinely selected sages, and Job's repudiation of Deuteronomic retribution as a proper way of understanding divine action in individual and collective life. These debates were not simply intellectual exercises pursued by a leisurely class of rich intellectuals, but rather encapsulated the expressions of sages who sought to gain influence over the Israelite and later Jewish communities.

Creation theology, central to the convictions of the sages, provided both a description of faith in God as creator of the world and humanity and in divine providence that directed in particular human life. Viewed as an ideological construct, creation became the order of righteousness that permeated reality and was captured in the writings of the sages. Wisdom, especially the teachings of the sages, was grounded in the regulation of the cosmos so that those who followed its instructions were successful in living in concert with the life-giving principle that governed life. If the traditional sages were right in their view of retribution, then the ones who suffered were in conflict with world order and had violated divine tenets. The truly righteous, according to this teaching, prospered. If the radicals are correct, however, then God, or at least the retributive theory of retribution, is at fault. The latter course would assist in shaping a rationale, then, that allowed at least some marginals who had suffered unjustly the possibility to enter positions of status and influence in the larger society.

THE SOCIAL ROLES OF THE PROFESSIONS OF SAGES AND SCRIBES

The Sage in Israelite and Jewish Wisdom

The term *ḥākām* (חכם) is difficult to define with precision. In general it is used as an adjective to describe anyone who possesses a particular skill or specialized knowledge. More specifically, however, it is also used to refer to a specialized class of scribes, counselors, legal officials, writers, teachers, and rhetors.

The Sage in the Israelite Court

The sages first appear as officials and scribes in the Israelite and later the Judahite courts and royal schools. This meant that the theology of the sages was shaped by the requirements of preparing youth for service in the royal bureaucracy, to legitimate the monarchy, and to articulate proper behavior at court. In addition, the theology reflected a conservative, political worldview in which justice permeated creation and society and was maintained by both the king and his advisors. This meant the king was viewed as the sage par excellence who used the gift of divine wisdom in ruling righteously and well. The preeminent sages served as counselors to kings and secretaries of various administrative units (temple, palace, legal court system, military, and taxation), while lesser ones in the capital were scribes engaged in the reading and writing of documents and correspondence, not only in Hebrew but also in Akkadian. At least a few Israelite scribes would have been able to read other West Semitic languages, Akkadian, hieroglyphics, and the hieratic script. They would have kept the archives of the kingdom, redacted texts, and composed the legal and sapiential texts as well as some of the narratives. Some sages were instructors in a palace school or served as tutors of youth who were training to become scribes and officials in the kingdom. The governors of local royal administrative districts also would have been served by scribes in carrying out local scribal tasks. It may be that an Egyptian court model influenced that of the early Israelite monarchy.

The Sage in the Temple

The sages of Israel were active also in the temple, which was under royal control and management. The temple scribes would have kept records of sacrifices and gifts, collected and distributed financial resources owned by the temple, and maintained archives of ritual texts. Of course, in addition to Jerusalem, there were other Jewish temples in Lachish and Samaria (Dan and Bethel). It is likely that temple sages played a part in the codification and interpretation of law codes, including both Deuteronomy and the Priestly Code. After the collapse of the monarchy, sages came under the oversight of the Zadokite high priesthood. Baruch and Ezra are two examples of sages involved in the social institution of the temple in their respective periods. In early Judaism, sages taught in the synagogues, where they interpreted the Torah and established a tradition that evolved into rabbinic Judaism.

The Sage and the School

Substantial evidence exists for schools and tutors in the literature of the ancient Near East and the empires and kingdoms of Greece and Rome. The Egyptian Kemyt and the descriptions of the gymnasium in the writings of Philo and Plutarch provide us substantial descriptions of the activities and curricula of the cultures surrounding Israel and Judah. The description of the education of Josephus also points to his own experience. Evidence for schools in First and Second Temple Israel and Judah is slight, but they would have been necessary for the teaching of culture; the performance of administrative, social, legal, and temple tasks; and the editing and transmission of literary records. "*LMLK*" jar stamps, the Gezer calendar, and bullae point to the scribal activities of sages in Israel and Judah as do the epigraphic materials (e.g., the numerous ostraca, the Siloam tunnel inscription, and the inscription of Uzziah at the entrance of a tomb).[2] The archive of Qumran points to a scribal community well skilled in the copying, editing, and writing of significant literary texts. Wisdom texts that were placed into collections that eventually entered into the canon and the deuterocanonical literature were largely those that had moral and educational value. These texts would have had their origins in scribal schools or would have been written by those who had studied in these educational settings. The education of youth would have required both their learning to read and write various types of texts and the assimilation of a moral and learned character that would equip them for serving in the court and the temple.

THE SAGES AND THE HISTORICAL PERIODS
OF ANCIENT ISRAEL

The First Temple Period

The sages appear in the monarchy as participants in the administration of the kingdom and the temple. Through various forms of education, ranging from schools to tutors, they acquired skills essential for the operation of the government and the temple: reading, writing, rhetoric, editing, and record keeping. These sages ranged from important officials in the royal court, serving as the major secretary of the king, the manager of his house (both domicile and palace), diplomats to foreign courts, and counselors to the monarch, to less lofty duties including financial record keeping, archiving of documents, judges and lawyers in the legal system, and commercial responsibilities over which the royal court had control. Other sages served in the temple administration in overseeing the maintenance of the structures, recording the sacrifices and gifts, and distributing portions of sacrifices to the priests. In the more remote cities, scribes would have been necessary for running the local governor's administration of the capital and the tribe or province. Their common worldview, moral virtues, and literary tradition point to a professional class of scribes.

The Babylonian Exile

While our knowledge of the exilic period in both Babylonia and Eretz Israel is quite limited, the captivity would have provided sages the opportunity to become quite familiar with the Mesopotamian mythical and other literary traditions. It is likely that many compositions were redacted and expanded during the exile, including an early form of the Priestly document and the book of Job. Job's significant parallels with Akkadian disputations could be explained by the presence of the poet in captivity. Theologically, the radical questioning of the justice of God emerged. This questioning centered on the traditional theology of righteousness and retribution that was occasioned by the conquest of the state.

The Persian Period

A major shift in the profession of the sages occurred during the first part of the Second Temple period, when Judah became part of the Persian satrapy of Abar Nahara. The clues are found in the literature of the school of the Chronicler (Ezra–Nehemiah and 1 and 2 Chronicles). The most important scribal figure in this literature is Ezra, who becomes a legendary exemplar of the scribes of this period. Ezra is fictionally presented not only as a Persian official who was in charge of codifying and implementing the law as the basis for Jewish social and religious life, but also as the ideal interpreter of the Torah of Moses. Ezra's law code, which perhaps refers to the Priestly narrative, was interpreted by a class of Levitical scribes under the direction of this sage of God Most High. This type of professional scribe combined the interpretation of the Torah with wisdom teaching, although under the direction of the high priestly families. In addition, scribes were active in the courts of officials, including that of the governor of Judah, and would have continued to serve in administrative and legal roles in the Second Temple period. The languages with which they worked would have been primarily Hebrew and Aramaic, indicating that the sages had to be at the very least bilingual. Their piety is expressed in the Torah psalms, which extol the law and obedience to its teachings.

The Period of Hellenization

The transition to Hellenistic rule brought about important changes in the scribal profession. Sages would have continued to teach in schools, as evidenced by the epilogue in Qoheleth and in the Qumran literature, and to prepare youth for roles in their respective communities. In Jerusalem and the district of Judah, Greek became the common language of the various echelons of Jewish society, although Aramaic and some Hebrew continued to be used. Qoheleth is best compared to the Greek skeptics, whose view of the world and human life was similar to his own despairing portrayal. His individualism is indicative of Greek humanism. Wisdom, while still part of social life and possibly even associated with sapiential schools, developed a more individualistic perspective that took to task many traditional teachings, including the knowledge and justice of the Deity, the participation in the temple cult, and the doctrine of retribution. The scribal community at Qumran composed, copied, and transmitted a variety of texts for use by the community. The literature helped to shape a new sapiential and apocalyptic reality among one Jewish sect, possibly Essenes. This type of sage, who came out of mantic wisdom, was now the one who not only taught the wisdom of the past and preserved the archaic traditions, but who was also a seer who had insight into the secret mysteries of the cosmos.

At the end of the Ptolemaic rule of Judah, Ben Sira continued the tradition of the sage who taught and interpreted the Torah in his own "house of study" or school. Only now wisdom was identified with the Torah, and select sages, including obviously himself, were inspired in their writing. This sage now spoke not only of following sapiential teaching and Torah in moral behavior, but also of supporting the temple and priesthood. Indeed, Wisdom, coming from the mouth of the Creator, chose Judah as the people among whom she took up residence, and she entered into the temple, where rituals and teaching coalesced. Ben Sira composed hymns to the Torah, piety, and especially creation in praising and exulting in God. In tracing the history of the pious among the ancestors, the encomium ends with Simeon II, the great high priest to whom Ben Sira was devoted, because of his office and his great deeds. Ben Sira's role as teacher in a school was carried out under the oversight of the Zadokite hierarchy.

The Alexandrian Sage in the Period of the Roman Empire

The final types of Jewish scribal professionals prior to the fall of the Roman Empire and the extermination of the Jewish community in Alexandria by Trajan in the early second century CE were the Jewish philosopher and rhetorician who combined various elements of Greek philosophy with Jewish religion in the Diaspora. The two best known Diaspora representatives are Philo Judaeus and the author of the Wisdom of Solomon. Middle Platonism and Jewish understandings of monotheism, the Torah, salvation history, and morality were combined to shape a new portrayal of sapiential literature. The rhetor who composed the Wisdom of Solomon was likely a teacher in a Hellenistic Jewish school that taught young Jews their traditions, major facets of Greek culture and language, and how to integrate the two into a new theological synthesis. The pressure of a pogrom led to the development of a belief in immortality for the righteous who remained faithful to their religion, while the articulation of an apology that defended Jewish religion and attacked pagan superstitions was designed to demonstrate their folly and to undercut their appeal.

INTERNATIONAL SAPIENTIAL INFLUENCE ON THE HISTORICAL THEOLOGY OF ISRAELITE AND JEWISH WISDOM

Introduction

It is impossible to understand the theology of the sages without an awareness of the impact of foreign cultures and religion. The people of Israel and Judah interacted with a variety of other peoples who had competing worldviews, often in direct contradiction. Yet it is also important to realize the influence these cultures and religions had on Israel and Judah. The sages of Israel, Judah, and early

Judaism were cosmopolitan scholars who viewed wisdom as an international phenomenon. This would have developed from travel to foreign courts, diplomatic service, and the knowledge of other languages for correspondence between monarchical administrations.

Egyptian Influence

One of the primary sources of influence on Israelite and Judahite wisdom was Egypt. This is particularly clear in the case of the Israelite collection of Prov. 22:17–24:22 and its dependency on Amenemopet. The vizier of the royal court who issued an instruction to his successor, and the monarch who advised his son in proper rule are features that appear in Israelite wisdom literature. Common emphases on creation, providence, and order (ma'at), and their different portrayals in mythological metaphors in Egyptian wisdom, along with the themes of the questioning of divine justice Woman Wisdom (Ma'at and Isis) as truth and justice, and the insight of the king are similar to those found in the wisdom of ancient Israel.

Another important case of Egyptian influence was the "testament of Qoheleth," which has the earmarks of Egyptian autobiographical tomb inscriptions. These inscriptions were instructions written by scribes for the tombs of nobles and addressed to the visitors of the deceased telling of his or her life lived in accordance with justice and exhorting them to conduct lives that are just and that celebrate life. Finally, the royal instructions of Egyptian monarchs who speak to their successors from the grave influenced the wisdom literature of Judah, especially Qoheleth.

Mesopotamian Influence

The closest parallels of the disputation of Job between Job and the three opponents and then between Job and Yahweh are the "Babylonian Theodicy" and the "Dialogue of Pessimism." The other parallel is the text *Ludlul bel nemeqi*, a first-person actualization of a lament in which the sufferer is finally saved from suffering and concludes with a praise of Marduk.

Persian Influence

Our knowledge of sages in Persia and their possible influence on Jewish sages is quite limited. It does appear that the Achaemenid court commissioned various native leaders to codify their laws (Udjahorresnet in Egypt and Ezra in Jerusalem).

Greco-Roman Influence

Jewish philosophical scribes found numerous parallels in the Greek and Roman world. Two schools were especially important in influencing Jewish wisdom: Skepticism for Qoheleth, and Middle Platonism for the Wisdom of Solomon.

Qoheleth's skeptical views of life and death and manner of determining what was true were similar to the Skeptics. The author of the Wisdom of Solomon knew enough about Middle Platonism to utilize some of its major tenets in the areas of cosmology, the World Soul, and important virtues. He also was familiar with several Greek mystery religions, including Isis and Dionysus, as well as late Greco-Egyptian religion and portrayals of ancient Syrian (= Canaanite) wisdom literature.

THE HISTORICAL THEOLOGY OF WISDOM

Wisdom and Metaphorical Theology

Creation theology in the wisdom traditions of Israel and the ancient Near East is not rendered by discursive prose and systematic formulation. The literary embodiments of creation theology include poems, narratives, instructions, and sayings. In addition, the rhetoric of each piece of literature operates with the content to form a minute esthesis, a world of beauty and life, that provides coherence and meaning and attracts would-be adherents to enter into this world of sapiential imagination. When speaking of creation, the sages usually filled these texts with the content and images of organizing metaphors and metaphor clusters that drew largely on the mythological traditions of Israel and the other cultures of the ancient Near East and Greece. These metaphors and metaphor clusters may be inferred from the linguistic construals of sapiential literature, for they are not always directly stated. The attention is placed on the activity of creation, rather than on the naming of the Creator in other than generic terms (God, "the God," "maker," and Yahweh). Nevertheless, the identification of the metaphorical referents of the language of God and creation is important for seeing how the sages actualized theological meaning. In order to activate and engage the imagination, the sages used metaphors for construing the acts of creation and providence. These included fertility, artistry, word, and battle.[3] The creation of humanity is viewed through the lens of human imagination that issued forth in metaphors that presented humans as the offspring or children of God, as infants given birth by the divine mother or aided by the divine midwife, a slave, and a ruler. These imply, then, that God is understood as creator, sustainer, king, judge, artist, warrior, parent, lover, husband, and sage and humans as those under divine sovereignty and care. Finally, the sages used their imagination to address the relationship between cosmology and anthropology. They did so through well-crafted and, at times, alluring metaphors of Woman Wisdom: a fertility goddess, the voice of God, teacher, queen of heaven, and consort and lover.

Creation and Providence: The Metaphor of Fertility

In the eastern Mediterranean, an important cluster of metaphors used to speak of world origins and maintenance is fertility.[4] The various elements of reality originated and continued to be sustained through the attraction and fecundity of goddesses. Gods were conceived and born as a result of sexual intimacy between creator and consort (theogonies), and this same sexual activity led to the forming of the seasons of fertility and sterility.[5] While this was a favorite metaphor among Israel's prophets in describing Israel as the sexual partner or wife of Yahweh (see Hos. 2; Jer. 3:1–4:2; Ezek. 18; Isa. 54:5–8), the sages adapted it to speak of the divine principle of Wisdom present in the makeup of the character of the Creator. For the sages, Yahweh is the "Lord of the womb" who ensured that reproduction would continue to provide life in the birth of future generations. Through the love and nurture of Wisdom and its incorporation in life, humans participated in the creative, generative power of reality.

The sages used the fertility metaphor to speak of Woman Wisdom as the lover and consort of God (cf. Wis. 7–9). Even as the divine lover and fertility goddess, Wisdom seeks to attract young students to her embrace (Prov. 7; 9:1–6).[6] In contrast to Folly, who is portrayed as a seductive harlot leading to death (7:6–27; 9:13–18), Wisdom brings life, fertility, and blessing to those who love her and follow her instruction. In the portrayal of divine activities, Yahweh is seen in the roles of the lover and consort of Woman Wisdom. She, in turn, as his beloved, becomes the instrument of creation and mediator between God and humanity (Prov. 8:2–31). Through God's love of Wisdom, life in the cosmos originated and continues. The wise sought to embrace Wisdom passionately and participated in the generative power of reality that sustained and continued life.

Creation and Providence: The Metaphor of Artistry

The sages appropriated from the mythological traditions of Israel and the surrounding culture the metaphor of the artisan. At times, the activities of creator deities are depicted as those of an architect or craftsman who builds the cosmos into a well-constructed house, an elegant palace, or a city for human habitation (Job 38:5–7). The sages of Israel used this mythic metaphor to describe the world as a house or building secured on firm foundations (38:6), with a roof (the firmament or sky; see 37:18) supported by cosmic pillars (i.e., the mountains; see 9:6).[7] Wisdom was the insight and skill of the divine artisan (Prov. 3:19–20).[8] Although God is rarely called "wise," it is clear that wisdom is a divine attribute that the sages used to speak of creation. As an attribute of God, Wisdom sometimes assumes the role of creator as the artificer of all things (Prov. 9:1–6; Wis. 7:22; 8:6).[9] In the first strophe of an elegant poem Woman Wisdom constructs her manse, that is, the cosmos supported by seven pillars (Prov. 9:1–6). She then invites the unlearned to enter into her house and partake of her cosmic banquet, that is, to take up the study of the wisdom tradition and learn to live wisely and well in her cosmic reality.

Creation and Providence: The Metaphor of Word

Another prominent metaphor for cosmology and providence is the divine word.[10] Language was at the center of the sages' activities: reading, writing, comprehending, and speaking. Indeed, each form utilized by the sage, in regard to both its beauty and its content, assists in ordering the world of the moral life. Language created a minute esthesis of beauty and content that together ordered the world. Thus it should not be surprising that the sages understood creation as a result of divine speech and providence as directed by the edicts of the Creator.[11] The spoken word (Job 28:26; 38:33), the divine spirit or breath (Sir. 24:1), command (Sir. 39:17), edict (Job 38:8–11), Torah (Ps. 19), and the thought that resides behind an action are related metaphors in the sages' depiction of creation and providence. God is the king who issues a royal decree separating chaos and cosmos, the sage whose eloquence orders the world and whose wisdom imagines and then brings into being creatures and the structures of life, and the poet whose elegant language fashions an esthesis of order, beauty, and justice. The divine spirit or *rûaḥ* gives life to the world and when withdrawn results in the withering and death of the creation and its inhabitants. The origins and maintenance of the cosmos, then, depend on the power of divine language encapsulated in Woman Wisdom.

Wisdom is both the imagination, skill, and talent of the poet to create beauty and the constructive reason of the sage that observes and posits coherence and order. Wisdom is the divine language that brings all things into existence and the moral character of God that guides those who desire life, reveals the divine will, and directs the sages to blessing (Prov. 1:20–33; 8:1–36; Wis. 1:7; 8:1–4; 9:17–18). For the sages, language possessed the power to create and to destroy. Wise teaching contained the potency to effectuate well-being, success, and vital existence, while each foolish word would lead to failure, suffering, and even death (Prov. 10:1, 20, 21; 12:6; 18:21). Language, both that of the Creator and that of the sages, contained the power to create and sustain a beneficent order of life, or, on the contrary, if spoken by the fool, could subvert order and lead to destruction. Through the rhetoric and content of the language of the sages, they participated in the maintenance of creation, social community, and life.

In Israel and other cultures of the ancient Near East, the creative and destructive power of language was at times associated with breath, considered to be the life force of creaturely existence and thus the vital, life-giving power that permeates all of the cosmos.[12] God's breath or spirit gives life and sustenance to all creatures (Ps. 104; also see Gen. 2:7 and Isa. 42:5). Elihu uses this tradition in speaking of the sovereignty of God and the utter dependency of creation upon God's vital breath (Job 34:14–15). Ben Sira speaks of Wisdom coming forth from the mouth of God and then permeating creation like a mist (Sir. 24). The author of the Wisdom of Solomon equates wisdom with the life-giving and sustaining spirit of God that is present in all of creation and in the souls of the righteous by which immortality is gained (1:6–7).[13]

The power of the divine edict is also associated with the creative and destructive potency of language. Justice is the divine force that permeates all of reality and keeps it from returning to chaos. Reality is regulated by divine laws that, combined together, constitute cosmic justice. Through obedience to laws and wisdom teachings, humans participate in the ordering of this reality. During the monarchy, kingship was legitimated by this tradition, for the king was responsible for laws and acts that reflected the justice that permeates the cosmos (cf. Prov. 16:12). Other institutions, including those of scribes and teachers, had a similar responsibility. The emphasis on proper speech by the sages points to the importance of this image. The sapiential tradition and its cluster of word metaphors were eventually identified with the written Torah (Pss. 19B; 119; Sir. 24). Torah and wisdom teaching became the sustaining power of creation.

Creation and Providence: The Metaphor of Conflict

A fourth metaphor for the origins and maintenance of world creation is battle.[14] Creation issues from the contest between the Divine Warrior and primeval chaos, often personified as a dragon residing in the cosmic waters (see Prov. 3:20; Job 38:8–11; Job 40–41). Through the defeat of chaos, the Creator ascends the throne as a cosmic ruler who then creates the world and issues decrees that determine human destiny, sustain creation, and order human society. This rule is not uncontested but continues to be opposed by the forces of chaos that seek to destroy the cosmic government of the Creator and to bring to an end the order of life. In this cluster of metaphors involving struggle, the Creator is both the divine warrior, who battles chaos for supremacy over the cosmos, and the victorious king, who assumes rule over the divine assembly and the entire cosmos and utters his decrees ordering life and keeping chaos at bay.

Creation and Anthropology: The Metaphors of Birth and Nurture

The sages drew from the literary cache of metaphors of fertility for speaking about God as creator and sustainer of humans.[15] An important metaphor for the creation of humanity is birth and nurture. Before the creation of the world, God engendered and gave birth to his child, Woman Wisdom, who dances before her divine parent and rejoices in the inhabited world (Prov. 8:22–31). In Job 10 God is the one who formed Job in the womb, bestowed steadfast love upon him, and cared for and sustained him. Job is now bewildered that his creator has turned against him, since God in an earlier time had given him life and nurtured him like a parent would a child. In Proverbs the voice of Woman Wisdom calls her children to follow her path in order to find success, peace, honor, and life. In the anthropological tradition, then, humans are described as the children of God, conceived in the womb, given birth, and nurtured throughout life by the divine parent, especially through wisdom.

Creation and Anthropology: The Metaphor of Artistry

The metaphor of artistry is also prominent in sapiential imaginings of human beings. Divine activities are portrayed as those of the weaver who knits together human bones and sinews and the potter who creates the first man from the soil. Job complains that Yahweh's own hands fashioned him. Later, after birth, God astonishingly turned against him to destroy him (Job 10; cf. 33:6 and 34:19). The Wisdom of Solomon (chaps. 13–15) uses the metaphor of artistry to attack the making of lifeless idols, because only God is the skillful artist who shapes human beings in the divine image. How ironic and tragic that humans made of the earth try to render their creator in lifeless images of clay. Israelite and later Jewish sages did not glory in the human body as the Greeks came to do. But the Israelite sages valued and honored human thought and life as things of wonderment and goodness.

Creation and Anthropology: The Metaphors of King and Slave

The literary traditions of the ancient Near East use metaphors not only to describe human origins, but also to depict human functions and destiny. Two of the most common are drawn from society: king and slave. In Israel humans, both male and female, were created in the image of God and received the divine commission to rule as God's royal surrogates over all creation (Gen. 1:26–28; cf. Ps. 8). Chosen by Woman Wisdom, kings and princes ruled over the earth and sustained its life-giving order through righteous rule (see Prov. 8). Elihu even goes a step further than Proverbs 8 to argue not only that God shows no partiality to kings and nobles over the poor (Job 34:18–20), but also will exalt the righteous, even those who are oppressed, to rule as kings (36:7). Job parodies the tradition of humanity's royal place in the cosmos, most elegantly articulated in Psalm 8, when he speaks of God's attack on the human creature (Job 7:17–21). Qoheleth's narrator is King Solomon, whose voice from the past speaks to tell a new generation of students that even he could not master life; thus how could they? Drawing on the tradition of human sovereignty in Genesis 1 and 9 as well as Psalm 8, Ben Sira speaks of God's giving humans dominion over creation, although the sage will still emphasize the dramatic difference between the majesty and power of God and the insignificance and weakness of humanity (Sir. 16:24–18:14). The sages took elements of the royal tradition and applied them to all those who sought wisdom's instruction. The word *māšāl* means not only the proverbial form in which the teachings of the wise were placed, but also the ability to "rule" or "master" life. The metaphor of humans ruling as kings over God's good creation affirmed that human nature was not corrupt, but rather intrinsically good. Having at least a measure of freedom, God gave humans the responsibility to go forth and rule over the good creation and to bring the social order into conformity not only with that of the cosmos but also with the divine will.

Job speaks metaphorically of humans as kings, only to discover in his own experience that slavery, not kingship, is the role and destiny of humanity. Job's revolt against the Creator, though finally abandoned, is a contest of sovereignty over the earth. Qoheleth also uses the royal metaphor in fashioning for Solomon a royal testament that speaks of his search, typical of every sage, to find the "good in life," even though he concludes that the mysterious Creator, not humans, rules over the cosmos. Qoheleth assumes the voice of the long-dead paragon of wisdom, King

Solomon, who takes his audience with him on his journey to discover what is the good in living.

The opposite metaphor for human destiny in the ancient Near East was slavery. In Mesopotamia especially, the gods decreed the fate of humanity and determined individual destinies. The lot assigned to human creatures was not an especially appealing one, for humanity's primary duty is to serve the gods. In Israel the metaphor of slave[16] was used on occasion to describe the relationship of humanity to God. The first man in the J creation story is created to "work" ('*ābad*) the garden, a role that becomes one of drudgery after the fall when humans must till the soil by the "sweat of their brow" until they return to the dust from which they were taken (Gen. 2–3).

As a metaphor for human existence, however, it was Job and Qoheleth who came to describe human existence in terms of slavery, an assertion that opposed the royal anthropology emerging in the exile (cf. P and Ps. 8). Although Qoheleth never seemed to entertain the possibility, Job engaged in a wholesale revolt against the rule of God (see Isa. 14:14b–21; Ezek. 28). Having experienced the drudgery and oppression of life, Job had had quite enough.

In speaking of humanity in images and activities associated with slaves, this common metaphor denies to humans significant freedom, making predestination and divine rule the dominant theological affirmation. In addition, the metaphor suggests that a largely corrupt human nature inclines people toward evil and denies them the ability to engage in actions that create and sustain a just order in the cosmos and human society. This metaphor renders the theological view of the radical sovereignty of God and the depravity of human nature.

Creation and Woman Wisdom: The Metaphor of the Fertility Goddess

The sages use a varied repertoire of metaphors drawn from the mythological texts of the various cultures of the eastern Mediterranean world to speak of Woman Wisdom. Her primary function is to serve as the mediator between heaven and earth and the one who leads humans to life and well-being. Wisdom is portrayed at times as a goddess of fertility. Early on she appears to be a goddess, although later she is the literary personification of a divine hypostasis. In Proverbs 8–9, Job 28, Sirach 24, and Wisdom 7–9, Woman Wisdom wears the garments of a variety of goddesses of fertility in both Israel and the other cultures of the eastern Mediterranean world: Anat, Asherah, Astarte, Hathor, Isis, and Ishtar/Inanna. She is responsible for the fertility of the soil; the rich produce of the orchards, vineyards, and fields; the fecundity of flocks, herds, and people; and the sustaining of life in the cosmos. At times she becomes the offspring of God, the first-born of divine creation, and the one in whom God delights. God's delighting in her enables the world of human habitation to continue to receive the life that the Creator continues to give to his followers.

Creation and Woman Wisdom: The Metaphor of the Voice of God

Wisdom becomes the incarnate word of God that gives life and redemption to the wise and provides the righteous in search of her with life-giving wisdom. Through her God is revealed to those who come to possess insight. Thus they are granted the means by which to learn the will of God and how to live in conformity with the teachings that will lead to success and life. At times, she becomes identified with the divine edict or law that governs society and provides the direction for the moral life. While on occasion hidden to those who search for her (Job 28), she nevertheless is known by God, who provides her insight to those who search her out.

Creation and Woman Wisdom: The Metaphor of the Teacher

Another metaphor for wisdom is that of the sage who teaches the simple virtues and ways to obtain happiness and success in life. To heed her warning (Prov. 1:20–33) makes life easy and secure, while to ignore her results in death. She is seen as the incarnation of the wisdom teacher composed by the sages for the incorporation of their values and beliefs as well as for the instruction of those who seek to follow her.

Creation and Woman Wisdom: The Queen of Heaven

As the queen of heaven she assumes the role of endowing rulers with wisdom, selecting monarchs and dynasties to rule their kingdoms, and ensuring that kings rule wisely and righteously in shaping and directing a society built on justice (Prov. 8:12–21). She constructs her cosmological temple in which she dwells and invites the untutored to come and partake of the banquet of life that she offers (9:1–6). She vies with Woman Folly for the hearts of human devotees and with the fertility goddesses of other cults who seek from the same audience followers who hope to find life in her (Prov. 9). She is the goddess who sings her own praises and seeks worshipers who are her followers (Sir. 24).

Creation and Woman Wisdom: Lover and Consort

Finally Woman Wisdom is the lover whom humans seek to embrace and to discover in their passionate fulfillment of desire the life that she offers to them in her teaching. She also is the consort of God who partakes of his divine character and sits enthroned beside him as his divine queen and mistress. Thus she willingly gives humans the knowledge that she possesses and the teaching for success in living that humans crave. In the Wisdom of Solomon Goddess Wisdom even becomes the means of immortality, for she enters into the souls of the righteous and sustains them beyond death to enjoy the fruits of life eternal.

Creation and Woman Wisdom: The Artisan

Woman Wisdom is finally depicted as an artisan (Wis. 7:21) who fashions the cosmos and makes it into a well-constructed house or building. She is the instrument of creation, the architect who carries out the divine plan for shaping reality, and the craftswoman who fashions nature (Prov. 3:19). Through her, Yahweh founds the earth, placing it on the pillars of the cosmos that provide it with stability and thus order. Through her, Yahweh establishes the heavens that are separate from the earth and the place of human dwelling.

A HISTORICAL OVERVIEW OF WISDOM THEOLOGY: CREATION, PROVIDENCE, ANTHROPOLOGY, AND WOMAN WISDOM

The Monarchy

Creation theology and providence were used in several ways. First, this theology with its emphasis on order ("righteousness") was used to legitimate the institution of kingship and the role of the king in establishing social justice. Second, the concept of justice in creation and society became the basis for righteous living according to wisdom instructions that incorporated the virtues and behavior necessary for living in concert with this divine order. Third, the legal institution was founded also on this order of justice. Through the righteous administration of justice, society was provided stability, order, and life. Fourth, and finally, the wisdom used by God in creating a world of justice and order came to be described as a goddess who orders the world of nature and life, maintains justice, chooses kings to rule over their kingdoms, requires of her royal consorts righteous rule, and builds her own temple, where she sits enthroned. She sends out her maidens to invite the foolish to come and learn from her in order to exist in harmony with the order of life and justice and to receive the blessing of an existence that is characterized by respect, honor, longevity, a good name, and family. Through the activation of the memory of the living, the wise will continue to exist. Through her indwelling, the righteous will eventually receive immortality.

The Babylonian Exile

The disruption of the social order in Judah by the Babylonian conquest became the basis for the questioning of divine justice. Has the Creator turned against his own human creature and enabled the wicked and the power of chaos to prevail over the righteous? This questioning of the justice of God brought into serious question not divine creation but rather the power of the Creator to sustain the created order in the face of chaos and even the integrity of God in ruling the world with justice. In either case, God was no longer worshiped as the righteous or powerful Deity sustaining creation and the social order based upon it. Even a positive reading of the content of the Yahweh speeches, which shift the blame for destruction from God to chaos and the wicked, points to the weakness of the Creator in eradicating the power of Leviathan, Behemoth, and their human incarnations. The appended poem on Woman Wisdom in Job 28 affirms the inability of humans to understand Wisdom, who is known only by God. Woman Wisdom is no longer the goddess who goes in search of followers to instruct in the ways of life. Rather, she is mysterious, incapable of being known, and hidden from human eyes. Only the Creator knows her and how to discover her secrets. Humans are instructed in the attached wisdom poem in chapter 28 that their only recourse is to fear God and turn from evil, the two major characteristics of the life of the Job of the narrative tale.

The Persian Period

In the activity and teachings of Ezra and in Psalm 19, wisdom now becomes identified with Torah. By the observation of the Torah, the divine teachings become known by the righteous sages. The teachings of the Torah, which are identified with those of the sages, become the focus of meditation, and its teachings become the basis for righteous and pious living. Through the Torah one comes to a knowledge of creation and the one who made all that exists. Now the Torah is to become the basis for social justice and righteous living for the community of the Jews. While wisdom is not personified as a goddess, it is now identified with the Torah, which becomes the basis for life and the foundation for creation in the Second Temple.

The Ptolemaic Period

In Qoheleth the Creator, who is to be feared but cannot be known, has now receded into the impenetrable darkness far removed from human insight and understanding. Creation is no longer a reality ruled over by a just Deity, but rather has become a nightmare world of constantly moving forces that betray no insight into "the God." While God is the giver of life, the ultimate fate of human beings is the tomb. Society is ruled by the unjust, while wisdom does not provide one the means by which to acquire well-being and to live in concert with a cosmic order. Indeed, the only order in reality is the constant movement of the forces of nature, wind, water, and the rising and setting sun. The one gift given by God to at least some humans is the ability to experience joy.

The Seleucid Period

In Ben Sira creation theology and providence, with some nuanced differences, return to a more traditional formulation. Wisdom permeates creation and is offered to humanity in the teachings of the sages and in the Torah. All things created by God have their proper place, time, and purpose for existence. Through the observance of the Torah, the fear of God, and wisdom humans are equipped to experience well-being and to live in concert with the created order. Creation is an object of beauty and wonder as well as justice that allows one to understand the nature and character of the Creator and to establish order in society. Woman Wisdom, who originates from the breath of God at creation, goes in search of a home and, instructed by God, takes up her residence in Israel, on the Temple Mount where she becomes identified with the liturgy and the offerings of the priest. Through the incorporation of her virtues, the heroes of the past experience life and salvation. Now the covenant and she have become one. The theocracy of God awaits its final culmination.

The Early Roman Empire

The appropriation of Middle Platonism provides the intellectual instrument needed by the author of the Wisdom of Solomon to speak of reason or wisdom as a World Soul, which allows the soul of the righteous to know how to live in justice. Wisdom is capable of residing as the spirit of God only in the souls of the righteous. While the wicked may prosper for a time, giving them the opportunity to repent, the righteous, even though they may die early, may rest assured that they are destined for immortality. Wisdom becomes the root of this everlasting existence and may be obtained by living a life in accordance with justice and cosmic order. Wisdom is also the guide of history, becoming the one who leads those who were righteous, even a sinful first man, to redemption. She then guides Moses, who takes Israel from Egypt in the exodus. Through the divine structuring of the cosmos, Wisdom enables the forces of nature to save Israel, while bringing destruction to the wicked Egyptians, their persecutors in the past and in the pogrom of Flaccus. Indeed, the means of the punishment of the wicked are transformed to become the instrumentalities of blessing for Israel.

CONCLUDING OBSERVATIONS

The Historical Theology of Wisdom

The thesis that wisdom searched for timeless ideas that transcended time and space cannot be maintained. This idealism does not reflect the changing understandings, social worlds, and scribal activities over the centuries of Israelite and early Jewish history. Wisdom indeed was strongly affected by the major currents of the historical and social transformation of larger Israel and Judaism. It also was influenced by the major centers of the empires and their wisdom, values, and rhetorical expressions. Egyptian instructions, biographies, wisdom and Isis hymns, Assyrian scribal legends, Babylonian contest literature, and Hellenistic encomia and protreptic discourse may be found in Israelite and early Jewish wisdom texts. This engagement could have occurred only within the context of international wisdom taught in wisdom schools and used in royal courts of the major empires that dominated Israel. The locus of the royal court, followed by that of the temple, occurred when the monarchy in Judah came to an end and the high priesthood assumed significant social control of the Jewish community in Jerusalem and part of Judah. The Qumran community, which rejected the corruption of the Jerusalem temple by Jason and Menelaus and the formation of the Sadducean party, became another locale for wisdom as it was joined to apocalyptic (see 4QInstruction). The different functions of the scribe also were shaped by the changing historical fortunes of the Jewish people. Thus the counselor, judge, and teacher in a royal court eventually became the scribe who edited and interpreted Scripture for which he/she was largely responsible.

The Importance of Wisdom for Old Testament Theology

First, we should recognize that the category of salvation history, including covenant and law at Sinai, cannot subsume the entire Old Testament under its confines. Many Old Testament texts, from Esther to the Song of Songs to numerous psalms, set forth a faith and a piety that are not grounded in a theology of election. A one-sided emphasis on salvation history, including the covenants and law of Sinai, excludes the theological understandings of a substantial part of the Old Testament and not simply the wisdom literature. Historically speaking, Israelite religion and piety were diverse enough to include expressions and practices that were based on theological understandings that were not limited to the nationalistic salvation of history and covenant.

Second, we need to remind ourselves that creation and providence are not secondary or unimportant theological affirmations in texts outside the wisdom literature. The creation of humanity and the universal thrust of the J narrative, the Priestly grounding of the Sabbath law in the creation and order of the cosmos, Jeremiah's depiction of the destruction of Judah by the enemy from the north in images of a return to chaos, Second Isaiah's theology that integrates a "new exodus" with a "new creation," and the Psalter's hymnic praise of God's majestic creation and rule over the cosmos (e.g., Ps. 104) are significant examples of the role that creation and providence play even in nonsapiential biblical texts.

Third, Israel's place in the cosmos and the relationship of the chosen people to the other nations are properly understood only by reference to the larger questions of the nature and character of the cosmos and of humanity. For the sages, divine activity and providence cannot be limited to Israel's election and history. Election may be properly understood only within the larger theological parameters of divine creation and providential rule over cosmos and history.

Fourth, revelation is not limited to special forms, for example, the prophetic word or the cultic celebration of the temple, but also includes a more general revelation that is open to all. Israel and human beings are taught by their observations of creation not only about nature but also about God, human life, and the world. Justice and the universality of Yahweh are based not only on the Torah or on the divine revelation to Israel but also on creation. The sages also recognize that there are contingencies in life that are not under human control or that cannot be anticipated. They reach the conclusion that there are mysteries in both the reality they experience and the world they imagine that reside beyond their capacity to know or to explain. God, of course, is the greatest mystery, whose nature cannot be directly known and whose actions are beyond human awareness.

Fifth, Wisdom recognizes the universal dominion of God and stresses the authority of its teachings. The tension between election theology and creation theology has been one of long-standing concern among biblical scholars.[17] In wisdom the nations are part of creation and the blessing of God. Universalism is most prevalent in those texts, which speak of God as the creator of the cosmos. Yahweh is the creator of all (Jer. 10:16; 51:19; Isa. 45:7; Job 38). The Creator maintains and delivers all that is created. Creation is "very good" (Gen. 1:31) and to be praised (Pss. 8 and 148). Even so, the sages are the ones who most frequently speak of God in universal terms. The ground of moral authority is not exclusively in Sinai and the Torah received from Yahweh, but in creation and wisdom, which derive from observation of the cosmos.[18] The sages impose upon the world and society a universal order of justice that then is to be realized in sapiential life. These teachings are more than simply good advice. They carry with them the weight and authority of the wisdom tradition and the Creator who originated and continues to sustain life and gave humans the gift of wisdom. Ben Sira and the Wisdom of Solomon are the two later sages who blend together universalism and the particularity of the chosen status of Israel. They affirm that it is especially Israel who is chosen by God, but this does not result in a rejection of the possibility of non-Jews to come to an understanding of God and to experience divine salvation.

Sixth, the sages are the ones who especially address the problem of theodicy, although others outside this social group do raise the issue (e.g., Habakkuk). Job, of course, questions the justice of God, a question that is never addressed directly, much less clearly answered, even in the Yahweh speeches. Qoheleth denies the justice of God and prefers to speak of a mysterious power residing outside the human ability to know or to influence. Ben Sira develops the "science of opposites" to argue that all things created in the world have their function, which ultimately results in the blessing of the righteous and the destruction of the wicked. The Wisdom of Solomon takes this a step further by arguing that each act of divine salvation reconstitutes the creation of the world in rewarding the righteous and punishing the wicked.

Seventh, the sages develop an important understanding of the beauty of the cosmos and its created elements. Qoheleth indicates that "the God" has created everything "beautiful in its time." The "king" then gives his own commentary on this traditional wisdom poem. His repetition in verse 9 of the programmatic question of 1:3 ("What remains to the laborer from his toil?") becomes for the implied audience a rhetorical question. Human activities fade from memory and disappear. Qoheleth then examines individual actions within the larger structure of time. He affirms the sapiential doctrine of the aesthetic, if not moral, goodness of creation by noting that everything God has created has an appropriate (*yāpâ*, יפה, literally "beautiful") time for existing. This may echo the divine evaluation of creation in Gen. 1:31 ("everything which he had made . . . was very good"), although the word in this latter text is *ṭôb*, טוב, "good." However, the problem for Qoheleth is that God denies even to sages any comprehension of the larger temporal order of the cosmos: God "has put eternity (*ʿōlām*, עלם)[19] into humanity's mind; yet they cannot discover what God does from the beginning to the end" (Qoh. 3:11–12). Not only are humans unable to influence the course of cosmic and historical events directed by God, they are also denied comprehension of the larger structure of time (the *ʿōlām*) within which these events occur (cf. 8:17 and 11:5). God governs the world in mystery and power. Consequently, the correlation of episodic, human action with divinely determined times is impossible. One may only ponder, but cannot clearly know, what has gone before and what is yet to come. Denied the comprehensive knowledge of the cosmic and historical components of time and the course of divine events in the past, present, and future, humanity is trapped in an opaque, mysterious, and ambiguous present unaware of what may or may not happen. Control over events and their outcome passes from human hands either to God or to mere chance. One may only rejoice in the "day of prosperity" and learn from the "day of adversity" that God is the one who structures time and determines the course of significant events (7:14). It is impossible even for sages to know the appropriate time for episodic events.[20] Thus all actions are accompanied by a high degree of chance.[21]

Ben Sira sings of the beauty of the works of God, noting that the divine language of judgment and wisdom also possesses within itself both beauty and the capacity to shape like a skilled poet works of wonderment and elegance (Sir. 42:22–25). Ben Sira states that there are things within creation that may be more beautiful than others, and yet all of them have a degree of grace that evokes human appreciation. Even so, the works of God are "beautiful" or "good," not simply in regard to their appearance, but also in terms of their function. Ben Sira articulates, then, a view that the world is an esthesis, an order that is both beautiful and filled with purpose. It is in both of these senses that God's works (both the activities and the objects of divine creation) are "beautiful" and "good." Each object of divine creation meets a specified need. All things taken together, within the totality of reality, point to an order that is both beautiful and moral and continues to be the same from the beginning of the world throughout all eternity. Continuing the cosmology of esthesis of the earlier poem, the fourth and longest strophe (43:1–22) praises the Creator for the wonders of sky and moisture that are objects of both beauty and purpose. Ben Sira praises the attractiveness and order of the heavens and the radiance and life-giving vitality of the various forms of moisture (see Job 38:4–38).

The sage in the Wisdom of Solomon discusses beauty in his section dealing with philosophical religion (13:1–9).[22] One of his arguments, which makes use of analogy, indicates that philosophers who worship nature should have made the correlation between the "goodness" and "greatness and beauty of created things" and the one who created them. This correlation should have allowed them to recognize something of the character of the Creator and to be aware of his superiority to what he has made.

Eighth, there remains the strong presence of skepticism, especially in Qoheleth. For this sage, the lack of any reference to the creation tradition of the world and the inability to discern divine activity undercuts both the theologies of salvation history and cultic ritual that represented and actualized in sacred drama the deeds of divine creation and redemption. In view of the ephemeral quality of human activity, Qoheleth encourages the celebration of joy during one's youth before old age and death, the final end of human beings, are inevitably experienced. In addition, the failure to perceive a coherent pattern for historical time, so evident in prophetic and historical texts in Israel, results in the fragmentation of experience and the loss of collective and individual identity.

The human quest for identity and self-understanding within a common tradition requires the integration of temporal phases (past, present, and future) into a coherent unity. Memory enables both the community and the individual to recall and sequence significant events from the past in order to explain the present and anticipate the future. Memory allows humans to tap the reservoirs of tradition to find root metaphors to convey meaning. And the anticipation of the future course of history, made possible by the unbounded horizon of the imagination, allows both the individual and the community to give informed direction to their actions. Memory and anticipation are creative acts of the imagination that organize and interpret experience. The individual and the community come to self-understanding through the narratives and poetry they construct. The incorporation of individual life within the larger tradition provides a meaning-structure in which self-understanding reaches culmination and produces coherence (cf., e.g., Ben Sira's "Praise of the Pious," chaps. 44–50). Thus individual life becomes part of the community's past experience, present existence, and anticipated future. At least these are the understandings of the traditional sages. The crisis for Qoheleth is the inevitable loss of collective (Qoh. 1:8–11) and individual (5:20) memory. With the loss of memory, experience does not achieve unity through time. Rather, experience fragments into disconnected pieces of isolated perceptions. All that remains is the immediacy of the present moment.[23]

Ninth, Ben Sira and the Wisdom of Solomon combine creation theology with salvation history. This combination points to the theological inventiveness of these two sages, who, for the first time in the wisdom tradition, unify the central traditions of salvation history and creation.

Tenth, the understanding of creation and history courses through the wisdom texts in significantly different ways. This is partly due to the fact that each text interacts with different historical and cultural milieus that dominated the ancient Near East at different times. Wisdom theology issues from and in turn engages history in different ways. Historical and social changes in the world of the sages require the recognition of the development of their responses in order to engage them.

A Final Word

In the future, Old Testament theologies should engage the traditions of ancient Israel by recognizing the contributions that history and the history of religions have to offer. In addition, these new constructions must recognize the significance of both creation and redemptive history for expressing Israelite and early Jewish faith. To focus exclusively or even primarily on the latter at the expense of the former is unacceptable. The integration of these two complexes of theological tradition, creation and salvation history, is a necessary step for including the entirety of the canonical and deuterocanonical literature within a comprehensive theology of the Old Testament. Further, wisdom should no longer be marginalized as the "unwanted bastard" of the Old Testament or caricatured as a pagan religious understanding that crept uninvited into the dwelling places of sacred Scripture. There is no theological or scholarly excuse for the exclusion of wisdom from the faith, piety, and understanding of ancient Israel and early Judaism. Finally, the theology of the sages, present in the canonical, deuterocanonical, and noncanonical literatures, deserves an important place in theologies of early Judaism. This may not be "Old Testament" theology, but the unyielding doctrine of a static canon, shaped by early first- and second-century communities dwelling in worlds that have long since disappeared, should not be allowed to dictate what is considered to be important in reconstructing wisdom's historical theology and the faith of the church.

The fundamental role of the sages in creating canonical writings, in editing texts that would become Scripture, and in sustaining the tradition of Judaism into the future should be a major consideration in any history of ancient Israel and early Judaism and the related theology that interacts with culture and events. Scribal editing in the late Persian and Greco-Roman periods should be thoroughly investigated in assessing the complexity of the roles and functions of the sages in ancient Israel and early Judaism. In this important area, I have offered only a few suggestions that need to be developed. A more detailed study of the sapiential redaction of the Hebrew Bible, the deuterocanonical literature, and the numerous texts of the Pseudepigrapha and other collections should be undertaken.[24] Finally, studies that focus on the development and variety of roles of the scribal profession, including this editorial role, also need to be written in order to identify the social functions and ideologies of those who shaped the theology of the wisdom traditions.[25]

Notes

Chapter 1: Introducing the Historical Theology of Wisdom Literature

1. See my volume, *The Collapse of History: Reconstructing Old Testament Theology* (OBT; Minneapolis: Fortress, 1994).
2. See my volume, *The Social History of Wisdom* (Atlanta: Society of Biblical Literature, forthcoming).
3. There are two notable exceptions, although neither presents a comprehensive overview. John J. Collins's book, *Jewish Wisdom in the Hellenistic Age* (OTL; Louisville: Westminster/John Knox, 1997), provides a significant history of Hellenistic wisdom, and C.-L. Seow's commentary on Qoheleth places this sage in the Persian period (*Ecclesiastes: A New Translation with Introduction and Commentary* [AB; New York: Doubleday, 1997]).
4. Leo G. Perdue, *Wisdom and Creation: The Theology of Wisdom Literature* (Nashville: Abingdon, 1994).
5. Gerhard von Rad, *Wisdom in Israel* (trans. James D. Martin; Nashville: Abingdon, 1972).
6. O. S. Rankin, *Israel's Wisdom Literature: Its Bearing on Theology and the History of Religion* (New York: Schocken, 1969).
7. See my *Reconstructing Old Testament Theology; After the Collapse of History* (OBT; Minneapolis: Fortress, 2005).
8. James Barr, *The Concept of Biblical Theology* (Minneapolis: Fortress, 2000) 133–37.
9. See Otto Eissfeldt, who clearly articulated the differences and similarities between these two approaches in "Israelitisch-jüdische Religionsgeschichte und alttestamentliche Theologie," *ZAW* 55 (1926) 1–12.
10. See Herbert Niehr, "Auf dem Weg zu einer Religionsgeschichte Israels und Judas. Annäherungen an einen Problemkreis," in *Religionsgeschichte Israels: Formale und Materiale Aspeckte*, ed. Bernd Janowski and Matthias Köckert (Gütersloh: Kaiser, 1999) 57–78. He adds that primary religions speak of the order of the cosmos and stress a hierarchical society, while secondary religions place in the foreground the personal relationship of humans to God and express themselves through confession. In contrast to theology, the purpose of the history of religions is to engage in reconstruction on the basis of material culture and texts and not in retelling biblical religion.
11. Rainer Albertz, *A History of Israelite Religion in the Old Testament Period* (2 vols.; OTL; Louisville: Westminster/John Knox, 1994).
12. Bernd Janowski, ed., *Religionsgeschichte Israels oder Theologie des Alten Testaments?* (Jahrbuch für biblische Theologie 10; Neukirchen-Vluyn: Neukirchener Verlag, 1995).

13. Barr, *Concept of Biblical Theology*, 135. Later he notes: "the history of religion must be accorded full recognition and importance by biblical theology. The two cannot be separated and works on the latter must recognize not only the material of the former but also the positive theological importance of its researches and results" (p. 138).

14. Two theologians especially emphasize reading the OT for its theological and normative significance for the church: Th. C. Vriezen, *An Outline of Old Testament Theology* (2nd ed.; Oxford: Blackwell, 1970); and Wilhelm Vischer, *The Witness of the Old Testament to Christ* (London: Lutterworth, 1949) (Zollikon: Evangelischer Verlag, 1946), in which he "Christianizes the Old Testament" in order to claim it for the church.

15. See Karel van der Toorn, *Family Religion in Babylonia, Ugarit, and Israel: Continuity and Changes in the Forms of Religious Life* (Leiden: Brill, 1996); Rainer Albertz, *Persönliche Frömmigkeit und offizielle Religion: Religionsinterner Pluralismus in Israel und Babylon* (CTM 9; Stuttgart: Calwer, 1978).

16. John H. Hayes and Frederick C. Prussner, *Old Testament Theology: Its History and Development* (Atlanta: John Knox, 1985) 264–67.

17. See Volkmar Fritz, *Studien zur Literatur und Geschichte des alten Israel* (Stuttgarter biblische Aufsatzbände 22; Stuttgart: Katholisches Bibelwerk, 1997).

18. Hayden White, *Metahistory: The Historical Imagination in Nineteenth-Century Europe* (Baltimore: Johns Hopkins University Press, 1975).

19. Karl Barth, *Church Dogmatics,* I/2 (2nd ed.; Edinburgh: T. & T. Clark, 1975) 303.

20. Hans-Jürgen Hermisson argues that both are needed for OT study (*Alttestamentliche Theologie und Religionsgeschichte Israels* [Forum Theologische Literature Zeitung 3; Leipzig: Evangelische Verlagsanstalt, 2000]). He contends that the history of Israelite religion enables one to recognize that Christian faith is based on historical events. Cf. Gerhard Ebeling, "Was heisst 'biblische theologie'?" *Wort und Glaube,* 1 (2nd ed.; Tübingen: Mohr, 1962) 69–89.

21. For the interpretation of Job as metaphorical theology see my *Wisdom in Revolt: Creation Theology in the Book of Job* (JSOTSup 121; Sheffield: Almond, 1991).

22. Garrett Green, "Myth, History, and Imagination: The Creation Narratives in Bible and Theology," *HBT* 12, no. 2 (1990) 23.

23. John Middleton Murry, *Countries of the Mind* (London: Oxford, 1931) 1–2.

24. "Metaphorical use of language differs in significant ways from literal use but is no less comprehensible, no more recondite, no less practical, and no more independent of truth and falsity than is literal use. Far from being a mere matter of ornament, it participates fully in the progress of knowledge: in replacing some stale 'natural' kinds with novel and illuminating categories, in contriving facts, in revising theory, and in bringing us new worlds" (Nelson Goodman, "Metaphor as Moonlighting," in *On Metaphor*, ed. Sheldon Sacks [Chicago: University of Chicago Press, 1979] 175).

25. See Eckart Otto, "Schöpfung als Kategorie der Vermittlung von Gott und Welt in biblischer Theologie," in *"Wenn nicht jetzt, wann dann?"* ed. Hans-Georg Geyer (Neukirchen-Vluyn: Neukirchener Verlag, 1983) 53–54.

26. Important studies include Ian Barbour, *Myths, Models and Paradigms* (New York: Harper & Row, 1974); Max Black, *Models and Metaphors* (Ithaca: Cornell University Press, 1962); George Lakoff and Mark Johnson, *Metaphors We Live By* (Chicago: University of Chicago Press, 1980); Paul Ricoeur, *The Rule of Metaphor* (Toronto: University of Toronto Press, 1977); Sacks, ed., *On Metaphor;* Phillip Wheelwright, *Metaphor and Reality* (Bloomington: Indiana University Press, 1962).

27. Paul Ricoeur, "The Metaphorical Process" *Semeia* 4 (1975) 78–79; Goodman, "Metaphor as Moonlighting," 175.

28. Ricoeur, "Metaphorical Process," 77–78. This seeming contradiction, says Ricoeur, gives new interpretive insight into meaning.

29. Wheelwright, *Metaphor and Reality*, 45–46.

30. Frederick Ferré, "Metaphors, Models, and Religion," *Soundings* 51 (1968) 331.

31. David Tracy, "Metaphor and Religion: The Test Case of Christian Texts," in *On Metaphor*, 80.

32. I. A. Richards, *The Philosophy of Rhetoric* (New York: Oxford University Press, 1936), 96. He proposes a model for metaphors in which the tenor and vehicle interact to develop meaning.

33. Wayne Booth, *A Rhetoric of Irony* (Chicago: University of Chicago Press, 1974) 22.

34. Ferré, "Metaphors, Models, and Religion," 330; Ricoeur, "Metaphorical Process," 78–79.

35. Sallie McFague, *Metaphorical Theology* (Philadelphia: Fortress Press, 1982).

36. Ricouer, "Metaphorical Process," 77–78.

37. Wheelwright, *Metaphor and Reality*, 45–46.

38. Goodman, "Metaphor as Moonlighting," 176.

39. Wheelwright, *Metaphor and Reality*, 33.

40. McFague, *Metaphorical Theology*, 41.

41. Fabien Blanquart, ed., *La Création dans l'Orient Ancien* (LD 127; Paris: Cerf, 1987); Richard J. Clifford, *Creation Accounts in the Ancient Near East and in the Bible* (CBQMS 26; Washington, DC: Catholic Biblical Association of America, 1994); Othmar Keel and Silvia Schroer, *Schöpfung: Biblische Theologien im Kontext altorientalischer Religion* (Göttingen: Vandenhoeck & Ruprecht, 2002).

42. Mircea Eliade, *Cosmos and History* (rev. ed.; Princeton: Princeton University Press, 1965).

43. For example, see Claus Westermann, *What Does the Old Testament Say about God?* (Atlanta: John Knox, 1979).

44. Rainer Albertz, *Weltschöpfung und Menschenschöpfung* (CTM 3; Stuttgart: Calwer, 1974).

45. Peter Doll, *Menschenschöpfung und Weltschöpfung in der alttestamentlichen Weisheit* (SBS 117; Stuttgart: Katholisches Bibelwerk, 1985). For salient criticisms of Westermann's dichotomy, see Clifford, *Creation Accounts*, 5–6; and J. C. de Moor, "El, the Creator," in *The Bible World: Essays in Honor of Cyrus H. Gordon*, ed. G. H. Rendsburg, et al. (New York: Ktav, 1980) 186, n. 75.

46. See Claus Westermann, *Creation* (Philadelphia: Fortress, 1974) 39–40. In my judgment, Westermann's dichotomy of creation (cosmology and anthropology) is not convincing.

47. Imagination is a feature of human thought that leads to the formation, organization, and interpretation of images. The mind projects the existence of something that is not immediate to sense perception. Memory enables the image to connect to the past, while projection may also posit its existence moving into the future. See the chapter on imagination in my *Collapse of History*, 263–98. Among the important studies on imagination and religion, see Mary Warnock, *Imagination* (Berkeley: University of California Press, 1976); Amos Wilder, *Theopoetic: Theology and the Religious Imagination* (Philadelphia: Fortress, 1976); Paul Ricoeur, "The Narrative Function," *Semeia* 13 (1978) 177–202; Gordon Kaufman, *The Theological Imagination: Constructing the Concept of God* (Philadelphia: Westminster, 1981); David Tracy, *Analogical Imagination* (New York: Crossroad, 1981); Garrett Green, *Imagining God: Theology and the Religious Imagination* (San Francisco: Harper & Row, 1989).

48. *Wisdom in Revolt*, 21–22.

Chapter 2: Salvation History, Covenant, Creation, and Providence

1. There are numerous helpful overviews of OT theology. See especially Barr, *Concept of Biblical Theology*; Jörg Jeremias, "Neuere Entwürfe zu einer 'Theologie des Alten Testaments,'" *VF* 48 (2003) 29–58; Ben C. Ollenburger, et al., eds., *Old Testament Theology: Flowering and Future* (rev. ed.; Sources for Biblical and Theological Study 1; Winona Lake, IN: Eisenbrauns, 2004); Perdue, *Collapse of History*; idem, *Reconstructing Old Testament Theology*; H. Graf Reventlow, "Modern Approaches to Old Testament Theology," in *The Blackwell Companion to the Hebrew Bible*, ed. Leo G. Perdue (Oxford: Blackwell, 2001) 221–40. A new series, the Library of Biblical Theology, ed. Leo G. Perdue (Nashville: Abingdon), is in progress and promises to produce volumes in OT theology, NT theology, biblical theology, and contemporary theology that will not only reconstruct the faiths of Israel, Judah, and early Christianity, but also will engage in dialogue with contemporary faith and culture. For a recent review of creation in OT theology, see Henning Graf Reventlow, "Creation as a Topic in Biblical Theology," in *Creation in Jewish and Christian Tradition*, ed. Henning Graf Reventlow and Yair Hoffman (Sheffield: Sheffield Academic Press, 202) 153–71.

2. Gerhard von Rad, "The Theological Problem of the Old Testament," *The Problem of the Hexateuch and Other Essays* (trans. E. W. Trueman Dicken; Edinburgh: Oliver & Boyd, 1966) 131–43. Only Ps. 19A and 104 do not present creation in soteriological terms. Von Rad argued, wrongly in my judgment, that these two psalms are on the periphery of the OT and likely have a foreign origin.

3. In following Karl Barth, Walther Zimmerli argued that in the initial article of the Christian creed, "Maker of heaven and earth," is first in the list of things to confess, but it is understood only in view of the second, i.e., Christology (*Old Testament Theology in Outline* [Atlanta: John Knox, 1978] 158).

4. Von Rad, "Theological Problem," noted the absence of creation in the so-called ancient historical credos (Deut. 26:5–9; Deut. 6; and Josh. 24). It is only in the later formulation found in Neh. 9 that creation becomes an integral part of the confession (9:6).

5. Bertil Albrektson, *History and the Gods: An Essay on the Idea of Divine Manifestation in the Ancient Near East and in Israel* (Lund: Gleerup, 1967).

6. Barth, *Church Dogmatics*, III/1, §41, III/2, §45, and III/3, §48.

7. Von Rad, "Theological Problem," 131–43.

8. George Ernest Wright, *God Who Acts: Biblical Theology as Recital* (SBT 1/8; London: SCM, 1952).

9. Von Rad, "Theological Problem," 142–43.

10. For a review of the understanding of wisdom in the writings of von Rad, see Samuel Amsler, "Gerhard von Rad et la Sagesse," in *La Sagesse biblique de l'Ancien au Nouveau Testament,* ed. Jacques Trublet (LD 160; Paris: Cerf, 1995) 209–16.

11. Von Rad, "Theological Problem," 140.

12. Von Rad, *Old Testament Theology* (trans. D. M. G. Stalker; 2 vols.; New York: Harper & Row, 1961–65) 1:418–52.

13. See von Rad, *Wisdom in Israel,* 307.

14. Ibid., 175.

15. Ibid., 157ff., 296–97.

16. Ibid., 307.

17. Von Rad, "Theological Problem," 142.

18. Von Rad, *Old Testament Theology,* 1:136–65.

19. Gerhard von Rad, "The Old Testament World View," in *Problem of the Hexateuch,* 164.

20. Claus Westermann, "Biblical Reflections on Creator-Creation," in *Creation in the Old Testament,* ed. B. W. Anderson (IRT 6; Philadelphia: Fortress, 1984) 90–101; idem, *Blessing in the Bible and the Life of the Church* (Philadelphia: Westminster, 1978); idem, *Creation* (Philadelphia: Fortress, 1974); idem, *Elements of Old Testament Theology* (Atlanta: John Knox, 1978); idem, *Genesis 1–11* (Continental Commentary; Minneapolis: Augsburg, 1984). Richard Clifford has also argued that creation is a significant theological theme in the Hebrew Bible as well as in the ancient Near East. He adds that this theme is not a late one in Israel (*Creation Accounts in the Ancient Near East and in the Bible* [CBQ 26; Washington D.C.: Catholic Biblical Association, 1994]).

21. Claus Westermann, "Creation and History in the Old Testament," *The Gospel and Human Destiny,* ed. Vilmos Vajta (Minneapolis: Augsburg, 1971) 23.

22. Westermann, *Elements of Old Testament Theology,* 53.

23. Westermann, "Creation and History," 12.

24. Westermann, *What Does the Old Testament Say about God?* 42.

25. Westermann, "The Blessing God and Creation," ibid., 39–52.

26. *The Epistle to the Romans* (trans. Edwyn C. Huskyns; London: Oxford University Press, 1936).

27. Walther Eichrodt, *Theology of the Old Testament* (trans. J. A. Baker; 2 vols.; OTL; Philadelphia: Westminster, 1961–67) 1:14.

28. Other theologians who have emphasized covenant include Patrick Miller, "Creation and Covenant," in *Israelite Religion and Biblical Theology,* ed. Patrick D. Miller (JSOTSup 267; Sheffield: Sheffield Academic Press, 2000) 470–91; Bernhard W. Anderson, *Contours of Old Testament Theology* (Minneapolis: AugsburgFortress, 1999).

29. Brevard Childs, *Old Testament Theology in a Canonical Context* (Philadelphia: Fortress, 1985); idem, *Biblical Theology of the Old and New Testaments* (Minneapolis: Fortress, 1992).

30. Childs, *Biblical Theology of the Old and New Testaments,* 70–71.

31. Ibid., 77–79.

32. Ibid., 85–88.

33. Ibid., 107–22.

34. See especially Perdue, *Collapse of History,* 155–86; Barr, *Concept of Biblical Theology,* 37–39, 47–51.

35. Theologians who have followed Childs's lead include, in particular, Rolf Rendtorff, *Theologie des Alten Testaments: Ein kanonischer Entwurf* (2 vols.; Neukirchen-Vluyn: Neukirchener Verlag, 1999–2001).

36. Similar theologies have been produced by Antonius H. J. Gunneweg, *Biblische Theologie des Altens Testaments: eine Religionsgeschichte Israels in biblisch-theologisches Sicht* [Stuttgart: Kohlhammer, 1993]); Horst Dietrich Preuss, *Old Testament Theology* (2 vols.; OTL; Louisville: Westminster/John Knox, 1995–1996); Otto Kaiser, *Der Gott des Alten Testaments; Wesen und Wirken, Theologie des Alten Testaments,* 3 vols. (Göttingen: Vandenhoeck & Ruprecht, 1993–2003). And while he denies he does OT theology, I would also place here Jon Levenson, *Creation and the Persistence of Evil: The Jewish Drama of Divine Omnipotence* (Princeton: Princeton University Press, 1994).

37. See especially "Schöpfung, Gerechtigkeit und Heil," *Altorientalische Welt in der alttestamentlichen Theologie* (Zurich: TVZ, 1974) 88. Hermann Spieckermann has used Schmid's approach in setting forth the major rubrics of OT theology:

"Schöpfung, Gerechtigkeit und Heil als Horizont alttestamentlicher Theologie," *ZTK* 100 (2003) 399–419.

38. See, e.g., Richard J. Clifford and John J. Collins, eds., *Creation in the Biblical Traditions* (CBQMS 24; Washington, DC: Catholic Biblical Association of America, 1992).

39. See Schmid, "Jahweglaube und altorientalisches Weltordnungsdenken," *Altorientalische Welt, 33*.

40. Schmid, "Schöpfung, Gerechtigkeit, und Heil," 18.

41. Ibid., 24.

42. See Rolf Knierim, "Cosmos and History in Israel's Theology," *The Task of Old Testament Theology* (Grand Rapids: Eerdmans, 1995) 171–224.

43. Walter Brueggemann, *The Theology of the Old Testament: Testimony, Dispute, Advocacy* (Minneapolis: Fortress, 1997) 145–64.

44. Ibid., 163.

45. Walter Brueggemann, *Finally Comes the Poet: Daring Speech for Proclamation* (Minneapolis: Fortress, 1989).

46. Walter Brueggemann, "A Shape for Old Testament Theology, I: Structure Legitimation," *CBQ* 47 (1985) 40.

47. Brueggemann, *Theology of the Old Testament*, 149.

48. See the survey and bibliography of my essay, "The Importance of Wisdom in Old Testament Theology," in *Das Alte Testament und die Kultur der Moderne: Beiträge des Symposiums 'Das Alte Testament und die Kultur der Moderne' anlässlich des 100. Geburtstags Gerhard von Rads (1901–1971) Heidelberg, 18.-21. Oktober 2001*, ed. Manfred Oeming, et al. (Münster: LTV, 2003) 71–98. Also see Collins, *Jewish Wisdom*; James L. Crenshaw, *Old Testament Wisdom: An Introduction* (rev. ed.; Louisville: Westminster John Knox, 1998); Maurice Gilbert, ed., *La Sagesse de l'Ancien Testament* (2nd ed.; BETL 51; Leuven: Leuven University Press, 1990); Roland Murphy, *The Tree of Life* (2nd ed.; Grand Rapids: Eerdmans, 1990); David J. A. Clines, Hermann Lichtenberger, and Hans-Peter Müller, eds., *Weisheit in Israel: Beiträge des Symposiums 'Das Alte Testament und die Kultur der Moderne" anlässlich des 100. Geburtstags Gerhard von Rads (1901–1971)* (Münster: LTV, 2003).

49. H.-P. Müller, "חכם," *TDOT* 4 (1980) 385.

50. Leo G. Perdue, "Wisdom in the Book of Job," in *In Search of Wisdom: Essays in Memory of John G. Gammie*, ed. Leo G. Perdue, et al. (Louisville: Westminster/John Knox, 1993) 73–80.

51. See José Vílchez-Líndez, "Panorama des recherches actuelles sur la Sagesse dans l'AT," in *Sagesse biblique*, 129–37.

52. Horst Dietrich Preuss, "Das Gottesbild der älteren Weisheit Israels," in *Studies in the Religion of Ancient Israel* (VTSup 23; Leiden: Brill, 1972) 117–45.

53. Preuss, *Old Testament Theology*, 2:203–8.

54. Ronald E. Clements, *Wisdom for a Changing World: Wisdom in Old Testament Theology* (Berkeley Lectures 2; Berkeley: Bibal, 1990).

55. Anderson, *Contours of Old Testament Theology*, 260.

56. Ibid., 239–50.

57. Ibid., 253.

58. Ibid., 261.

59. Murphy, *Tree of Life*, 124.

60. Anderson, *Contours of Old Testament Theology*, 263.

61. Ibid., 264.

62. Murphy, *Tree of Life*, 138.

63. Anderson refers to Kathleen O'Connor, who indicates that in Prov. 8 Wisdom "is a separate being that partakes of the reality that she symbolizes, so that ulti-

mately she is indistinguishable from the Creator" ("Wisdom Literature and Experience of the Divine," in *Biblical Theology: Problems and Perspectives*, ed. S. J. Kraftchick, et al. [Nashville: Abingdon, 1995] 188). Anderson criticizes this view by noting that the poem describes Wisdom as subject to God.

64. Anderson, *Contours of Old Testament Theology*, 258.

65. Jutta Hausmann, "'Weisheit' im Kontext alttestamentlicher Theologie: Stand und Perspektiven gegenwärtiger Forschung," in *Weisheit ausserhalb der kanonischen Weisheitsschriften*, ed. Bernd Janowski (Gütersloh: Kaiser, 1996) 9–19.

66. Ibid., 18.

Chapter 3: The Book of Proverbs

1. Among the numerous studies of Proverbs, see Claudia V. Camp, *Wisdom and the Feminine in the Book of Proverbs* (Decatur, GA: Almond Press, 1985); Claus Westermann, *Wurzeln der Weisheit: Die ältesten Sprüche Israels und anderer Völker* (Göttingen: Vandenhoeck & Ruprecht, 1990); Raymond Van Leeuwen, "The Book of Proverbs," *NIB* 5 (1997) 19–264; Richard Clifford, *Proverbs: A Commentary* (OTL; Louisville: Westminster, 1999); Michael V. Fox, *Proverbs 1–9: A New Translation with Introduction and Commentary* (AB; New York: Doubleday, 2000); Leo G. Perdue, *Proverbs* (Interpretation; Louisville: Westminster/John Knox, 2000). For the theology of creation in Proverbs, see especially Lennart Boström, *The God of the Sages: The Portrayal of God in the Book of Proverbs* (Stockholm: Almqvist & Wiksell International, 1990).

2. See Boström, *God of the Sages*, 46–89.

3. Boström's understanding that Proverbs is not theological in a strict sense is, in my judgment, a disputable assertion, unless one restricts the understanding of theology to a systematic formulation. If so, then nothing in the Hebrew Bible is theological (*God of the Sages*, 47).

4. John Taylor, "The Third Intermediate Period (1069–664 BC)," in *The Oxford History of Ancient Egypt*, ed. Ian Shaw (Oxford: Oxford University Press, 2000) 330–68; Alan B. Lloyd, "The Late Period (664–332 BC)," in ibid., 369–94. Also see *The Prehistory of the Balkans; and the Middle East and the Aegean World, Tenth to Eighth Centuries B.C.*, ed. John Boardman et al. (2nd ed.; Cambridge: Cambridge University Press, 1982); Nicolas Christoph Grimal, *A History of Ancient Egypt* (Oxford: Blackwell, 1992) 311–33. The Egyptian chronology follows Shaw, *Oxford History of Ancient Egypt*, 479–83.

5. See Shaye J. D. Cohen, "Solomon and the Daughter of Pharaoh: Inter-marriage, Conversion, and the Impurity of Women," *JANES* 16–17 (1984–85) 23–37. Most historians have identified this pharaoh as Siamun (978–959 BCE). See A. R. Green, "Solomon and Siamun: A Synchronism between Early Dynastic Israel and the Twenty-First Dynasty of Egypt," *JBL* 97 (1978) 353–67.

6. See Tryggve N. D. Mettinger, *Solomonic State Officials: A Study of the Civil Government Officials of the Israelite Monarchy* (Lund: Gleerup, 1971); E. W. Heaton, *Solomon's New Men: The Emergence of Ancient Israel as a Nation State* (New York: Pica, 1974); Gusta W. Ahlström, *Royal Administration and National Religion in Ancient Palestine* (SHANE 1; Leiden: Brill, 1982).

7. See Kenneth A. Kitchen, "Shishak's Military Campaign in Israel Confirmed," *BAR* 15 (1989) 32–33.

8. Lloyd, "Late Period," 381–82.

9. For an overview of Egyptian wisdom literature, see the volume of essays edited by Antonio Loprieno, *Ancient Egyptian Literature: History and Forms* (Leiden: Brill, 1996). For the translations of texts, see Günter Burkard, et al., eds., *Texte aus der Umwelt des Alten Testaments 3: Weisheitstexte, 2 Mythen und Epen*

(Gütersloh: Mohn, 1991) 191–94; Miriam Lichtheim, *Late Egyptian Wisdom Literature in the International Context* (OBO 52; Göttingen: Vandenhoeck & Ruprecht, 1983); Emma Brunner-Traut, *Lebensweisheit der Alten Ägypter* (Herderbücheri 1236; Freiburg: Herder, 1985); Ronald J. Williams, "Egyptian Literature (Wisdom)," *AB* 2 (1992) 395–99; Erick Hornung and Othmar Keel, eds., *Studien zu altägyptischen Lebenslehren* (OBO 28; Göthingen: Vanderhoeck & Ruprecht, 1979); J. D. Ray, "Egyptian Wisdom Literature," in *Wisdom in Ancient Israel*, ed. John Day, et al. (Cambridge: Cambridge University Press, 1995) 17–29. The important Egyptian wisdom texts are translated in the three volumes by Miriam Lichtheim, *Ancient Egyptian Literature* (Berkeley: University of California Press, 1973–80).

10. That is, *ma'at*. See the study by C.-J. Bleeker, "L'idée de l'ordre cosmique dans l'ancienne Égypte," *RHPR* 42 (1962) 193–200.

11. "The Instruction of Ptahhotep," ll. 84–94 (*ANET*, 421).

12. Merikare, ll. 131–32; *ANET*, 417. See Winfried Barta, "Der anonyme Gott der Lebenslehren," *ZÄS* 103 (1976) 79–89.

13. Hellmut Brunner, *Die Weisheitsbücher der Ägypter: Lehren für das Leben* (Zurich: Artimus & Winckler, 1998) 11–45.

14. For Egyptian schools and education, see Eberhard Otto, "Bildung und Ausbildung in Alten Ägypten," *ZÄS* 8 (1956) 41–48; Hellmut Brunner, *Altägyptische Erziehung* (Wiesbaden: Harrassowitz, 1957).

15. See Ronald J. Williams, "Scribal Training in Ancient Egypt," *JAOS* 92 (1972) 214–21; idem, "The Sages in Ancient Egypt," *JAOS* 101 (1981) 1–19; Ursula Kaplony-Heckel, "Schüler und Schulwesen in der ägyptischen Spätzeit," *Studien zur altägyptischen Kultur* 1 (Hamburg: H. Buske, 1974) 227–46; Edward Wente, "The Scribes of Ancient Egypt," *CANE* 4 (1995) 2211–21; Nili Shupak, *Where Can Wisdom Be Found? The Sage's Language in the Bible and in Ancient Egyptian Literature* (OBO 130; Göttingen: Vandenhoeck & Ruprecht, 1993); Adelheid Schlott, *Schrift und Schreiber im Alten Ägypten* (Munich: Beck, 1989).

16. K. T. Zauzich, "Demotische Fragmente zum Ahikar-Roman," in *Folia Rara*, ed. Herbert Franke, Walther Heissig, and Wolfgang Treue (Verzeichnis der orientalischen Handschriften in Deutschland Supplementband 19; Wiesbaden: Steiner, 1976) 180–85.

17. One development in recent scholarship has questioned the historical existence of the united monarchy; cf., e.g., Thomas L. Thompson, *Early History of the Israelite People: From the Written and Archaeological Sources* (SHANE 4; Leiden: Brill, 1992); Philip Davies, *In Search of "Ancient Israel"* (Sheffield: JSOT Press, 1992); Diana V. Edelman, ed., *The Fabric of History* (Sheffield: JSOT Press, 1991); Volkmar Fritz and Philip R. Davies, *The Origins of the Ancient Israelite States* (Sheffield: Sheffield Academic Press, 1996). This so-called minimalist view argues that a biblical text is historical only when confirmed by archaeology and/or ancient Near Eastern sources. For discussions and critical responses, see Ian W. Provan, "Ideologies, Literary and Critical," *JBL* 114 (1995) 585–606; William G. Dever, *What Did the Biblical Writers Know, and When Did They Know It? What Archaeology Can Tell Us about the Reality of Ancient Israel* (Grand Rapids: Eerdmans, 2001); William W. Hallo, "The Limits of Skepticism," *JAOS* 110 (1990) 187–99.

18. See Mettinger, *Solomonic State Official* 45–41, 58–62, 66–69, 107–10, and 140–57. For overviews of Egyptian influence on Syria-Palestine, see Raphel Giveon, *The Impact of Egypt on Canaan* (Göttingen: Vandenhoeck & Ruprecht, 1978).

19. Nili Shupak, "The 'Sitz im Leben' of the Book of Proverbs in the Light of a Comparison of Biblical and Egyptian Wisdom Literature," *RB* 94 (1989) 98–119.

20. D. B. Redford, *Egypt, Canaan, and Israel in Ancient Times* (Princeton: Princeton University Press, 1992) 385.

21. Ibid.

22. Shupak, "Sitz im Leben," 107.

23. Ibid., 102.

24. Ibid.

25. *Qesem* refers to "divination," indicating that the king's decisions are comparable to the knowledge normally obtained by diviners.

26. *Tô'ēbâ* is a frequent term in Deuteronomy (13:15; 17:4; etc.) and Proverbs (3:22; 11:1–20; 12:22; 15:8–9, 26; 20:10–23; etc.) and means "abomination," usually in reference to something abhorrent to Yahweh.

27. See Michael Carisik, "Who Were the 'Men of Hezekiah' (Proverbs xxv 1)?" *VT* 44 (1994) 289–300.

28. Raymond Van Leeuwen argues that 25:2–27 is a proverb poem addressed to courtiers (*Context and Meaning in Proverbs 25–27* [SBLDS 96; Atlanta: Scholars Press, 1988]).

29. Hellmut Brunner, "Gerechtigkeit als Fundament des Thrones," *VT* 8 (1958) 426–28.

30. James L. Crenshaw, "A Mother's Instruction to Her Son (Proverbs 31:1–9)," *Perspectives in Religious Studies* 15 (1988) 9–22. For studies of the queen and the queen mother, see Athalya Brenner, *The Israelite Woman: Social Role and Literary Type in Biblical Narrative* (Sheffield: JSOT Press, 1985); Zafrira Ben-Barak, "The Status and Right of the *Gĕbîrâ*," *JBL* 110 (1991) 23–34; Ktziah Spanier, "The Queen Mother in the Judaean Royal Court: Maacah," in *A Feminist Companion to Samuel and Kings*, ed. Athalya Brenner (2nd ed.; Feminist Companion to the Bible 7; Sheffield: Sheffield Academic Press, 1994) 188–91; idem, "The Northern Israelite Queen Mother in the Judaean Court: Athaliah and Abi," in *Boundaries of the Ancient Near Eastern World: A Tribute to Cyrus H. Gordon*, ed. Meir Lubetzky, et al. (JSOTSup 273; Sheffield: Sheffield Academic Press, 1998) 136–49; Susan Ackermann, "The Queen Mother and the Cult in the Ancient Near East," in *Women and Goddess Traditions: In Antiquity and Today*, ed. Karen L. King (Studies in Antiquity and Christianity; Minneapolis: Fortress, 1997) 179–209; Nancy R. Bowen, "The Quest for the Historical *Gĕbîrâ*," *CBQ* 63 (2001) 597–618. Perhaps the sociopolitical position and functions of the queen mother helped to shape the description of Woman Wisdom.

31. For detailed studies of the queen and queen mother in Egypt, see Lana Troy, *Patterns of Queenship in Ancient Egyptian Myth and History* (Acta Universitatis Upsaliensis, Boreas, Uppsala Studies in Ancient Mediterranean and Near Eastern Civilizations 14; Uppsala: University of Uppsala Press, 1986); Silke Roth, *Die Königsmutter des alten Ägypten von der Frühzeit bus zum Ende der 12. Dynastie* (Ägypte und Altes Testament: Studien zu Geschichte, Kultur und Religion Ägyptens und des Alten Testaments 46; Wiesbaden: Harrassowitz, 2001).

32. Harold C. Washington, *Wealth and Poverty in the Instruction of Amenemope and the Hebrew Proverbs* (SBLDS 142; Atlanta: Scholars Press, 1994).

33. D. C. Simpson, "The Hebrew Book of Proverbs and the Teaching of Amenophis," *JEA* 12 (1926) 232–39.

34. Our knowledge of schools and education in ancient Israel, prior to Ben Sira, is limited and often inferential. Friedemann Golka's strong criticism of the evidence and argument for royal wisdom and schools in Israel is overstated to an extreme ("Die israelitischen Weisheitsschule oder 'des Kaisers neue Kleider,'" *VT* 33 [1983] 257–70; idem, *The Leopard's Spots: Biblical and African Wisdom in Proverbs* [Edinburgh: T. & T. Clark, 1993]). For a more recent assessment of

the evidence and the arguments, see James L. Crenshaw, *Education in Ancient Israel* (ABRL; New York: Doubleday, 1998) 85–113. Drawing on the evidence of Lemaire, he also concludes that the epigraphic evidence is enough to support the existence of schools at least as early as the eighth century BCE. He thinks that guilds and schools educated scribes prior to the collapse of the monarchy. Also see G. I. Davies, "Were There Schools in Ancient Israel?" in *Wisdom in Ancient Israel*, 199–211; E. W. Heaton, *The School Tradition of the Old Testament* (Oxford: Oxford University Press, 1994). David W. Jamieson-Drake on the basis of social and anthropological methods argues that by the eighth century Judah became a centralized state with its capital, Jerusalem, being the administrative center, requiring then a school to train scribes (*Scribes and Schools in Monarchic Judah: A Socio-Archaeological Approach* [JSOTSup 109; Sheffield: Almond, 1991]). By contrast, Stuart Weeks argues that both the epigraphic and the biblical evidence for the existence of schools in ancient Israel is rather weak and at the least negates the notion of "an integrated school system" (*Early Israelite Wisdom* [Oxford: Clarendon, 1994] 132–56).

35. See André Lemaire, *Les écoles et la formation de la Bible dans l'ancien Israel* (OBO 39; Göttingen: Vandenhoeck & Ruprecht, 1981); idem, "Sagesse et écoles," *VT* 34 (1984) 270–81; H.-J. Hermisson, *Studien zur israelitischen Spruchweisheit* (WMANT 28; Neukirchen-Vluyn: Neukirchener Verlag, 1968) 97–136; Bernhard Lang, "Schule und Unterricht im alten Israel," in *Sagesse de l'Ancien Testament*, 186–201. Pottery sherds on which were written schoolboy exercises have been identified at several locations (Gezer, Lachish, Arad, Kadesh-Barnea, Kuntilat Ajrud), which date from the twelfth century BCE and later.

36. Shupak, *Where Can Wisdom Be Found?* 350–51.

37. Several collections are arranged differently in the LXX: 30:1–14 occurs before 24:23, while 30:15–31:9 is placed after 24:34. This indicates that chaps. 24–31 were fluid in their placement in the larger book.

38. The sages' emphasis on proper speaking points to both the content and the literary beauty of sapiential language. See Walter Bühlmann, *Vom Rechten Reden und Schweigen: Studien zu Proverbien 10–31* (OBO 12; Göttingen: Vandenhoeck & Ruprecht, 1976).

39. See Christa Bauer Kayatz, *Studien zu Proverbien 1–9. Eine form- und motivgeschichtliche Untersuchung unter Einbeziehung ägyptischen Vergleichsmaterials* (WMANT 22; Neukirchen-Vluyn: Neukirchener Verlag, 1966). J. N. Aletti, "Seduction et parole en Proverbes I–IX," *VT* 27 (1977) 129–44; Carol A. Newsom, "Woman and the Discourse of Patriarchal Wisdom": A Study of Proverbs 1–9," *Gender and Difference in Ancient Israel,* ed. Peggy L. Day (Minneapolis: Fortress, 1989) 142–60.

40. See Kayatz, *Studien zu Proverbien 1–9.*

41. See Bernhard Lang, *Die weisheitliche Lehrrede* (SBS 54; Stuttgart: Katholisches Bibelwerk, 1971) 29. Also see R. N. Whybray, *Wisdom in Proverbs* (SBT 1/45; London: SCM, 1965). Those who date Prov. 1–9 in the postexilic period include Roland Murphy, "The Kerygma of the Book of Proverbs," *Int* 20 (1966) 4; Georg Fohrer, *Introduction to the Old Testament* (Nashville: Abingdon, 1968) 219.

42. For a study of Woman Wisdom's role as metaphor, see Claudia V. Camp, "Woman Wisdom as Root Metaphor: A Theological Consideration," in *The Listening Heart*, ed. Kenneth G. Hoglund, et al. (JSOTSup 58; Sheffield: Sheffield Academic Press, 1987) 45–76.

43. Newsom, "Woman and the Discourse of Patriarchal Wisdom."

44. Leo G. Perdue, "Wisdom Theology and Social History in Proverbs 1–9," *Wisdom, You Are My Sister*, ed. Michael L. Barré (CBQMS 29; Washington, DC: Catholic Biblical Association of America, 1997) 78–101.

45. Murphy, "Kerygma," 3–14. He notes that life in Proverbs is characterized by length of days (3:16; 28:16), a good name (10:7; 22:1), and abundant resources (22:4).

46. Raymond C. Van Leeuwen, "Liminality and World View in Proverbs 1–9," in *Paraenesis: Act and Form*, ed. Leo G. Perdue and John G. Gammie, *Semeia* 50 (1990) 111–44.

47. Otto Plöger, *Sprüche Salomos* (BKAT 17; Neukirchen-Vluyn: Neukirchener Verlag, 1981) 8–10.

48. *Protrepsis*, or exhortation, is issued to youths to study under a teacher who will teach them philosophy as a way of life (see my essay, "The Social Character of Paraenesis and Paranetic Literature," in *Paraenesis: Act and Form*, ed. Lee G. Perdue and John G. Gammie, *Semeia* 50 (1990) 5–39.

49. The expression occurs fourteen times in Proverbs. The word "beginning" (*rēʾšît*, ראשית) indicates that the "fear of Yahweh" is the necessary precondition of wisdom and its human quest, and the "foundation" of the sapiential tradition (Perdue, *Proverbs,* 36).

50. For comprehensive treatments of "fear of the Lord," see J. Becker, *Gottesfurcht im Alten Testament*; Johannes Marböck, "Im Horizont der Gottesfurcht," 47–70.

51. Numerous scholars have seen this "poem" as the combining of two separate ones: vv. 13–18 and 19–20 (e.g., R. B. Y. Scott, *Proverbs. Ecclesiastes* [AB; Garden City, NY: Doubleday, 1965], 45–46).

52. See my *Wisdom and Cult: A Critical Analysis of the Views of Cult in the Wisdom Literatures of the Ancient Near East* (SBLDS 30; Missoula, MN: Scholars Press, 1977) 299–312; Plöger, *Sprüche Salomos*, 36. Also see Arndt Meinhold, "Gott und Mensch in Proverbien 3," *VT* 37 (1987) 468–77.

53. See Erhard S. Gerstenberger, *Psalms,* vol. 1 (FOTL 14; Grand Rapids: Eerdmans, 1988) 16–19.

54. For detailed discussions of Woman Wisdom, see Gerlinde Baumann, *Die Weisheitsgestalt in Proverbien 1–9* (FAT 16; Tübingen: Mohr [Siebeck] 1996) 1–57; Bernhard Lang, *Frau Weisheit: Deutung einer biblischen Gestalt* (Düsseldorf: Patmos, 1975), 147–76.

55. Several scholars have seen in Woman Wisdom evidence of an Israelite goddess prior to the development of monotheism in Israel (Bernhard Lang, *Wisdom and the Book of Proverbs; A Hebrew Goddess Redefined* [New York: Pilgrim, 1986]; Camp, "Woman Wisdom as Root Metaphor," 45–76).

56. Gertie Englund, "Gods as a Frame of Reference: On Thinking and Concepts of Thought in Ancient Egypt," in *The Religion of the Ancient Egyptians: Cognitive Structures and Popular Expressions*, ed. Gertie Englund (Stockholm: Almqvist & Wiksell, 1989) 23. See Jan Assmann, *Maʿat: Gerechtigkeit und Unsterblichkeit im Alten Ägypten* (Munich: Beck, 1990).

57. Kayatz notes examples of the goddess Maʿat holding a symbol of life in one hand and a scepter symbolizing wealth and honor in the other (*Studien zu Proverbien 1–9*, 105).

58. Fertility religions describe the affections of goddesses and humans for one another.

59. Berend Gemser, *Sprüche Salomos* (2nd ed.; HAT 10; Tübingen: Mohr [Siebeck], 1963) 29.

60. See Judith M. Hadley, *The Cult of Asherah in Ancient Israel and Judah: The Evidence for a Hebrew Goddess* (Cambridge: Cambridge University Press, 2000).

61. Van Leeuwen, "Proverbs," 53. The children of the "Woman of Worth" call her "blessed" (31:28; cf. 3:13, 18; 8:32, 34), her gifts are of great value (31:10, 18; cf. 3:14–15; 8:11, 19), and nothing desirable is equal to her (31:10; cf. 3:15; 8:11).

62. See Norman Habel, "The Symbolism of Wisdom in Proverbs 1–9," *Int* 26 (1972) 131–57.

63. Prov. 3:19 closely compares to Jer. 10:12 (= 51:15), likely due to scribal redaction.

64. Othmar Keel, *The Symbolism of the Biblical World: Ancient Near Eastern Iconography and the Book of Psalms* (trans. Timothy J. Hallett; repr. Winona Lake, IN: Eisenbrauns, 1997) 16–26.

65. See Mary K. Wakeman, *God's Battle with the Monster* (Leiden: Brill, 1973); Foster McCurley, *Ancient Myths and Biblical Faith: Scriptural Transformations* (Philadelphia: Fortress, 1983) 11–71; Levenson, *Creation*.

66. See "The Creation Epic," *ANET*, 67. For a discussion of the chaos monster's defeat, see Hermann Gunkel, *Creation and Chaos in the Primeval Era and the Eschaton: A Religio-Historical Study of Genesis 1 and Revelation 12* (The Bible Resources Series; Grand Rapids: Eerdman, 2006).

67. See Gemser, *Sprüche Salomos*, 30.

68. See James G. Williams, "Proverbs and Ecclesiastes," in *The Literary Guide to the Bible*, ed. Robert Alter and Frank Kermode (Cambridge: Harvard University Press, 1987) 263–76.

69. See M. Gilbert, "Le discours de la sagesse en Proverbes 8," in *Sagesse de l'Ancien Testament*, 202–18; Patrick Skehan, "Structures in Poems on Wisdom: Proverbs 8 and Sirach 24," *CBQ* 41 (1979) 365–79.

70. Van Leeuwen ("Proverbs," 89) notes that many of the terms in Prov. 8 connect it to other passages in Prov. 1–9, thus indicating "that the book's teaching is grounded in cosmic wisdom" (e.g., 1:4 = 8:12; 1:7 = 8:13).

71. Keel, *Symbolism*, 16–26.

72. See Norman Habel's study of the "way" (*derek*, דרך; "Symbolism," 131–57). Using Ricoeur's understanding of "symbol," Habel argues that *derek* ("way") points to three "symbolic zones": personal experience (Prov. 4–6), Yahwistic religion and covenant (Prov. 1–3), and cosmological reflection (Prov. 7–9).

73. The "entrance of the portals" refers to the outer threshold of the main gate to a city.

74. The complex of the temple and house represents the summit of the cosmos in which life and the maintenance of order are sustained and empowered to continue. The building and maintenance of a "house" are metaphorical actions of cosmogony and providence.

75. See Yigal Shiloh, *Excavations at the City of David* (Jerusalem: Institute of Archaeology, Hebrew University, 1984).

76. Van Leeuwen ("Proverbs," 89) remarks: "In sum, the city is the culture-shaped world of humans, a reflection in miniature of the world itself where Lady Wisdom has been active from the beginning (8:22–31), and where she presently speaks to all humans (8:4, 31) in their condition of moral and spiritual ambiguity (8:5)."

77. Ibid.

78. This imagery suggests strongly a close association between wisdom and law.

79. One location mentioned in 1:20–33, but not repeated here, is the "square" (*rĕḥôb*, רחוב). While open to a variety of uses, the square or plaza is the place where business dealings were pursued (see Neh. 8:1, 3, 16) and where people gathered for various types of public assembly (2 Chr. 29:4; 32:6; Ezra 10:9). It is also a setting for sapiential teaching and lectures.

80. Wisdom is personified as a goddess initiating her cult in 9:1–6 and as an Israelite wife in 31:10–31. For the latter, see especially Thomas P. McCreesh, "Wisdom as Wife: Proverbs 31:10–31," *RB* 92 (1985) 25–46.

81. Creation also was personified as the "voice" of God speaking words that revealed the glory and handiwork of the Creator (see Ps. 19:4).

82. The sage who creates this poem draws heavily on the myth of the goddesses Ma'at and Isis in Egyptian religion.

83. See K.-H. Bernhardt, *Das Problem der altorientalischen Königs-Ideologie im Alten Testament* (VTSup 8: Leiden: Brill); Henri Frankfort, *Kingship and the Gods: A Study of Ancient Near Eastern Religion as the Integration of Society and Nature* (Chicago: University of Chicago Press, 1948); Winfried Barta, "Königsdogma," *LÄ* III (1980) 485–94; *The Sacral Kingship; Contributions to the Central Theme of the VIIIth International Congress for the History of Religions (Rome, April 1955)* (Numen Sup 4; Leiden: Brill, 1959).

84. For a discussion of the theology of kingship and in particular the legitimation of the dynasty of David, see Albertz, *History of Israelite Religion,* 1:114–26.

85. See Katherine Sakenfeld, *The Meaning of Ḥesed in the Hebrew Bible: A New Inquiry* (HSM 17; Missoula, MT: Scholars Press, 1978).

86. See Roland Murphy, "Wisdom and Eros in Prov. 1–9," *CBQ* 50 (1988) 600–603.

87. P. A. H. de Boer, "The Counsellor," in *Wisdom in Israel and in the Ancient Near East: FS H. H. Rowley,* ed. M. Noth and D. Winton Thomas (VTSup 3; Leiden: Brill, 1955). 42–71.

88. Among the important studies of this poem, see Othmar Keel, *Die Weisheit spielt vor Gott* (Göttingen: Vandenhoeck & Ruprecht, 1974); Herbert Donner, "Die religionsgeschichtlichen Ursprünge von Prov. Sal. 8, 22–31," *ZÄS* 82 (1957) 8–18; J. N. Aletti, "Proverbes 8:22–31: Étude et structure," *Bib* 57 (1976) 25–37; R. B. Y. Scott, "Wisdom in Creation: The *'Āmôn* of Proverbs VIII 30," *VT* 10 (1960) 213–23; Gale A. Yee, "An Analysis of Prov. 8:22–31 according to Style and Structure," *ZAW* 94 (1982) 58–66.

89. See Jan Assmann, *Ägypten—Theologie und Frömmigkeit einer frühen Hochkultur* (Stuttgart: Kohlhammer, 1991), especially 211, Coffin Text 80; Donner, "Die religionsgeschichtlichen Ursprünge," 8–18.

90. The verb *qānâ* (קנה) may mean "acquire" or "obtain" as in the sense of acquiring wisdom (Prov. 1:5; 4:5, 7) or "purchase" as in buying a male Hebrew slave (Exod. 21:2). In several texts, however, the verb means "create," as in God creating heaven and earth (Gen. 14:19, 22) or human beings (Gen. 4:1; Ps. 139:13). In the case of creating, the specific nuance is that of procreating as in Deut. 32:6, where God created, i.e., fathered, Israel. "Create" fits the sense of the entire text, especially since the verb *ḥûl* (חול) is used in vv. 24 and 25 ("to writhe in birth pains"). For *qnh* as an epithet of God as creator, also see the inscription *qn 'rṣ* ("creator of the earth") found on the Western Hill in Jerusalem and the Phoenician inscription of Karatepe, *'l qn 'rṣ* ("El, creator of the earth"). For El as creator, see the studies of Patrick Miller, "El, the Creator of the Earth," *BASOR* 239 (1980) 43–46; J. C. de Moor, "El, the Creator," in *The Bible World: Essays in Honor of Cyrus H. Gordon,* ed. Gary Rendsburg, et al. (New York: Ktav, 1980) 171–87.

91. Prov. 8:24, 25. The verb *ḥûl* (חול) reflects the activity of writhing in birth pains (Deut. 32:18; Job 39:1; Pss. 29:9; 51:7; 90:2). The verb in Prov. 8:24 and 25 is passive, "I was brought forth" or "I was given birth," with Yahweh likely the mother.

92. See Job 40:19, where Behemoth, a chaos monster, is the "first [or best] of El's works" of creation. *Derek* (דרך) is placed in parallel to *pĕ'ālāyw* (פעליו, "things made"), a term referring to various types of works or actions, including creation and God's activities as creator (Job 36:3; Prov. 16:4; Isa. 45:9, 11).

93. See the struggle for this birthright between Jacob and Esau in Gen. 25:24–26 and 38:27–30). For a full discussion of the privileges of the firstborn, see Roland de Vaux, *Ancient Israel,* vol. 1: *Social Institutions* (repr. New York: McGraw-Hill, 1965) 40–41.

94. The Masoretic pointing, *layyām* (לְיָם), reads "to the sea." However, repointing the consonants allows one to read *lĕyām* ("to Yamm").

95. See Scott, "Wisdom in Creation," 213–33.

96. The word *'āmôn* occurs elsewhere only in Jer. 52:15, where it refers to a group of artisans. A related term, *'ommān*, appears in Cant. 7:2, possibly meaning "master workman." The term is suggestive of Akkadian *ummanu*, "master worker," "skilled laborer," and "counselor, advisor." If this meaning is followed, then Wisdom is the coworker with Yahweh in creation and his advisor.

97. See Yahweh's "rejoicing" (*ša'ăsu'îm*, שעשעים; "delights") over his dear son Ephraim (Jer. 31:20; cf. Isa. 66:12). The verb *śāḥaq* (שחק) also means "to play with," "to play" (Zech. 8:5), and "to dance" (2 Sam. 6:5, 21).

98. See Keel, *Weisheit spielt vor Gott*; Samuel Terrien, "The Play of Wisdom: Turning Point in Biblical Theology," *HBT* 3 (1981) 125–53.

99. For a discussion of death in the OT, see Ludwig Wächter, *Der Tod im Alten Testament* (Arbeiten zur Theologie 8; Stuttgart: Calwer, 1964).

100. See H.-J. Kraus, *Die Verkündigung der Weisheit* (Biblische Studien 2; Neukirchen Kreis Moers: Buchhandlung des Erziehungsvereins, 1951).

101. Eliade notes that traditional societies seek through mythic celebration to return to those formative acts of creation in the beginning of time in order to secure and empower the present (*Cosmos and History*).

102. Gale A. Yee, "The Theology of Creation in Proverbs 8:22–31," in *Creation in the Biblical Traditions*, 90.

103. Albertz, *Weltschöpfung und Menschenschöpfung*; Doll, *Menschenschöpfung und Weltschöpfung*; H. J. Hermisson, "Observations on the Creation Theology in Wisdom," in *Israelite Wisdom: FS Gammie*, 43–57; Walther Zimmerli, "The Place and Limit of the Wisdom in the Framework of the Old Testament Theology," *SJT* 17 (1964) 146–58.

104. It is noteworthy that Woman Wisdom is not only portrayed as a goddess and a teacher of wisdom. She is also incarnate in the "woman of worth" in Prov. 31:10–31. See Christine Roy Yoder, "The Woman of Substance (אשת-חיל): A Socioeconomic Reading of Proverbs 31:10–31," *JBL* 122 (2003) 427–47. Her most important conclusion is that "the woman of worth" may reflect "real women in the Persian period."

105. Gemser, *Sprüche Salomos*, 55. For a detailing of themes in this collection, see Udo Skladny, *Die ältesten Spruchsammlungen in Israel* (Göttingen: Vandenhoeck & Ruprecht, 1962).

106. Bühlmann, *Vom Rechten Reden und Schweigen*.

107. The topic of rich and poor is a common one in this collection (10:15; 11:28; 13:7, 18, 23; 14:20, 21, 31; 17:5; 18:23; 19:4, 7, 17, 22; 21:13; 22:2, 7, 16; cf. 3:27–28; 23:4–5, 28:6, 11; 30:7–9). For an overview see Raymond Van Leeuwen, "Wealth and Poverty: System and Contradiction in Proverbs," *Hebrew Studies* 33 (1992) 25–36; Washington, *Wealth and Poverty*; R. N. Whybray, *Wealth and Poverty in the Book of Proverbs* (JSOTSup 99; Sheffield: JSOT Press, 1990); J. David Pleins, "Poverty in the Social World of the Wise," *JSOT* 37 (1987) 61–78.

108. De Vaux, *Ancient Israel* 1:21–22.

109. Ibid., 21–22, 37–38.

110. Ibid., 72–74.

111. See Washington, *Wealth and Poverty*.

112. Van Leeuwen, "Wealth and Poverty," 33.

113. See Alfred Dünner, *Die Gerechtigkeit nach dem Alten Testament* (Schriften zur Rechtslehre und Politik 42; Bonn: H. Bouvier, 1963) 63–64.

114. Skladny notes: "The responsibility of humans to both their fellow human beings and to Yahweh and his order result from the recognition of their creaturely status" (*Die ältesten Spruchsammlungen*, 27).

115. The term *dal* (דל) occurs fifteen times in this collection, seven times in chaps. 25–29, and twice in 22:22. The word *'ebyôn* (עביון) is found three times in Proverbs (30:14; 31:9, 20), all in relationship to *'ānî* (עני); also see Deut. 15:11; 24:11, 15; Job 24:12; Isa. 3:14, 15. These three terms for "poor" are found forty-two times in Proverbs, predominantly in 10:1–22:16.

116. The term *'ōśēh* may mean "creator," and the verb *'āśâ* (עשה) also may connote "to create" (Gen. 1:7, 16, 25; 3:1; Job 9:9; 31:15; 40:19; Prov. 14:31; 17:5, 7).

117. For important discussions of theodicy, see Levenson, *Creation*. Also see Crenshaw, "Introduction: The Shift from Theodicy to Anthropodicy," in *Theodicy in the Old Testament*, ed. Crenshaw (IRT 4; Philadelphia: Fortress, 1983) 1–16; idem, *Whirlpool of Torment: Israelite Traditions of God as an Oppressive Presence* (OBT; Philadelphia: Fortress, 1984); idem, *Defending God: Biblical Responses to the Problem of Evil* (Oxford: Oxford University Press, 2005).

118. Leo G. Perdue, "Cosmology and the Social Order," in *Sage in Israel*, 457–78.

119. See Hermisson, *Studien zur israelitischen Spruchweisheit*, 46.

120. This verb and its pronominal suffix also may be translated "its counterpart" (see Boström, *God of the Sages*, 60–61).

121. See von Rad, *Wisdom in Israel*, 138–43.

122. Hans Heinrich Schmid, *Gerechtigkeit als Weltordnung Hintesgrund und Geschichte der alttestamentlichen Gerechtigkeitsbegriffes* (Tübingen: Mohr [Siebeck], 1968).

123. "Gerechtigkeit als Fundament des Thrones," 426–28. Cf. Miriam Lichtheim, *Maat in Egyptian Autobiographies and Related Studies* (OBO 120; Göttingen: Vandenhoeck & Ruprecht, 1992).

124. De Vaux, *Ancient Israel*, 1:195–209.

125. Boström, *God of the Sages*, 62.

126. Scott, *Proverbs. Ecclesiastes*, 110.

127. Perdue, "Wisdom in the Book of Job," in *In Search of Wisdom*, 73–76.

128. Van Leeuwen, "Proverbs," 186.

129. Scott (*Proverbs Ecclesiastes*, 128) offers three possibilities of the meaning of "meet together": "This may mean (a) that they share a common humanity, (b) that God has willed their station in life, and may reverse it, or (c) that personal worth is more important then wealth. . . ." I lean toward the first meaning.

130. H. Schmoldt, "עתק," *TDOT* 11 (2001) 456; i.e., "moved from one place to another." Thus the term would suggest the activity of "editing." The LXX translates the verb as *exegrapsanto* (ἐξεγραψάντο), "copied." The "men of Hezekiah" working as scribes in the eighth century BCE correlates with the epigraphic evidence.

131. Glendon Bryce ("Another Wisdom 'Book' in Proverbs," *JBL* 91 [1972] 145–57) has argued that 25:2–27 is a sayings collection that deals with the relationship of the ruler (vv. 6–15) and the wicked (vv. 16–26).

132. Perdue, *Proverbs*, 246–49.

133. Van Leeuwen argues that these chapters consist of a proverb poem addressed to courtiers (25:2–27), a proverb poem dealing with the fool (26:1–12), a proverb poem focusing on the sluggard (26:13–16), a proverb poem that develops the themes of chap. 25 (26:17–18), a collection of miscellaneous proverbs (27:1–22), and an admonitory poem addressed to a shepherd, possibly meaning the king (27:23–27). See his *Context and Meaning*.

134. See Georg Sauer, *Die Sprüche Agurs* (BWANT 4; Stuttgart: Kohlhammer, 1963); Paul Franklyn, "The Sayings of Agur in Proverbs 30: Piety or Scepticism?" *ZAW* 95 (1983) 238–51.

135. An Akkadian word, *maš*, postulated on the basis of Assyrian *maš'ayya*, the "Masa'aean," may refer to an Arabian tribe.

136. See 31:1–9, an instruction to Lemuel that originates in the court or ruling counsel of the Arabic tribe of Massa.

137. "Words" (*dĕbārîm*, דברים) on occasion refers to the content and various forms of language present in sapiential collections (Prov. 4:20, 31:1; Qoh. 1:1).

138. Other examples of the possible blending of prophecy and wisdom are Amos (Hans Walter Wolff, *Amos' Geistige Heimat* [WMANT 18; Neukirchen-Vluyn: Neukirchener Verlag, 1964]) and Isaiah (J. William Whedbee, *Isaiah and Wisdom* [Nashville: Abingdon, 1971]).

139. Hans Peter Müller, "Mantische Weisheit und Apokalyptik," in *Congress Volume: Uppsala 1971* (VTSup 22; Leiden: Brill, 1972) 268–93. In addition, see my "Wisdom and Apocalyptic: The Case of Qoheleth," in *Wisdom and Apocalypticism in the Dead Sea Scrolls and in the Biblical Tradition*, ed. Florentino García Martínez (BETL 168; Leuven: Leuven University Press, 2003) 231–58.

140. The translation of the middle part of v. 1 is notoriously difficult (*lĕ'îtî'ēl*, לאיתיאל), leading to many different proposals. Other translations include: "I am not God, I am not God"; "God is not with me, God is not with me"; "Surely God is with me, surely God is with me"; "To Ithiel, to Ithiel and Ucal" (two addressees of the collection?); and "there is no God."

141. The plural *qĕdōšîm* (קדשים) plausibly refers to the members of the divine council (Job 5:1; 15:15; Ps. 89:6, 8).

142. *Wisdom in Revolt.*

143. See my *Wisdom in Revolt*, 70–72.

144. This is true of Yahweh's rhetorical questions to his human antagonist, Job.

145. See "*apkallu*," *Chicago Assyrian Dictionary*, 1/2:171–73; Erica Reiner, "The Etiological Myth of the 'Seven Sages,'" *Or* 30 (1961) 1–11.

146. See the same question in "The Dialogue of Pessimism," *BWL*, 139–49; and Gilgamesh, *ANET*, 79.

147. This is a rejection of the claims of apocalyptic's heavenly journeys of seers.

148. Rykle Borger, "Die Beschwörungsserie *bit meseri* und die Himmeltfahrt Henochs," *JNES* 33 (1974) 193–95.

149. See Frederick Greenspahn, "A Mesopotamian Proverb and Its Biblical Reverberations," *JAOS* (1994) 33–38.

150. See Raymond van Leeuwen, "Proverbs 30:21–23 and the Biblical World Upside Down," *JBL* 105 (1986) 599–610.

151. While *nābāl* (נבל) usually refers to the fool (Prov. 17:7, 21; Job 30:8), it may also mean a person of low social rank (2 Sam. 3:33). See C. H. Toy, *A Critical and Exegetical Commentary on the Book of Proverbs* (ICC; Edinburgh: T. & T. Clark, 1899) 533.

152. See Helmer Ringgren, "Sprüche," in Ringgren, Walther Zimmerli, and Otto Kaiser, *Sprüche/Prediger; Das Hohe Lied/Klagelieder, Das Buch Esther* (3rd rev. ed.; ATD 16; Göttingen: Vandenhoeck & Ruprecht, 1981) 116; Toy, *Proverbs*, 352.

153. Brevard Childs, "The Enemy from the North and the Chaos Tradition," *JBL* 78 (1959) 187–98.

154. Michel Foucault points to the intrinsic relationship between knowledge and power. For Foucault, every text reflects the social ideology of its community that gave it form and substance and is set on achieving what is in its best interests. See *The Archaeology of Knowledge and the Discourse on Language* (New York: Pantheon, 1982); and *Power* (ed. James Faubian; London: Penguin, 2002).

Chapter 4: Exilic Wisdom and the Babylonian Sapiential Tradition: The Book of Job

1. See *Wisdom in Revolt*.
2. For Mesopotamia see Wolfram von Soden, *The Ancient Orient: An Introduction to the Study of the Ancient East* (Grand Rapids: Eerdmans, 1985); A. Leo Oppenheim, *Ancient Mesopotamia: Portrait of a Dead Civilization* (rev. ed. Erica Reiner; Chicago: University of Chicago Press, 1996). For works on the Neo-Babylonian Empire and Judah, see Oded Lipschits and Joseph Blenkinsopp, eds., *Judah and the Judeans in the Neo-Babylonian Period* (Winona Lake, IN: Eisenbrauns, 2003); David S. Vanderhooft, *The Neo-Babylonian Empire and Babylon in the Latter Prophets* (HSM 59; Atlanta: Scholars Press, 1999).
3. See Hans-Peter Müller, ed., *Babylonien und Israel: Historische, religiöse und sprachliche Beziehungen* (Darmstadt: Wissenschaftliche Buchgesellschaft, 1991).
4. See Peter R. Ackroyd, "Interpretation of the Babylonian Exile: A Study of 2 Kings 20, Isaiah 38–39," *SJT* 27 (1974) 329–52; Yigael Shiloh, "Judah and Jerusalem in the Eighth-Sixth Centuries B.C.E.," in *Recent Excavations in Israel: Studies in Iron Age Archaeology*, ed. Seymour Gitin and William G. Dever (ASOR 49; Winona Lake, IN: Eisenbrauns, 1989) 97–105; Daniel L. Smith, *The Religion of the Landless: The Social Context of the Babylonian Exile* (Bloomington, IN: Meyer-Stone, 1990); T. C. Mitchell, "The Babylonian Exile and the Restoration of the Jews in Palestine (586–c. 500 B.C.)" in *Cambridge Ancient History*, vol. III/2: *The Assyrian and Babylonian Empires and Other States of the Near East, from the Eighth to the Sixth Centuries B.C.*, ed. John Boardman, et al. (2nd ed.; Cambridge: Cambridge University Press, 1991) 410–60; Robert P. Carroll, "The Myth of the Empty Land," *Semeia* 59 (1992) 79–93; Bustenay Oded, "Observations on the Israelite/Judaean Exiles in Mesopotamia during the Eighth-Sixth Centuries B.C.E.," in *Immigration and Emigration within the Ancient Near East*, ed. Karel van Lerberghe and Antoon Schoors (OLA 65; Leuven: Peeters, 1995) 205–12; H. M. Barstad, *The Myth of the Empty Land: A Study in the History and Archaeology of Judah During the "Exilic" Period* (Symbolae Osloenses Fascicle Sup 28; Oslo: Scandinavian University Press, 1996); Daniel L. Smith-Christopher, *A Biblical Theology of Exile* (OBT; Minneapolis: Fortress, 2002).
5. This language is taken from the Chronicler's image of the land that was "emptied" or "lay in waste" (see 2 Chr. 36:17–21). For the minimalist position, see Barstad, *Myth of the Empty Land*; idem, "After the 'Myth of the Empty Land': Major Challenges in the Study of Neo-Babylonian Judah," in *Judah and the Judeans*, 3–20. See the responses to this position in this same collection: Lisbeth S. Fried, "The Land Lay Desolate: Conquest and Restoration in the Ancient Near East," 21–54; Bustenay Oded, "Where Is the 'Myth of the Empty Land' to Be Found? History versus Myth," 55–74.
6. Peter Frei and Klaus Koch, *Reichsidee und Reichsorganisation im Perserreich* (2nd ed.; OBO 55; Göttingen: Vandenhoeck & Ruprecht, 1996). Cf. Jon L. Berquist, *Judaism in Persia's Shadow: A Social and Historical Approach* (Minneapolis: Fortress, 1995).
7. See the essays that are critical of these views in James W. Watts, ed., *Persia and Torah: The Theory of Imperial Authorization of the Pentateuch* (SBLSymS 17; Atlanta: SBL, 2001).
8. John Bright, *A History of Israel* (3rd ed.; Philadelphia: Westminster, 1981); John H. Hayes and J. Maxwell Miller, eds., *Israelite and Judaean History* (OTL; Philadelphia: Westminster, 1977); Ephraim Stern, *Archaeology of the Land of the Bible*, vol. 2: *The Assyrian, Babylonian, and Persian Periods, 732–332 BCE* (ABRL; New York: Doubleday, 2001).

9. Lawrence Stager, "The Fury of Babylon: Ashkelon and the Archaeology of Destruction," *BAR* 22, no. 1 (1996) 69.

10. William Schniedewind, "In Search of the Exile," SBL Annual Meeting, Boston, 1999. Quoted in Smith-Christopher, *Biblical Theology of Exile*, 47, n. 59. Schniedewind notes that some 80 percent of the cities, towns, and villages were either destroyed or abandoned in the sixth century BCE, while 42 percent of the Persian cities were new. See the study by Vanderhooft, *Neo-Babylonian Empire*, who is also critical of Barstad's thesis. He argues, in contrast to Barstad, that the first half of the sixth century BCE witnessed significantly reduced economic activity. In addition, Stern and Vanderhooft point to the substantial archaeological evidence for the destruction of Judah during the early part of the sixth century. Indeed, Stager's excavation at Ashkelon points to a significant destruction of the city, likely the one by Nebuchadrezzar II in 604, that was followed by a period of nonoccupation for seventy to eighty years ("The Fury of Babylon: Ashkelon and the Archaeology of Destruction," *BAR* 22 [1996] 69; cf. Amélie Kuhrt, *The Ancient Near East* [2 vols.; New York: Routledge, 1997] 2:593; Stern, *Archaeology*, 2:326).

11. Christopher-Smith, *Biblical Theology of Exile*, 47.

12. Carroll, "Myth of the Empty Land."

13. Smith-Christopher, *Biblical Theology of Exile*, 32.

14. Ran Zadok, *The Jews in Babylonia during the Chaldean and Achaemenian Periods according to the Babylonian Sources* (Haifa: University of Haifa, 1979).

15. Peter R. Ackroyd, *Exile and Restoration* (OTL; Philadelphia: Westminster, 1968) 32.

16. Oded, "Observations." The Murashu documents mention slave status for some exiles.

17. R. McCormick Adams, *Heartland of Cities: Surveys of Ancient Settlement and Land Use on the Central Floodplain of the Euphrates* (Chicago: University of Chicago Press, 1981).

18. Smith-Christopher, *Biblical Theology of Exile*, 66–67.

19. Bustenay Oded, "Judah and the Exile," *Israelite and Judaean History*, 483.

20. Oded, "Observations."

21. See Jean Lévêque, *Job et son Dieu: Essai d'exégèse et de théologie biblique* (2 vols.; Paris: Gabalda, 1970), especially 1:13–16; idem, "Chapitre III: Sagesse et paradoxe dans le livre de Job," *Sagesse biblique*, 99–128.

22. See Samuel Terrien, "Quelques remarques sur les affinités de Job avec le Deutéro-Esaïe," *Volume du Congrès: Génève 1965* (VTSup 15; Leiden: Brill, 1966) 295–310.

23. For introductions to the Babylonian wisdom traditon, see *BWL*, and Jean Bottéro, *Mesopotamia: Writing, Reasoning, and the Gods* (Chicago: University of Chicago Press, 1992).

24. *BWL*, 1.

25. Denning-Bolle (*Wisdom in Akkadian Literature*, 34–39) provides a detailed list of words for "wisdom/wise" in Akkadian with numerous textual examples.

26. Ibid., 38–39.

27. For wisdom and priestly religion see my chapter on Mesopotamia in *Wisdom and Cult*, 85–133. For wisdom and esoteric knowledge, see the essays in Florentino García Martínez, ed., *Wisdom and Apocalyptic* (BETL 168; Leuven: Leuven University Press, 2003).

28. See the Myth of Atra-ḫasis, discussed below.

29. Berossus provides a late account of the many areas of study in which the sages were involved (S. M. Burstein, *The Babyloniaca of Berossus* [Malibu: Undena,

1978]). See W. G. Lambert, "Ancestors, Authors, and Canonicity," *JCS* 11 (1957) 1–14; Samuel Noah Kramer, *Sumerians: Their History, Culture, and Character* (Chicago: University of Chicago Press, 1963), 165–248; Adam Falkenstein, "Die babylonische Schule," *Saeculum* 4 (1953) 125–37; Benno Landsberger, "Scribal Concepts of Education," in *City Invincible*, ed. Carl H. Kraeling and Robert M. Adadms (Chicago: University of Chicago Press, 1958), 94–123; D. E. Weisberg, *Guild Structure and Political Allegiance in Early Achaemenid Mesopotamia* (Baltimore: Johns Hopkins University Press, 1967); A. Leo Oppenheim, "The Position of the Intellectual in Mesopotamian Society," *Wisdom, Revelation, and Doubt: Perspectives on the First Millennium BC*, 37–46; A. W. Sjöberg, "The Old Babylonian Edubba," in *Sumerological Studies in Honor of Thorkild Jacobsen on His Seventieth Birthday*, ed. S. Lieberman (Assyriological Studies 20; Chicago: University of Chicago Press, 1975) 159–79.

30. For Sumer see S. N. Kramer, "Sumerian Wisdom Literature: A Preliminary Survey," *BASOR* 122 (1951) 28–31; E. Gordon, "A New Look at the Wisdom of Sumer and Akkad," *BO* 17 (1960) 122–52; J. J. A. van Dijk, *La sagesse suméro-akkadiene* (Leiden: Brill, 1953). For Akkadian wisdom forms see *BWL*. See Willem H. Ph. Römer, *Weisheitstexte, Mythen und Epen*, vol. 1: *Weisheitstexte* (TUAT 3: Gütersloh-Mohn, 1990) 17ff.

31. See Wolfram von Soden, "'Weisheittexte' in akkadischer Sprache," in *Weisheitstexte*, 143–57; Hallo, *Context of Scripture*, 1:492–95; Benno Landsberger, "Die babylonische Theodizee," *Zeitschrift für Assyriologie* 43 (1936) 32–76; J. J. Stamm, "Die Theodizee in Babylon und Israel," *JEOL* 9 (1944) 99–107; Georgio Buccellati, "Tre saggi sulla sapienza mesopotamica, III. La teodicea: Condanna dell'abulia politica," *OrAnt* 11 (1972) 161–78.

32. *BWL*, 63–64, dates it from around 1000 BCE.

33. For the questioning of divine justice, see Dorthea Sitzler, "*Vorwurf gegen Gott*": *Ein religiöses Motiv im Alten Orient (Ägypten und Mesopotamien)* (Studies in Oriental Religions 32; Wiesbaden: Harrassowitz, 1995).

34. Jean Nougayrol, "Une version ancienne du 'Juste Souffrant,'" *RB* 59 (1952) 1–43. Also see Jean Bottéro, "Juste souffrant (R.S. 25.46)," *Ugaritica* V, ed. Jean Nougayrol, et al. (Paris: Librairie Orientaliste Paul Guethner, 1968) 265–99; idem, "Le problème du mal en Mesopotamie ancienne: Prologue à une étude du 'juste souffrant,'" *Recherches et documents du Centre Thomas More* (1977) Document 76/7.

35. For a detailed study of dialogues in Akkadian wisdom, see Denning-Bolle, *Wisdom in Akkadian Literature*, 85–175; also see her essay, "Wisdom and Dialogue in the Ancient Near East," *Numen* 34 (1987) 214–34. In addition see the Sumerian "A Man and His God," and a number of Akkadian texts, "Dialogue between Two Gods," "Dialogue between a Teacher and his Student," a variety of contests involving a dialogue between two or three speakers to discuss who or what is the best or better among the things or actions compared.

36. See *BWL*, 21–62; von Soden, *Weisheitstexte*, 110–35; *COS*, 1:486–92.

37. Von Soden, *Weisheitstexte*, 135–40.

38. See Jacob Klein, "'Personal God' and Individualized Prayer in Sumerian Religion," *Archiv für Orientforschung Beiheft* 19 (1982) 295–306.

39. *ANET*, 589–91; Römer, *Weisheitstexte*,102–9; *COS*, 1:485. For three school dialogues, see *COS*, 1:589–93.

40. *BWL*, 139–49; von Soden, *Weisheitstexte*, 158–63; *COS*, 1:495–96. E. A. Speiser ("The Case of the Obliging Servant," *JCS* 8 [1954] 98–105) interprets this text as satire.

41. See James M. Lindenberger, *The Aramaic Proverbs of Ahiqar* (Baltimore: Johns Hopkins University Press, 1983); Ingo Kottsieper, *Die Sprache der Ahiqarsprüche*

(BZAW 194; Berlin: de Gruyter, 1990); idem, "Die Geschichte und die Sprüche des weisen Achiqar," in J. Assmann, et al., *Weisheitstexte,* vol. 2: *Religiöse Texte, Lieder und Gebete* (TUAT 3: Gütersloh: Mohn, 1991) 320–47.

42. Kottsieper dates the sayings no later than the beginning of the seventh century BCE, if not earlier (*Weisheitstexte,* 2:320–47); cf. Lindenberger, *Aramaic Proverbs of Ahiqar,* 20.

43. See Jonas Greenfield, "Background and Parallel to a Proverb of Ahiqar," in *Hommages à André Dupont-Sommer,* ed. A. Caquot and M. Philonenko (Paris: Adrien-Maisonneuve, 1971) 49–59.

44. Manfried Dietrich, "Babylonische Sklaven auf der Schreiberschule: Anspielungen auf Ṭup šarrūtu-Lehrverträge in OIP 114,83 und YOS 19,110," *Veenhof Anniversary Volume,* ed. W. H. Van Soldt (Leiden: Nederlands Instituut voor het Nabije Oosten, 2001) 67–81.

45. Lindenberger, *Aramaic Proverbs of Ahiqar,* 13.

46. The translation comes from ibid., 68.

47. A number of scholars have understood Job's opponents as professional sages. For example, see Viktor Maag, *Hiob: Wandlung und Verarbeitung des Problems in Novelle, Dialogdichtung und Spätfassungen* (FRLANT 128; Göttingen: Vandenhoeck & Ruprecht, 1982) 125. Others disagree: Rainer Albertz, "The Sage and Pious Wisdom in the Book of Job: The Friends' Perspective," in *Sage in Israel,* 243–61.

48. See Samuel Terrien, "Job as a Sage," in *Sage in Israel,* 231–61.

49. See 2 Sam. 13:4.

50. Albertz, "Sage and Pious Wisdom," 247.

51. Albertz, "Der sozialgeschichtliche Hintergund des Hiobbuches und der 'Babylonischen Theodizee,'" in *Die Botschaft und die Boten,* ed. Jörg Jeremias and Lothar Perlitt (Neukirchen-Vluyn: Neukirchener Verlag, 1981) 349–72.

52. *Those Who Ponder Proverbs: Aphoristic Thinking and Biblical Literature* (Sheffield: Almond Press, 1981).

53. Jacques Vermeylen, *Job, ses amis et son Dieu: La legende de Job et ses relectures postexiliques* (Leiden: Brill, 1986) 72–79.

54. Albertz ("Sage and Pious Wisdom," 249–50) placed Job, prior to his cataclysmic fall, in the "pious circles of the upper class." While not considering him to be a professional sage, Albertz does note that Job is the teacher who "gives counsel" (*yāʿaṣ,* יעץ; 26:3, 29:21), teaches (*yārâ;* ירה; 6:24; 8:10), and "transmits knowledge/perceives" (*yāda,* ידע; *bîn,* בין; 6:24; 26:3). His opponents "provide guidance and instruction" (*yāsar,* יסר; *yākaḥ,* יכח, hiphil; *mûsār,* מוסר; *tôkaḥat,* תוחכה; 4:3, 6, 25–26; 15:2; 19:5; 20:3; 32:12).

55. Norman C. Habel, "In Defense of God the Sage," in *The Voice from the Whirlwind: Interpreting the Book of Job,* ed. Leo G. Perdue and W. Clark Gilpin (Nashville: Abingdon, 1992) 21–38.

56. Claus Westermann, *The Structure of the Book of Job* (trans. Charles A. Muenchow; Philadelphia: Fortress, 1981).

57. Hartmut Gese, *Lehre und Wirklichkeit in der alten Weisheit* (Tübingen: Mohr [Siebeck], 1958).

58. Heinz Richter, *Studien zu Hiob* (Theologische Arbeiten 11; Berlin: Evangelische Verlaganstalt, 1955) 131; Berend Gemser, "The *Rîb-* or Controversy-Pattern in Hebrew Mentality," in *Wisdom in Israel and in the Ancient Near East,* 120-37.

59. Georg Fohrer, *Das Buch Hiob* (KAT 16; Gütersloh: Mohn, 1963).

60. Denning-Bolle, *Wisdom in Akkadian Literature,* 136–58; John Gray, "The Book of Job in the Context of Near Eastern Literature," *ZAW* 82 (1970) 251–69; Moshe Weinfeld, "Job and Its Mesopotamian Parallels—A Typological Analysis," in *Text and Context: Old Testament and Semitic Studies for F. C. Fensham,* ed. W. Claassen (JSOTSup 48; Sheffield: Sheffield Academic Press, 1988) 217–26.

61. Cf. Norman Habel, *The Book of Job* (OTL; Philadelphia: Westminster, 1985); David J. A. Clines, *Job 1–20* (WBC 17; Waco: Word, 1989).

62. For example, see Carol A. Newsom, "The Book of Job," *NIB* 5 (1997) 321.

63. The Egyptian "Protests of the Eloquent Peasant" is translated and interpreted in Lichtheim, *Ancient Egyptian Literature,* 1:169–84.

64. "The Poor Man of Nippur" is translated in Benjamin R. Foster, *From Distant Days: Myths, Tales, and Poetry of Ancient Mesopotamia* (Bethesda, MD: CDL, 1995), 357–62; von Soden, *Weisheitstexte,* 174–80.

65. Harry Hoffner Jr., *COS,* 1:153–55.

66. See Erhard S. Gerstenberger, "The Psalms," in *Old Testament Form Criticism,* ed. John Hayes (San Antonio: Trinity University Press, 1977), 179–223; idem, *Psalms* 1 (FOTL 14; Grand Rapids: Eerdmans, 1988) 14–15.

67. Foster, *From Distant Days,* 295–97.

68. *BWL,* 21–62.

69. See Loren R. Mack-Fisher, "A Survey and Reading Guide to the Didactic Literature of Ugarit: Prolegomenon to a Study on the Sage," in *Sage in Israel,* 67–80; idem., "The Scribe (and Sage) in the Royal Court at Ugarit," ibid., 109–15.

70. *ANET,* 601–4 (see Perdue, *Wisdom and Cult,* 105–6). Also see Jean-Jacques Glassner, "The Use of Knowledge in Ancient Mesopotamia," *CANE* 3 (1995) 1816. See also F. Nötscher, "Biblische und Babylonische Weisheit," *BZ* 6 (1962) 120–26.

71. Foster, *From Distant Days,* 295–97.

72. Lichtheim, *Ancient Egyptian Literature,* 1:169–84.

73. Ibid., 163–69.

74. Franz Hesse, *Hiob* (ZBK; Zurich: Theologische Verlag, 1978) 7–12; Victor Maag, *Hiob: Wandlung und Verarbeitung des Problems in Novelle, Dialogdichtung und Spätfassungen* (FRLANT 128; Göttingen: Vandenhoeck & Ruprecht, 1982) 13–19; Markus Witte, *Vom Leiden zur Lehre: Der dritte Redegang (Hiob 21–27) und die Redaktionsgeschichte des Hiobbuches* (BZAW 230; Berlin: de Gruyter, 1994).

75. See also Habel, *Job,* 37.

76. Fohrer, *Introduction to the Old Testament,* 327–29.

77. Jean Lévêque, "L'Argument de la Création dans le livre de Job," in P. Beauchamp, et al., *La Création dans l'Orient ancien* (LD 127; Paris: Cerf, 1987), 261–99.

78. Hans-Peter Müller, "Die weisheitliche Lehrerzählung im Alten Testament und seiner Umwelt," *WO* 9 (1977) 77–98.

79. See Plath's discussion of the "fear of God" (*Furcht Gottes*).

80. "The satan" refers to either an opponent in a law court or a prosecutor (Ps. 109:6), not a personal name as in 1 Chr. 21:1 and Zech. 3:1. See Peggy L. Day, *An Adversary in Heaven: SĀTĀN in the Hebrew Bible* (HSM 43; Atlanta: Scholars Press, 1988).

81. See Leo G. Perdue, "Job's Assault on Creation," *HAR* 10 (1987) 295–315.

82. See Gerstenberger, *Psalms.*

83. See Otto Piper, "Light, Light and Darkness," *IDB* 3 (1962) 130–31.

84. See Yahweh's curse of the soil in Gen. 3:17.

85. Dermot Cox, "The Desire for Oblivion in Job 3," *SBFLA* 23 (1973) 37–49; idem, *The Triumph of Impotence* (Analecta Gregoriana 212; Rome: Universita Gregoriana, 1978); Valerie Forstman Pettys, "Let There Be Darkness: Continuity and Discontinuity in the 'Curse' of Job 3," *JSOT* 98 (2002) 89–104.

86. Eichrodt, *Theology of the Old Testament,* 2:69–70.

87. See Michael Fishbane, "Jeremiah IV 23–26 and Job III 3–13: A Recovered Use of the Creation Pattern," *VT* 21 (1971) 151–62.

88. "Day" and "night" are an important word pair in creation texts: Gen. 1:5ff.; 8:22; Pss. 74:16; 136:7–9; Jer. 31:35.
89. See Apophis, who threatens the sun god Re in Egyptian mythology (*ANET,* 7–8), Tiamat in Akkadian mythology ("Enuma eliš"; *ANET,* 67–68), and Yamm and Lotan in the Baal Cycle (*ANET,* 137–41).
90. See P. D. Miller Jr., *The Divine Warrior in Early Israel* (HSM 5; Cambridge: Harvard University Press, 1973).
91. For Yahweh's fight with Leviathan, see Isa. 27:1; Ps. 74:12–17; Job 40:25–41:26; Ps. 104:25–26.
92. Yamm, the ruler of the primeval ocean, does battle with Baal for the rulership of the earth (see Exod. 15; Job 7:12; 38:8–11; Ps. 46; Hab. 3:15).
93. "Arouse" on occasion means "to stand to engage in battle" (Judg. 5:12; Isa. 51:9–12).
94. *ANET,* 64.
95. Thus Albertz, "Der sozialgeschichtliche Hintergrund," 63–91.
96. His description of his status as a slave may reflect the social and civil status of the exiles in Babylon (see the Murashu documents). For the Murashu archive and family firm, see Matthew W. Stolper, *Entrepreneurs and Empire: The Murašû Archive, the Murašû Firm, and Persian Rule in Babylonia* (Leiden: Nederlands Historisch-Archaeologisch Press, 1988); and Michael David Coogan, *West Semitic Personal Names in the Murašû Documents* (HSM 7; Missoula, MT: Scholars Press, 1976).
97. Friedrich Horst, *Hiob* (BKAT 16. Neukirchen-Vluyn: Neukirchener Verlag, 1969) 64. See Josh. 7:19; Amos 4:13; 5:8; 8:8; 9:5–6; Jer. 13:15–16; 1 Sam. 6:5; Ps. 118:17–21.
98. See the reference to the authority of tradition by Eliphaz in 15:18–19 (cf. Bildad in 8:8–10).
99. Perdue, "Wisdom and Apocalyptic: The Case of Qoheleth."
100. Artur Weiser, *Das Buch Hiob* (7th ed.; ATD; Göttingen: Vandenhoeck & Ruprecht, 1980) 52.
101. This phrase is an idiom that means to "make supplication" to Yahweh (Gen. 25:22, Exod. 18:15; Amos 5:5; Ezek. 14:10; Ps. 77:3; 2 Chr. 1:5).
102. See Diethelm Conrad, "Der Gott Reschef," *ZAW* 83 (1971) 157–83; W. J. Fulco, *The Canaanite God Rešep* (New Haven: American Oriental Society, 1976).
103. See Jörg Jeremias, *Theophanie: Die Geschichte einer alttestamentlichen Gattung* (WMANT 10; Neukirchen-Vluyn: Neukirchener Verlag, 1965).
104. Cf. the laments of accusation (e.g., Pss. 10; 13; 44; 74).
105. According to *Enuma eliš,* the lot of human beings is menial service to the gods (*ANET,* 68).
106. See de Vaux, *Ancient Israel,* 1:80–90; Walther Zimmerli and Joachim Jeremias, *The Servant of God* (SBT 1/20; Naperville, IL: Allenson, 1965).
107. Hans Walter Wolff, *Anthropology of the Old Testament* (trans. Margaret Kohl; Philadelphia: Fortress, 1974) 10–11.
108. See Pss. 74:13; 148:7; Isa. 27:1; 51:9; Ezek. 28:3; 32:2). Yamm and "dragon" are a word pair in Ps. 74:13.
109. See *Enuma eliš* in *ANET,* 60–98, 501–12.
110. Humanity's place in creation is discussed in Eichrodt, *Theology of the Old Testament,* 2:118–19; Wolff, *Anthropology of the Old Testament,* 159–60.
111. See Karl Budde, *Das Buch Hiob* (2nd ed.; Göttinger Handkommentar zum Alten Testament; Göttingen: Vandenhoeck & Ruprecht, 1913) 42; Robert Gordis, *The Book of Job* (New York: Jewish Theological Seminary of America, 1978) 522.
112. Jeremias, *Theophanie,* 151.
113. *Ṣedeq* (צדק) in legal settings refers to innocence, while *ṣādaq* (צדק) means being declared innocent (e.g., Isa. 43:9, 26; Ps. 143:1–2) by a judge.

114. Isa. 2:4; Mic. 4:3.
115. In juridical settings, this verb has a forensic meaning (Isa. 29:1; Amos 5:1). The "mediator" is to resolve conflict (Gen. 21:25ff.; Amos 5:10) (G. Mayer, "יכח," *TDOT* 6 [1990] 66). Those who mediate may be the judge, an outside party, or the parties involved in the dispute.
116. Reading *lū'* ("would") for MT's *lō'* ("not") in v. 33. See William Irwin, "Job's Redeemer," *JBL* 81 (1962) 217–29. M. B. Dick ("The Legal Metaphor in Job 31," *CBQ* 41 [1979] 37–50) argues that Job wishes for an arbiter to settle the dispute, before coming to trial.
117. Hesse, *Hiob*, 85.
118. See Wolff, *Anthropology of the Old Testament*, 26–27.
119. Cf. Khnum, who in Egyptian religion is the divine potter creating human beings ("The Divine Attributes of Pharaoh," 11.16–17, *ANET*, 431).
120. Katharine Doob Sakenfeld, *The Meaning of ḥesed in the Hebrew Bible: A New Inquiry* (HSM 17; Missoula, MT: Scholars Press, 1978).
121. A vision of death often concludes Jobs speeches (7:21; 14:20–22; 17:13–16; 21:32–33).
122. See my essay, "Creation in the Dialogues between Job and His Opponents," in *Das Buch Hiob und seine Interpretationen,* ed. Thomas Krüger, et al. (ATANT 88; Zurich: TVG, 2007).
123. See A. De Guglielmo, "Job 12:7–9 and the Knowability of God," *CBQ* 6 (1944) 476–82.
124. Contrast Jeremiah, whose wording is to "tear down and rebuild" (Jer. 1:10).
125. For *'ēṣâ* (עצה) as wise planning by sages, especially monarchs and his close advisors, often in a political context, see de Boer, "Counsellor."
126. *HALOT,* 1:45. This plural noun, difficult to define, may mean "members of ancient families."
127. Alfred Jepsen, "אמן," *TDOT* 1 (1974) 294–98, trusted ones (*ne'ĕmānîm*, נאמנים). See Prov. 25:13; Isa. 8:2; Jer. 42:5; Neh. 13:13; 1 Sam. 22:14.
128. *HALOT,* 1:78, "mighty ones" (*'āpîqîm*, אפיקים) is the possible meaning of this *hapax legomenon*.
129. *HALOT,* 2:844–47; "the depths" (*'ămūqôt*, עמקות; Ps. 64:7; Qoh. 7:24), and the "impenetrable darkness" (*ṣalmāwet*, צלמות; Job 3:5; 10:22; 16:16; 24:17; 28:3; 34:22).
130. This recurrent metaphor for human existence reflects Marduk's decree of slavery for human existence in *Enuma eliš* VI (*ANET*, 68).
131. See Keel, *Symbolism,* figs. 46, 47, 48, 479, and 480.
132. See Thorkild Jacobsen, *Treasures of Darkness,* 22–74; McCurley, *Ancient Myths and Biblical Faith,* 75–78; Jean Bottéro, *Religion in Ancient Mesopotamia* (Chicago: University of Chicago Press, 2001) 155–58. For detailed studies of the goddess, see Helgard Balz-Cochois, *Inanna: Wesenbild und Kult einer unmütterlichen Göttin* (Gütersloh: Mohn, 1992); W. W. Hallo, *The Exaltation of Inanna* (New York: AMS Press, 1982).
133. See Gen. 2–3 and Ezek. 28.
134. See, e.g., Othmar Keel and Christoph Uehlinger, *Gods, Goddesses, and Images of God in Ancient Israel* (Minneapolis: Fortress, 1992), 26–29.
135. See W. G. Lambert and Alan Rid Millard, *Atra-Ḥasis: The Babylonian Story of the Flood* (Oxford: Clarendon, 1969).
136. *Yālad* (ילד) means "to father" or "to give birth," while *ḥûl* (חול) connotes to "give birth" or "have offspring" (Isa. 51:2; Job 39:1). God is a mother who "gives birth" to the earth (Ps. 90:2), Israel (Deut. 32:18), and Wisdom (Prov. 8:24).
137. Wisdom (Prov. 8:22) also presents herself as the "first" of God's "ways," i.e., first in origins and rank, a similar claim attributed to the primal man in Job 15:7 (cf.

Sir. 25:24; 49:16). In Job 40:19 Yahweh says Behemoth (a metaphor for chaos) is "the first" of the divine acts of creation.

138. For myths of primordial sages, see Reiner, "Etiological Myth of the 'Seven Sages,'" 1–11; Benjamin Foster, "Wisdom and the Gods in Ancient Mesopotamia," *Or* 43 (1976) 344–54; William H. Shea, "Adam in Ancient Mesopotamian Tradition," *Andrews University Seminary Studies* 15 (1977) 27–41.

139. Frankfort, *Kingship and the Gods*, 215–333.

140. Fohrer, *Hiob*, 375; Gordis, *Job*, 276; Pope, *Job*, 181.

141. Conrad E. L'Heureux, *Rank among the Canaanite Gods: El, Ba'al, and the Repha'im* (HSM 21; Missoula, MT: Scholars Press, 1979) 201–27. The Rephaim are noble charioteers and warriors ruling in the underworld.

142. Abaddon, "place of destruction," is either a synonym for Sheol or a region within the netherworld (Prov. 15:11; 27:20; Job 28:22; 31:12). See Nicholas Tromp, *Primitive Conceptions of Death and the Nether World in the Old Testament* (BibOr 21; Rome: Pontifical Biblical Institute Press, 1969) 80.

143. See Norman Habel, "He Who Stretches Out the Heavens," *CBQ* 34 (1972) 417–30.

144. Perdue, *Wisdom in Revolt*.

145. Leo G. Perdue, "Revelation and the Problem of the Hidden God in the Second Temple," *Shall Not the Judge of All the Earth Do What Is Right?* ed. David Penchansky and Paul L. Redditt (Winona Lake, IN: Eisenbrauns, 2000) 201–22.

146. Horst Dietrich Preuss, "Jahwes Antwort an Hiob und die sogenannte Hiobliteratur des alten Vorderen Orients," in *Beiträge zur alttestamentlichen Theologie*, ed. Herbert Donner, et al. (Göttingen: Vandenhoeck & Ruprecht, 1977) 338.

147. Kubina, *Gottesreden im Buche Hiob: eine Beitrage zur Diskussion um die Einheit von Hiob 38,1–42,6* (Freiburger Theologische Studien 115; Freiburg im Breisgau: Herder, 1979) 131–42. She notes that rhetorical questions belong to the repertoire of legal interrogation.

148. *Yasad* (יסד) refers to Yahweh laying the foundations of the earth (cf. Pss. 24:2; 78:69; 89:12; 102:26; Isa. 48:13; Amos 9:6). As founder, Yahweh holds proprietary rights over the earth for all time and to secure the earth against collapse (R. Mosis, *TDOT* 6 [1990] 116–17).

149. *Měmaddêhā* (ממדיה) refers to the measurements of a building, for example, the tabernacle and ark (Exod. 26:2–8; 36:9, 15), the palace of Solomon (1 Kgs. 9:11; 6:36; 7:12), Ezekiel's vision of the temple (Ezek. 40–48), and Nehemiah's walls (Neh. 3:2, 4, 5). At times, Yahweh's acts of creation include "measuring" (Jer. 31:37; Job 28:25; Isa. 40:12). See H.-J. Fabry, *TDOT* 8 (1997) 123–31.

150. *Nāṭâ* (נטה) is the act of "stretching or laying out" a measuring line. See Isa. 44:13.

151. *Qāw* (קו) is a measuring line used by builders (Isa. 28:17; 34:17; Jer. 31:39; Ezek. 47:31).

152. *Hoṭěbā'û* (הטבעו) means "to be sunk or planted" (Exod. 15:4, Prov. 8:25; Jer. 38:22).

153. The plural term *'ădānêhā* (אדניה) probably refers to the bases of the earth, i.e., the sturdy ground, pedestal, or rocks upon which a structure is placed (Exod. 26:19–40:18; Num. 3:36–37; 4:31–32; Cant. 5:15).

154. *Yārâ* (ירה) means "to set up or lay," in this case, a cornerstone (see Gen. 31:51 for the setting up a heap of stones as a commemorative symbol). "The Job passage may involve a technical architectural term: 'lay foundation stones,' 'set up foundation stones,' i.e., lay a firm foundation for the building" (S. Wagner, *TDOT* 6 [1990] 333).

155. *'eben pinnātâ* (אבן פנתה) is here the "cornerstone" or "angle joint" of a wall (see Isa. 28:16).

156. *Rān* (רן) refers to a cry of exultation or rejoicing (Isa 14:7; 35:10; 44:23; 48:20; 49:13; 51:11; 54:1; 55:12; Pss. 30:6; 42:5).

157. *Yarî'û* (יריעו) means in this context "rejoice, cheer, shout in jubilation" (Isa. 44:23; Zeph. 3:14; Zech. 9:9; Ps. 65:13).

158. The term *gîaḥ,* (גיח) refers to "bubbling or gushing" of a spring or river (see Job 40:23; Ezek. 32:2). In this context it is a metaphor for the breaking of the placenta at birth.

159. *Ḥătullātô* (חתלתו) is cognate with Ugaritic *ḥtl* and refers to a "swaddling band."

160. *ANET,* 67.

161. This term is a legal statute or ordinance, and parallels "law" (*tôrâ,* תורה) or "commandment" (*mišpāṭ,* משפט). See H. Ringgren, *TDOT,* 5:141–47.

162. Jacobus van Dijk, "The Amarna Period and the Later New Kingdom," *The Oxford Dictionary of Ancient Egypt,* ed. Ian Shaw (Oxford: Oxford University Press, 2000) 273.

163. Compare to the Akkadian sun god, Shamash, whose light discerns wicked acts that become the basis for judgment (*BWL,* 121–38).

164. This metaphor portrays death as a city in which the dead dwell.

165. The canals and causeways were an engineering marvel in the ancient world by providing courses for river and floodwaters through and around cities, as was the case with Babylon.

166. See Gordis, *Job,* 453.

167. See Baal in particular, but also other fertility deities, including Marduk.

168. The mythology of the constellations as gods or fallen heroes is a frequent theme.

169. Othmar Keel, *Jahwes Entgegnung an Ijob* (FRLANT 121; Göttingen: Vanderhoeck & Ruprecht, 1978) 65, 71–72.

170. See Weiser, *Hiob,* 258. These terms are found in theophanic texts, including Hab. 3.

171. For a discussion of El and Baal in Canaanite religion, see Ulf Oldenburg, *The Conflict between El and Ba'al in Canaanite Religion* (Numen Sup; Leiden: Brill, 1969); Herbert Niehr, *Der höchste Gott: Alttestamentlicher JHWH-Glaube in Kontext syrisch-kanaanäischer Religion des 1. Jahrtausends v. Chr.* (BZAW 190; Berlin: de Gruyter, 1990); John Day, *Yahweh and the Gods and Goddesses of Canaan* (JSOTSup 265; Sheffield: Sheffield Academic Press, 2000).

172. These four terms are frequently used to describe the aura of the royal majesty of rulers, especially Yahweh: *gā'ôn* (גאון, Exod. 15:7; Isa. 24:14; Mic. 5:3; Isa. 13:11; 14:11), *gōbah* (גבה, Ps. 138:6; Job 41:26), *hôd* (הוד, Hab. 3:3; Pss. 8:2; 148:13; Job 37:22; Sir. 10:5; Dan. 11:21; Pss. 21:6; 45:4), and *hādār* (הדר, Pss. 21:6; 45:4–5; 96:6; 104:1; 111:3).

173. The term "praise" (*yādâ,* ידה) refers to hymnic praise of Yahweh for one or both of two reasons: creation and salvation history.

174. The pairing of these two mythical creatures compares to the five pairs of wild animals in the first speech. Gunkel rightly notes that these two creatures are mythic monsters that oppose Yahweh's rule over creation (*Schöpfung und Chaos,* 48–49).

175. For an overview of the mythical themes and images in Job, see Gisella Fuchs, *Mythos und Hiobdichtung* (Stuttgart: Kohlhammer, 1993).

176. Fohrer, *Hiob,* 523; Gordis, *Job,* 571.

177. Bernard Couroyer, "Qui est Behemoth?" *RB* 82 (1975) 418–43.

178. Keel, *Jahwes Entgegnung an Ijob,* 127–28; Kubina, *Die Gottesreden im Buche Hiob,* 44.

179. See Keel and Schroer, *Schöpfung,* 123–33.

180. G. J. Botterweck, *TDOT* 2 (1975) 6–20; Keel, *Jahwes Entgegnung an Ijob,* 127–28; E. Ruprecht, "Das Nilpferd im Hiobbuch: Beobachtungen zu der

sogennanten zweiten Gottesrede," *VT* 21 (1971) 209–31; Torgny Säve-Söderbergh, *On Egyptian Representations of Hippopotamus Hunting as a Religious Motive* (Horae Soederblomianae 3; Uppsala: Gleerup, 1953).

181. "To cut a covenant" is the common idiom for covenant making in the Priestly document (see, e.g., Gen. 26:28).

182. See the pieces of glyptic art that portray the theme of the "Lord of the animals" in Keel, *Jahwes Entgegnung an Ijob*, 86–87.

183. The LXX and Qumran Targum read *māsas* (מסס, "to melt, be poured out") for MT *mā'as* (מאס, "to despise, reject, protest").

184. Gen. 18:27 and Job 30:19 indicate that the expression "dust and ashes" points to that which is insignificant or worthless. Abraham in the first passage confesses he is but "dust and ashes" when he stands in judgment of Yahweh, who is planning to destroy Sodom and Gomorrah, including both the wicked and the righteous.

185. The Masoretic notes indicate that this is one of the *tiqqûnê sōpĕrîm* ("correction of the scribes"). A later scribal copyist has changed "they declared God guilty" in 32:3 to "they declared Job guilty."

186. See Habel, *Job*, 450–51.

187. See Roland Murphy, *Wisdom Literature* (FOTL 13; Grand Rapids: Eerdmans, 1981) for the literary forms in Job.

Chapter 5: Scribalism and the Torah in the Wisdom Tradition

1. Pierre Briant, *From Cyrus to Alexander: A History of the Persian Empire* (Winona Lake, IN: Eisenbrauns, 2002); M. A. A. Dandamaev, *A Political History of the Achaemenid Empire* (Leiden: Brill, 1997); M. A. A. Dandamaev and V. G. Kukonin, *The Culture and Social Institutions of Ancient Iran* (Cambridge: Cambridge University Press, 1989); Kenneth G. Hoglund, *Achaemenid Imperial Administration in Syria-Palestine and the Missions of Ezra and Nehemiah* (Atlanta: Scholars Press, 1992); H. Sancisi-Weerdenburg, Amélie Kuhrt, and M. Cool Root, eds., *Achaemenid History* (Nederlands Instituut voor het Nabije Oosten; Leiden: Brill, 1994); Amélie Kuhrt, *The Ancient Near East, c. 300–330 BC* (2 vols.; New York: Routledge, 1995) 2:647–701. For the historical background of the Jewish community in the Persian period, see Herbert Donner, *Geschichte des Volkes Israel und seiner Nachbarn in Grundzügen* (2 vols.; Grundrisse zum Alten Testament 4/1–2; Göttingen: Vandenhoeck & Ruprecht, 1984–86) 405–20; Peter R. Ackroyd, "The Jewish Community in Palestine in the Persian Period," in *The Cambridge History of Judaism*, vol. 1, *Introduction; the Persian Period*, ed. W. D. Davies and Louis Finklestein (Cambridge: Cambridge University Press, 1984) 130–61; Ephraim Stern, "The Persian Empire and the Political and Social History of Palestine in the Persian Empire," in *Cambridge History of Judaism*, 1:70–87; Josef Wiesehöfer, *Ancient Persia* (London: Tauris, 2001).

2. See "The Cyrus Cylinder," *ANET,* 315–16, which praises the magnanimous policies of Cyrus in rebuilding temples and holy cities and allowing all exiled peoples to return to their homeland (see János Harmatta, "The Literary Patterns of the Babylonian Edict of Cyrus," *Acta Antiqua Academiae Scientiarum Hungaricae* 19 [1971] 217–31). Cyrus also ingratiated himself by returning the divine images, which Nabonidus had removed, to their cities.

3. This policy was not always followed by later Achaemenid rulers. Herodotus reports that Darius I deported people from Libya to Bactria (Herodotus 4.204; 5.13–16; 6.20).

4. See, e.g., Joseph Blenkinsopp, *Ezra–Nehemiah: A Commentary* (OTL; Philadelphia: Westminster, 1989) 307–8.

5. See the essay by Smith-Christopher, "Reassessing the Historical and Social Impact of the Babylonian Exile (597/587–539 B.C.E.)," *Exile: Old Testament, Jewish, and Christian Conceptions,* ed. J. M. Scott (Leiden: Brill, 1997) 7–36. He notes that of the forty-two times the term "decree" (*te'ēm* or *pitgām*) occurs, fourteen are in Ezra 1–7, nine in Esther, and nine more in Daniel. Most of these are authoritative directives of foreign rulers dealing with Judah.

6. See the essays in James W. Watts, ed., *Persia and Torah: The Theory of Imperial Authorization of the Pentateuch* (SBLSym 17; Atlanta: SBL, 2001).

7. Also see Joel P. Weinberg, *Citizen-Temple Community* (Sheffield: Sheffield Academic Press, 1992); P. R. Bedford, *Temple Restoration in Early Achaemenid Judah* (Leiden: Brill, 2001). These policies were not implemented to benefit only the Jews, but also other conquered countries throughout the empire. This system of local semi-autonomous government combined with imperial control encouraged economic growth by means of local production coupled with international trade administered by the empire; see Josette Elayi and Jean Sapin, *Beyond the River: New Perspectives on Transeuphratene* (JSOTSup 250; Sheffield: Sheffield Academic Press, 1998).

8. For the self-interests served by Persian imperial policies, see Hoglund, *Achaemenid Imperial Administration.*

9. See Josephus (*Ant.* 11.1–18), who indicates that Cyrus allowed the Jews to return to Judah after reading Isaiah's prophecy.

10. See Ephraim Stern, *Archaeology of the Land of the Bible,* vol. 2: *The Assyrian, Babylonian, and Persian Periods (732–332 BC)* (ABRL; New York: Doubleday, 2001).

11. See the essays in *Persia and Torah.*

12. Stern, "Persian Empire," 78–86.

13. The Behistun Inscription, the Inscription of Naqsh-I Rustam, and the Inscription of Persepolis make no reference to Abar Nahara. Since Babylon is listed, this city may have been part of Abar Nahara until Xerxes I (486–465) removed it to form another satrapy.

14. Seth Schwartz, *Imperialism and Jewish Society, 200 B.C.E. to 640 C.E.* (Princeton: Princeton University Press, 2001) 20–21.

15. Elias J. Bickerman, "The Babylonian Captivity," in *Cambridge History of Judaism,* 1:342–58.

16. Morton Smith, "Jewish Religious Life in the Persian Period," *The Cambridge History of Judaism* 1:222.

17. See the discussion by Morton Smith, *Palestinian Parties and Politics That Shaped the Old Testament* (New York: Columbia University Press, 1971) 90.

18. For example, Levine, *Jerusalem,* 10–11; Dandamaev, *Political History,* 63–64.

19. The dates for these two leaders, their actions, and their relationship to each other continues to be debated. See H. G. W. Williamson, *Israel in the Books of Chronicles* (Cambridge: Cambridge University Press, 1977); Blenkinsopp, *Ezra-Nehemiah;* Sara Japhet, *1 & 2 Chronicles* (OTL; Louisville: Westminster/John Knox, 1993).

20. *ANET,* 315–16. For example, see A. B. Lloyd, "The Inscription of Udahorresnet: A Collaborator's Testament," *JEA* 68 (1982) 166–80; Joseph A. Blenkinsopp, "The Mission of Udjahorresnet and Those of Ezra and Nehemiah," *JBL* 106 (1987) 409–21.

21. Quoted by Edwin M. Yamauchi, *Persia and the Bible* (Grand Rapids: Baker Book House, 1996) 259.

22. Lawrence Schiffman, *Who Was a Jew? Rabbinic and Halakhic Perspectives on the Jewish-Christian Schism* (Hoboken, NJ: Ktav, 1985) 14–17; Christine Hayes, "Intermarriage and Impurity in Ancient Jewish Sources," *HTR* 92 (1999) 3–36.

23. See Smith, *Palestinian Parties and Politics*, 82–125.

24. Consult the essay by W. Lee Humphreys, "The Motif of the Wise Courtier in the Book of Proverbs," in *Israelite Wisdom: Theological and Literary Essays in Honor of Samuel Terrien*, ed. John G. Gammie, et al. (Missoula, MT: Scholars Press, 1978) 177–90.

25. See Robert Carroll, "Coopting the Prophets: Nehemiah and Noadiah," in *Priests, Prophets and Scribes: Essays on the Formation and Heritage of Second Temple Judaism in Honour of Joseph Blenkinsopp*, ed. E. C. Ulrich, et al. (JSOTSup 149; Sheffield: Sheffield Academic Press, 1992) 87–99. While the status of the prophets declined in the civil religion of Judaism, popular religiosity may have warmed to them.

26. See Stolper, *Entrepreneurs and Empire,* 151. Also compare the situation in Babylonia set forth by M. A. Dandamaev, "Achaemenid Babylonia," in *Ancient Mesopotamia*, ed. I. M. Diakonoff (Moscow: Nauka, 1969) 308. Interest rates grew enormously by the end of the fifth century BCE. See R. P. Maloney, "Usury and Restrictions on Interest-Taking in the Ancient Near East," *CBQ* 36 (1974) 1–20. Nehemiah seems to be chastising the wealthy for charging 1 percent per month (Neh. 5:11). The Torah prohibited the wealthy charging interest in order to profit from those who were in dire circumstances. See Ephraim Neufeld, "The Prohibition Against Loans at Interest in Ancient Hebrew Laws," *HUCA* 26 (1955) 355–412.

27. See Frank Crüsemann, *The Torah: Theology and Social History of Old Testament Law* (Minneapolis: Fortress, 1996).

28. See Smith, "Jewish Religious Life in the Persian Period," *The Cambridge History of Judaism*, 1:219–78; Lester Grabbe, *Judaic Religion in the Second Temple Period: Belief and Practice from the Exile to Yavneh* (London: Routledge, 2000).

29. A Jewish drachma dating ca. 370 BCE has on one side a legend that contains the word "Judea" and portrays a bearded male head in a Corinthian helmet. The other side presents a deity in a Greek *chitōn* (χιτών), seated in a winged wheel and holding an Egyptian falcon on one of his arms. This god has a satyr's mask. One possible interpretation is that the deity is Yahweh seated on his chariot (winged wheel; cf. Ezek. 1–2), the mask of a satyr indicates the significance of Yahweh as the God of wine, and the falcon symbolizes the Egyptian sun god, Horus. This is clear evidence of Jewish polytheism or at least the adaptation of pagan symbolism to portray religious beliefs.

30. For the excavation of this shrine and its interpretation, see Olga Tufnell, *Lachish (Tell ed Duweir)* (Oxford: Oxford University Press, 1953); Yohanan Aharoni, *Investigations at Lachish: The Sanctuary and the Residency,* 5 (Tel Aviv: Gateway, 1975), 3ff., who argued that Tufnell's site was Hellenistic, but still pointed to an adjacent building as a temple.

31. Martin Hengel, "'Schriftauslegung' und 'Schriftwerdung' in der Zeit des Zweiten Tempels," in *Kleine Schriften*, vol. 2: *Judaica, Hellenistica et Christiana*, ed. Jorg Frey and Dorothea Betz (WUNT 109; Tübingen: Mohr, 1999) 20–35.

32. See Michael Fishbane, "From Scribalism to Rabbinism," in *Sage in Israel,* 440–43.

33. Nahman Avigad, *Bullae and Seals from a Post-Exilic Judaean Archive* (Qedem 4; Jerusalem: Hebrew University of Jerusalem, Institute of Archaeology, 1976). Also see Helga Weippert, *Palästina in vorhellenistischer Zeit* (HO, Archäologie, Vorderasien 2.1; Munich: Beck, 1988) 695.

34. Joseph Blenkinsopp, "The Sage, the Scribe, and Scribalism in the Chronicler's Work," in *Sage in Israel,* 307–15; Hengel, "'Schriftauslegung' und 'Schriftwerdung,'" 20–35; Moshe Weinfeld, *Deuteronomy and the Deuteronomic School* (Oxford: Oxford University Press, 1972).

35. J. Kenneth Kuntz, "The Canonical Wisdom Psalms of Ancient Israel—Their Rhetorical, Thematic, and Formal Dimensions," in *Rhetorical Criticism: Essays in Honor of James Muilenburg*, ed. Jared J. Jackson and Martin Kessler (PTMS 1; Pittsburgh: Pickwick, 1974) 186–222; J. Reindl, "Weisheitliche Bearbeitung von Psalmen: Ein Beitrag zum Verständnis der Sammlung des Psalters," in *Congress Volume: Vienna 1980*, ed. J. A. Emerton (VTSup 32: Leiden: Brill, 1981) 339–56; Anthony Ceresko, "The Sage in the Psalms," in *Sage in Israel*, 217–30; J. Clinton McCann, "Wisdom's Dilemma: The Book of Job, the Final Form of the Book of Psalms, and the Entire Bible," in *Wisdom, You Are My Sister*, 18–30.

36. Louis Ginzberg, *The Legends of the Jews*, vol. 4; *From Joshua to Esther* (repr. Baltimore: Johns Hopkins University Press, 1998) 359. According to Ginzberg Ezra is not only a member of the Great Assembly, but also directed it. This depiction of Ezra in Ezra–Nehemiah may have been in its origins a didactic legend.

37. Fishbane, "From Scribalism to Rabbinism," 441. This compares to Ps. 119:18 in which the psalmist-sage prays for divine illumination in the interpretation of the Torah.

38. In rabbinic tradition Ezra is also mentioned as among the earliest members of the Great Synagogue, thus connecting him with the sages and the rabbis. In *b. Qidd.* 30a the scribes were called *sōpĕrîm*, because they counted all of the letters of the Torah. Thus there is a line of scribes that includes copyists, supported by the temple, who were also likely priests (see *y. Šeqal.* 4:2 and *b. Ketub.* 106a), exegetes, and teachers (*m. 'Or.* 3:9) of both Torah and Mishnah (*m. Ned.* 9:2; *m. Qidd.* 4:13).

39. If Artaxerxes II were meant, then the date of the beginning of the mission of Ezra would be ca. 398 BCE.

40. See the classic study of Hans Heinrich Schaeder, *Esra der Schreiber* (BHT 5; Tübingen: Mohr, 1930). Blenkinsopp and many others have argued that Schaeder's view needs modification, since he considers the decree of Artaxerxes I to be historical. Instead, there is strong evidence that the decree has undergone significant editing by the Chronicler ("Sage, Scribe, and Scribalism," 312–14).

41. He also is called a "priest" (*kāhănā*, כהנא, Ezra 7:12) in the letter of Artaxerxes. Then, in the "official" degree of Artaxerxes, once more Ezra is a "priest" (7:21).

42. For *māhîr* (מהיר) see H. Ringgren, *TDOT* 8 (1997) 141–42.

43. Ceresko, "Sage in the Psalms," 218–30.

44. See Anthony R. Ceresko, "The ABCs of Wisdom in Psalm XXXIV," *VT* 35 (1985) 99–104.

45. Herman L. Jansen, *Die spätjüdische Psalmdichtung* (SNVAO II 3; Oslo: Dybwad, 1937); Kuntz, "Canonical Wisdom Psalms," 186–222; idem, "Wisdom Psalms and the Shaping of the Hebrew Psalter," in *For a Later Generation: The Transformation of Tradition in Israel, Early Judaism, and Early Christianity*, ed. R. A. Angell et al. (Harrisburg: Trinity Press International, 2000) 144–60; Avi Hurvitz, "Wisdom Vocabulary in the Hebrew Psalter: A Contribution to the Study of 'Wisdom Psalms,'" *VT* 38 (1988) 41–51; R. W. Whybray, "The Wisdom Psalms," in *Wisdom in Ancient Israel*, ed. Day, 152–60; Samuel Terrien, "Wisdom in the Psalter," in *In Search of Wisdom*, 51–72; James L. Crenshaw, "Wisdom Psalms?" *Currents in Research: Biblical Studies* 8 (2000) 9–17; idem, "Gold Dust or Nuggets? A Brief Response to J. Kenneth Kuntz," *Currents in Biblical Research* 1 (2003) 155–58; J. Kenneth Kuntz, "Reclaiming Biblical Wisdom Psalms: A Response to Crenshaw," *Currents in Biblical Research* 1 (2003) 145–54. Crenshaw rejects the category, while Jacques Trublet, critical of the classification, notes that while there may not have been sapiential psalms as a generic classification, there are those that come close lexically and semantically to certain sapiential passages ("Chapitre V: Le corpus sapiential et le Psautier," in *Sagesse biblique*, 139–74).

46. Weinfeld, *Deuteronomy and the Deuteronomic School*.

47. For a detailed discussion of method in the identification of wisdom psalms, including those that speak primarily of the Torah, see my forthcoming volume, *Wisdom Literature. A Social, Historical, and Literary Introduction* (Grand Rapids: Eerdmans).

48. See Gerald H. Wilson, *The Editing of the Hebrew Psalter* (SBLDS 76; Chico, CA: Scholars Press, 1985); Gerald T. Sheppard, *Wisdom as a Hermeneutical Construct: A Study in the Sapientializing of the Old Testament* (BZAW 151; Berlin: de Gruyter, 1980).

49. The root *rš'* is found seventy-eight times in Proverbs (adjective, noun, and verb): Prov. 2:22, 3:25, 33, 4:14, 19; 5:22; 9:7; 10:3, 6, 7, 11, 16, 20, 24, 25, 27, 28, 30, 32; etc.

50. See Prov. 1:3, 13:21; 23:17.

51. Prov. 1:22; 9:7, 8; 15:12; 24:9; etc.

52. "Meditating" (*hāgâ*, הגה) is found in Pss. 63:7; 77:13; 143:5. The noun form, "meditation" (*hegyôn*, הגיון), occurs in Ps. 19:15 and refers to the sage's mediation on Torah that is expressed in a thanksgiving to God for the gift of the divine law.

53. See *BWL*, 127ff., for a hymn to Shamash as the sun god, the god of justice, overseeing and judging the world as he makes his way across the heavens.

54. Following the note in *BHK* that reads בים (*bayyām*, "in the sea") in place of MT בהם (*bāhem*, "in them").

55. Michael Fishbane, *The Exegetical Imagination: On Jewish Thought and Theology* (Cambridge: Harvard University Press, 1998) 151–72.

56. See André Robert, "Le psaume CXIX et les Sapientiaux," *RB* 48 (1939) 5–20; Alfons Deissler, *Psalm 119 (118) und seine Theologie* (Munich: Karl Zink, 1955); Jon Levenson, "The Sources of Torah: Psalm 119 and the Modes of Revelation in Second Temple Judaism," in *Ancient Israelite Religion*, ed. Patrick D. Miller Jr., et al. (Philadelphia: Fortress, 1987) 559–74; David Noel Freedman, *Psalm 119: The Exaltation of Torah* (BJS 6; Winona Lake, IN: Eisenbrauns, 1999).

57. Fishbane, *Biblical Interpretation in Israel*, 332–34, 539–42. See M. Gertner, "Midrashim in the New Testament," *JSS* 7 (1962) 276. Fishbane notes that all eight verses of the psalm beginning with the letter פ share the language of the Priestly blessing in Num. 6:23–27.

58. See my essay, "Ben Sira and the Prophets," in *Intertextual Studies in Ben Sira and Tobit: Essays in Honor of Alexander A. Di Lella, O.F.M.*, ed. Jeremy Corley and Vincent Skemp (CBQMS 38; Washington, DC: Catholic Biblical Association of America, 2005) 132–54.

59. David Daube, *Studies in Biblical Law* (Cambridge: Cambridge University Press, 1947) 47.

60. Fishbane, "From Scribalism to Rabbinism," 447.

61. This second verb, *kûn*, refers to the establishment of the pillars of the earth in the act of creation.

62. For a discussion of the tradition of the creation of humanity and its later expression, the creation of the individual, see Rainer Albertz, *Weltschöpfung und Menschenschöpfung* (Calwer Theologische Monographien: Reihe A, Bibelwissenschaft 3; Stuttgart: Calwer, 1974).

Chapter 6: Wisdom and Egyptian and Hellenistic Skepticism: The Book of Qoheleth

1. Günther Hölbl, *A History of the Ptolemaic Empire* (London: Routledge, 2001); Werner Huss, *Ägypten in hellenistischer Zeit. 332–30 v. Chr.* (Munich: Beck, 2001). Also see Dov Gera, *Judaea and Mediterranean Politics 219–161 B.C.E.* (Brill's Series in Jewish Studies 3; Leiden: Brill, 1998).

2. Schwartz, *Imperialism and Jewish Society*, 1–2.

3. See Martin Hengel, *Jews, Greeks, and Barbarians: Aspects of the Hellenization of Judaism in the Pre-Christian Period* (Philadelphia: Fortress, 1980) 33–44.

4. See Huss, *Ägypten in hellenistischer Zeit*, 381–488.

5. Hölbl, *History of the Ptolemaic Empire*, 134.

6. Peter Kaplony, "Demotische Chronik," *LÄ* 1 (1975) 1056–60.

7. Miriam Lichtheim, *Ancient Egyptian Literature* 3 (Berkeley: University of California Press, 1980), 159–84; idem, *Late Egyptian Wisdom Literature*, 13–92; Burkard, *Weisheitstexte*, 2:222–50; Hellmut Brunner, *Die Weisheitsbücher der Ägypter: Lehren für das Leben* (Zurich: Artenis & Winckler, 1998) 257–91; Thomas Krüger, *Qoheleth: A Commentary* (Hermeneia; Minneapolis: Fortress, 2004): 1–5.

8. Williams, "Egyptian Literature (Wisdom)," 397. Gemser agrees it is not prior to the fifth century ("The Instructions of 'Onchsheshonqy and Biblical Wisdom Literature," in *Congress Volume: Oxford, 1959* [VTSup 7; Leiden: Brill, 1960] 106).

9. Lichtheim, *Ancient Egyptian Literature*, 3:159–84; idem, *Late Egyptian Wisdom Literature*, 13–92; Burkard, *Weisheitstexte*, 2:222–50; Brunner, *Weisheitsbücher der Ägypter*, 257–91.

10. Zauzich, "Demotische Fragmente zum Ahikar-Roman," *Folia Rara*, 180–85. A copy of the sixth century BCE was found in Elephantine.

11. See Lichtheim, *Late Egyptian Wisdom Literature*, 93–106; Burkard, *Weisheitstexte*, 2:277–80.

12. Lichtheim, *Ancient Egyptian Literature*, 3:184–217; idem, *Late Egyptian Wisdom Literature*, 107–234; Burkard, *Weisheitstexte*, 2:280–319; Brunner, *Weisheitsbücher der Ägypter*, 295–349.

13. Aksel Volten, ed., *Das demotische Weisheitsbuch, Studien und Bearbeitung* (Copenhagen: E. Munksgaard, 1941); also see his *Kopenhagener Texte zum demotischen Weisheitsbuch* (Analecta Aegyptiaca 2; Copenhagen: Munksgaard, 1941).

14. See Williams, "Egyptian Literature (Wisdom)," 397. Williams notes that there were additional demotic wisdom texts.

15. George B. Kerford, "The Sage in Hellenistic Philosophical Literature," in *Sage in Israel*, 319–28. See especially F. L. Vatai, *Intellectuals in Politics in the Greek World from Early Times to the Hellenistic Age* (London: Croom Helm, 1984); A. A. Long and D. N. Sedley, *The Hellenistic Philosophers* (New York: Cambridge University Press, 1987).

16. Ronald F. Hock, "Paul and Graeco-Roman Education," in *Paul in the Graeco-Roman World: A Handbook*, ed. J. Paul Sampley (Harrisburg: Trinity Press International, 2003) 198–227. In addition, see Raffaella Cribiore, *Writing, Teachers, and Students in Graeco-Roman Egypt* (Atlanta: Scholars Press, 1996); Teresa Morgan, *Literate Education in the Hellenistic and Roman Worlds* (New York: Cambridge University Press, 1998).

17. Alan Mendelson, *Secular Education in Philo of Alexandria* (HUCM 7; Cincinnati: Hebrew Union College Press, 1982), 1.

18. See Hock, "Paul and Graeco-Roman Education," whose essay contains a substantial bibliography on Greek education.

19. Morgan, *Literate Education*.

20. Hock, "Paul and Graeco-Roman Education," 204.

21. Euripides 4, frg. 980. See the classic study by Martin P. Nilsson, *Geschichte der griechischen Religion* (2 vols.; Munich: Beck, 1955).

22. Louis Robert, "Un corpus des inscriptions juives," *REJ* 101 (1937) 73–86.

23. H. A. Harris, *Greek Athletics and the Jews* (Cardiff: University of Wales Press, 1976).

24. Robert Doran, "The High Cost of a Good Education," in *Hellenism in the Land of Israel*, ed. John J. Collins and Gregory E. Sterling (Christianity and Judaism in Antiquity 13; Notre Dame: University of Notre Dame Press, 2001) 94–115. Important studies are those by Martin P. Nilsson, *Die hellenistiche Schule* (Munich: Beck, 1955); H. I. Marrou, *A History of Education in Antiquity* (New York: Sheed & Ward, 1956). Also see Jean Delorme, *Gymnasion: Étude sur les monuments consacrés à l'éducation en Grèce (dès origins à l'empire romain)* (Paris: Boccard, 1960) 253–315; Chrysis Pélékidis, *Histoire de l'éphbie attique dès origines à 31 avant Jésus Christ* (Paris: Boccard, 1962); Rafaella Cribiore, *Gymnastics of the Mind: Greek Education in Hellenistic and Roman Egypt* (Princeton: Princeton University Press, 2001); idem, *Writing, Teachers, and Students*; Morgan, *Literate Education*; Daniel Kah and Peter Scholz, *Das hellenistische Gymnasion* (Wissenskultur und gesellschaftlicher Wandel 8; Oldenbourg: Akademie Verlag, 2004).

25. Hengel, *Jews, Greeks and Barbarians*.

26. See especially J. M. Modrzejewski, *The Jews of Egypt: From Rameses II to Emperor Hadrian* (Princeton: Princeton University Press, 1995) 21–44; Huss, *Ägypten in hellenistischer Zeit*, 449–50; idem, "Die Juden im ptolemäischen Ägypten," *Artibus: Kulturwissenschaft und deutsche Philologie des Mittelalters und der Frühen Neuzeit, FS Dieter Wuttke*, ed. Stephan Füssell, Gert Hübner, and Joachim Knape (Wiesbaden: Harrassowitz, 1994) 1–31.

27. *CPJ*, 1–3; P. M. Fraser, *Ptolemaic Alexandria* 1–3 (Oxford: Clarendon, 1972); Kasher, *Jews in Hellenistic and Roman Egypt*; William Horbury and Noy Dov, *Jewish Inscriptions of Graeco-Roman Egypt* (Cambridge: Cambridge University Press, 1992); Dorothy Sly, *Philo's Alexandria* (London: Routledge, 1996).

28. Moses Hadas, *The Third and Fourth Books of Maccabees* (New York: Harper, 1953); Hugh Anderson, "3 Maccabees," *OTP*, 2:509–29; André Paul, "Le Troisième Livre des Macchabées," *ANRW*, 20.1, 2, 298–336; Johannes Tromp, "The Formation of the Third Book of Maccabees," *Henoch* 17 (1995) 311–28.

29. BGU 1211, cited in F. W. Walbank, *The Hellenistic World* (Brighton, Sussex: Harvester, 1981) 211–12; J. M. G. Barclay, *Jews in the Mediterranean Diaspora from Alexander to Trajan (323 BCE–117 CE)* (Edinburgh: T. & T. Clark, 1996) 32.

30. See especially Modrzejewski, *Jews of Egypt*, 21–44; Huss, *Ägypten in hellenistischer Zeit*, 449–50; idem, "Die Juden im ptolemäischen Ägypten."

31. See Ephraim Stern, "The Beginning of the Greek Settlement in Palestine in the Light of the Excavations at Tel Dor," *Recent Excavations in Israel: Studies in Iron Age Archaeology*, ed. Seymour Gitin and William G. Dever (AASOR 49; Winona Lake, IN: Eisenbrauns, 1982) 107–24. Also see Gideon Fuks, "A Mediterranean Pantheon: Cults and Deities in Hellenistic and Roman Ashkelon," *Mediterranean Historical Review* 15 (1999) 27–48.

32. Stern, "Beginning of the Greek Settlement," in *Recent Excavations in Israel*, 107–24.

33. See Aryeh Kasher, "Jerusalem Cathedra," in *Jerusalem* (Detroit: Wayne State University Press, 1982) 63–78; idem, *Jews and Hellenistic Cities in Eretz-Israel: Relations of the Jews in Eretz-Israel with the Hellenistic Cities during the Second Temple Period (332 BCE–70 CE)* (Tübingen: Mohr [Siebeck], 1990).

34. Martin Hengel, *Judaism and Hellenism* 1 (London: SCM Press, 1974) 104–5. Also see idem, *Jews, Greeks, and Barbarians*, 49–82; idem, "Jerusalem als jüdische und hellenistische Stadt," *Kleine Schriften*, vol. 2: *Judaica, Hellenistica et Christiana* (WUNT 109; Tübingen: Mohr, 1999) 114–56.

35. Gregory E. Sterling, "Judaism between Jerusalem and Alexandria," in *Hellenism in the Land of Israel*, appendix, 279–90. Sterling's study focuses on Jerusalem between 175 and 135 BCE.

36. Susan Sherwin-White and Amélie Kuhrt, *From Samarkhand to Sardis* (Berkeley: University of California Press, 1993). The Greeks prided themselves for their supposed superiority over other nations and cultures.

37. Shimon Applebaum, "Jewish Urban Communities and Greek Influences," *Judaea in Hellenistic and Roman Times* (Leiden: Brill, 1989) 30–46.

38. Shimon Applebaum, "Hellenistic Cities of Judaea and Its Vicinity—Some New Aspects," in *The Ancient Historian and His Materials: Essays in Honour of C. E. Stevens*, ed. Barbara Levick (Franborough, Hants: Gregg, 1975) 59–73.

39. The *agoranomos* referred to both the administration of the market of a city and to its overseer in a Greek city. These overseers or administrators "kept order in the market, saw to the quality of goods, and collected market dues (*Athenaion politeia* 51.1)." See *OCD*, 43. They also assured the supply of food.

40. Applebaum, "Jewish Urban Communities," 31.

41. Ibid., 32.

42. For technological developments and the introduction of new agricultural products, see Hengel, *Judaism and Hellenism*, 1:46–47; Mikhail Ivanovich Rostovtzeff, *The Social and Economic History of the Hellenistic World* (2 vols.; Oxford: Clarendon, 1941) 2:1186–97.

43. See Gera's *Judaea and Mediterranean Politics*, 6–58; as well as his essay, "On the Credibility of the History of the Tobiads," in *Greece and Rome in Eretz Israel*, ed. Aryeh Kasher, et al. (Center for Eretz Israel Research of Yah Izhak Ben-Zvi and the University of Haifa and of Tel Aviv University; Jerusalem: Israel Exploration Society, 1990) 21–38. He concludes that the story in Josephus in these two places originated from a source that is propaganda written by a Jew of Ptolemaic Egypt to encourage confidence among the Jews in Egypt of this period and to encourage them to engage in important service to the Ptolemiaic kings.

44. Applebaum, "Jewish Urban Communities," 37.

45. For a convenient list of Greco-Jewish literature in Jerusalem, inscriptions in Jerusalem, ossuaries in Jerusalem, Greek manuscripts in the Judean Desert, Greco-Jewish literature in Alexandria, and nonliterary Jewish texts from or dealing with Alexandria, see Sterling, "Judaism between Jerusalem and Alexandria," 279–90.

46. See the appendix, "Jews with Greek or Roman Names," in Harris, *Greek Athletics and the Jews*, 102–6.

47. Unfortunately, there is no comprehensive survey of Greek inscriptions from the Hellenistic period until the seventh century CE. However, a team is working on cataloguing, drawing/photographing, printing, translating, and commenting on Greek inscriptions from this period. This will involve about six thousand to seven thousand Greek texts. For the present, see Saul Lieberman, *Greek in Jewish Palestine* (New York: Feldheim, 1965); Pieter W. van der Horst, *Ancient Jewish Epitaphs: An Introductory Survey of a Millennium of Jewish Funerary Epigraphy (300 B.C.E.–700 C.E.)* (Kampen: Kok Pharos, 1991); J. W. van Henten and P. W. van der Horst, eds., *Studies in Early Jewish Epigraphy* (Leiden: Brill, 1994); P. W. van der Horst, "Greek in Jewish Palestine in the Light of Jewish Epigraphy," in *Japheth in the Tents of Shem: Studies on Jewish Hellenism in Antiquity* (Contributions to Biblical Exegesis and Theology 32; Leuven: Peeters, 2002) 9–26.

48. Lieberman, *Greek in Jewish Palestine*; Rachel Hachlili, *Ancient Jewish Art and Archaeology in the Land of Israel* (HO 35; Leiden: Brill, 1988) 103. Lea Roth-Gerson indicates that more than a third of the synagogue inscriptions in Palestine are in Greek (*The Greek Inscriptions from the Synagogue in Eretz-Israel* [Jerusalem: Yad Izhak Ben Zvi, 1987]). This is also true of Samaritan synagogues (van der Horst, "Greek in Jewish Palestine," 17).

49. See van der Horst, *Japheth*, 12.

50. Lieberman, *Greek in Jewish Palestine*, 16.
51. See Hengel, *Kleine Schriften*, vol. 1: *Judaica et Hellenistica* (Tübingen: Mohr, 1996) 1–90.
52. See Francis T. Fallon, "Theodotus," *OTP*, 2:785–931; Carl F. Holladay, *Fragments from Hellenistic Jewish Authors*, vol. 2: *Poets: The Epic Poets Theodotus and Philo and Ezekiel the Tragedian* (SBLTT 30; Pseudepigrapha series 12; Atlanta: Scholars Press, 1989); John J. Collins, "The Epic of Theodotus and the Hellenism of the Hasmoneans," *HTR* 73 (1980) 91–104.
53. Harold A. Attridge, "Philo the Epic Poet," *OTP*, 2:781–84; Yehoshua Gutman, "Philo the Epic Poet," *Scripta Hierosolymitana* 1 (Jerusalem: Magnes, 1954) 36–63.
54. See especially B. Z. Wacholder, *Eupolemus: A Study of Judaeo-Greek Literature* (Cincinnati: Hebrew Union College Press, 1974); Carl R. Holladay, *Fragments from Hellenistic Jewish Authors*, vol. 1: *Historians* (SBLTT 20; Pseudepigrapha series 10; Chico, CA: Scholars Press, 1983) 90–156.
55. Van der Horst, *Japheth*, 26.
56. See especially Levine, *Jerusalem*, 45–90.
57. See Eric Gruen, *Heritage and Hellenism: The Reinvention of Jewish Tradition* (Berkeley: University of California Press, 1998) xv; John J. Collins, "The Hellenization of Jerusalem in the Pre-Maccabean Era," *International Rennert Guest Lecture Series* 6 (Jerusalem: Ingeborg Rennert Center for Jerusalem Studies, 1999).
58. See his *Aegyptiaca*, partially preserved in Diodorus Siculus, *Bibliotheca historica* 40.3.4–7. Also see Pseudo-Hecataeus, *On the Jews*, written during the first half of the second century BCE.
59. Nahman Avigad, *Jewish City Excavations in the Old City of Jerusalem, Conducted by Nahman Avigad, 1969–1982*, ed. Hillel Geva (Jerusalem: Israel Exploration Society, 2000); Th. A. Busink, *Der Tempel in Jerusalem von Salomo bis Herodes* (2nd ed.; Leiden: Brill, 1980); Hengel, "Jerusalem als jüdische und hellenistiche Stadt," 128–52; van Henten and van der Horst, eds., *Studies in Early Jewish Epigraphy*; Tal Ilan, "New Ossuary Inscriptions from Jerusalem," *Scripta Classica Israelica* 9 (1991/1992) 149–59; H.-P. Kuhnen, *Palästina in griechisch-römischer Zeit* (*HO*, Archäologie, Vorderasien II/2; Munich: Beck, 1990); Levine, *Jerusalem*.
60. Diodorus Siculus, *Bibliotheca historica* 40.3.8.
61. See Hengel, *Judaism and Hellenism*, 1:76. Greek tutors may have been present in the house of the high priest as early as the third century. This would help to explain why Jason, the son of the high priest Simeon II, was a leading hellenizer.
62. See Arie Kindler, "Silver Coins Bearing the Name of Judea from the Early Hellenistic Period," *IEJ* 24 (1974) 73–76; D. T. Ariel, "A Survey of Coin Finds in Jerusalem," *SBFLA* 32 (1982) 273–326; Dan Barag, "The Coinage of Yehud and the Ptolemies," in *Studies in Honor of Arie Kindler*, ed. Dan Barag (Jerusalem: Israel Numismatic Society, 1999) 27–38.
63. D. T. Ariel, *Excavations at the City of David 1978–1985* (Qedem 30; Jerusalem: Institute of Archaeology, Hebrew University, 1990). For stamped handles and pottery from the Persian and Hellenistic periods in Jerusalem, see his "Locally Stamped Handles and Associated Body Fragments of the Persian and Hellenistic Periods," in *Excavations at the City of David 1978–1985 Directed by Yigal Shiloh*, vol. 6: *Inscriptions* (Qedem 41; Jerusalem: Institute of Archaeology, Hebrew University, 2000) 137–94.
64. *CPJ*, 1:115–30.
65. Hengel, "Jerusalem als jüdische und hellenistische Stadt," 128–32.
66. See ibid., 129.

67. *Judaism and Hellenism*, 1:3. See also the helpful discussions by G. Delling, "Die Begegnung zwischen Hellenismus und Judentum," *ANRW*, 20.1, 2, 3–39; Erich S. Gruen, *Heritage and Hellenism*; Lee I. Levine, *Judaism and Hellenism in Antiquity: Conflict or Confluence?* (Seattle: University of Washington Press, 1998).

68. Martin Hengel, "Judaism and Hellenism Revisited," in *Hellenism in the Land of Israel*, 6–37.

69. Peter Schäfer, *The History of the Jews in the Graeco-Roman World* (2nd ed.; London: Routledge, 2003) 1.

70. Hengel, *Jews, Greeks, and Barbarians*, 51–54.

71. See the essay by John J. Collins, "Cult and Culture: The Limits of Hellenization in Judea," in *Hellenism in the Land of Israel*, 38–61.

72. Studies of Hellenistic Judea include John J. Collins, *Between Athens and Jerusalem* (2nd ed.; Biblical Resource Series; Grand Rapids: Eerdmans, 2000); idem and Sterling, eds., *Hellenism in the Land of Israel*; Hengel, *Judaism and Hellenism*; idem, *Jews, Greeks, and Barbarians*; Louis H. Feldman, *Jew and Gentile in the Ancient World* (Princeton: Princeton University Press, 1993); Tcherikover, *Hellenistic Civilization*.

73. See especially the Zeno papyri and the accounts of the Tobiads by Josephus in *Ant.* 12.4.1–11 for the economic and administrative involvement of Jews in Hellenistic Egypt.

74. Hengel, *Jews, Greeks, and Barbarians*, 120–21. See Hengel, *Judaism and Hellenism*, 1:115–30; Rainer Braun, *Kohelet und die frühhellenistische Popularphilosophie* (BZAW 130; Berlin: de Gruyter, 1973); Dominic Rudman, *Determinism in the Book of Ecclesiastes* (Sheffield: Sheffield Academic Press, 2001), who points to a comparison with Stoic philosophy.

75. "Qoheleth" (1:1; 7:27; 12:8, 9) is not a personal name, but an office, likely meaning a collector of sayings or one who assembles (students in his school).

76. Hengel, "Judaism and Hellenism Revisited," 20–21. "God" (*ĕlōh* אלהים *îm*, אים) is used by Qoheleth forty times. He does not use the word "Yahweh" or any other divine name. Most of the time the noun is accompanied by the definite article. This is Qoheleth's way of referring to an impersonal, remote, yet universal Deity.

77. "Influence from the Greek world of ideas is seen in Koheleth more than in any other Old Testament work" (Hengel, *Judaism and Hellenism*, 1:115).

78. Hengel, *Jews, Greeks, and Barbarians*, 120–21.

79. Personal correspondence, October 13, 2003.

80. Braun, *Kohelet*, 45–55.

81. Norbert Lohfink, *Qoheleth* (Continental Commentaries, Old Testament; Minneapolis: Fortress, 2003) 14–15.

82. Hartmut Gese, "Die Krisis der Weisheit bei Koheleth," in *Les Sagesses du Proche-Orient Ancien Bibliothèque des Centres d'Études supérieures spécialisés* (Paris: Presses Universitaires de France, 1963) 139–51.

83. Frank Crüsemann, "The Unchangeable World: The 'Crisis of Wisdom' in Koheleth," in *God of the Lowly*, ed. Willy Schottroff and Wolfgang Stegemann (Maryknoll, NY: Orbis, 1984) 57–77; Aare Lauha, "Die Krise des Religiösen Glaubens bei Kohelet," in *Wisdom in Israel and in the Ancient Near East*, 183–91; Hans-Peter Müller, "Neige der althebräischen 'Weisheit': Zum Denken Qohäläts," *ZAW* 90 (1978) 238–64.

84. Tcherikover, *Hellenistic Civilization*, 59–75. See Polybius, *Hist.* 5.86.10.

85. Greek autobiography appears in such writings as Xenophon's *Anabasis*, Isocrates' *Antidosis*, Demosthenes' *On the Crown*, and Plato's *Seventh Letter*. The memoir began to appear in the third century BCE (see the Sicyonian statesman Aratus). See *OCD*, 241–42. However, these vary significantly from Qoheleth's testament.

86. See Jan Bergman, "Discours d'adieu—Testament—Discours poshume: Testaments juifs et enseignements égyptien," in *Sagesse et Religion*, 21–50; Jan Assmann, "Schrift, Tod und Identität: Das Grab als Vorschule der Literatur im alten Ägypten," in *Schrift und Gedächtnis: Beiträge zur Archäologie der literarischen Kommunikation*, ed. Aleida Assmann, et al. (Munich: W. Fink, 1983); Miriam Lichtheim, *Ancient Egyptian Autobiographies Chiefly of the Middle Kingdom: A Study and an Anthology* (OBO 84; Göttingen: Vandenhoeck & Ruprecht, 1988); Eberhard Otto, *Die biographischen Inschriften der Ägyptischen Spätzeit* (Probleme der Ägyptologie 2; Leiden: Brill, 1954); Olivier Perdu, "Ancient Egyptian Biographies," *CANE* 4 (1995): 2243–54; Andrea M. Gnirs, "Die Ägyptische Autobiographie," in *Ancient Egyptian Literature: History and Forms*, 191–241; Jan Assmann, "Der literarische Aspekt des Ägyptischen Grabes und seine Funktion im Rahmen des 'Monumentalen Diskurses,'" in *Ancient Egyptian Literature: History and Forms*, 97–104; Shannon Burkes, *Death in Qoheleth and Egyptian Biographies of the Late Period* (SBLDS 170; Atlanta: Society of Biblical Literature, 1999) 171–208.

87. Otto, *Biographischen Inschriften*, 70–71. See inscriptions 46, 58b, 58c, 127, etc.

88. Ibid., inscriptions 10c, 10h, 3e, 19, 46, 58, etc.

89. See Jan Bergman, "Gedanken zum Thema 'Lehre-Testament-Grab-Name,'" in *Studien zu Altägyptischen Lebenslehren*, 73–104.

90. Otto, *Die Biographischen Inschriften*.

91. Ibid., 61.

92. See Otto's translation of the text on the statue of Neb-neteru: "The exit from life is sorrow, signifying want from what was yours formerly and emptiness of possessions. It means sitting in the hall of unconsciousness awaiting the announcement of a morning that never comes. It offers as compensation an eye that weeps—take care, for it comes! It means knowing nothing and sleep when the sun is in the East. It means thirst for beer! Therefore, the West itself answers: 'Give . . . to the one who follows his heart! The heart is a god. Desire is its shrine. It rejoices when the body's members are in a festive mood" (ibid., inscription 5; cf. inscription 57).

93. Michael Fox argues that Qoheleth is the composer of the epilogue and the author of the book (*Qohelet and His Contradictions* [JSOTSup 71: Sheffield: Almond, 1989] 311–21). Harold Fisch argues that the epilogue (12:9–14) derives from the same person who edited the rest of the book ("Qohelet: A Hebrew Ironist," in *Poetry with a Purpose: Biblical Poetics and Interpretation* [Bloomington: Indiana University Press, 1988] 158–78). I tend to agree with Fisch.

94. See Taimhotep, who tells her husband: "O (my) brother, husband, friend, high priest: do not weary of drink, food, deep drinking, and loving. Make a holiday! Follow your heart day and night! Do not set sorrow in your heart. What are the years which are not on earth?" This translation is taken from Burkes, *Death in Qoheleth*, 192–93.

95. For an introduction to Hellenistic skepticism, see A. A. Long, *Hellenistic Philosophy: Stoics, Epicureans, Sceptics* (New York: Scribner, 1974).

96. Wilhelm Nestle, "Der Pessimismus und sein Überwindung bei den Griechen," *Neues Jahrbuch für die klassische Altertumswissenschaft* 24 (1921) 81–97.

97. See Homer, *Iliad* 12.449. Noted by Braun, *Kohelet*, 15.

98. See Hesiod, *Theogony*, which often speaks of mortal humans in the midst of his contrasting description of the mighty and eternal gods (590–91, 765–66). The lyrical writing of Theognis, an elegiac poet of Megara in the mid-sixth century, BCE, is preserved within a larger collection of expanded poetry attributed to him. However, the expansions are due to his work's incorporation into a larger collection of several elegiac anthologies. His work, likely intended for reading in the symposia, set forth the view that Sophocles' plays portray the final end of

human existence as death and the grave, although he does portray humans as the master of their own fate. Euripides' eighteen tragedies that have been preserved depict humans railing against the unchangeable fate of humans brought about by divine tyranny. This final destiny of every person is the tomb.

99. See Theognis, *Work and Days*.

100. See Sophocles and Euripides.

101. Braun, *Kohleth*, 27–31.

102. In addition to Sextus Empiricus, see Diogenes Laertius (9.79–80) of the third century CE.

103. John Glucker, *Antiochus and the Late Academy* (Hypomnemata, Untersuchungen zur Antike und zu ihrem Nachleben 56; Göttingen: Vandenhoeck & Ruprecht, 1978); Martin Ostwald and J. P. Lynch, "The Growth of Schools and the Advance of Knowledge," in *Cambridge Ancient History*, vol. 6: *The Fourth Century B.C.*, ed. D. M. Lewis, et al. (2nd ed.; Cambridge: Cambridge University Press, 1994), 592–633.

104. Malcolm Schofield summarizes the three major assertions of Arcesilaus against Stoic epistemology as follows: (1) "there is no true impression such that there could not be a false impression indistinguishable from it. From this he further argued (2) that in that case if the wise person assents, what he will be holding is an opinion—since cognition is impossible. And he held (3) that it is necessary for the wise person not to hold opinions, and so not to assent" ("Academic Epistemology," *The Cambridge History of Hellenistic Philosophy* [Cambridge: Cambridge University Press, 1999] 344).

105. The influence of Hellenism on Qoheleth has been argued by Harry Ranston, "Koheleth and the Early Greeks," *JTS* 24 (1923) 160–69; idem, *Ecclesiastes and the Early Greek Wisdom Literature* (London: Epworth, 1925), Martin Hengel, "The Political and Social History of Palestine from Alexander to Antiochus III (333–187 BCE)," in *Cambridge History of Judaism*, vol. 2: *The Hellenistic Age*, ed. W. D. Davies and Louis Finkelstein (Cambridge: Cambridge University Press, 1989) 35–78; idem, "The Interpenetration of Judaism and Hellenism in the Pre-Maccabean Period," in ibid., 167–228.

106. Braun, *Kohelet*, 170.

107. Philip Mitsis, *Epicurus' Ethical Philosophy: The Pleasures of Invulnerability* (Ithaca, NY: Cornell University Press, 1988).

108. See Christine Schams, *Jewish Scribes in the Second-Temple Period* (JSOTSup 291; Sheffield: Sheffield Academic Press) 73–83.

109. Roland E. Murphy, "The Sage in Ecclesiastes and Qoheleth the Sage," in *Sage in Israel*, 263–71.

110. Walther Zimmerli, "Das Buch des Predigers Salomo," in Helmer Ringgren and Walther Zimmerli, *Sprüche/Prediger* (ATD 16; Göttingen: Vandenhoeck & Ruprecht, 1962) 123–351.

111. Fishbane, *Biblical Interpretation in Ancient Israel*, 29–32.

112. Sheppard, *Wisdom as a Hermeneutical Construct*, 126.

113. For *limmad* as a scribal, sapiential activity that was assumed later by the Levites, see 2 Chr. 17:7–9.

114. The *'am* could be understood in several ways: "people" (Gen. 11:6), "population" of a land or city (Ruth 4:4, 9), "people" in general (Num. 21:6), and a "group" of people (Deut. 18:3).

115. This "knowledge" in a school setting would refer to the curriculum taught to students.

116. Murphy (*Tree of Life*, 49) and Seow (*Ecclesiastes*, 20) date the book in the late Persian period. However, Collins (*Jewish Wisdom in the Hellenistic Age*, 14–15), James L. Crenshaw, *Ecclesiastes: A Commentary* (OTL; Louisville: Westminster/John

Knox Press, 1988) 49–50; Lohfink (*Qoheleth*, 4–6), Thomas Krüger, *Qohelet: A Commentary* (Hermeneia; Minneapolis: Fortress, 2004), 19; and W. Sibley Towner ("The Book of Ecclesiastes," *NIB* 5 [1997] 271) point to the third century BCE, during the period of Ptolemaic rule of Palestine. Krüger (*loc. cit.*) is even more specific when he argues for a date close to the beginning of the reign of Ptolemy V Epiphanes (205–180 BCE). For a consideration of the manuscript fragments of Qumran and their impact on the question of date, see my essay, "Wisdom and Apocalyptic: The Case of Qoheleth." Here I suggest that the book may date as late as the end of the third century BCE. This argument is based on several factors: the lateness of the Hebrew (see Anton Schoors, *The Preacher Sought to Find Pleasing Words: A Study of the Language of Qoheleth* [OLA 41; Leuven: Peeters, 1992]); Ben Sira's critical response to Qoheleth (see Krüger, *Koheleth*, 53–55; Johann Marböck, *Untersuchungen zur Weisheitstheologie bei Ben Sira* [BBB 37; Bonn: Hanstein, 1971] 281–82); the dating of the Qumran fragments (4QQoh), the earliest of which can be traced back to 175 to 150 BCE; and the similarities to certain views inherent in Greek philosophy, in particular those of the Skeptics in the New Academy. The importance of sapiential texts and the manuscripts of Qoheleth from Qumran for examining the history of the redaction of this book may be seen in two essays by Armin Lange: "In Diskussion mit dem Tempel: Zur Auseinandersetzung zwischen Kohelet und weisheitlichen Kreisen am Jerusalemer Tempels," in *Qoheleth in the Context of Wisdom*, ed. Antoon Schoors (BETL 136; Leuven: Peeters, 1998) 113–59; idem, "Eschatological Wisdom in the Book of Qohelet and the Dead Sea Scrolls," in *The Dead Sea Scrolls Fifty Years after Their Discovery: Proceedings of the Jerusalem Congress, July 20–25, 1997*, ed. Lawrence H. Schiffman, et al. (Jerusalem: Israel Exploration Society and Shrine of the Book, 2000) 817–25.

117. See my article, "The Testament of David and Egyptian Royal Instructions," in *Scripture in Context*, vol 2: *More Essays on the Comparative Method*, ed. W. W. Hallo, James C. Moyer, and L. G. Perdue (Winona Lake, IN: Eisenbraun, 1983), 79–96.

118. See especially Oswald Loretz, *Qohelet und der Altes Orient* (Freiburg: Herder, 1964) 167–73; Roland E. Murphy, *Wisdom Literature* (FOTL 13; Grand Rapids: Eerdmans, 1981) 125–49.

119. For the different translations of the word, see Crenshaw, *Ecclesiastes*, 32–34.

120. See Diethelm Michel, *Untersuchungen zur Eigenart des Buches Qohelet. Mit einem Anhang: Reinhard Lehmann, Bibliographie zu Qohelet* (BZAW 183; Berlin: de Gruyter, 1989); Fox, *Qohelet and His Contradictions*; Towner, "Ecclesiastes," 269–70.

121. Walther Zimmerli, "Das Buch Kohelet—Traktat oder Sentenzensammlung?" *VT* 24 (1974) 221–30. Zimmerli thinks it is more than simply a loose collection of different sayings, as is the case with Proverbs. Other possibilities have been proposed: the Cynic-Stoic diatribe (e.g., Braun, *Kohelet*, 36, 179); a type of school book used for the instruction of youths (Lohfink, 12–13); a wisdom teaching (Krüger, *Qohelet*, 11–14); and a reflective internal discourse (Roland Murphy, *Ecclesiastes* [WBC 23A; Dallas: Word, 1992]).

122. E.g., Aarre Lauha, *Kohelet* (BKAT 19; Neukirchen-Vluyn: Neukirchener Verlag, 1978) 5.

123. There are several examples of first-person narratives in Israelite and Jewish wisdom texts: Prov. 4:3–9; 24:30–34; Sir. 33:16–18; and Ps. 73.

124. Schwartz, *Imperialism and Jewish Society*, 29–30.

125. Braun, *Kohelet*, 153–59.

126. See Ragnar Höistad, *Cynic Hero and Cynic King: Studies in the Cynic Conception of Man* (Lund: Bloms, 1948).

127. Loretz (*Qoheleth und der Alte Orient*, 148, 161, 212–13) and von Rad (*Wisdom in Israel*, 226) have argued that the royal testament was the literary form for the entire book of Qoheleth. Others limit this form to 1:12–2:26.

128. See Eckhard von Nordheim, *Die Lehre der Alten* (2 vols.; Arbeiten zum Literatur und Geschichte des Hellenistischen Judentum 13, 20; Leiden: Brill, 1980–85).

129. For a list of Egyptian sapiential texts ascribed to famous sages in the past, see "In Praise of Learned Scribes," *ANET*, 431–32 (Chester Beatty IV verso ii 5-iii 11) probably dating ca. 1300 BCE. For texts exhorting youths to be scribes and speaking of the superiority of the scribal profession, see Lichtheim, *Ancient Egyptian Literature*, 2:167–78.

130. Sheppard argues that the composer of the epilogue is a commentator who, like Ben Sira, seeks to establish a relationship between wisdom and the Torah ("The Epilogue to Qoheleth as Theological Commentary," *CBQ* 39 [1977] 182–89).

131. The setting of death for instructions is a common one. See my essay, "Paraenesis and the Death of the Sage," in *Paraenesis: Act and Form*, 81–109.

132. See Karl-Heinz Bernhardt, *Das Problem der altorientalischen Königs Ideologie im Alten Testament* (VTSup 8; Leiden: Brill, 1961); Kalugila, *Wise King*.

133. See Addison Wright, "The Riddle of the Sphinx: The Structure of the Book of Qoheleth," *CBQ* 30 (1968) 313–34.

134. Klaus Seybold, *TDOT* 3 (1978) 313–20. Seybold gives *hebel* (הבל) a rather wide semantic range. He argues that the terms often paralleled to *hebel* in the Bible are *rîq* (ריק, "empty"), *tōhû* (תהו, "emptiness, nothingness"), *šeqer* (שקר, "lie"), *ʾāwen* (און, "delusion, illusion, fraud"), *šāwʾ* (שוא, "emptiness"), *lōʾ hôʿîlû* (לא הועילו, "worthless, good for nothing"), and especially *rûaḥ* (רוח, "wind, breath, spirit"). Of the semantic field for *rûaḥ*, *hebel* shares the meanings of "wind, breath, storm" and "breath of life." See now Douglas B. Miller, *Symbol and Rhetoric in Ecclesiastes: The Place of Hebel in Qohelet's Work* (Academia Biblica 2; Atlanta: Society of Biblical Literature, 2002). Miller notes that the word is indeed polyvalent, but in some sense always relates to the key meaning of "vapor."

135. Crenshaw, *Ecclesiastes*, 23; Rudi Kroeber, *Der Prediger* (Schriften und Quellen der Alten Welt 13; Berlin: Akademie Verlag, 1963) 122; Lauha, *Kohelet*, 18.

136. Michael Fox, "The Meaning of *Hebel* for Qohelet," *JBL* 105 (1986): 409–27.

137. W. E. Staples, "Vanity of Vanities," *Canadian Journal of Theology* 1 (1955) 141–56.

138. Seow, *Ecclesiastes*, 112; Kurt Galling, *Prediger Salomon* (2nd ed., HAT 18; Tübingen: J. C. B. Mohr, 1969), 79; Robert Gordis, *Koheleth the Man and His World: A Study of Ecclesiastes* (3rd augm. ed: New York: Schocken Books, 1968) 20; Scott, *Proverbs. Ecclesiastes*, 202; Loretz, *Qohelet und der alte Orient*, 223.

139. Another term for "breath" is *nĕšāmâ* (נשמה), which God breathes into human beings at creation, making them a "living being" (i.e., *nepeš*, נפש). See Gen. 2:7; Job 33:4; 34:14.

140. For *rĕʿût* (רעות) see 2:11, 17, 26; 4:4; and 6:9.

141. Marcus Jastrow, *A Dictionary of the Targumim, the Talmud Babli and Yerushalmi, and the Midrashic Literature* (repr. New York: Judaica Press, 1985) 1486. See Zimmerli, "Predigers Salomo," 48.

142. The word *yitrôn* occurs ten times in Qoheleth (1:3; 2:11, 13; 3:9; 5:8, 15; 7:12; 10:10, 11), while *yôtēr* is present seven times (2:15; 6:8, 11; 7:11, 16; 12:9, 12), and *môtār* (מותר) once (3:19; see Prov. 14:23; 21:5).

143. *Ecclesiastes*, 113.

144. See Edwin Good, "The Unfilled Sea: Style and Meaning in Ecclesiastes 1:2–11," in *Israelite Wisdom: Theological and Literary Essays in Honor of Samuel Terrien*, ed.

John G. Gammie, et al. (Missoula, MT: Scholars Press, 1978) 59–73; R. N. Whybray, "Ecclesiastes 1:5–7 and the Wonders of Nature," *JSOT* 41 (1988) 105–12.

145. Ernst Jenni sees *'ōlām* (עלם) as meaning "an extensive expanse of time" ("Das Wort *'ōlām* im Alten Testament," *ZAW* 64 [1952] 197–248; 65 [1953] 1–35).

146. See my essay, "Cosmology and the Social Order in the Wisdom Tradition," in *Sage in Israel*, 457–78.

147. Young-Jin Min, "How Do the Rivers Flow? (Ecclesiastes 1:7)," *BT* 42 (1991) 229.

148. Israel's wisdom literature is clearly monotheistic, save for the figure of Woman Wisdom, who takes on the attributes of a goddess similar to Ma'at and Isis. Qoheleth's emphasis is on "the God." The definite article adds to the sense of the powerful creator and sovereign who is removed from human understanding.

149. Crüsemann notes that God in Qoheleth has become an impersonal power that cannot be known or influenced ("Unchangeable World," 59).

150. Rudi Kroeber, *Der Prediger*, Hebräisch und Deutsch (Berlin: Akademie-Verlag, 1963) 124; O. S. Rankin, "The Book of Ecclesiastes," *IB* 5 (1956) 17.

151. Graham S. Ogden notes that this unceasing activity of humans parallels the cosmic movements of nature and points to the lack of completion or fulfillment ever being obtained ("The Interpretation of *dwr* in Ecclesiastes 1.4," *JSOT* 34 [1986] 92). Also see Johannes Pedersen, "Scepticisme israélite," *RHPR* 10 (1930) 345.

152. Aarre Lauha, "Kohelets Verhältnis zur Geschichte," in *Die Botschaft und die Boten*, 393–401.

153. See 3:21, which is skeptical about the mythic (post-diluvian *apkallu*s and later the apocalyptic descriptions of seers (in Qoheleth's case, breath, *rûaḥ*, רוח) "going upward" (presumably to heaven).

154. See Lauha, "Kohelets Verhältnis zur Geschichte," 393–401. Zimmerli argues that Qoheleth points not to an unchangeable world but rather to the limits of human existence and knowledge ("'Unveränderbare Welt' oder 'Gott ist Gott'? Ein Plädoyer für die Unaufgebbarkeit der Predigerbuches in der Bibel," in *"Wenn nicht jetzt wann dann?"* 103–14).

155. Crüsemann, "Unchangeable World," 57–77.

156. The verb *lidrôš* (לדרוש) means "to inquire" for something that is true or even normative (Exod. 18:15; Isa. 9:12; Job 5:8; Ezra 7:10; 1 Chr. 10:14; 22:19). However, *lātûr* (לתור) refers to searching out something or an idea that is new (Num. 10:33; 13:16–17; Deut. 1:33). For a discussion of the nuances of these two infinitives, see Seow, *Ecclesiastes*, 144.

157. The word *'inyān* (ענין) occurs only in Qoheleth: 1:13; 2:23, 26; 3:10; 4:8; 5:2, 13; and 8:16. The term indicates a task that induces "restlessness, obsession, anxiety, worry" (Seow, *Ecclesiastes*, 121).

158. The verb *la'ănôt* (לענות), in the sense of "to be busy," occurs only twice in the Hebrew Bible, here in 1:13 and 3:10. The word suggests to be preoccupied with an activity that causes unease or anxiety.

159. Qoheleth uses this term forty-seven times and adds "in my heart" (i.e., "mind") twenty-six times.

160. For *śimḥâ* (שמחה) see E. Ruprecht, *TLOT* 3 (1997) 1272–77.

161. This noun occurs seven times in the book (2:10, 21; 3:22; 5:17, 18; 9:6, 9). *Ḥēleq* (חלק) normally refers to an inheritance, but Qoheleth uses it to speak of the destiny of human beings in general, and the experience of joy in particular.

162. This verb means "to become master of" (Neh. 5:15; Esth. 9:1; Eccl. 8:9).

163. Von Rad, *Wisdom in Israel*, 139.

164. Ibid., 138–43.

165. Wolff, *Anthropology of the Old Testament*, 89–92.

166. This noun is found in Neh. 2:6; Esth. 9:27, 31; and Sir. 43:7, and refers to the cosmic order of time, while *'ēt* has to do with the time associated with specific events.

167. For Qoheleth, "the all" (*hakkol*, הכל) refers on occasion to cosmic reality or "all things" ("heaven and earth," humans and creatures, society and nature; cf. 1:2, 14; 2:11, 17; 3:19), while *ḥēpeṣ* (חפץ) at times refers to individual events or matters (3:17; 5:7; 8:6).

168. See the argument by Bernhard Lang that there are still choices humans can make ("Ist der Mensch hilflos?" *TQ* 159 [1979] 109–24).

169. Reading the root as "eternity." Other suggestions are "darkness," the "desire for eternity," and the "world." Several have emended the word to read *hā'āmāl*, "toil"; see H. Louis Ginsberg, *Studies in Koheleth* (New York: The Jewish Theological Seminary, 1950); Fox, *Qoheleth and His Contradictions*, 194.

170. See Kurt Galling, "Das Rätsel der Zeit," *ZTK* 58 (1961) 1–15.

171. Daniel Lys, "L'Être et le temps," in *Sagesse de l'Ancien Testament*, 249–58.

172. See Stephen Crites, "The Narrative Quality of Experience," *JAAR* 39 (1971) 291–311.

173. This literary strategy compares with "The Dialogue of Pessimism" from Babylonian wisdom literature (see J. A. Loader, *Polar Structures in the Book of Qoheleth* [BZAW 152; Berlin: de Gruyter, 1979]). There were also apocalyptic scribes in Judea and likely in Jerusalem as is demonstrated by the existence of *1 Enoch* from the third century BCE (chaps. 1–36; 72–82). See Michael E. Stone, *Scriptures, Sects and Visions: A Profile of Judaism from Ezra to the Jewish Revolts* (Cleveland: Collins, 1980) 27–35; James C. VanderKam, *Enoch and the Growth of an Apocalyptic Tradition* (Washington, DC: Catholic Biblical Association, 1984) 79–88, 111–14.

174. Hertzberg sees 3:20 as an approximate citation of Gen. 3:19. Indeed, both Gordis and he argue that Qoheleth knew the Genesis creation tradition in its final form (H. W. Hertzberg, *Der Prediger*, [KAT 17/4; Gütersloh: Mohr, 1963] 46, 227–30; Gordis, *Koheleth*, 43). Also see C. C. Forman, "Koheleth's Use of Genesis," *JSS* 5 (1960) 256–63.

175. *'ereṣ* (ארץ) also occasionally refers to the underworld (e.g., Job 10:21–22).

176. John J. Collins, "The Sage in the Apocalyptic and Pseudepigraphic Literature," *Seers, Sibils, and Sages in Hellenistic-Roman Judaism* (JSJSup 54; Leiden: Brill, 1997) 339–50 = *Sage in Israel*, 343–54. Collins agrees with Müller that Enoch and Daniel were "mantic sages" ("Mantische Weisheit und Apokalyptik"), but regards both 4 Ezra and 2 Baruch to be "visionary sages." Collins notes that the major difference between the visionary sage and the sage in the traditional wisdom literature in the Bible was in the former's claim to special revelation in dreams, visions, and in some cases heavenly ascents.

177. See Hellmut Brunner, "Gerechtigkeit as Fundament des Thrones," *VT* 8 (1958) 426–28; Schmid, *Gerechtigkeit als Weltordnung*.

178. For a discussion of Qoheleth's debate with sapiential tradition, see Roland Murphy, "Qohelet's 'Quarrel' with the Fathers," in *From Faith to Faith*, ed. D. Y. Hadidian (PTMS 31; Pittsburgh: Pickwick, 1979) 235–45.

179. Important studies of the temple include: Karl Rupprecht, *Der Tempel von Jerusalem* (BZAW 144; Berlin: de Gruyter, 1976); Volkmar Fritz, *Tempel und Zelt: Studien zum Tempelbau in Israel und zu dem Zeltheiligtum der Priesterschrift* (Neukirchen-Vluyn: Neukirchener Verlag, 1977); Busink, *Tempel von Jerusalem*.

180. Eglon Pfeiffer, "Die Gottesfurcht im Buche Kohelet," in *Gottes Wort und Gottes Land*, ed. H. G. Reventlow (Göttingen: Vandenhoeck & Ruprecht, 1965) 133–58.

181. See 2 Chr. 1:11, which speaks of the divine gifts of possessions, wealth, and honor bestowed on Solomon. Crenshaw notes that the verb *'ākal* (אכל, "to eat")

most likely means "to enjoy," since what is "eaten" includes riches, possessions, and honor (*Ecclesiastes*, 126).

182. For discussions of Qoheleth's views of God, see H.-P. Müller, "Wie sprach Qohälät von Gott?" *VT* 128 (1968) 507–21; Leo Gorssen, "La cohérence de la conception de dieu dans l'Ecclésiaste," *ETL* 46 (1970) 282–324.

183. Kroeber, *Prediger*, 29.

184. Loader notes that Qoheleth engages in polemics against traditional wisdom by turning its own topoi and forms against it (*Polar Structures*).

185. The topos of the "foreign woman" is a common one in wisdom texts (Prov. 2:16–19; 5:1–6; 6:24–35; 7:6–27; Ani, III, 13–14; Ptahhotep 275–76; Papyrus Insinger 8.5–6).

186. A proverb quoted by Qoheleth that by means of hyperbole affirms that human beings are universally wicked (Galling, *Prediger Salomon*, 109; Kroeber, *Prediger*, 148). Cf. 7:20 and 1 Kgs. 8:46.

187. The word translated "devices" occurs only here and in 2 Chr. 26:15, where it means "war machines." Qoheleth may be using the term as a metaphor for evil, destruction, or even death.

188. J. Bergman, et al., "יד," *TDOT* 5 (1986) 393–426. In addition to "hand" as a part of the human body, other meanings of the word include "personal responsibility" (Exod. 32:4; Prov. 6:17) and "possession, control" (Exod. 22:3; Deut. 3:8). In addition, the theological meaning is often "power" (Isa. 10:13; Job 30:21), "protection" (1 Kgs. 18:46; Isa. 49:2), or even "hostile divine power" (Job 13:21; 40:32).

189. Graham Ogden, "Qoheleth XI 1–6," *VT* 33 (1983) 222–30.

190. Reading "in" (*bĕ*, ב) with many Hebrew mss. and the Targum in the place of MT's "like" (*kĕ*, כ).

191. Von Rad, *Wisdom in Israel*, 139.

192. Ibid., 138–43.

193. See Graham S. Ogden, "Qoheleth XI 7–XII 8: Qoheleth's Summons to Enjoyment and Reflection," *VT* 34 (1984) 27–38.

194. R. E. Clements, "זכר," *TDOT* 4 (1980) 64–82. *Zākar* (זכר) often refers to humans remembering God (Deut. 8:18; Judg. 8:34; Ps. 78:35) and particularly divine deeds (Isa. 63:11–14; Ezek. 23:19, 27).

195. See Denis Buzy, "Le portrait de la vieillesse (Ecclésiaste xii, 1–7)," *RB* 41 (1932) 329–40; Michael V. Fox, "Aging and Death in Qohelet 12," *JSOT* 42 (1988) 55–77; Maurice Gilbert, "La description de la vieillesse en Qohelet xii 1–7, est-elle allégorique?" in *Congress Volume: Vienna 1980*, ed. J. A. Emerton (VTSup 32; Leiden: Brill, 1981) 96–109; John F. A. Sawyer, "The Ruined House in Ecclesiastes 12: A Reconstruction of the Original Parable," *JBL* 94 (1975) 519–31.

196. Crüsemann notes that "the deterioration of old age and the picture of its obnoxiousness that is given in 12:1–8 represent a typical reversal of segmentary thinking, since the elderly no longer embody the human ideal" ("Unchangeable World," 69).

197. Jacob Neusner, *The Mishnah: A New Translation* (New Haven: Yale University Press, 1988) 678. Abot 3:1.

198. *Gešem* (גשם) is used in Gen. 7:11–12 and 8:2–3 to refer to the rains which inundated the earth during the primeval flood (cf. Ezek. 38:22).

199. Prov. 7:6. An alternative interpretation is aristocratic ladies awaiting the return of their heroic warriors with spoil (Judg. 5:28).

200. Galling, *Prediger Salomon*, 122–23.

201. Certainly Qoheleth's abandonment of traditional Yahwism had its parallels in the Greek world, in which the ancient Olympian deities were renounced and replaced with human philosophies and mystery religions.

202. The symposium (*symposion*, συμποσία, "drinking together"), literally a "drinking party," was a scripted social gathering where men drank together, conversed, and enjoyed themselves in a setting that enhanced conviviality. See William J. Slater, ed., *Dining in a Classical Context* (Ann Arbor: University of Michigan Press, 1991).

Chapter 7: Hellenistic Wisdom in Judah: The Book of Ben Sira

1. See the bibliographical essay by Friederich V. Reiterer, "Die immateriellen Ebenen der Schöpfung bei Ben Sira (1980–1996)," in *The Book of Ben Sira in Modern Research: Proceedings of the First International Ben Sira Conference 28–31 July 1996 Soesterberg, Netherlands*, ed. P. C. Beentjes (BZAW 255; Berlin: de Gruyter, 1997) 48–54. Also see Friedrich V. Reiterer, et al., eds., *Bibliographie zu Ben Sira* (Berlin: de Gruyter, 1998).

2. See Gera, *Judaea and Mediterranean Politics*; Sherwin-White and Kuhrt, *From Samarkhand to Sardis*; and Amélie Kuhrt and Susan Sherwin-White, eds., *Hellenism in the East: The Interaction of Greek and Non-Greek Civilizations from Syria to Central Asia after Alexandria* (Berkeley: University of California Press, 1987).

3. Sherwin-White and Kuhrt, *From Samarkhand to Sardis*, 47–48.

4. Tcherikover, *Hellenistic Civilization*, 61–62.

5. Avigad, *Jewish Quarter Excavations*; Eilat Mazar, et al., *Excavations in the South of the Temple Mount: The Ophel of Biblical Jerusalem*, vol. 1 (Jerusalem: Hebrew University, 1989). Also see Benjamin Mazar, et al., "Jerusalem" in *New Encyclopedia of Archaeological Excavations in the Holy Land* 2, ed. Ephraim Stern (trans. George Lamb; 4 vols., Jerusalem: Israel Exploration Society and Carta, 1993) 2:698–767; Levine, *Jerusalem*.

6. H. I. Marrou, *A History of Education in Antiquity* (New York: Sheed & Ward, 1956) 95. There is little information about Jewish education in Ben Sira's period. The first information comes from two legends in the Jerusalem Talmud that place these stories after the beginning of the first century BCE (e.g., *b. Baba Batra* 21a). See S. Safrai, "Education and the Study of the Torah," in *The Jewish People in the First Century*, ed. Safrai and M. Stern (CRINT 1/2; Assen: Van Gercam, 1976), 2:947–48.

7. Alexander Di Lella, "Conservative and Progressive Theology: Sirach and Wisdom," *CBQ* 28 (1966) 139–54.

8. Several recent studies relate different features of Ben Sira's thought to Stoicism, especially the doctrine of providence. See Otto Kaiser, "Die Rezeption der stoischen Providenz bei Ben Sira," *JNSL* 24 (1998) 41–54; and the dissertation of his student, Ursel Wicke-Reuter, *Göttliche Providenz und menschliche Verantwortung bei Ben Sira und in der Frühen Stoa* (BZAW 298; Berlin: de Gruyter, 2000). See the latter's essay, "Ben Sira und die Frühe Stoa: Zum Zusammenhang von Ethik und dem Glauben an eine göttliche Providenz," in *Ben Sira's God: Proceedings of the International Ben Sira Conference Durham—Upshaw College 2001*, ed. Renate Egger-Wenzel (BZAW 321; Berlin: de Gruyter, 2002) 268–81. Also see S. L. Mattila, "Ben Sira and the Stoics: A Reexamination of the Evidence," *JBL* 119 (2000) 473–501.

9. Joseph Blenkinsopp, *Sage, Priest, Prophet: Religious and Intellectual Leadership in Ancient Israel* (LAI; Louisville: Westminster/John Knox, 1996), 19.

10. John J. Collins, *The Apocalyptic Imagination* (2nd ed.; Biblical Resource Series; Grand Rapids: Eerdmans, 1998) 145–76; idem, "Wisdom, Apocalypticism and the Dead Sea Scrolls," in *'Jedes Ding hat seine Zeit. . . .' Studien zur israelitischen und altorientalischen Weisheit*, ed. Anja A. Diesel, et al. (BZAW 241; Berlin: de Gruyter, 1996) 19–32; idem, *Apocalypticism in the Dead Sea Scrolls* (London:

Routledge, 1997); idem, "Apocalypticism and Literary Genre in the Dead Sea Scrolls," in *The Dead Sea Scrolls after Fifty Years: A Comprehensive Assessment*, ed. Peter W. Flint and James C. VanderKam (2 vols.; Leiden: Brill, 1998–99) 2:403–30; Lawrence H. Schiffman and James C. VanderKam, eds. *Encyclopedia of the Dead Sea Scrolls* (2 vols.; New York: Oxford, 2000); Adriaan van der Woude, "Wisdom at Qumran," in *Wisdom in Ancient Israel: Essays in Honour of J. A. Emerton*, ed. John Day, Robert P. Gordon, and H. G. M. Williamson (Cambridge: Cambridge University Press, 1995) 244–56; Armin Lange, "Die Bedeutung der Weisheitstexte aus Qumran," in *Weisheit in Israel*, 129–44; Florentino García Martínez, ed., *Wisdom and Apocalypticism in the Dead Sea Scrolls and in the Biblical Tradition* (BETL 168; Leuven: Leuven University Press, 2003); John J. Collins, Gregory E. Sterling, and Ruth A. Clements, eds., *Sapiential Perspectives: Wisdom Literature in Light of the Dead Sea Scrolls* (STDJ 51; Leiden: Brill, 2004); Matthew Goff, *Discerning Wisdom* (Wisdom Literature in the Old Testament 1; Leiden: Brill, 2007).

11. The date of the origins of this sect is widely debated. Frank Moore Cross (*The Ancient Library of Qumran* [3rd ed.; Minneapolis: Fortress, 1995]) championed the early date. However, numerous scholars, on the basis of paleography and material culture at the community, have placed the date at a later period; see especially Matthew Goff, *The Worldly and Heavenly Wisdom of 4QInstruction* (STDJ 50; Leiden: Brill, 2003) 231.

12. The Essene hypothesis has been advocated by numerous scholars, including Cross (*Ancient Library of Qumran*) and Hartmut Stegemann (*Die Essener, Qumran, Johannes der Täufer: Ein Sachbuch* [3rd ed.; Vienna: Herder, 1994]). For a criticism of this hypothesis, see Norman Golb, *Who Wrote the Dead Sea Scrolls? The Search for the Secret of Qumran* (New York: Scribner, 1995). The yaḥad (יחד) in the scrolls points not to a single community, but to numerous ones that comprised the sect.

13. See E. P. Sanders, "Aristocrats and Sadducees," *Judaism: Practice and Belief 63 BCE–66 CE* (London: SCM, 1992) 317–40.

14. See Daniel J. Harrington, *Wisdom Texts from Qumran: The Literature of the Dead Sea Scrolls* (London: Routledge, 1996); Torleif Elgvin, "Wisdom with and without Apocalyptic," in *Sapiential, Liturgical and Poetical Texts from Qumran*, ed. Daniel K. Falk and Florentino García Martínez (Proceedings of the Third Meeting of the International Organization for Qumran Studies Oslo 1998; Brill: Leiden, 2000) 15–38; Charlotte Hempel, *The Wisdom Texts from Qumran and the Development of Sapiential Thought*, ed. Charlotte Hempel, Armin Lange, and Hermann Lichtenberger (BETL 159; Leuven: Leuven University Press, 2002); Goff, *Wisdom in the Dead Sea Scrolls*.

15. See 4Q416 I–IV par. 4Q417 1 I–II par. 4Q418 7–10; 4Q418 126 II and 127; Lange, "Bedeutung der Weisheitstexte," 131–32.

16. Harrington, *Wisdom Texts from Qumran*, 48–49; see idem, "The *Rāz Nihyeh* in a Qumran Wisdom Text (1Q26, 4Q415–418, 423)," *RevQ* 17 (1996) 549–53. Also see Armin Lange, *Weisheit und Prädestination: Weisheitliche Urordnung und Prädestination in den Textfunden von Qumran* (STDJ 18; Leiden: Brill, 1995) 62, 91; Matthew J. Goff, "The Mystery of Creation in 4QInstruction," *DSD* 10 (2003) 163–86.

17. Harrington, *Wisdom Texts from Qumran*, 83. Eschatology is an important theme in the Book of Mysteries (1Q27 1; 4Q300 3); see Lange, "Bedentung der Weisheitstexte," 15.

18. This Persian-derived term means "secret" or "mystery." As Goff notes, it most frequently communicates the idea of revelation of secretive knowledge of divine origin in early Jewish texts (e.g., Dan. 2:18–19, 27–30, 47; 4:6; *1 Enoch* 103:2).

See "Mystery of Creation," 165. He concludes that the idiom refers to the divine determination of reality, both creation and history, that is revealed to the chosen (cf. 4Q417 1 i 18–19). Indeed, in his view, the idiom could just as easily be translated as the "eternal mystery" or "the mystery that exists always" (p. 169).

19. Torlief Elgvin, "Wisdom and Apocalypticism in the Early Second Century B.C.E.—The Evidence of 4QInstruction," in *Dead Sea Scrolls Fifty Years after Their Discovery: Proceedings of the Jerusalem Congress, July 20–25, 1997*, ed. L. H. Schiffman, et al. (Jerusalem: Israel Exploration Society and Shrine of the Book, 2000) 239. According to Elgvin, the expression *rāz nihyeh* is the "pre-existent sapiential order of creation," viewed through the lens of apocalyptic.

20. Goff, "Mystery of Creation," 179. This equating of *rāz* and the act of creation is also found in the *Hodayot* (e.g., 1QH 5:19).

21. Lawrence Schiffman, "4QMysteries: A Preliminary Translation," in *Proceedings of the Eleventh World Congress of Jewish Studies: Division A* (Jerusalem: World Union of Jewish Studies, 1994) 199–206; "4QMysteries[b], a Preliminary Edition," *RevQ* 16 (1993) 203–23; idem, "4QMysteries[a]: A Preliminary Edition and Translation," in *Solving Riddles and Untying Knots: Biblical, Epigraphic, and Semitic Studies in Honor of Jonas C. Greenfield*, ed. Ziony Zevit, Seymour Gitin, and Michael Sokoloff (Winona Lake, IN: Eisenbrauns, 1995) 207–26.

22. For a detailed list of wisdom texts from Qumran, see Lange, "Weisheitstexte aus Qumran," 3–30; and the appendix, 435–42.

23. Goff, "Mystery of Creation," 184–86.

24. Th. Middendorp, *Die Stellung Jesus Ben Siras zwischen Judentum und Hellenismus* (Leiden: Brill, 1973). For Ben Sira's knowledge of Greek philosophy, in particular Stoicism, see Raymond Pautrel, "Ben Sira et le Stoïcisme," *RSR* 51 (1963) 535–49; Hengel, *Judaism and Hellenism*, 1:146–50, 159–62; Johannes Marböck, *Weisheit im Wandel: Untersuchungen zur Weisheitstheologie bei Ben Sira* (BBB 37; Bonn: Peter Hanstein, 1971) 143–45. He perhaps was familiar with Isis aretalogies, as argued by Hans Conzelmann, "The Mother of Wisdom," in *The Future of Our Religious Past*, ed. James M. Robinson (New York: Harper & Row, 1971) 230–43; Marböck, *Weisheit im Wandel*, 48–54; Burton L. Mack, *Logos und Sophia: Untersuchungen zur Weisheitstheologie im hellenistischen Judentum* (SUNT 10; Göttingen: Vandenhoeck & Ruprecht, 1973) 40–42.

25. See Wolfgang Roth, "On the Gnomic-Discursive Wisdom of Jesus ben Sirach," *Semeia* 17 (1980) 59–79.

26. For a detailed discussion of Ben Sira as a learned scribe and teacher belonging to the priestly class, see Stadelmann, *Ben Sira als Schriftgelehrter*. The idea that he is from the priestly class is based on his staunch support of the temple (Sir. 24), the panegyric eulogy to Simeon II (Sir. 50), the emphasis on the Torah and the equation of it with wisdom, and the support of cultic religion (e.g., Sir. 31:21–32:26 = LXX 34:18–35:20; Perdue, *Wisdom and Cult*, 188–211). However, Ben Sira makes no claim that he has a priestly lineage. He rather is a learned scribe and wisdom teacher who strongly supports the Zadokite priesthood. The school in which Ben Sira taught may have been under the oversight of the Zadokites. For a discussion of Ben Sira's teaching in his private house, see Oda Wischmeyer, *Die Kultur des Buches Jesus Sirachs* (BZNW 77; Berlin: de Gruyter, 1995); Schams, *Jewish Scribes*.

27. This invitation is found in the acrostic poem at the end of the book. This poem also is partially present in the Psalms Scroll, leading some to question Ben Sira's authorship of the poem.

28. Yigael Yadin, *The Ben Sira Scroll from Masada with Introduction, Emendations, and Commentary* (Jerusalem: Israel Exploration Society, 1965).

29. See Lee I. Levine, *The Ancient Synagogue: The First Thousand Years* (New Haven: Yale University Press, 2000) 133.

30. For the list of synagogues see *CPJ*, 1:8; 3:9, 13, 22, 24–25, 27–28, 117, 125–27.

31. Other synagogues in Judah predated the Roman sacking of Jerusalem, including Chorazin, Qumran, Gedala, Kiriat Sefer, Magdala, Shuafat, and the recent Hasmonean one found in Jericho (Ehud Netzer, "A Synagogue from the Hasmonean Period Recently Exposed in the Western Plain of Jericho," *IEJ* 49 [1999] 203–21).

32. Adolf Deissmann, "Appendix V: The Synagogue Inscription of Theodotus at Jerusalem," *Light from the Ancient East: The New Testament Illustrated by Recently Discovered Texts of the Graeco-Roman World* (New York: Harper, 1928) 439–41 and fig. 80.

33. In my view Sanders has not made a convincing case that Ben Sira could read demotic texts (see Jack T. Sanders, *Ben Sira and Demotic Wisdom* [SBLMS 28; Chico, CA: Scholars Press, 1983]).

34. Lichtheim, *Late Egyptian Wisdom Literature*, 106.

35. See ibid., 104–6.

36. See ibid., 1–12.

37. André Barucq, "Une veine de spiritualité sacerdotale et sapientielle dans l'égypte ancienne," in *À la rencontre de Dieu: Mémorial Albert Gélin*, ed. André Barucq (Bibliothèque de la faculté catholique de théologie de Lyon 8; Le Puy Mappus, 1961) 193–202.

38. See Williams, "Egyptian Literature (Wisdom)," 397.

39. Lichtheim, *Ancient Egyptian Literature*, 3:159–84; idem, *Late Egyptian Wisdom Literature*, 13–92; Brunner, *Weisheitsbücher der Ägypter*, 257–91.

40. Lichtheim, *Late Egyptian Wisdom Literature*, 103–6. Also see Ulrich Wilcken, *Urkunden der Ptolemaerzeit* 1 (Berlin: de Gruyter, 1927) 127 and 133–34.

41. Williams, "Egyptian Literature (Wisdom)," 397.

42. Lichtheim, *Late Egyptian Wisdom Literature*, 92.

43. See Lichtheim, *Ancient Egyptian Literature* 3:184–217; idem, *Late Egyptian Wisdom Literature*, 107–234.

44. See Williams, "Egyptian Literature (Wisdom)," 397.

45. See Collins, *Between Athens and Jerusalem*, 33–37; Max Küchler, *Frühjüdische Weisheitstraditionen: Zum Fortgang weisheitlichen Denkens im Bereich des frühjüdischen Jahweglaubens* (OBO 26; Freiburg: Universitätsverlag, 1979) 117–21; Emilio Gabba, *Greek Knowledge of Jews up to Hecataeus of Abdera* (Berkeley: Center for Hermeneutical Studies, 1981); P. M. Fraser, *Ptolemaic Alexandria*, vol. 2 (Oxford: Clarendon, 1972) 960–61, n. 94.

46. See David G. Burke, *The Poetry of Baruch* (SBLSCS 10; Chico, CA: Scholars Press, 1982); Emanuel Tov, *The Book of Baruch also Called I Baruch (Greek and Hebrew)* (SBLTT 8; Missoula, MT: Scholars Press, 1975); idem, *The Septuagint Translation of Jeremiah and Baruch* (HSM 8; Missoula, MT: Scholars Press, 1976); P.-M. Bogaert, "Le personnage de Baruch et l'histoire du livre de Jérémie: Aux origines du livre deutéronocanonique de Baruch," *Studia Evangelica* 7, ed. E. A. Livingstone (TU 126; Berlin: Akademie Verlag, 1982) 73–81. Now see Reinhard Kratz, "Ezra—Priest and Scribe," in *Scribes, Sages, and Seers*, ed. Leo G. Perdue (FRLANT; Göttingen: Vandenhoeck & Ruprecht, forthcoming).

47. Stone, "Ideal Figures and Social Content: Priest and Sage in the Early Second Temple Age," in *Ancient Israelite Religion*, 575–86; John J. Collins, "The Sage in the Apocalyptic and Pseudepigraphic Literature," in *Sage in Israel*, 343–54.

48. See, e.g., Burke, *Poetry of Baruch*, 23–26.

49. C. A. Moore, "Toward Dating the Book of Baruch," *CBQ* 36 (1974) 312–20.

50. For a discussion of the issue of a Hebrew original, see Burke, *Poetry of Baruch*, 65–324.

51. Walter Harrelson, "Wisdom Hidden and Revealed according to Baruch (Baruch 3.9–4.4)," in *Priests, Prophets and Scribes*, ed. Eugene Ulrich, et al. (JSOTSup 149; Sheffield: Sheffield Academic Press, 1992) 158–71.

52. Attridge, "Historiography," 171–76; Doran, "First Book of Maccabees," 1–178; Bezalel Bar-Kochba, *Judas Maccabeus* (Cambridge: Cambridge University Press, 1988); Joseph Sievers, *The Hasmoneans and Their Supporters: From Mattathias to the Death of John Hyrcanus* (South Florida Studies in the History of Judaism 6; Atlanta: Scholars Press, 1991).

53. See Bar-Kochba, *Judas Maccabeus*; Seth Schwartz, "Israel and the Nations Roundabout: 1 Maccabees and the Hasmonean Expansion," *JJS* 42 (1991) 16–30.

54. Fergus Millar, "The Problem of Hellenistic Syria," in *Hellenism in the East*, 110.

55. In addition to Christian Habicht, *Jüdische Schriften aus hellenistisch-römische Zeit, Makkabäerbuch* (Gütersloh: Gütersloher Verlagshaus, 1979), other studies of this history include: Robert Doran, "2 Maccabees and 'Tragic History,'" *HUCA* 50 (1979) 107–14; idem, *Temple Propaganda: The Purpose and Character of 2 Maccabees* (Washington, DC: Catholic Biblical Association of America, 1981); idem, "2 Maccabees," *IB* 4:179–299; Thomas Fischer, *Seleukiden und Makkabäer: Beiträge zur Seleukidengeschichte und zu den politischen Ereignissen Judäa während der 1. Hälfte des 2. Jahrhunderts v. Chr.* (Bochum: N. Brockmeyer, 1980).

56. Second Maccabees has been preserved in two Greek uncials, Alexandrinus (fifth century CE) and Venetus (eighth century CE) and in numerous Greek minuscules.

57. Habicht, *2. Makkabäer*, 169.

58. Sherwin-White and Kuhrt, *From Samarkhand to Sardis*, 60–61.

59. Hengel, *Judaism and Hellenism*, 1:132–57; Marböck, *Weisheit im Wandel*; Küchler, *Frühjüdische Weisheitstraditionen*; E. J. Schnabel, *Law and Wisdom from Ben Sira to Paul* (WUNT 2/16; Tübingen: Mohr Siebeck, 1985); John G. Gammie, "The Sage in Sirach," in *Sage in Israel*, 355–72; Schams, *Jewish Scribes*, 98–106.

60. Michael E. Stone, "Ideal Figures and Social Context: Priest and Sage in the Early Second-Temple Age," *Selected Studies in Pseudepigrapha and Apocrypha: With Special Reference to the Armenian Tradition* (SVTP 9; Leiden: Brill, 1991) 259–70.

61. Compare to the Egyptian "Satire of the Trades" (*ANET*, 432–34).

62. Rudolph Smend, *Die Weisheit des Jesus Sirach erklärt* (Berlin: Reimer, 1906) 345–46; Gordis, "Social Background," 77–118. For Ben Sira's positive view of wealth, see 3:17–18; 10:27; 13:24; 14:11–16; 25:3; 34:3; 40:18; 44:6; 47:18.

63. Blenkinsopp, *Sage, Priest, Prophet*, 17.

64. Mack points to two ways that Ben Sira has reinterpreted prophetic inspiration: "First, it has been evoked as a moment that occurs in the context of prayer for mercy, thus verifying the scholar's piety and making the claim for superior understanding. Second, this moment itself has been cast as the bridge between research and authorship" (*Wisdom and the Hebrew Epic*, 99).

65. *Judaism and Hellenism*, 1:131–62.

66. Ibid., 247. See Marböck, *Weisheit im Wandel*, 83.

67. Johannes Marböck, "Kohelet und Sirach," in *Das Buch Kohelet*, ed. Ludger Schwienhorst-Schönberger (BZAW 254; Berlin: de Gruyter, 1995) 275–301.

68. See James L. Crenshaw, "The Book of Sirach," *NIB* 5 (1997) 628.

69. The Hebrew Bible refers a number of times to scribes as interpreters of Scripture: Jer. 18:18; Isa. 7:26; 22:26; 44:23–24; Hos. 4:6; Mic. 3:11; Zeph. 3:4; Hag. 2:10–13; 2 Chr. 15:3; 17:7–9; 19:5–10; 35:3. Deuteronomy 33:9b–10 speaks of Levites who taught the law, and Mal. 2:7–9 indicates that priests had the responsibility of instruction (see *Let. Aris.* 130–70; *Jub.* 32:1, 3, 9; 45:16;

the *T. Levi* 4, 8). Ben Sira also speaks of the sage's duty of interpreting and teaching the biblical texts (39:1–11).

70. See Johannes Marböck, "Sir. 38,24–39,11: Der schriftgelehrte Weise," in *Sagesse de l'Ancien Testament*, 293–316.

71. See my essay, "Ben Sira and the Prophets."

72. Benjamin G. Wright, "The Discourse of Riches and Poverty in the Book of Ben Sira," *SBLSP 1998* (Atlanta: Scholars Press, 1998) 559–78; Wischmeyer, *Kultur*, 181.

73. Hengel, "'Schriftauslegung' und 'Schriftwerdung'" 38–39.

74. Middendorp, *Stellung Jesu Ben Siras*, 136.

75. Wischmeyer, *Kultur*, 174–200.

76. Also see 2 Chr. 13:22; 24:27. For the late biblical and rabbinic meaning of *midrāš*, see Gary G. Porton, "Defining Midrash," in *The Study of Ancient Judaism*, ed. Jacob Neusner (2 vols.; New York: Ktav, 1981) 1:55–92. The term came to mean the literature that interpreted Scripture.

77. Wichmeyer, *Kultur*, 177.

78. See Stadelmann, *Ben Sira als Schriftgelehrter*, 296ff.

79. For a detailed list of references to the Hebrew prophets in Ben Sira, see Stadelmann, *Ben Sira als Schriftgelehrter*, 177–270. Also see Middendorp, *Stellung Jesus ben Siras*, 6–71; J. L. Koole, "Die Bibel des Ben-Sira," *OTS* 14 (1965) 374–96.

80. Schams, *Jewish Scribes*, 312–21.

81. Schams argues that there were scribes involved in the resistance movement against Antiochus IV Ephiphanes who fought to enable Jews to continue to study and practice their traditions and laws (*Jewish Scribes*, 314).

82. Patrick W. Skehan and Alexander A. Di Lella, *The Wisdom of Ben Sira* (AB 39; Garden City, NY: Doubleday, 1987) 21–30. For Greek forms, see Theodore C. Burgess, *Epideictic Literature* (Chicago: University of Chicago Press, 1902); and Stanley E. Porter, *Handbook of Classical Rhetoric in the Hellenistic Period 330 BC–400 AD* (Leiden: Brill, 1997).

83. Aristotle, *Rhet.* 2.20, 1393a23–1394a18. See Thomas R. Lee, *Studies in the Form of Sirach 44–50* (SBLDS 75; Atlanta: Scholars Press, 1986); Mack, *Wisdom and the Hebrew Epic*.

84. For the apostrophe see Stanley K. Stowers, "Apostrophe, προσωποπιία, and Paul's Rhetorical Education," in *Early Christiantiy and Classical Culture: Comparative Studies in Honer of Abraham J. Malherbe,* ed. John Fitzgerald et al. (SNT 110; Leiden: Brill, 2003) 351–69.

85. See Gammie and Perdue, eds., *Paraenesis: Act and Form.*

86. Conzelmann, "Mother of Wisdom," 230–43; Marböck, *Weisheit im Wandel*, 48–54; Mack, *Logos und Sophia.*

87. See Johann Marböck, "Structure and Redaction History of the Book of Ben Sira: Review and Prospects," in *Ben Sira in Modern Research*, 62–79; W.-W. Jungling, "Der Bauplan des Buches Jesus Sirach," in *"Den Armen eine frohe Botschaft."* FS *Franz Franphaus*, ed. J. Hainz (Frank am Main: Peter Lang, 1997) 89–105; Georg Sauer, "Gedanken über den thematischen Aufbau des Buches Ben Sira," in *Treasures of Wisdom: Studies in Ben Sira and the Book of Wisdom: FS Maurice Gilbert*, ed. Núria Calduch-Benages and Jacques Vermeylen (BETL 143; Leuven: Leuven University Press, 1999) 51–61.

88. The book does not appear to possess a detailed literary structure, in spite of several efforts to uncover one (see Collins, *Jewish Wisdom*, 45–46).

89. James C. VanderKam, *An Introduction to Early Judaism* (Grand Rapids: Eerdmans, 2001) 117.

90. See the argument by D. S. Williams, "The Date of Ecclesiasticus," *VT* 44 (1994) 563–66.

91. Collins, *Jewish Wisdom*, 18; Smend, *Weisheit des Jesus Sirach*, 3–4; Skehan and Di Lella, *Wisdom of Ben Sira*, 134.

92. For a brief overview of the Hebrew, Greek, and other translations, see Skehan and Di Lella, *Wisdom of Ben Sira*, 55–62.

93. Important discussions of the textual history of Ben Sira include Hans Peter Rüger, *Text und Textform im hebräischen Sirach* (BZAW 112; Berlin: de Gruyter, 1970); Skehan and Di Lella, *Wisdom of Ben Sira*, 51–82; B. G. Wright, *No Small Difference: Sirach's Relationship to Its Hebrew Parent Text* (SBLSCS 26; Atlanta: Scholars Press, 1989). For the printing of the extant Hebrew mss., see Pancratius Cornelis Beentjes, *The Book of Ben Sira in Hebrew: A Text Edition of All Extant Hebrew Manuscripts and a Synopsis* (VTSup 68; Leiden: Brill, 1997). For a comprehensive review of examinations of the texts of Ben Sira and the listing of comparative columns, see Friedrich V. Reiterer, *Zählsynopse zum Buch Ben Sira* (Fontes et Subsidia ad Bibliam pertinentes 1; Berlin: de Gruyter, 2003) 1–86. Reiterer presents his own reversification in order to provide a more convenient way of referring to the passages of Ben Sira (pp. 87–247).

94. I use the abbreviations of Skehan and Di Lella, *Wisdom of Ben Sira*. Joseph Ziegler, *Sapientia Iesu Filii Sirach* (Septuaginta 12/2; Göttingen: Vandenhoeck & Ruprecht, 1965), labels them GrI and GrII.

95. "Genizah" means "storeroom" for the keeping of worn manuscripts no longer used.

96. ~~*Sapientia Iesu Filii Sirach.*~~

97. Beentjes, *Book of Ben Sira in Hebrew.*

98. See *Gottes Weisheit unter uns: Zur Theologie des Buches Sirach: FS Johannes Marböck*, ed. Irmtraud Fischer (HBS 6; Freiburg: Herder, 1995).

99. Marböck, *Weisheit im Wandel.*

100. Josef Haspecker, *Gottesfurcht bei Jesus Sirach* (AnBib 30; Rome: Pontifical Biblical Institute, 1967).

101. See Johann Marböck, "Gesetz und Weisheit: Zum Verständnis des Gesetzes bei Jesus Ben Sira," *BN* NF 20 (1976) 1–21.

102. Küchler, *Frühjüdische Weisheitstraditionen*, 40–45.

103. Collins, *Jewish Wisdom*, 225.

104. See James L. Crenshaw, "The Problem of Theodicy in Sirach: On Human Bondage," in *Theodicy in the Old Testament* (IRT 4; Philadelphia: Fortress, 1983) 47–64; G. L. Prato, *Il problema della teodicea in Ben Sira: Composizione dei contrari e richiamo alle origini* (AnBib 65; Rome: Pontifical Biblical Institute, 1975); Johannes Marböck, "Gerechtigkeit Gottes und Leben nach dem Sirachbuch: Ein Antwortversuch in seinem Kontext," in *Gerechtigkeit und Leben im hellenistischer Zeitalter*, ed. J. Jeremias (BZAW 296; Berlin: de Gruyter, 2001) 21–52.

105. Küchler, *Frühjüdische Weisheitstraditionen*, 33–61.

106. Marböck, *Weisheit im Wandel*, 34.

107. This text has not been preserved in Hebrew. GII, the expanded Greek text, has added to GI vv. 5, 7, and the second half of v. 10.

108. Haspecker, *Gottesfurcht bei Jesus Sirach.*

109. Crenshaw, "Book of Sirach," 647.

110. See André Wénin, "De la création à l'alliance sinaïtique: La logique de Si 16,26–17,14," in *Treasures of Wisdom*, 147–58.

111. R. A. F. MacKenzie, *Sirach* (Old Testament Message; Wilmington, DE: Michael Glazier, 1983) 77. This text (16:26–18:14) is taken entirely from the LXX. This misogynistic text suggests that Eve was responsible for the introduction of disobedience.

112. See Alonso Schökel, "Vision of Man in Sirach 16:24–17:14," *Israelite Wisdom*, 235–45.

113. Ibid.

114. Skehan and Di Lella, *Wisdom of Ben Sira*, 282.
115. W. O. E. Oesterley, *The Wisdom of Jesus the Son of Sirach, or Ecclesiasticus* (Cambridge Bible for Schools and Colleges; Cambridge: Cambridge University Press, 1912) 113.
116. See 1 Kgs. 3:1–14 and Isa. 11:1–9. For a lengthy discussion, see Kalugila, *Wise King*.
117. In 15:14 Ben Sira indicates that God created the human being (*ʾādām*, אדם) in the beginning and placed him under the power of his "inclination" (*yēṣer*, יצר), an idea that derives from the Jewish understanding of the presence of two *yods* in *yiṣer* (ייצר, "and he formed") in human nature (see Gen. 2:7; *Gen. Rab.* 14:4). The *yēṣer haṭṭôb* (יצר הטוב) is the "good inclination" and the *yēṣer hārāʿ* (יצר הרע) is the "evil inclination" in the human will (see Gen. 6:5; 8:21). In rabbinic Judaism *yēṣer* (יצר) is the internal force that initiates human action (*b. Ber.* 61b).
118. Haspecker regards the "fear of God" as the fundamental theme of the book (*Gottesfurcht bei Jesus Sirach*). The expression is found more than sixty times and holds a prominent place in the interpretation of the teaching.
119. See especially Marböck, *Weisheit im Wandel*; idem, "Gesetz und Weisheit: Zum Verständnis des Gesetzes bei Jesus Sira," *BZ* 20 (1976) 1–21.
120. Skehan and Di Lella, *Wisdom of Ben Sira*, 285.
121. See Maurice Gilbert, "L'éloge de la Sagesse (Siracide 24)," *RTL* 5 (1974) 326–48.
122. MacKenzie (*Sirach*, 101) notes concerning this hymn in Sir. 24: "It is a hymn of self-praise by a divine being, a goddess who describes her own beauty, virtues, and readiness to bless and help humanity." For a discussion of Greek aretologies of Isis, see Conzelmann, "Mother of Wisdom"; Marböck, *Weisheit im Wandel*, 454. Other aretologies include those of Plutarch (*Moralia*, 5.351–84) and Apuleius (*Metamorphoses* 11). Conzelmann argues that the background for Woman Wisdom is the Egyptian Isis.
123. For hymns in general, see Claus Westermann, *Praise and Lament in the Psalms* (Atlanta: John Knox, 1981); Patrick Miller, *Interpreting the Biblical Psalms* (Philadelphia: Fortress, 1986); Gerstenberger, *Psalms*, vol. 1; Hans-Joachim Kraus, *Psalms 1–59* (trans. Hilton C. Oswald; Continental Commentary; Minneapolis: Augsburg, 1988).
124. For the literary structure of the poem, see Gilbert, "L'éloge de la Sagesse."
125. Ben Sira is the first sage to teach that wisdom is the active principle in both creation and history. See Edmond Jacob, "Wisdom and Religion in Sirach," in *Israelite Wisdom*, 247–60 (originally, "Sagesse et religion chez Ben Sira," in *Sagesse et Religion*, 83–98).
126. Sauer, "Gedanken," 51.
127. Ibid., 61.
128. See E. Theodore Mullen, *The Divine Council in Canaanite and Early Hebrew Literature* (HSM 24; Chico, CA: Scholars Press, 1980).
129. See Burton Mack, "Wisdom Myth and Mythology," *Int* 24 (1970) 46–60.
130. For a detailed examination of the relationship between Logos and Sophia, see Mack, *Logos und Sophia*. Ben Sira is only a step away from the Jewish view of the preexistence of Torah and its embodiment in creation and the Jewish law.
131. Cf. *1 Enoch* 42:1–2, where Wisdom, failing to find an earthly abode, is given a home in heaven.
132. See C. T. R. Hayward, "Sacrifice and World Order: Some Observations on Ben Sira's Attitude on the Temple Service," in *Sacrifice and Redemption*, ed. S. W.

Sykes (Durham Essays in Theology; Cambridge: Cambridge University Press, 1991) 22–34.

133. One should note that in the first-person poem in 51:13–28, Ben Sira speaks of his search for Wisdom. The Hebrew text uses language of erotic love to describe his engagement with her. See Takamitsu Muraoka, "Sir 51:13–30: An Erotic Hymn to Wisdom?" *JSJ* 10 (1979) 166–78; Celia Deutsch, "The Sirach 51Acrostic: Confession and Exhortation," *ZAW* 94 (1982) 400–409.

134. *Sifre Deut.* 37; *b. Pesaḥ.* 54a, b; *Gen. Rab.* 1:1. See the essay by Gabriele Boccaccini, "The Preexistence of the Torah: A Commonplace in Second Temple Judaism or a Later Rabbinic Development?" *Henoch* 17 (1995) 329–48.

135. See E. J. Schnabel, *Law and Wisdom from Ben Sira to Paul* (WUNT 2/16; Tübingen: Mohr [Siebeck], 1985) 40–41.

136. Leonidas Kalugila, *Wise King: Studies in Royal Wisdom as Divine Revelation in the Old Testament and Its Environment* (CBOT 15; Lund: CWK Gleerup, 1980). See Ezek. 28:1–10.

137. See G. L. Prato, "La lumière interprète de la sagesse dans la tradition textuelle de Ben Sira," in *Sagesse de l'Ancien Testament*, 317–46. Prato traces the theme of light throughout Ben Sira to point to the metaphorical connection between the cosmos and ethics.

138. Ben Sira is the first sage to teach that wisdom is the active principle in both creation and history. See Edmond Jacob, "Wisdom and Religion in Sirach," in *Israelite Wisdom*, 247–60.

139. See Werner Dommershausen, "Zum Vergeltungsdenken des Ben Sira," in *Wort und Geschichte: FS K. Elliger*, ed. Hartmut Gese and H. P. Rüger (AOAT 18; Neukirchen-Vluyn: Neukirchener Verlag, 1973) 37–43; Oda Wischmeyer, "Gut und Böse: Antithetisches Denken im Neuen Testament und bei Jesus Sirach," in *Treasures of Wisdom*, 129–36.

140. This text is not well preserved in the Hebrew. Ms. E is the only Hebrew textual witness, and it is corrupt, with words and letters on the left edge of the manuscript missing. The translation follows ms. E, with some dependence on GI in difficult places. While the Old Latin has preserved the proper sequence of chapters, two sections in the Greek manuscripts have exchanged places.

141. See Prato, *Problema*; Crenshaw, "Problem of Theodicy in Sirach," 47–64.

142. Wischmeyer, "Gut und Böse: Antithetisches Denken im Neuen Testament und bei Jesus Sirach," *Treasures of Wisdom*, 129–36.

143. The Hebrew is corrupt. The Greek verb ἤγγισεν (ēngisen, "to draw near") is likely a translation of qārēb (קרב, "to draw near," or in Hiphil, "to bring near"). This verb at times serves as a cultic term for approaching God or the sphere of the holy. See J. Kühlewein, *TLOT* 3 (1997) 1164–69.

144. David Winston argues that this doctrine of opposites indicates Ben Sira's dependence on Stoic philosophy ("Theodicy in Ben Sira and Stoic Philosophy," in *Of Scholars, Savants, and Their Texts*, ed. Ruth Link-Salinger [New York: Lang, 1989] 239–49).

145. See the detailed study of Jan Liesen, *Full of Praise: An Exegetical Study of Sir 39,12–35* (JSJSup 64; Leiden: Brill, 2000). His major thesis is that the poem in places reflects the author's activities, elsewhere the disciple's activities, and then an unnamed actor's activities who turns out to be God.

146. Wisdom psalms, hymnic in form and content with creation as their theme, are Pss. 8; 19A; 104 (if the last one is a wisdom psalm); see Avi Hurvitz, "Wisdom Vocabulary in the Hebrew Psalter: A Contribution to the Study of 'Wisdom Psalms,'" *VT* 38 (1988) 41–51; Kuntz, "Canonical Wisdom Psalms."

147. See my *Wisdom and Cult.*

148. Prato, *Problema della teodicea*; Crenshaw, "Problem of Theodicy," 47–64.

149. Reiterer, "Die immateriellen Ebenen der Schöpfung bei Ben Sira," in *Treasures of Wisdom*, 91–127.

150. Smend, *Weisheit des Jesus Sirachs*, 396.

151. Núria Calduch-Benages, "God, Creator of All (Sir 43:27–33)," in *Ben Sira's God*, 79–100.

152. See the other places in Ben Sira where the same sequence of creation and history occurs: 1:1–8/1:9–18; 16:24–30/17:1–11; 24:1–7/24:8–21; 39:12–35/40:1–11.

153. See in particular Theodore Burgess, *Epideictic Literature* (Chicago: University of Chicago Press, 1902); Mack, *Wisdom and the Hebrew Epic*, e.g., 130–34; Lee, *Form of Sirach 44–50*; R. N. Whybray, "Ben Sira and History," in *Treasures of Wisdom*, 137–45; J. L. Ska, "L'éloge des Pères dans le Siracide (Sir. 44–50) et le canon de l'Ancient Testament," in *Treasures of Wisdom*, 181–93; Ronald N. Whybray, "Ben Sira and History," in *Treasures of Wisdom*, 137–45; Teresa R. Brown, "God and Men in Israel's History: God and Idol Worship in Praise of the Fathers (Sir. 44–50)," in *Ben Sira's God*, 214–20; Alon Goshen-Gottstein, "Ben Sira's Praise of the Fathers: A Canon-Conscious Reading," in *Ben Sira's God*, 235–67.

154. Collins, *Between Athens and Jerusalem*, 32.

155. For a comprehensive overview, see Robert Doran, "Jewish Hellenistic Historians before Josephus," *ANRW*, 20.1, 2, 246–97.

156. Arnaldo Momigliano, *Alien Wisdom: The Limits of Hellenization* (Cambridge: Cambridge University Press, 1975) 98; Ben Zion Wacholder, *Eupolemus: A Study of Judea-Greek Literature* (Monographs of the Hebrew Union College 3; Cincinnati: Hebrew Union College Press, 1974) 12. While recognizing the diversity of Judaism at this time, von Rad does not allow for the engagement of Ben Sira with the larger Hellenistic world of philosophy, culture, religion, and language. While noting changes in the wisdom movement, he chooses instead to interpret Ben Sira completely within the sapiential tradition of ancient Israel (*Wisdom in Israel* [Nashville: Abingdon, 1972] 258, n. 24). This is true as well of J. D. Martin, "Ben Sira—A Child of His Time," in *A Word in Season: Essays in Honour of William McKane*, ed. J. D. Martin and P. R. Davies (JSOTSup 42; Sheffield: JSOT Press, 1986) 141–61.

157. Another form to which some interpreters point is the midrash. Mack speaks of Sir. 44–50 as a "proto-midrash" in that it "anthologizes both in the sense of collecting and combining disparate descriptive details and in the sense of using the language of the scriptural accounts anthologically" (*Wisdom and the Hebrew Epic*, 15). In my view, the "Praise of the Pious" is not midrash or "proto-midrash." Instead it possesses the classic features of the Greek encomium that Ben Sira has used to narrate the salvation of the nation through the redemptive acts of God mediated through the pious and righteous ancestors.

158. Burgess, *Epideictic Literature*.

159. Thomas R. Lee, *Form of Sirach 44–50* (SBLDS 75; Atlanta: Scholars Press, 1986), 84.

160. Ibid., 82–93.

161. Burgess, *Epideictic Literature,* 113. There were numerous examples of encomia that existed at the time of Ben Sira's book edited and "published" in the early second century BCE.

162. Lee, *Form of Sirach 44–50*, 99.

163. For studies of this Greek form (*paradeigma*, παραδείγμα = Latin *exemplum*), see Marsh H. McCall Jr., *Ancient Rhetorical Theories of Simile and Comparison* (Cambridge: Harvard University Press, 1969) 189; Adolf Lumpe, "Exemplum," *Reallexikon für Antike und Christentum* 6, ed. Theodor Klausner (Stuttgart: Anton Hiersemann, 1966) 1229–57.

164. Lee suggests that the *paradeigmata* in this section in Ben Sira may be used in one of two ways: an encomiastic genealogy or a section furnishing the formal syncretistic element in the encomium (*Form of Sirach 44–50*).
165. Ibid., 206.
166. The criticism of Solomon breaks the pattern by emphasizing his sins leading to the rebellion following his death (47:19–21).
167. See Mack, *Wisdom and the Hebrew Epic*, 37–65.
168. See ibid., Appendix A, 189–93. He argues that the hymn on creation and the "Praise of the Pious" belong together: "Now I will remember God's works/praise pious men." Indeed, he thinks that the connection of the two makes an important statement. Both literary pieces are held together by the theme of the revelation of "glory."
169. Ibid., Appendix D, 205–14.
170. Ibid., 199–203.
171. Ibid., 16–36.
172. Ibid., 19.
173. Ibid., 56–65.
174. Ibid., 65. See Maurice Gilbert, "L'action de grâce de Ben Sira (Sir 51, 1–12)," in *Ce Dieu qui vient: Mélanges offerts à Bernard Renaud* (LD 159; Paris: Cerf, 1995) 231–42; Johannes Marböck, "Der Hohepriester Simon in Sir 50: Ein Beitrag zur Bedeutung von Priestertum und Kult im Sirachbuch," in *Treasures of Wisdom*, 215–29.
175. Johannes Marböck, "Structure and Redaction History of the Book of Ben Sira: Review and Prospects." *Book of Ben Sira in Modern Research*, 61–79. For the literary connections between the hymn in 42:15–43:33 and the encomium in chaps. 44–50, see P. C. Beentjes, "The 'Praise of the Famous' and Its Prologue: Some Observations on Ben Sira 44:1–15 and the Question on Enoch in 44:16," *Bijdragen* 45 (1984) 374–83.
176. Marböck, "Hohepriester Simon in Sir 50," 218–25.
177. Ibid., 224.

Chapter 8: Wisdom and Alexandrian Hellenism: The Wisdom of Solomon

1. See Erich S. Gruen, *The Hellenistic World and the Coming of Rome* (Berkeley: University of California Press, 1984).
2. The chronology of this period is conveniently outlined by Modrzejewski, *Jews of Egypt*, 233–36. For a discussion of Hellenism's impact on the Wisdom of Solomon, see J. M. Reese, *Hellenistic Influence on the Book of Wisdom and Its Consequences* (AnBib 41; Rome: Pontifical Biblical Institute, 1970).
3. Bezalel Porten, "Settlement of the Jews at Elephantine and the Arameans at Syene," in *Judah and the Judeans in the Neo-Babylonian Period*, ed. Oded Lipschits and Joseph Blenkinsopp (Winona Lake, IN: Eisenbrauns, 2003), 451–70.
4. In addition to Elephantine and the "land of Onias" near Leontopolis that had Jewish military colonies and adjacent Jewish lands, land grants to soldiers included Krokodilopolis, Alexandria, Kerkeosiris, Samaria-Kerkesephis, Apias, Trikomia, Hephaistias, and areas close to the Nile in the Herakleopolite nome (Hibey Papyrus I 96; *CPJ* 1:18).
5. William Horbury and David Noy, *Jewish Inscriptions of Graeco-Roman Egypt* (Cambridge: Cambridge University Press, 1992). This volume contains a large number of the Jewish inscriptions from Egypt between the third century BCE and the sixth century CE. Also see Jan Willem van Henten and Pieter Willem van der Horst, eds., *Studies in Early Jewish Epigraphy* (AGAJU 21; Leiden: Brill, 1994).

6. Porten, *Archives from Elephantine*; idem and Ada Yardeni, eds., *Textbook of Aramaic Documents from Ancient Egypt*, vol. 1: *Letters* (Winona Lake, IN: Eisenbrauns, 1987); idem, eds., *Textbook of Aramaic Documents from Ancient Egypt*, vol. 2: *Contracts* (Winona Lake, IN: Eisenbrauns, 1989); idem, eds., *Textbook of Aramaic Documents from Ancient Egypt*, vol. 3: *Literature, Accounts, Lists* (Winona Lake, IN: Eisenbrauns, 1999); idem, eds., *Textbook of Aramaic Documents from Ancient Egypt*, vol. 4: *Inscriptions* (Winona Lake, IN: Eisenbrauns, 1999).

7. For a more reasonable assessment of numbers, see the essay by Diana Delia, "The Population of Roman Alexandria," *Transactions of the American Philological Association* 118 (1988) 275–92. She estimates the Jewish population was approximately 180,000 of the 500,000–600,000 inhabitants of Alexandria during the first century CE. Josephus estimates the entire population of Roman Egypt, not including Alexandria, to be 7.5 million people (*J. W.* 2.385). Delia estimates that of the 8 million total, 6.5 million were Egyptians, and 1.5 million were Greek-speaking immigrants. Possibly 300,000 of the population were Jewish.

8. See Shimon Applebaum, "The Organization of the Jewish Communities in the Diaspora," in *The Jewish People in the First Century*, ed. Shemuel Safrai and Menahem Stern (CRINT 1/1; Assen: Van Gorcum, 1974) 464–503. Jews were recognized as an ethnic and cultic community, but not a semiautonomous civic entity (*Let. Aris.* 310 uses the word *politeuma*, perhaps of the Jews, but in an ambiguous manner). With the Roman Empire, Jews were no longer allowed to be governed internally by an ethnarch.

9. See Gregory E. Sterling, "Judaism between Jerusalem and Alexandria," in *Judaism in the Land of Israel*, ed. John J. Collins and Gregory E. Sterling (Notre Dame: University of Notre Dame Press, 2001) 266.

10. Tcherikover, *Hellenistic Civilization*, 299.

11. See Cribiore, *Writing, Teachers*; Kah and Scholz, *Hellenistische Gymnasion*.

12. For a series of important essays on Hellenistic Judaism in the Roman period, see *ANRW* 20.1, 2.

13. See Tcherikover, *Hellenistic Civilization*; Momigliano, *Alien Wisdom*.

14. It is clear from the literature of the Diaspora that the upper-class Jews were educated in Greek grammar, philosophy, and literature. The use of Greek names and the references to Hellenistic law indicated that Hellenism was part of the identity of aristocratic Jews. See Feldman, *Jew and Gentile*; *CPJ*, 1:38–39.

15. In the foreword to Modrzejewski, *Jews of Egypt*, xi.

16. See Barclay, *Jews in the Mediterranean Diaspora*, 48–81; Martin Goodman, "Judaea," in *Cambridge Ancient History*, vol. 10: *The Augustan Empire, 43 B.C.–A.D. 69*, ed. Alan K. Bowman, et al. (2nd ed.; Cambridge: Cambridge University Press, 1996), especially 774–81.

17. See E. M. Smallwood, *Philonis Alexandrini Legatio ad Gaium* (2nd ed.; Leiden: Brill, 1970) 11–12.

18. See E. M. Smallwood, *The Jews under Roman Rule* (Studies in Judaism in Late Antiquity 20; Leiden: Brill, 1976).

19. *CPJ*, 1:150–51.

20. Among the studies of early anti-Judaism, originating in Alexandria, see Peter Schäfer, *Judeophobia: Attitudes toward the Jews in the Ancient World* (Cambridge: Harvard University Press, 1997); Jan N. Sevenster, *The Roots of Pagan Anti-Semitism* (NovTSup 41; Leiden: Brill, 1975) 89–144.

21. Modrzejewski, *Jews of Egypt*, 136–37.

22. Gruen, *Diaspora*, 64; Feldman, *Jew and Gentile in the Ancient World*.

23. For the text with notes and introduction, see Manahem Stern, *Greek and Latin Authors on Jews and Judaism* (Jerusalem: Israel Academy of Sciences and Humanities, 1974–1985) 62–85.

24. Gerald P. Verbrugghe and John M. Wickersham, *Berossos and Manetho, Introduced and Translated: Native Traditions in Ancient Mesopotamia and Egypt* (Ann Arbor: University of Michigan Press, 1996). Also see Alan Lloyd, "Manetho and the Thirty-First Dynasty," in *Pyramid Studies and Other Essays Presented to I. E. S. Edwards*, ed. John Baines, et al. (London: Egypt Exploration Society, 1988) 154–60.

25. For the text, with introduction and notes, see Stern, *Greek and Latin Authors*, 148–49.

26. Diodorus Siculus made similar accusations (40.3.4). See Stern, *Greek and Latin Authors*, 167–89. His description concerning the Jews was part of the larger narrative of the taking of Jerusalem by Pompey in 63 BCE.

27. For the text see Josephus, *Contra Apion*; Tatianus, *Oratio ad Graecos* 38; Clement of Alexandria, *Strom.* 1.21; and Eusebius, *Praep. ev.* 10.10.16.

28. See David L. Balch, "Josephus, *Against Apion* II.145–296," *SBLSP 1975*, ed. George MacRae (2 vols.; Missoula, MT: Scholars Press, 1975) 1:187–92. This rhetorical form, which was used to revile nations and cities, is used both by Apion and by his opponent, Josephus (*C.Ap.* 1.220–21). See the discussion by Menander of Laodicea, *How One Praises Cities* 353.8–30.

29. Feldman, *Jew and Gentile*, 96, 126–28, 143, 224, 229–39, 505, n. 58.

30. Stern, *Greek and Latin Authors*, 390.

31. Posidonius of Apamea in Syria (ca. 135–51 BCE) was a Stoic philosopher who taught in Rhodes. According to Josephus, he charged Jews with outrageous behavior, including the idea that the Jews worshiped an ass in their temple, sacrificed annually on their altar a fattened Greek, and hated all other nationalities, especially the Greeks. Posidonius seems to have included these accusations in his history of the Seleucids (Stern, *Greek and Latin Authors*, 141–47; Feldman, *Jew and Gentile*, 126). Cicero (ca. 106–43 BCE) was a prominent Roman orator, lawyer, and philosopher who lived during the period of transition from the republic to the empire. A noted xenophobe, Cicero held in contempt the Jews and other plebians in the empire, since he regarded himself to be one of the optimates of Roman society. Jews had a powerful voice in Roman politics in part due to their strong sense of communal existence (*quanta concordia*) that led to their support of one another when conditions warranted. For him, the strong Jewish presence in the public assemblies was in part due to their desire for political power. He characterized Jewish religion as a *barbara superstitio* that sought to undercut Roman religion (Cicero, *Flac.* [59 BCE]; see Stern, *Greek and Latin Authors*, 193–206). The Roman lyric poet Horace (65–8 BCE), expressed his anti-Judaism in the form of biting satire that he used to lampoon Jewish religious practices (*Sat.* 1.5.100; l.9.69–78). Chaeremon of Alexandria, who lived during the first century CE, was a Stoic philosopher and grammarian, as well as a member of the elite priesthood devoted to Serapis. His unique retelling of the exodus story appears to confuse the Jews with the Hyksos who were driven out of Egypt (Josephus, *C. Ap.* 1.289). Speaking as an Alexandrian Greek, Lysimachus expressed his disgust for the Jews and criticized the influence of Jewish military leaders in the army of Cleopatra III. His version of the exodus follows essentially that of Manetho (Josephus, *C. Ap.* 1.305–11). The Roman historian Tacitus (55–117 CE) contrived his own version of the exodus, explaining it as due to the expulsion of plague-infected inhabitants of Egypt, who, led by Moses, journeyed across the desert, conquered Canaan, and built their own cities. He condemned the religion of the Jews as an abominable set of rituals and the sacrifice and eating of animals held sacred by others. They were characterized as indolent, lascivious, antisocial, avaricious, and despisers of the gods (*Histories* 5.2–5).

32. See Stern, *Greek and Roman Authors*, 1:261–315, for the text, introduction, and notes. He thinks there is considerably more material from Strabo's *Historica Hypomnemata* in books 13 and 14 of the *Antiquities* of Josephus than the Jewish historian admits to have cited (p. 262).

33. For the views of Moses in this period on into the early Roman Empire, see John Gager, *Moses in Graeco-Roman Paganism* (SBLMS 16; Nashville: Scholars Press, 1972).

34. Feldman, *Jew and Gentile*, 238.

35. Among writers who were favorably disposed to the Jews and Judaism are the following. Hecataeus of Abdera, active during the reign of Ptolemy I (ca. 300 BCE), wrote a history of Egypt (*On the Egyptians*) in which he included remarks about Judaism. While transmitting some criticism of the Jews, he also at times speaks well of them. The oldest reference to Hecataeus is found in *Let. Aris.* 31. Here he indicated that historians, poets, and other literati ignored the Jews because their way of life was "so sacred and religious" (cf. Josephus, *Ant.* 12.38; Eusebius, *Praep. ev.* 8.3.3). He explained that when the Jews were driven out of Egypt, they came to Palestine and founded the city of Jerusalem. Jews were monotheists and rejected idols due to their unwillingness to depict their deity in anthropomorphic terms. Their ethical teachings are praised for requiring support for the poor and repudiating the exposing of infants. He speaks of the prominence of priests in the religion and the importance of law, comparable to legal materials in Egypt. Both of these points are of greater significance than the laws of the Greeks. He admired Jews for having destroyed pagan temples and for refusing to participate in restoring the temple of Bel in Babylon. Finally, he explained that Moses introduced a course of life that, later on, perhaps due to the Babylonian exile, became antisocial and disallowed contact with foreigners (Stern, *Greek and Latin Authors*, 1:20–44). Clearchus of Soli was a disciple of Aristotle who regarded the Jews as philosophers. Around 300 BCE, he introduced in one of his dialogues a Jew from Coele-Syria, who was described as "Hellenic not in speech only, but also in mind," and as engaging in a conversation with Aristotle. Clearchus was especially impressed with the Jew's manner of life (*diaita*), that is, having to do with his diet (Josephus, *C. Ap.* 1.76–183; see Stern, *Greek and Latin Authors*, 1:47–52). Varro (ca. 116–27 BCE) refers to Judaism (no. 72 a-b) in his *Res Divinae*, which is part of the *Antiquitates Rerum Humanarum et Divinarum*. He is impressed that Judaism did not allow idolatry, a prohibition similar to the pristine religion of ancient Rome. The Jewish criticism of cult images is grounded in Greco-Roman philosophy. However, Varro notes that the downside of anti-idolatry is that it detracts from the fear of the gods (see Stern, *Greek and Latin Authors*, 1:207–12). Pompeius Trogus (end of the first century BCE, and the beginning of the first century CE) was a Roman historian who wrote a Latin history of the Macedonian-Hellenistic states. He passed on the traditional Egyptian argument that they were lepers forced to leave Egypt, after the Egyptians had been warned in an oracle that they were responsible for the plague. Joseph was praised by Trogus for his intelligence and talent, traits also attributed to the Jews as a whole. The Jews had no dealings with other peoples, not because of misanthropy, but due to the fact that they remembered they had spread the infection and thus did not wish to become odious to their neighbors. Because of their religion and justice, Trogus argued, the Jews became incredibly "powerful" (*coaluere*; also possible of being translated as "united" and "increased") (see Stern, *Greek and Latin Authors*, 1:332–43).

36. Stern, *Greek and Latin Authors*, 1:264.

37. Ibid., 1:167. See pp. 181–85 (esp. no. 63).

38. For the texts of Hecataeus preserved primarily in Diodorus Siculus and Josephus (which include Pseudo-Hecataeus), together with introduction and notes, see Küchler, *Frühjüdische Weisheitstraditionen*, 120–21.

39. Holladay, *Fragments* 1:289. Bar-Kochva also considers *On the Jews* to be a pious forgery (*Pseudo-Hecataeus 'On the Jews': Legitimizing the Jewish Diaspora* [Berkeley: University of California Press, 1996]). Bar-Kochva thinks that this writer represented moderate conservative Jews of Alexandria who were opposed to the religious practices of Hellenistic Judaism. He sought to legitimize Jewish residence in Egypt during a period of the expansion of the Jewish community and its economic prosperity.

40. Holladay, *Fragments*, 1:189–243; Attridge, "Historiography," 166–68; John J. Collins, "Artapanus," *OTP*, 2:889–903; Robert Doran, "The Jewish Hellenistic Historians before Josephus," *ANRW*, 20.1, 2, 257–63.

41. *Apologia* are a form of Greek rhetoric used by several Jewish writers during the Hellenistic period in order to present Judaism in a form that would make it palatable to both Jews and Gentiles. See Mark Edwards, Martin Goodman, and Simon Price, in association with Christopher Rowland, eds., *Apologetics in the Roman Empire: Pagans, Jews, and Christians* (Oxford: Oxford University Press, 1999); Elisabeth Schüssler Fiorenza, ed., *Aspects of Religious Propaganda in Judaism and Early Christianity* (University of Notre Dame Center for the Study of Judaism and Christianity in Antiquity 2; Notre Dame: University of Notre Dame Press, 1976).

42. Holladay, *Fragments*, 1:193. This liberal and tolerant sentiment strongly contrasts with the views of the Jewish historian Theodotus, who, writing likely in Judea during the rule of John Hyrcanus, presented a very narrow, legalistic view of Judaism.

43. Collins, *Between Athens and Jerusalem*, 39. He dates Artapanus at the end of the third century BCE, thus shortly before Ben Sira's composition. Collins argues convincingly for an Egyptian origin for the author of this romance history, although he is not convinced that he carried out his work in Alexandria.

44. Holladay, *Fragments*, 1:190.

45. The Ethiopians were so taken with Moses that they began to practice circumcision.

46. Collins, *Between Athens and Jerusalem*, 42. Artapanus explains that euhemerism is the idea that the gods were deified kings who benefited humanity. Thus they were worshiped in gratitude for their beneficence.

47. Carl Howard Jacobsen, *The Exagoge of Ezekiel* (New York: Cambridge University Press, 1983); R. G. Robertson, "Ezekiel the Tragedian," *OTP*, 2:803–7.

48. See especially the study of Emanuel Tov that deals with Greek translations, in particular the LXX, "Die griechischen Bibelübersetzungen," *ANRW*, 20.1, 2, 121–89. He notes that the LXX translation was likely produced at different times; the Torah first, followed by the prophets and wisdom books. The translation was likely begun in the third century BCE and concluded by the end of the second century BCE. The language suggests a Hellenistic Egyptian setting in which the translators lived.

49. See Sidney Jellicoe, "The Occasion and Purpose of the Letter of Aristeas: A Re-Examination," *NTS* 12 (1966) 144–50; George Howard, "The Letter of Aristeas and Diaspora Judaism," *JTS* 22 (1971) 337–48; R. J. H. Shutt, "Letter of Aristeas," *OTP* 2:7–34.

50. Barclay, *Jews in the Mediterranean Diaspora*, 138–50.

51. Howard's view is that the "letter" was written in part to respond to conservative Jews in Jerusalem who claimed one could practice true Judaism only by studying the Torah from the Hebrew Bible preserved in Jerusalem. Aristeas wished to

show that the translation was as accurate and inspired as the original. The apology was directed not to the Greeks but rather to the Jews of Jerusalem and its environs ("Letter of Aristeas," 348).

52. Viktor Tcherikover, *Hellenistic Civilization and the Jews* (New York: Athenaeum, 1970) 61.
53. Barclay, *Jews in the Mediterranean Diaspora*, 149.
54. See Ben Sira's description of the sage in 38:34b–39:11.
55. Barclay, *Jews in the Mediterranean Diaspora*, 141.
56. Rappaport, "When Was the Letter of Aristeas Written?" 37–50.
57. Shutt, *OTP* 2:10.
58. Adela Yarbro Collins, "Aristobulus," *OTP* 2:831–42; Carl H. Holladay, *Fragments from Hellenistic Jewish Authors*, vol. 3: *Aristobulus* (SBLTT 39; Pseudepigrapha series 13; Atlanta: Scholars Press, 1995); Nikolaus Walter, *Der Thoraausleger Aristobulos: Untersuchungen zu seinen Fragmenten und zu pseudepigraphischen Resten der jüdisch-hellenistischen Literatur* (Berlin: Akadamie Verlag, 1964).
59. Clement of Alexandria preserved fragments 2–5, which were more paraphrases than quotations (*Strom.* 1, 5, 6).
60. Collins, *Between Athens and Jerusalem*, 188. The Peripatetic school met in a public space called the lyceum, in a sanctuary of the god Apollo that was located just outside the city wall of Athens. This school was more of a place than a group of philosophers adhering to a common tradition that was shaped and transmitted by disciples. Aristotle was the first philosopher associated with this school, which also had a gymnasium. It was a location for philosophers, including traveling Sophists, to gather, discuss, and lecture.
61. An Aristobulus is mentioned in 2 Macc. 1:10–2:18. If this letter's reference is historically authentic, then it could link this Aristobulus with the Hasmoneans, especially Judas Maccabeus. This would mean then that the Ptolemy mentioned would be Ptolemy VI Philometor.
62. See David Dawson, *Allegorical Readers and Cultural Revision in Ancient Alexandria* (Berkeley: University of California Press, 1992).
63. E. R. Goodenough, *The Politics of Philo Judaeus* (New Haven: Yale University Press, 1938) 52–74; idem, *Introduction to Philo Judaeus* (2nd ed.; Oxford: Blackwell, 1962); H. A. Wolfson, *Philo: Foundations of Religious Philosophy in Judaism, Christianity, and Islam* (2nd ed.; 2 vols.; Cambridge: Harvard University Press, 1948); Samuel Sandmel, *Philo's Place in Judaism* (augm. ed.; New York: Ktav, 1971); idem, *Philo of Alexandria: An Introduction* (New York: Oxford University Press, 1979); David Winston, *Logos and Mystical Theology in Philo of Alexandria* (Cincinnati: Hebrew Union College Press, 1985); Ellen Birnbaum, *The Place of Judaism in Philo's Thought: Israel, Jews, and Proselytes* (BJS 290; Atlanta: Scholars Press, 1996); Sly, *Philo's Alexandria*; Barclay, *Jews in the Mediterranean Diaspora*, 158–80; Collins, *Between Athens and Jerusalem*, 131–38; David Winston, *The Ancestral Philosophy: Hellenistic Philosophy in Second Temple Judaism*, ed. Gregory E. Sterling (BJS 331; Providence: Brown Judaic Studies, 2001).
64. See David Winston, "Was Philo a Mystic?" in *Ancestral Philosophy*, 151–70. Winston gives the basic understanding of mysticism as "a timeless apprehension of the transcendent through a unifying vision that gives bliss or serenity and normally accrues upon a course of self-mastery and contemplation" (p. 151). Winston asserts that in Philo one finds these characteristic features of mysticism: knowledge of God, which is humanity's greatest bliss; humanity's nothingness; the soul's yearning for God; the attachment to God, who alone is the true actor; contemplative prayer; a timeless union of a humanity with the "All" of existence; serenity that derives from this union; and ecstasy in the state of mysticism (p. 170).

65. Barclay also examines Philo in his chapter 6, "Cultural Convergence," *Jews in the Mediterranean Diaspora*, 125–80.
66. Sly, *Philo's Alexandria*, 7.
67. See Jacob Neusner, *Early Rabbinic Judaism* (Leiden: Brill, 1975) 100–136.
68. Sly, *Philo's Alexandria*, 136–37.
69. See Harris, *Greek Athletics and the Jews*; Alan Mendelson, *Secular Education in Philo of Alexandria* (HUCM 7; Cincinnati: Hebrew Union College Press, 1982).
70. Barclay, *Jews in the Mediterranean Diaspora*, 161.
71. This metaphor is also found in rabbinic writings. See Ephraim Urbach, *The Sages: Their Concepts and Beliefs* (2nd ed.; 2 vols.; Jerusalem: Magnes, 1979) 2:200–201.
72. Winston, "Was Philo a Mystic?" 159.
73. There are numerous, other mediators between God and the world, including Moses and angels.
74. Collins, *Between Athens and Jerusalem*, 132.
75. Peder Borgen, "Philo of Alexandria," 251. *Jewish Writings of the Second Temple Period: Apocrypha, Pseudepigrapha, Qumran Sectarian Writings, Philo, Josephus*, ed. Michael E. Stone (Compendia rerum Iudaicarum, ad Novum Testamentum 2; Philadelphia: Fortress, 1984), 251.
76. Goodenough, *Politics of Philo Judaeus*, 52–74; Wolfson, *Philo*, 2:322–438; Collins, *Between Athens and Jerusalem*, 133–38; Ray Barraclough, "Philo's Politics, Roman Rule and Hellenistic Judaism," *ANRW*, 21.1, 2, 417–553.
77. *Mos.* 2.238–41. See Goodenough, *Introduction to Philo Judaeus*, 85.
78. See Douglas Young, ed., *Theognis, Ps.-Phocylides, Chares, Anonymi aulodia, fragmentum teleiambicum* (2nd ed.; Leipzig: Teubner, 1971).
79. See the translation and introduction by P. W. van der Horst, "Pseudo-Phocylides," *OTP* 2:565–82 (cf. his *Sentences of Pseudo-Phocylides, with Introduction and Commentary* [VTSup 4; Leiden: Brill, 1978]). Other studies are those of Walter T. Wilson, *The Mysteries of Righteousness: The Literary Composition and Genre of the Sentences of Pseudo-Phocylides* (Texte und Studien zum antiken Judentum 40; Tübingen: Mohr, 1994); Johannes Thomas, *Der jüdische Phokylides: Formgeschichtliche Zugänge zu Pseudo-Phokylides und Vergleich mit der neutestamentlichen Paränese* (Göttingen: Vandenhoeck & Ruprecht, 1992).
80. See Pieter van der Horst, "Pseudo-Phocylides Revisited," *JSP* 3 (1988) 19.
81. The *Testaments of the Twelve Patriarchs*, written sometime after 200 BCE, began to be formed during the reign of the Seleucid rulers and continued to be edited as late as early Christianity in the second century CE (see Jürgen Becker, *Untersuchungen zur Entstehungsgeschichte der Testamente der zwölf Patriarchen* [AGAJU 8: Leiden: Brill, 1970]; idem, *Die Testamente der zwölf Patriarchen* [JSHRZ 3; Gütersloh: Mohn, 1980]). It also contains substantial parenetic materials, while ignoring obvious Jewish features.
82. Tjitze Baarda, "The Sentences of the Syriac Menander," *OTP* 2:583–606; Küchler, *Frühjüdische Weisheitstraditionen*, 303–18. Although the writings of this sage are lost, he was apparently one of the students of Eratosthenes (276/275–195/194 BCE). The Greek original was likely written in the second century BCE.
83. Peter Schäfer, *Judeophobia: Attitudes toward the Jews in the Ancient World* (Cambridge: Harvard University Press, 1997).
84. Hengel is opposed to using the term "syncretism" or "assimilation" to characterize hellenization and the Jews (*Judaism and Hellenism*, 1:114). He suggests that a more appropriate term is "acculturation."
85. For the debate about the exodus in Jewish and anti-Jewish literature that best explains why the author devoted so much space to this theme in redemption

history, see Claude Aziza, "L'utilisation polémique du récit de l'exode chez les écrivains alexandrins (Ivème siècle ap. J.-C.)," *ANRW*, 20.1, 2, 41–65. He deals especially with Lysimachus, Chaeremon, and Apion.

86. The contention that Hellenistic Jewish literature sought to convert non-Jews to Judaism has been advocated by a number of scholars, including Feldman, *Jew and Gentile*, 293. However, it is doubtful that Jewish literature written in Greek had this as an important purpose. See Victor Tcherikover, "Jewish Apologetic Literature Reconsidered," *Eos* 48 (1956) 169–93; Martin Goodman, *Mission and Conversion: Proselytizing in the Religious History of the Roman Empire* (Oxford: Clarendon, 1994).

87. Michael Kolarcik, "The Book of Wisdom," *NIB* 5 (1997) 439–40.

88. Gruen, *Diaspora*, 77.

89. Peter Dalbert, *Die Theologie der hellenistisch-jüdischen Missionsliteratur unter Ausschluss von Philo und Josephus* (Hamburg-Volksdorf: Reich, 1954) 14–15.

90. For the classic study of Middle Platonism, see John Dillon, *The Middle Platonists: 80 B.C. to A.D. 220* (Ithaca: Cornell University Press, 1977). Important works on rhetoric and rhetors include D. L. Clark, *Rhetoric in Greco-Roman Education* (New York: Columbia University Press, 1957); David Ross, ed., *Ars Rhetorica: Aristotle* (Oxford: Oxford University Press, 1959); G. A. Kennedy, *The Art of Persuasion in Greece* (Princeton: Princeton University Press, 1963); Thomas Cole, *The Origins of Rhetoric in Ancient Greece* (Ancient Society and History; Baltimore: Johns Hopkins University Press, 1991).

91. "It was to be a kind of University, modeled on the Athenian schools of philosophers. The hope was that men of eminence would be attracted to Alexandria from the rest of the Greek world. Under the second and third Ptolemies a very brilliant company of scholars, scientists, and poets were to be found at the Alexandrian court" (E. V. Bevan, *The House of Ptolemy* [repr. Chicago: Argonaut, 1968] 124).

92. See especially the essay by David Winston, "The Sage as Mystic in the Wisdom of Solomon," in *Sage in Israel*, 383–97.

93. See Hermann von Lips, "Jüdische Weisheit und griechische Tugendlehre: Beobachtungen zur Aufnahme der Kardinaltugenden in hellenistisch-jüdischen Texten (Aristeasbrief, Sapientia Salomonis, 4. Makkabäerbuch)," in *Weisheit, Ethos und Gebot: Weisheits- und Dekalogtraditionen in der Bibel und im frühen Judentum*, ed. Henning Graf Reventlow (Neukirchen-Vluyn: Neukirchener Verlag, 2001), 29–60.

94. For a discussion of immortality and resurrection, especially as regards this text, see Paul Beauchamp, "Sagesse de Salomon: De l'argumentation médicale à la réssurection," in *Sagesse biblique*, 175–86.

95. Winston, "Sage as Mystic," 397.

96. W. K. C. Guthrie, *A History of Greek Philosophy*, vol. 3: *The Fifth-Century Enlightenment* (Cambridge: Cambridge University Press, 1969) 27; H. G. Liddell and R. Scott, "σοφία," *A Greek-English Lexicon* (9th ed.; Oxford: Clarendon, 1953) 1621–22.

97. Guthrie, *History of Greek Philosophy*, 3:32.

98. Barclay, *Jews in the Mediterranean Diaspora*, 181.

99. See the classic study of Franz Cumont, *Oriental Religions in Roman Paganism* (New York: Dover, 1956).

100. Sly, *Philo's Alexandria*, 103–19.

101. Hans-Joseph Klauck, *Die religiöse Umwelt des Urchristentums*, vol 1: *Stadt- und Hausreligion, Mysterienkulte, Volksglaube* (Kohlhammer Studienbücher Theologie 9, 1; Stuttgart: Kohlhammer, 1995) 77–128.

102. See Euripides, *Bacchae*.

103. See Apuleius, *Golden Ass.*
104. Michael Grant, *A Social History of Greece and Rome* (New York: Charles Scribner's Sons, 1992) 5–26. Grant writes concerning women in the Hellenistic world: "But religion was the women's great strength. It had always been so, but now priestesses were abundant and honored on a scale that had not been seen hitherto. And never previously had there been a goddess like Isis, Egyptian but widely exported elsewhere, who was the immensely important patron of the whole female sex, passionately worshipped by women, praised for giving them equal strength to men, and even for encouraging wives to feel superior and give orders to their husbands, who had promised them obedience. Once again the powerful Ptolemaic queens had a lot to do with this. Not only were they deified themselves, but they also were intimately associated and even identified with Isis, whose example and instruction encouraged their consciousness of their power" (p. 26). This contrasts dramatically with the misogyny of Ben Sira.
105. Susan Pomeroy, *Women in Hellenistic Egypt* (New York: Schocken, 1984).
106. See especially Dillon, *Middle Platonists.*
107. For a crisp and clear overview of the Platonic thinking of Philo, see Dillon, *Middle Platonists*, 139–83. The standard work of Philo is that of Wolfson, *Philo.*
108. For a discussion of the various literary genres used in this book, see Reese, *Hellenistic Influence*, 90–121.
109. Winston, "Sage as Mystic," 383–97.
110. Hellenistic elements included the original composition of the piece in Greek, the four cardinal virtues of Stoicism (self-control, intelligence, justice, and courage; 8:7), the harmony of the elements (chap. 19), the argument from design (13:1–5), the Stoic ideal of a world soul, and the Platonic conception of the immortality of the soul. See especially Chrysostome Larcher, *Études sur le Livre de la Sagesse* (Études bibliques; Paris: Gabalda, 1969) 201–2; Reese, *Hellenistic Influence.*
111. Modrzejewski, *Jews of Egypt*, 67; Collins, *Between Athens and Jerusalem*, 13.
112. Winston indicates that it is difficult to determine which of the two is dominant ("Review of," *CBQ* 48 [1986] 527).
113. This use of Greek rhetorical forms does not suggest that the writer was especially sophisticated in the elite culture of Greek rhetoric. His work was the more common type of protreptic uttered by a moral teacher. However, he must have studied with a teacher or teachers of Greek rhetoric, knew well the LXX, and was conversant with many of the major literary forms of Hellenistic philosophy and literature.
114. Winston, *Wisdom of Solomon,* 18–20; Reese, *Hellenistic Influence*, 117–18. Reese notes: "The protreptic, then, is not a formal treatise on the abstract aspects of philosophy, but an appeal to follow a meaningful philosophy as a way of life."
115. Burgess, *Epideictic Literature*, 229–30; Stanley E. Porter, ed., *Handbook of Classical Rhetoric in the Hellenistic Period, 330 B.C.–A.D. 400* (Leiden: Brill, 1997); Stanley K. Stowers, *Letter Writing in Graeco-Roman Antiquity* (Library of Early Christianity; Philadelphia: Westminster, 1986) 92.
116. See Wolfson, *Philo*, 1:73–74.
117. John G. Gammie, "Paraenetic Literature: Toward the Morphology of a Secondary Genre," in *Paraenesis: Act and Form*, 52.
118. See the relevant literature in Collins, *Jewish Wisdom*, 154–57.
119. See Johannes Pedersen, "Wisdom and Immortality," in *Wisdom in Israel and in the Ancient Near East*, 238–46.
120. Kolarcik, "Book of Wisdom," 437.
121. Addison Wright, "The Structure of the Book of Wisdom," *Bib* 48 (1967) 165–84; idem, "The Structure of Wisdom 11–19," *CBQ* 27 (1965) 28–34. For

another analysis of the structure, see James M. Reese, "Plan and Structure in the Book of Wisdom," *CBQ* 27 (1965) 391–99.

122. "Structure of the Book of Wisdom," 168–69.

123. The critical Greek text used is Ziegler, *Sapientia Salomonis*. Also see Peter Arzt, et al., eds., *Sprachlicher Schlüssel zur Sapientia Salomonis (Weisheit)* (2nd ed.; Institut für Neutestamentliche Bibelwissenschaft Salzburg 1, Sapientia Salomonis; Salzburg: Verlag Institut für Ntl. Bibelwissenschaft, 1997).

124. While there is little evidence to identify the provenance of the book, the origins in Alexandria are supportable at least implicitly. The emphasis on the exodus and the polemic against idolatry and animal worship would suggest an Egyptian origin.

125. For discussions of possible dates of composition, ranging from the late second century BCE to the first century CE, and the probable location of Alexandria, see Winston, *Wisdom of Solomon*, 12–25. Winston points to the early first century CE as the period of composition on the basis of the occurrence of numerous Greek words and phrases that do not appear in Greek literature before this period. This text is also similar to some of Philo's ideas.

126. Samuel Cheon, *The Exodus Story in the Wisdom of Solomon: A Study in Biblical Interpretation* (JSPSup 23; Sheffield: Sheffield Academic Press, 1997).

127. Winston, *Wisdom of Solomon*, 20–25.

128. Collins, *Jewish Wisdom*, 196.

129. Ibid., 201.

130. Texts are found in Wilhelm Dittenberger, *Sylloge Inscriptionum Graecorum*, vol. 3 (3rd ed.; Chicago: Ares, 1999) 390ff., no. 1267 (from Ios); Wilhelm Peek, *Der Isishymnos von Andros und Verwandte Texte* (Berlin: Weidmannsche Buchhandlung, 1930) 15–22, 122–25 (from Kyme and Ios), 129 (from Cyrene), 135 (from Gomphoi in Thessalien); Jan Bergman, *Ich bin Isis: Studien zum memphitischen Hintergrund der griechischen Isisaretologien* (Acta Universitatis Upsaliensis, Historia Religionum 3; Lund: Berlingska Boktryckeriet, 1968) 301–4 (from Kyme and Esna). See John S. Kloppenborg, "Isis and Sophia in the Book of Wisdom," *HTR* 75 (1982) 57–84.

131. Marco Nobile, "La thématique eschatologique dans le livre de la Sagesse en relation avec l'apocalyptique," in *Treasures of Wisdom*, 303–12.

132. See Michael Kolarcik, *The Ambiguity of Death in the Book of Wisdom 1–6: A Study of Literary Structure and Interpretation* (AnBib 127; Rome: Pontifical Biblical Institute, 1991).

133. Vittorio D'Alario, "La réflexion sur le sens de la vie en Sg 1–5: Une réponse aux questions de Job et de Qohélet," in *Treasures of Wisdom*, 313–30.

134. For a general introduction see Collins, *Apocalyptic Imagination*. For the Wisdom of Solomon see Pierre Grelot, "L'eschatologie de la Sagesse et les apocalypses juives," in *Á la Rencontre de Dieu: Mémorial Albert Gelin* (Bibliothèque de la faculté catholique de théologie de Lyon 8; Le Puy: Mappus, 1961) 165–78.

135. For examples of royal testaments see "The Instruction of Amenemhet" and "The Instruction for King Merikare" from Egypt, "The Counsel of a Prince" from Mesopotamia, and the instruction of Solomon by David in 1 Kgs. 2:1–9 (see Leo G. Perdue, "The Testament of David and Egyptian Royal Instructions," in *Scripture in Context*, vol. 2: *More Essays on the Comparative Method*, ed. William W. Hallo, James C. Moyer, and Leo G. Perdue [Winona Lake, IN: Eisenbrauns, 1983] 79–96).

136. See Wisdom's love of humanity in Prov. 8:17–18.

137. For a detailed discussion see Helmer Ringgren, *Word and Wisdom: Studies in the Hypostatization of Divine Qualities and Functions in the Ancient Near East* (Lund: H. Ohlssons, 1947).

138. The teacher does not distinguish between "soul" (*psychē*, ψυχή), "mind" (*nous*, νοῦς), or "spirit" (*pneuma*, πνεῦμα). See A. T. S. Goodrick, *The Book of Wisdom with Introduction and Notes* (New York: Macmillan, 1913) 87.

139. The noun "immortality" (*athanasia*, ἀθανασία) occurs five times in this text: 3:4; 4:1; 8:13, 17; 15:3; while the adjective *athanatos* (ἀθανατός) occurs in 1:15. The concept of the immortality of the soul is given classic definition by Plato in his theory of ideas (see Winston, *Wisdom of Solomon*, 26–27). The author of the Wisdom of Solomon also suggests at one point the preexistence of immortal souls (8:19–20). The belief in the immortality of the soul or the resurrection of the dead, at least those who are righteous, develops only in the beginnings of early Judaism (Dan. 12:2–3; 2 Macc. 7:9).

140. Hermann Spieckermann regards the theme of immortality and its various features as the major contribution of the Wisdom of Solomon to biblical theology ("Die Gerechten Seelen sind in Gottes Hand: Die Bedeutung der Sapientia Salomonis für die Biblische Theologie," in *Vergegenwärtigung des Alten Testaments: FS Rudolph Smend*, ed. Christoph Bultmann, et al. (Göttingen: Vandenhoeck & Ruprecht, 2002) 345–68.

141. Winston, *Wisdom of Solomon*, 101. See 5:16; 6:21; 9:3.

142. See Hans Hübner, "Die Sapientia Salomonis und die antike Philosophie," in *Die Weisheit Salomos im Horizont biblischer Theologie*, ed. Hans Hübner (Neukirchen-Vluyn: Neukirchener Verlag, 1993) 55–81; Reider, *Book of Wisdom*, 54.

143. For discussions of death in this book see Kolarcik, *Ambiguity of Death*; Richard J. Taylor, "The Eschatological Meaning of Life and Death in the Book of Wisdom I-V," *ETL* 42 (1966) 72–137.

144. Or "creatures."

145. Cf. the battle between Baal and Mot (death) in Ugaritic literature, a battle that is reflected in theological metaphor in the OT (e.g., Isa 25:7). In classical mythology Hades (Pluto) is the ruler of the underworld who abducted and married Persephone.

146. See 4Q218. The Greek adjectival form of this term is present in 12:1 and 18:4. Incorruption is assured by obedience to the Jewish laws.

147. See Mathias Delcor, "L'immortalité de l'âme dans le livre de la Sagesse et dans les documents de Qumran," *Nouvelle revue théologique* 77 (1955) 614–30; Roland E. Murphy, "'To Know Your Might Is the Root of Immortality,'" *CBQ* 25 (1963) 88–93.

148. See Quintilian, *Institutio Oratoria* 9.2.30–33. In this rhetorical form, Quintilian explains that we present the thoughts of our adversaries or engage in dialogue with others. Stowers notes that this form, which is introduced by an apostrophe or reference to imaginary opponents, is at times indicated by modulating the voice in speaking the words of the adversaries (cf. Stowers, "Apostrophe, προσωποπία," 351–69).

149. Larcher, *Études sur la Sagesse*, 217. He notes that, unlike the Stoics, who identify the soul as a fire that gives life to nature and is identical to reason that permeates the cosmos, the wicked give a materialistic explanation to thought and breath as a kind of combustion caused by the beating of the heart (pp. 218–19).

150. See John P. Weisengoff, "The Impious of Wisdom 2," *CBQ* 11 (1949) 40–65.

151. See Goodrick, *Book of Wisdom*, 100.

152. See, e.g., 3 Maccabees and Philo's antagonism toward Hellenistic Egyptians in his treatises *In Flaccum* and *De Legatione ad Gaium*.

153. Barclay, *Jews in the Mediterranean Diaspora*, 186.

154. Another possibility is Cain's jealousy that leads him to murder his brother Abel (Gen. 4:1–16).

155. Also see Josephus, *Ant.* 1.1.4; and *3 Bar.* 4:8.

156. For a gestation period of ten (lunar) months, see 4 Macc. 16:17; Philo, *Leg.* 1.4; Plutarch, *Num.* 12; Virgil, *Ecl.* 14.61; Pliny, *Nat.* 7.5. The teacher reflects the idea that conception occurs by the coagulation of menstrual blood, mixed with male sperm. See Larcher, *Études sur la Sagesse*, 445–46.

157. Larcher, *Études sur la Sagesse*, 444.

158. See ibid., 443–44.

159. See 13:2 and 19:18. The four major elements that comprise reality and are active agents in the cosmos according to Greek thought were earth, air, fire, and water.

160. Larcher thinks the reference may be to psychological impulses considered to be an area within the human passions (*Études sur la Sagesse*, 445).

161. See 14:2.

162. See Mack, *Logos und Sophia*; Reider, *Book of Wisdom*, 115.

163. See Ringgren, *Word and Wisdom*.

164. Larcher, *Études sur la Sagesse*, 516–17.

165. Cf. the metaphor of Israel as the wife and lover of God in Hos. 1–3 and Jer. 2.

166. Cf. the royal prayers of David in 1 Chr. 29:10–19 and Solomon in 1 Kgs. 8:22–53 = 2 Chr. 6:12–42.

167. A primary use of the verb *kataskeuazō* (κατασκευάζω) is to refer to the "constructing" of ships (14:2) and buildings. See Frederick William Danker (ed.), *A Greek-English Lexicon of the New Testament and Other Early Christian Literature* (3rd ed.; Chicago: University of Chicago Press, 2000) 527.

168. Goodrick, *Book of Wisdom*, 215–16.

169. Some have seen v. 15 as referring to something comparable to the Platonic duality of mortal body and immortal soul (Plato, *Phaed.* 81c). Cf. Philo, *Gig.* 31. See Larcher, *Études sur la Sagesse*, 595–96; Winston, *Book of Wisdom*, 207.

170. For a discussion of salvation in this text, see Damien Noël, "Chapitre VII: Quelle sotériologie dans le livre de la Sagesse?" in *Sagesse biblique*, 187–96.

171. See Mack's discussion of the relationship of Wisdom and soteriology (*Logos und Sophia*, 72–73).

172. Perdue, "Social Character of Paraenesis," 16–17.

173. Armin Schmitt, "Struktur, Herkunft und Bedeutung der Beispielreihe in Weish 10," *BZ* 21 (1977) 1–22. He argues that this list of redeemed follows not the summaries of salvation history in the OT, but rather the literary conventions of Hellenistic literature.

174. John Collins argues that the book of Wisdom shares with apocalyptic a "cosmological conviction," i.e., the path to salvation resides in understanding the structure of the universe and living accordingly. Apocalyptic, however, rejected Wisdom's claim that there is order in the present creation. Apocalyptic looked forward to a new order formed by the transformation of the old ("Cosmos and Salvation: Jewish Wisdom and Apocalypticism in the Hellenistic Age," *Seers, Sibils, and Sages*, 317–38).

175. See Abraham Malherbe, "Hellenistic Moralists and the New Testament," *ANRW*, 26.1, 2, 267–333.

176. See André Dupont-Sommer, "Adam 'Père du Monde' dans la Sagesse de Salomon (10, 1–21)," *RHR* 119 (1939) 182–203.

177. Michael Kolarcik, "Creation and Salvation in the Book of Wisdom," in *Creation in the Biblical Traditions*, 97–107.

178. See Cheon, *Exodus Story*.

179. Barclay, *Jews in the Mediterranean Diaspora*, 182.

180. See the Third *Sibylline Oracle*, which presents a literary attack directed against the Egyptians as an immoral and barbaric people who even worship cats and snakes (*Sib. Or.* 3.29–45, 314–18, 596–600).

181. The criticism directed against the Egyptians in Alexandria is one reason for the teacher's emphasis on their punishment and devastation during the events of the exodus and the Red Sea. It is notable that the poet Ezekiel the Tragedian wrote a Greek tragedy based on the theme of the exodus and directed strong criticism not only against the pharaoh but also against the wicked Egyptians. See Eusebius, *Praep. ev.* 9.28.2; 29.14; Jacobson, *Exagoge of Ezekiel*, 50–67; Holladay, *Fragments*, 2:344–405.

182. See Robert T. Siebeneck, "The Midrash of Wisdom 10–19," *CBQ* 22 (1960) 178.

183. Johannes Fichtner, *Weisheit Salomos* (HAT 6; Tübingen: J. C. B. Mohr, 1938), 42–43.

184. See Edmund Stein, "Ein jüdisch-hellenistischer Midrasch über den Auszug aus Ägypten," *MGWJ* 78 (1934) 559–60.

185. See Peter T. van Rooden, "Die antike Elementarlehre und der Aufbau von Sapientia Salomonis 11–19," in *Tradition and Re-Interpretation in Jewish and Early Christian Literature*, ed. J. W. van Henten, et al. (Studia Post-Biblica 36; Leiden: Brill, 1986) 81–96.

186. Winston, *Book of Wisdom*, 227.

187. See M.-J. Lagrange, "Le Livre de la Sagesse," *RB* 16 (1907) 85–104.

188. See Job 28:25 and Isa 40:12, 26.

189. For the Dyonisian mystery religion, see Martin Nilsson, *The Dionysiac Mysteries of the Greek and Roman Age* (New York: Arno, 1975).

190. Cf. Josephus, *C. Ap.* 1.224–25; 2.66, 85–86; *Let. Aris.* 138.

191. See Maurice Gilbert, *La critique des dieux dans le Livre de la Sagesse* (AnBib 13; Rome: Pontifical Biblical Institute, 1973); Friedo Ricken, "Gab es eine hellenistische Vorlage für Weish 13–15?" *Bib* 49 (1968) 54–86.

192. Exod. 3:14. See Goodrick, *Book of Wisdom*, 275.

193. Georg Ziener, *Die theologische Begriffssprache im Buche der Weisheit* (BBB 11; Bonn: Peter Hanstein, 1956) 128–29. Also see Georg Picht, "The God of the Philosophers," *JAAR* 48 (1980): 61–79.

194. The feminine form of the noun was applied to Wisdom (8:6).

195. Joseph Reider, *Book of Wisdom* (New York: Harper & Brothers, 1957) 160.

196. See Hermann Eising, "Der Weisheitslehrer und die Göttesbilder," *Bib* 40 (1959) 393–408.

197. Horst Dietrich Preuss, *Verspottung fremder Religionen im Alten Testament* (BWANT 92; Stuttgart: Kohlhammer, 1971) 265.

198. This is probably human wisdom that involves the knowledge and skill of a craftsperson (cf. Exod. 28:3; 31:3, 6; 35:26, 31, 35), not the cosmic Wisdom of God that shapes the world and human beings (Wis. 8:6).

199. See Walter Burkert, *Ancient Mystery Cults* (Cambridge: Harvard University Press, 1987); Hans-Josef Klauck, *The Religious Context of Early Christianity: A Guide to Greco-Roman Religions* (Minneapolis: Fortress, 2003), 81–152; 1:77–128. This could refer to the mystery religion of Horus/Seth/Isis.

200. Winston notes that this principle was articulated by the Stoics, allowing the gods to act so as not to violate nature's laws (*Wisdom of Solomon*, 325).

201. See Ernest G. Clarke, *The Wisdom of Solomon* (Cambridge Bible Commentary; Cambridge: Cambridge University Press, 1973) 126; Ziener, *Theologische Begriffssprache*, 148–49.

202. Winston, *Wisdom of Solomon*, 333.

203. Michael Kolarcik, "Universalism and Justice in the Wisdom of Solomon," in *Treasures of Wisdom*, 289–301.

204. Ibid., 291.

205. Ibid., 295–301.
206. Werner Foerster, *TDNT* 3 (1965) 1025–27.
207. See Ringgren, *Word and Wisdom*.
208. Larcher, *Études sur la Sagesse*, 516–17.
209. See Ringgren, *Word and Wisdom*.
210. Some have seen v. 15 as referring to something comparable to the Platonic duality of mortal body and immortal soul (Plato, *Phaedo* 81c). Cf. Philo, *Gig.* 31. See the discussions in Goodrick, *Book of Wisdom*, 221; Larcher, *Études sur la Sagesse*, 595–96; Winston, *Book of Wisdom*, 207.
211. Cf. the royal prayer of David in 1 Chr. 29:10–19 and of Solomon in 1 Kgs. 8:22–53 = 2 Chr. 6:12–42.
212. Schäfer, *Judeophobia*; Gruen, *Diaspora*, chaps. 1–2.
213. Walter Vogels, "The God Who Creates Is the God Who Saves: The Book of Wisdom's Reversal of the Biblical Pattern," *Église et Théologie* 22 (1991) 315–35.

Chapter 9: The Historical Theology of Wisdom Literature: Conclusions

1. Perdue, *Social History of Wisdom*.
2. André Lemaire, *Inscriptions hébraïques introduction, traduction, commentaire* (Littératures anciennes du Proche orient 9; Paris: Cerf, 1977).
3. Westermann, *Elements of Old Testament Theology*, 89. Also see Clifford and Collins, "Introduction: The Theology of Creation Traditions," in *Creation in the Biblical Traditions*, 11; Perdue, *Wisdom and Creation*.
4. See *Enuma eliš* (Mesopotamia, *ANET*, 12–17), the Baal Cycle (Canaan, *ANET*, 129–42), and the Osiris-Horus myth (Egypt, *ANET*, 60–118, 501-7).
5. See McCurley, *Ancient Myths and Biblical Faith*, 73–124; Keel, *Symbolism*, 201–2.
6. Bernhard Lang, *Frau Weisheit*. A revised version in English is *Wisdom and the Book of Proverbs: A Hebrew Goddess Redefined* (New York: Pilgrim, 1986).
7. Cf. Isa. 40:12 and 48:13.
8. See Ps. 104:24.
9. Cf. my discussion of Prov. 8:30 in *Wisdom and Creation*, 89–91.
10. See Lorenz Dürr, *Die Wertung des Göttlichen Wortes im Alten Testament und im Antiken Orient* (MVAG 42; Leipzig: Hinrichs, 1938).
11. For example, Thorkild Jacobsen notes: "The creative power of the word underlies all Mesopotamian religious literature" (*Treasures of Darkness: A History of Mesopotamian Religion* (New Haven: Yale University Press, 1976) 15.
12. See the "Instruction for King Meri-ka-Re," *ANET*, 417. For other Egyptian examples see Viktor Notter, *Biblischer Schöpfungsbericht und ägyptische Schöpfungsmythen* (SB 568; Stuttgart: KBW-Verlag, 1974) 145–49.
13. God's breath brings destruction to the wicked (see Ps. 18:15; Exod. 15:8).
14. McCurley, *Ancient Myths and Biblical Faith*, 12–57.
15. See Job 32:22; 35:10; 36:3. Qoheleth may refer to God as "your creator" (12:1).
16. The word *'ebed* means both "slave" and "servant."
17. Jon D. Levenson, "The Universal Horizon of Biblical Particularism," in *Ethnicity and the Bible*, ed. Mark Brett (Biblical Interpretation Series 19; Leiden: Brill, 1996) 143–69.
18. James L. Crenshaw, "Wisdom and Authority: Sapiential Rhetoric and Its Warrants," in *Congress Volume: Vienna 1980*, ed. J. A. Emerton (VTSup 32; Leiden: Brill, 1981) 10–29.
19. Reading the root as "eternity."

20. See James Crenshaw, "The Eternal Gospel," in *Essays in Old Testament Ethics*, ed. James L. Crenshaw and John T. Willis (New York: Ktav, 1974) 25–55; Kurt Galling, "Das Rätsel der Zeit, im Urteil Kohelets (Koh 3:1–15)," *2TK* 58 (1961) 1–15.
21. Daniel Lys, "L'Être et le temps," in *Sagesse de l'Ancien Testament*, 249–58.
22. The argument that Gentiles should know the moral law by their observation of nature is also made by the Third Sibyl (see Collins, *Between Athens and Jerusalem*, 162).
23. See Crites, "Narrative Quality of Experience," 291–311.
24. Armin Lange plans to address the role of sages in the shaping of the canonical form of the Hebrew Bible with a volume for my series, Wisdom Literature in the Old Testament (Leiden: Brill, forthcoming).
25. I am writing this type of volume, *The Sage*, for Westminster/John Knox scheduled for 2007. Also see two collections of essays, *Sage in Israel*, and my new edited collection, *Scribes, Sages, and Seers*.